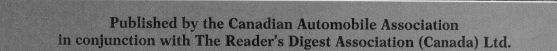

DRIVE NORTH AMERICA

Published by the Canadian Automobile Association
in conjunction with The Reader's Digest Association (Canada) Ltd.

Credits and Acknowledgments

Editor: Kenneth Winchester
Art Director: Pierre Léveillé
Designers: Michel Rousseau, Anne A. Racine (assistant)
Text Research: Caroline Miller (senior researcher), Heather Pengelley
Photo Research: Rachel Irwin (chief), Michelle Turbide
Copy Preparation: Francis R. Legge

Senior Staff Editor: Ian Walker
Planning Manager: Horst D. Dornbusch

Coordination: Nicole Samson-Cholette
Production: Holger Lorenzen

Contributing Writers: Keith Bellows, Kent and Donna Dannen, Nancy Seifer
Map Research: Mary Ashley

Color Separation: Herzig Somerville Limited
Typesetting: Reader's Digest Text Processing Center
Printing: Ronalds Printing
Binding: Harpell's Press Co-operative
Binding Material: Columbia Finishing Mills Limited
Paper: Rolland Inc.

Maps Copyright © The H. M. Goushā Company
Box 6277
San Jose, Calif. 95150

The credits and acknowledgments that appear on page 384 are
herewith made a part of this copyright page.

First Edition
ISBN 0-88850-112-9
83 84 85 / 5 4 3

Colorado River, Colorado

Contents

Manitoba
166

Ontario
172

Québec
310

Newfoundland
336

Prince Edward Island

New Brunswick
Nova Scotia
330

New
Dakota
150

Minnesota
142

Michigan

South
Dakota

Wisconsin
192

Michigan
184

Michigan

Maine
320

Vermont

New Hampshire
304

Massachusetts
Rhode Island
294

New York
282

Connecticut

Nebraska

Iowa

Illinois
200

Indiana

Ohio
208

Pennsylvania
268

New Jersey
276

Maryland

Delaware

Kansas
118

Missouri

West
Virginia
256

Virginia

Kentucky
222

North Carolina
248

Oklahoma

Arkansas
108

Tennessee
230

South
Carolina

Texas
94

Mississippi

Louisiana

Alabama

Georgia

Florida
238

How To Use this Book

The **Index Map** of North America on pages 4 and 5 (*see A, right*) and the adjacent **Contents** list are designed to help you locate the places you wish to find. For further convenience, an **Alphabetical Index** of provincial and state maps is featured on page 7.

Two- and four-page **Highlights** features (*B*) introduce each region, providing a summary of things to do and places to see. Each attraction described in the text is keyed to its map location for easy lookup.

Following the Highlights pages are the regional **Road Maps** (*C*). With each province or state, there is an index including most cities and towns, and a list of counties and county seats. You can pinpoint a place simply by using the map page number and the alphanumeric grid (the system of letters across the top and bottom of each map and numbers down both sides). Most provinces and states require more than one map for coverage, so each map includes a "locator" panel with a tan-colored insert to show the area that is fully covered on those two pages. This locator also indicates page numbers for adjacent maps.

When you reach the edge of a map, page numbers and grid coordinates direct you to the next map, and the continuation of the road you are following. If two sets of coordinates appear on the edge of a map, then the roads in *one grid* of the map you are using continue on *two grids* on the other map.

The **City Map** section (*D*) begins on page 340 (with a separate **City Map Index** on page 383). The 124 small-scale "in-and-out" maps and the 12 large-scale "close-up" maps are arranged alphabetically by state and province.

Metric measurements (except tons and acres) appear on Canadian maps and Highlights features. United States measurements follow the imperial system. You will find a conversion scale on each road map.

A. Index Map of North America

B. Highlights Feature

C. Regional Road Map

D. City Map Section

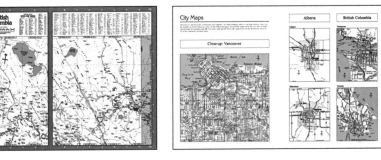

HIGHWAY MARKERS

INTERSTATE **30** UNITED STATES **40** STATE AND PROVINCIAL **34** TRANS-CANADA **6**

QUEBEC AUTOROUTE **10** YELLOWHEAD **4** COUNTY **26** **26** **M**

MEXICO FEDERAL **6** ONTARIO SECONDARY (500 and over) **500** GREAT RIVER ROAD

Highway markers correct at time of publication but subject to change.

DISTANCES

SHOWN AS MILES ON UNITED STATES MAPS AND KILOMETRES ON CANADIAN MAPS.

ONE MILE EQUALS 1.6 KILOMETRES

ONE KILOMETRE EQUALS .6 MILES

DISTANCE BETWEEN TOWNS AND JUNCTIONS 3 / 4

DISTANCE BETWEEN DOTS • 35 • • 35 •

SELECTED POINT TO POINT DISTANCES SHOWN IN RED VANCOUVER 494 Miles / 795 km PRINCE GEORGE

ROAD CLASSIFICATIONS

CONTROLLED ACCESS HIGHWAYS
In some states interchange numbers are mileposts.

TOLL HIGHWAYS

OTHER DIVIDED HIGHWAYS

PRINCIPAL THROUGH HIGHWAYS

OTHER THROUGH HIGHWAYS

CONNECTING HIGHWAYS

LOCAL ROADS In unfamiliar areas inquire locally before using these roads

Divided **4** Undivided
Interchanges
Service Areas

Paved

Paved

Paved   Gravel

Paved   Gravel

Paved   Gravel   Dirt

SPECIAL FEATURES

STATE AND PROVINCIAL PARKS
With Campsites ⛺ Without Campsites ⛺

RECREATION AREAS
With Campsites ▲ Without Campsites △

SELECTED REST AREAS
With Toilets Without Toilets

PORTS OF ENTRY
Open 24 Hours Inquire Locally

AIRPORTS
Airline Stops Military Other ✈

POINTS OF INTEREST

SCENIC ROADS

SKI AREAS

TIME ZONE

MAJOR MTN. ROADS

CLOSED IN WINTER (United States only) Closed in Winter

COUNTY LINES

TOURIST INFORMATION

BOAT RAMPS

COVERED BRIDGES

POPULATION SYMBOLS

⊛ Capitals   ⊗ 2,500 to 5,000   ▫ 25,000 to 50,000

○ Under 1,000   ◉ 5,000 to 10,000   ▣ 50,000 to 100,000

◎ 1 000 to 2,500   ◉ 10,000 to 25,000   ▣ 100,000 and over

Alphabetical Index

New York City

Cancan Girls and Dancing Lights in the Eldorado of the North

Alaska/Yukon/Northwest Territories

A weathered symbol of Alaska, this totem survives in a park near Ketchikan.

Denali, "The Great One," is the name Indians gave to Alaska's 20,320-foot Mount McKinley. Laced with more than a dozen glaciers and visible from 150 miles on a clear day, it is North America's loftiest peak and the highlight of **Denali National Park (11, F-5)**. Also in the park are the multicolored slopes of Polychrome Pass, raft trips on the Nenana River and the nightly magic of the aurora borealis—the northern lights.

Some 120 miles from the Arctic Circle, almost at the northern limit of Alaska's interior road network, is **Fairbanks (11, E-4)**. Alaskaland's Goldrush Town has a re-created turn-of-the-century mining camp, the retired stern-wheeler *Nenana,* and an Athabascan Indian village. The stern-wheelers *Discovery I* and *II* cruise past deserted cabins and Indian fish wheels along the Chena and Tanana rivers. Nearby is **Cripple Creek.** A refurbished ghost town of frontier buildings, it features floor shows at the Malemute Saloon and accommodation in the Hotel and Bunkhouse, built in 1906 to serve prospectors drawn to the area's goldfields.

Anchorage (11, G-5) lies on the coast. Rimmed with snowy mountains, it was once a tent city for construction gangs on the Alaska Railroad. Alaskan history and crafts are showcased at the Anchorage Historical and Fine Arts Museum. Displays cover early Russian colonization; English, Spanish and French exploration; and the deeds of whalers and prospectors. Earthquake Park, an affluent neighborhood until buried in a 1964 earthquake, offers dramatic views of the tides that flood Cook Inlet.

South of the city limits is the Portage Glacier, which has calved the icebergs that drift in the blue-green waters of Portage Lake. To the west a road cuts through the Kenai National Moose Range (home of some 5,000

giant Kenai moose) and leads to **Kenai (10, C-5)**, a native village where the Russians established a fur-trade post in 1791. One of the oldest (1895) of Alaska's Russian Orthodox churches stands here, its trio of sky-blue onion domes mounted by golden crosses.

In **Skagway (11, H-1)**, gold-rush spirit still lingers along the boardwalks of Broadway. False-fronted buildings recall the days of '98 when gold hunters (many now buried in the town's Goldrush Graveyard) packed saloons and gambling dens. Eagle Hall stages a lively show complete with garter auction and cancan dancing. The Soapy Smith Museum, named for an 1890s confidence man and outlaw, displays newspapers, photographs, and other relics of the town's heyday.

Winding streets and wooden stairs hug the hillsides of **Juneau (10, D-3)**, the state capital and site of an 1880 gold strike. A four-story totem at the head of Seward Street portrays the casts of characters in four separate Indian myths. At the Alaska State Museum are gold-rush memorabilia, totem poles, masks, canoes, and the arts and artifacts of aboriginal tribes that lived 2,000 years ago. St. Nicholas Russian Orthodox Church (1894), an octagonal clapboard building with traditional onion-shaped dome, houses a unique collection of Russian icons.

Ferries from Juneau service the island communities of **Sitka (10, D-4)** and **Ketchikan (10, D-3)**. Sitka National Historical Park, where Russian forces defeated the Tlingit Indians in an 1804 battle, displays native crafts in a lush evergreen forest dotted with ancient totem poles. Near Ketchikan, totem poles depict the legends of the Tlingits and other Indian tribes at Totem Bight Historical Site. Set on the banks of the salmon-rich Ketchikan Creek, the Tongass Historical Society Museum holds such articles as bentwood boxes, a Chilkat blanket of cedar bark and mountain goat wool, and a 19th-century Tlingit shirt with mother-of-pearl buttons.

The ghosts of a gold-rush past crowd the streets of **Dawson (11, E-2)**, the Yukon's "City of Gold" in 1897–98. Here, along creaking boardwalks, once strolled Silent Sam Bonifield, Swiftwater Bill Gates, Glass-Eyed Annie and Overflowing Flora. A whirl with a dance-hall girl cost $1, champagne went for $40 a bottle, and $2,000 in gold dust could ride on the turn of a card. Much of the town has been restored to its former glory. Today cancan girls kick high at Diamond Tooth Gertie's Gambling Hall, Canada's only legalized casino, and in summer the Palace Grand Theatre stages The Gaslight Follies. More than 25,000 artifacts in the Dawson City Museum recall the town's rich past. The stern-wheeler *Keno,* once a common sight on the Yukon River, is preserved in Dawson, as is the log cabin in which Robert Service penned his novel *The Trail of '98.*

Upriver is **Whitehorse (11, G-1)**, the Yukon's capital and largest city, and a former

Wild grandeur (above) and the absence of civilization are the lure of Northern travel.

The Dempster Highway (below) approaches the Richardson Mountains. Canada's most northerly road winds 728 kilometres between Dawson and Inuvik.

Homesick soldiers erected the first signposts at Watson Lake, Yukon (above).

At Button Point, N.W.T. (below), an Inuit practices a traditional string game.

Diamond Tooth Gertie's Gambling Hall re-creates Dawson's gold-rush past, where the motto was "never refuse a drink or kick a dog."

staging point for gold seekers. Recalling those days each February, residents don period costumes and hold dogsled and snowshoe races during the Sourdough Rendezvous. Sam McGee's Cabin, where Robert Service wrote *The Cremation of Sam McGee*, has been relocated here from Lake Laberge. A log church (1900) in Whitehorse has an altar frontal of beaded caribou hide and contains vestry minutes written by Service. Also here are a three-story log cabin and the *Klondike*, the last stern-wheeler to ply the Yukon River. The MacBride Museum exhibits a 1,174-kilogram copper nugget—the largest ever found in the Yukon.

Linking Whitehorse and Skagway is the White Pass and Yukon Route, a spectacular rail journey that retraces the White Pass Trail to the Klondike goldfields. The train climbs narrow-gauge track to 889-metre Log Cabin and crosses a bridge spanning Dead Horse Gulch (named for the nearly 3,000 horses that died here during the gold rush).

A road links Whitehorse to **Carcross (11, H-1)** where George Carmack, Skookum Jim and Tagish Charlie launched the prospecting trip that triggered the Klondike Gold Rush. Skookum Jim, Tagish Charlie and Carmack's wife are buried in Carcross cemetery. Also in "the town that discovered the Klondike" are a White Pass and Yukon stagecoach and *Tutshi*, an old stern-wheeler beached since 1955.

Another road leads west from Whitehorse to the wild grandeur of **Kluane National Park (11, G-2)**. Canada's second largest national park is a wilderness of rock and ice surrounding Canada's highest peak, 5,951-metre Mount Logan, and 409-square-kilometre Kluane Lake, the Yukon's largest.

Straddling the border between the Northwest Territories and Alberta is **Wood Buffalo National Park (10, C-1)**, established in 1922 to protect North America's last herd of wood bison. More than a million ducks and geese populate the poorly drained bogs, meandering streams and silty river channels of the Peace–Athabasca Delta.

Outside the park, at **Fort Smith (10, C-1)**, the Northern Life Museum houses dinosaur bones; early Indian and Inuit tools and utensils; a printing press brought north in 1873; and paintings, photographs and mementos of trappers, traders and missionaries.

West of the park, the 1,513-kilometre Mackenzie Highway tracks north through muskeg and dense forest, and past duck-filled sloughs and lakes. Near **Hay River (10, C-2)** the highway passes Alexandra Falls, a 90-metre-wide torrent plunging 33 metres, and 15-metre-high Louise Falls, which tumbles into a rapid-filled gorge.

On the northern margin of Great Slave Lake, only 500 kilometres south of the Arctic Circle, is the skyline of **Yellowknife (10, B-2)**, capital of the Northwest Territories. Traces of its rough-and-ready past as a gold-boom settlement remain at Old Town, a jumble of wooden shanties along the shoreline. In the Prince of Wales Northern Heritage Center, the history and culture of the North come alive in dioramas, slide displays and exhibits of Dene and Inuit artifacts.

Yellowknife takes abundant advantage of its location. During the Caribou Carnival each March, contests include igloo building, log sawing, snowshoeing and skiing, and a three-day dogsled race on Great Slave Lake. In June, competitors take to the links in uninterrupted daylight for the Midnight Golf Tournament, and each September, judges at the County Fair North of Sixty rate flowers and vegetables grown during the long hours of summer daylight.

At **Inuvik (10, A-4)**, accessible from the Yukon by the Dempster Highway, entrants compete in traditional Indian and Inuit sports during the Northern Games. Canada's highest road—passable only in winter—links Inuvik with **Tuktoyaktuk.** Here soil-covered mounds of solid ice (pingos) bulge from the tundra under permafrost pressure. One has been hollowed to create a natural freezer; another, a curling rink. At the Nanuk Cooperative Workshop, Inuit women make cushions and mukluks, and fashion parkas from muskrat, seal and wolf.

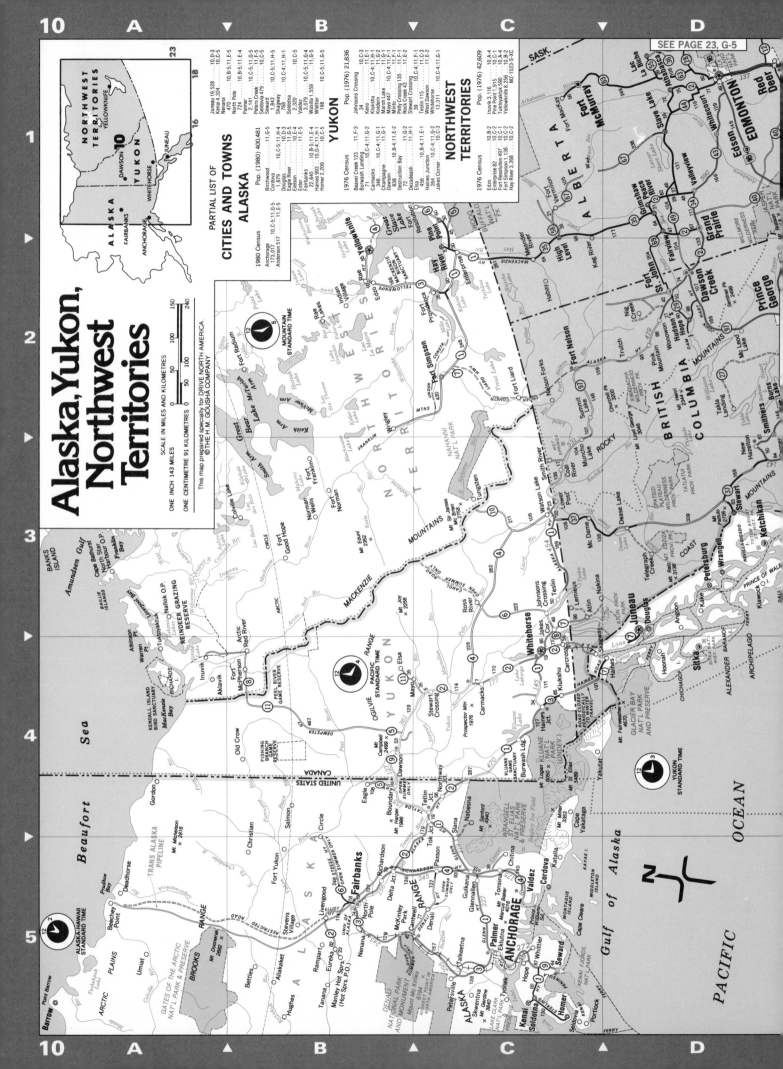

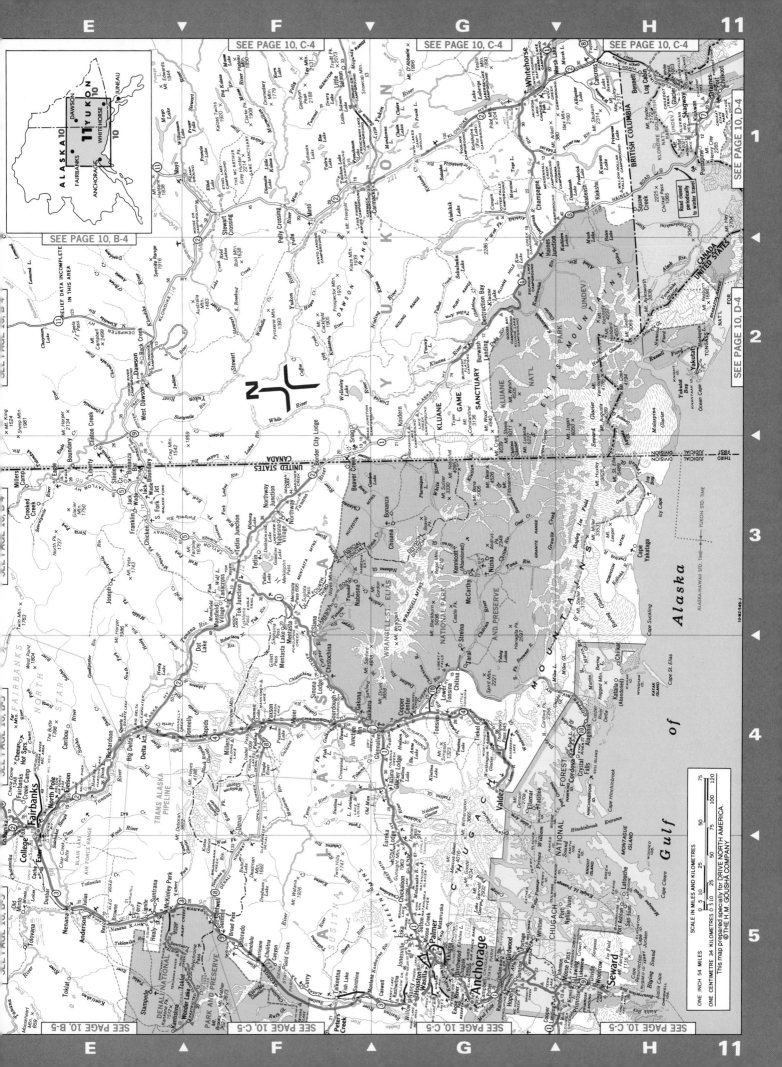

On the Shores of the Pacific:
Totems and a Touch of Old England

British Columbia

Canada's westernmost province brings striking contrast to the eye. Slung between two mountain ranges—the historic Rockies and the mist-shrouded Coast Mountains—and washed by the Pacific, it covers almost a million square kilometres of ranchland and forest, shoreline and island.

Some of British Columbia's finest scenery is found in its five national parks and 370 provincial preserves. **Pacific Rim National Park (17, G-3),** on the west coast of Vancouver Island, is a spectacular blend of foaming breakers, rocky headlands and craggy islands. The main attraction is Long Beach, an 11-kilometre crescent of hard-packed sand threaded with trails that lead to weathered rock arches and water-blasted blowholes. Boat tours take visitors to rocks frequented by basking Steller's sea lions.

Della Falls plummets 440 metres to Della Lake in **Strathcona Provincial Park (17, F-3),** home to Vancouver Island's last elk herd and British Columbia's tallest tree (a 93-metre giant fir).

Once a roistering fur-trade post, genteel **Victoria (17, G-2)** today lends a touch of England to the wild grandeur of the Pacific Coast, with its double-decker buses, Victorian mansions, and high teas in the Empress Hotel. Buildings in the English Village include replicas of Shakespeare's birthplace and Anne Hathaway's thatched cottage. At night, the soft glow of hidden lamps illuminates the paths of Butchart Gardens, a rock amphitheater ablaze by day with flowering plants, shrubs and trees.

Totem poles, cedar dugout canoes and a replica of a 19th-century Kwakiutl Indian house in Thunderbird Park represent the rich culture of the Pacific coast tribes. Nearby, at the imposing British Columbia Parliament Buildings, a statue of Capt. George Vancouver crowns the copper-covered dome of the main building. The Provincial Museum and Archives contain wildlife dioramas, a replica of Captain Cook's HMS *Discovery* and paintings by West Coast artist Emily Carr.

The story of logging, the province's main industry, is told at the British Columbia Forest Museum in **Duncan (17, G-2).** Between May and September, a 1910 steam engine chuffs along 2.5 kilometres of narrow-gauge track, over a 92-metre trestle, past donkey engines, a sawmill, and a fire tower.

The spectacular setting of **Vancouver (17, F-1)** between the Coast Mountains and the Pacific provides "innumerable pleasing landscapes," as Captain Vancouver noted in 1792. Visitors can ride an aerial tramway to the top of Grouse Mountain for a splendid panorama of Vancouver, its harbor and surrounding mountains.

Scenic drives and hiking trails wind through giant stands of cedar, hemlock and Douglas fir in Stanley Park, a quiet refuge minutes from downtown Vancouver. The park contains a collection of totem poles, a small zoo, an aquarium, and the Nine

Salmon, herring and shrimp boats crowd the port of Tofino.

O'Clock Gun. This muzzle-loading cannon has boomed out the time each evening at Hallelujah Point (named in honor of the Salvation Army) since 1894.

Even telephone booths wear pagoda-style roofs in Vancouver's Chinatown, second largest in North America (after San Francisco's). Waterfront buildings in the former slum of Gastown have been restored and refurbished as boutiques, antique shops, pubs, cafés and art galleries. At the University of British Columbia, the ultramodern Museum of Anthropology houses a major collection of massive Indian carvings and totem poles. Swaying high above the Capilano River gorge is the world's longest suspended footbridge (137 metres). At the Vancouver Public Aquarium, killer and beluga whales, dolphins and rare sea otters are among some 6,000 specimens on view. The prize exhibit at the Maritime Museum is the RCMP schooner *St. Roch,* which in 1940–42 became the first vessel to navigate the Northwest Passage from west to east.

The Crown Colony of British Columbia was inaugurated on November 19, 1858, at **Fort Langley (17, F-1),** a Hudson's Bay Company post completed in 1841. The original warehouse (1840) remains. Re-created buildings include the Big House, which contains

This haunting figure of a little girl carved in stone graces Butchart Gardens, a former quarry near Victoria transformed into a year-round flower bowl.

officers' quarters, guest rooms and a community hall, and an artisans' building. Sentries in period costume patrol the palisades.

The Seaview Highway weaves through breathtaking scenery along Howe Sound north of Vancouver before turning inland at **Squamish (17, F-1).** In summer, the restored steam locomotive *Royal Hudson* pulls a sightseeing excursion train along the same cliff-hugging route. The renowned ski slopes of nearby Whistler Mountain are covered with snow from November to May. The Diamond Head Trail in **Garibaldi Provincial Park** leads to The Gargoyles, weirdly shaped volcanic formations sculpted by erosion.

Farther north along the coast is **Prince Rupert (14, B-5).** Here Indian art, artifacts and handicrafts are displayed at the Museum of Northern British Columbia. These include horn, shell and wood spoons, and a Tsimshian princess' blanket fringed with puffin bills. Two large totem poles stand outside.

Towering totem poles are the centerpieces of 'Ksan, a reconstructed Gitksan Indian village near **Hazelton (14, D-4).** The village's six longhouses, dugout canoes, fish traps and smokehouses make it a showplace of the region's Indian culture. Gitksan crafts are sold in one longhouse; tools, costumes and carvings are displayed in another.

An 1873 census of Vancouver (above) recorded a population of 65, mostly loggers and mill workers. Today, with almost half a million people, it is one of Canada's dynamic cities.

Vancouver's Stanley Park.

Victoria's double-decker buses and stately Empress Hotel are two city trademarks.

A fur warehouse, a clerk's house and a fish cache remain at **Fort St. James (15, F-5)**, built in 1806 by explorers Simon Fraser and John Stuart. Adjoining the fort is a Carrier Indian reservation—"Carrier" because widows here once carried around the ashes of their dead husbands.

Barkerville (18, B-5), the Gold Rush Capital of the Cariboo in the 1860s, is now a living museum of restored or reconstructed buildings. Period entertainment is staged at the Theatre Royal, and visitors can drink at Kelly's and Denny's saloons or sample sourdough bread and stew at the Wake-Up Jake Coffee Saloon and Lunch House.

At **Fort Steele (19, F-1)**, in the province's southeastern corner, visitors may ride a stagecoach, pan for gold, and tour 40 buildings that recall the Kootenay Gold Rush of 1864. (Some of the buildings have been restored; others are reconstructions.) Named for the Mounties' legendary Sam Steele, the "Lion of the Yukon" who established the province's first North West Mounted Police post here in 1887, Fort Steele includes a schoolhouse, police barracks, a drugstore and general store and three churches.

Farther north in **Kootenay National Park (18, D-2)** on the eastern slope of the Rockies, the Banff–Windermere Parkway weaves between the sheer walls of Sinclair Canyon and over Vermilion Pass (1,650 metres), the summit of the Continental Divide. Trails link the highway with Marble Canyon, its gray walls streaked with white marble, and the Paint Pots—three ponds stained yellow, red and orange by oxide-bearing springs. Two park-operated mineral pools at Radium Hot Springs are open year-round.

Glacier-fed Takakkaw Falls in **Yoho National Park (18, D-2)** plunges 380 metres into the Yoho River. Wapta Falls cascades to the Kicking Horse River in a 60-metre-wide sheet of water. Yoho (a Cree exclamation of awe and wonderment) contains 30 peaks higher than 3,000 metres.

The Selkirk Mountains in **Glacier National Park (18, D-3)** cradle more than 100 glaciers, including dozens in the Asulkan Valley which provide superb skiing. In neighboring **Mount Revelstoke National Park** a trail crosses alpine meadows spangled with alpine flowers and passes the "Icebox"—a sheltered crevice that retains snow year-round.

Gulf Island-Hopping Via British Columbia Ferry

The best way for motorists to explore British Columbia's tranquil Gulf Islands is to take one of the fast, reliable car ferries operated by the provincial government. At Tsawwassen, 24 kilometres south of Vancouver, boats depart daily for Galiano, Mayne, Pender, Saturna and Saltspring islands. Gabriola Island can be reached from Nanaimo.

Saltspring, the largest Gulf Island, was settled in the 1850s by California blacks—many of them escaped slaves—who became successful farmers. Today this rural retreat is a haven for potters, wood-carvers, weavers and quilt-makers.

At Mayne Island the sea's handiwork is the main attraction. A 180-kilogram fountain at Mary Magdalene Church was exquisitely molded by the sea from a single block of stone.

Another sculpted masterpiece is found on Gabriola Island, where wind and water have hollowed out a spectacular 90-metre-long sandstone headland in Gabriola Provincial Park.

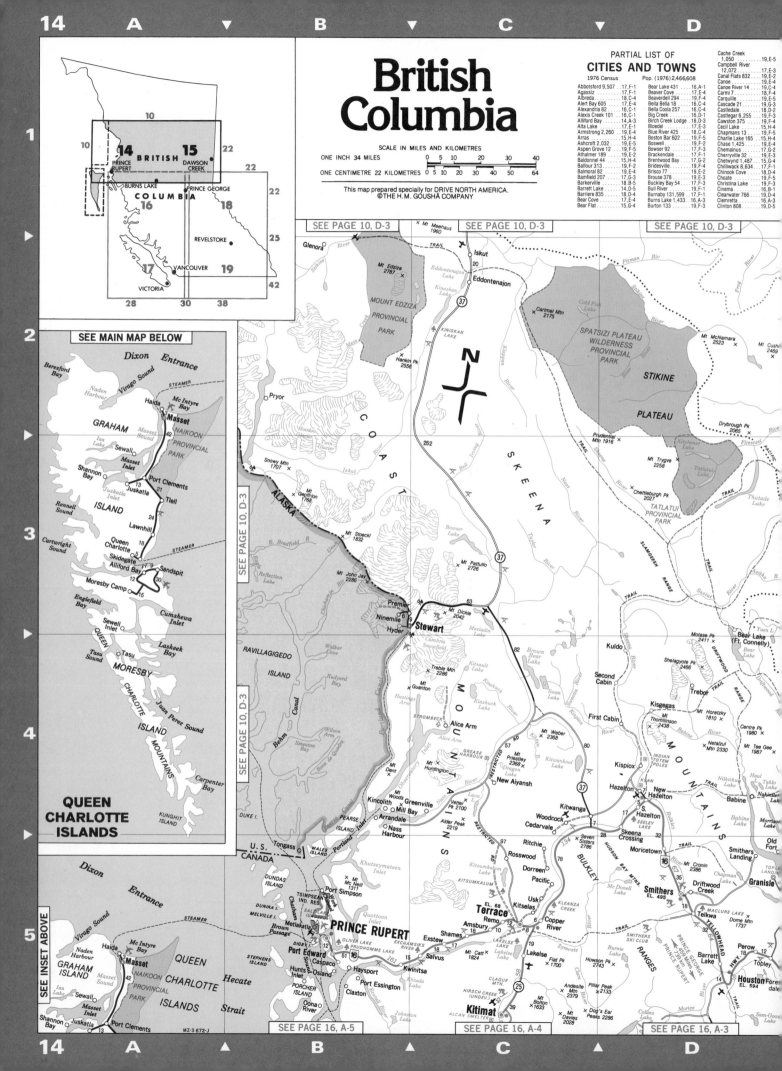

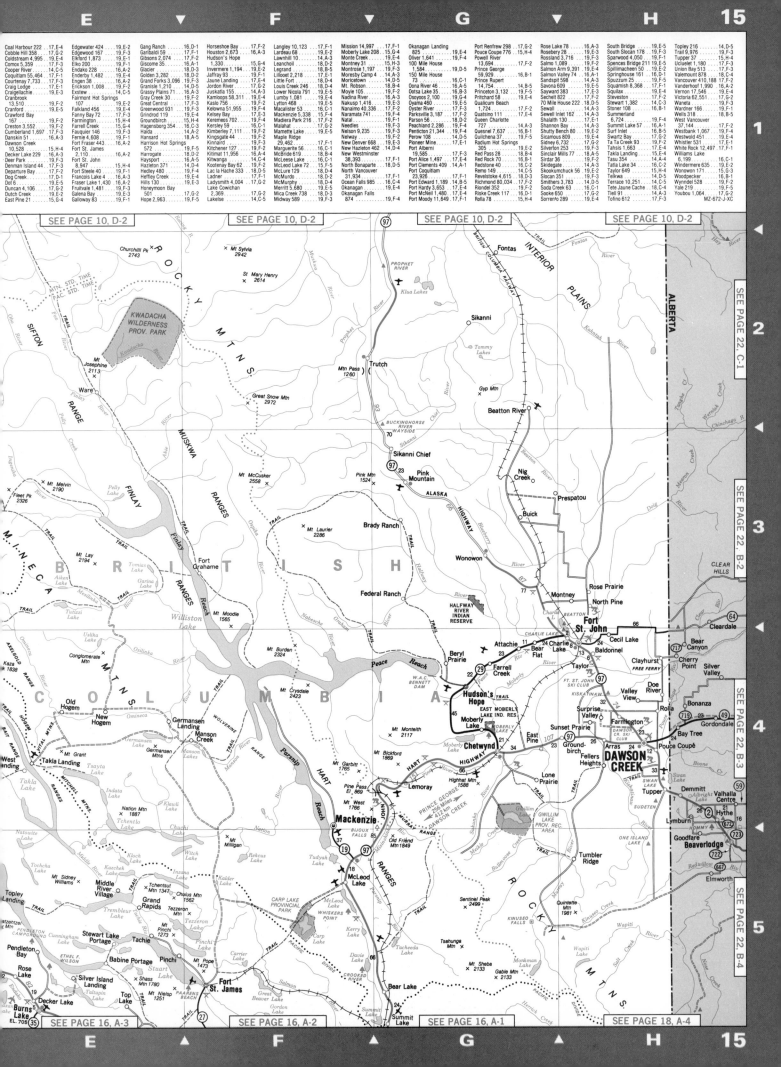

15

Coal Harbour 222 ...17,E-4	Edgewater 424 ...19,E-2	Gang Ranch ...16,D-1	Horseshoe Bay ...17,F-2
Cobble Hill 358 ...17,G-2	Edgewood 167 ...19,F-3	Garibaldi 59 ...17,F-1	Houston 2,673 ...16,A-3
Coldstream 4,995 ...19,E-4	Elkford 1,873 ...19,E-1	Gibsons 2,074 ...17,F-2	Hudson's Hope ...15,H-4
Comox 5,359 ...17,F-3	Elko 200 ...19,F-1	Giscome 35 ...16,A-1	Invermere 1,194 ...19,E-2
Cooper River ...14,C-5	Endako 228 ...16,A-2	Glacier ...19,E-2	Jaffray 93 ...19,F-1
Coquitlam 55,464 ...17,F-1	Enderby 1,482 ...19,E-4	Golden 3,282 ...19,E-2	Jaune Landing ...17,E-4
Courtenay 7,733 ...17,F-3	Engen 38 ...16,A-2	Grand Forks 3,096 ...19,F-3	Jordon River ...17,G-2
Craig Lodge ...19,E-1	Erickson 1,008 ...19,F-2	Granisle 1,210 ...14,B-5	Juskatla 155 ...14,A-3
Craigellachie ...19,E-3	Estevan ...14,C-5	Grassy Plains 71 ...16,A-3	Kamloops 58,311 ...19,E-4
Cranbrook 13,510 ...19,F-2	Fairmont Hot Springs 572 ...19,F-2	Gray Creek 30 ...19,F-2	Kaslo 756 ...19,F-2
Cranford ...19,E-5	Falkland 456 ...19,E-4	Great Central ...17,F-3	Kelowna 51,955 ...19,F-4
Crawford Bay 167 ...19,F-2	Fanny Bay 72 ...17,F-3	Greenwood 931 ...19,F-3	Kelsey Bay ...17,E-3
Creston 3,552 ...19,F-2	Farmington ...15,H-4	Grindrod 119 ...19,E-4	Keremeos 702 ...19,F-4
Cumberland 1,697 ...17,F-3	Farrell Creek ...15,G-4	Groundbirch ...15,G-4	Kersley 59 ...16,D-1
Danskin 51 ...16,A-3	Fauquier 146 ...19,F-3	Hagensborg 354 ...16,C-1	Kimberley 7,111 ...19,F-2
Dawson Creek 10,528 ...15,H-4	Fernie 4,608 ...19,F-1	Haida ...14,A-3	Kingsgate 44 ...19,F-2
Deer Park ...19,F-2	Fort Fraser 443 ...16,A-2	Hansard ...18,A-5	Kinnaird ...19,F-3
Denman Island 44 ...17,F-3	Fort St. James 2,110 ...16,A-2	Harrison Hot Springs ...19,F-5	Kitchener 127 ...19,F-2
Departure Bay ...17,F-3	Fort St. John 8,947 ...15,H-4	Harrogate ...19,E-2	Kitimat 11,956 ...14,B-4
Dog Creek ...17,D-1	Fort Steele 40 ...19,F-2	Haysport ...14,A-4	Kitwanga ...14,C-4
Dot 6 ...19,E-5	Francois Lake 4 ...16,A-3	Hazelton 371 ...14,D-4	Kootenay Bay 62 ...19,F-2
Duncan 4,106 ...17,G-2	Fraser Lake 1,430 ...16,A-2	Hedley 480 ...19,F-3	Lac la Hache 333 ...18,D-5
Dutch Creek ...19,F-2	Fruitvale 1,481 ...19,F-2	Heffley Creek ...19,E-4	Ladner ...17,F-1
East Pine 21 ...15,G-4	Galena Bay ...19,E-3	Hills 130 ...19,F-3	Ladysmith 4,004 ...17,G-2
	Galloway 83 ...19,F-1	Honeymoon Bay 501 ...17,G-2	Lake Cowichan 2,369 ...17,G-2
		Hope 2,963 ...19,F-5	Lakelse ...14,C-5

Langley 10,123 ...17,F-1	Mission 14,997 ...17,F-1	Okanagan Landing 825 ...19,E-4	Port Renfrew 298 ...17,G-2
Lardeau 68 ...19,E-2	Moberly Lake 208 ...15,G-4	Oliver 1,641 ...19,F-4	Pouce Coupe 776 ...15,H-4
Lawnhill 10 ...14,A-3	Monte Creek ...19,E-4	Oona River 46 ...14,B-5	Powell River 13,694 ...17,F-2
Leanchoil ...19,E-2	Montney 31 ...15,H-3	Ootsa Lake 35 ...16,B-3	Prince George 59,929 ...16,B-1
Legrand ...18,B-5	Montrose 1,197 ...19,F-2	Osoyoos 2,100 ...19,F-4	Prince Rupert 14,754 ...14,B-5
Lilloolet 2,218 ...17,E-1	Moresby Camp 4 ...14,A-3	Oyama 460 ...19,E-4	Princeton 3,132 ...19,F-3
Little Fort ...18,D-4	Moricetown ...14,D-5	Oyster River ...17,F-3	Pritchard 58 ...19,E-4
Louis Creek 246 ...18,D-4	Mt. Robson ...18,C-3	Parksville 3,187 ...17,F-2	Qualicum Beach 1,724 ...17,F-2
Lower Nicola 791 ...19,F-5	Moyle 105 ...19,F-2	Parson 56 ...19,E-2	Quatsino 111 ...17,E-4
Lumby 1,081 ...19,E-4	Nadina River ...16,A-3	Peachland 2,286 ...19,F-4	Queen Charlotte 727 ...14,A-3
Lytton 468 ...19,E-5	Nakusp 1,416 ...19,E-3	Penticton 21,344 ...19,F-4	Quesnel 7,637 ...16,B-5
Macalister 53 ...16,C-1	Nanaimo 40,336 ...17,F-2	Perow 108 ...14,D-5	Quilchena 37 ...19,E-5
Mackenzie 5,338 ...15,H-5	Naramata 741 ...19,F-4	Pioneer Mine ...17,F-1	Radium Hot Springs 305 ...19,E-2
Madiera Park 216 ...17,F-2	Natal ...19,F-1	Port Alberni 19,585 ...17,F-3	Red Pass 20 ...18,B-4
Malahat ...17,G-2	Needles ...19,F-3	Port Alice 1,497 ...17,E-4	Red Rock 70 ...16,B-1
Mamette Lake ...19,E-5	Nelson 9,235 ...19,F-2	Port Clements 409 ...14,A-1	Redstone 40 ...16,C-2
Maple Ridge 29,462 ...17,F-1	Nelway ...19,F-2	Port Coquitlam 23,926 ...17,F-1	Remo 149 ...14,C-5
Marguerite 56 ...16,C-1	New Denver 668 ...19,E-3	Port Edward 1,189 ...14,B-5	Revelstoke 4,615 ...18,D-3
McBride 619 ...18,B-4	New Hazelton 462 ...14,D-4	Port Hardy 3,653 ...17,E-4	Richmond 80,034 ...17,F-1
McLeese Lake ...16,C-1	New Westminster 38,393 ...17,F-1	Port McNeill 1,480 ...17,E-4	Riondel 352 ...19,F-2
McLeod Lake 72 ...15,H-5	North Bonaparte ...18,D-5	Port Moody 11,649 ...17,F-1	Riske Creek 117 ...16,D-1
McLure 129 ...18,D-4	North Vancouver 31,934 ...17,F-1		Rolla 78 ...15,H-4
McMurdo ...18,D-2	Ocean Falls 985 ...16,C-4		
McMurphy ...18,D-4	Okanagan 4 ...19,E-4		
Merritt 5,680 ...19,E-5	Okanagan Falls 874 ...19,F-4		
Mica Creek 738 ...18,D-3			
Midway 589 ...19,F-3			

Rose Lake 78 ...16,A-3	South Bridge ...19,E-5	Topley 216 ...14,D-5
Roseberry 28 ...19,E-3	South Slocan 178 ...19,F-3	Trail 9,976 ...19,F-2
Rossland 3,716 ...19,F-2	Spallumcheen ...19,E-2	Tupper 37 ...15,H-4
Salmo 1,089 ...19,F-2	Sparwood 4,050 ...19,F-1	Ucluelet 1,180 ...17,F-3
Salmon Arm 9,391 ...19,E-4	Spences Bridge 211 ...19,E-5	Union Bay 513 ...17,F-3
Salmon Valley 74 ...16,A-1	Spillimacheen 50 ...19,E-2	Valemount 878 ...18,C-4
Sandspit 598 ...14,A-3	Springhouse 161 ...16,D-1	Vancouver 410,188 ...17,F-1
Savona 609 ...19,E-5	Spuzzum 25 ...19,F-5	Vanderhoof 1,990 ...16,A-2
Sayward 383 ...17,E-3	Squamish 8,368 ...17,F-1	Vernon 17,546 ...19,E-4
Sechelt 822 ...17,F-2	Squilax ...19,E-4	Victoria 62,551 ...17,G-2
70 Mile House 222 ...18,D-5	Steveston ...17,F-1	Waneta ...19,F-2
Sewall ...14,A-3	Stewart 1,382 ...14,C-3	Wardner 166 ...19,F-1
Sewell Inlet 162 ...14,A-3	Stoner 108 ...16,B-1	Wells 318 ...18,B-5
Shalalth 130 ...17,E-1	Summerland ...19,F-4	West Vancouver 37,144 ...17,F-1
Shannon Bay ...14,A-3	Summit Lake 57 ...16,A-1	Westbank 1,067 ...19,F-4
Shutty Bench 80 ...19,F-2	Surf Inlet ...16,C-2	Westwold 451 ...19,E-4
Sicamous 809 ...19,E-4	Swartz Bay ...17,G-2	Whistler 531 ...17,F-1
Sidney 6,732 ...17,G-2	Tahsis 1,663 ...17,E-4	White Rock 12,497 ...17,F-1
Silverton 253 ...19,F-3	Takla Landing ...15,E-4	Williams Lake 6,199 ...16,C-1
Sinclair Mills 71 ...18,A-5	Tasu 354 ...14,A-4	Windermere 635 ...19,E-2
Sirdar 36 ...19,F-2	Tatla Lake 34 ...16,C-2	Wonowon 171 ...15,G-3
Skidegate ...14,A-3	Taylor 649 ...15,H-4	Woodpecker ...16,B-1
Skookumchuck 56 ...19,F-2	Telkwa ...14,D-5	Wynndel 528 ...19,F-2
Slocan 351 ...19,F-3	Terrace 10,251 ...14,C-5	Yale 219 ...19,F-5
Smithers 3,783 ...14,D-5	Tete Jaune Cache ...18,C-4	Youbou 1,064 ...17,G-2
Soda Creek 63 ...16,C-1	Tiell 91 ...14,A-3	
Sooke 650 ...17,G-2	Tofino 612 ...17,F-3	
Sorrento 289 ...19,E-4		MZ-672-J-XC

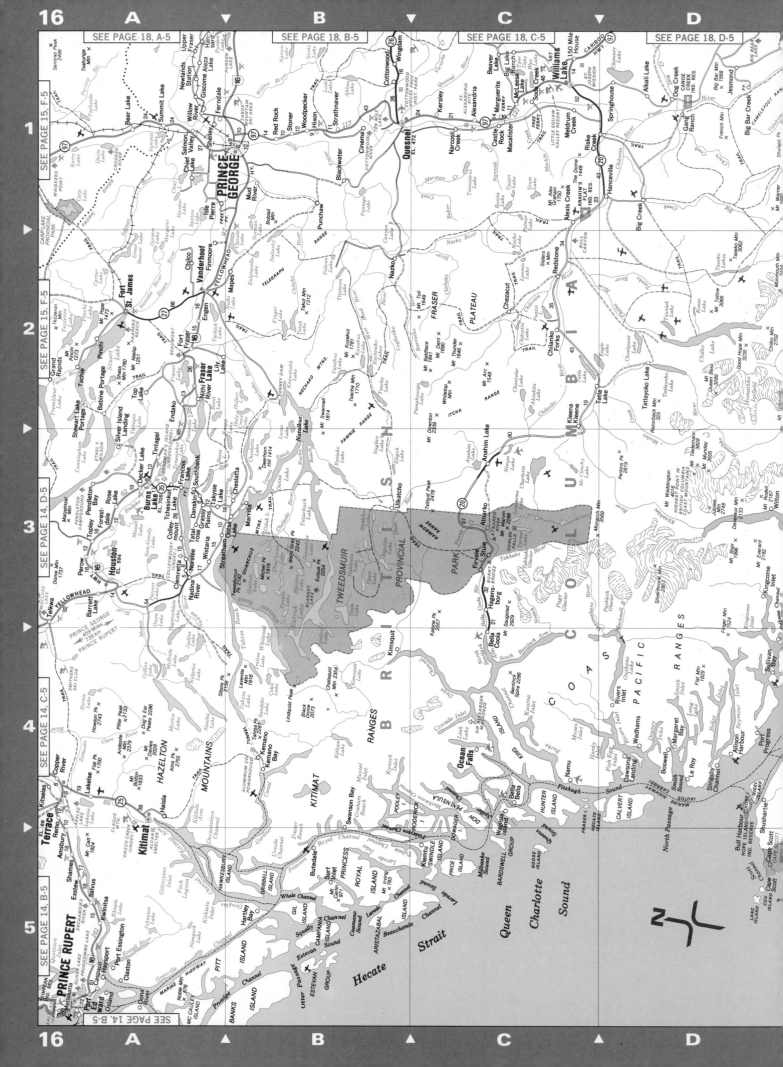

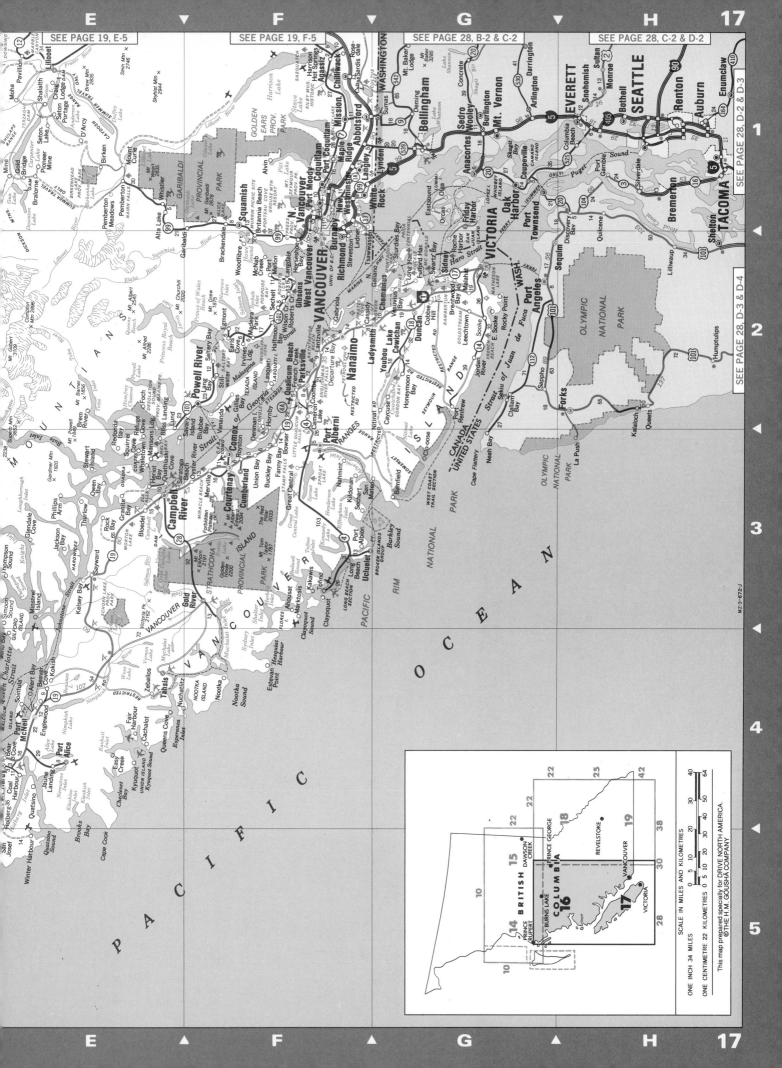

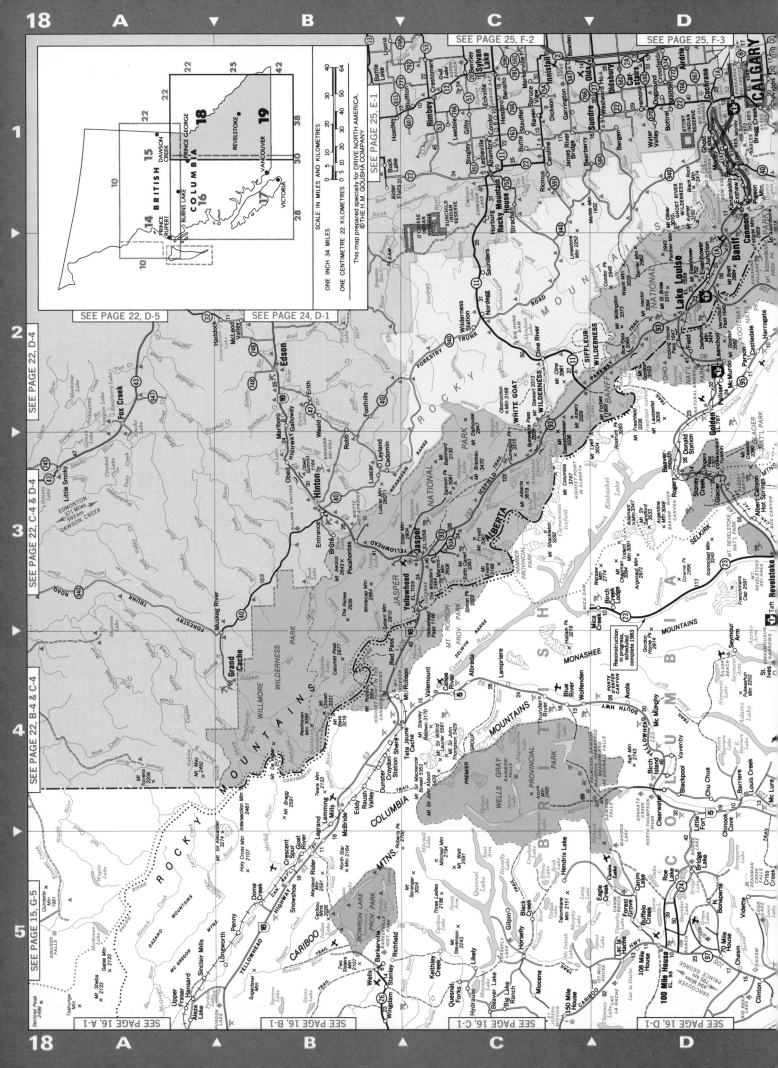

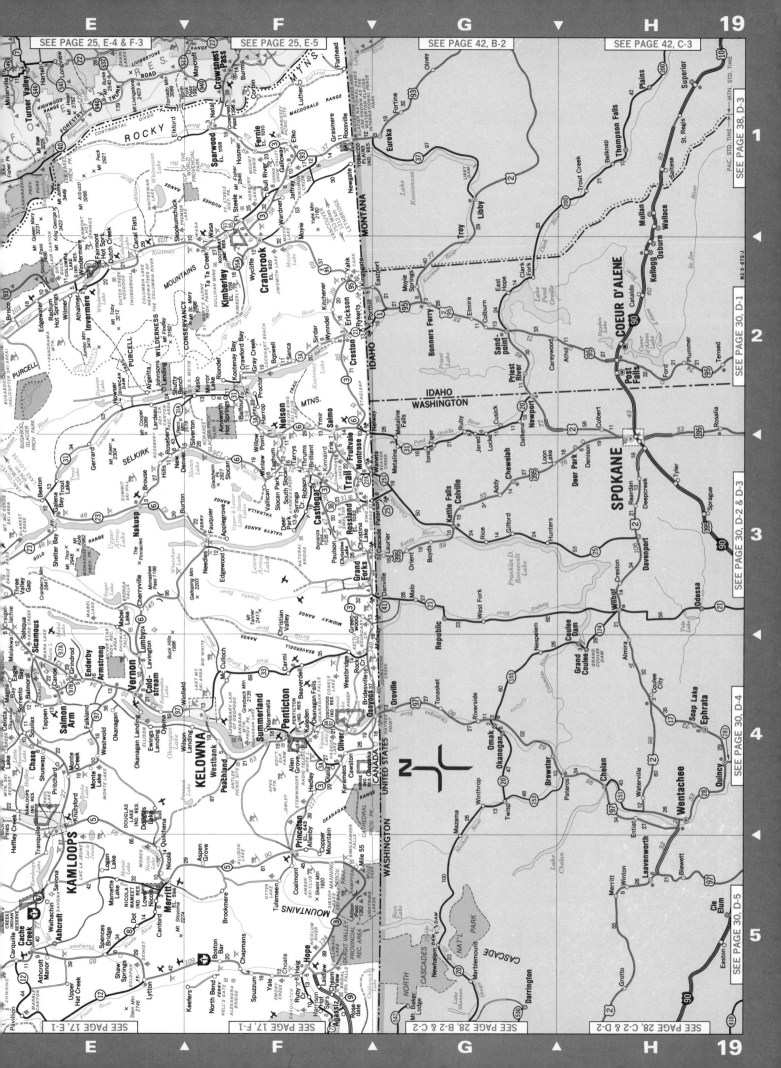

Soaring Peaks, Booming Cities and Eerie, Exquisite Badlands

Alberta

Frontier only a century ago, Alberta today is energized by oil and gas, sunshine and scenery. Along its border with British Columbia rises the high spine of the Rocky Mountains. Eastward stretches a broad tableland: in the south, rolling farmland; in the middle, parkland cut by wide river valleys; to the north, great expanses of lake-strewn forest and fertile prairie.

The most attractive area of Alberta's Cypress Hills (the range extends into Saskatchewan) has been preserved in 200-square-kilometre **Cypress Hills Provincial Park (25, H-4)**. Hiking trails wind through wildflower meadows, tranquil valleys, and cool forests of white spruce and lodgepole pine. Self-guided automobile tours lead to points of interest throughout the park.

In contrast with the tranquil park is the busy city of **Medicine Hat (25, H-4)**. Vast natural gas reserves here prompted Rudyard Kipling, in 1907, to describe this as a place with "all hell for a basement." At Altaglass, visitors may watch craftsmen shape fine glass ornaments and sculpture. In July, the three-day Medicine Hat Exhibition and Stampede attracts circuit cowboys from all over North America.

A cairn at the junction of the St. Mary and Oldman rivers marks the site of **Fort Whoop-Up (25, F-4)**, where traders peddled illicit liquor to the Indians in the 1870s. The fort was put out of business by the newly formed North West Mounted Police in 1874.

Built in 1909, the High Level Bridge spanning the Oldman River in **Lethbridge (25, F-4)** is the world's longest (more than one kilometre) for its height; it rises 93.7 metres from the riverbed. The University of Lethbridge, a striking modern structure on the banks of the Oldman, was built as a Centennial project. At the Nikka Yuko Centennial Garden is a 16th-century-style pavilion of cypress wood.

A replica of the first North West Mounted Police fort stands at the edge of nearby **Fort Macleod (25, F-4)**. Buildings in the reconstructed fort include a museum with early NWMP weapons and uniforms, a law office, blacksmith shop, chapel and medical center.

A concrete crow nesting in a tree is the symbol of **Blairmore (25, E-5)**, the first settlement in the Crowsnest Pass—although that name probably originated not with birds but with Crow Indians. Between Blairmore and Bellevue is the scar of the great Frank Slide, which claimed 70 lives and all but obliterated the town of Frank in the 1903 disaster.

Calgary's skyline (above) symbolizes Alberta's oil-fueled prosperity. Towers of a different kind characterize Sentinel Pass in Banff National Park (right). The glass pyramids of Muttart Conservatory (below) are a striking addition to Edmonton.

A boardsailor catches the wind at Bow Lake (left). At the Calgary Stampede (below), the thrill of the chuckwagon race.

Few places in Canada can equal the dramatic contrast of landscapes in **Waterton Lakes National Park (25, F-5)**, where snow-capped peaks rise abruptly from rolling grasslands. More than 180 kilometres of hiking trails meander through the park, linking such features as Red Rock Canyon and Cameron Falls.

Kananaskis Provincial Park (25, E-3) has changed little since explorer John Palliser came here in 1858. Outstanding scenery includes six large lakes, ice caps, remnant valley glaciers, alpine tundra and waterfalls. The 2.5-kilometre self-guided Resource Trail winds through a portion of the Kananaskis Forest Experiment Station.

The skyline of **Calgary (25, E-3)** continual-

nial Planetarium, where images of the stars and planets are projected onto a 20-metre-wide domed screen. An Avro CF-100, a Vampire jet and a Sikorsky helicopter are among the restored aircraft in the Aero-Space Museum of Calgary.

Eerie but exquisite are the rock formations of the Red Deer Badlands, described by artist A. Y. Jackson as "the most paintable valley in western Canada." **Drumheller (25, F-3)** and the city of **Red Deer (25, F-2)** are popular bases for exploring the badlands.

Banff National Park (24, D-3) offers a wide variety of ways to enjoy its natural splendors. One starting point is Banff townsite: park headquarters and year-round re-creation center for tourists, horseback riders, hikers and mountain climbers. The Parks Canada Natural History Museum here displays specimens of wildlife native to the park. Indian lore and customs are shown in dioramas at the Luxton Museum, built to resemble a fur-trade post. Annual events include the summer-long Festival of the Arts.

The 230-kilometre Icefields Parkway, one of the world's great highways, runs between Lake Louise and Jasper townsite. Following in turn the Bow, Mistaya, North Saskatchewan, Sunwapta and Athabasca rivers, and crossing the Bow and Sunwapta passes, the route presents a panorama of peaks, glaciers, waterfalls and canyons.

Adjoining Banff National Park at the Columbia Icefield, **Jasper National Park (24, C-1)** sweeps northwest along the Continental Divide. The most spectacular gateway is Sunwapta Pass on the Icefields Parkway, where a flower-carpeted meadow provides a view of 3,491-metre Mount Athabasca. At Summit Viewpoint, forested ridges frame the hanging glaciers of Mount Kitchener (3,505 metres) and the Stutfield Glacier. The breathtaking scenery is often enhanced by the sight of wildlife foraging beside the road.

Edmonton (23, F-5), Alberta's capital and Canada's most northerly major city, is a booming metropolis astride the North Saskatchewan River. During Klondike Days in July, the city relives the gold fever of '98 as

stores don false fronts, pubs become saloons, and Edmontonians stroll around in their Klondike finery.

Several other local attractions recall the city's frontier past. Fort Edmonton Park has two small-town streets re-creating the city of 1905 and 1920, and a reconstruction of Fort Edmonton. The first structure built outside the fort, the George McDougall House (1872), has been restored and is now a museum. At Canada's Aviation Hall of Fame, visitors are transported into the past by means of aeronautical artifacts, model aircraft and dioramas. Western art and artifacts are exhibited in four galleries at the Provincial Museum and Archives.

Polar Park, east of Edmonton, has been described as a zoo in reverse—where the visitors are fenced in and the more than 4,000 animals roam free. An even larger nature preserve is **Elk Island National Park (23, F-5)**, named for the large wapiti (elk) herds that once roamed the area. Set in the Beaver Hills, Elk Island has North America's smallest and largest land mammals—the pygmy shrew and the plains bison.

A showcase for Alberta's rich Ukrainian heritage is the Pysanka Festival, held in early July at **Vegreville (23, G-5)**. A striking attraction of this community is its giant pysanka (Easter egg), built to honor the early pioneers.

Rolling foothills, a patchwork of forests and plains and some of the world's richest farmland are found in northern Alberta. Here the broad Peace River has cut the Alberta prairie to a depth of 300 metres in places and forms a valley 3 to 11 kilometres wide. Sweeping vistas of the valley can be seen along the Shaftesbury Trail (Secondary Highway 684), a scenic road that parallels the river southwest of the town of **Peace River (22, C-3)**.

From Grimshaw, the Mackenzie Highway reaches north across 940 kilometres of prairie and forest to Fort Simpson, N.W.T. At Hay River, a secondary highway turns east to Fort Smith—gateway to Wood Buffalo National Park. One of the world's largest parks, it protects the world's only nesting ground of the whooping crane.

ly climbs against the horizon, rimmed 100 kilometres to the west by the Rocky Mountains. But the white-collar city reverts to jeans and Stetsons each July during the Calgary Stampede, ten days of street dances, parades, rodeos and fireworks.

Images of the Old West can be found year-round at the Glenbow Museum with its extensive collection of historic documents, movies, diaries, paintings and artifacts. In Prairie Park are the wooden foundations of Fort Calgary (1875) and a log cabin (c. 1880) that is Calgary's oldest building on its original site. Heritage Park, a re-created pioneer community, has a 200-passenger stern-wheeler and a train pulled by a steam locomotive.

Past and present are combined in Centen-

Alberta's Valley of the Dinosaurs

The Red Deer Badlands, millions of years ago the domain of the dinosaur, is a wild and wind-scoured expanse of hoodoos, bluffs and gullies between Red Deer and Brooks. Some of the most impressive badlands scenery—and one of the world's richest fossil beds—lies within Dinosaur Provincial Park. Within the multi-hued rock layers are the remains of plants, clams, snails, crocodiles, turtles, fish—and dinosaurs. There could be the bones of as many as 400 dinosaurs buried in the soft, eroding rock here. To date, some 30 species have been identified, from the Albertosaurus, a smaller version of the Tyrannosaurus, to the duckbilled Edmontosaurus, a four-ton creature with a body the size of a bus. These immense beasts thrived on lush, subtropical vegetation. To prevent damage to the fossils, a restricted zone has been created. There are bus tours and conducted hikes into this zone in summer. Also in the preserve is Prehistoric Park, where life-size dinosaur models are displayed.

The Drumheller and District Museum exhibits the skeleton of an Ice Age bison which has embedded in its skull a rounded stone believed to be the first evidence of man in Alberta.

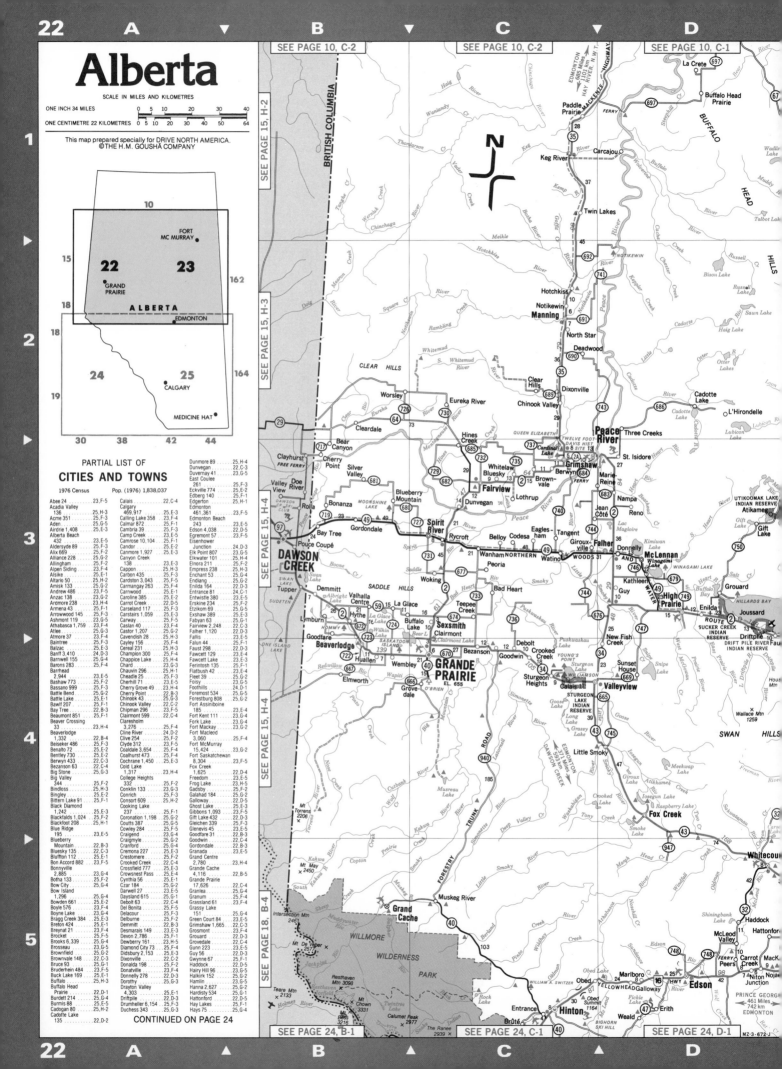

Alberta

SCALE IN MILES AND KILOMETRES

ONE INCH 34 MILES

ONE CENTIMETRE 22 KILOMETRES

0 5 10 20 30 40 (miles)
0 5 10 20 30 40 50 64 (kilometres)

This map prepared specially for DRIVE NORTH AMERICA.
© THE H.M. GOUSHA COMPANY

PARTIAL LIST OF CITIES AND TOWNS

1976 Census   Pop. (1976) 1,838,037

Place	Ref
Abee 24	23,F-5
Acadia Valley 136	25,H-3
Acme 351	25,F-3
Aden	25,G-5
Airdrie 1,408	25,E-3
Alberta Beach 432	23,E-5
Aldersyde 89	25,F-3
Alix 669	25,F-2
Allingham	25,F-2
Alpen Siding	25,E-1
Alsike	25,E-2
Altario 50	25,H-2
Amisk 133	25,G-2
Andrew 486	23,F-5
Aromore 238	23,H-4
Armena 43	25,F-1
Arrowwood 145	25,F-3
Ashmont 119	23,F-4
Athabasca 1,759	23,F-4
Atlee	25,G-3
Atmore 37	23,F-4
Baintree	25,F-3
Balzac	25,E-3
Banff 3,410	24,D-3
Barnwell 155	25,G-4
Barons 283	25,F-4
Barrhead 2,944	23,E-5
Bashaw 773	25,F-2
Bassano 999	25,F-3
Battle Bend	25,G-2
Battle Lake	25,E-1
Bawlf 207	25,F-2
Bay Tree	22,B-3
Beaumont 851	25,F-1
Beaver Crossing 33	23,H-4
Beaverlodge 1,332	22,B-4
Beiseker 486	25,F-3
Benalto 72	25,E-2
Bentley 730	25,E-2
Berwyn 433	22,C-3
Bezanson 63	22,C-4
Big Stone	25,G-3
Big Valley 344	25,F-2
Bindloss	25,H-3
Bingley	25,E-2
Bittern Lake 91	25,F-1
Black Diamond 1,242	25,E-3
Blackfalds 1,024	25,F-2
Blackfoot 208	25,H-1
Blue Ridge 195	23,E-5
Blueberry Mountain	22,B-3
Bluesky 135	22,C-3
Bluffton 112	25,E-1
Bon Accord 822	23,F-5
Bonnyville 2,885	23,G-4
Botha 133	25,F-2
Bow City	25,G-4
Bow Island 1,296	25,G-4
Bowden 661	25,E-2
Boyle 576	23,F-4
Boyne Lake	23,G-4
Bragg Creek 384	25,E-3
Breton 424	25,E-1
Breynat 21	23,F-4
Brocket	25,F-5
Brosseau	23,G-5
Brownfield	25,G-2
Brownvale 148	22,C-3
Bruce 93	25,G-1
Bruderheim 484	23,F-5
Buck Lake 169	25,E-1
Buffalo	25,H-3
Buffalo Head Prairie	22,D-1
Burdett 214	25,G-4
Burmis 88	25,E-5
Cadogan 80	25,H-2
Cadotte Lake 135	22,D-2
Calais	22,C-4
Calgary 469,917	25,E-3
Calling Lake 358	23,F-4
Calmar 872	25,F-1
Cambria 39	25,F-3
Camp Creek	23,E-5
Camrose 10,104	25,F-1
Candor	24,D-3
Canmore 1,927	25,E-3
Canyon Creek 138	23,E-3
Cappon	25,H-3
Carbon 435	25,F-3
Cardston 3,043	25,F-5
Carmangay 263	25,F-4
Carnwood	25,E-1
Caroline 385	25,E-1
Carrot Creek	22,D-5
Carseland 117	25,F-3
Carstairs 1,059	25,E-3
Carway	25,F-5
Caslan 40	23,F-4
Castor 1,207	25,G-2
Cavendish 28	25,H-3
Cayley 156	25,F-3
Cereal 231	25,H-3
Champion 300	25,F-4
Chappice Lake	25,H-4
Chard	23,G-3
Chauvin 296	25,H-1
Cheadle 25	25,F-3
Cherhill 71	23,E-5
Cherry Grove 49	23,H-4
Cherry Point	22,B-3
Chinook 43	25,G-3
Chinook Valley	22,C-2
Chipman 296	23,F-5
Clairmont 599	22,C-4
Claresholm 3,276	25,F-4
Cline River	24,D-2
Clive 254	25,F-2
Clyde 312	23,F-5
Coaldale 3,654	25,F-4
Coalhurst 473	25,F-4
Cochrane 1,450	25,E-3
Cold Lake 1,317	23,H-4
College Heights 332	25,F-2
Conklin 133	23,G-3
Conrich	25,F-3
Consort 609	25,H-2
Cooking Lake 237	25,F-1
Coronation 1,198	25,G-2
Coutts 387	25,G-5
Cowley 284	25,F-5
Craigend	23,G-4
Craigmyle	25,G-3
Cranford	25,G-4
Cremona 227	25,E-3
Crestomere	25,F-2
Crooked Creek	22,C-4
Crossfield 777	25,E-3
Crowsnest Pass	25,E-5
Cynthia 56	25,E-1
Czar 184	25,G-2
Darwell 27	23,E-5
Daysland 615	25,G-1
Debolt 63	22,C-4
Del Bonita	25,F-5
Delacour	25,F-3
Delburne 664	25,F-2
Demmitt	22,B-3
Desmarais 149	23,E-3
Devon 2,786	25,F-1
Dewberry 161	23,H-5
Diamond City 73	25,F-4
Didsbury 2,153	25,E-3
Dixonville	22,C-2
Donalda 198	25,F-2
Donatville	23,F-5
Donnelly 278	22,D-3
Dorothy	25,G-3
Drayton Valley 4,303	25,E-1
Driftpile	23,E-3
Drumheller 6,154	25,F-3
Duchess 343	25,G-3
Dunmore 89	25,H-4
Dunvegan	22,C-3
Duvernay 41	23,G-5
East Coulee 261	25,F-3
Eckville 774	25,E-2
Edberg 140	25,F-1
Edgerton	25,H-1
Edmonton 461,361	23,F-5
Edson 4,038	22,D-5
Egremont 57	23,F-5
Eisenhower Junction	24,D-3
Elk Point 807	23,G-5
Elkwater 101	25,H-4
Elnora 211	25,F-2
Empress 238	25,H-3
Enchant 53	25,G-4
Endiang	25,G-2
Enilda 164	22,D-3
Entrance 81	24,C-1
Entwistle 380	23,E-5
Erskine 234	25,F-2
Etzikom 69	25,G-5
Exshaw 389	25,E-3
Fabyan 63	25,G-1
Fairview 2,248	22,C-3
Falher 1,120	22,D-3
Fallis	23,E-5
Falun 44	25,F-1
Faust 298	22,D-3
Fawcett 129	23,E-4
Fawcett Lake	23,E-3
Ferintosh 135	25,F-1
Flatbush 42	23,E-4
Fleet 39	25,G-2
Foisy	23,G-5
Foothills	24,D-1
Foremost 534	25,G-5
Forestburg 808	25,G-2
Fort Assiniboine 185	23,E-4
Fort Kent 111	23,G-4
Fork Lake	23,G-4
Fort Mackay	23,G-2
Fort Macleod 3,060	25,F-4
Fort McMurray 15,424	23,G-2
Fort Saskatchewan 8,304	23,F-5
Fox Creek 1,625	22,D-4
Freedom	23,E-5
Frog Lake	23,H-5
Gadsby	25,F-2
Galahad 184	25,G-2
Galloway	22,D-5
Ghost Lake	25,E-3
Gibbons 1,093	23,F-5
Gift Lake 432	22,D-3
Gleichen 339	25,F-3
Glenevis 45	23,E-5
Goodfare 31	22,B-3
Goodwin	22,C-4
Gordondale	22,B-3
Granada	23,E-5
Grand Centre 2,780	23,H-4
Grande Cache 4,116	22,B-5
Grande Prairie 17,626	22,C-4
Granlea	25,G-4
Granum	25,F-4
Grassland 61	23,F-4
Grassy Lake 151	25,G-4
Green Court 84	23,E-5
Grimshaw 1,665	22,C-3
Grosmont	23,F-4
Grouard	22,D-3
Grovedale	22,C-4
Gunn 223	23,E-5
Guy 56	22,D-3
Gwynne 67	25,F-1
Haddock	22,D-5
Hairy Hill 96	23,G-5
Halkirk 152	25,F-2
Hamlin	23,G-5
Hanna 2,627	25,G-2
Hardisty 534	25,G-1
Hattonford	23,E-5
Hay Lakes 435	25,F-1
Hays 75	25,G-4

CONTINUED ON PAGE 24

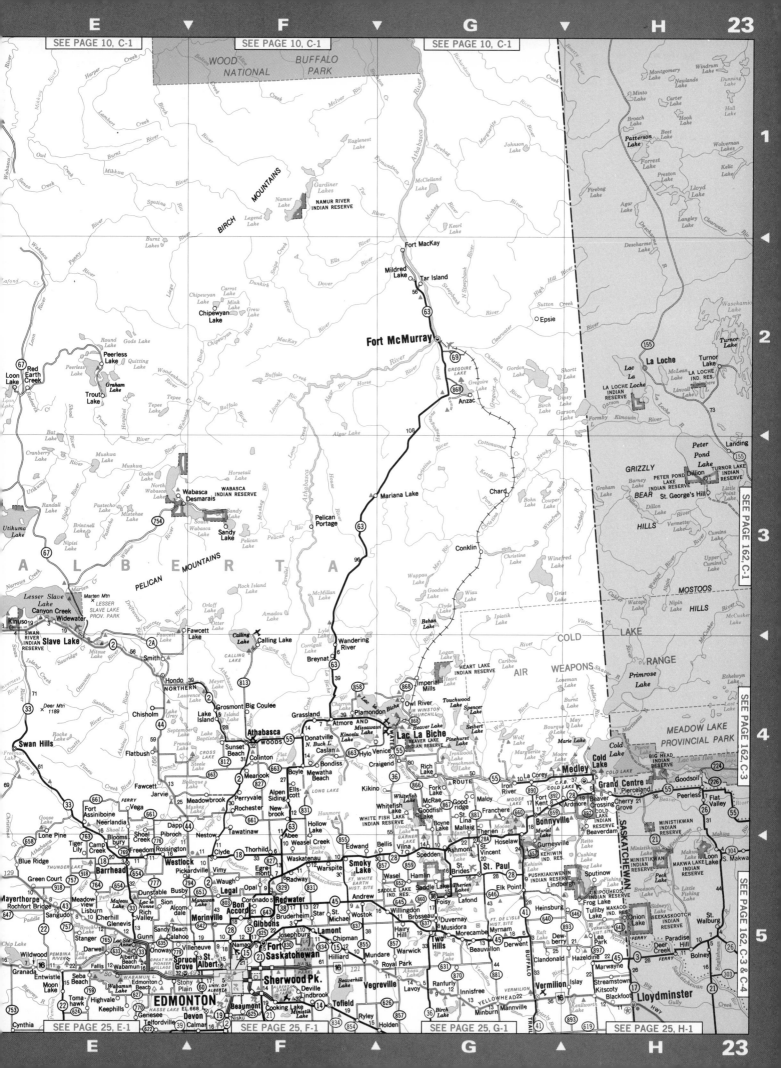

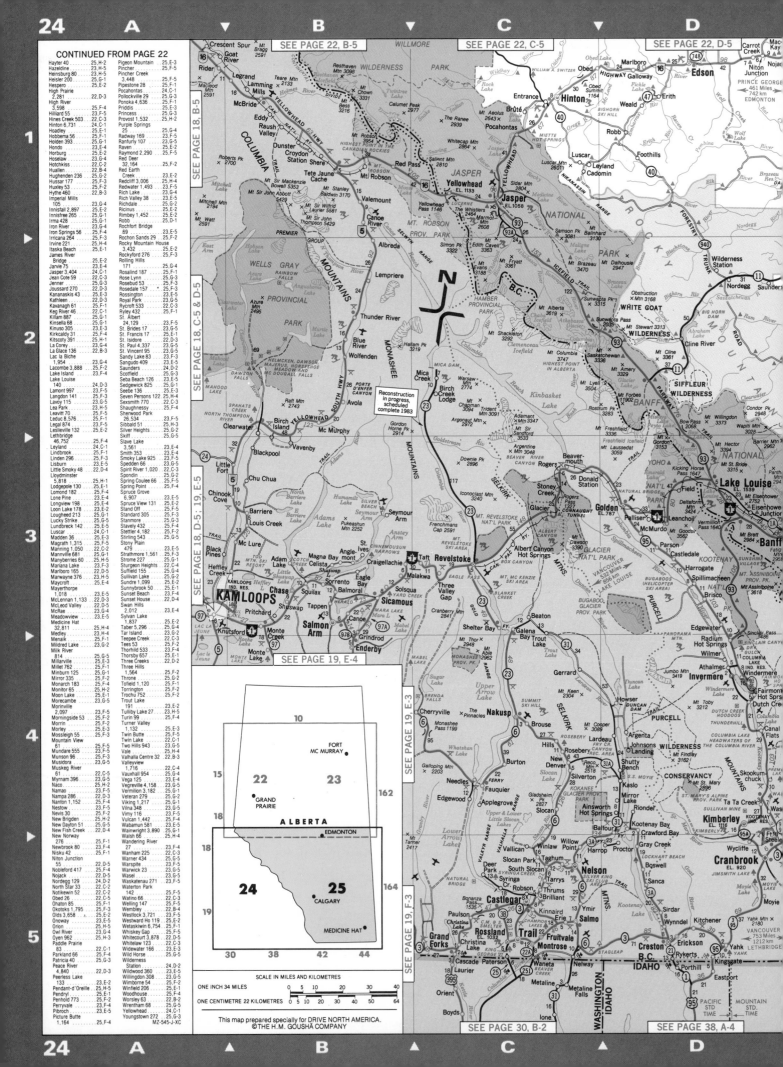

Rain Forests and Realms of Ice in the Historic Northwest

Washington/Oregon

Washington is a divided state, cleaved from north to south by the Cascade Mountains. These volcanic peaks—occasionally ribboned by glaciers—have affected the Evergreen State's climate to a splendid end. For on both sides of the range, Washington presents a superb showcase of natural wonders.

Where Washington thrusts a rocky thumb into the Pacific lies 1,400-square-mile **Olympic National Park (28, C-4).** Here are tall mountains overrun with glaciers, a 50-mile stretch of some of the wildest beach in the country, and a rain forest as green and dim as an Amazon jungle, dripping beneath the heaviest rainfall in North America. State Highway 112 runs along the north shore of the Olympic Peninsula between **Port Angeles (28, C-4)** and **Neah Bay (28, B-5),** passing

Salmon is prepared in the traditional way (right) at Tillicum Village near Seattle. Sunlight filters dimly through the Hall of Mosses (below) in Olympic National Park.

Seattle's Space Needle and burgeoning skyline.

The Mountain that Blew its Top

It was in May 1980 that Washington's Mount St. Helens erupted unexpectedly, blasting away almost a cubic mile of its conical summit and taking 60 lives. Slowly, life is returning to the landscape of gray ash and debris. Such plants as fireweed, lupine, bracken fern and avalanche lily have stabilized the barren slopes. Foresters are planting seedlings to replace the timber flattened by the blast. Birds, insects and small animals are finding new homes amid the devastation.

At an information center near **Toledo (29, F-3),** visitors will find maps indicating which roads to take to view the ravaged land. One of the best spots to observe the steaming crater—from a distance—is off Highway 12 near **Morton (29, F-2).** Here is a safe view of the mountain that gave North Americans of this century a first-hand demonstration of volcanic destruction and rebirth.

26

Agate and Crescent beaches and climbing to several high overlooks.

There are loftier peaks in the United States, but none that so dominates its landscape as **Mount Rainier (28, E-2)**. A gleaming ice cap gives the great mountain its shining summit, visible from 100 miles. No mountain in the United States (excluding Alaska) is topped with more glaciers—a 40-square-mile mass of ice and snow that conceals all but Rainier's most rugged peaks and ridges. More than 300 miles of trails lace surrounding Mount Rainier National Park.

The ice-covered volcanic cone of **Mount Baker (28, B-2)** rises 10,778 feet. Like Mount Rainier and Mount Hood, it is a landmark for hundreds of miles around. The jagged profile of Liberty Bell Mountain, at the eastern entrance of nearby **North Cascades National Park (28, B-1)**, is typical of the multitude of snowy peaks in this wilderness of magnificent alpine scenery.

When explorer David Thompson reached the mouth of the Columbia River in 1811, its waters were free-flowing and untamed—second only to the Mississippi in volume. Today the river has been harnessed by the 550-foot-high **Grand Coulee Dam (30, C-3)**, the largest concrete dam in the world. Lapping against the flanks of the dam is Lake Franklin D. Roosevelt, a summer playground stretching 151 miles to the Canadian border.

Throughout Washington are reminders of a time when the state's wild beauty was the domain of Indian tribes and, later, of fur traders and pioneers. In **Tacoma (28, D-3)**, human figures, a grizzly bear, a killer whale and a huge eagle are carved into the 105-foot-high Tacoma totem pole, thought to be the tallest in the United States. The Museum of Native American Culture, in **Spokane (30, D-1)**, features the most extensive collection of Indian art and artifacts in the Northwest.

Fort Walla Walla Park (31, F-2), a 96-acre park and museum complex, occupies the site of the original fort, established in 1856. Several original and restored buildings, and a mid-19th-century pioneer village—which includes a schoolhouse, a country store, a pioneer cabin and a smithy—re-create the past here. Visitors to **San Juan Island National Historical Park (28, B-3)**, accessible by ferry from Anacortes, can view restored British and American buildings occupied during the comic-opera 1859 Pig War—sparked when a "British" pig uprooted an "American" potato patch. The 17-room Meeker Mansion in **Puyallup (29, E-2)** is the former home of the "Hop King of the World." Constructed by Ezra Meeker, an Iowa pioneer who in 1852 crossed the plains with his family on the Oregon Trail, the building boasts six tiled Victorian fireplaces and a widow's walk.

Visitors to **Seattle (28, D-3)** can trace the city's first hundred years at the Museum of History and Industry, step underground to storefronts and interiors spared by the fire of 1889, or browse through some 300 vegetable, fruit, fish and flower stalls at three-block-long Pike Place Market.

The Columbia River slices through Oregon and Washington. Sometimes savage, sometimes tamed by huge dams, the river is nowhere more spectacular than where it surges through 60-mile-long Columbia Gorge. An expressway parallels the gorge, but the old scenic highway offers a more leisurely trip. It climbs to Crown Point, a rocky promontory 725 feet above the river, and skirts 620-foot-high Multnomah Falls, Oregon's highest waterfall. Also in the gorge is 1,450-foot-wide Bonneville Dam, which has created a lake 48 miles long. Near the dam, salmon vault a series of fish ladders in a battle against the current.

Settled in 1844, **Portland (32, B-3)** has grown to be Oregon's largest city. It is a place of contrasts, where snow-covered mountains rise to the north and east—with 11,235-foot Mount Hood as the focal point—but the temperate effects of the Japanese Current produce a mild climate. Roses and rhododendrons grow here in profusion (a summer rose festival has been held since 1909); the city is also an educational, cultural and outdoor recreation center.

Oregon City (32, C-3), nearby, was once an important way station on the storied Oregon Trail. The Dr. John McLoughlin House is a stately throwback to that fur-trading era. As a chief factor for the Hudson's Bay Company, McLaughlin oversaw its western territory for 22 years. His house, built in 1845, is a showplace of period furniture.

Other echoes of early Oregon history can be heard at **Astoria (32, A-4)**. Explorers Lewis and Clark, exhausted after an 18-month overland journey, wintered here in 1805–06. Fort Clatsop, their stronghold, has been re-created. South from Astoria, the 400-mile Oregon Coast unfolds—a stretch of wave-sculpted headlands, rocky reefs and sandy beaches backed by 4,000-foot mountains and paralleled by Highway 101. This scenic drive skirts 72 state parks and more than 20 splendid beaches along the route—and the Old Yaquina Lighthouse, now a museum and one of the oldest lighthouses (1871) on the North Pacific coast. North of **Florence (33, E-4)** are the Sea Lion Caves, a favorite haunt of these playful creatures and of the cormorants that wheel and dive overhead. Visitors to the Dolly Wares Doll Museum nearby can savor remembrances of childhood through its collection of some 2,500 rare and unusual dolls. East of Highway 101, at **Corvallis (32, D-3)**, the Horner Museum on the campus of Oregon State University displays Victorian antiques, Indian basketry and musical instruments dating from 1870 to 1930.

Below Florence, stark headlands soften into a 40-mile stretch of sand dunes. The dunes extend three miles inland and reach heights of 90 feet, often engulfing trees in their path. **Cape Arago (33, F-5)** marks the start of the most rugged stretch of the Oregon Coast. The weatherbeaten terrain continues to **Cape Blanco (33, G-5)**, a flat, grassy terrace jutting two miles seaward, Oregon's most westerly point.

In the foothills of the Siskiyou Mountains is **Jacksonville (33, H-3)**, born of a nearby gold boom in the 1850s. Visitors can still pan for gold in the area, or take a stroll into the past—passing 19th-century white frame churches, trim clapboard and brick homes and the Odd Fellows Hall, built in 1855. The hall contains a structural curiosity: a foot of earth between roof and ceiling that was intended to prevent damage from Indian fire arrows.

Northeast of Jacksonville lies **Crater Lake (33, G-2)**, one of the world's scenic jewels. "The vast loneliness of the place, the sparkling water so many feet below, the beautiful view . . . are too great to be described," wrote prospector John Wesley Hillman in 1853. "One must see them to appreciate them." Today, thousands of visitors do just that. Many take the 33-mile drive around the rim of the lake, formed by the collapsed cone of an extinct volcano. The lake shimmers in the sunlight—eerie, often incandescent in its blueness, its waters broken only by Phantom Ship and Wizard islands.

A breaker erupts amidst creamy surf off Oregon's Cape Kiwanda.

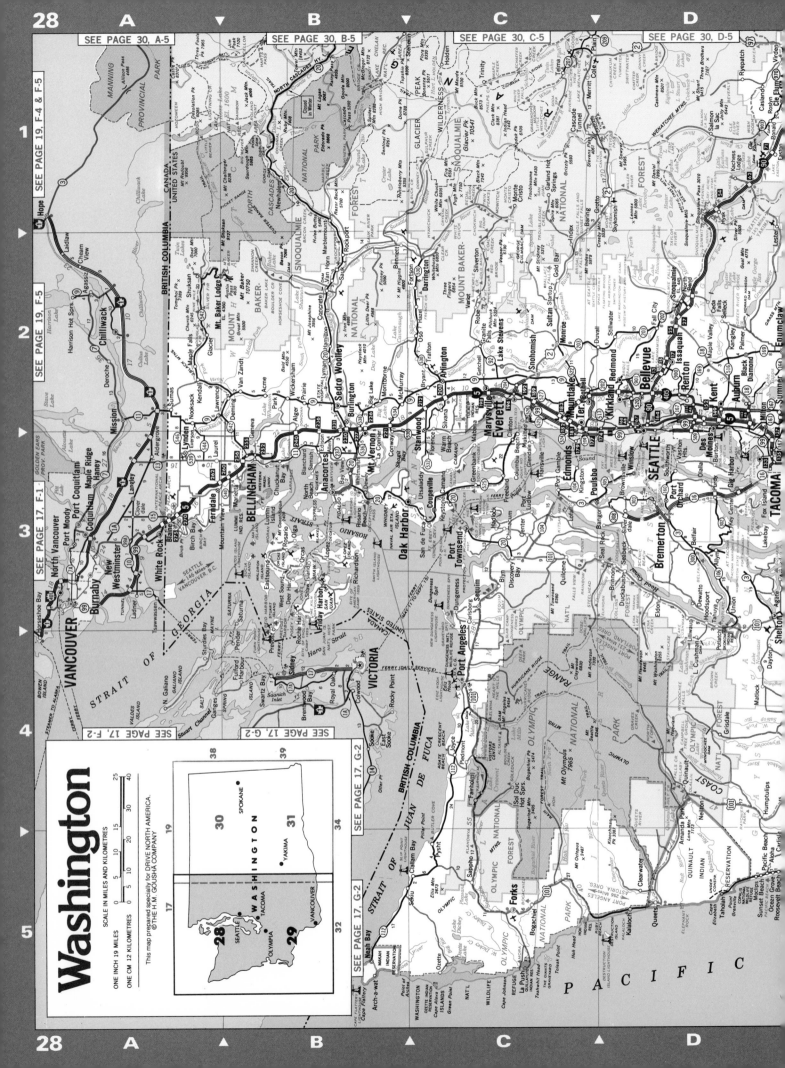

SEE PAGE 30, A-5   SEE PAGE 30, B-5   SEE PAGE 30, C-5   SEE PAGE 30, D-5

SEE PAGE 19, F-4 & F-5
SEE PAGE 19, F-5
SEE PAGE 17, F-1
SEE PAGE 17, F-2
SEE PAGE 17, G-2
SEE PAGE 17, G-2

Washington

SCALE IN MILES AND KILOMETRES

ONE INCH 19 MILES
ONE CM 12 KILOMETRES

This map prepared specially for DRIVE NORTH AMERICA.
©THE H.M. GOUSHA COMPANY

PACIFIC

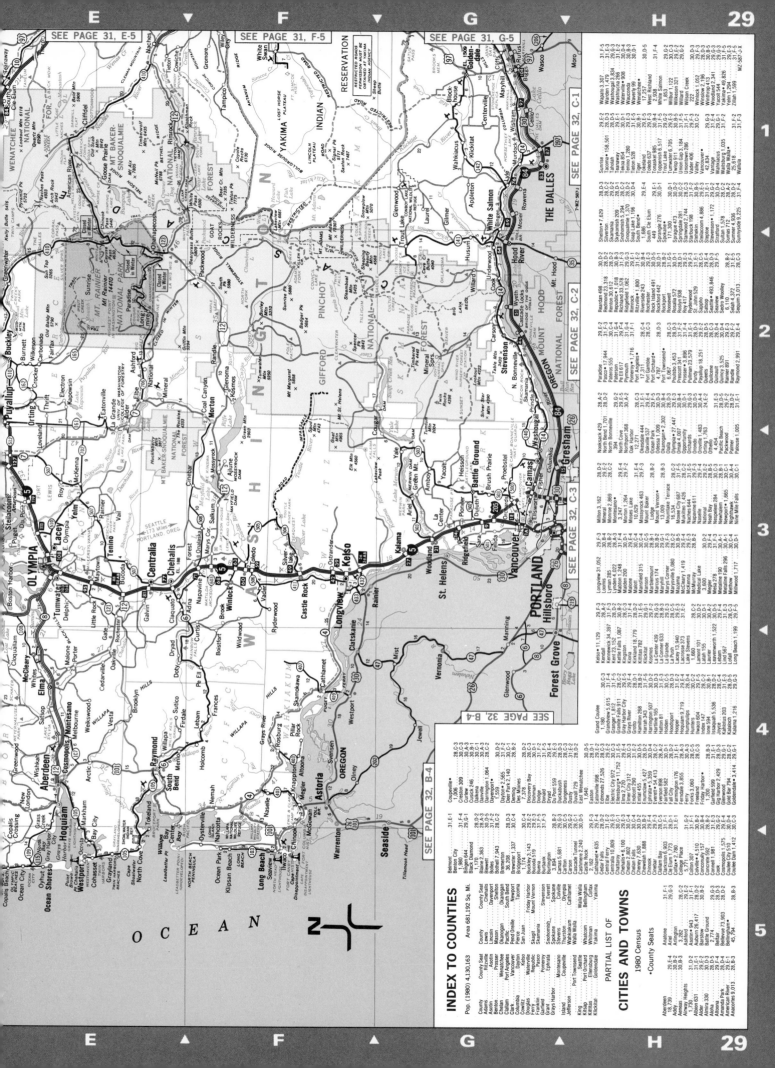

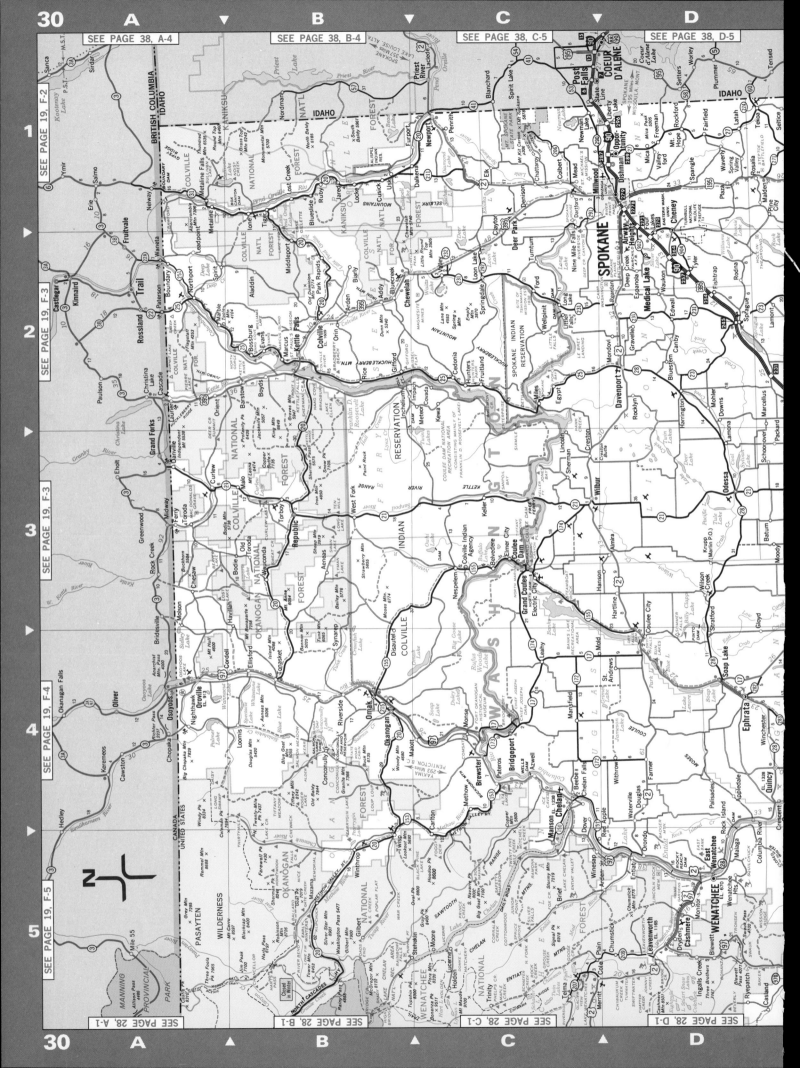

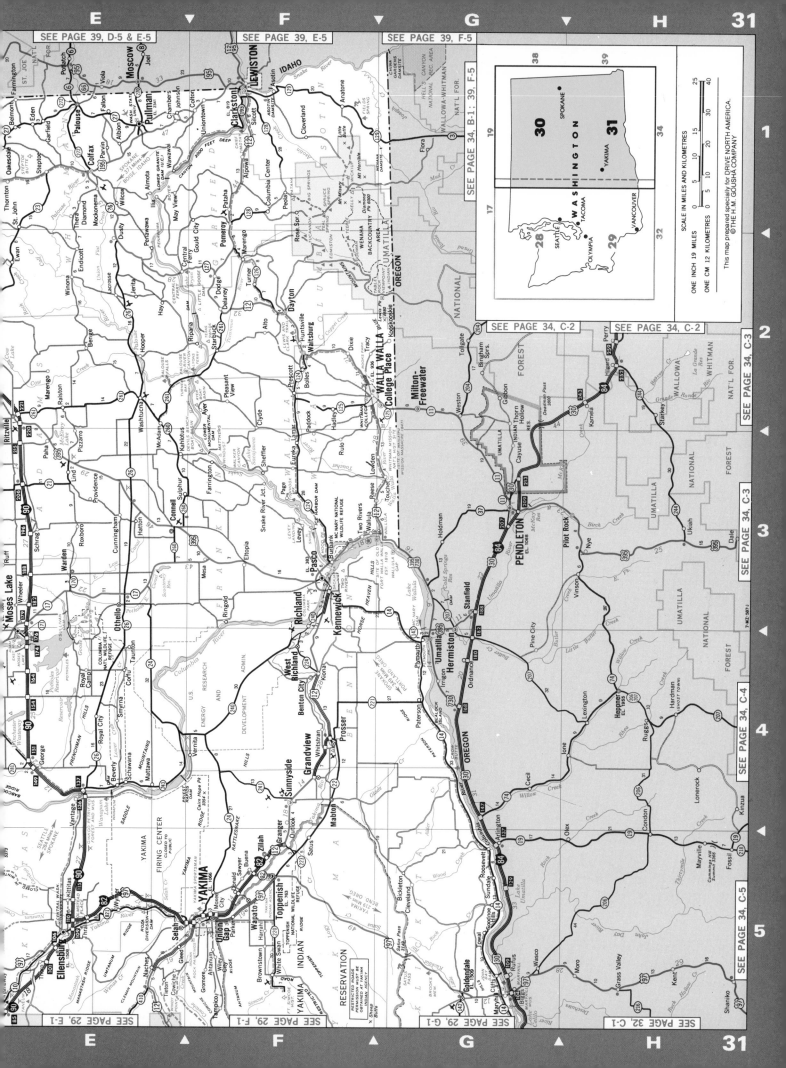

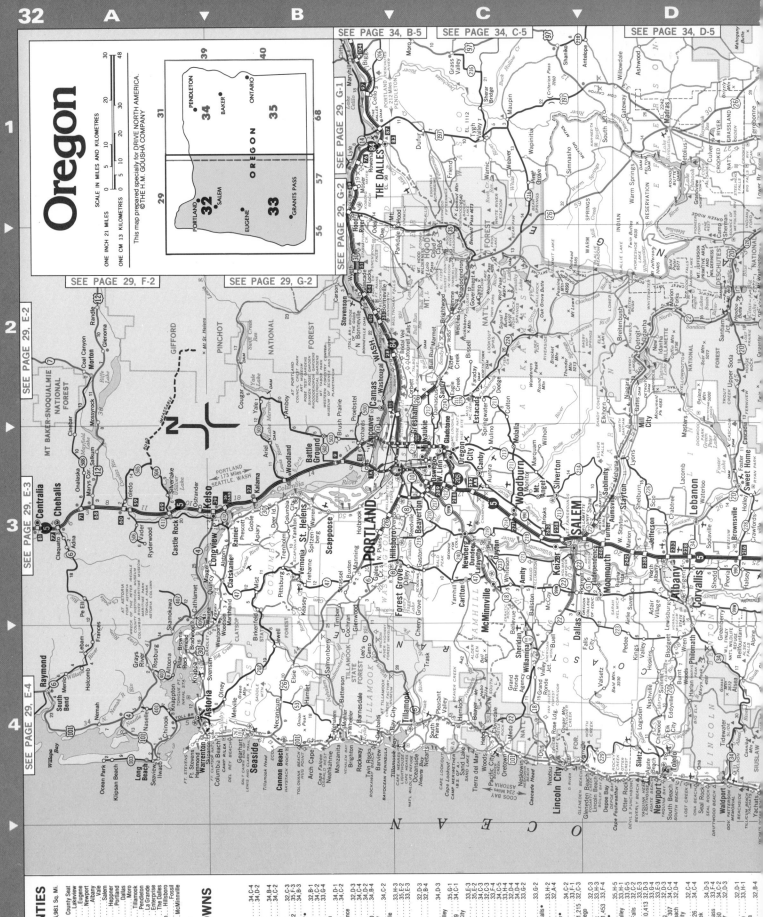

Oregon

SCALE IN MILES AND KILOMETRES

This map prepared specially for DRIVE NORTH AMERICA.
©THE H.M. GOUSHA COMPANY

ONE INCH 21 MILES
ONE CM 13 KILOMETRES

SEE PAGE 34, B-5 SEE PAGE 34, C-5 SEE PAGE 34, D-5

SEE PAGE 29, F-2 SEE PAGE 29, G-2

SEE PAGE 29, G-1
SEE PAGE 29, G-2

SEE PAGE 29, E-2
SEE PAGE 29, E-3
SEE PAGE 29, E-4

INDEX TO COUNTIES

Pop. (1980) 2,632,663   Area 96,981 Sq. Mi.

County	County Seat	County	County Seat
Baker	Baker	Lake	Lakeview
Benton	Corvallis	Lane	Eugene
Clackamas	Oregon City	Lincoln	Newport
Clatsop	Astoria	Linn	Albany
Columbia	St. Helens	Malheur	Vale
Coos	Coquille	Marion	Salem
Crook	Prineville	Morrow	Heppner
Curry	Gold Beach	Multnomah	Portland
Deschutes	Bend	Polk	Dallas
Douglas	Roseburg	Sherman	Moro
Gilliam	Condon	Tillamook	Tillamook
Grant	Canyon City	Umatilla	Pendleton
Harney	Burns	Union	La Grande
Hood River	Hood River	Wallowa	Enterprise
Jackson	Medford	Wasco	The Dalles
Jefferson	Madras	Washington	Hillsboro
Josephine	Grants Pass	Yamhill	McMinnville
Klamath	Klamath Falls		

PARTIAL LIST OF CITIES AND TOWNS

1980 Census
•County Seats

Adams 240	Heppner•	34, C-4
Adrian 965	Herford	35, E-1
Agate Beach	Hermiston	34, D-2
Albany 26,546	Hilgard	33, E-1
Algoma	Hillsboro• 27,664	32, C-3
Alfalfa	Hines 1,632	35, G-3
Amity 1,092	Hood River• 4,329	34, B-5
Antelope 39	Hot Lake	34, D-3
Applegate	Hubbard	32, D-3
Arch Cape	Hugo	33, G-3
Arlington 521	Huntington 539	34, D-1
Ashland 14,943	Imbler 292	34, A-4
Astoria•	Independence 4,024	32, C-3
Athena 965	Ione 345	34, C-4
Aumsville 1,432	Ironside	34, D-4
Aurora 523	Island City 477	34, B-4
Azalea	Jacksonville 2,030	33, H-3
Baker•	Jamieson	35, F-1
Bandon 2,311	Jasper	33, E-2
Barview 986	Jefferson 1,702	32, C-3
Bay City 986	Jewell	32, C-3
Beaver	John Day 2,012	35, E-2
Beaverton 30,582	Jordan Valley 473	35, G-1
Bellevue	Joseph 999	34, C-1
Bend• 17,263	Junction City 3,320	33, E-2
Blodgett	Kamela	33, E-3
Bly	Keizer 22,868	32, C-3
Boardman	Kellogg	33, F-2
Bonanza 270	Kent	34, C-5
Brighton	Kerby	33, H-1
Brightwood	Kernville	32, D-2
Brogan	Kimberly	34, D-3
Brookings 3,384	Kirk	33, H-4
Brothers	Klamath Agency	33, H-4
Brownsville 3,579	Klamath Falls• 16,661	33, H-4
Burns• 3,579	Knappa	32, A-4
Burnt Woods	La Grande• 11,354	34, B-4
Butte Falls 252	Lafayette 1,215	32, C-3
Camas Valley	Lake Oswego 22,868	32, C-3
Cannon Beach 1,187	Lakecreek	33, H-3
Canyon City• 639	Lakeside 1,453	33, F-1
Carlton 1,302	Lakeview• 2,770	33, H-5
Carpenterville	Langlois	33, G-1
Cascade Locks 838	Latourell Falls	33, E-3
Cascadia	Leaburg	33, E-3
Celilo	Lebanon 10,413	32, D-3
Central Point 6,357	Leland	33, G-4
Charleston	Leona	33, H-4
Chemult	Lewisburg	32, D-4
Cheshire	Lincoln Beach	32, C-4
Chiloquin 778	Lincoln City 5,469	32, D-2
Chitwood	Lonerock 26	34, C-3
Coaledo	Long Creek 252	34, D-3
Columbia	Lookingglass	33, F-2
	Lostine 250	34, B-2
	Lyons 877	32, D-3
	Madras• 2,235	33, F-4
	Malin 539	33, H-1
	Manzanita 443	32, B-4

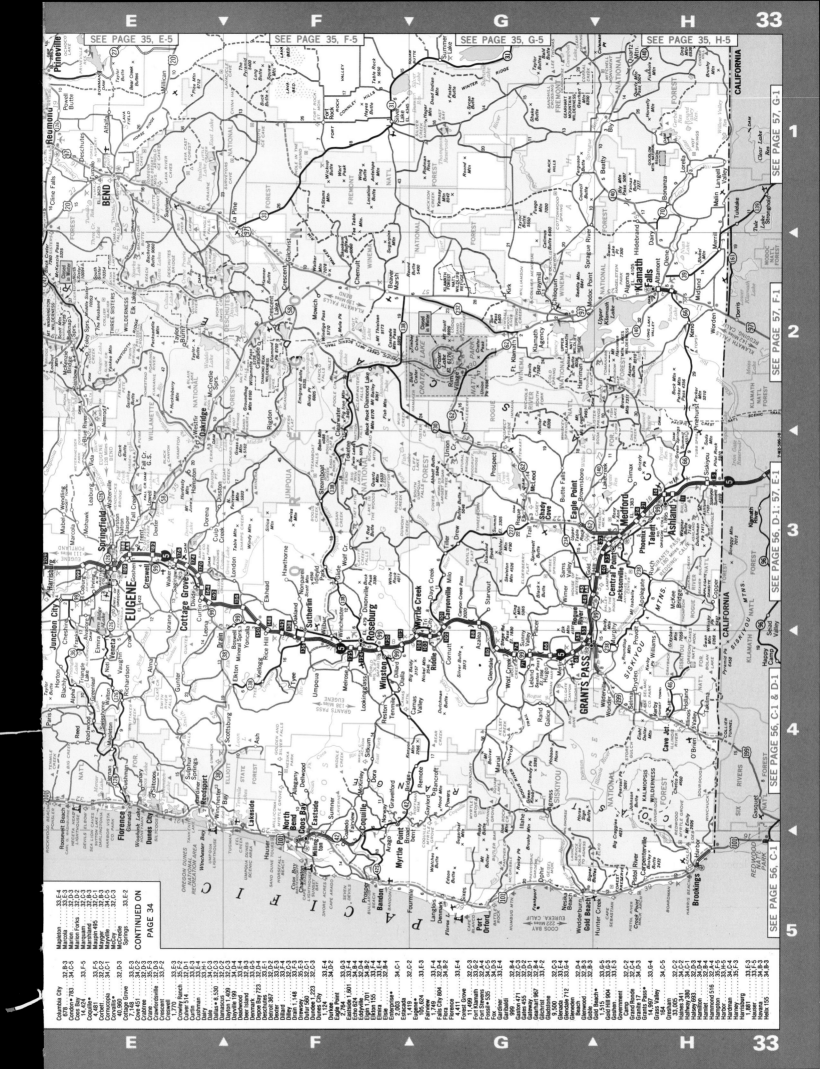

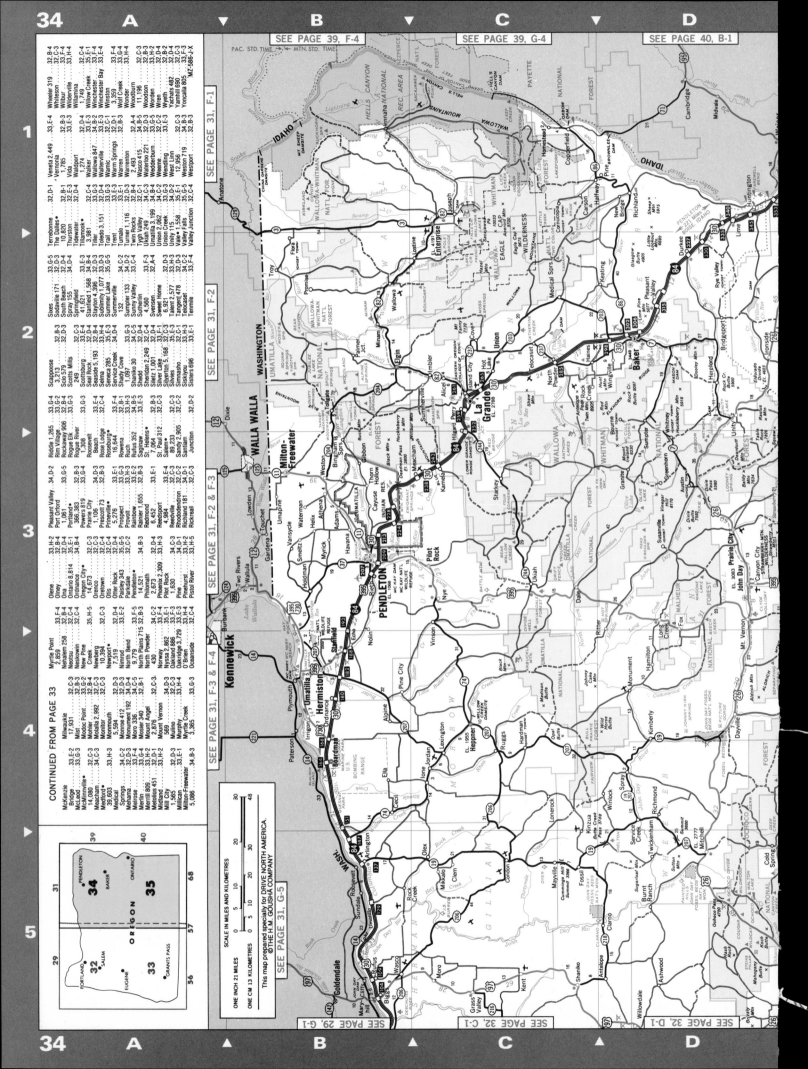

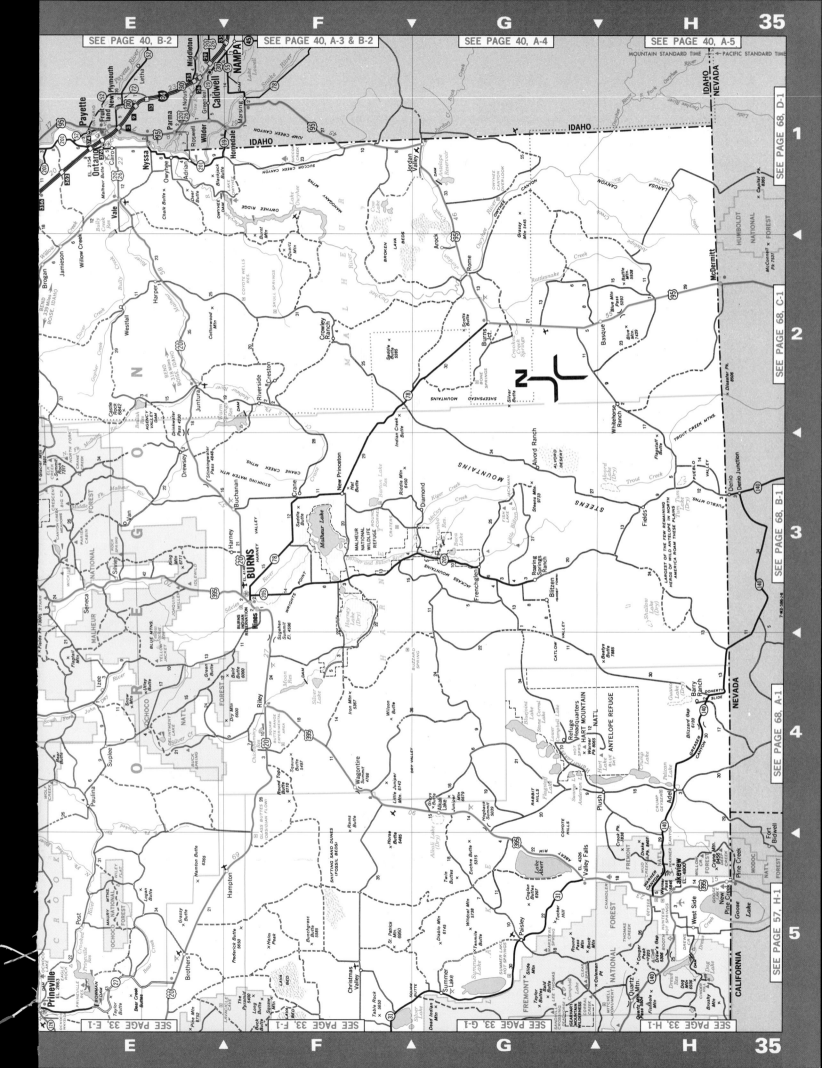

Beneath the 'Teeth of the World'— a Faithful Geyser, a Famous Battle

Idaho/Montana/Wyoming

When Abraham Lincoln in 1863 had to find a governor for newly created Idaho Territory, no one wanted the post. Indeed, some governors who were appointed never showed up. But today millions of visitors flock to the three states carved from that huge territory— Idaho, Montana and Wyoming—attracted by mountain grandeur, open spaces, and a wild-and-woolly cowboy-and-Indian past.

Idaho is the thirteenth largest state and one of the most thinly populated. In the southeast, bleak, black lava flows cover much of the landscape. **Craters of the Moon National Monument (41, E-3),** which contains a wide variety of these volcanic features, is perhaps most impressive in spring, when vivid wildflowers carry the bright banner of life onto the barren lava. More than 100 hot springs also percolate to the surface in this area.

In the remote and mountainous corner where Idaho meets Oregon lies **Hells Canyon of the Snake River (39, F-5),** a gash 75 miles long and with an average depth of 5,500 feet from rim to river. At its deepest, from the summit of He Devil Peak in the Seven Devils range to the bottom of the gorge is a dizzying 7,900 feet. White sturgeon, prehistoric survivors which may weigh 200 to 300 pounds, find refuge in the protected waters of the canyon.

Boise (40, B-2), the capital of Idaho and its largest city, is a modern industrial city today. But reminders of the city's gold-rush beginnings are evident in the abandoned mines and ghost towns in the 3-million-acre Boise National Forest nearby. The sleek, contemporary Boise Gallery of Art houses a permanent collection that includes American, European and Oriental paintings and sculpture, with special emphasis on the work of Idaho artists. Exhibits on early Indian and pioneer life, and a miniature railroad are featured in the Idaho State Historical Museum. The city's midsummer Basque Festival is a celebration by the largest assemblage of Basques outside of Spain and France. Basque immigrants came to the Boise area at the turn of the century to herd sheep.

The generally wild scenery of northern Idaho becomes tamer around the 108-mile shoreline of **Coeur d'Alene Lake (38, C-5).** Its hilly shores are deeply indented with bays, and a promenade at Coeur d'Alene offers water sports facilities. The name comes from French fur traders, who joked that hard-bargaining local Indians were so tough they had the "heart of an awl." To the north, **Lake Pend Oreille (38, B-4)** offers an ideal combination of scenic beauty and excellent fishing for Dolly Varden trout.

Montana was home to the area's most celebrated painter and sculptor—"cowboy artist" Charles Russell. The artist came west in the 1880s, to a land where "the big hills wear white robes and where the teeth of the world tear holes in the clouds." Such landscapes can still be seen, as can Russell's art—hon-

The colorful formations of Idaho's Salmon Falls Creek gorge climax with 40-foot-high Balanced Rock (above). A mountain goat kid (left) peers cautiously at visitors to Glacier National Park, Montana.

Cowboy Chronicler of the Real West

A two-story frame house in Great Falls, Montana, now the C. M. Russell Museum, was the home of renowned cowboy artist Charles M. Russell until his death in 1926. Next door is the studio where Russell did most of his work—a log cabin made from telephone poles. A stunning collection of his paintings and bronzes— including the watercolor *Attack on the Red River Carts (above)*—vividly recaptures the reality of the cowboy-and-Indian West.

ored at his original log cabin studio in **Great Falls (44, C-4)** and at an adjacent museum.

Just upstream along the Missouri River, **Ulm Pishkun State Monument (44, C-4)** provides a fine view of the country that was background for many Russell paintings. (Pishkun is Blackfeet for "buffalo jump"; it was here that Indian hunting parties drove whole herds of bison over cliffs.)

Bison, pronghorn antelope, elk, bighorn sheep, deer and other wildlife graze in abundance at the National Bison Range north of **Missoula (42, D-2).** The spectacular Mission

Mountains are a backdrop to glacial lakes that are habitat for thousands of ducks and geese. **Flathead Lake (42, C-2)** with its scenic east shore drive, is the largest natural freshwater lake in the western United States. Also in the area is Hungry Horse Dam, uppermost of a series of dams controlling the Columbia River system, which holds back a 34-mile-long reservoir along the Flathead Range.

Farther north are the mountains whose captivating beauty symbolizes Montana, the "mountainous land." **Glacier National Park (42, A-2)** adjoins Canada's Waterton Lakes

National Park. A half-dozen large lakes stretch from the park's lowland edges into the mountainous interior. Several hundred other lakes, large and small, line deep canyons and nestle in gigantic cups of lofty valleys, forests sloping up from their shores. On the eastern mountainsides are stands of Engelmann spruce and Douglas fir. The western slopes are heavily blanketed with red cedar, hemlock, larch and lodgepole pine. Grinnell, the largest of the park's 60 glaciers, covers 300 acres and contains ice 400 feet thick. Going-to-the-Sun Road offers a superb view of Triple Divide Peak, whose waters flow to three oceans: the Pacific by the Columbia River, the Arctic by Hudson Bay, the Gulf of Mexico via the Mississippi system. En route, motorists may glimpse mountain goats, bighorn sheep—even black and grizzly bears.

Montana's Crow Indian Reservation is the site of perhaps the most famous event in Plains Indian history. Here, in 1876, along the cottonwood-shaded banks of the Little Bighorn River, Lt. Col. George Armstrong Custer made his legendary last stand—a rout of some 260 soldiers of the 7th Cavalry by almost 3,000 Sioux and Cheyenne warriors. **Custer Battlefield National Monument (47, F-4)** commemorates the battle.

Wyoming shares three outstanding features with Montana: Bighorn Canyon, Beartooth Highway, and Yellowstone National Park. **Bighorn Canyon National Recreation Area (47, F-4)** is a 71-mile-long lake backed up by Yellowtail Dam in Montana. Above the water rise the precipitous walls of Bighorn Canyon—more than 1,000 feet high at Devil's Canyon Overlook. The surrounding Bighorn Mountains are dominated by 13,165-foot Cloud Peak and deeply incised by gorges cut by Tensleep and Shell creeks. Hiking trails wend through pastures past the mysterious Indian "Medicine Wheel," a stone circle 80 feet in diameter. Nearby **Sheridan (50, A-1)** is a business center for ranching and mining. Its multigabled Sheridan Inn is a national historical landmark. Constructed in 1893, the building was once partly owned by Buffalo Bill Cody. From its porch, the famous scout auditioned local cowboys, sharpshooters and rodeo riders for his Wild West show. The Bradford-Brinton Memorial Ranch, more typical of a Vermont village than a Wyoming ranch, displays Indian artifacts, antiques, wagons, buggies and saddles.

The Beartooth Highway leads to **Yellowstone National Park (48, B-4)** the world's first national park. Famous for such features as Mammoth Hot Springs, Grand Prismatic Spring, and Old Faithful Geyser, Yellowstone also has superb lakes and waterfalls, as well as canyons, mountains and standing petrified trees. The Grand Canyon of the Yellowstone is an awesome gorge of 1,000-foot walls dappled with shades of orange, brown, red, gray, pink and white. The Lower Falls drop more than 300 feet into a gorge where ospreys nest on rock pinnacles and several small geysers spout. Wildlife is plentiful—moose, bighorn sheep, elk, deer, bison, pronghorn antelope, and the park's notorious black and grizzly bears.

Grand Teton National Park (48, C-4) is much smaller than Yellowstone, but within its boundaries is a concentration of scenic grandeur unmatched on the continent. The Tetons themselves—dominated by 13,770-foot Grand Teton, its snow-streaked spire reflected in Jackson Lake—are almost overpowering in their splendor. Jackson Hole, lush with wildflower meadows, makes a perfect theater from which to view the mountains. Through the valley winds the Snake River, its tributaries dammed here and there into placid ponds by beavers. At the National Elk Refuge at **Jackson (48, C-5)**, visitors on horse-drawn sleds can travel amid thousands of elk from December through March.

Wyoming's four corners have several interesting features. Yellowstone holds down the northwest, while **Devils Tower (50, A-1)**, the first national monument (1906), dominates the northeast. The volcanic pillars which make up this western outpost of the Black Hills rise 865 feet above the pines and prairie. Black-tailed prairie dogs are the most common—and entertaining—wildlife attraction.

In the southwest corner is **Fossil Butte National Monument (49, F-5)**. Fish fossils dating back some 45 million years can be found here—the densest such concentration in the United States.

Wyoming visitors frequently confuse **Laramie (51, F-2)**, in southeast Wyoming, with **Fort Laramie National Historic Site (51, E-1)**. The town, the fort, and the mountains between them were named for an otherwise forgotten French fur trapper. Fort Laramie National Monument is a reconstruction of an important post on the Oregon Trail, later a hub of army operations in the Plains Indian Wars. There are remains of 22 structures, many of them restored. "Old Bedlam," a two-story building, contained post headquarters and officers' quarters.

The Wild West tradition is a major part of Wyoming's image as "the Cowboy State." The Buffalo Bill Historical Center in **Cody (48, A-3)** is one of the nation's most important repositories of this legacy. Mementos ranging from Buffalo Bill's clothing, guns and saddles to posters advertising his wild west show trace the career of this colorful character who played a unique role in the taming of the West. In the Whitney Gallery of Western Art, an outstanding collection of painting and sculpture documents the life and times of cowboys, Indians and pioneers.

A 145-foot-high gold-leaf dome caps the impressive seat of Wyoming government in **Cheyenne (51, G-1)**. On display in the rotunda are specimens of two of the state's most important wildlife species, the elk and the buffalo. "Big Boy," at 1,208,750 pounds the biggest steam locomotive ever built, rests proudly in the city park.

The first men to see Minerva Terrace at Yellowstone's Mammoth Hot Springs (above) described it as a mountain that was turning itself inside out. They were partly right: water seeping through rock rich in calcium carbonate has built up the colorful terraces.

The colors are struck at Wyoming's Fort Laramie (left). For 41 years the post safeguarded the Oregon Trail.

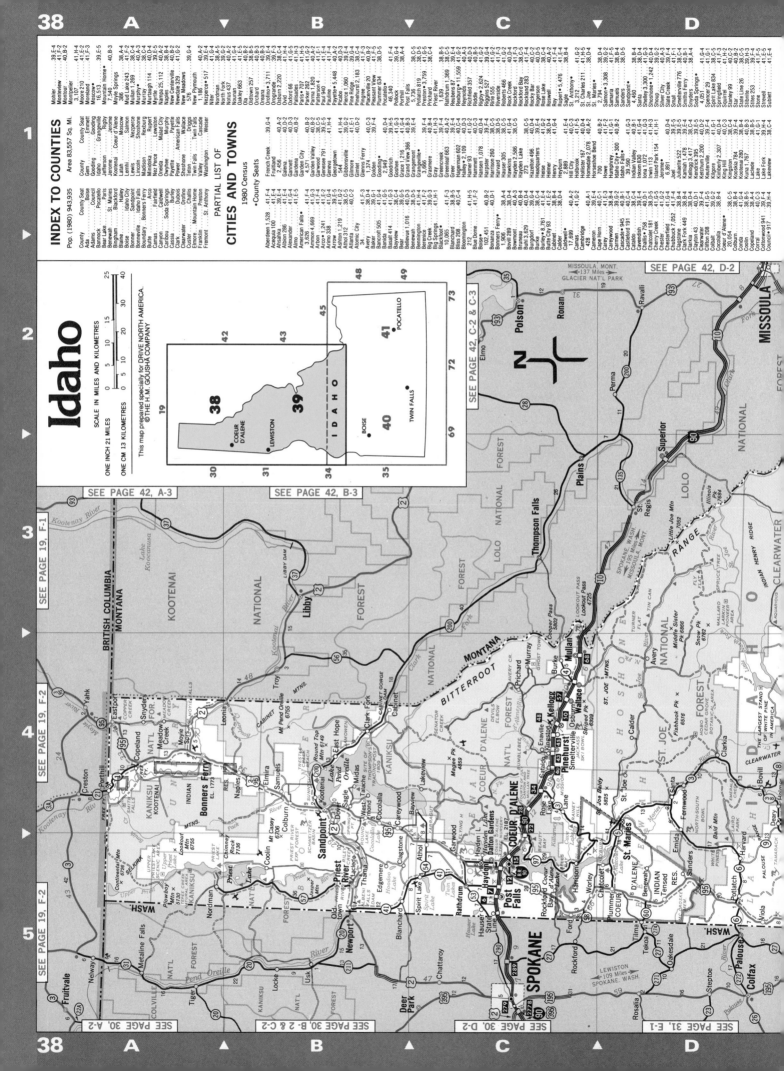

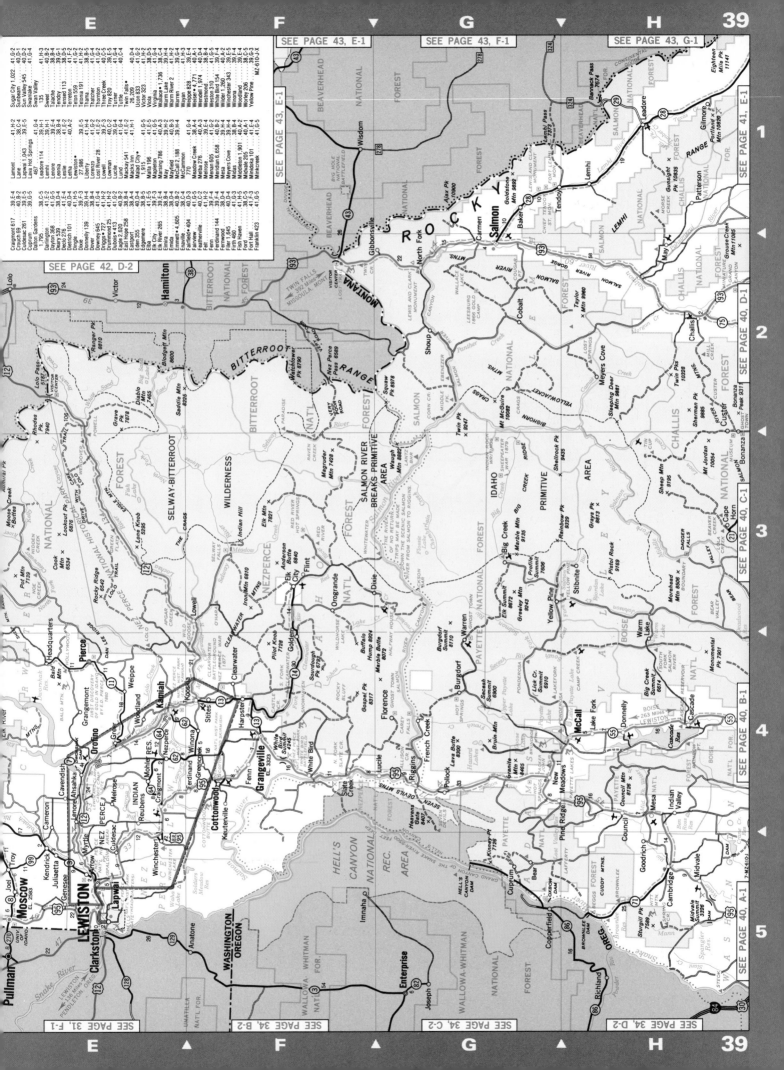

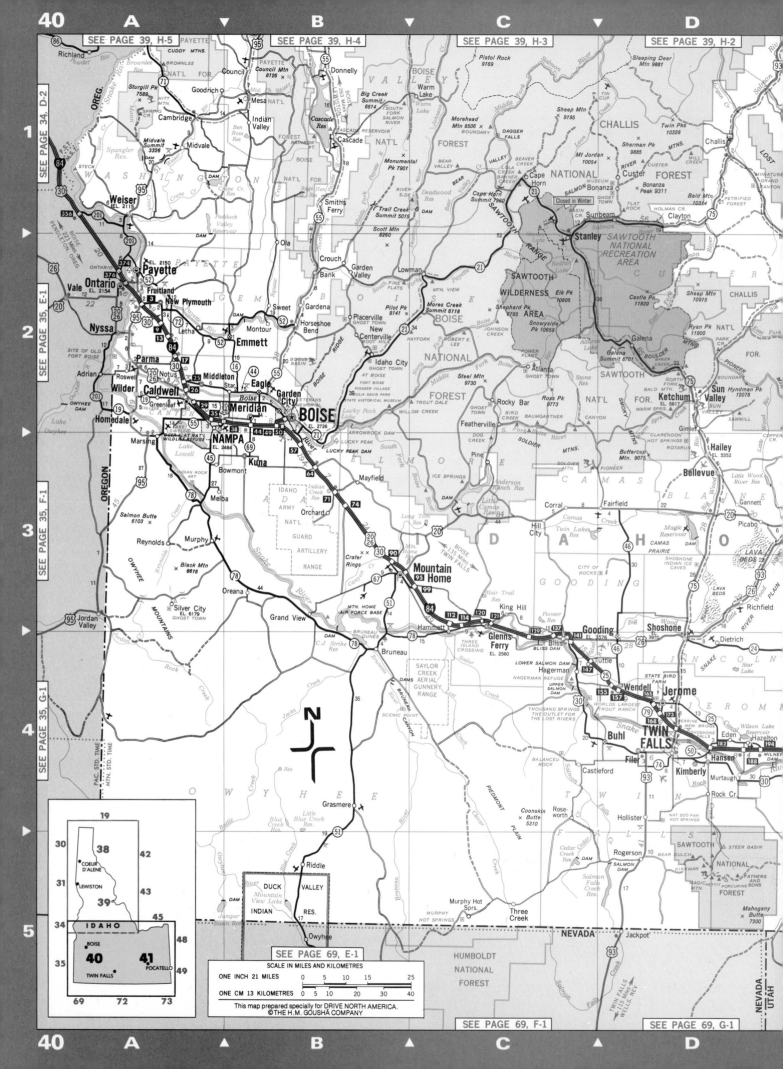

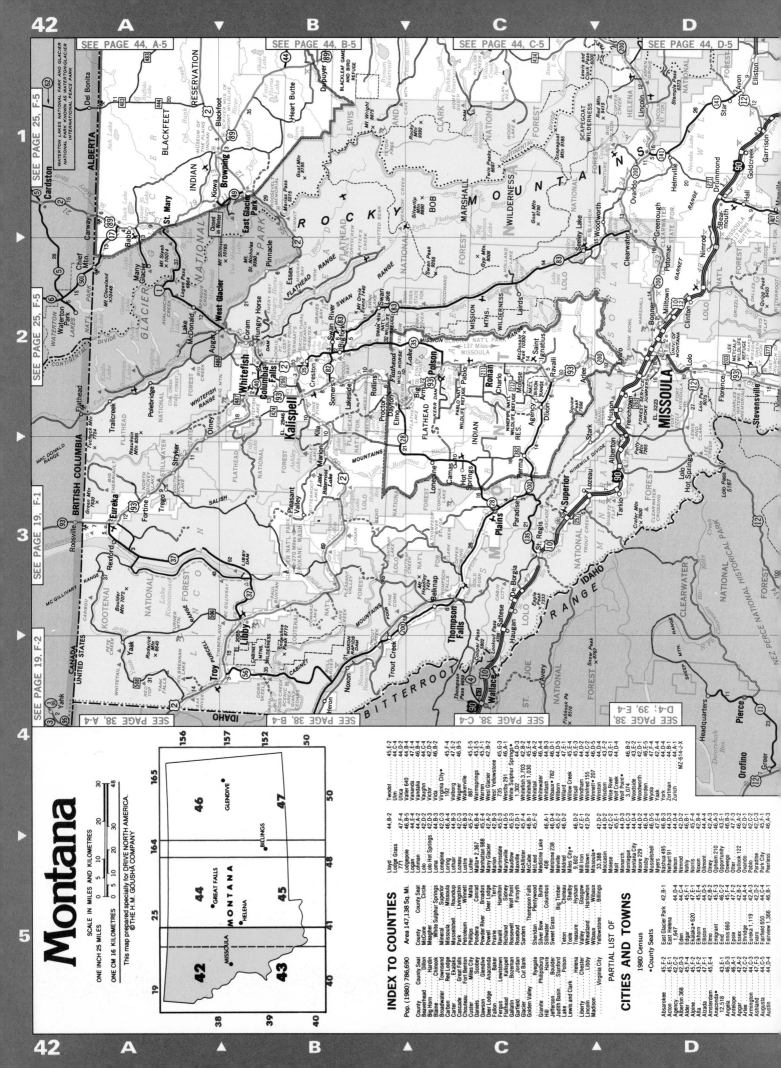

Montana

SCALE IN MILES AND KILOMETRES

ONE INCH 25 MILES
ONE CM 16 KILOMETRES

This map prepared specially for DRIVE NORTH AMERICA.
© THE H. M. GOUSHA COMPANY

INDEX TO COUNTIES

Pop. (1990) 786,690   Area 147,138 Sq. Mi.

PARTIAL LIST OF

CITIES AND TOWNS

1980 Census
• County Seats

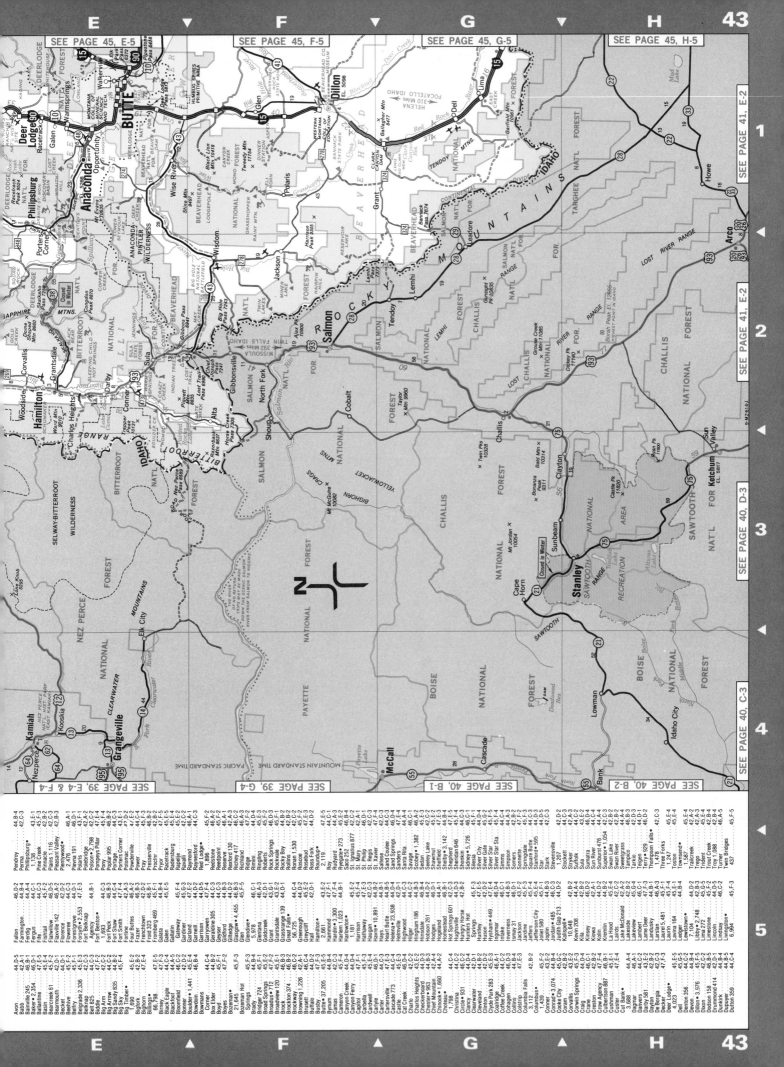

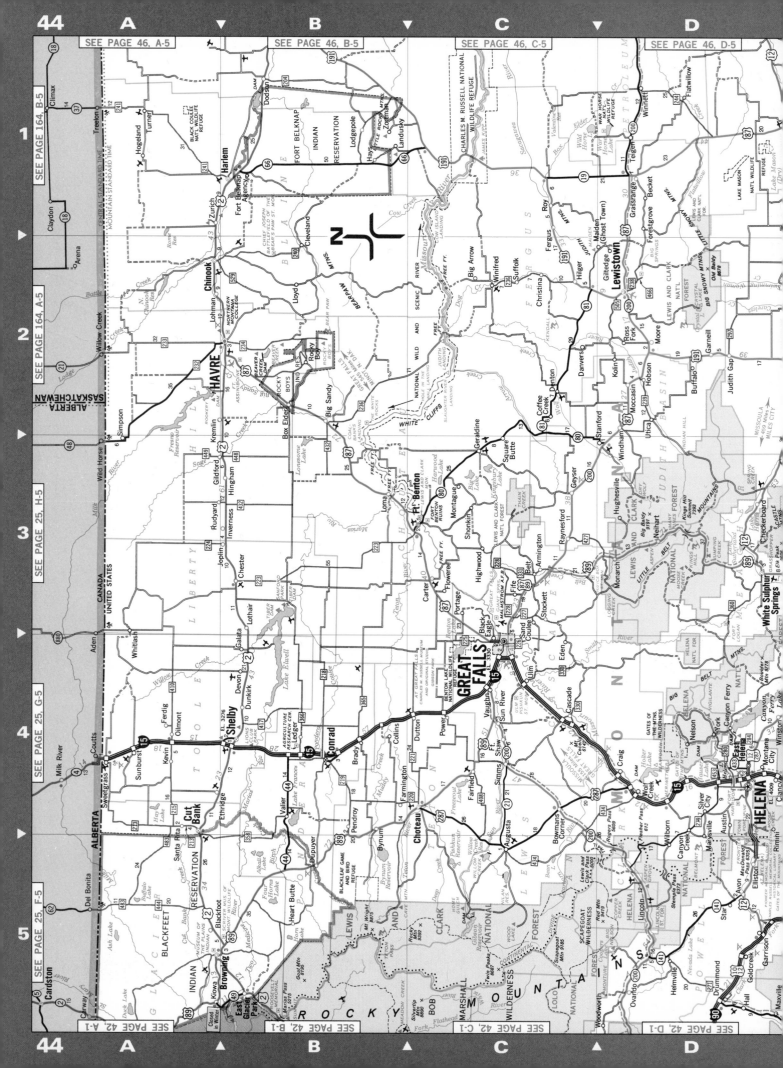

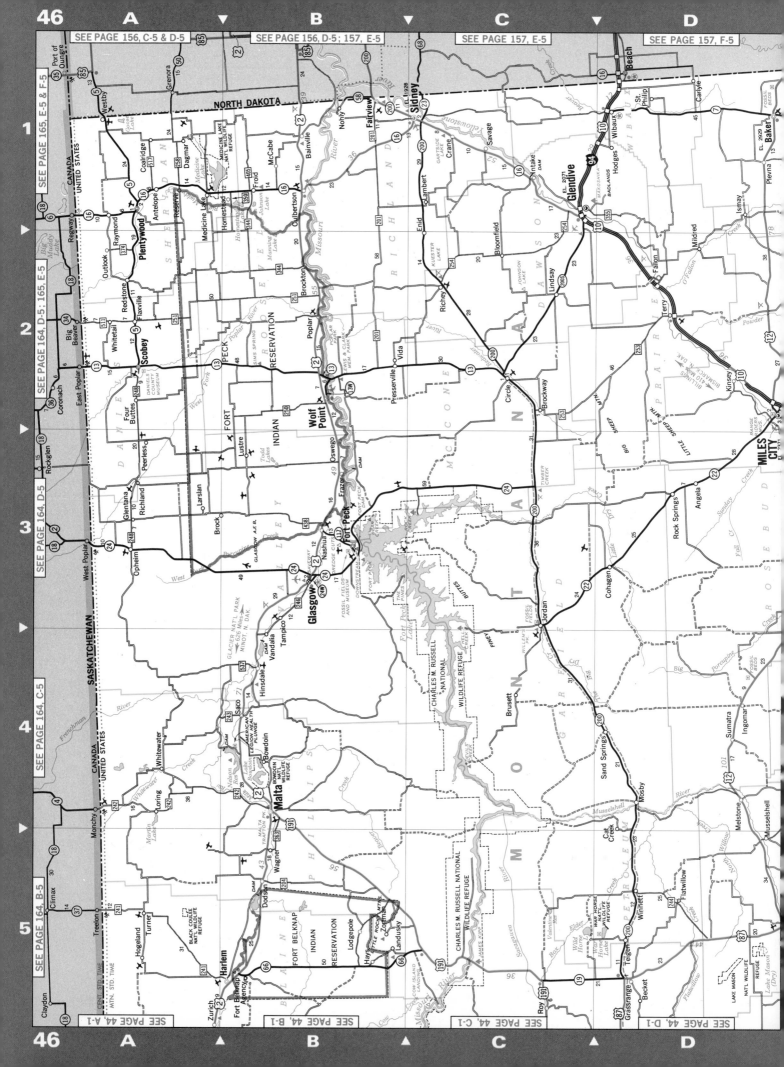

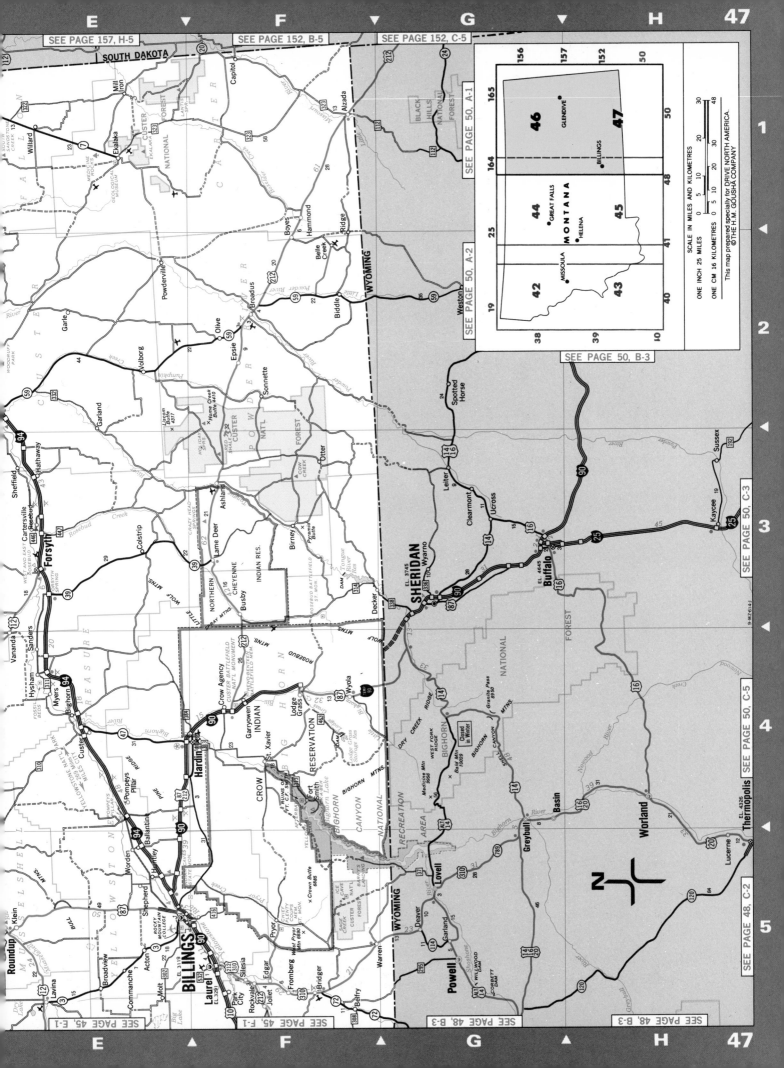

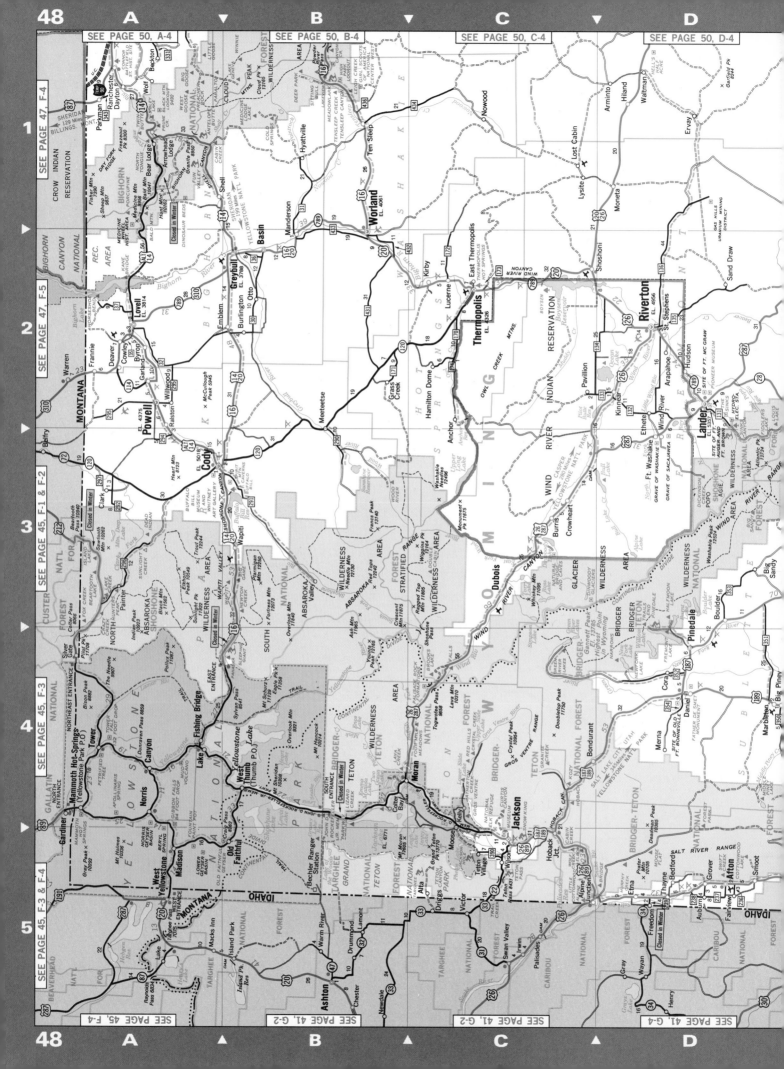

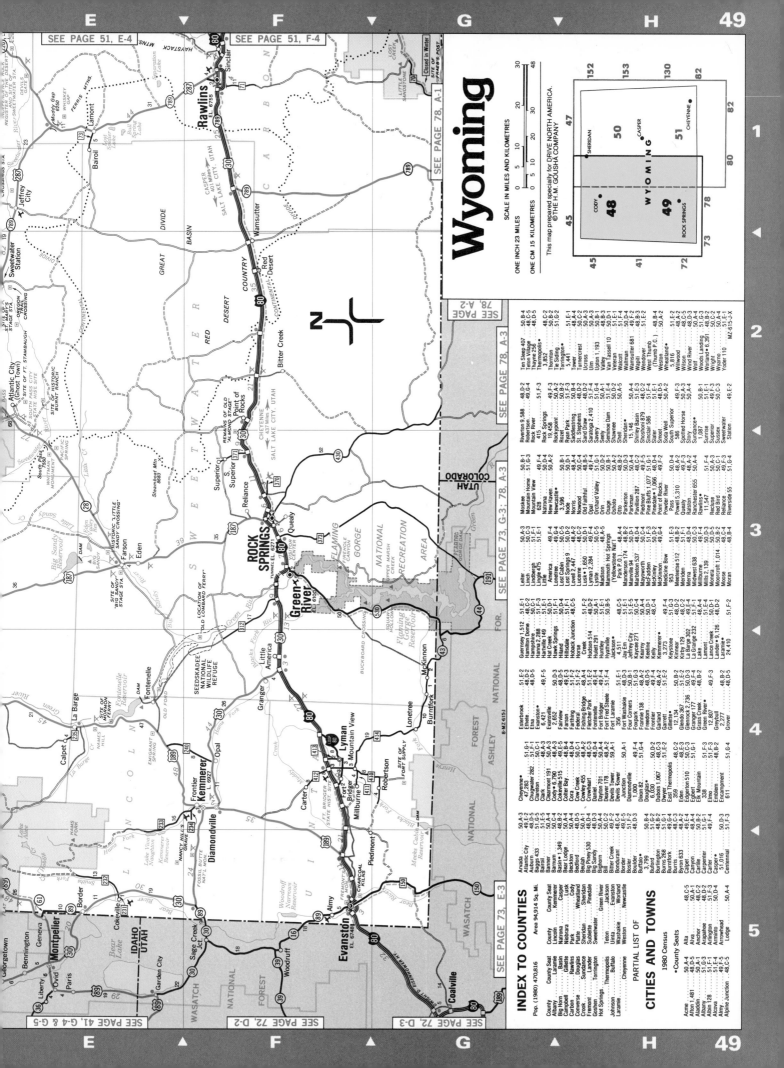

Wyoming

SCALE IN MILES AND KILOMETRES

ONE INCH 23 MILES
ONE CM 15 KILOMETRES

This map prepared specially for DRIVE NORTH AMERICA.
© THE H.M. GOUSHA COMPANY

8-MZ-615-J

INDEX TO COUNTIES

Pop. (1980) 470,816   Area 94,914 Sq. Mi.

County	County Seat
Albany	Laramie
Big Horn	Basin
Campbell	Gillette
Carbon	Rawlins
Converse	Douglas
Crook	Sundance
Fremont	Lander
Goshen	Torrington
Hot Springs	Thermopolis
Johnson	Buffalo
Laramie	Cheyenne
Lincoln	Kemmerer
Natrona	Casper
Niobrara	Lusk
Park	Cody
Platte	Wheatland
Sheridan	Sheridan
Sublette	Pinedale
Sweetwater	Green River
Teton	Jackson
Uinta	Evanston
Washakie	Worland
Weston	Newcastle

PARTIAL LIST OF CITIES AND TOWNS

1980 Census
• County Seats

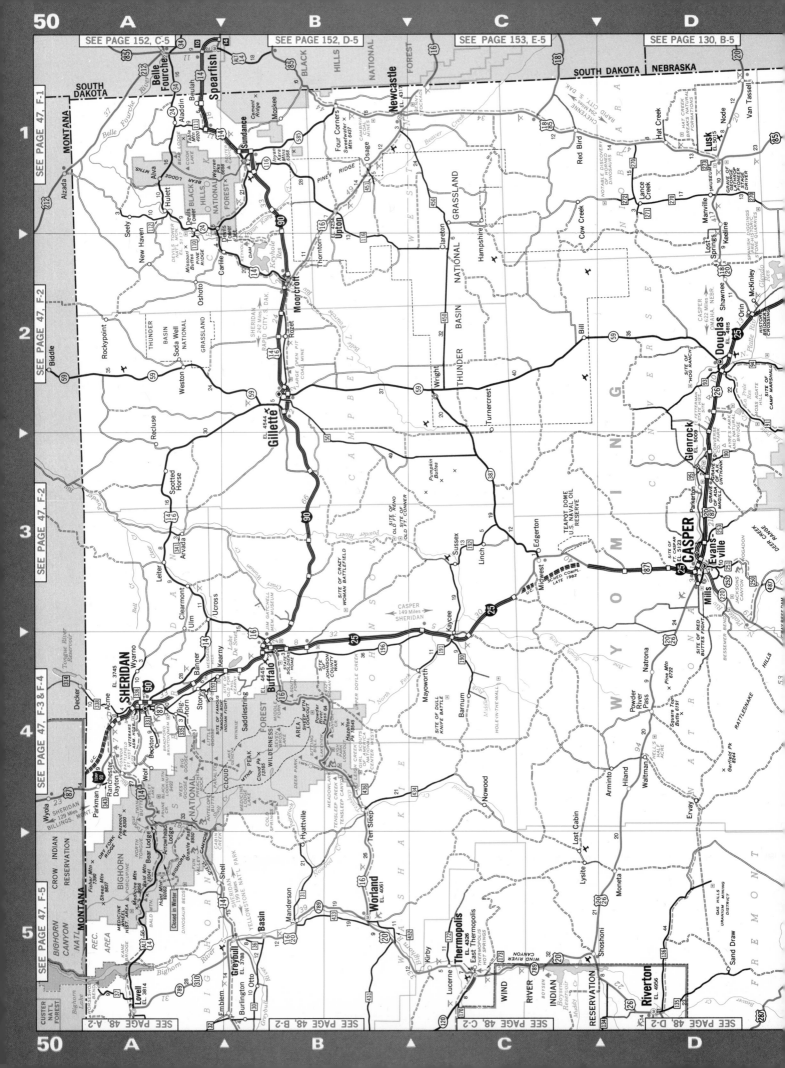

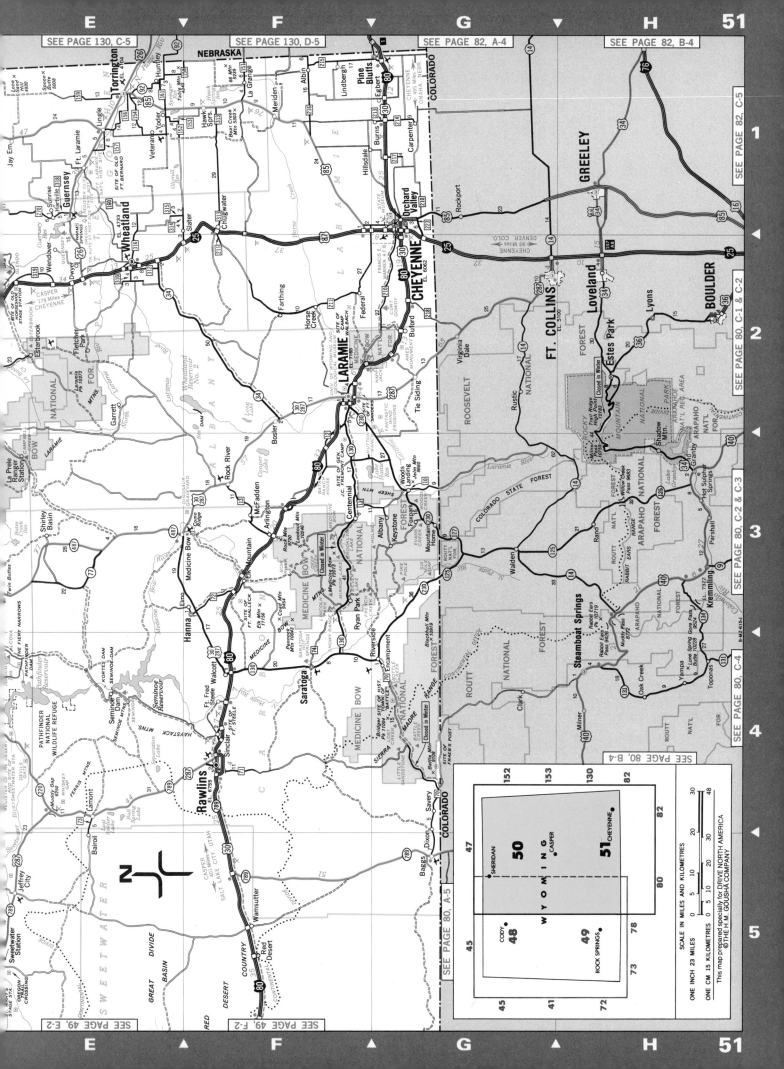

The Golden West:
Death Valley to Disneyland

California

Within California's borders, only 80 miles apart, are Mount Whitney and Death Valley, the highest and lowest points in the lower 48 states. Skyscrapers and Spanish missions, wilderness parks and glittering resorts, vineyards and volcanoes, Death Valley and Disneyland—all can be found in this West Coast vacationland.

Many travelers consider **San Francisco (58, C-3)** to be the most beautiful city in the United States. The city sprawls over 50 square miles of rumpled hills with such evocative names as Russian, Nob and Telegraph. Gleaming office buildings tower over Victorian townhouses—and contrast with the distinctive architecture of the largest Chinatown in the Western world.

More than 1,000 city acres are set aside in Golden Gate Park for recreation. There are outdoor attractions—wooded trails, botanical gardens, an arboretum—as well as galleries, museums and a Japanese Tea Garden. Although visitors might expect the California Palace of the Legion of Honor in Lincoln Park to be a hall of fame, it is actually an art museum. More than 40 bronze, plaster, and marble sculptures by Rodin—including his famous *Thinker*—make up one of the finest such collections in the United States.

Broadway, Bush, Kearney and Stockman streets form the borders of Chinatown. Its main street is Grant Avenue, a parade of colorful tearooms, temples, theaters, nightclubs, and shops filled with exotic fare. At the foot of Polk Street is another famous neighborhood, Fisherman's Wharf, with its galleries, landscaped plazas and abundant seafood. Among several historic vessels moored here is the *Balclutha*, an 1886 square-rigger.

Alcatraz Island has sheltered a famous prison, an immigrant station and a missile base. Today it is a park where hikers, picnickers and anglers find rustic refuge from San Francisco, all within view of the city and its striking bridges.

Across the bay in **Oakland (58, B-3)**, the Oakland Mormon Temple stands like a Shangri-la vision with its shining white walls and golden spires. Nearby, traditional Buddhist and Shinto symbolism graces the design of Lakeside Park's Japanese garden.

Much of the University of California at **Berkeley (58, C-3)**, with its white granite buildings, luxuriant vegetation and hilly setting above San Francisco Bay, has the air of a Mediterranean village. Among more than 8,000 plant species at the university's Botanical Garden in Strawberry Canyon is the world's most complete array of cacti. Exhibits in the University Art Museum include Oriental art objects, European paintings, and 20th-century American works.

On clear days, sunlight splinters through a graceful arcade of tall trees in **Muir Woods National Monument (58, B-3)**, a short drive from San Francisco. Towering redwoods and low-growing ferns thrive side by side along the park's main trail, where markers identify various trees and shrubs. At **Point Reyes National Seashore (58, B-2)**, surf advances and retreats endlessly on a broad triangular peninsula of granite. Inland, hills of vineyards surrounding **Napa (58, C-2)** form the heart of California's wine country.

Redwood National Park (56, C-1) preserves a 90-square-mile remnant of the great redwood forest that once blanketed two million acres of northern California. The oldest of these, the world's tallest trees, is some 2,000 years old. To the east is another ancient giant, 14,162-foot **Mount Shasta (57, F-3)**. Perpetually clad in glacial snows, the extinct volcano looms above misty evergreen forests, gleaming lakes and lava-covered rocks. To the south is **Lassen Peak (57, F-3)**. Half a century ago this mountain exploded and spewed forth rivers of lava. Now snowfields and virgin forest mantle its slopes.

Surrounded by a landscaped park with trees and plants from around the world, the monumental state capitol in **Sacramento (58, D-2)** is capped by an impressive dome. Spacious rooms, magnificent fireplaces and many fine period furnishings contribute to the Victorian charm of the Governor's Mansion. The Crocker Art Museum—the oldest west of the Mississippi—was established in 1873 by Judge Edwin Bryant Crocker to house his more than 700 paintings, 1,600 drawings and 400 prints.

California routes 41, 120 and 140 converge on the western end of **Yosemite National Park (59, F-3)**, delivering one of the world's most astonishing vistas. The sheer granite face of El Capitan dominates the lower valley, rising more than 3,000 feet from its floor. At its foot the Merced River flows—fast or slow, depending on the season—and its tributaries cascade into the abyss. Within the park are half of the country's highest falls. The most splendid is Yosemite, which plunges 2,425 feet in two dramatic leaps—the height of 13 Niagaras. The highest single drop is Ribbon Falls, which spills 1,612 feet.

In 1885 Senator and Mrs. Leland Stanford set aside 8,800 acres and established Stanford University in **Palo Alto (58, C-3)** as a memorial to their son. Superb Venetian mosaics adorn the university's Memorial Church; New Testament themes are depicted in its more than 50 stained-glass windows. The Hoover Institution on War, Revolution and Peace is one of the world's largest repositories of books, papers and documents relating to global conflicts.

A crew of carpenters worked day and night, seven days a week, for 38 years to build the bizarre Winchester Mystery House in **San Jose (58, C-3)**. The house had nine rooms when it was bought by Sarah Winchester, eccentric heiress to the Winchester arms fortune. When she died in 1922, it had 160 rooms, 2,000 doors, 10,000 windows, 50 staircases—one leading nowhere—and an intriguing secret passage. Another of San Jose's unusual attractions is the Rosicrucian

The landmark Ghiradelli sign (right) welcomed ships into San Francisco Bay for decades, until World War II doused its lights. Now it glows again over Ghiradelli Square, a delightful complex of restaurants, galleries and shops. This view is over the waters of the bay past the steps of Aquatic Park.

From sunny Marin County the Golden Gate Bridge (below) arches into San Francisco fog. The city's most famous landmark is one of the longest single-span suspension bridges ever built. With sidewalks for pedestrians and bicyclists, its total length is 8,981 feet, while the main span between the two towers is 4,200 feet.

Egyptian Museum, a replica of an Egyptian temple. The museum exhibits mummies, sarcophagi, jewelry, textiles, ancient scrolls and statues of gods and pharaohs.

South of Carmel, Route 1 climbs and plunges through endless curves, while the sea hurls itself at the foot of the cliffs known as Big Sur. The view at **Point Lobos State Reserve (58, C-5)**, with its perilous coastline guarded by offshore rocks and whirling eddies, has been called "the greatest meeting of land and water in the world." The rocks are the nesting grounds for countless seabirds, including endangered brown pelicans. Farther out to sea California gray whales can be seen during their November-to-April migrations. Some 30 miles south of Point Lobos is **Pfeiffer–Big Sur State Park (58, C-5)**, a densely wooded preserve of sycamore, cottonwood and alder.

Touring Wine Country

Wine is the lifeblood of the Napa Valley, and a winery tour along Highway 29 or the scenic Silverado Trail is a pleasant way to explore this sunny region of vineyards and Victorian towns.

The grand old estates of Beringer and Charles Krug date back to the 1800s; today there are more than 100 wineries in the valley. Large, modern operations such as those of Robert Mondavi and The Christian Brothers, with their state-of-the-art technology and well planned tours, provide an excellent introduction to Napa wine making. Smaller houses, such as Freemark Abbey or the award-winning Stag's Leap, add depth and lore. But no wine tour is complete without a visit to a champagne house. The new, French-owned Domaine Chandon is a good choice. So, too, at the other end of the valley, is Schramsberg, maker of the champagne that former U.S. President Richard Nixon served on his historic trip to China.

No superlative can take true measure of the living giants that connect earth and sky in Redwood National Park (above). The oldest of these trees—still green and growing—bear as many as 2,000 annual rings and rise to a height of 300 feet.

San Simeon's sparkling Neptune Pool (left) was a gathering place for the rich and famous. Ten feet deep and 104 feet long, the pool is framed with Etruscan-style colonnades and a Greco-Roman temple facade.

Rising above a 1,600-foot hill overlooking the Pacific, the white twin towers of **San Simeon (60, C-2)** stand as an extravagant monument to a prodigal man. Publisher William Randolph Hearst spent as much as $4 million a year for 30 years filling this sprawling estate with art treasures from around the world. The man, and the resulting grandiose hodgepodge that he called home, became the basis for the film *Citizen Kane*.

The Mission Santa Barbara in **Santa Barbara (61, E-4)** was founded in 1786. Its present twin-towered church was completed in 1820, one of the most beautiful of all California missions. On display are religious vestments, living quarters furnished in period style, and an altar built by Indians soon after the mission was founded. The grounds of the Santa Barbara Botanic Gardens invite visitors to stroll in a splendid mountain-backed canyon setting. Five miles of trails meander through a variety of California's habitats, each with distinctive trees, shrubs

53

A familiar face greets visitors to the Magic Kingdom. Beyond, Sleeping Beauty Castle heralds the happy realm of Fantasyland.

Surf batters and sun bronzes on California beaches (above), which range from wide strips of sand to rocky headlands.

and flowers. Redwoods flourish along the Gardens' Mission Creek.

Greek and Roman statues, 18th-century French furniture and decorative arts, and English, Italian and Dutch paintings of the 15th to 18th centuries are part of the distinguished works shown in the J. Paul Getty Museum in **Malibu (61, F-5).** Rembrandt's *St. Bartholomew*, Veronese's *Baptism* and Rubens' *Hunt of Diana* are three of the museum's most famous works.

Orky, the largest killer whale in captivity, and Bubbles, a pilot whale, are among the disarming denizens of **Hanna-Barbera's Marineland (61, G-5).** Dolphins, sea elephants, walruses and more than 100 other kinds of sea creatures live here. The world's biggest fishbowl, a four-story tank, contains more than 3,000 fish. Regular shows—featuring whales and sea lions—are presented at two stadiums.

Los Angeles (61, G-4), founded by Spanish settlers in 1781 as "The City of Angels," covers 464 square miles. Over the years, some residents came for the climate, some to take jobs in the new factories, others to make their name on the Silver Screen. Today Los Angeles is the third largest city in the United States, with almost three million Angelenos, and has attractions that range far beyond the film industry. Museums, parks, colorful markets and churches are only a few of its enticements.

European and English paintings as well as temporary exhibits line the walls of the Art Galleries of the University of California at Los Angeles. But the prize spectacle is a spacious garden containing sculptures. Landscaped with gracefully winding walks, it holds 37 major works by eminent 20th-century artists. The modern Los Angeles County Museum of Art, flanked by pools with fountains, holds ancient Egyptian, Indian and Oriental works, as well as medieval, Renaissance and Baroque paintings and sculpture, and outstanding examples of glassmaking art.

El Pueblo de Los Angeles reflects the architectural development of the city since 1815 and includes the two-story brick Pelanconi House (1860) and the brick and cut stone Garnier Building (1890). Almost 70 stalls, shops and restaurants attract visitors to brick-paved Olvera Street with its strong Mexican influence.

Death Valley's Zabriskie Point is a study in remarkable colors and textures.

54

The Byzantine-style St. Sophia Cathedral, modeled after the Hagia Sophia in Istanbul and dedicated in 1952, is one of America's most beautiful Greek Orthodox churches. Its interior is brilliantly decorated with paintings large and small, gold-leafed carvings and 21 massive crystal chandeliers. In colorful contrast to the cathedral are the Watts Towers, an eccentric construction of pipes, broken bottles, seashells, bed frames and other paraphernalia rising 100 feet.

The Music Center of Los Angeles County offers a full range of programs in the performing arts. The 2,000-seat Ahmanson Theater schedules musicals, ballets and dramas, while the Mark Taper Forum provides 750 seats for intimate lectures and recitals. The huge Dorothy Chandler Pavilion hosts symphony orchestra concerts, operas, and the annual Oscar presentations. Stars of a different kind can be seen from the Griffith Observatory, where visitors can peer through a twin refracting telescope.

More than 2,000 animals, including some 50 endangered species, inhabit the Los Angeles Zoo. A walk-through flight cage is a haven for bird-watchers, and youngsters crowd the Children's Zoo with its farm animals and baby animal nursery. Moored in **Long Beach (61, G-5)** is the Cunard liner *Queen Mary*, retired in 1967 after a 14,500-mile journey around Cape Horn.

Within a few years of his retirement in 1910, railway executive Henry Edwards Huntington built his library in **San Marino (61, G-4)** into one of the finest rare book collections in the country. Among the library's 5½ million precious volumes are a 1410 manuscript of Chaucer's *Canterbury Tales*, a Gutenberg Bible, and the earliest editions of Shakespeare. The Art Gallery displays a collection of English paintings; in the Botanical Gardens visitors may wander across broad lawns through acres of camellias to the Japanese, Shakespeare and Desert gardens.

A fabulous world of fact and fantasy springs to life at Disneyland in **Anaheim (61, G-5)**, where dozens of imaginative attractions appeal to old and young alike. The classic Disney characters—Mickey Mouse, Donald Duck and all the rest—are here, as well as a thrilling variety of rides and displays. A 2½-hour guided tour introduces visitors to all seven "lands" in the Magic Kingdom, from Main Street 1890 to Tomorrowland.

Almost overrun with bright flowers, cascading vines and gnarled trees, the mission at **San Juan Capistrano (61, H-5)** is famous for the regular appearance of its migrating swallows. The mission's adobe chapel (1778) with its gilded altar has been completely restored.

San Diego (63, H-4), renowned for its idyllic climate, has long been popular as a resort. Founded by Spain and ruled for many years by Mexico, it still possesses a distinctive Spanish colonial appearance, best seen in the historic Old Town. Balboa Park is San Diego's cultural and recreational heart. The California-Pacific International Exposition was held here in 1935–36; many exposition buildings have been preserved. Serra Museum sits atop Presidio Hill, known as the "Plymouth Rock of the West." It was here in 1769 that Father Junipero Serra established the first mission in California. South of nearby **Oceanside** the Pacific coast is dotted with white sand beaches backed by high bluffs. The surf is generally mild, making it safe for swimming.

The world's largest collection of mammals, birds and reptiles is housed in the San Diego Zoological Garden. The more than 3,000 animals include such rare creatures as a pygmy chimpanzee, a lion-tailed macaque and a green tree python. The children's zoo has a glass-enclosed nursery for baby primates, a rodent tunnel, walk-through bird displays, a seal pool and a tortoise ride.

There is plenty in **Death Valley National Monument (62, B-4)** to remind a visitor of the "valley of the shadow of death" in the 23rd Psalm. Temperatures here have reached as high as 134°F. The valley floor descends to 280 feet below sea level near Badwater—the lowest dry land in the Western Hemisphere. But only 15 miles away, Telescope Peak looms 11,000 feet above sea level.

Recurring rumors of gold and silver—most of them false—induced many to ignore the valley's fearsome reputation. In the 1920s one enterprising prospector, known as Death Valley Scotty, even convinced a Chicago millionaire to finance the construction of an ornate, sprawling castle at the northern end of the valley. Scotty's Castle still stands, its richly decorated rooms open to visitors, as the desert's most incongruous landmark.

Highlights of the northern end of the valley include the giant Ubehebe Crater, half a mile across and 500 feet deep, and the Race Track, where desert winds push large rocks across the surface as if they were giant snails moving under their own power. In the south, Dantes View gives the most dramatic panorama in the valley—a mile down to the glittering salt plains around Badwater.

Fifty miles east of Fresno, and reaching to the towering majesty of 14,495-foot Mount Whitney, lies a stretch of America's most primeval land, preserved in two adjacent national parks: **Kings Canyon (59, G-4)**, a rugged and breathtaking expanse of granite mountains furrowed by mile-deep canyons; and **Sequoia (59, G-5)**, home of the General Sherman Tree—the largest living thing on earth.

"Lights! Camera! Action! Cue the Red Sea!"

At Hollywood's Universal Studios visitors witness special effects created to fool the camera and the moviegoer, and watch a flash flood, a colonial mansion that burns on cue, and the parting of the Red Sea. Burbank Studios (Warner Brothers, Columbia Pictures and several independents) offers a more intimate look at the making of movies and television, including props and special-effects shops, and a historical back lot.

California

SCALE IN MILES AND KILOMETRES

ONE INCH 21 MILES
0 5 10 15 20 25

ONE CM 13 KILOMETRES
0 5 10 15 20 30 40

This map prepared specially for DRIVE NORTH AMERICA.
©THE H.M. GOUSHÁ COMPANY

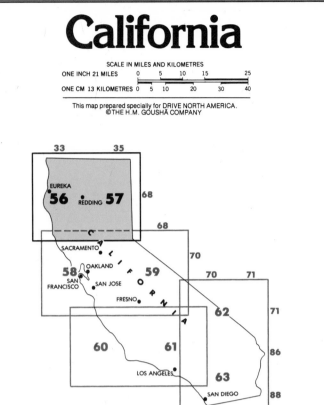

INDEX TO COUNTIES

Pop. (1980) 23,668,652   Area 158,693 Sq. Mi.

PARTIAL LIST OF
CITIES AND TOWNS

1980 Census

•County Seats

CONTINUED ON PAGE 60

CALIFORNIA HIGHWAY PATROL
EMERGENCY TELEPHONE

To report an ACCIDENT or
TRAFFIC EMERGENCY outside
cities, or on city freeways
where there are no call boxes,
dial Operator and ask for

ZEnith 1-2000

On city streets
CALL LOCAL POLICE

9-M2-527-J

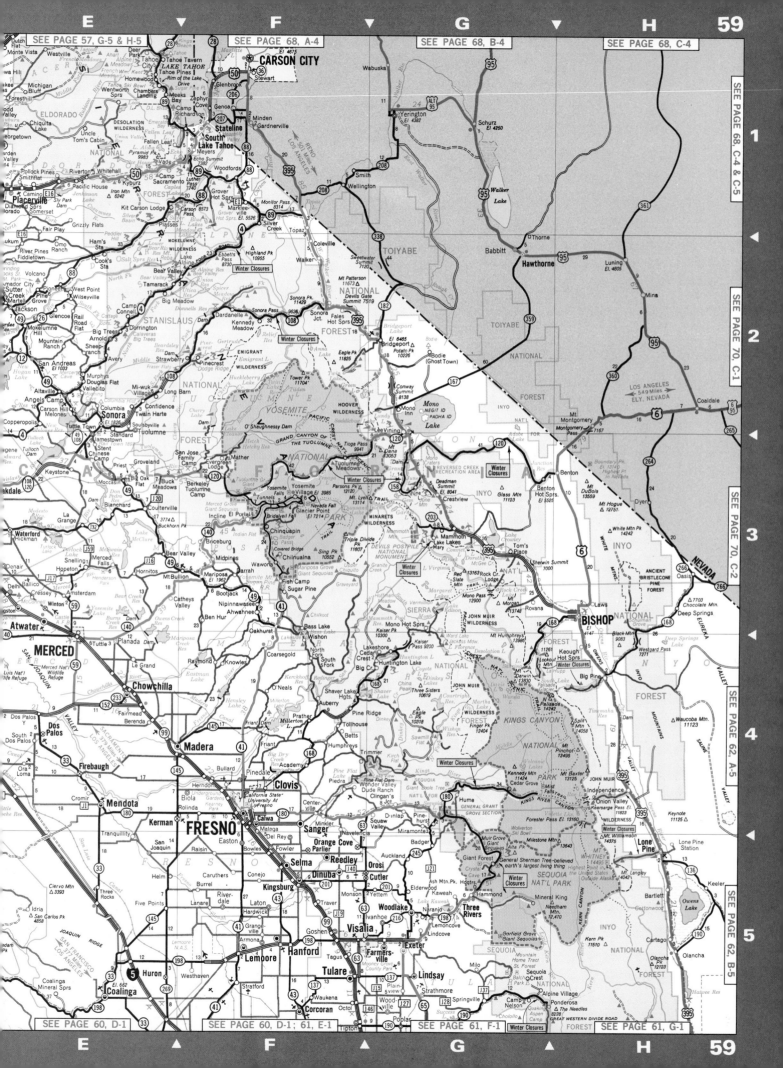

SEE PAGE 58, C-5
SEE PAGE 58, D-5
SEE PAGE 59, E-5

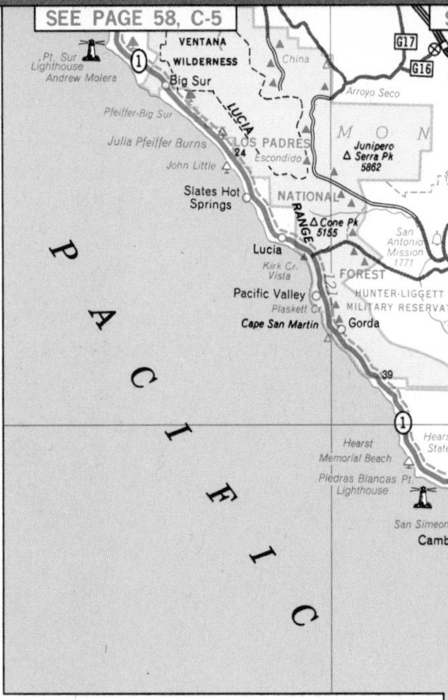
PACIFIC
Big Sur
VENTANA WILDERNESS
Pt. Sur Lighthouse
Andrew Molera
Pfeiffer-Big Sur
Julia Pfeiffer Burns
LOS PADRES
Slates Hot Springs
NATIONAL
RANGE
FOREST
Cone Pk 5155
Lucia
Pacific Valley
Plaskett Cr.
Cape San Martin
Gorda
HUNTER-LIGGETT MILITARY RESERVATION
Junipero Serra Pk 5862
Arroyo Seco
China

Greenfield
King City
San Lucas
San Ardo
Jolon
Lockwood
Bradley
San Antonio Res.
CAMP ROBERTS
San Miguel
Estrella
Paso Robles
El. 721
Templeton
Creston
Atascadero
Cayucos
Morro Bay
Cambria
Cambria Pines
Harmony
San Simeon
Hearst San Simeon State Hist. Mon.
Piedras Blancas Pt. Lighthouse
Point Estero
Baywood Park
Los Osos
SAN LUIS OBISPO
Santa Margarita
Avila Beach
Edna
Pismo Beach
Grover City
Oceano
Arroyo Grande
San Luis Obispo Bay
Nipomo
SANTA MARIA
Guadalupe
Point Sal
Orcutt
Casmalia
VANDENBERG AIR FORCE BASE MISSILE TEST CENTER
Lompoc
Surf
Point Arguello Lighthouse
Jalama
Los Alamos
Buellton
Solvang
Santa Ynez
Los Olivos
Gaviota
Las Cruces
Tajiguas
Naples
Point Conception Lighthouse
Coalinga
Coalinga Mineral Sprs
Huron
Avenal
Kettleman City
Parkfield
Cholame
Shandon
Whitley Gardens
Cushing
Pozo
La Panza
Cottonwood Pass 2000
Orchard Pk 3134
Devils Den
NATIONAL FOREST
LOS PADRES
Sisquoc
Garey
Timber Pk 4758
OCEAN
SAN FRANCISCO 418 Miles
LOS ANGELES
SAN FRANCISCO 377 Miles LOS ANGELES
SAN JOSE 367 Miles LOS ANGELES

CONTINUED FROM PAGE 56

Fallbrook 63,G-5
Fallen Leaf 59,E-1
Famoso 61,E-2
Farmersville
5,544 ......59,G-5
Farmington 58,D-3
Feather Falls 57,G-4
Fellows 61,E-2
Felton 58,C-4
Ferndale 1,367 ......56,C-3
Fieldbrook 56,C-2
Fields Landing 56,C-3
Fillmore 9,602 ......61,F-4
Firebaugh 3,740 ......59,E-4
Fish Camp 59,F-3
Five Points 59,E-5
Florin 58,D-2
Folsom 11,003 ......58,D-1
Fontana 37,109 ......61,H-4
Ford City 61,E-2
Foresthill 59,E-1
Forestville 58,B-2
Forks of Salmon 56,D-2
Fort Bidwell 57,H-1
Fort Bragg 5,019 ......56,C-5
Fort Dick 56,C-1
Fort Jones 544 ......57,E-1
Fortuna 7,591 ......56,C-3
Fowler 2,496 ......59,F-5
Franklin 58,D-2
Frazier Park 61,F-3
Freedom 58,C-4
Fremont 131,945 ......58,C-3
French Camp 58,D-3
French Gulch 57,E-3
Freshwater 56,C-2
Fresno• 218,202 ......59,F-4
Friant 59,F-4
Fullerton
102,034 ......61,G-4
Furnace Creek 62,B-4
Galt 5,514 ......58,D-2
Garberville 56,C-4
Garden Grove
123,351 ......61,G-5
Garden Valley 59,E-1
Gaviota 60,D-4
Gazelle 57,E-1
Georgetown 59,E-1
Gerber 57,E-4
Geyserville 58,B-1
Giant Forest 59,G-5
Gilroy 21,641 ......58,D-4
Glen Ellen 58,B-2
Glendale
139,060 ......61,G-4
Glendora
38,654 ......61,G-4
Glenn 57,F-4
Glennville 61,F-2
Gold Run 57,G-5
Goleta 61,E-4
Gonzales 2,891 ......58,D-5
Gorman 61,F-3
Goshen 59,F-5
Graeagle 57,G-4
Grangeville 59,F-5
Grapevine 61,F-3
Grass Valley
6,697 ......57,G-5
Graton 58,B-2
Greenfield
4,181 ......58,D-5
Greenfield 61,F-2
Greenview 57,E-1
Greenville 57,G-3
Greenwood 58,D-1
Gridley 3,982 ......57,F-5
Grimes 57,F-5
Groveland 59,E-3
Grover City
8,827 ......60,D-2
Guadalupe
3,629 ......60,D-3
Gualala 58,A-1
Guerneville 58,B-2
Guinda 58,C-1
Gustine 3,142 ......58,D-4
Half Moon Bay
7,282 ......58,B-3
Hamburg 56,D-1
Hamilton City 57,F-4
Hammond 59,G-5
Hanford•
20,958 ......59,F-5
Happy Camp 56,D-1
Harold 61,G-3
Harris 56,D-4
Hayfork 56,D-3
Hayward
94,167 ......58,C-3
Healdsburg
7,217 ......58,B-1
Heber 63,H-2
Hemet 23,211 ......61,H-4
Herlong 57,H-3
Hermosa Beach
18,070 ......61,G-4
Hesperia 63,E-5
Highland 63,F-5
Hillsborough
10,451 ......58,C-3
Hilt 57,E-1
Hollister• 11,488 ......58,D-4
Hollywood 61,G-4
Hollywood Beach 61,E-4
Hollywood
by the Sea 61,E-4
Holtville 4,399 ......63,H-2
Honeydew 56,C-3
Hoopa 56,D-2
Hopland 58,B-1
Hornbrook 57,E-1
Hornitos 59,E-3
Hughson 2,943 ......58,D-3
Humphreys 59,F-4
Huntington Beach
170,505 ......61,G-5
Huntington
Lake 59,G-4
Huntington Park
46,223 ......61,G-4
Huron 2,768 ......60,D-1
Idyllwild 63,F-4
Imperial 3,451 ......63,H-2
Imperial Beach
22,689 ......63,H-4
Independence• 59,H-4
Indian Falls 57,G-4
Indio 21,611 ......63,F-3
Inglewood
94,245 ......61,G-4
Inyokern 61,G-2
Ione 2,207 ......58,D-2
Isleton 914 ......58,D-2
Ivanhoe 59,G-5
Jackson• 2,331 ......59,E-2
Jacumba 63,H-3
Jamestown 59,E-3
Jamul 63,H-4
Jenner 58,B-2
Johannesburg 61,G-2
Johnstonville 57,G-3
Jolon 60,C-1
Julian 63,H-4
Keddie 57,G-4
Kelley
Hot Springs 57,G-1
Kellogg 58,B-1
Kelseyville 58,B-1
Kelso 62,D-3
Kerman 4,002 ......59,E-4
Kernville 61,F-2
Kettleman City 60,D-1
Keyes 58,D-3
Keystone 59,E-3
King City 5,495 ......58,D-5
Kingsburg
5,115 ......59,F-5
Klamath 56,C-1
Knights Landing 58,C-1
Korbel 56,C-2
La Grange 59,E-3
La Habra 45,232 ......61,G-4
La Jolla 63,H-5
La Mesa 50,342 ......63,H-4
Laguna Beach
17,860 ......61,G-5
Lagunitas 58,B-2
Lake Alpine 59,F-2
Lake
Arrowhead 63,F-5
Lake Elsinore
5,982 ......63,F-5
Lake Hughes 61,F-3
Lake Isabella 61,F-2
Lake Mary 59,G-3
Lakehead 57,E-2
Lakeport• 3,675 ......56,D-5
Lakeshore 59,G-4
Lakeside 63,H-4
Lakeview 63,F-4
Lamont 61,F-2
Lanare 59,F-5
Lancaster
48,027 ......61,G-3
Las Cruces 60,D-3
Lathrop 58,D-3
Laton 59,F-5
Laytonville 56,D-4
Le Grand 59,E-4
Lebec 61,F-3
Lee Vining 59,G-2
Lemoncove 59,G-5
Lemon Grove
20,780 ......63,H-4
Lemoore 8,832 ......59,F-5
Lenwood 63,E-4
Leucadia 63,H-5
Likely 57,G-2
Lincoln 4,132 ......58,D-1
Linden 58,D-2
Lindsay 6,924 ......59,G-5
Litchfield 57,H-3
Little River 56,C-5
Little Shasta 57,E-1
Littlerock 61,G-3
Live Oak 3,103 ......57,F-5
Livermore
48,349 ......58,C-3
Livingston 5,326 ......59,E-3
Locke 58,D-2
Lockeford 58,D-2
Lockwood 60,C-1
Lodi 35,221 ......58,D-2
Lodoga 57,E-5
Loleta 56,C-3
Lompoc 26,267 ......60,D-3
Lone Pine 59,H-5
Long Barn 59,E-2
Long Beach
361,334 ......61,G-4
Longville 57,G-3
Loomis 58,D-1
Los Alamos 60,D-3
Los Altos
25,769 ......58,C-3
Los Angeles•
2,966,763 ......61,G-4
Los Banos
10,341 ......58,D-4
Los Gatos 26,593 ......58,C-4
Los Molinos 57,F-4
Los Olivos 60,D-3
Los Osos 60,C-2
Lost Hills 61,E-2
Lower Lake 58,B-1
Loyalton 1,030 ......57,H-4
Lucerne 57,E-5
Lucerne Valley 63,E-4
Lynwood
48,548 ......61,G-4
Macdoel 57,F-1
Madeline 57,G-2
Madera• 21,732 ......59,F-4
Madison 58,C-1
Magalia 57,F-4
Mammoth Lakes 59,G-3
Manchester 58,A-1
Manhattan Beach
31,542 ......61,F-4
Manteca 24,925 ......58,D-3
Manzanita Lake 57,F-3
Maricopa 946 ......61,E-3
Marina 20,647 ......58,C-4
Mariposa• 59,F-3
Markleeville• 59,F-1
Marshall 58,B-2
Martinez•
22,582 ......58,C-2
Marysville•
9,898 ......57,F-5
Maxwell 57,F-5
McArthur 57,F-2
McCloud 57,E-2
McFarland
5,151 ......61,E-2
McKinleyville 56,C-2
McKittrick 61,E-2
Meadow Valley 57,G-4
Mecca 63,G-3
Meiners Oaks 61,E-4
Mendocino 56,C-5
Mendota 5,038 ......59,E-4
Menlo Park
25,673 ......58,C-4
Merced• 36,499 ......59,E-3
Merced Falls 59,E-3
Meridian 57,F-5
Mesa Grande 63,G-4
Middletown 58,B-1
Mill Creek 57,F-3
Mill Valley
12,967 ......58,B-3
Milpitas
37,820 ......58,C-3
Milton 58,D-2
Mineral 57,F-3
Mira Loma 61,H-4
Mira Monte 61,E-4
Miramar 63,H-4
Modesto•
106,105 ......58,D-3
Mohawk 57,G-4
Mojave 61,G-3
Mokelumne
Hill 59,E-2
Monrovia
30,531 ......61,G-4
Montague 1,285 ......57,E-1
Montalvo 61,E-4
Montara 58,B-3
Monte Rio 58,B-2
Montebello
52,929 ......61,G-4
Montecito 61,E-3
Monterey 27,558 ......58,C-5
Monterey Park
54,338 ......61,G-4
Moorpark 61,F-4
Morgan Hill
17,060 ......58,C-4
Morro Bay 9,064 ......60,C-2
Moss Landing 58,C-4
Mount Bullion 59,F-3
Mount Eden 58,C-3
Mount Shasta
2,837 ......57,E-2
Mountain Center 63,G-4
Mountain View
58,655 ......58,C-3
Murphys 59,E-2
Murrieta 63,G-5
Napa• 50,879 ......58,C-2
Naples 60,D-4
National City
48,772 ......63,H-4
Needles 4,120 ......63,E-1
Nelson 57,F-4
Nevada City•
2,431 ......57,G-5
New Almaden 58,C-4
New Cuyama 61,E-3
Newark 32,126 ......58,C-3
Newbury Park 61,F-4
Newcastle 58,D-1
Newhall 61,F-4
Newman 2,785 ......58,D-3
Newport Beach
63,475 ......61,G-5
Nice 57,E-5
Niland 63,G-2
Nipomo 60,D-3
Norco 21,126 ......61,H-4
Norden 57,H-5
North Palm Sprs. 63,F-4
North San Juan 57,G-5
North Shore 63,G-3
Norwalk
85,232 ......61,G-4
Novato 43,916 ......58,B-2
Nubieber 57,G-2
Oak View 61,E-4
Oakdale 8,474 ......59,E-3
Oakhurst 59,F-3
Oakland•
339,288 ......58,C-3
Oakley 58,C-2
Oakville 58,C-2
Oasis 59,H-3
Oceano 60,D-3
Oceanside
76,698 ......63,G-5
Ocotillo Wells 63,G-3
Oildale 61,F-2
Ojai 6,816 ......61,E-4
Olancha 59,H-5
Old River 61,E-2
Olema 58,B-2
Olivehurst 57,F-5
Ontario 88,820 ......61,H-4
Orange 91,788 ......61,G-5
Orange Cove
4,026 ......59,F-5
Orcutt 60,D-3
Ordbend 57,F-4
Orick 56,C-2
Orland 3,976 ......57,E-4
Oro Grande 63,E-5
Orosi 59,G-5
Oroville• 8,683 ......57,F-4
Oxnard 108,195 ......61,E-4
Pacific Beach 63,H-5
Pacific Grove
15,755 ......58,C-5
Pacifica 36,866 ......58,B-3
Pala 63,G-4
Palermo 57,F-5
Palm Desert
11,801 ......63,F-3
Palm Springs
32,271 ......63,F-4
Palmdale 1,2277 ......61,G-3
Palo Alto
55,225 ......58,C-3
Palo Cedro 57,E-3
Palomar
Mountain 63,G-4
Paradise 22,571 ......57,F-4
Parker Dam 63,E-1
Parlier 2,680 ......59,F-5
Pasadena
119,374 ......61,G-4
Paskenta 57,E-4
Paso Robles
9,163 ......60,C-2
Patterson 3,866 ......58,D-3
Pauma Valley 63,G-4
Pearblossom 61,G-3
Penryn 58,D-1
Pentz 57,F-4
Pepperwood 56,C-3
Perkins 58,D-2
Perris 6,740 ......63,F-5
Pescadero 58,C-4
Petaluma 33,834 ......58,B-2
Philo 56,D-5
Piedmont 10,498 ......58,C-3
Pilot Hill 58,D-1
Pine Creek 57,H-1
Pine Grove 59,E-2
Pine Valley 63,H-4
Pinedale 59,F-4
Pinole 14,253 ......58,C-2
Pioneer 59,E-2
Piru 61,F-4
Pismo Beach
5,364 ......60,D-2
Pittsburg 33,034 ......58,C-2
Pixley 61,E-1
Placerville•
6,739 ......59,E-1
Planada 59,E-4
Pleasant Hill
25,124 ......58,C-2
Pleasanton
35,160 ......58,C-3
Plymouth 699 ......59,D-2
Point Arena 425 ......58,A-1
Point Reyes
Station 58,B-2
Pomona 92,742 ......61,G-4
Pond 61,E-2
Pope Valley 58,C-1
Poplar 61,F-1
Port Chicago 59,C-2
Port Hueneme
17,803 ......61,E-4
Porterville
19,707 ......61,F-1
Portola 1,885 ......57,H-4
Potter Valley 56,D-5
Poway 63,H-4
Prather 59,F-4
Princeton 57,F-5
Proberta 57,E-4
Project City 57,E-3
Quartz Hill 61,G-3
Quincy• 57,G-4
Raisin 59,F-5
Ramona 63,H-4
Rancho
Cordova 58,D-1
Rancho Mirage
6,281 ......63,F-3
Randsburg 61,G-2
Ravendale 57,H-2
Red Bluff• 9,490 ......57,E-3
Red Mountain 61,H-2
Redding• 41,995 ......57,E-3
Redlands 43,619 ......63,F-4
Redonda Beach
57,102 ......61,G-4
Redwood City•
54,965 ......58,C-3
Reedley 11,071 ......59,F-5
Rialto 35,615 ......63,F-5
Richmond
74,676 ......58,C-3
Richvale 57,F-5
Ridgecrest 15,929 ......61,G-2
Rincon Springs 63,G-4
Rio Dell 2,687 ......56,C-3
Rio Linda 58,D-1
Rio Oso 58,D-1
Rio Vista 3,142 ......58,C-2
Ripon 3,509 ......58,D-3
Riverbank 5,695 ......58,D-3
Riverdale 59,F-5
Riverside•
170,876 ......63,F-5
Riverton 59,E-1
Robbins 58,C-1
Rocklin 7,344 ......58,D-1
Rockport 56,C-4
Rodeo 58,C-2
Rohnert Park
22,965 ......58,B-2
Rolinda 59,F-4
Rosamond 61,G-3
Rosedale 61,F-2
Roseville
24,347 ......59,D-1
Ross 2,682 ......58,B-2
Round Mountain 57,F-2
Rumsey 58,C-1
Running Springs 63,F-4
Rutherford 58,C-2
Ryde 58,D-2
Sacramento•
275,741 ......58,D-2
St. Helena 4,898 ......58,C-2
Salida 58,D-3
Salinas• 80,479 ......58,C-4
Samoa 56,C-2
San Andreas• 59,E-2
San Anselmo
11,927 ......58,B-2
San Ardo 60,C-1
San Bernardino•
118,057 ......63,F-5
San Bruno
35,417 ......58,B-3
San Carlos
24,710 ......58,C-3
San Clemente
27,325 ......61,H-5
San Diego•
875,504 ......63,H-4
San Fernando
17,731 ......61,F-4
San Francisco•
678,974 ......58,B-3
San Gregorio 58,C-3
San Jacinto
7,098 ......63,F-4
San Joaquin
1,930 ......59,E-5
San Jose•
636,550 ......58,C-3
San Juan Bautista
1,276 ......58,D-4
San Juan Capistrano
18,959 ......61,H-5
San Leandro
63,952 ......58,C-3
San Lucas 60,C-1
San Luis Obispo•
34,252 ......60,D-2
San Luis Rey 63,G-5
San Marcos
17,479 ......63,G-4
San Martin 58,C-4
San Mateo
77,561 ......58,C-3
San Miguel 60,C-1
San Pablo 19,750 ......58,C-2
San Pedro 61,G-5
San Rafael•
44,700 ......58,B-2
Sanger 12,558 ......59,F-4
Santa Ana•
203,713 ......61,G-5
Santa Barbara•
74,542 ......61,E-4
Santa Clara
87,746 ......58,C-3
Santa Cruz•
41,483 ......58,C-4
Santa Margarita 60,D-2
Santa Maria
39,685 ......60,D-3
Santa Monica
88,314 ......61,F-4
Santa Paula
20,552 ......61,E-4
Santa Rita 58,C-4
Santa Rosa•
83,205 ......58,B-2
Santa Susana 61,F-4
Santa Ynez 61,D-3
Santa Ysabel 63,G-4
Santee 63,H-4
Saratoga 29,261 ......58,C-4
Saticoy 61,E-4
Sattley 57,H-4
Saugus 61,F-4
Sausalito 7,090 ......58,B-3
Schellville 58,C-2
Scotia 56,C-3
Seal Beach
25,975 ......61,G-5
Seaside 36,567 ......58,C-5
Sebastopol 5,500 ......58,B-2
Seeley 63,H-2
Selma 10,942 ......59,F-5
Shafter 7,010 ......61,E-2
Shandon 60,D-2
Shasta 57,E-3
Shaver Lake Hgts. 59,F-4
Sheerpranch 59,E-2
Shell Beach 60,D-2
Sheridan 58,D-1
Shingle Springs 58,D-1
Shoshone 62,C-3
Sierra City 57,G-4
Sierraville 57,H-5
Simi Valley
77,500 ......61,F-4
Simmler 60,D-2
Sisquoc 60,D-3
Sloat 57,G-4
Smartville 57,F-5
Smith River 56,C-1
Snelling 59,E-3
Soda Springs 57,H-5
Solana Beach 63,H-5
Soledad 5,928 ......58,D-5
Solemint 61,F-4
Solvang 60,D-3
Somes Bar 56,D-1
Sonoma 6,054 ......58,B-2
Sonora• 3,239 ......59,E-2
Soquel 58,C-4
Soulsbyville 59,E-2
South Gate
66,784 ......61,G-4
South Lake Tahoe
20,681 ......59,F-1
South San Francisco
49,393 ......58,B-3
Springville 61,F-1
Standard 59,E-2
Stewarts Point 58,A-1
Stinson Beach 58,B-3
Stirling City 57,F-4
Stockton•
149,779 ......58,D-2
Stonyford 57,E-5
Stratford 61,E-1
Strathmore 61,F-1
Suisun City
11,087 ......58,C-2
Summerland 61,E-4
Summit City 57,E-3
Sun City 63,G-5
Sunland 61,G-4
Sunnymead 63,F-5
Sunnyvale
106,618 ......58,C-3
Sunol 58,C-3
Sunset Beach 61,G-5
Susanville•
6,520 ......57,G-3
Sutter 57,F-5
Sutter Creek
1,705 ......59,E-2
Taft 5,316 ......61,E-2
Tahoe City 57,H-5
Tahoe Vista 57,H-5
Tajiguas 60,D-4
Tecate 63,H-4
Tehachapi 4,126 ......61,F-2
Tehama 365 ......57,E-4
Temecula 63,G-4
Templeton 60,C-2
Tennant 57,F-1
Terminous 58,D-2
Termo 57,H-2
Terra Bella 61,F-1
Thermal 63,G-3
Thornton 58,D-2
Thousand Oaks
77,797 ......61,F-4
Three Points 61,F-3
Three Rivers 59,G-5
Tipton 61,E-1
Tollhouse 59,F-4
Tomales 58,B-2
Tom's Place 59,G-3
Topanga 61,F-4
Topanga Beach 61,F-4
Torrance
131,497 ......61,G-5
Tracy 18,428 ......58,D-3
Tranquility 59,E-5
Tres Pinos 58,D-4
Trinidad 379 ......56,C-2
Trinity Center 57,E-2
Trona 62,C-5
Trowbridge 58,D-1
Truckee 57,H-5
Tulare 22,475 ......61,E-1
Tulelake 783 ......57,F-1
Tuolumne 59,E-2
Turlock 26,291 ......58,D-3
Turner 58,D-3
Tustin 32,073 ......61,G-5
Twain 57,G-4
Twentynine
Palms 63,F-3
Ukiah• 12,035 ......56,D-5
Union City
39,406 ......58,C-3
Upland 47,647 ......61,H-4
Upper Lake 56,D-5
Vacaville 43,367 ......58,C-2
Valerie Jean 63,G-3
Vallecito 59,E-2
Vallejo 80,188 ......58,C-2
Valley Center 63,G-4
Valley Ford 58,B-2
Valley Springs 59,E-2
Venice 61,F-4
Ventura•
74,474 ......61,E-4
Vernalis 58,D-3
Victorville
14,220 ......63,E-5
Vidal 63,F-1
Vina 57,F-4
Visalia• 49,729 ......59,F-5
Vista 35,834 ......63,G-5
Volta 58,D-4
Vorden 58,D-2
Walnut Creek
53,643 ......58,C-3
Walnut Grove 58,D-2
Warm Springs 58,C-3
Wasco 9,613 ......61,E-2
Waterford 2,683 ......59,E-3
Waterloo 58,D-2
Watsonville
23,543 ......58,C-4
Waukena 61,E-1
Weaverville• 56,D-3
Weed 2,879 ......57,E-1
Weott 56,C-3
West Butte 57,F-5
West Covina
80,094 ......61,G-4
West Point 59,E-2
West
Sacramento 58,D-2
Westley 58,D-3
Westmorland
1,590 ......63,H-2
Westwood 57,G-3
Wheatland
1,474 ......58,D-1
Whittier 68,872 ......61,G-4
Williams 1,655 ......57,E-5
Willits 4,008 ......56,D-5
Willow Creek 56,D-2
Willow Ranch 57,H-1
Willows• 4,777 ......57,E-4
Wilmington 61,G-5
Windsor 58,B-1
Winterhaven 63,H-1
Winters 2,652 ......58,C-2
Winton 59,E-3
Woodbridge 58,D-2
Wooden Valley 58,C-2
Woodford 61,F-2
Woodfords 59,F-1
Woodlake 5,375 ......59,G-5
Woodland•
30,235 ......58,C-1
Woodside 5,291 ......58,C-3
Woodville 61,E-1
Yermo 63,E-4
Yolo 58,C-1
Yorba Linda
28,254 ......61,G-4
Yosemite
Village 59,F-3
Yountville 2,893 ......58,C-2
Yreka• 5,916 ......57,E-1
Yuba City•
18,736 ......57,F-5
Yucaipa 63,F-4
Yucca Valley 63,F-4
Zamora 58,C-1

MZ-527-J-X2

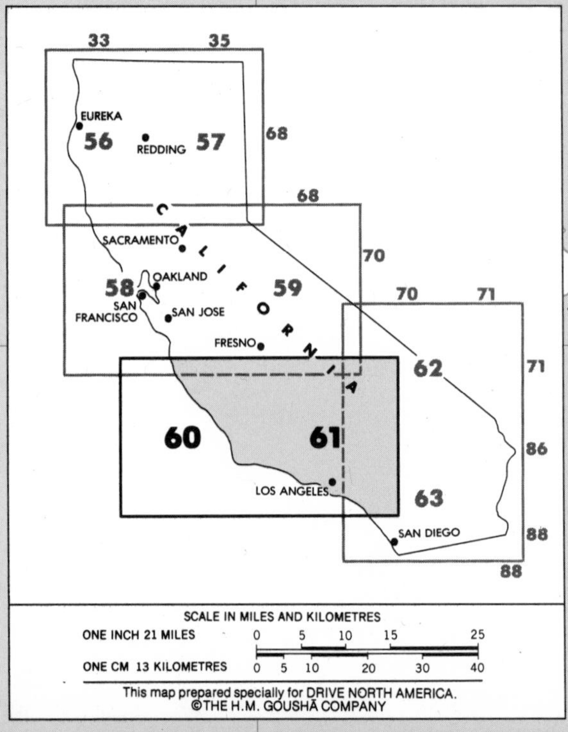
33
35
EUREKA
56
REDDING
57
68
CALIFORNIA
SACRAMENTO
70
58
OAKLAND
59
SAN FRANCISCO
SAN JOSE
FRESNO
70
71
62
71
60
61
86
LOS ANGELES
63
SAN DIEGO
88
88
SCALE IN MILES AND KILOMETRES
ONE INCH 21 MILES
0 5 10 15 25
ONE CM 13 KILOMETRES
0 5 10 20 30 40

This map prepared specially for DRIVE NORTH AMERICA.
©THE H.M. GOUSHA COMPANY

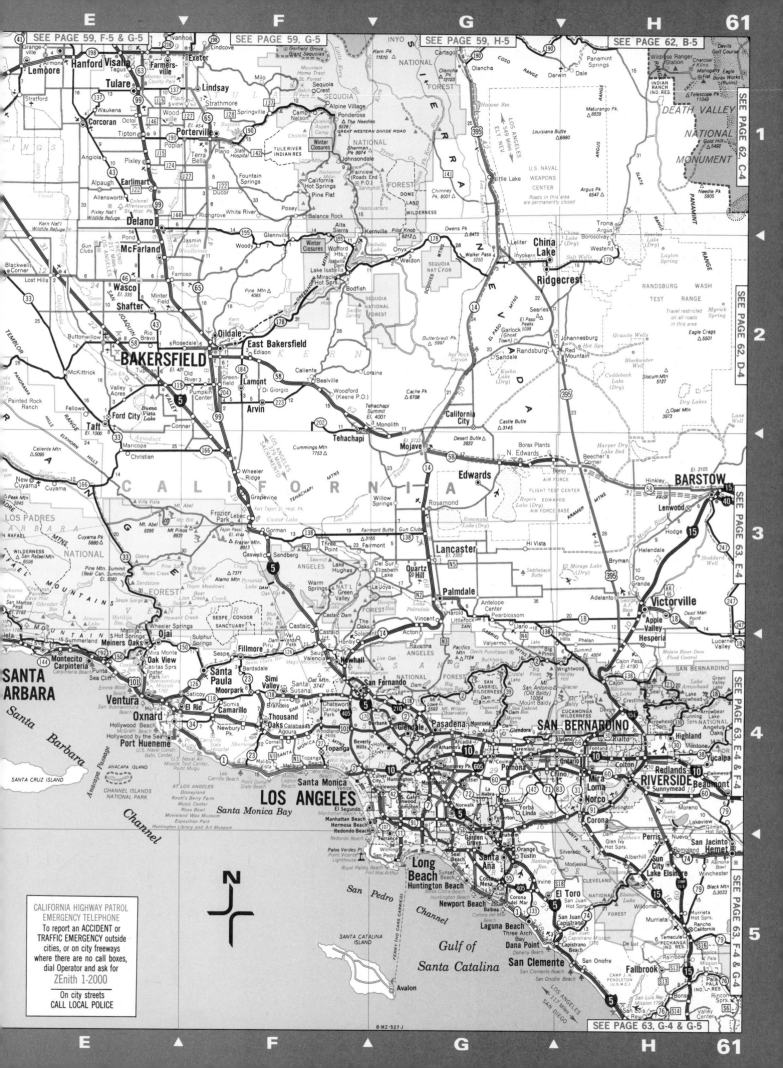

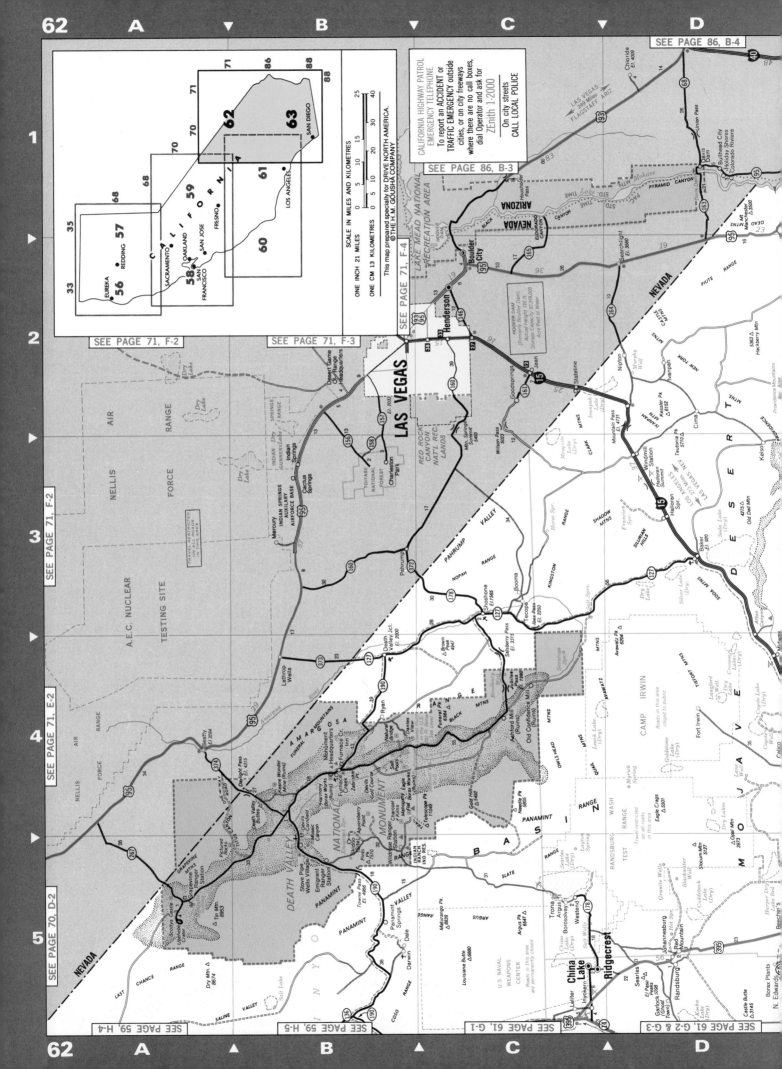

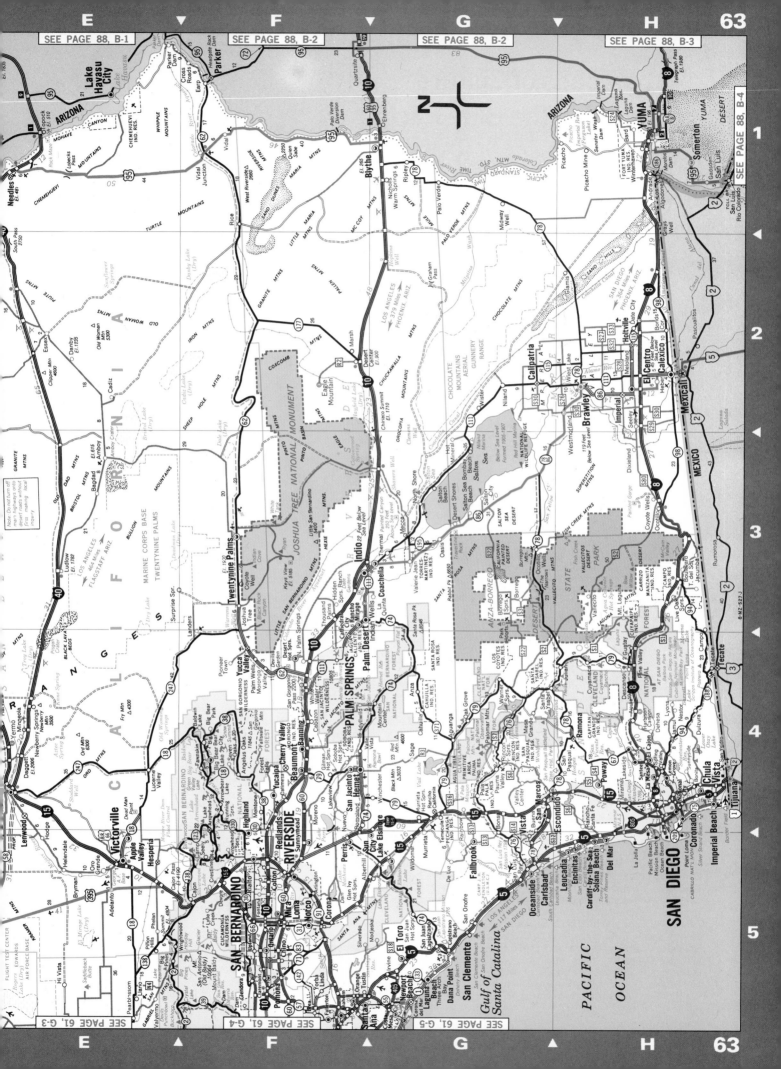

A Crossroads of Culture Anchored in the Blue Pacific

Hawaii

Three faces of Hawaii's beauty: Lava spews forth from fiery Kilauea Volcano (left); Flower leis garland two lovely wahines (right) wearing their traditional, colorful dress, the muumuu; Diamond Head, an extinct volcano, looms above the palm-fringed crescent of Waikiki Beach.

Mark Twain called them the "loveliest fleet of islands anchored in any ocean." Hawaii, the largest island in this archipelago of volcanic peaks, is dominated by the central peaks of Mauna Loa and Mauna Kea. In **Hawaii Volcanoes National Park (65, D-5)**, the highest drive in the Pacific climbs to 11,150 feet through an eerie landscape of lava flows that have spilled from the slopes of 13,680-foot Mauna Loa. Lava still bubbles through scarred earth in Kilauea Crater, a vast cauldron on the volcano's east flank. At Kalapana Black Sand Beach, coconut fronds fringe an expanse of black sand and ledges formed when lava from Mauna Loa seethed into the ocean and hardened. To the north is **Hilo (65, D-4)**, where heavy rains nourish the orchids for which the area is famous.

Skirting the southwestern slope of Mauna Loa, Highway 11 passes Pacific seascapes, macademia nut plantations, coffee plantations, lava flows. At **Kailua (65, C-5)** is the Hulihee Palace, built by governor John Adams Kuakini in 1838.

Kauai—The Garden Isle—brims with the tropical beauty of lush, often impenetrable jungle, shimmering rice paddies, and pineapple and sugarcane fields. Rising from the heart of the island, 5,170-foot Mount Waialeale soaks up almost 500 inches of rain annually—the wettest spot on earth. Runoff from the peak feeds a hundred waterfalls and at least six main rivers, one of which carved **Waimea Canyon (65, A-3)**, 10 miles long and 1½ miles wide. From the Kalalau overlook, at the northern end of the canyon, is a vista of sheer green cliffs plunging into the blue Pacific.

On Kauai's east coast, a launch ride carries visitors three miles up the Wailua River, Hawaii's only navigable waterway, to the **Fern Grotto (65, B-3)**, a cool cave lavishly festooned with ferns.

Maui's **Haleakala National Park (65, B-5)** lies like a moonscape of cinder slopes and lava rock. Rare wildlife such as the nene, Hawaii's state bird, and silversword plants, unique to this volcanic area, are found on the slopes of Haleakala Crater.

During the 19th-century heyday of American whaling, **Lahaina (65, A-4)** was a thriving seaport. Several historic sites from the period have survived: the white stucco home of missionary Dwight Baldwin, dating from the 1830s; Hale Pa'i, the missionaries' printing house; and Lahainaluna High School, the oldest school west of the Rockies (1831).

On Molokai, legend and history cling to **Halawa Valley (65, C-3)**, once settled by Hawaiian farmers and fishermen, now deserted except for a few houses, an old church, and ancient burial grounds. Jungle overruns taro plots, blankets the valley cliffs, and often hides hiking trails to 500-foot Hipuapua and 250-foot Moaula waterfalls.

At **Palaau State Park (65, C-3)**, visitors gaze down sheer 2,000-foot cliffs to Kalaupapa Peninsula, site of a leper colony once ministered to by the Belgian priest Father Damien. Visitors ride mules down steep trails to today's settlement, which can be toured.

Stretched out between the fluted green slopes of Oahu's Koolau Range and the Pacific, **Honolulu (65, B-2)** defies the notion that East and West never meet. Buddhist temples share a place with Christian churches, Chinese markets thrive along with suburban malls, museums display Polynesian crafts and Renaissance art. Foremost of the city's architectural attractions is the ornate Victorian Iolani Palace (1882), the only royal palace in the United States. Exhibits in the Bishop Museum range from exotic tropical flora and fauna to ancient surfboards and carved images of Hawaiian gods.

A short distance from Honolulu, the mountainous Round Top Drive provides bird's-eye views of Oahu's south coast as far as **Diamond Head (65, C-2)**. Among the world's most famous landmarks, the near-perfect volcanic crater on the edge of Waikiki Beach typifies the exotic beauty of all the Hawaiian Islands.

West of Honolulu is **Pearl Harbor (65, B-2)**, where a bridgelike memorial spans the submerged hulk of the U.S.S. *Arizona*. The battleship sank with a loss of 1,177 lives in the 1941 Japanese attack on the U.S. Pacific fleet.

Hawaii's ethnic diversity is celebrated at the Polynesian Cultural Center in **Laie (65, B-1)**. Displays showcase the arts, crafts, clothing, customs, cooking and sports of these far-flung islands—and capture the essence of Hawaii, a crossroads of culture.

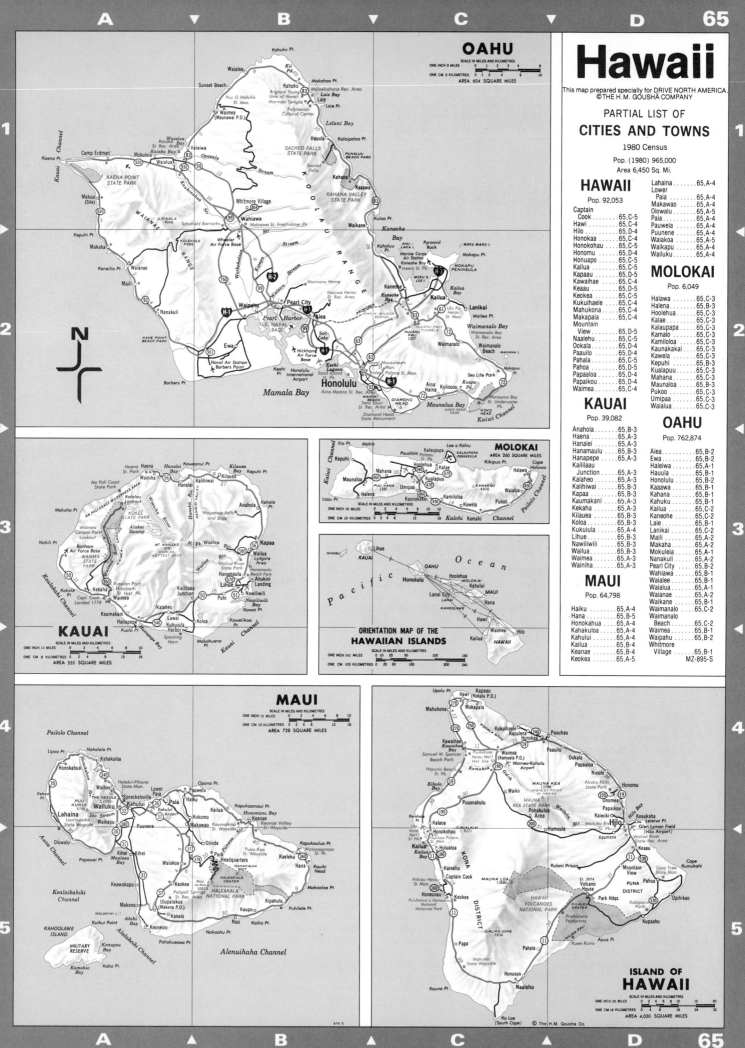

Hawaii

This map prepared specially for DRIVE NORTH AMERICA.
© THE H.M. GOUSHA COMPANY

PARTIAL LIST OF
CITIES AND TOWNS

1980 Census

Pop. (1980) 965,000
Area 6,450 Sq. Mi.

HAWAII

Pop. 92,053

Captain Cook	65,C-5
Hawi	65,C-4
Hilo	65,D-4
Honokaa	65,C-4
Honokohau	65,C-5
Honomu	65,D-4
Honuapo	65,C-5
Kailua	65,C-5
Kapaau	65,D-5
Kawaihae	65,C-4
Keaau	65,D-5
Keokea	65,C-5
Kukuihaele	65,C-4
Mahukona	65,C-4
Makapala	65,C-4
Mountain View	65,D-5
Naalehu	65,C-5
Ookala	65,C-4
Paauilo	65,C-4
Pahala	65,C-5
Pahoa	65,D-5
Papaaloa	65,D-4
Papaikou	65,D-4
Waimea	65,C-4

KAUAI

Pop. 39,082

Anahola	65,B-3
Haena	65,A-3
Hanalei	65,A-3
Hanamaulu	65,B-3
Hanapepe	65,A-3
Kalihiwai Junction	65,A-3
Kalaheo	65,A-3
Kalihiwai	65,B-3
Kapaa	65,B-3
Kaumakani	65,A-3
Kekaha	65,A-3
Kilauea	65,B-3
Koloa	65,B-3
Kukuiula	65,A-3
Lihue	65,B-3
Nawiliwili	65,B-3
Wailua	65,B-3
Waimea	65,A-3
Wainiha	65,A-3

MAUI

Pop. 64,798

Haiku	65,A-4
Hana	65,B-5
Honokahua	65,A-4
Kahakuloa	65,A-4
Kahului	65,A-4
Kailua	65,B-4
Keanae	65,B-5
Keokea	65,A-5

Lahaina	65,A-4
Lower Paia	65,A-4
Makawao	65,A-4
Olowalu	65,A-5
Paia	65,A-4
Pauwela	65,A-4
Puunene	65,A-4
Waiakoa	65,A-5
Waikapu	65,A-4
Wailuku	65,A-4

MOLOKAI

Pop. 6,049

Halawa	65,C-3
Halena	65,B-3
Hoolehua	65,C-3
Kalae	65,C-3
Kalaupapa	65,C-3
Kamalo	65,C-3
Kamiloloa	65,C-3
Kaunakakai	65,C-3
Kawela	65,C-3
Kepuhi	65,B-3
Kualapuu	65,C-3
Mahana	65,C-3
Maunaloa	65,B-3
Pukoo	65,C-3
Umipaa	65,C-3
Waialua	65,C-3

OAHU

Pop. 762,874

Aiea	65,B-2
Ewa	65,B-2
Haleiwa	65,A-1
Hauula	65,B-1
Honolulu	65,B-2
Kaaawa	65,B-1
Kahana	65,B-1
Kahuku	65,B-1
Kailua	65,C-2
Kaneohe	65,C-2
Laie	65,B-1
Lanikai	65,C-2
Maili	65,A-2
Makaha	65,A-2
Mokuleia	65,A-1
Nanakuli	65,A-2
Pearl City	65,B-2
Wahiawa	65,B-1
Waialee	65,B-1
Waialua	65,A-1
Waianae	65,A-2
Waikane	65,B-1
Waimanalo Beach	65,C-2
Waimea	65,B-1
Waipahu	65,B-1
Whitmore Village	65,B-1

MZ-895-S

All-Night Casinos and a 'Sleeping Rainbow'

Utah/Nevada

An empty, forbidding land of shimmering deserts and fantastically eroded canyons—this is how many travelers think of Utah and Nevada. And although these desert states do have green zones fed by mountain waters, the image of stark grandeur holds true.

Utah, the "National Park State," contains five of the nation's finest parks within a 200-mile circle in the southern part of the state. **Zion National Park (74, B-5)** derives its awesome cliffs from petrified sand dunes. Sandstone, deposited by a retreating prehistoric sea, rises 2,000 feet in canyon walls, arches, and massive monoliths. The reverence these features inspired in early explorers is reflected in many of the names—Altar of Sacrifice, Great White Throne, Temple of Sinawava. The same explorers predicted that only winged immortals would set foot atop the pinnacle of Angels Landing. But now a steep 2½-mile trail winds to the rock's summit, part of a well-developed trail system. West of Zion is **Grafton,** perhaps Utah's most photogenic ghost town.

Bryce Canyon National Park (74, C-4) is not really a canyon, but a 20-mile-long escarpment indented by a dozen natural amphitheaters. These notches are festooned with hoodoos—wind-carved spires, walls, arches, and other outcrops—painted shades of red, yellow, purple and white by the leaching of iron and manganese.

Nearby **Cedar Breaks National Monument (74, B-4)** has the same spectacular geology as Bryce. In winter, when park roads are closed except to visitors on snowmobiles or cross-country skis, the hues of Cedar Breaks contrast strikingly with the glittering snow. In summer, the vibrant rocks are complemented by vivid patches of wildflowers.

Capitol Reef National Park (75, E-3) was called "land of the sleeping rainbow" by Paiute Indians. Its jagged ramparts blocked frontier travel, and Australian prospectors called it a reef, after the coral barriers at sea. Fluted sandstone domes eroded by rain inspired the name capitol.

Canyonlands National Park (75, G-3) is a wilderness of 2,000-foot-deep gorges carved by the Green and Colorado rivers. One of the last explored regions of America, Canyonlands is seen in two parts by most motorists. To the north is Island in the Sky, a 25,000-acre peninsula surrounded by canyons (except for a 60-foot-wide isthmus called The Neck, over which the road passes). The southern part of Canyonlands is reached by a 36-mile spur past Newspaper Rock, a large display of Indian petroglyphs.

The world's greatest concentration of natural arches is in **Arches National Park (75, G-2).** While many arches, balanced rocks and other outcrops can be viewed along the road, the prize features—Landscape Arch, Double Arch, Delicate Arch—are best seen along short walking trails.

Utah also has a wealth of natural bridges. (Natural bridges span watercourses; arches

Bronze pioneers (above) *commemorate Utah's past at Temple Square, Salt Lake City.*

Checkerboard Mesa (right), *a giant of eroded sandstone, dominates Zion National Park.*

A paleontologist at Dinosaur National Park (below) *painstakingly unearths the fossilized bones of a Diplodocus, the largest of all dinosaur species.*

do not.) Bridges in various stages of erosion can be seen from a loop road through **Natural Bridges National Monument (75, F-4).** But the largest and most symmetrical natural bridge in the Southwest is **Rainbow Bridge (75, E-5).** This massive bridge of weathered pink sandstone is the largest known natural span in the world.

Bodies of water in desert regions are always spectacular, and **Lake Powell (75, E-5),** nearly 200 miles long and with 1,800 miles of shoreline, is a playground for every kind of water sport. The reservoir was formed by Glen Canyon Dam backing up the Colorado River.

Perched in an arid valley at 4,300 feet, **Salt Lake City (72, D-3),** was founded in 1847 by Mormon emigrants from Illinois. Salt Lake Temple, a monumental granite structure with three richly ornamented towers, dominates the 10-acre grounds within the walls of Temple Square. The Church Muse-

Neon blazes day and night in Las Vegas (above), luring millions to this gambling mecca. Vintage Fords and Cadillac Roadsters crowd Harrah's Automobile Collection, Reno (right).

um displays the plow used to turn over the first acre of land in the Salt Lake valley, pianos hauled across the plains by oxen, and the area's first printing press. Salt Lake Tabernacle, famed for its acoustics and 11,000-pipe organ, is the home of the Mormon Tabernacle Choir. Other church-related sites in Salt Lake City include the Beehive House (once the home of Mormon leader Brigham Young) and Brigham Young Forest Farm Home, a pioneer showplace dating back to 1863.

On the campus of the University of Utah are the Utah Museum of Natural History, with such exhibits as life-size wildlife dioramas and the skeletons of three dinosaurs. Nearby is the Utah Museum of Fine Arts. The Thomas Kearns Mansion and Carriage House, for 20 years the official residence of Utah governors, now houses the Utah Historical Society.

Great Salt Lake is the largest saline lake in the Western Hemisphere—a shrinking remnant of a huge freshwater lake that existed during the Ice Age. The broad salt flats west of the lake exemplify the probable fate of Great Salt Lake itself.

Mormons first farmed near **Provo (72, D-4)** in 1849. The city is now an agricultural and manufacturing center surrounded by impressive scenery such as Provo Canyon and 12,000-foot Mount Timpanogos. Museums of earth sciences, fine arts, life sciences,

and archeology attract visitors to Brigham Young University.

On the Utah–Colorado border, **Dinosaur National Monument (73, G-4)** displays a frieze of 140-million-year-old fossil bones. From a gallery opposite the quarry wall, visitors can watch as paleontologists uncover still more fossils embedded in solid rock.

Nevada's largest city, **Las Vegas (71, F-4)**, is North America's casino and nightclub capital. In this city that never sleeps are The Strip, a glittering three-mile stretch of hotels and nightclubs, and the downtown Casino Center, which covers three blocks of Fremont Street and is illuminated by 43 miles of neon tubing and some two million light bulbs.

Contrasting with colorful Las Vegas is the monumental symmetry of **Hoover Dam (71, F-4)**, rising 726 feet from bedrock. The bulwark stretches 1,244 feet across Black Canyon, its wall 660 feet thick at the base, a mere 45 feet at the top. Behind it the Colorado River backs up for 110 miles to form Lake Mead, one of the world's largest manmade lakes and a popular recreation area.

Reno (68, A-4), Nevada's second largest city, is a lively resort town set in a lush valley at the base of the Sierra Nevada. Harrah's Automobile Collection is the world's largest; more than 1,100 of the 1,500 cars in the collection are on display. At the Fleischmann Atmospherium-Planetarium, films relating to planets, galaxies, oceans and natural phenomena, past and present, are shown. Ski resorts and the scenery of Lake Tahoe are within a short drive.

In 1864, over the objections of the more populous Virginia City, **Carson City (68, A-4)** remained the capital of Nevada when it became a state. The discovery of the fabled Comstock Lode—which yielded both gold and silver—boosted the economy, and the thriving town became the social center of the area. A self-guided walking tour passes the silver-domed Capitol, Bliss Mansion,

Governor's Mansion, and Bowers Mansion with its ornate chandeliers, marble statues and elaborate antique furnishings. A mint, now the Nevada State Museum, coined almost $50 million between 1870 and 1893.

During the 1860s and 1870s, the glory years of the silver rush, **Virginia City (68, A-4)** was the queen city of Nevada. Its former stature is still reflected in the architecture of such buildings as MacKay Mansion (1860), Piper's Opera House, the Gothic St. Mary's in the Mountains (1868), and the Castle (1868), known as the "House of Silver Doorknobs."

Austin (68, D-4), too, was a silver boomtown. It was noted for its camel pack trains and local pony express, and for the Grindley Sack of Flour auctions in which one R. C. Grindley, by repeatedly auctioning a single sack of flour, raised $275,000 to help Civil War wounded. Much of the flavor of this period is retained in the historic district in the center of town.

Belmont (68, D-5) fared worse than Austin. The ghost town was once the flourishing seat of Nye County. It now holds a population of three, and a few lonely buildings from its heyday. Among the early structures still intact are a two-story brick courthouse and the Cosmopolitan Saloon, a weathered relic of the bonanza days.

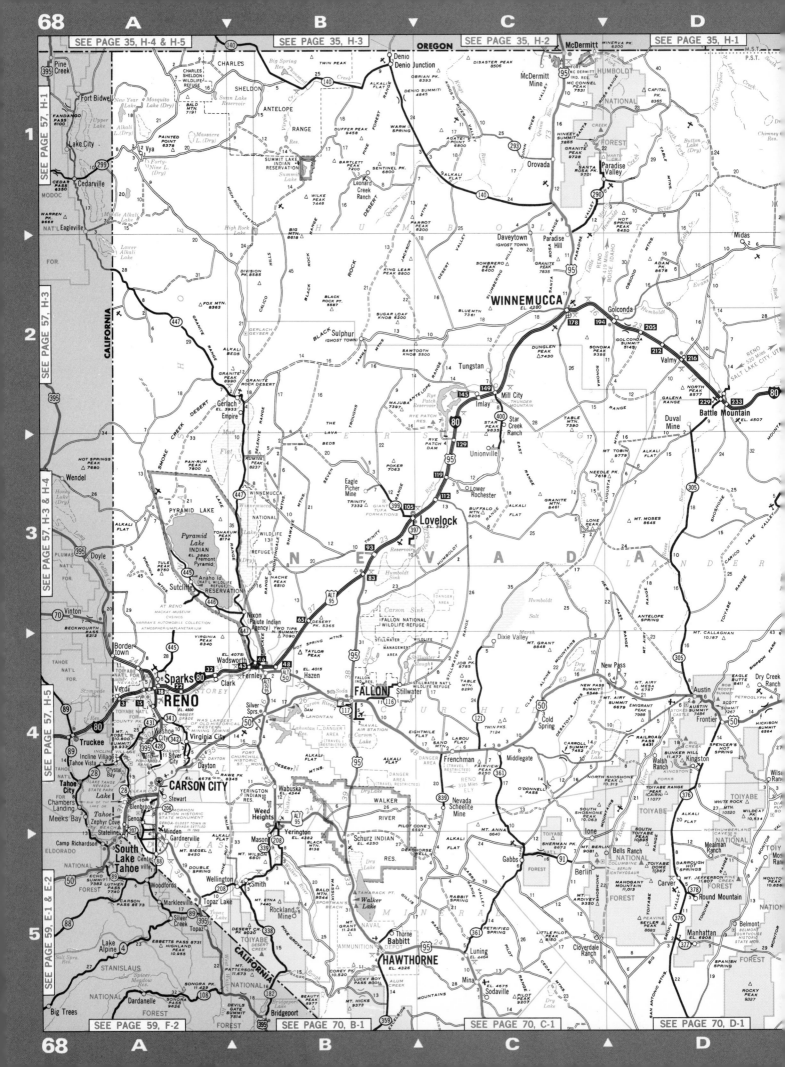

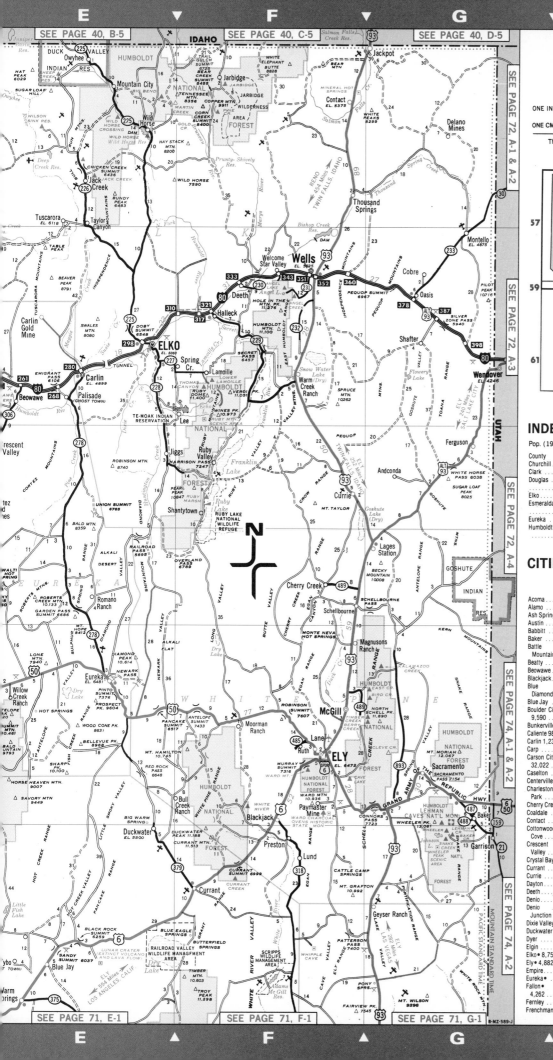

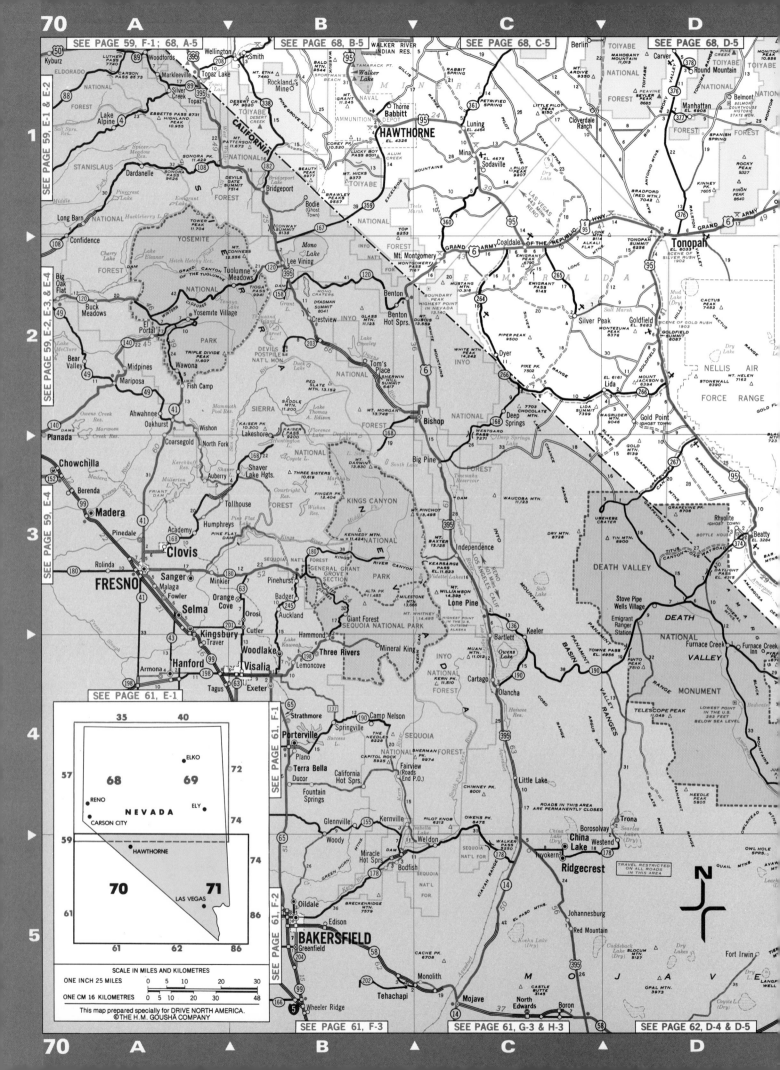

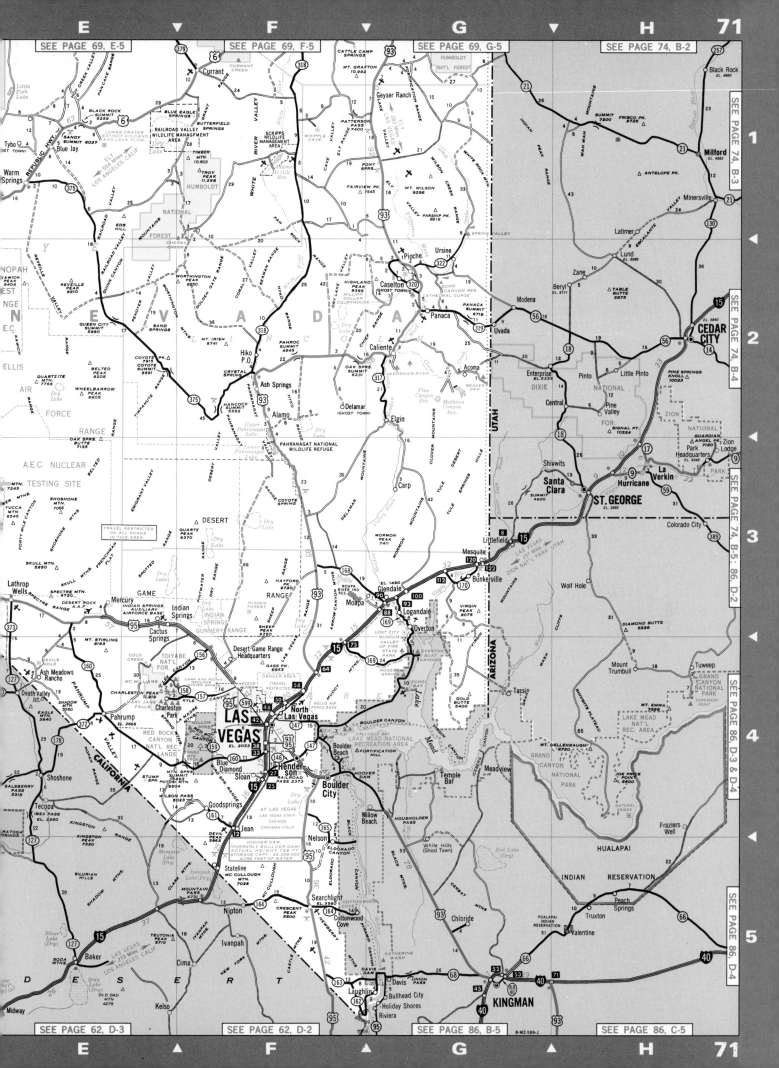

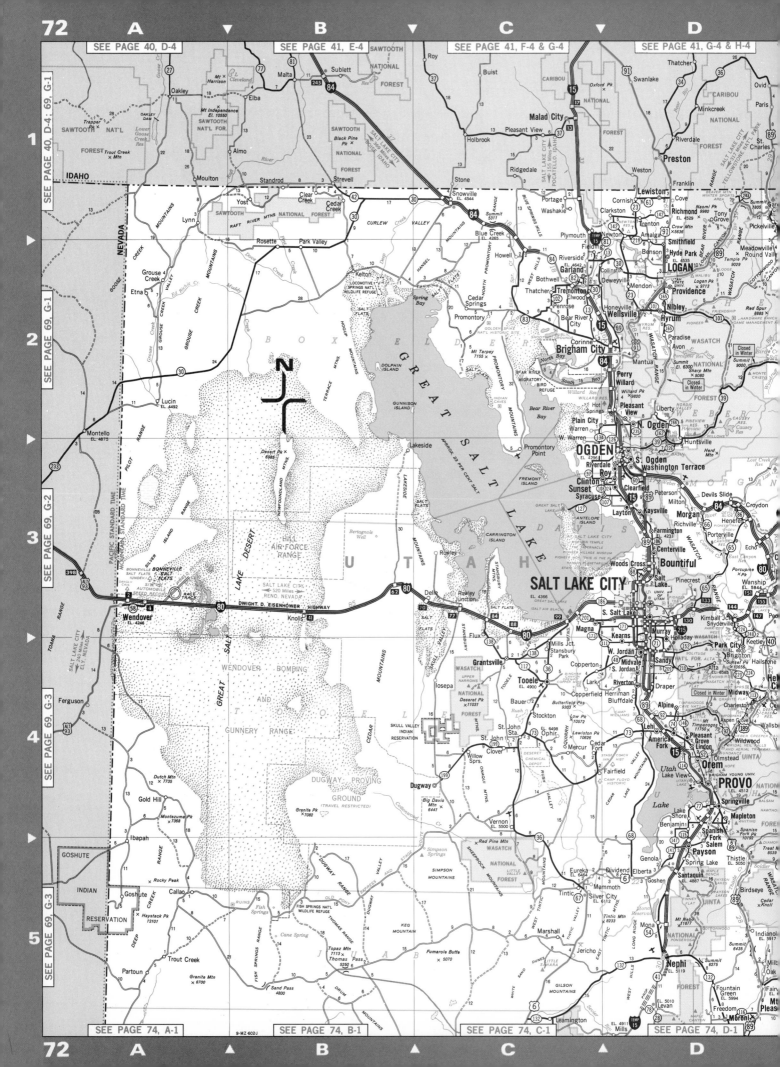

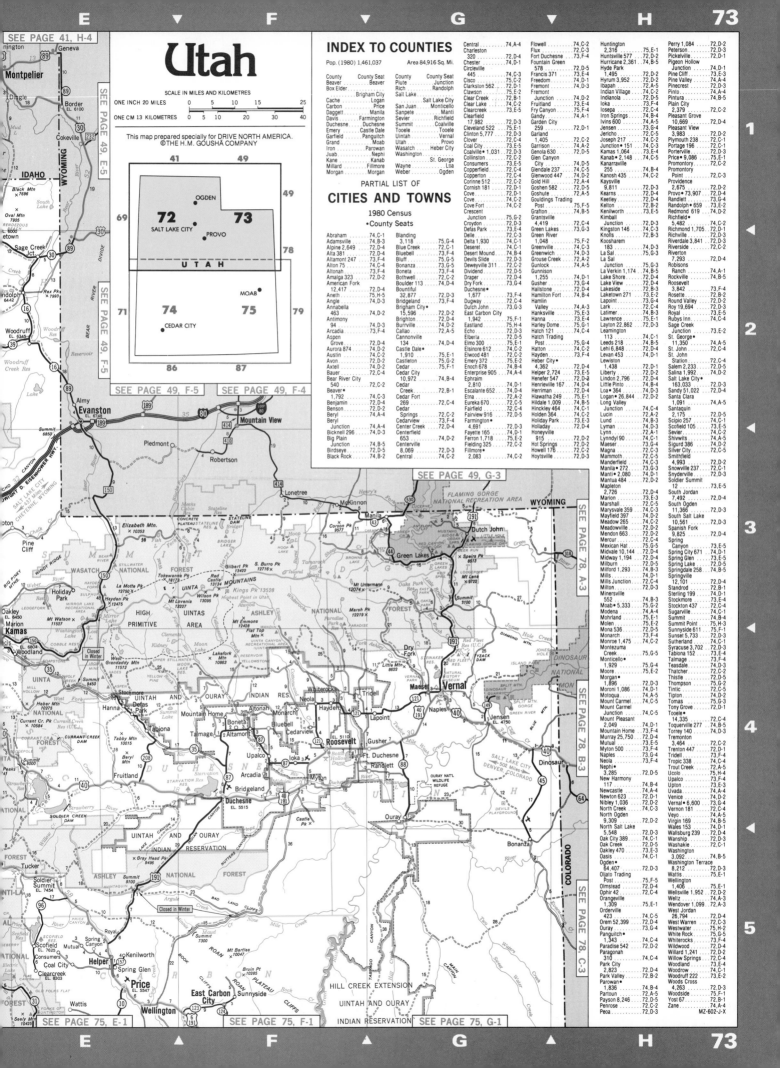

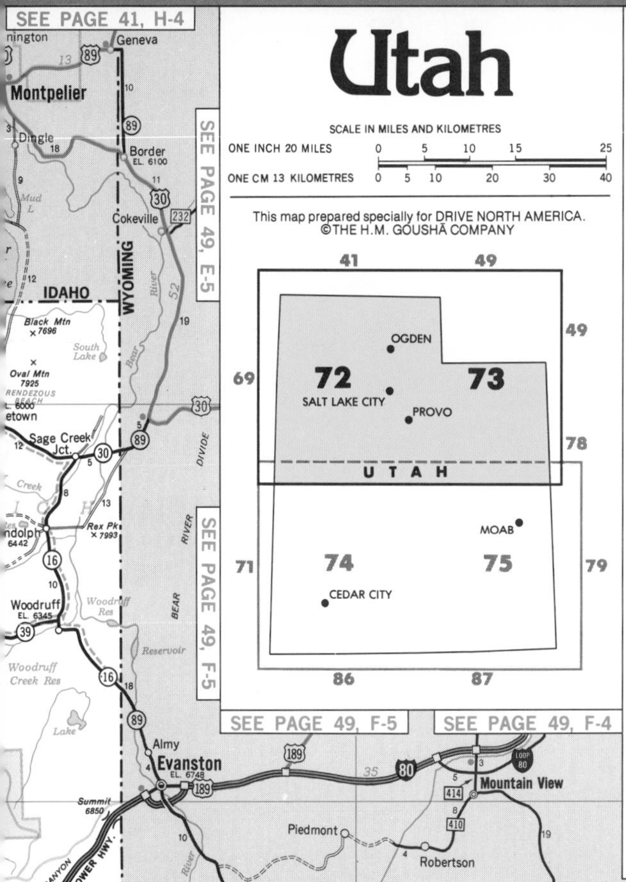
Utah
SCALE IN MILES AND KILOMETRES
ONE INCH 20 MILES
ONE CM 13 KILOMETRES
This map prepared specially for DRIVE NORTH AMERICA.
©THE H.M. GOUSHĀ COMPANY
SEE PAGE 41, H-4
SEE PAGE 49, E-5
SEE PAGE 49, F-5
SEE PAGE 49, F-4
OGDEN
SALT LAKE CITY
PROVO
MOAB
CEDAR CITY
UTAH
IDAHO
WYOMING
Montpelier
Geneva
Border
Cokeville
Evanston
Kamas
Woodland
Holiday Park
Marion
Oakley

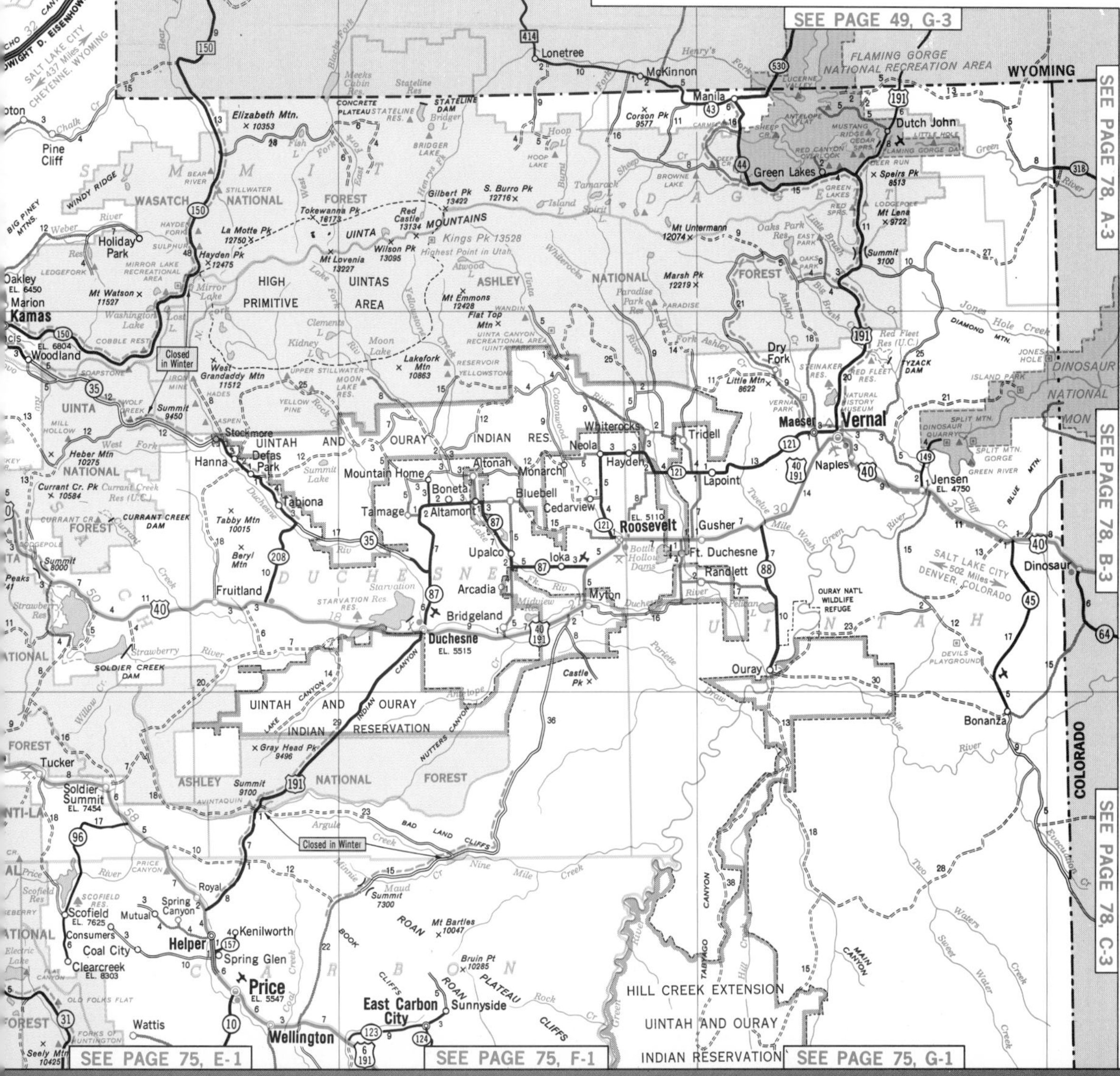
SEE PAGE 49, G-3
SEE PAGE 78, A-3
SEE PAGE 78, B-3
SEE PAGE 78, C-3
SEE PAGE 75, E-1
SEE PAGE 75, F-1
SEE PAGE 75, G-1
FLAMING GORGE NATIONAL RECREATION AREA
WYOMING
COLORADO
Mountain View
Lonetree
McKinnon
Manila
Dutch John
Green Lakes
HIGH UINTAS PRIMITIVE AREA
UINTA MOUNTAINS
Kings Pk 13528
ASHLEY NATIONAL FOREST
DINOSAUR NATIONAL MONUMENT
Vernal
Maeser
Naples
Jensen
Roosevelt
Duchesne
Myton
Fruitland
Tabiona
Hanna
Stockmore
Altamont
Ioka
Randlett
Ouray
Bonanza
UINTAH AND OURAY INDIAN RESERVATION
Soldier Summit
Scofield
Helper
Price
Wellington
East Carbon City
Sunnyside
Wattis
HILL CREEK EXTENSION
Closed in Winter

INDEX TO COUNTIES

Pop. (1980) 1,461,037 Area 84,916 Sq. Mi.

County	County Seat	County	County Seat
Beaver	Beaver	Piute	Junction
Box Elder	Brigham City	Rich	Randolph
Cache	Logan	Salt Lake	Salt Lake City
Carbon	Price	San Juan	Monticello
Daggett	Manila	Sanpete	Manti
Davis	Farmington	Sevier	Richfield
Duchesne	Duchesne	Summit	Coalville
Emery	Castle Dale	Tooele	Tooele
Garfield	Panguitch	Uintah	Vernal
Grand	Moab	Utah	Provo
Iron	Parowan	Wasatch	Heber City
Juab	Nephi	Washington	St. George
Kane	Kanab	Wayne	Loa
Millard	Fillmore	Weber	Ogden
Morgan	Morgan		

PARTIAL LIST OF

CITIES AND TOWNS

1980 Census

•County Seats

Abraham . . . 74,C-1
Adamsville . . . 74,B-3
Alpine 2,649 . . . 72,D-4
Alta 381 . . . 72,D-4
Altamont 247 . . . 73,F-4
Alton 75 . . . 74,C-4
Altonah . . . 73,F-4
Amalga 323 . . . 72,D-2
American Fork 12,417 . . . 72,D-4
Aneth . . . 75,H-5
Angle . . . 74,D-3
Annabella 463 . . . 74,D-2
Antimony 94 . . . 74,D-3
Arcadia . . . 73,F-4
Aspen Grove . . . 72,D-4
Aurora 874 . . . 74,D-2
Austin . . . 74,C-2
Avon . . . 72,D-2
Axtell . . . 74,D-2
Bauer . . . 72,C-4
Bear River City 540 . . . 72,C-2
Beaver• 1,792 . . . 74,C-3
Benjamin . . . 72,D-4
Benson . . . 72,D-2
Beryl . . . 74,A-4
Beryl Junction . . . 74,A-4
Bicknell 296 . . . 74,D-3
Big Plain Junction . . . 74,B-5
Birdseye . . . 72,D-5
Black Rock . . . 74,B-2
Blanding 3,118 . . . 75,G-4
Blue Creek . . . 72,C-1
Bluebell . . . 73,F-4
Bluff . . . 75,G-5
Bonanza . . . 73,G-5
Boneta . . . 73,F-4
Bothwell . . . 72,C-2
Boulder 113 . . . 74,D-4
Bountiful 32,877 . . . 72,D-3
Bridgeland . . . 73,F-4
Brigham City• 15,596 . . . 72,D-2
Brighton . . . 72,D-4
Burrville . . . 74,D-2
Callao . . . 72,A-5
Cannonville 134 . . . 74,D-4
Castle Dale• 1,910 . . . 75,E-1
Castleton . . . 75,G-2
Cedar . . . 75,F-1
Cedar City 10,972 . . . 74,B-4
Cedar Creek . . . 72,B-1
Cedar Fort 269 . . . 72,C-4
Cedar Springs . . . 72,C-2
Cedarview . . . 73,F-4
Center Creek . . . 72,D-4
Centerfield 653 . . . 74,D-2
Centerville 8,069 . . . 72,D-3
Central . . . 74,C-2
Central . . . 74,A-4
Charleston 320 . . . 72,D-4
Chester . . . 74,D-1
Circleville 445 . . . 74,C-3
Cisco . . . 75,C-2
Clarkston 562 . . . 72,D-1
Clawson . . . 75,E-2
Clear Creek . . . 72,B-1
Clear Lake . . . 74,C-2
Clearcreek . . . 73,E-5
Clearfield 17,982 . . . 72,D-3
Cleveland 522 . . . 75,E-1
Clinton 5,777 . . . 72,D-3
Clover . . . 72,C-4
Coal City . . . 73,E-5
Coalville• 1,031 . . . 72,D-3
Collinston . . . 72,C-2
Consumers . . . 73,E-5
Copperfield . . . 72,C-4
Copperton . . . 72,C-4
Corinne 512 . . . 72,C-2
Cornish 181 . . . 72,D-1
Cove . . . 72,D-1
Cove . . . 74,C-2
Cove Fort . . . 74,C-2
Crescent Junction . . . 75,G-2
Croydon . . . 72,D-3
Defas Park . . . 73,E-4
Delle . . . 72,C-3
Delta 1,930 . . . 74,C-1
Deseret . . . 74,C-1
Desert Mound . . . 74,B-4
Devils Slide . . . 72,D-3
Deweyville 311 . . . 72,C-2
Dividend . . . 72,D-5
Draper . . . 72,D-4
Dry Fork . . . 73,G-4
Duchesne• 1,677 . . . 73,F-4
Dugway . . . 72,C-4
Dutch John . . . 73,G-3
East Carbon City 1,942 . . . 75,F-1
Eastland . . . 75,H-4
Echo . . . 72,D-3
Elberta . . . 72,D-5
Elmo 300 . . . 75,E-1
Elsinore 612 . . . 74,C-2
Elwood 481 . . . 72,C-2
Emery 372 . . . 75,E-2
Enoch 678 . . . 74,B-4
Enterprise 905 . . . 74,A-4
Ephraim 2,810 . . . 74,D-1
Escalante 652 . . . 74,D-4
Etna . . . 72,A-2
Eureka 670 . . . 72,C-5
Fairfield . . . 72,C-4
Fairview 916 . . . 72,D-5
Farmington• 4,691 . . . 72,D-3
Fayette 165 . . . 74,D-1
Ferron 1,718 . . . 75,E-2
Fielding 325 . . . 72,C-2
Fillmore• 2,083 . . . 74,C-2
Flowell . . . 74,C-2
Flux . . . 72,C-3
Fort Duchesne . . . 73,F-4
Fountain Green 578 . . . 72,D-5
Francis 371 . . . 73,E-4
Freedom . . . 74,D-1
Fremont . . . 74,D-3
Fremont Junction . . . 74,D-2
Fruitland . . . 73,E-4
Fry Canyon . . . 75,F-4
Gandy . . . 74,A-1
Garden City 259 . . . 72,D-1
Garland 1,405 . . . 72,C-2
Garrison . . . 74,A-2
Genola 630 . . . 72,D-5
Glen Canyon City . . . 74,D-5
Glendale 237 . . . 74,C-5
Glenwood 447 . . . 74,D-2
Gold Hill . . . 72,A-4
Goshen 582 . . . 72,D-5
Goshute . . . 72,A-5
Gouldings Trading Post . . . 75,F-5
Grafton . . . 74,B-5
Grantsville 4,419 . . . 72,C-4
Green Lakes . . . 73,G-3
Green River 1,048 . . . 75,F-2
Greenville . . . 74,C-3
Greenwich . . . 74,D-3
Grouse Creek . . . 72,A-2
Gunlock . . . 74,A-5
Gunnison 1,255 . . . 74,D-1
Gusher . . . 73,G-4
Hailstone . . . 72,D-4
Hamilton Fort . . . 74,B-4
Hamlin Valley . . . 74,A-3
Hanksville . . . 75,E-3
Hanna . . . 73,E-4
Harley Dome . . . 75,G-1
Hatch 121 . . . 74,C-4
Hatch Trading Post . . . 75,G-4
Hatton . . . 74,C-2
Hayden . . . 73,F-4
Heber City• 4,362 . . . 72,D-4
Helper 2,724 . . . 73,E-5
Henefer 547 . . . 72,D-3
Henrieville 167 . . . 74,D-4
Herriman . . . 72,D-4
Hiawatha 249 . . . 75,E-1
Hildale 1,009 . . . 74,B-5
Hinckley 464 . . . 74,C-1
Holden 364 . . . 74,C-2
Holiday Park . . . 73,E-3
Holladay . . . 72,D-4
Honeyville 915 . . . 72,D-2
Hot Springs . . . 72,D-2
Howell 176 . . . 72,C-2
Hoytsville . . . 72,D-3
Huntington 2,316 . . . 75,E-1
Huntsville 577 . . . 72,D-2
Hurricane 2,361 . . . 74,B-5
Hyde Park 1,495 . . . 72,D-2
Hyrum 3,952 . . . 72,D-2
Ibapah . . . 72,A-5
Indian Village . . . 74,C-2
Indianola . . . 72,D-5
Ioka . . . 73,F-4
Iosepa . . . 72,C-4
Iron Springs . . . 74,B-4
Ivins 600 . . . 74,A-5
Jensen . . . 73,G-4
Jericho . . . 72,C-5
Joseph 217 . . . 74,C-2
Junction• 151 . . . 74,C-3
Kamas 1,064 . . . 73,E-4
Kanab• 2,148 . . . 74,C-5
Kanarraville 255 . . . 74,B-4
Kanosh 435 . . . 74,C-2
Kaysville 9,811 . . . 72,D-3
Kearns . . . 72,D-4
Keetley . . . 72,D-4
Kelton . . . 72,B-2
Kenilworth . . . 73,E-5
Kimball Junction . . . 72,D-3
Kingston 146 . . . 74,C-3
Knolls . . . 72,B-3
Koosharem 183 . . . 74,D-3
La Sal . . . 75,G-3
La Sal Junction . . . 75,G-3
La Verkin 1,174 . . . 74,B-5
Lake Shore . . . 72,D-4
Lake View . . . 72,D-4
Lakeside . . . 72,B-3
Laketown 271 . . . 73,E-2
Lapoint . . . 73,G-4
Lark . . . 72,C-4
Latimer . . . 74,B-3
Lawrence . . . 75,E-1
Layton 22,862 . . . 72,D-3
Leamington 113 . . . 74,C-1
Leeds 218 . . . 74,B-5
Lehi 6,848 . . . 72,D-4
Levan 453 . . . 74,D-1
Lewiston 1,438 . . . 72,D-1
Liberty . . . 72,D-2
Lindon 2,796 . . . 72,D-4
Little Pinto . . . 74,B-4
Loa• 364 . . . 74,D-3
Logan• 26,844 . . . 72,D-2
Long Valley Junction . . . 74,C-4
Lucin . . . 72,A-2
Lund . . . 74,B-3
Lyman . . . 74,D-3
Lynn . . . 72,A-1
Lynndyl 90 . . . 74,C-1
Maeser . . . 73,G-4
Magna . . . 72,C-3
Mammoth . . . 72,C-5
Manderfield . . . 74,C-3
Manila• 272 . . . 73,G-3
Manti• 2,080 . . . 74,D-1
Mantua 484 . . . 72,D-2
Mapleton 2,726 . . . 72,D-4
Marion . . . 73,E-3
Marshall . . . 72,C-5
Marysvale 359 . . . 74,C-3
Mayfield 397 . . . 74,D-2
Meadow 265 . . . 74,C-2
Meadowville . . . 72,D-2
Mendon 663 . . . 72,D-2
Mercur . . . 72,C-4
Mexican Hat . . . 75,G-5
Midvale 10,144 . . . 72,D-4
Midway 1,194 . . . 72,D-4
Milburn . . . 72,D-5
Milford 1,293 . . . 74,B-3
Mills . . . 74,D-1
Mills Junction . . . 72,C-4
Milton . . . 72,D-3
Minersville 552 . . . 74,B-3
Moab• 5,333 . . . 75,G-2
Modena . . . 74,A-4
Mohrland . . . 75,E-1
Molen . . . 75,E-2
Mona 536 . . . 72,D-5
Monarch . . . 73,F-4
Monroe 1,475 . . . 74,C-2
Montezuma Creek . . . 75,G-5
Monticello• 1,929 . . . 75,G-4
Moore . . . 75,E-2
Morgan• 1,896 . . . 72,D-3
Moroni 1,086 . . . 74,D-1
Motoqua . . . 74,A-5
Mount Carmel . . . 74,C-5
Mount Carmel Junction . . . 74,C-5
Mount Pleasant 2,049 . . . 74,D-1
Mountain Home . . . 73,F-4
Murray 25,750 . . . 72,D-4
Mutual . . . 73,E-5
Myton 500 . . . 73,F-4
Naples . . . 73,G-4
Neola . . . 73,F-4
Nephi• 3,285 . . . 72,D-5
New Harmony 117 . . . 74,B-4
Newcastle . . . 74,A-4
Newton 623 . . . 72,D-1
Nibley 1,036 . . . 72,D-2
North Creek . . . 74,C-3
North Ogden 9,309 . . . 72,D-2
North Salt Lake 5,548 . . . 72,D-3
Oak City 389 . . . 74,C-1
Oak Creek . . . 72,D-5
Oakley 470 . . . 73,E-3
Oasis . . . 74,C-1
Ogden• 64,407 . . . 72,D-3
Oljato Trading Post . . . 75,F-5
Olmstead . . . 72,D-4
Ophir 42 . . . 72,C-4
Orangeville 1,309 . . . 75,E-1
Orderville 423 . . . 74,C-5
Orem 52,399 . . . 72,D-4
Ouray . . . 73,G-4
Panguitch• 1,343 . . . 74,C-4
Paradise 542 . . . 72,D-2
Paragonah 310 . . . 74,C-4
Park City 2,823 . . . 72,D-4
Park Valley . . . 72,B-2
Parowan• 1,836 . . . 74,B-4
Partoun . . . 72,A-5
Payson 8,246 . . . 72,D-5
Penrose . . . 72,C-2
Peoa . . . 72,D-3
Perry 1,084 . . . 72,D-2
Peterson . . . 72,D-3
Pickelville . . . 72,D-1
Pigeon Hollow Junction . . . 74,D-1
Pine Cliff . . . 73,E-3
Pine Valley . . . 74,A-4
Pinecrest . . . 72,D-3
Pinto . . . 74,A-4
Pintura . . . 74,B-5
Plain City 2,379 . . . 72,C-2
Pleasant Grove 10,669 . . . 72,D-4
Pleasant View 3,983 . . . 72,D-2
Plymouth 238 . . . 72,C-1
Portage 196 . . . 72,C-1
Porterville . . . 72,D-3
Price• 9,086 . . . 75,E-1
Promontory . . . 72,C-2
Promontory Point . . . 72,C-3
Providence 2,675 . . . 72,D-2
Provo• 73,907 . . . 72,D-4
Randlett . . . 73,G-4
Randolph• 659 . . . 73,E-2
Redmond 619 . . . 74,D-2
Richfield• 5,482 . . . 74,C-2
Richmond 1,705 . . . 72,D-1
Richville . . . 72,D-3
Riverdale 3,841 . . . 72,D-3
Riverside . . . 72,C-2
Riverton 7,293 . . . 72,D-4
Robisons Ranch . . . 74,A-1
Rockville . . . 74,B-5
Roosevelt 3,842 . . . 73,F-4
Rosette . . . 72,B-2
Round Valley . . . 72,D-2
Roy 19,694 . . . 72,D-3
Royal . . . 73,E-5
Rubys Inn . . . 74,C-4
Sage Creek Junction . . . 73,E-2
St. George• 11,350 . . . 74,A-5
St. John . . . 72,C-4
St. John Station . . . 72,C-4
Salem 2,233 . . . 72,D-5
Salina 1,992 . . . 74,D-2
Salt Lake City• 163,033 . . . 72,D-3
Sandy 51,022 . . . 72,D-4
Santa Clara 1,091 . . . 74,A-5
Santaquin 2,175 . . . 72,D-5
Scipio 257 . . . 74,C-1
Scofield 105 . . . 73,E-5
Sevier . . . 74,C-2
Shivwits . . . 74,A-5
Sigurd 386 . . . 74,D-2
Silver City . . . 72,C-5
Smithfield 4,993 . . . 72,D-2
Snowville 237 . . . 72,C-1
Snyderville . . . 72,D-3
Soldier Summit 12 . . . 73,E-5
South Jordan 7,492 . . . 72,D-4
South Ogden 11,366 . . . 72,D-3
South Salt Lake 10,561 . . . 72,D-3
Spanish Fork 9,825 . . . 72,D-4
Spring Canyon . . . 73,E-5
Spring City 671 . . . 74,D-1
Spring Glen . . . 73,E-5
Spring Lake . . . 72,D-5
Springdale 258 . . . 74,B-5
Springville 12,101 . . . 72,D-4
Standrod . . . 72,B-1
Sterling 199 . . . 74,D-1
Stockmore . . . 73,E-4
Stockton 437 . . . 72,C-4
Sugarville . . . 74,C-1
Summit . . . 74,B-4
Summit Point . . . 75,H-3
Sunnyside 611 . . . 75,F-1
Sunset 5,733 . . . 72,D-3
Sutherland . . . 74,C-1
Syracuse 3,702 . . . 72,D-3
Tabiona 152 . . . 73,E-4
Talmage . . . 73,F-4
Teasdale . . . 74,D-3
Thatcher . . . 72,C-2
Thistle . . . 72,D-5
Thompson . . . 75,G-2
Tintic . . . 72,C-5
Tipton . . . 74,D-2
Tomas . . . 75,G-3
Tony Grove . . . 72,D-1
Tooele• 14,335 . . . 72,C-4
Toquerville 277 . . . 74,B-5
Torrey 140 . . . 74,D-3
Tremonton 3,464 . . . 72,C-2
Trenton 447 . . . 72,D-1
Tridell . . . 73,F-4
Tropic 338 . . . 74,C-4
Trout Creek . . . 72,A-5
Ucolo . . . 75,H-4
Upalco . . . 73,F-4
Upton . . . 73,E-3
Uvada . . . 74,A-4
Venice . . . 74,D-2
Vernal• 6,600 . . . 73,G-4
Vernon 181 . . . 72,C-4
Veyo . . . 74,A-5
Virgin 169 . . . 74,B-5
Wales 153 . . . 74,D-1
Wallsburg 239 . . . 72,D-4
Wanship . . . 72,D-3
Washakie . . . 72,C-1
Washington 3,092 . . . 74,B-5
Washington Terrace 8,212 . . . 72,D-3
Wattis . . . 75,E-1
Wellington 1,406 . . . 75,E-1
Wellsville 1,952 . . . 72,D-2
Weltz . . . 74,A-3
Wendover 1,099 . . . 72,A-3
West Jordan 26,794 . . . 72,D-4
West Warren . . . 72,C-3
Westwater . . . 75,H-2
White Rock . . . 75,G-5
Whiterocks . . . 73,F-4
Wildwood . . . 72,D-4
Willard 1,241 . . . 72,D-2
Willow Springs . . . 72,C-4
Woodland . . . 73,E-4
Woodrow . . . 74,C-1
Woodruff 222 . . . 73,E-2
Woods Cross 4,263 . . . 72,D-3
Woodside . . . 75,F-1
Yost 67 . . . 72,B-1
Zane . . . 74,A-4

MZ-602-J-X

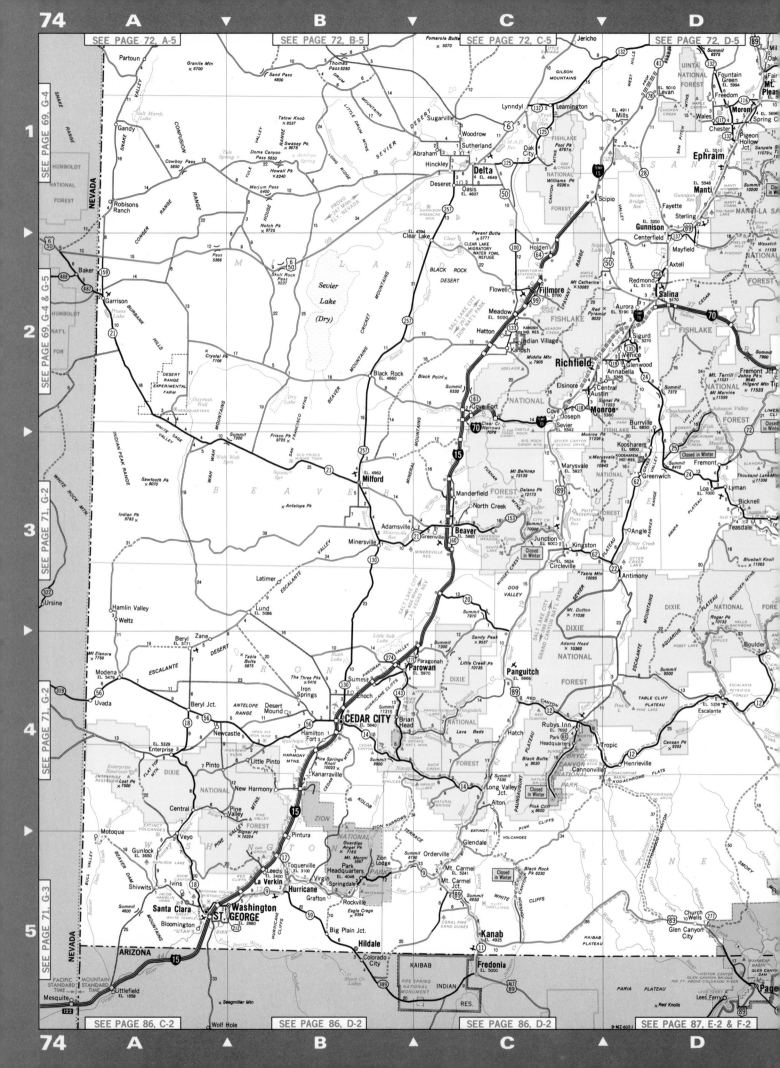

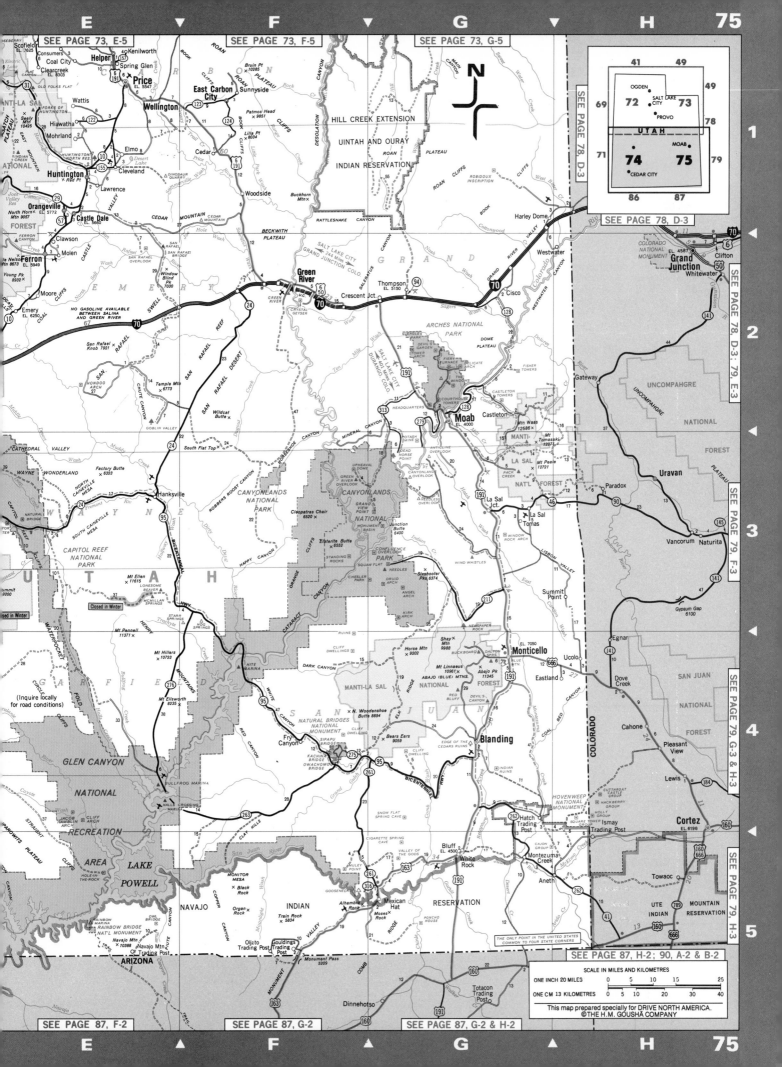

Ghosts of the Gold Rush
Haunt Ski Trails and Hot Springs

Colorado

Some fifty peaks, rising to 14,000 feet and more, cast their shadow over the center of Colorado. To the east, high plains stretch toward the horizon, supporting cattle and crops. To the west, the Colorado River and its tributaries slice through dry plateau country rich in oil and natural gas.

Colorado's most popular natural attraction is **Rocky Mountain National Park (80, B-2),** a 410-square-mile wilderness of jagged mountaintops, alpine lakes and valleys, forests, glaciers and perpetual snowfields. The mountains nurture such wildlife as elk, mule deer, and bighorn sheep. Trail Ridge Road, the highest through highway in the United States, climbs to 12,183 feet and crosses alpine tundra for 11 of its 48 miles between Estes Park and Grand Lake. At Farview Curve is a splendid view of the Never Summer Mountains. Far below is the birthplace of the Colorado River, the prime creator of Arizona's Grand Canyon, on its way to the Gulf of California.

A spectacular introduction to Rocky Mountain National Park for travelers from the east, **Big Thompson Canyon** is traversed by a road that leads steadily upward alongside the rushing Big Thompson River. **Estes Park,** gateway to the mountains, is at the head of the canyon. To the north, the Cache la Poudre (hide the powder) River has cut a narrow valley through Roosevelt National Forest in **Cache la Poudre Canyon.**

Indian Peaks marks one end of the 50-mile-wide gold and silver seam that extends through the mountains to the southwest corner of the state. These precious metals spurred the growth of Colorado during the gold rush of 1859 and the silver rush of 1870. **Denver (80, C-1),** the state capital, flourished with these bonanzas. The dome of its 272-foot-high capitol building, covered with gold, is a tribute to this rich past. The dome contrasts strikingly with the steel-and-glass skyscrapers that crowd downtown Denver. In the three-block Civic Center are a number of handsome public buildings and monuments. Particularly remarkable is sculptor Alexander Phimister Proctor's bronze "Bronco Buster," which appears to defy gravity. The massive City and County Building, occupying an entire city block, is built in modified Roman style. The curved front is colonnaded with Doric columns that rival the largest ever erected in Greece and Rome. Nearby, the Denver Art Museum houses some 20,000 art objects from all major historical periods and cultures. Exhibits in the Forney Transportation Museum include automobiles, carriages, railroad engines, airplanes and fire-fighting equipment. Other historical attractions are the Colonial-style Governor's Mansion and the 1890 Molly Brown House, home of the famous heroine of the play "Unsinkable Molly Brown." The U.S. Mint, thought to hold some $2.5 billion in gold, can be visited. The sweeping concrete and plexiglass Boettcher Memorial Conservatory is the main feature

of the 20-acre Denver Botanic Gardens. There are Japanese and herb gardens, and seasonal displays of annuals and perennials.

Although mining towns in the mountains often died when the ore gave out, ghosts did not take over everywhere. With the rising value of gold and silver, some mines, such as those in the Cripple Creek district, have reopened. **Central City** and **Georgetown (80, C-2)** preserve their mining heritage for tourists. Summer throngs in Central City's honky-tonk commercial district echo those of the boomtown's early years. More genteel Georgetown has restored many of its Victorian gingerbread homes, and the handsome Hotel de Paris (1875).

Leadville (80, D-3) began as a mining camp when gold was discovered at nearby California Gulch in 1860, but its real prosperity came with the discovery of vast silver deposits. Buildings from the town's heyday are reminders of the life-styles enjoyed by the few who struck it rich. Though its straight-lined exterior seems rather stark, the interior of Healy House, built in 1878, is a trove of relics epitomizing Victorian elegance. Red velvet and gilt, and hand-carved furniture and mirrors backed with diamond dust abound. A stained-glass window shaped remarkably like a human eye accounts for the name of the House with the Eye Museum. When the Tabor Opera House opened in

1879, many claimed it was the biggest and best west of the Mississippi. The stage today remains set as though for a performance.

Other mining towns such as Dillon, Breckenridge and Aspen have found new life as ski resorts. **Vail (80, C-3),** the world's largest one-mountain ski resort, was developed by World War II veterans who had trained nearby for mountain fighting.

The geologic upheaval that brought precious minerals to the earth's surface also peppered the region with hot springs. Glenwood, Hot Sulphur, Pagosa, and Steamboat Springs have lured visitors from far and wide into the luxury of a good hot soak. **Idaho Springs (80, C-2)** also boasts a colorful mining history and is the gateway to the highest highway in the United States, which winds to the top of Mount Evans (14,264 feet).

Even in 1871 hot springs were popular—so

Challenging runs and deep powder lure skiers to Aspen (left). White water raftsmen (below) battle a turbulent stretch of the 277-mile Colorado River.

Colorado gold crowns the Capitol, Denver.

Six centuries separate the heydays of mining camp Ashcroft (above), now a ghost town, and the cliffside Anasazi Indian ruins of Mesa Verde National Park (left).

much so that one developer named his resort **Colorado Springs (81, E-1),** despite the fact that there were no springs there. On a plateau backed by towering mountains is the U.S. Air Force Academy, a space-age complex of glass, aluminum and marble buildings. In the Pioneers' Museum, carriages, portraits, and early photographs recall the history of the Colorado Springs region. One of the world's best collections of mounted tropical insects, including a 17-inch specimen from New Guinea, draws visitors to the May Natural History Museum.

Strange red rock formations called the Garden of the Gods cover much of the western edge of Colorado Springs, and Pike National Forest, dominated by **Pikes Peak,** lies just beyond. Visitors can ascend by car—over a toll road up Ute Pass—or by cog railway from Manitou Springs. To the west, **Florissant Fossil Beds National Monument (81, E-2),** preserves fossilized animals and plants buried 35 million years ago by volcanic eruptions.

The 36-mile **Gold Camp Road** traverses rugged mountain scenery to the site of what were, 80 years ago, the richest gold workings in the world. Visitors can go down into the Mollie Kathleen mine for a glimpse into the past and the hard life of the miner.

Sheer walls of red granite, whose color changes with the sun, rise 1,000 feet above the Arkansas River in dizzying Royal Gorge near **Canon City (81, F-2).** The gorge can be viewed from the suspension bridge that crosses it—said to be the world's highest—and from an aerial tramway, cable car or walkway.

The southern Colorado skyline is marked by the San Juan Mountains, an awesome jumble of 14,000-foot peaks raised by ancient volcanoes. During the cataclysm, valuable minerals were forced to the surface, giving rise to such mining towns as Telluride, Silverton, Ouray and Trinidad. To transport this wealth from the mountains, narrow-gauge railroads were constructed. The Cumbres & Toltec Scenic Railroad still links **Antonito (81, H-3)** and Chama, New Mexico. The "Silverton" threads the gorge of the Animas River between **Durango (79, H-2)** and **Silverton (79, G-1).**

Great Sand Dunes National Monument (81, G-2) rises like a mirage from the almost treeless San Luis Valley. The dunes run 10 miles along the flank of the Sangre de Cristo Mountains, many of whose peaks are snow-topped year round—a visual blend of Sahara and Switzerland. For centuries, winds sweeping across the valley floor have picked up sand anchored only by sparse grasses and sagebrush. As the winds rise over the Sangre de Cristo range, they lose velocity, and rain sand at the foot of the mountains. The resulting accumulation has produced dunes 700 feet high.

While not as dry as the San Luis Valley, the plateau country of western Colorado receives little rain. This tableland, cut by steep canyons, was inhabited for 1,300 years by the Anasazi Indians. At **Mesa Verde National Park (79, H-3),** visitors can see excavated ruins of 1,000-year-old pit houses and "pueblos in the sky" the Anasazi built on mesa tops and in natural caves. The largest, the Cliff Palace, contains 200 rooms and 23 ceremonial kivas (chambers). Spruce Tree House, situated in a cave in Spruce Tree Canyon, is a complex of 114 living and storage rooms and eight kivas built over the course of about 100 years. The best-preserved and third-largest cliff dwelling in the park, it can be seen on a self-guided tour. Four separate dwelling areas nestle in the Fewkes Canyon Ruins. Symmetrical Fire Temple was probably used for ceremonies; it is visible from the drive above. New Fire House holds two caves with living rooms and three kivas, while Oak Tree House encompasses 30 living areas and seven kivas. A virtual ruin, Mummy House derives its name from the preserved body of a child found there. In summer, park rangers conduct tours of these ancient buildings—man's earliest apartment houses.

No canyon in North America is at once as deep, narrow, and darkly forbidding as the **Black Canyon of the Gunnison River (79, E-1).** Taking its name from the gloom of its shadowed depths, this chasm starts near Colorado's Blue Mesa Dam and carries the turbulent Gunnison River plunging 2,150 feet on its journey to its confluence with the North Fork River, some 50 miles westward. Chasm Wall has an almost vertical drop of 1,800 feet, and Colorado's greatest cliff, the Painted Wall, has a sheer 2,250 feet from rim to river. Cougars and Rocky Mountain bighorn sheep prowl the canyon's lonelier reaches.

The main branch of the Colorado River cuts several deep canyons as it wends from the west side of Rocky Mountain National Park through the ranchland of the western slope, past oil shale cliffs on the edge of the Roan Plateau. Across the Grand Valley's irrigated croplands and orchards, tributaries of the Colorado have carved fanciful buttresses and delicate spires in the gorges of **Colorado National Monument (98, D-3). Grand Mesa (79, E-2),** a 10,000-foot-high tableland to the east, is the world's largest flattop mountain.

Colorado shares one of its finest canyons with Utah in **Dinosaur National Monument (78, B-3)** at Echo Park, where the Yampa joins the Green River in a canyon nearly 3,000 feet deep. An overlook, a short walk from the end of the road at Harpers Corner, gives a superb view of the canyon. The quarry and wall of fossils for which the park is named is near Jensen, Utah.

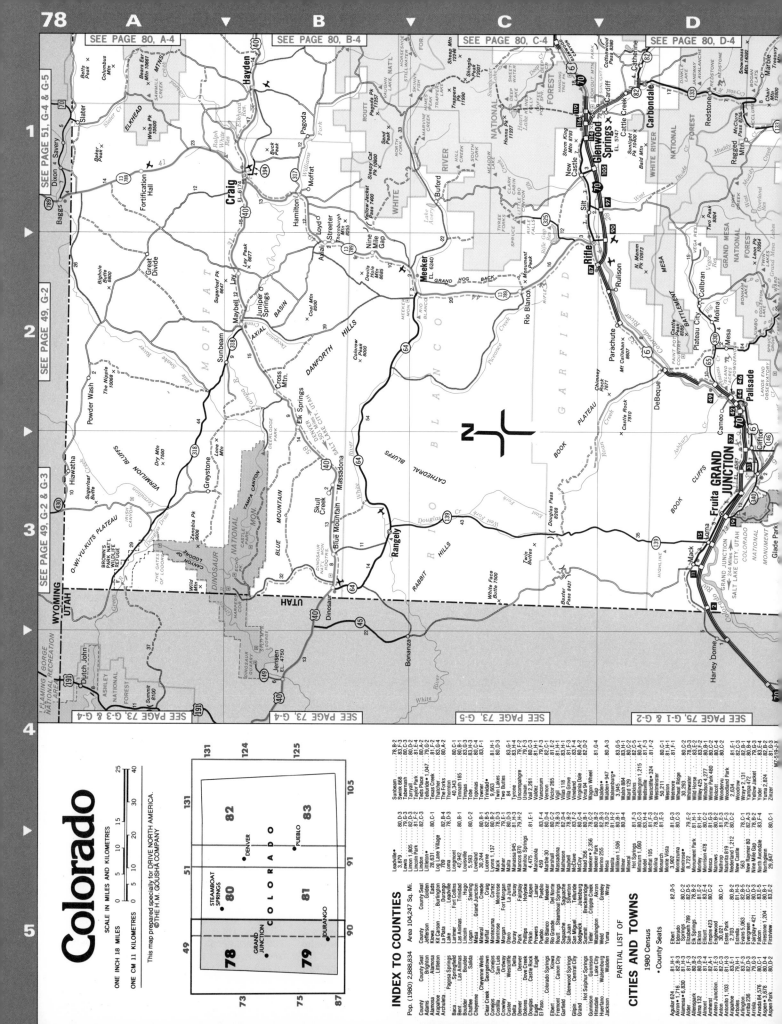

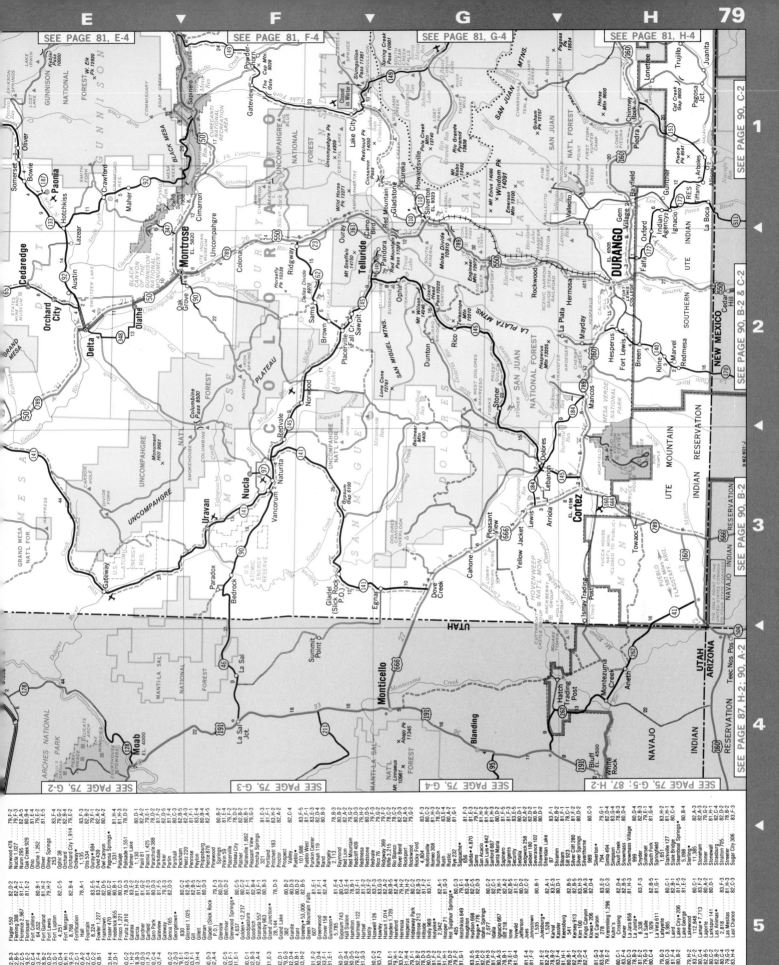

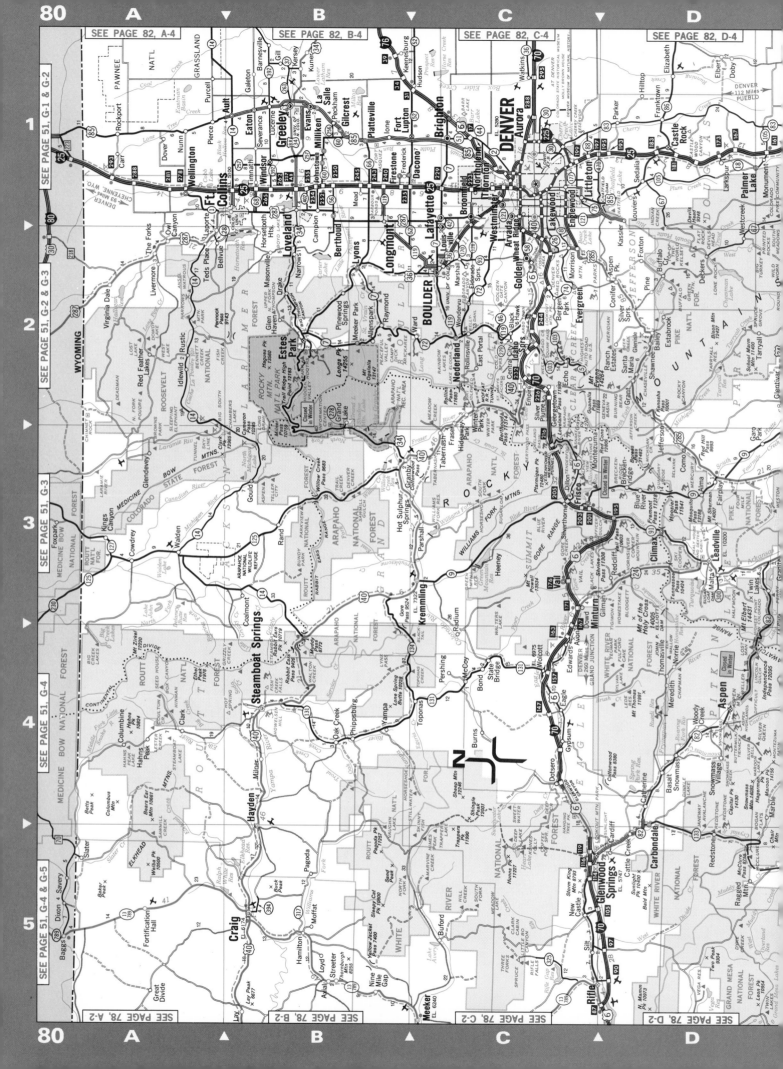

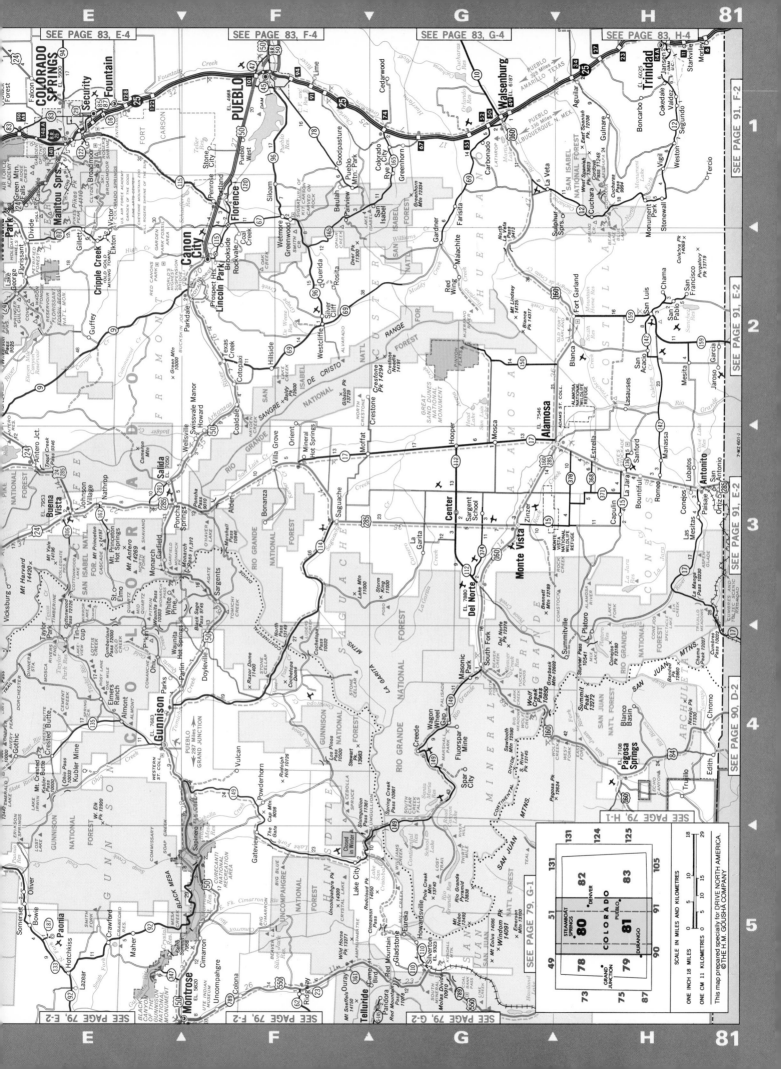

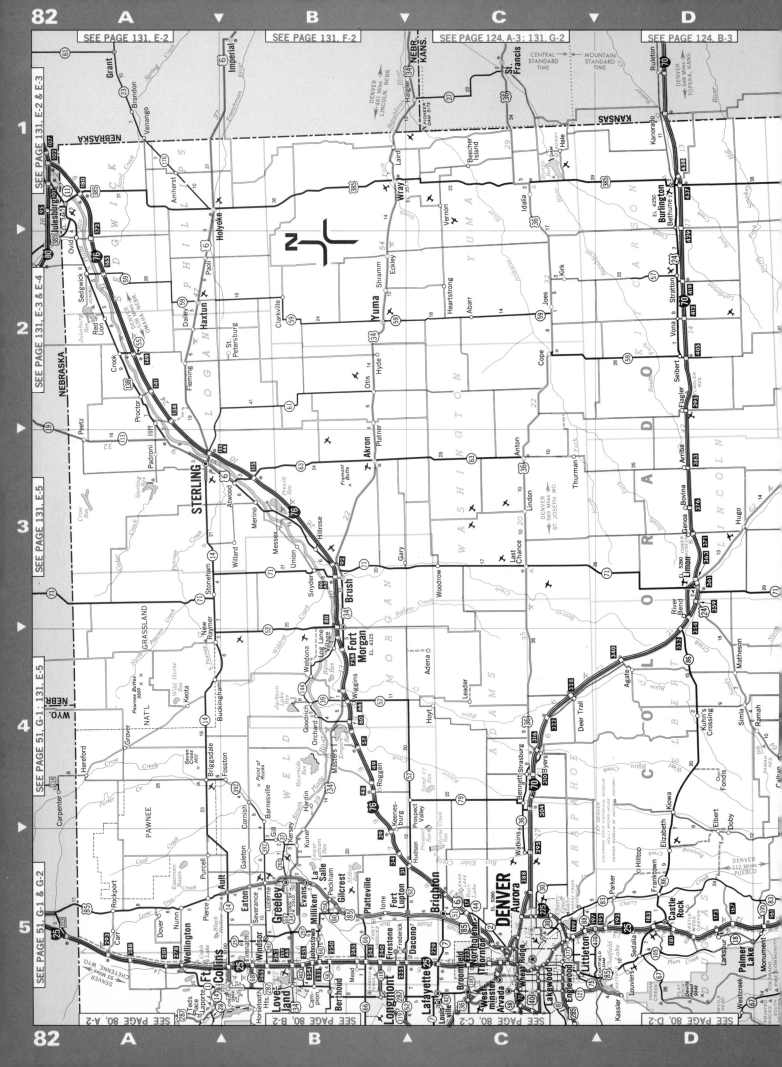

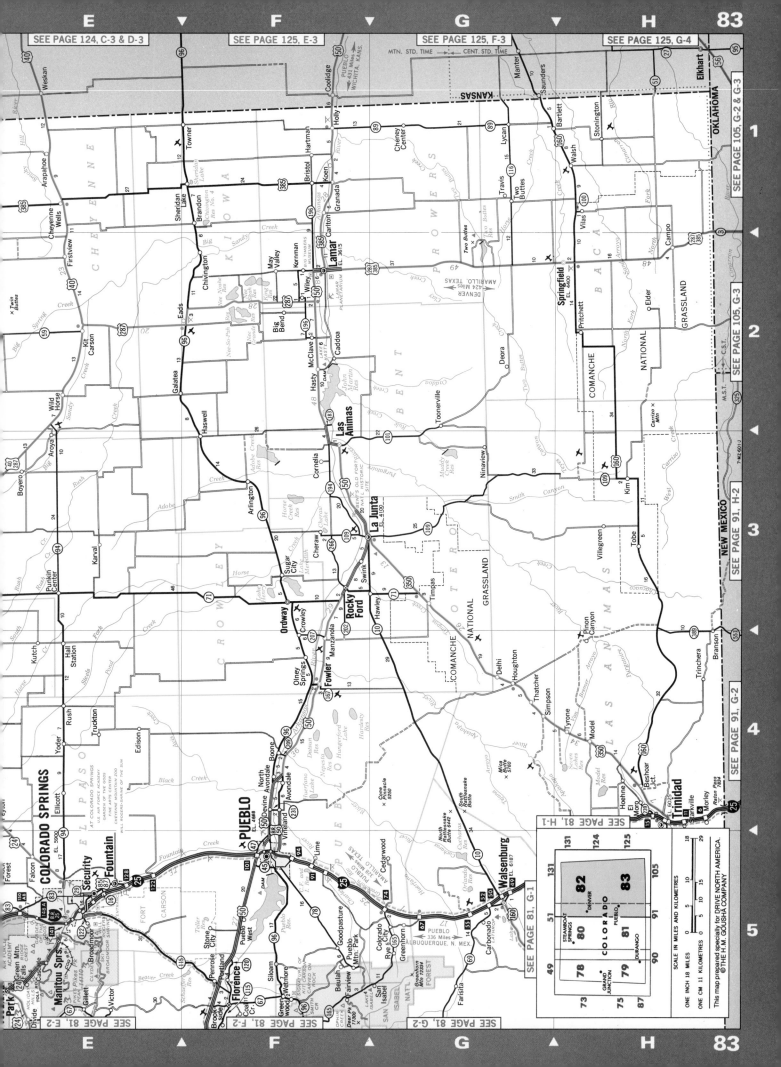

Canyons, Kachina Dolls and a Forest of Stone

Arizona/New Mexico

Arizona is known as the "Grand Canyon State." A mile deep and 10 miles wide where the road runs along the South Rim, **Grand Canyon National Park (87, E-3)** is, indeed, the essence of grandeur. The sheer immensity of the canyon, half as old as the earth itself, creates an overwhelming sense of wildness.

West of Grand Canyon Village, seven miles of the rim road are serviced by a free shuttle that departs every 12 to 15 minutes, from May to September. From the South Rim to the less crowded North is a scenic drive of some 200 miles, through the Navajo Indian Reservation and Kaibab National Forest. Here, the canyon view is even more striking because of the nearness of the towers and buttes within the gorge.

Around 1065, Sunset Crater was thrust up from the volcanic San Francisco Mountains. Today the cinder cone rises 1,000 feet above ponderosa pines, black sand dunes, and fields of lava in **Sunset Crater National Monument (87, E-4).** When nature's pyrotechnics had ceased, Sinagua Indian farmers ventured into the devasted area. The ghostly

Chapel of the Holy Cross, Sedona

ruins of their settlement are protected in **Wupatki National Monument (87, E-4).**

Indian culture, both ancient and contemporary, and the natural history of the Colorado Plateau are depicted in the Museum of Northern Arizona in **Flagstaff (87, E-5).** Of particular interest are a replica of a Hopi kiva (a circular, partly subterranean worship center), ceremonial kachina dolls and a room hung with Navajo rugs.

East of **Clarkdale (87, E-5)** stands the fortresslike pueblo of Tuzigoot National Monument, constructed in the early 12th century and occupied for 300 years. A museum exhibits bone and stone implements, mosaic pendants, pottery, basketry, and other artifacts excavated here. North of **Camp Verde (89, E-1)** is Montezuma Castle National Monument, where 800 years ago Sinagua

Indians constructed a five-story apartment house in a cavity 70 feet up the face of a cliff.

The soaring cliffs around **Sedona (87, E-5)** are complemented by the rock-buttressed Chapel of the Holy Cross, a shrine rooted between two spurs of red sandstone. Built in 1956, the rose-hued chapel seems a natural outcrop of its setting in Oak Creek Canyon.

One of Arizona's most unusual attractions is London Bridge, in the planned community of **Lake Havasu City (88, B-1).** Transported from Britain in 1968 and rebuilt here, the massive stone landmark proudly defies the nursery-rhyme warning of "falling down."

Arizona's northeast corner is an arid country of deserted Indian cliff dwellings such as those at **Canyon de Chelly National Monument (87, H-3).** A rim drive with five scenic overlooks skirts the south side of the reserve, which was an ancient stronghold of the Navajos and is still Indian territory. Highlights include a beautiful Indian ruin—the White House, reached by a mile-long trail—the Mummy Cave, and the vertical Spider Rock.

Petrified Forest National Park (87, H-5) dates back some 200 million years, when fallen trees collected in backwaters of prehistoric rivers. Covered by silt, which prevented rotting, the trees were slowly permeated by groundwater. This water replaced the wood with silica, creating a forest of stone from the smallest twig to massive trunks still rooted in the rock.

Phoenix (89, E-2), Arizona's capital, is the Southwest's prototype boomtown. In only 100 years it has expanded from a cotton-growing community of 30 to a cosmopolitan city of 700,000. The dignified Arizona State Capitol, set in a park beautifully landscaped with cactus as well as trees and flowers, was the territorial capitol before it became the statehouse in 1912. Indian artifacts, both ancient and modern, are among the prize possessions of the Heard Museum. The museum's unique collection of more than 400 ceremonial kachina dolls occupies a separate room. Treasures in the Phoenix Art Museum include priceless Chinese tomb figures from the Tang dynasty.

Pioneer life of the 19th-century Southwest is re-enacted at Pioneer Arizona, a cluster of 26 buildings ranging from an 1861 ranch to a miner's camp. Ranch animals are also part of the village setting. More exotic animals— white rhinos, Arabian oryx, DeBrazza's monkeys—are featured in the 123-acre Phoenix Zoo.

In southern Arizona, the branching saguaro cactus of the Sonoran Desert has come to symbolize all American deserts. Saguaros are displayed with 6,000 other plant species from deserts around the world at the Boyce Thompson Southwestern Arboretum, a state park west of **Superior (89, F-2).**

Desert creatures in surroundings simulating their natural habitats are the specialty of the Arizona–Sonora Desert Museum in **Tucson (89, F-4).** The animals, all indige-

nous to the Southwest, include bighorn sheep, coyotes, bobcats, beavers and mountain lions. Displays in the Orientation Room explain the fragile ecology of the desert; a tunnel exhibit explores the intricacies of underground life.

The remains of a 10,000-year-old mammoth, along with the spearpoints used to kill it, are among displays in the Arizona State Museum on the campus of the University of Arizona. The wide-ranging collection of the university's Museum of Art covers many centuries and styles, including Renaissance and contemporary American.

With the early Spanish explorers of the Southwest came missionaries who strove to convert the scattered tribes and pueblos to Christianity. A remnant of this era is the ruined 18th-century mission at **Tumacacori (89, F-5),** which was brought down by Apache raids. Parts of the baroque church remain: the dome, plastered walls, painted decorations and the ceiling of the sacristy. South of Tucson, **Mission San Xavier del Bac** survived. Franciscans completed this domed and arched church in 1797.

Less noble ambitions lured silver prospector Ed Schieffelin, who called his 1877 strike **Tombstone (89, G-5)** because it was predict-

ed that Apaches would kill him before he staked a claim. Marshall Wyatt Earp and Doc Holliday tried to keep order here, but Boothill Graveyard is filled with reminders of murders and hangings.

New Mexico's capital, **Santa Fe (91, E-4)**, is perhaps the most successful blend of Anglo, Spanish and Indian cultures in the Southwest. Many artists have made their homes and studios along the narrow streets where the houses still follow the Spanish-Pueblo style. The Palace of the Governors, completed in 1610, is the oldest public building in the United States. Now a museum and library, it contains displays of Indian farming practices, and of arts and crafts such as weaving and jewelry making. Outside, Indian craftsmen sell turquoise and silver jewelry, baskets, pottery and other handicrafts. Nearby is the Cristo Rey Church. Considered to be the largest adobe structure in the Southwest, the church resembles a citadel, with walls 2 to 7 feet thick. The lower walls of the Oldest House in the U.S.A., made of primitive, puddled adobe, are the last remains of the Analco

Uniformed "recruits" (above) re-enact a Civil War battle at Phoenix's Pioneer Arizona, a living-history museum.

The delicate, colorful sand paintings of New Mexico's Navajo Indians (right) have been used for centuries in rituals to influence weather and cure the sick.

J. B. Priestley called Arizona's Grand Canyon (left) "A Landscape Day of Judgement." Rocks over a billion years old are bared by erosion in the mile-deep gorge, seen here from the South Rim. At sunset, massive buttes glow gold against turquoise skies. At dawn the landscape is bathed in pastels.

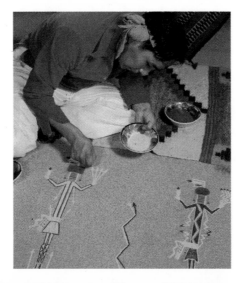

Pueblo, dating from 1200. The rest of the house dates from the early 1600s, as does the nearby San Miguel Mission. Visitors may ring San Miguel's 780-pound bell—made of gold, silver, copper and iron. The bell was cast in Spain in 1356.

At the Fine Arts Museum, works by George Bellows, Robert Henri, and other American artists associated with Santa Fe and Taos are displayed along with modern and traditional Indian art. The Fine Arts Museum is part of the Museum of New Mexico, as are the Laboratory of Anthropology and the Museum of International Folk Art. Other works of Indian artists, from more than 400 different tribes, form the permanent collection of the Institute of American Indian Arts Museum. Some 600 sand paintings and 2,000 recorded legends and chants are preserved in the Wheelwright Museum.

Santa Fe provides a convenient base for visiting the pueblos of northern New Mexico. Some of these pueblos—**Santo Domingo, San Ildefonso, Santa Clara**—have nurtured artists whose jewelry or ceramics have earned international repute. Others, such as those in **Coronado** and **Jemez** state monuments and **Bandelier National Monument**, have lain in ruins for centuries.

Among the most picturesque of the Rio Grande pueblos is **Taos (91, E-3)**. Here New Mexico's highest mountains form the backdrop for the home of more than 500 Indian families. The two well-preserved multilevel pueblos are believed to be 800 years old. The Mission of San Geronimo de Taos stands near ruins of the original mission, (1617), which was all but destroyed by the U.S. Army in 1847. In the town of Taos is a thriving art colony, and a museum dedicated to mountain man Kit Carson.

Northwest of Taos, the narrow-gauge Cumbres & Toltec Scenic Railroad has chuffed between **Chama (90, D-3)** and Antonito, Colorado, for more than a century. The 64-mile scenic route passes over breathtaking Toltec Gorge and through Cumbres Pass—at 10,022 feet, one of the world's highest railroad crossings.

For centuries, **El Morro National Monument (90, B-5)** has marked a spring for desert travelers, many of whom carved names and messages on the soft rock. Another landmark of the Four Corners region—where New Mexico, Colorado, Arizona and Utah meet— is **Ship Rock (90, B-3)**, a volcanic plug soaring 1,700 feet above the desert floor.

Near **Alamogordo (93, E-3)** is White Sands National Monument, 145,000 acres of gypsum dunes that look exactly like snowdrifts. Across the mountains and evergreen forests of the Mescalero Apache Reservation lies **Lincoln (93, E-2)**, scene of the 1878 Lincoln County War between ranchers and farmers. The two-story Old Lincoln County Courthouse contains the jail from which the young William Bonney, alias Billy the Kid, made a notorious escape in 1881.

On the Texas–New Mexico border, beneath the Chihuahuan desert of the Guadalupe Mountains is **Carlsbad Caverns National Park (93, G-4)**, considered the world's most magnificent cave system. The main chamber alone could hold the U.S. Capitol—in one corner. Stalactites and stalagmites, and a resident swarm of bats—which issue from the entrance each evening in summer—are prime attractions.

Multi-storied adobe dwellings at Taos Pueblo, New Mexico

85

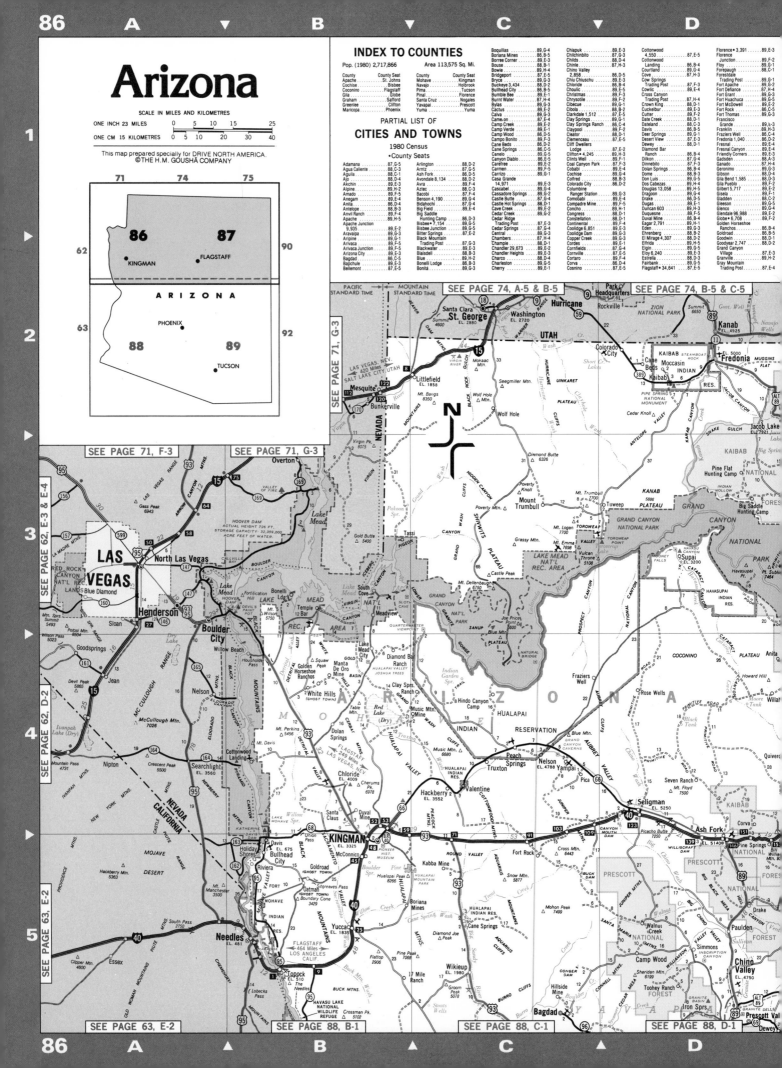

Arizona

SCALE IN MILES AND KILOMETRES

ONE INCH 23 MILES
ONE CM 15 KILOMETRES

0 5 10 15 25
0 5 10 20 30 40

This map prepared specially for DRIVE NORTH AMERICA.
©THE H.M. GOUSHA COMPANY

86 87
KINGMAN FLAGSTAFF

A R I Z O N A

88 89
PHOENIX
TUCSON

INDEX TO COUNTIES

Pop. (1980) 2,717,866   Area 113,575 Sq. Mi.

County	County Seat
Apache	St. Johns
Cochise	Bisbee
Coconino	Flagstaff
Gila	Globe
Graham	Safford
Greenlee	Clifton
Maricopa	Phoenix
Mohave	Kingman
Navajo	Holbrook
Pima	Tucson
Pinal	Florence
Santa Cruz	Nogales
Yavapai	Prescott
Yuma	Yuma

PARTIAL LIST OF CITIES AND TOWNS

1980 Census
•County Seats

Adamana ...87,G-5
Agua Caliente ...88,C-3
Aguila ...88,C-1
Ajo ...88,D-4
Akchin ...89,E-3
Alpine ...89,H-2
Amado ...89,F-5
Anegam ...89,E-4
Anita ...86,D-4
Antelope ...88,B-3
Anvil Ranch ...89,F-4
Apache ...89,H-5
Apache Junction 9,935 ...89,E-2
Aripine ...89,G-1
Arivaca ...89,F-5
Arivaca Junction ...89,F-5
Arizona City ...89,E-3
Bagdad ...86,C-5
Bapchule ...89,E-3
Bellemont ...87,E-5

Arlington ...88,D-2
Arntz ...87,G-5
Ash Fork ...86,D-5
Avondale 8,134 ...88,D-2
Avra ...88,C-3
Aztec ...88,C-4
Bacobi ...87,F-4
Benson 4,190 ...89,G-4
Bidahochi ...87,F-3
Big Field ...89,E-4
Big Saddle Hunting Camp ...86,D-3
Bisbee• 7,154 ...89,G-5
Bisbee Junction ...89,G-5
Bitter Springs ...87,E-2
Black Mountain Trading Post ...87,G-3
Blackwater ...89,E-3
Blaisdell ...89,E-4
Blue ...89,H-2
Bonelli Lodge ...86,B-3
Bonita ...89,G-3

Boquillas ...89,G-4
Boriana Mines ...86,B-5
Borree Corner ...89,E-3
Bouse ...88,B-1
Bowie ...89,H-4
Bridgeport ...89,G-2
Bryce ...89,G-3
Buckeye 3,434 ...88,D-2
Bullhead City ...86,B-5
Bumble Bee ...89,E-1
Burnt Water ...87,G-3
Bylas ...89,G-3
Cactus ...89,G-3
Calva ...89,G-3
Cameron ...87,E-2
Camp Creek ...89,E-2
Camp Verde ...89,F-2
Camp Wood ...86,D-5
Campo Bonito ...89,F-3
Cane Beds ...86,D-2
Cane Springs ...86,C-5
Canyon Diablo ...87,F-2
Carefree ...89,E-2
Carmen ...89,F-5
Carrizo ...89,G-1
Casa Grande 14,971 ...89,E-3
Cascabel ...89,G-4
Cassadore Springs ...89,G-2
Castle Butte ...87,F-3
Castle Hot Springs ...88,D-1
Cave Creek ...89,E-2
Cedar Creek ...89,G-1
Cedar Ridge ...87,E-2
Central ...89,G-3
Chambers ...87,G-4
Champie ...88,D-1
Chandler 29,673 ...89,E-2
Chandler Heights ...89,E-2
Charco ...89,E-4
Charleston ...89,G-5
Cherry ...89,E-1

Chiapuk ...89,E-3
Chilchinbito ...87,G-3
Childs ...88,D-4
Chinle ...87,H-3
Chino Valley 2,858 ...86,D-5
Chiu Chiuschu ...89,E-4
Chloride ...86,B-4
Choulic ...89,E-4
Christmas ...89,F-3
Chrysotile ...89,F-2
Cibecue ...89,G-1
Cibola ...88,B-1
Clarkdale 1,512 ...87,E-5
Clay Springs ...86,C-4
Claypool ...89,F-2
Cleator ...89,E-1
Clemenceau ...87,E-5
Cliff Dwellers Lodge ...87,E-2
Clifton• 4,245 ...89,H-3
Clints Well ...89,F-1
Coal Canyon Park ...87,F-3
Cochise ...89,G-4
Colfred ...88,B-3
Colorado City ...86,D-2
Columbine Ranger Station ...89,G-3
Comobabi ...89,E-4
Compadre Mine ...89,F-5
Concho ...87,G-4
Congress ...88,D-1
Constellation ...89,E-1
Continental ...89,F-5
Coolidge 6,851 ...89,E-3
Coolidge Dam ...89,G-3
Copper Creek ...89,F-3
Cordes ...89,E-1
Cornfields ...87,G-4
Cornville ...87,E-5
Cortaro ...89,E-4
Corva ...86,D-4
Cosnino ...87,E-5

Cottonwood 4,550 ...87,E-5
Cottonwood Landing ...86,B-4
Courtland ...89,G-4
Cove ...87,H-3
Cow Springs ...87,F-3
Cowlic ...89,E-4
Cross Canyon ...87,H-4
Crown King ...88,D-1
Cuckelbur ...89,E-3
Cutter ...89,F-2
Date Creek ...88,C-5
Dateland ...88,C-3
Davis ...86,B-5
Deer Springs ...87,E-3
Desert View ...87,E-2
Dewey ...88,D-1
Diamond Bar Ranch ...86,B-4
Dilkon ...87,G-4
Dinnebito ...87,F-3
Dolan Springs ...86,B-4
Dome ...88,B-4
Don Luis ...89,G-5
Dos Cabezas ...89,H-4
Douglas 13,058 ...89,H-5
Dragoon ...89,G-4
Drake ...86,D-5
Duacon ...89,F-3
Dugas ...89,E-1
Duncan 603 ...89,H-3
Duquesne ...89,F-5
Duval Mine ...89,F-4
Eagar 2,791 ...89,H-2
Eden ...89,G-3
Ehrenberg ...88,B-2
El Mirage 4,307 ...88,D-2
Elfrida ...89,G-5
Elgin ...89,G-5
Eloy 6,240 ...89,E-3
Estrella ...88,D-3
Fairbank ...89,G-5
Flagstaff• 34,641 ...87,E-5

Florence• 3,391 ...89,E-3
Florence Junction ...89,F-2
Floy ...89,G-1
Forepaugh ...88,C-1
Forestdale Trading Post ...89,G-2
Fort Apache ...89,G-2
Fort Defiance ...87,H-4
Fort Grant ...89,G-3
Fort Huachuca ...89,G-5
Fort McDowell ...89,E-2
Fort Rock ...86,C-4
Fort Thomas ...89,G-3
Francisco Grande ...89,E-3
Franklin ...89,H-3
Fredericks Well ...86,B-4
Fredonia 1,040 ...86,D-2
Fresnal Canyon ...89,E-4
Fresnal Canyon ...89,E-4
Friendly Corners ...89,E-3
Gadsden ...89,E-4
Ganado ...87,H-4
Geronimo ...89,G-3
Gibson ...88,B-4
Gila Bend 1,585 ...88,D-3
Gila Pueblo ...89,G-2
Gilbert 5,717 ...89,E-2
Gisela ...89,F-1
Gladden ...88,C-1
Gleeson ...89,G-4
Glenco ...89,G-4
Glendale 96,988 ...88,D-2
Globe• 6,708 ...89,F-2
Golden Horseshoe Ranchos ...86,B-4
Goldroad ...86,B-5
Goodwin ...88,D-1
Goodyear 2,747 ...88,D-2
Grand Canyon Village ...87,E-5
Granite ...89,H-2
Gray Mountain Trading Post ...87,E-4

SEE PAGE 71, G-3
SEE PAGE 74, A-5 & B-5
SEE PAGE 74, B-5 & C-5
SEE PAGE 71, F-3
SEE PAGE 71, G-3
SEE PAGE 62, E-3 & E-4
SEE PAGE 62, D-2
SEE PAGE 63, E-2

SEE PAGE 63, E-2
SEE PAGE 88, B-1
SEE PAGE 88, C-1
SEE PAGE 88, D-1

Greasewood ...87,G-4
Greasewood
Greaterville ...87,H-X
Green Valley ...89,F-4
Greer ...88,D-4
Gu Vo ...88,D-4
Gunsight ...88,D-X
Guthrie ...89,H-3
Hackberry ...86,C-4
Hannagan
  Meadow ...89,H-2
Hano ...87,G-4
Happy Jack ...87,E-5
Hardshell ...89,F-5
Harshaw ...88,D-2
Hassayampa ...88,D-2
Havana Nakya ...86,C-5
Hay Hollow ...88,D-X
Hayden 1,205 ...89,F-3
Hayden Junction ...89,F-3
Helvetia ...89,F-4
Hereford ...89,G-5
Higley ...89,E-2
Hillside ...88,D-1
Hillside Mine ...86,C-5
Hindo Canyon
  Camp ...86,C-4
Holbrook 5,785 ...87,G-4
Hope ...88,D-X
Hookers
  Hot Springs ...89,G-4
Hotevilla ...87,F-4
Houck ...87,H-4
House Rock ...87,E-2
Huachuca City
  1,661 ...89,G-5
Humboldt ...88,D-1
Hunt ...87,H-5
Hunters Point ...87,H-4

Hyder ...88,C-3
Indian
  Hot Springs ...89,G-1
Indian Pine ...89,G-1
Indian Wells ...87,G-4
Inscription House
  Trading Post ...87,F-3
Inspiration ...89,F-2
Iron Springs ...88,D-1
Jackrabbit ...89,E-3
Jacob ...89,H-2
Jacob Lake ...86,D-2
Jakes Corner ...89,F-1
Jaynes ...89,F-4
Jerome 420 ...87,E-5
Johnson ...89,G-4
Joseph City ...87,G-4
Kabba Mine ...86,C-5
Kaibab ...87,G-2
Kaibab Lodge ...87,F-2
Kaibito ...87,F-3
Kearns Canyon ...87,G-4
Kearny 2,646 ...89,F-3
Kelvin ...89,F-3
Kim Li Chee ...87,H-4
Kingman ★
  9,257 ...86,B-5
Kings Ranch ...89,E-3
Kirkland ...88,D-1
Kirkland
  Junction ...88,D-1
Klagetoh ...87,H-4
Klondyke ...89,G-4
Kohatk ...89,E-3
Kohls Ranch ...89,F-1
Komatke ...89,E-2
Kupk ...88,D-3
La Palma ...89,E-3
La Paz (Ruins ...88,B-2
Laguna ...88,B-3

Lake Havasu
  City 15,737 ...88,B-1
Lake Mead City ...86,B-4
Lakeside ...89,G-1
Laveen ...89,E-2
Lees Ferry ...87,E-2
Leupp ...87,F-4
Lewis Springs ...89,G-5
Liberty ...89,E-2
Liguria ...88,D-1
Linden ...89,G-1
Litchfield ...89,E-2
Litchfield Park ...88,D-2
Littlefield ...86,C-2
Lochiel ...89,F-5
Long Valley ...89,F-1
Low Mountain ...87,G-3
Lukachukai ...87,H-3
Lukeville ...88,D-4
Lupton ...87,H-4
Madera Canyon ...89,F-5
Mammoth 1,906 ...89,F-3
Manta de Oro
  Mine ...88,B-4
Marana Farms ...89,E-4
Marana 1,574 ...89,F-4
Marble Canyon ...87,E-2
Maricopa ...89,E-3
Marinette ...89,E-2
Marble Lake ...88,B-4
Mayer ...88,D-1
McConnico ...86,B-5
McNary ...89,G-1
McNeal ...89,H-5
McVay ...88,C-3
Meadview ...86,B-3
Menegers Dam ...88,D-4
Mesa 152,453 ...89,E-2
Mexican Hay ...89,G-1
Mexican Water ...87,G-2
Miami 2,716 ...89,F-2
Midland City ...89,F-2
Mishongnovi ...87,G-4
Mobile ...88,D-3

Moccasin ...86,D-2
Moenkopi ...87,F-4
Mohawk ...88,C-3
Montezuma ...89,F-3
Morenci ...87,F-4
Mormon Lake ...87,F-5
Morristown ...88,D-2
Mount Trumbull ...86,C-2
Mountain View ...89,F-4
Mowry ...89,F-5
Music Mountain
  Mine ...86,C-4
Naahtee ...89,G-1
Naco ...89,G-5
Navajo ...87,H-4
Navajo Station ...87,G-4
Nazlini ...87,H-4
Nelson ...86,C-4
New River ...88,D-2
Nogales ★ 15,683 ...89,F-5
Nolia ...89,E-4
North Komelik ...89,E-3
North Rim ...87,E-3
Nutrioso ...89,H-1
Oak Springs ...88,D-3
Oatman ...86,B-5
Ocotillo ...89,E-2
Octave ...88,D-1
Olberg ...89,E-2
Oracle ...89,F-4
Oracle Junction ...89,F-4
Oraibi ...87,F-4
Oro Blanco
  Ranch ...89,F-5
Oro Valley
  1,489 ...89,F-4
Overgaard ...89,F-1
Page 4,907 ...87,E-2
Palm Springs ...89,E-2
Palo Alto Ranch ...89,G-2
Palo Verde ...88,D-2
Palomines ...89,G-5
Pan Tak ...89,E-3
Pantano ...89,F-4

Paradise ...89,H-4
Parker 2,542 ...88,B-1
Parker Creek ...89,F-1
Parks ...87,E-4
Patagonia 980 ...89,F-5
Paulden ...88,D-1
Payson 5,068 ...89,F-1
Peach Springs ...86,C-4
Pearce ...89,H-4
Peeples Valley ...88,D-1
Peoria 12,251 ...89,E-2
Perkinsville ...87,E-5
Perryville ...88,D-2
Phantom Ranch ...87,E-3
Phoenix ★
  764,911 ...89,E-2
Pia Oik ...89,E-2
Pica ...89,H-3
Picacho ...89,E-3
Pima 1,599 ...89,G-3
Pine ...89,F-1
Pine Flat
  Hunting Camp ...86,D-3
Pine Springs ...89,H-4
Pinedale ...89,G-1
Pinetop ...89,G-1
Piñon ...87,G-3
Pirtleville ...89,H-5
Pinion ...88,D-4
Planet Ranch ...88,B-1
Point of Pines ...89,G-2
Polacca ...87,G-4
Poland ...88,D-1
Pomerene ...89,G-4
Portal ...89,H-4
Poston ...88,B-1
Prescott ★ 20,055 ...88,D-1
Prescott Valley 2,284 ...88,D-1
Punkin Center ...89,F-2
Quartzsite ...88,B-2

Queen Creek ...89,E-2
Queens Well ...89,E-4
Quijotoa ...89,E-3
Quiotobaquito ...88,D-4
Quivero ...86,D-4
Radium
  Hot Springs ...88,B-3
Rainbow Valley ...88,B-3
Raso ...89,E-4
Ray ...89,F-3
Red Lake ...87,F-3
Red Lake ...87,E-4
Red Mesa ...87,G-2
Red Rock
  Trading Post ...87,H-3
Red Rock ...89,F-4
Redington ...89,G-4
Regal Mine ...89,E-4
Rillito ...89,F-4
Rimrock ...87,E-5
Rittenhouse ...89,G-2
Riverside ...89,F-3
Riviera ...86,B-5
Rock House ...89,H-4
Rock Point
  Trading Post ...87,G-2
Rock Ridge ...89,F-2
Roll ...88,B-3
Roosevelt ...89,F-2
Roosevelt
  Indian School ...89,G-2
Rose Wells ...86,D-4
Rough Rock ...87,G-3
Rowood ...88,D-4
Ruby ...89,F-5
Sacacton ...89,E-3
Sacate ...89,E-2
Safford ★ 7,010 ...89,H-3
Sahuarita ...89,F-4
St. David ...89,G-4
St. Johns ★ 3,343 ...89,H-1

St. Michaels ...87,H-4
Salina Springs ...87,G-3
Salome ...88,C-2
San Carlos ...89,G-2
San Jose ...89,H-5
San Luis 1,943 ...88,B-4
San Manuel 5,761 ...89,F-4
San Pedro ...89,H-4
San Simon ...89,H-4
San Vincente ...89,E-4
Sanders ...87,H-4
Santa Cruz ...88,B-4
Santa Rosa ...89,E-3
Santa Rosa Ranch ...89,E-4
Sasabe ...89,E-5
Sawmill ...87,H-4
Sawmill ...89,G-2
Scottsdale
  88,364 ...89,E-2
Sedona ...87,E-5
Seligman ...86,D-4
Sells ...89,E-4
Sentinel ...88,C-3
Seven Ranch ...86,D-4
Seven Springs ...89,E-1
Sheldon ...89,H-3
Shonto ...87,F-3
Show Low 4,298 ...89,G-1
Shumway ...89,G-1
Sichomovi ...87,G-4
Sierra Vista ...89,G-5
Sil Vaya ...89,E-3
Sikul Himatk ...89,E-3
Sil Nakya ...89,E-3
Silver Bell ...89,E-4
Silver Creek ...89,H-1

Simmons ...88,D-5
Skull Valley ...88,D-1
Smoke Signal ...87,G-3
Snowflake
  3,510 ...89,G-1
Soldiers Camp ...89,F-4
Solomon ...89,H-3
Sombrero Butte ...89,F-4
Somerton 5,761 ...88,B-4
Sonoita ...89,F-5
South Komelik ...89,E-5
South Tucson ...89,F-4
Springerville
  1,452 ...89,H-1
Stanfield ...89,E-3
Stanton ...88,D-1
Steamboat
  Trading Post ...87,G-3
Stone Cabin ...88,D-3
Stoneman Lake ...87,E-5
Stoval ...88,C-3
Strawberry ...89,F-1
Sun City ...89,E-2
Sundad ...88,C-3
Sunflower ...89,F-2
Sunnyside ...89,G-5
Sunrise Springs ...87,G-4
Sunrise
  Trading Post ...86,D-3
Supai ...86,D-3
Superior 4,600 ...89,F-2
Sup Oidak ...89,E-3
Surprise 3,723 ...88,D-2
Swansea ...88,B-1
Swift Trail
  Junction ...89,H-3
Tacna ...88,B-3
Tachee ...87,G-3

Tempe 106,743 ...89,E-2
Temple Bar ...86,B-3
Thatcher 3,374 ...89,H-3
The Gap ...87,E-3
Tilton ...87,E-5
Tolleson 4,433 ...88,D-2
Tombstone ...89,G-5
Tonalea ...87,F-3
Tonopah ...88,D-2
Toohey Ranch ...86,D-5
Topock ...86,B-5
Toreva ...87,G-4
Tortilla Flat ...89,F-2
Totacon
  Trading Post ...87,H-3
Totopitk ...88,D-3
Toyei ...87,G-4
Truxton ...86,C-4
Tuba City ...87,F-3
Tubac ...89,F-5
Tucson ★
  330,537 ...89,F-4
Tumacacori ...89,F-5
Turkey Flat ...89,E-5
Tuweep ...86,C-3
Twin Buttes ...89,F-4
Two Guns ...87,F-5
Tyson ...88,B-1
Valentine ...86,C-4
Vail ...89,F-4
Valle ...86,D-4
Valley Farms ...89,E-3
Ventana ...89,E-3
Verde Hot
  Springs ...89,F-1
Vernon ...89,H-1
Vicksburg ...88,C-2
Vicksburg Jct. ...88,C-2

Vulture Mine ...88,D-2
Waddell ...88,D-2
Wagoner ...88,D-1
Walker ...88,D-1
Walnut Creek ...86,D-5
Walpi ...87,G-4
Warren ...89,F-5
Washington ...89,F-5
Webb ...89,H-3
Wellton 911 ...88,B-4
Wenden ...88,C-2
Whipple ...88,D-1
White Cone ...87,G-4
White Hills ...86,B-4
Whiteriver ...89,G-2
Whitlow ...88,D-1
Wide Ruins ...87,H-4
Wikieup ...86,C-5
Wilhoit ...88,D-1
Willcox 3,243 ...89,H-4
Willow Beach ...86,B-4
Window Rock ...87,H-4
Winkelman 1,060 ...89,F-3
Winona ...87,F-5
Winslow 7,921 ...87,F-5
Wintersburg ...88,D-2
Wittmann ...88,D-2
Wolf Hole ...86,C-2
Woodruff ...87,G-5
Woolaroc ...89,F-3
Wooley ...88,D-1
Yampai ...86,C-4
Yarnell ...88,D-1
York ...89,H-3
Young ...89,F-1
Youngtown 2,254 ...88,D-2
Yucca ...86,B-5
Yuma ★ 42,433 ...88,B-4
Zeniff ...87,G-5
17 Mile Ranch ...88,B-5

MZ-588-J-X

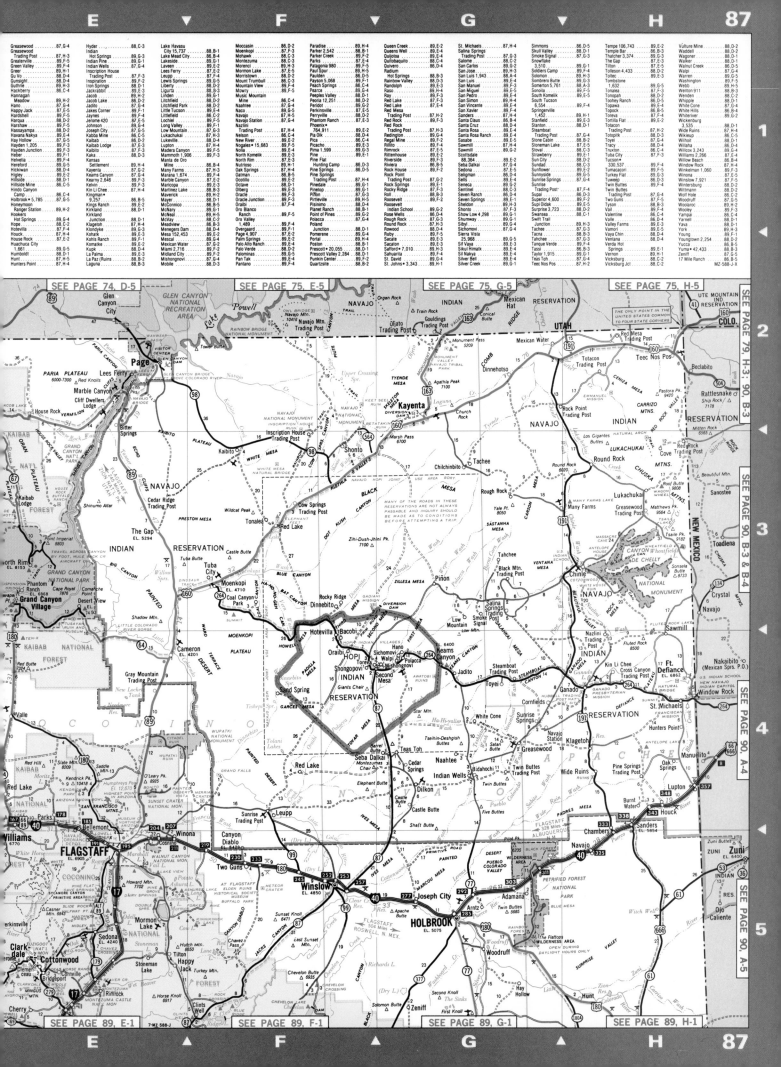

SEE PAGE 74, D-5   SEE PAGE 75, E-5   SEE PAGE 75, G-5   SEE PAGE 75, H-5
SEE PAGE 79, H-3 ; 90, B-3
SEE PAGE 90, B-3 & B-4
SEE PAGE 90, A-4
SEE PAGE 90, A-5
SEE PAGE 89, E-1   SEE PAGE 89, F-1   SEE PAGE 89, G-1   SEE PAGE 89, H-1

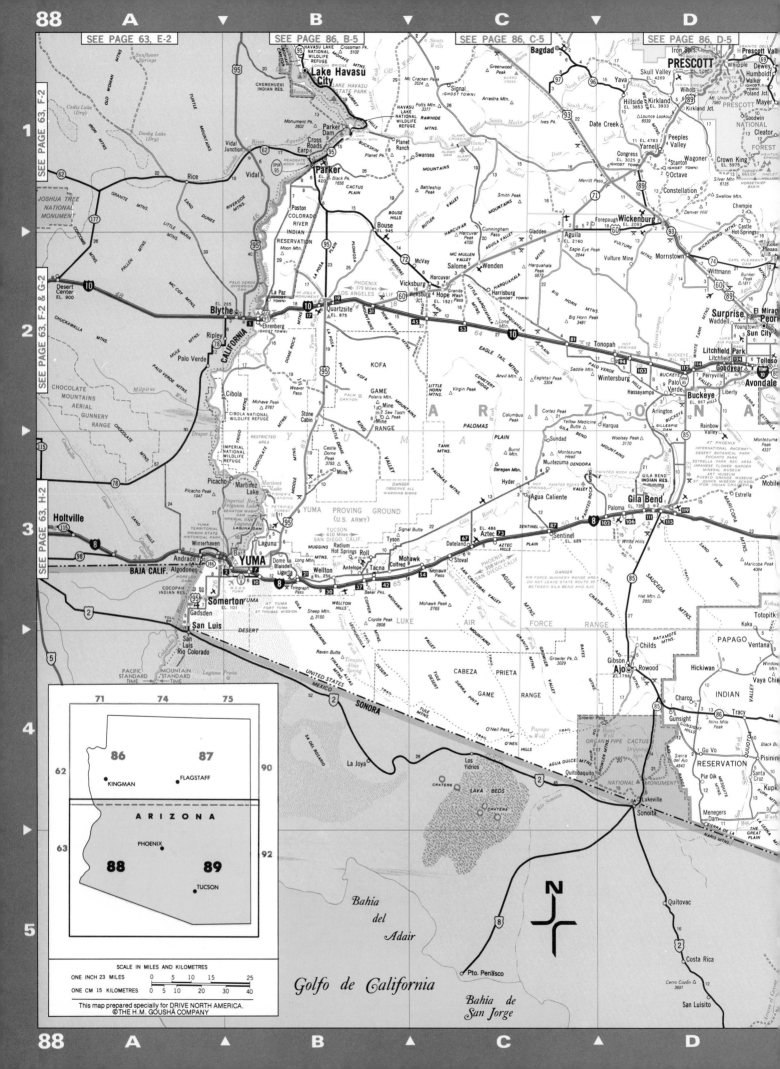

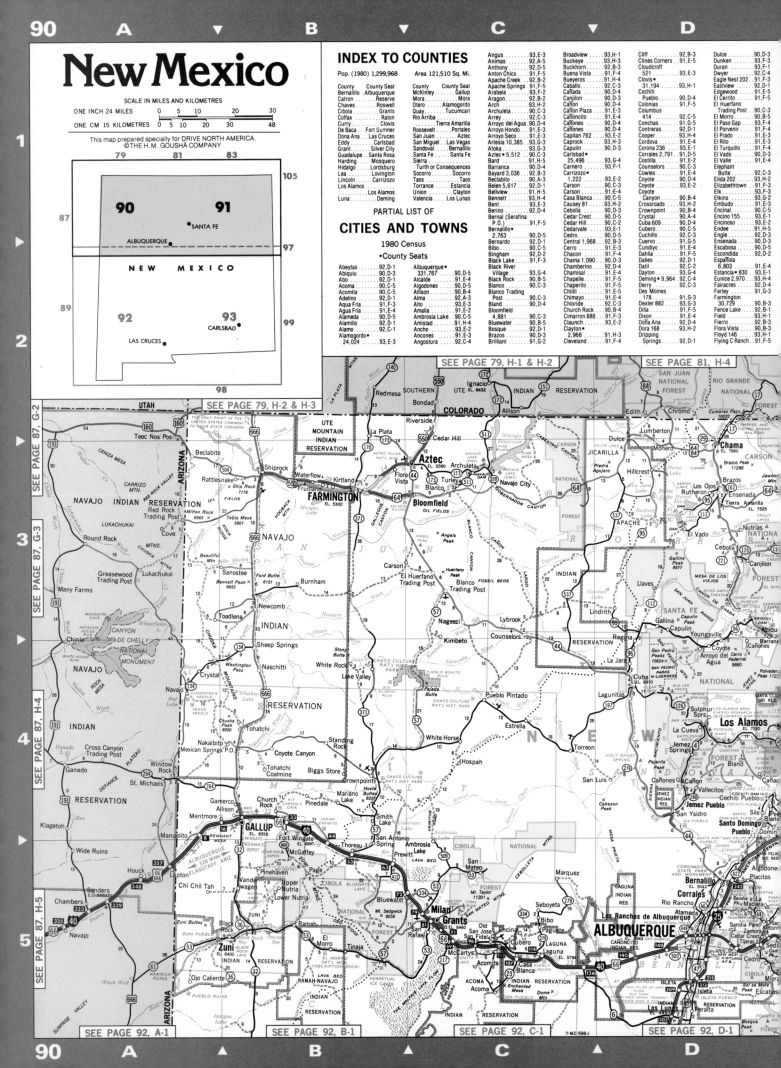

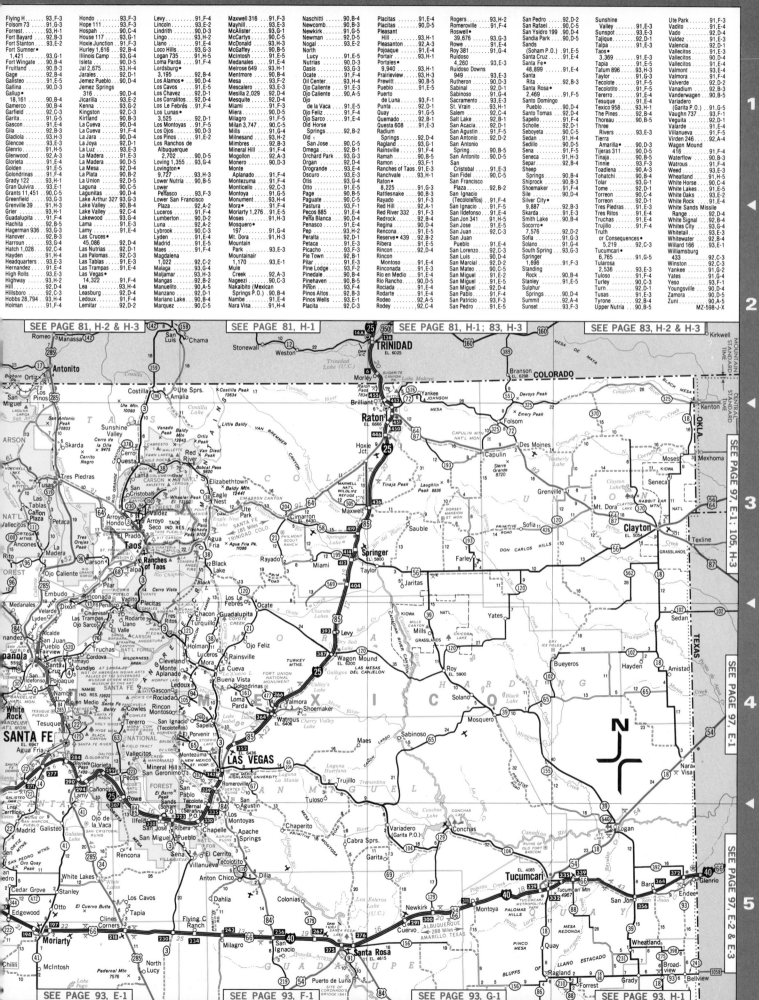

Flying H . . . 93,F-3
Folsom 73 . . . 91,G-3
Forrest . . . 93,H-1
Fort Bayard . . . 92,B-3
Fort Stanton . . . 93,E-2
Fort Sumner• 1,421 . . . 93,G-1
Fort Wingate . . . 90,B-4
Fruitland . . . 90,B-3
Gage . . . 92,B-4
Galisteo . . . 91,E-5
Gallina . . . 90,D-3
Gallup• 18,161 . . . 90,B-4
Gamerco . . . 90,B-4
Garfield . . . 92,C-3
Garita . . . 91,G-5
Gascon . . . 91,E-4
Gila . . . 92,B-3
Gladiola . . . 93,H-3
Glencoe . . . 93,E-3
Glenrio . . . 91,H-5
Glenwood . . . 92,A-3
Glorieta . . . 91,E-4
Golden . . . 91,E-5
Golondrinas . . . 91,F-4
Grady 122 . . . 93,H-1
Gran Quivira . . . 93,E-1
Grants 11,451 . . . 90,C-5
Greenfield . . . 93,G-3
Grenville 39 . . . 91,H-3
Grier . . . 93,H-1
Guadalupita . . . 91,F-4
Hachita . . . 92,B-5
Hagerman 936 . . . 93,G-3
Hanover . . . 92,B-3
Harroun . . . 93,G-4
Hatch 1,028 . . . 92,C-4
Hayden . . . 91,H-4
Headquarters . . . 93,E-3
Hernandez . . . 91,E-4
High Rolls . . . 93,E-3
Highway . . . 93,H-2
Hill . . . 92,D-4
Hillsboro . . . 92,C-3
Hobbs 28,794 . . . 93,H-4
Holman . . . 91,F-4
Hondo . . . 93,F-3
Hope 111 . . . 93,F-3
Hospah . . . 90,C-4
House 117 . . . 93,G-1
Hoxie Junction . . . 91,F-3
Hurley 1,616 . . . 92,B-4
Illinois Camp . . . 93,G-4
Isleta . . . 90,D-5
Jal 2,675 . . . 93,H-4
Jarales . . . 92,D-1
Jemez Pueblo . . . 90,D-4
Jemez Springs 316 . . . 90,D-4
Jicarilla . . . 93,E-2
Kenna . . . 93,G-2
Kingston . . . 92,C-3
Kirtland . . . 90,B-3
La Cueva . . . 90,D-4
La Cueva . . . 91,F-4
La Jara . . . 90,D-4
La Joya . . . 92,D-1
La Luz . . . 93,E-3
La Madera . . . 91,E-3
La Madera . . . 90,D-5
La Mesa . . . 92,D-4
La Plata . . . 90,B-2
La Union . . . 92,D-5
Laguna . . . 90,C-5
Lagunitas . . . 90,D-4
Lake Arthur 327 93,G-3
Lake Valley . . . 90,B-4
Lake Valley . . . 92,C-4
Lakewood . . . 93,G-4
Lama . . . 91,E-3
Lamy . . . 91,E-4
Las Cruces• 45,086 . . . 92,D-4
Las Nutrias . . . 92,D-1
Las Palomas . . . 92,C-3
Las Tablas . . . 91,E-3
Las Trampas . . . 91,E-4
Las Vegas• 14,322 . . . 91,F-4
Lea . . . 93,H-4
Leasburg . . . 92,D-4
Ledoux . . . 91,F-4
Lemitar . . . 92,D-2
Levy . . . 91,F-4
Lincoln . . . 93,E-2
Lindrith . . . 90,D-3
Lingo . . . 93,H-2
Llano . . . 91,E-4
Loco Hills . . . 93,G-3
Logan 735 . . . 91,H-5
Loma Parda . . . 91,F-4
Lordsburg• 3,195 . . . 92,B-4
Los Alamos• . . . 90,D-4
Los Cavos . . . 91,E-5
Los Chavez . . . 92,D-1
Los Corralitos . . . 92,D-4
Los Le Febrés . . . 91,F-4
Los Lunas• 3,525 . . . 92,D-1
Los Montoyas . . . 91,F-5
Los Ojos . . . 90,D-3
Los Pinos . . . 91,E-2
Los Ranchos de Albuquerque 2,702 . . . 90,D-5
Loving 1,355 . . . 93,G-4
Lovington• 9,727 . . . 93,H-3
Lower Nutria . . . 90,B-5
Lower Peñasco . . . 93,F-3
Lower San Francisco Plaza . . . 92,A-2
Luceros . . . 91,F-4
Lumberton . . . 90,D-2
Luna . . . 92,A-2
Lybrook . . . 90,C-3
Lyden . . . 91,E-4
Madrid . . . 91,E-5
Maes . . . 91,F-4
Magdalena 1,022 . . . 92,C-2
Malaga . . . 93,G-4
Maljamar . . . 93,H-3
Mangas . . . 92,B-2
Manuelito . . . 90,A-5
Manzano . . . 92,D-1
Mariano Lake . . . 90,B-4
Marquez . . . 90,C-5
Maxwell 316 . . . 91,F-3
Mayhill . . . 93,E-3
McAlister . . . 93,G-1
McCartys . . . 90,C-5
McDonald . . . 93,H-3
McGaffey . . . 90,B-5
McIntosh . . . 91,E-5
Medanales . . . 91,E-4
Melrose 649 . . . 93,H-1
Mentmore . . . 90,B-4
Mesa . . . 93,F-2
Mescalero . . . 93,E-3
Mesilla 2,029 . . . 92,D-4
Mesquite . . . 92,D-4
Miami . . . 91,F-3
Miera . . . 90,D-5
Milagro . . . 91,F-5
Milan 3,747 . . . 90,C-5
Mills . . . 91,G-4
Milnesand . . . 93,H-2
Mimbres . . . 92,B-3
Mineral Hill . . . 91,F-4
Mogollon . . . 92,A-3
Monero . . . 90,D-3
Monte Aplanado . . . 91,F-4
Montezuma . . . 91,F-4
Monticello . . . 92,C-3
Montoya . . . 91,G-5
Monument . . . 93,H-4
Mora• . . . 91,F-4
Moriarty 1,276 . . . 91,E-5
Moses . . . 91,H-3
Mosquero• 197 . . . 91,G-4
Mt. Dora . . . 91,H-3
Mountain Park . . . 93,E-3
Mountainair 1,170 . . . 93,E-1
Mule Creek . . . 92,A-3
Nageezi . . . 90,C-3
Nakaibito (Mexican Springs P.O.) . . . 90,B-4
Nambe . . . 91,E-4
Nara Visa . . . 91,H-4
Naschitti . . . 90,B-4
Newcomb . . . 90,B-3
Newkirk . . . 91,G-5
Newman . . . 92,D-5
Nogal . . . 93,E-2
North Lucy . . . 91,E-5
Nutrias . . . 90,D-3
Oasis . . . 93,G-3
Ocate . . . 91,F-4
Oil Center . . . 93,H-4
Ojo Caliente . . . 91,E-3
Ojo Caliente . . . 90,A-5
Ojo de la Vaca . . . 91,E-5
Ojo Feliz . . . 91,F-4
Ojo Sarco . . . 91,E-4
Old Horse Springs . . . 92,B-2
Old San Jose . . . 90,C-5
Omega . . . 92,B-1
Orchard Park . . . 93,G-3
Organ . . . 92,D-4
Orogrande . . . 93,E-4
Oscuro . . . 93,E-3
Otis . . . 93,G-4
Otto . . . 91,E-5
Page . . . 90,B-5
Paguate . . . 90,C-5
Pastura . . . 93,F-1
Pecos 885 . . . 91,E-4
Peña Blanca . . . 90,D-4
Penasco . . . 91,E-4
Pep . . . 93,H-2
Peralta . . . 92,D-1
Petaca . . . 91,E-3
Picacho . . . 93,F-3
Pie Town . . . 92,B-1
Pilar . . . 91,E-3
Pine Lodge . . . 93,F-2
Pinedale . . . 90,B-4
Pinehaven . . . 90,B-5
Piñon . . . 93,F-4
Pinos Altos . . . 92,B-3
Pinos Wells . . . 93,E-1
Placita . . . 92,C-3
Placitas . . . 91,E-4
Placitas . . . 90,D-5
Pleasant Hill . . . 93,H-1
Pleasanton . . . 92,A-3
Pojoaque . . . 91,E-4
Portair . . . 93,H-1
Portales• 9,940 . . . 93,H-1
Prairieview . . . 93,H-3
Prewitt . . . 90,B-5
Pueblo . . . 91,E-5
Puerto de Luna . . . 93,F-1
Punta . . . 92,D-1
Quay . . . 91,G-5
Quemado . . . 92,B-1
Questa 608 . . . 91,E-3
Radium Springs . . . 92,D-4
Ragland . . . 93,G-1
Rainsville . . . 91,F-4
Ramah . . . 90,B-5
Ramon . . . 93,F-1
Ranches of Taos . . . 91,E-3
Ranchvale . . . 93,H-1
Raton• 8,225 . . . 91,G-3
Rattlesnake . . . 90,B-3
Rayado . . . 91,F-3
Red Hill . . . 92,A-1
Red River 332 . . . 91,F-3
Redrock . . . 92,B-4
Regina . . . 90,D-4
Rencona . . . 91,E-5
Reserve• 439 . . . 92,B-2
Ribera . . . 91,E-5
Rincon . . . 92,D-4
Rincon Montoso . . . 91,E-4
Rinconada . . . 91,E-3
Rio en Medio . . . 91,E-4
Rio Rancho . . . 90,D-5
Rociada . . . 91,E-4
Rodarte . . . 91,E-4
Rodeo . . . 92,A-5
Rodey . . . 92,C-4
Rogers . . . 93,H-2
Romeroville . . . 91,F-4
Roswell• 39,676 . . . 93,G-3
Rowe . . . 91,E-4
Roy 381 . . . 91,G-4
Ruidoso 4,260 . . . 93,E-3
Ruidoso Downs 949 . . . 93,E-3
Rutheron . . . 90,D-3
Sabinal . . . 92,D-1
Sabinoso . . . 91,G-4
Sacramento . . . 93,E-3
St. Vrain . . . 93,H-1
Salem . . . 92,C-4
Salt Lake . . . 92,B-1
San Acacia . . . 92,D-1
San Agustin . . . 91,F-5
San Antonio . . . 92,D-2
San Antonio Spring . . . 90,B-5
San Antonito . . . 90,D-5
San Cristobal . . . 91,E-3
San Fidel . . . 90,C-5
San Francisco Plaza . . . 92,B-2
San Ignacio (Tecoloteños) . . . 91,F-4
San Ignacio . . . 91,F-5
San Ildefonso . . . 91,E-4
San Jon 341 . . . 91,H-5
San Jose . . . 91,E-5
San Juan . . . 92,C-3
San Juan Pueblo . . . 91,E-4
San Lorenzo . . . 92,C-3
San Luis . . . 90,D-4
San Marcial . . . 92,D-2
San Mateo . . . 90,C-5
San Miguel . . . 91,E-2
San Miguel . . . 91,E-5
San Miguel . . . 92,D-4
San Pablo . . . 91,F-4
San Patricio . . . 93,F-3
San Pedro . . . 91,E-5
San Pedro . . . 92,D-2
San Rafael . . . 90,C-5
San Ysidro 199 . . . 90,D-4
Sandia Park . . . 90,D-5
Sands (Soham P.O.) . . . 91,E-5
Santa Cruz . . . 91,E-4
Santa Fe• 48,899 . . . 91,E-4
Santa Rita . . . 92,B-3
Santa Rosa• 2,469 . . . 91,F-5
Santo Domingo Pueblo . . . 90,D-4
Santo Tomas . . . 92,D-4
Sapello . . . 91,F-4
Scholle . . . 92,D-1
Seboyeta . . . 90,C-5
Sedan . . . 91,H-4
Sedillo . . . 90,D-5
Sena . . . 91,F-5
Seneca . . . 91,H-3
Separ . . . 92,B-4
Sheep Springs . . . 90,B-4
Shiprock . . . 90,B-3
Shoemaker . . . 91,F-4
Sile . . . 90,D-4
Silver City• 9,887 . . . 92,B-3
Skarda . . . 91,E-3
Smith Lake . . . 90,B-4
Socorro• 7,576 . . . 92,D-2
Sofia . . . 91,G-3
Solano . . . 91,G-4
South Spring . . . 93,G-3
Springer 1,696 . . . 91,F-3
Standing Rock . . . 90,B-4
Stanley . . . 91,E-5
Sulphur Springs . . . 90,D-4
Summit . . . 92,A-4
Sunset . . . 93,F-3
Sunshine Valley . . . 91,E-3
Sunspot . . . 93,E-3
Tajique . . . 92,D-1
Talpa . . . 91,E-3
Taos• 3,369 . . . 91,E-3
Tapia . . . 91,E-5
Tatum 896 . . . 93,H-3
Taylor . . . 91,G-3
Tecolote . . . 91,F-5
Tecolotito . . . 91,F-5
Tererro . . . 91,E-4
Tesuque . . . 91,E-4
Texico 958 . . . 93,H-1
The Pines . . . 92,B-4
Thoreau . . . 90,B-5
Three Rivers . . . 93,E-3
Tierra Amarilla• . . . 90,D-3
Tijeras 311 . . . 90,D-5
Tinaja . . . 90,B-5
Tinnie . . . 93,F-3
Toadlena . . . 90,A-3
Tohatchi . . . 90,B-4
Tolar . . . 93,G-1
Tome . . . 92,D-1
Torreon . . . 90,C-4
Torreon . . . 92,D-1
Tres Piedras . . . 91,E-3
Tres Ritos . . . 91,E-4
Truchas . . . 91,E-4
Trujillo . . . 91,F-4
Truth or Consequences• 5,219 . . . 92,C-3
Tucumcari• 6,765 . . . 91,G-5
Tularosa 2,536 . . . 93,E-3
Tuloso . . . 91,F-4
Turley . . . 90,C-3
Turn . . . 92,D-1
Tusas . . . 91,E-3
Tyrone . . . 92,B-4
Upper Nutria . . . 90,B-5
Ute Park . . . 91,F-3
Vadito . . . 91,E-4
Vado . . . 92,D-4
Valdez . . . 91,E-3
Valencia . . . 92,D-1
Vallecitos . . . 91,E-3
Vallecitos . . . 90,D-4
Vallecitos . . . 91,E-4
Valmont . . . 93,E-4
Valmora . . . 91,F-4
Valverde . . . 92,D-2
Vanadium . . . 92,B-3
Vanderwagen . . . 90,B-5
Variadero (Garita P.O.) . . . 91,G-5
Vaughn 737 . . . 93,F-1
Veguita . . . 92,D-1
Valarde . . . 91,E-4
Villanueva . . . 91,F-5
Virden 246 . . . 92,A-4
Wagon Mound 416 . . . 91,F-4
Waterflow . . . 90,B-3
Watrous . . . 91,F-4
Weed . . . 93,E-3
Wheatland . . . 91,H-5
White Horse . . . 90,C-4
White Lakes . . . 91,E-5
White Oaks . . . 93,E-2
White Rock . . . 91,E-4
White Sands Missile Range . . . 92,D-4
White Signal . . . 92,B-4
Whites City . . . 93,G-4
Whitetail . . . 93,E-3
Whitewater . . . 92,B-4
Willard 166 . . . 93,E-1
Williamsburg 433 . . . 92,C-3
Winston . . . 92,C-3
Yankee . . . 91,G-2
Yates . . . 91,G-4
Yeso . . . 93,F-1
Youngsville . . . 90,D-4
Zamora . . . 90,D-5
Zuni . . . 90,A-5

MZ-598-J-X

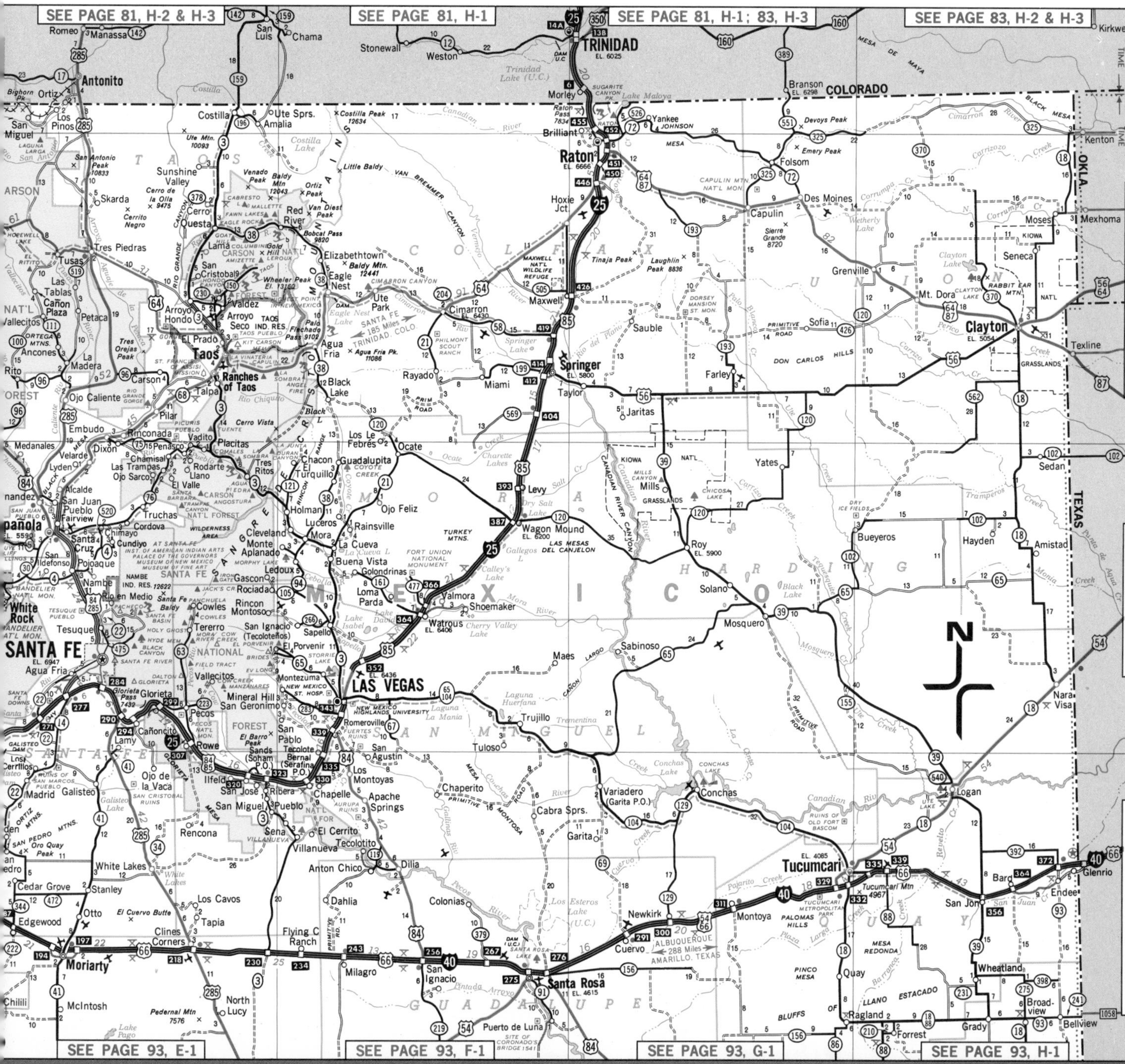

SEE PAGE 81, H-2 & H-3
SEE PAGE 81, H-1
SEE PAGE 81, H-1; 83, H-3
SEE PAGE 83, H-2 & H-3
TRINIDAD
EL. 6025
COLORADO
MOUNTAIN STANDARD TIME
CENTRAL STANDARD TIME
Antonito
Chama
Raton
EL. 6666
Clayton
EL. 5054
OKLA.
TEXAS
SEE PAGE 97, E-1; 105, H-3
SEE PAGE 97, E-1
SEE PAGE 97, E-2 & E-3
Taos
Ranchos de Taos
Springer
EL. 5800
Cimarron
Eagle Nest
Maxwell
Wagon Mound
EL. 6200
SANTA FE
EL. 6947
LAS VEGAS
EL. 6436
Tucumcari
EL. 4085
Santa Rosa
EL. 4615
Moriarty
Mosquero
Roy
EL. 5900
Conchas
Logan
Nara Visa
San Jon
Glenrio
ALBUQUERQUE 288 Miles
AMARILLO, TEXAS
SEE PAGE 93, E-1
SEE PAGE 93, F-1
SEE PAGE 93, G-1
SEE PAGE 93, H-1

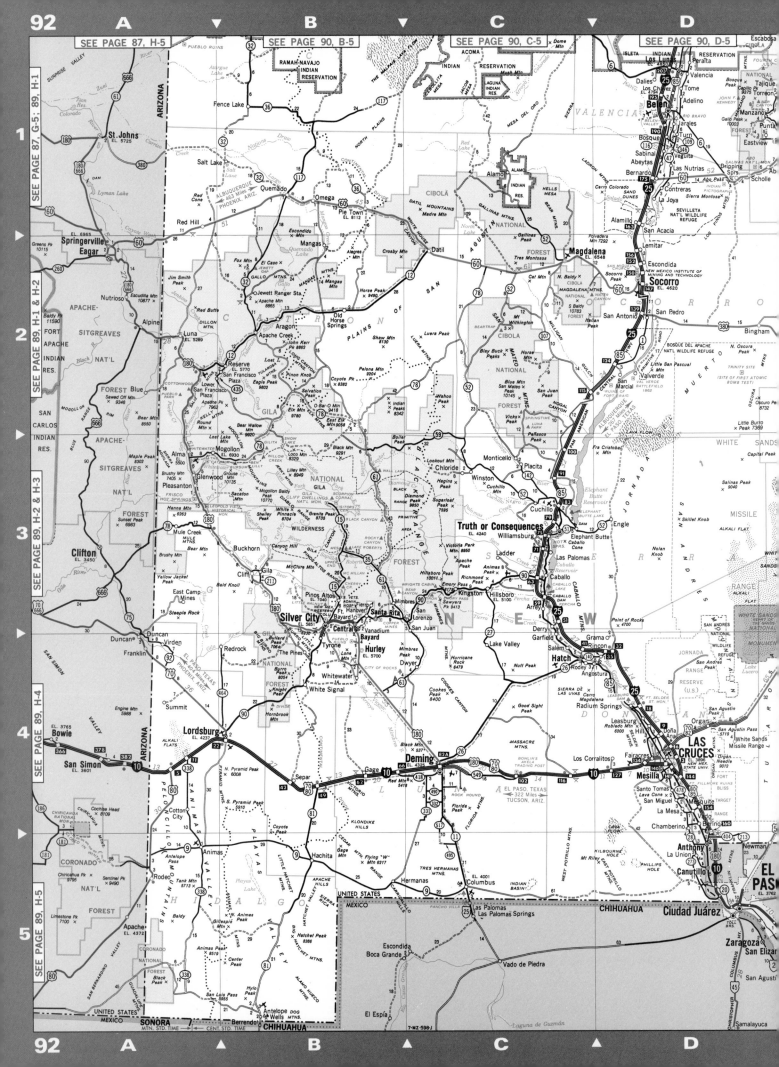

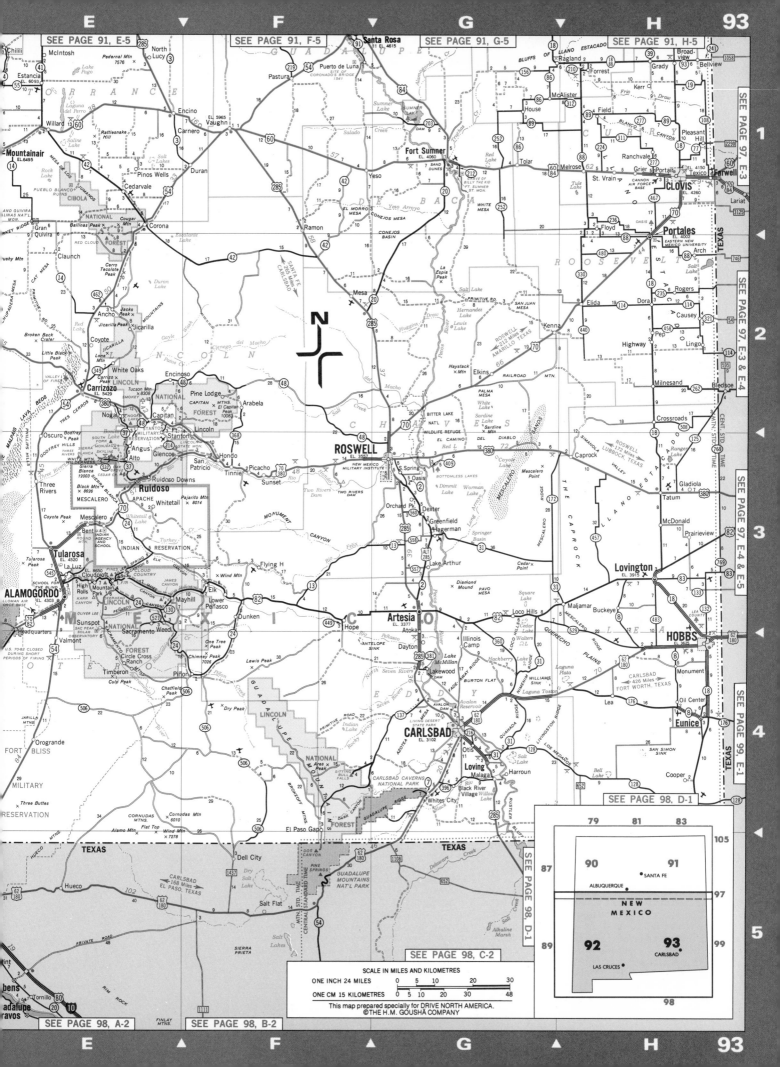

Echoes of the Alamo,
and the Oil Capital of the World

Texas/Oklahoma

Texas and Oklahoma occupy so much geography that any single picture of these states is certain to be incomplete. West of the Pecos River, Texas lives up to its rugged image. In **Guadalupe Mountains National Park (98, C-1)** sunlight yellows the cliffs of Guadalupe Peak, at 8,751 feet the highest point in Texas. The park is part of a fossil reef, once underwater, that was built about 250 million years ago. Now canyons shelter cacti, hardwood groves, evergreens—and such animals as elk and bobcats.

Settlers in Texas came first to this part of the state, building frontier outposts such as **El Paso (98, A-1)** along the Rio Grande. The city's Ysleta Mission, founded in 1682 by Spanish padres and Tigua Indians, is believed to be the oldest in Texas.

Texas' "Big Bend" is a curve in the Rio Grande, 1,106 square miles of which are protected in **Big Bend National Park (98, D-4).** Most of the park is Chihuahuan desert, studded with creosote bush, mesquite, ocotillo and prickly pear cactus. The Rio Grande, here serene and slow-moving, cuts three deep canyons in the arid landscape.

As might be expected, the Texas State Capitol in **Austin (100, D-5),** 300 feet high from basement to the top of the dome, is one of the biggest of all state capitols. At the University of Texas, the Lyndon B. Johnson Library holds an overwhelming 31 million documents relating to the 36th president's career from 1935 to 1969. Johnson's birthplace in **Stonewall (100, C-5)** has been restored and furnished with many of the belongings of his parents and grandparents, as has his boyhood home in **Johnson City.**

Dating from 1718, when the Spanish first established Mission San Antonio de Valero (the Alamo), bilingual **San Antonio (102, C-1)** has a varied cultural flavor and rich history. On March 6, 1836, 188 rebel Texans—including Davy Crockett and Jim Bowie—were massacred at the crumbling Alamo mission after a 13-day siege by 2,000 Mexican soldiers. "Remember the Alamo!" became the battle cry that carried Texans on to victory at the

Late afternoon sun strikes gold from the skyline of Dallas (above). Anglo-Americans first settled here in 1841. Since then, Swiss, German, French and other immigrant groups intermingled to transform the city into a cosmopolitan center for the arts, banking, insurance, fashion—and friendly rival to Houston. Cowboys in Stetsons (right) are as familiar a sight as bankers in gray flannel.

A delicate facade of Renaissance-style limestone carvings adorns the Mission San José in San Antonio, called the "Queen Mission of New Spain."

Battle of San Jacinto. Artifacts relating to the mission and to Texas history are displayed in the Alamo Museum.

Winding stone stairways lead to the rustic but sophisticated Paseo del Rio (River Walk) along the San Antonio River. Terraced and landscaped with a variety of trees and shrubs —including wild olive, cypress, palm and jasmine—the walk offers a tranquil promenade only a short distance from downtown San Antonio.

More than 30 miles of clean and sandy beach stretch westward from **Galveston (103, G-1).** Many fishing piers are built well out into the water, the surf-fishing is highly rated, and deep-water catches from boats offshore include sailfish, marlin, king mackerel and red snapper. North of **Corpus Christi (103, E-3)** the rare whooping crane has chosen the vast Aransas National Wildlife Refuge as its wintering ground (it breeds in northern Canada).

Houston (103, G-1), Texas' largest city and the headquarters of the NASA Space Center, began as a riverboat landing in 1836. In the spring of that year, 910 Americans defeated a larger Mexican force here in a mere 18 minutes. The 570-foot limestone monument of San Jacinto Battleground Park pays tribute to the event, which led to the annexation of Texas by the United States. A more familiar Houston landmark is the Astrodome, an en-

gineering marvel and the world's first enclosed, domed sports arena.

Twenty-four American period rooms with furniture and accessories dating from the early 17th century comprise the Bayou Bend Collection, the largest in the Southwest devoted to the decorative arts. Exhibits in the Museum of Fine Arts range from Rodin sculptures to works by contemporary artists such as Pollock and Motherwell.

Lavish use of marble and wood lends a luxurious air to the handsome Texas Hall of State in **Dallas (101, E-2),** where bronze statues of famous Texans line the Hall of Heroes. The Dallas Museum of Fine Arts collection of 20th-century American paintings features Hopper's *Light-House Hill* and Pollock's *Cathedral.* Rare animals such as the klipspringer, dik-dik, suni and slender-horned gazelle inhabit the Dallas Zoo. A three-level tropical rain forest is home to colorful free-flying birds, and a landscaped pool belongs to stilt-legged flamingos. The Dallas Garden

Carbine in hand, Buffalo Bill strikes a dashing pose at Oklahoma City's National Cowboy Hall of Fame (above). Western history and lore is recorded here in paintings, life-size dioramas, a stagecoach, a gun shop, an Indian village and a chuck wagon. A room-size relief map, using light and sound, tracks the historic trails pioneers followed westward.

A towering oil derrick, symbol of Oklahoma's petroleum wealth, pierces the haze near the town of Corn. Such oil finds once fueled boundary disputes between Oklahoma and Texas.

Center has formal and informal gardens laced with lagoons, and an Herb and Scent Garden, designed for the blind.

Foremost among the museums and galleries of **Fort Worth (100, D-2)** is the Amon Carter Museum. The bronze front doors open into a gallery two stories high dominated by the paintings, drawings, and bronzes of Frederic Remington and Charles M. Russell.

To a visitor driving through the nearly featureless farmland of southwestern Oklahoma, the sudden upthrust of the Wichita Mountains, rising 2,500 feet in a series of folds and faults, comes as a surprise. **Wichita Mountains Wildlife Refuge (105, E-2)** protects several hundred plains bison, remnants of some 60 million buffalo that moved in wide waves across the grasslands in the 19th century.

Near the park's eastern boundary in **Lawton (105, E-1)** is Fort Sill, a site steeped in Western history and legend. Established in 1869 as a cavalry fort, the enormous compound served soldiers, settlers, missionaries and homesteaders. The post cemetery is regarded as the Indian "Arlington" because of the many chiefs buried here, among them the great Apache leader Geronimo. Scouts, warriors, educators, statesmen and tribal leaders are honored in the National Hall of Fame for Famous American Indians in nearby **Anadarko (104, D-1)**.

Like many public buildings, the state capitol in **Oklahoma City (106, D-5)** is a classic structure with a pillared portico—but it is unique. On the grounds are several working oil wells. Tales of pioneers, cowboys and Indians come to life in the National Cowboy Hall of Fame and Western Heritage Center. The Rodeo Hall of Fame—crammed with saddles, buckles, boots, spurs and trophies—honors champion riders.

Driven from their southeastern homes in the early 19th century, the Cherokee, Chickasaw, Choctaw, Creek and Seminole Indians resettled in Oklahoma. The Five Civilized Tribes Museum in **Muskogee (106, C-2)**, housed in the 1875 Union Indian Agency Building, preserves the traditions of the tribes. In 1878 in **Okmulgee (106, C-3)**, Creek Indians drew up a constitution and constructed the handsome Creek Indian Nation Council House now a museum. Tsa-La-Gi (Cherokee Cultural Center) near **Park Hill (106, C-1)** is the setting of a re-created 18th-century Cherokee village and the Cherokee National Museum.

The oil boom that transformed **Tulsa (106, B-3)** into "the oil capital of the world" made Thomas Gilcrease a millionaire before the age of 21. His good fortune enabled him to amass the 5,000 examples of American painting and sculpture, Indian artifacts, historic documents and letters, and rare books now housed in the Thomas Gilcrease Institute of American History and Art. Among Tulsa's architectural attractions are several striking churches, including the Boston Avenue Church (1929), built on a cathedral scale in unusual art deco style. A chapel crowns its 200-foot tower.

The town of **Claremore (106, B-2)**, northeast of Tulsa, is famous as the home of cowboy humorist Will Rogers. Although Oklahoma's favorite son was born ten miles away in **Oologah**, he claimed Claremore as home because, he said, "nobody but an Indian could pronounce Oologah."

Texas' Treasure Island

Padre Island National Seashore (103, E-4), on one of the world's great barrier islands, is a gleaming strip of sand and surf that extends from Corpus Christi to Port Isabel and separates the blue waters of the Gulf of Mexico from the mainland of Texas. To summer visitors, it may seem that the vast dome of sky arching over the beaches and dunes is always clear and sunny. But in the mid-16th century treacherous weather destroyed three treasure-laden Spanish galleons attempting to pass this "graveyard of the Gulf." Many other ships met the same stormy fate and their wrecks lie here still, some beneath the waves off Padre Island, others under the shifting sands.

Those who stroll the beaches may dream of gold doubloons, but the island's real treasure is its wildlife. Coyotes, gophers, ground squirrels and kangaroo rats share the dunes and grasslands with 12 species of snakes, including two types of rattlesnakes. Even inexperienced birdwatchers will recognize some of the area's more spectacular inhabitants—the majestic great blue heron and the white pelican. More than 350 species of birds, from meadowlark to marsh hawk, have been recorded here.

Some islanders are trying to establish a nesting place on a remote beach for the huge Atlantic ridley sea turtles. They hope that some of the turtles hatched here will return when mature, in seven years, to lay their own eggs.

Ila Loetscher—South Padre Island's "Turtle Lady"—provides temporary homes in plastic wading pools for ailing sea turtles.

95

Texas

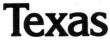

SCALE IN MILES AND KILOMETRES
ONE INCH 28 MILES 0 5 10 20 30
ONE CM 18 KILOMETRES 0 5 10 20 30 48

This map prepared specially for DRIVE NORTH AMERICA.
©THE H.M. GOUSHA COMPANY

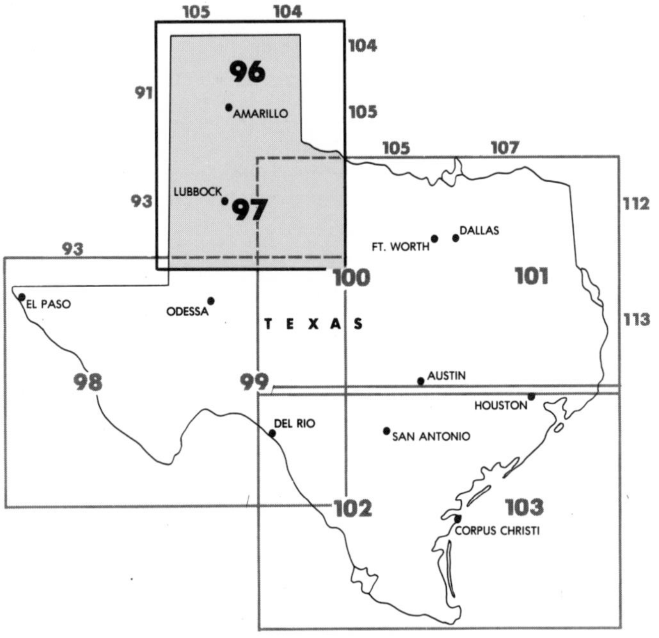
105
104
96
AMARILLO
91
104
105
105
107
112
93
LUBBOCK
97
FT. WORTH
DALLAS
93
100
101
EL PASO
ODESSA
T E X A S
113
98
99
AUSTIN
HOUSTON
DEL RIO
SAN ANTONIO
102
103
CORPUS CHRISTI

INDEX TO COUNTIES

Pop. (1980) 14,228,383 Area 267,339 Sq. Mi.

County	County Seat
Anderson	Palestine
Andrews	Andrews
Angelina	Lufkin
Aransas	Rockport
Archer	Archer City
Armstrong	Claude
Atascosa	Jourdanton
Austin	Bellville
Bailey	Muleshoe
Bandera	Bandera
Bastrop	Bastrop
Baylor	Seymour
Bee	Beeville
Bell	Belton
Bexar	San Antonio
Blanco	Johnson City
Borden	Gail
Bosque	Meridian
Bowie	Boston
Brazoria	Angleton
Brazos	Bryan
Brewster	Alpine
Briscoe	Silverton
Brooks	Falfurrias
Brown	Brownwood
Burleson	Caldwell
Burnet	Burnet
Caldwell	Lockhart
Calhoun	Port Lavaca
Callahan	Baird
Cameron	Brownsville
Camp	Pittsburg
Carson	Panhandle
Cass	Linden
Castro	Dimmitt
Chambers	Anahuac
Cherokee	Rusk
Childress	Childress
Clay	Henrietta
Cochran	Morton
Coke	Robert Lee
Coleman	Coleman
Collin	McKinney
Collingsworth	Wellington
Colorado	Columbus
Comal	New Braunfels
Comanche	Comanche
Concho	Paint Rock
Cooke	Gainesville
Coryell	Gatesville
Cottle	Paducah
Crane	Crane
Crockett	Ozona
Crosby	Crosbyton
Culberson	Van Horn
Dallam	Dalhart
Dallas	Dallas
Dawson	Lamesa
De Witt	Cuero
Deaf Smith	Hereford
Delta	Cooper
Denton	Denton
Dickens	Dickens
Dimmit	Carrizo Springs
Donley	Clarendon
Duval	San Diego
Eastland	Eastland
Ector	Odessa
Edwards	Rocksprings
El Paso	El Paso
Ellis	Waxahachie
Erath	Stephenville
Falls	Marlin
Fannin	Bonham
Fayette	La Grange
Fisher	Roby
Floyd	Floydada
Foard	Crowell
Fort Bend	Richmond
Franklin	Mount Vernon
Freestone	Fairfield
Frio	Pearsall
Gaines	Seminole
Galveston	Galveston
Garza	Post
Gillespie	Fredericksburg
Glasscock	Garden City
Goliad	Goliad
Gonzales	Gonzales
Gray	Pampa
Grayson	Sherman
Gregg	Longview
Grimes	Anderson
Guadalupe	Seguin
Hale	Plainview
Hall	Memphis
Hamilton	Hamilton
Hansford	Spearman
Hardeman	Quanah
Hardin	Kountze
Harris	Houston
Harrison	Marshall
Hartley	Channing
Haskell	Haskell
Hays	San Marcos
Hemphill	Canadian
Henderson	Athens
Hidalgo	Edinburg
Hill	Hillsboro
Hockley	Levelland
Hood	Granbury
Hopkins	Sulphur Springs
Houston	Crockett
Howard	Big Spring
Hudspeth	Sierra Blanca
Hunt	Greenville
Hutchinson	Stinnett
Irion	Mertzon
Jack	Jacksboro
Jackson	Edna
Jasper	Jasper
Jeff Davis	Fort Davis
Jefferson	Beaumont
Jim Hogg	Hebbronville
Jim Wells	Alice
Johnson	Cleburne
Jones	Anson
Karnes	Karnes City
Kaufman	Kaufman
Kendall	Boerne
Kenedy	Sarita
Kent	Jayton
Kerr	Kerrville
Kimble	Junction
King	Guthrie
Kinney	Brackettville
Kleberg	Kingsville
Knox	Benjamin
La Salle	Cotulla
Lamar	Paris
Lamb	Littlefield
Lampasas	Lampasas
Lavaca	Hallettsville
Lee	Giddings
Leon	Centerville
Liberty	Liberty
Limestone	Groesbeck
Lipscomb	Lipscomb
Live Oak	George West
Llano	Llano
Loving	Mentone
Lubbock	Lubbock
Lynn	Tahoka
Madison	Madisonville
Marion	Jefferson
Martin	Stanton
Mason	Mason
Matagorda	Bay City
Maverick	Eagle Pass
McCulloch	Brady
McLennan	Waco
McMullen	Tilden
Medina	Hondo
Menard	Menard
Midland	Midland
Milam	Cameron
Mills	Goldthwaite
Mitchell	Colorado City
Montague	Montague
Montgomery	Conroe
Moore	Dumas
Morris	Daingerfield
Motley	Matador
Nacogdoches	Nacogdoches
Navarro	Corsicana
Newton	Newton
Nolan	Sweetwater
Nueces	Corpus Christi
Ochiltree	Perryton
Oldham	Vega
Orange	Orange
Palo Pinto	Palo Pinto
Panola	Carthage
Parker	Weatherford
Parmer	Farwell
Pecos	Fort Stockton
Polk	Livingston
Potter	Amarillo
Presidio	Marfa
Rains	Emory
Randall	Canyon
Reagan	Big Lake
Real	Leakey
Red River	Clarksville
Reeves	Pecos
Rufugio	Refugio
Roberts	Miami
Robertson	Franklin
Rockwall	Rockwall
Runnels	Ballinger
Rusk	Henderson
Sabine	Hemphill
San Augustine	San Augustine
San Jacinto	Coldspring
San Patricio	Sinton
San Saba	San Saba
Schleicher	Eldorado
Scurry	Snyder
Shackelford	Albany
Shelby	Center
Sherman	Stratford
Smith	Tyler
Somervell	Glen Rose
Starr	Rio Grande City
Stephens	Breckenridge
Sterling	Sterling City
Stonewall	Aspermont
Sutton	Sonora
Swisher	Tulia
Tarrant	Fort Worth
Taylor	Abilene
Terrell	Sanderson
Terry	Brownfield
Throckmorton	Throckmorton
Titus	Mount Pleasant
Tom Green	San Angelo
Travis	Austin
Trinity	Groveton
Tyler	Woodville
Upshur	Gilmer
Upton	Rankin
Uvalde	Uvalde
Val Verde	Del Rio
Van Zandt	Canton
Victoria	Victoria
Walker	Huntsville
Waller	Hempstead
Ward	Monahans
Washington	Brenham
Webb	Laredo
Wharton	Wharton
Wheeler	Wheeler
Wichita	Wichita Falls
Wilbarger	Vernon
Willacy	Raymondville
Williamson	Georgetown
Wilson	Floresville
Winkler	Kermit
Wise	Decatur
Wood	Quitman
Yoakum	Plains
Young	Graham
Zapata	Zapata
Zavala	Crystal City

PARTIAL LIST OF

CITIES AND TOWNS

1980 Census

•County Seats

Abbott 359 ... 101,E-3
Abernathy 2,904 ... 97,F-4
Abilene• 98,315 ... 100,B-3
Agua Dulce 934 ... 102,D-3
Alamo 5,831 ... 102,D-5
Alamo Heights 6,252 ... 102,C-1
Alba 568 ... 101,F-2
Albany• 2,450 ... 100,B-2
Alice• 20,961 ... 102,D-3
Alpine• 5,465 ... 98,D-3
Alto 1,203 ... 101,G-3
Alvarado 2,701 ... 101,E-3
Alvin 16,515 ... 103,G-1
Alvord 874 ... 100,D-2
Amarillo• 149,230 ... 97,F-2
Amherst 971 ... 97,E-4
Anahuac• 1,840 ... 103,G-1
Anderson• ... 101,F-5
Andrews• 11,061 ... 99,E-1
Angleton• 13,929 ... 103,G-2
Anna 855 ... 101,E-2
Annona 471 ... 101,G-1
Anson• 2,831 ... 100,B-2
Anton 1,180 ... 97,F-4
Aransas Pass 7,173 ... 103,E-3
Arcadia ... 103,G-1
Archer City• 1,862 ... 100,C-1
Arlington 160,123 ... 101,E-2
Arp 939 ... 101,G-3
Asherton 1,574 ... 102,B-2
Aspermont• 1,357 ... 97,G-5
Athens• 10,197 ... 101,F-3
Atlanta 6,272 ... 101,H-2
Aubrey 948 ... 101,E-2
Austin• 345,496 ... 100,D-5
Avery 520 ... 101,G-1
Avinger 671 ... 101,G-2
Azle 5,822 ... 100,D-2
Baird• 1,696 ... 100,B-3
Ballinger• 4,207 ... 100,B-3
Balmorhea 568 ... 98,D-2
Bandera• 947 ... 102,C-1
Bangs 1,716 ... 100,C-3
Barrett ... 103,G-1
Barstow 637 ... 98,D-2
Bartlett 1,567 ... 100,D-5
Bastrop• 3,789 ... 101,E-5
Bay City• 17,837 ... 103,F-2
Baytown 56,923 ... 103,G-1
Beaumont• 118,102 ... 101,H-5
Beckville 945 ... 101,G-3
Beeville• 14,574 ... 102,D-2
Bellevue 352 ... 100,D-1
Bellmead 7,569 ... 101,E-4
Bells 846 ... 101,E-1
Bellville• 2,860 ... 103,F-1
Belton• 10,660 ... 100,D-4
Benavides 1,978 ... 102,C-3
Benjamin• 257 ... 100,B-1
Bessmay ... 101,H-5
Big Lake• 3,404 ... 99,F-2
Big Sandy 1,258 ... 101,G-2
Big Spring• 24,804 ... 99,F-1
Big Wells 939 ... 102,B-2
Bishop 3,706 ... 102,D-3
Blanco 1,179 ... 100,C-5
Blanket 388 ... 100,C-3
Bloomburg 419 ... 101,H-2
Blooming Grove 823 ... 101,E-3
Blossom 1,487 ... 101,F-1
Blue Ridge 442 ... 101,E-2
Blum 357 ... 100,D-3
Boerne• 3,229 ... 102,C-1
Bogata 1,508 ... 101,G-1
Bonham• 7,338 ... 101,F-1
Booker 1,219 ... 97,G-1
Borger 15,837 ... 97,F-2
Boston• ... 101,G-1
Bovina 1,499 ... 97,E-3
Bowie 5,610 ... 100,D-1
Boyd 889 ... 100,D-2
Brackettville• 1,676 ... 99,G-4
Brady• 5,969 ... 100,B-4
Brazoria 3,025 ... 103,F-2
Breckenridge• 6,921 ... 100,C-2
Bremond 1,025 ... 101,E-4
Brenham• 10,966 ... 101,F-5
Bridge City 7,667 ... 101,H-5
Bridgeport 3,737 ... 100,D-2
Bronte 983 ... 99,G-1
Brookshire 2,175 ... 103,F-1
Brownfield• 10,387 ... 97,E-4
Brownsboro 582 ... 101,F-3
Brownsville• 84,997 ... 102,D-5
Brownwood• 19,203 ... 100,C-3
Bryan• 44,337 ... 101,F-5
Bryson 579 ... 100,C-2
Buda 597 ... 100,D-5
Buffalo 1,507 ... 101,F-4
Bullard 681 ... 101,F-3
Burkburnett 10,688 ... 100,C-1
Burleson 11,734 ... 100,D-2
Burnet• 3,410 ... 100,D-5
Byers 556 ... 100,D-1
Caddo Mills 1,060 ... 101,F-2
Caldwell• 2,953 ... 101,E-5
Calvert 1,732 ... 101,E-4
Camden ... 101,G-4
Cameron• 5,721 ... 101,E-4
Camp Wood 728 ... 102,B-1
Campbellton ... 102,D-2
Canadian• 3,491 ... 97,G-1
Canton• 2,845 ... 101,F-2
Canutillo ... 98,A-1
Canyon• 10,724 ... 97,F-2
Carbon 281 ... 100,C-3
Carrizo Springs• 6,886 ... 102,B-2
Carrollton 40,591 ... 101,E-2
Carthage• 6,447 ... 101,G-3
Castroville 1,821 ... 102,C-1
Catarina ... 102,B-3
Cedar Hill 6,849 ... 101,E-2
Celeste 716 ... 101,F-2
Celina 1,520 ... 101,E-2
Center• 5,827 ... 101,H-3
Centerville• 779 ... 101,F-4
Channing• 304 ... 97,E-2
Charlotte 1,443 ... 102,C-2
Chico 890 ... 100,D-2
Childress• 5,817 ... 97,G-3
Chillicothe 1,052 ... 97,H-3
Cisco 4,517 ... 100,C-3
Clairemont• ... 97,G-5
Clarendon• 2,220 ... 97,G-2
Clarksville• 4,917 ... 101,G-1
Claude• 1,112 ... 97,F-2
Clear Lake City ... 103,G-1
Cleburne• 19,218 ... 101,D-3
Cleveland 5,977 ... 101,G-5
Clifton 3,063 ... 100,D-3
Clute 9,577 ... 103,G-2
Clyde 2,562 ... 100,B-3
Coahoma 1,069 ... 99,F-1
Cockrell Hill 3,262 ... 101,E-2
Coldspring• 569 ... 101,G-5
Coleman• 5,960 ... 100,B-3
College Station 37,272 ... 101,F-5
Collinsville 860 ... 101,E-1
Colorado City• 5,405 ... 99,G-1
Columbus• 3,923 ... 103,E-1
Comanche• 4,075 ... 100,C-3
Comfort ... 102,C-1
Commerce 8,136 ... 101,F-2
Conroe• 18,034 ... 101,F-5
Coolidge 810 ... 101,E-3
Cooper• 2,338 ... 101,F-1
Copperas Cove 19,469 ... 100,D-4
Corpus Christi• 231,999 ... 103,E-3
Corrigan 1,770 ... 101,G-4
Corsicana• 21,712 ... 101,E-3
Cotulla• 3,912 ... 102,C-2
Crandall 831 ... 101,E-2
Crane• 3,622 ... 99,E-2
Crawford 610 ... 100,D-4
Crockett• 7,405 ... 101,F-4
Crosbyton• 2,289 ... 97,F-4
Cross Plains 1,240 ... 100,C-3
Crowell• 1,509 ... 100,B-1
Crystal City• 8,334 ... 102,B-2
Cuero• 7,124 ... 103,E-2
Cumby 647 ... 101,F-2
Cushing 518 ... 101,G-3
Daingerfield• 3,030 ... 101,G-2
Daisetta 1,177 ... 101,G-5
Dalhart• 6,854 ... 97,E-1
Dallas• 904,078 ... 101,E-2
Darrouzett 444 ... 97,G-1
Dawson 747 ... 101,E-3
Dayton 4,908 ... 101,G-5
De Kalb 2,217 ... 101,G-1
De Leon 2,478 ... 100,C-3
Decatur• 4,104 ... 100,D-2
Del Rio• 30,034 ... 99,G-4
Denison 23,884 ... 101,E-1
Denton• 48,063 ... 101,E-2
Denver City 4,704 ... 97,E-5
Deport 724 ... 101,F-1
Detroit 805 ... 101,F-1
Devine 3,756 ... 102,C-2
Diboll 5,227 ... 101,G-4
Dickens• 409 ... 97,G-4
Dickinson 7,505 ... 103,G-1
Dilley 2,579 ... 102,C-2
Dimmit• 5,019 ... 97,E-3
Dodd City 286 ... 101,F-1
Dodson 185 ... 97,H-3
Donna 9,952 ... 102,D-5
Dublin 2,723 ... 100,C-3
Dumas• 12,194 ... 97,F-1
Eagle Lake 3,921 ... 103,F-1
Eagle Pass• 21,407 ... 99,G-5
Early 2,313 ... 100,C-3
Earth 1,512 ... 97,E-3
Eastland• 3,747 ... 100,C-3
Ector 573 ... 101,E-1
Edcouch 3,092 ... 102,D-5
Eden 1,294 ... 99,H-2
Edgewood 1,413 ... 101,F-2
Edinburg• 24,075 ... 102,D-5
Edna• 5,650 ... 103,E-2
El Campo 10,462 ... 103,F-1
El Paso• 425,259 ... 98,A-1
Eldorado• 2,061 ... 99,G-3
Electra 3,755 ... 100,C-1
Elgin 4,535 ... 100,D-5
Elkhart 1,317 ... 101,F-3
Elsa 5,061 ... 102,D-5
Emory• 813 ... 101,F-2
Ennis 12,110 ... 101,E-3
Estelline 258 ... 97,G-3
Euless 24,002 ... 101,E-2
Fabens ... 98,A-2
Fairfield• 3,505 ... 101,F-3
Fairview 893 ... 101,E-2
Falfurrias• 6,103 ... 102,D-4
Falls City 580 ... 102,D-2
Farmersville 2,360 ... 101,E-2
Farwell• 1,354 ... 97,E-3
Fayetteville 356 ... 103,E-1
Ferris 2,228 ... 101,E-2
Flatonia 1,070 ... 103,E-1
Florence 744 ... 100,D-4
Floresville• 4,381 ... 102,D-2
Floydada• 4,193 ... 97,F-4
Follett 547 ... 97,H-1
Forney 2,483 ... 101,E-2
Fort Davis• ... 98,D-3
Fort Stockton• 8,688 ... 99,E-2
Fort Worth• 385,141 ... 100,D-2
Franklin• 1,349 ... 101,E-4
Frankston 1,255 ... 101,F-3
Fredericksburg• 6,412 ... 100,C-5
Freeport 13,444 ... 103,G-2
Freer 3,213 ... 102,C-3
Friona 3,809 ... 97,E-3
Frisco 3,420 ... 101,E-2
Fritch 2,299 ... 97,F-2
Frost 564 ... 101,E-3
Gail• ... 97,F-5
Gainesville• 14,081 ... 101,E-1
Galveston• 61,902 ... 103,G-1
Ganado 1,770 ... 103,E-2
Garden City• ... 99,F-1
Garland 138,857 ... 101,E-2
Garrison 1,059 ... 101,G-3
Gatesville• 6,260 ... 100,D-4
George West• 2,627 ... 102,D-3
Georgetown• 9,468 ... 100,D-5
Giddings• 3,950 ... 101,E-5
Gilmer• 5,167 ... 101,G-2
Gladewater 6,548 ... 101,G-2
Glen Rose• 2,075 ... 100,D-3
Godley 614 ... 100,D-3
Goldsmith 409 ... 99,E-1
Goldthwaite• 1,783 ... 100,C-4
Goliad• 1,990 ... 103,E-2
Gonzales• 7,152 ... 102,D-1
Gordon 516 ... 100,C-2
Goree 524 ... 100,B-1
Gorman 1,258 ... 100,C-3
Graford 495 ... 100,C-2
Graham• 9,055 ... 100,C-2
Granbury• 3,332 ... 100,D-3
Grand Prairie 71,462 ... 101,E-2
Grand Saline 2,709 ... 101,F-2
Grandfalls 635 ... 99,E-2
Grandview 1,205 ... 101,E-3
Granger 1,236 ... 100,D-5
Grapeland 1,634 ... 101,F-4
Grapevine 11,801 ... 101,E-2
Greenville• 22,161 ... 101,F-2
Gregory 2,739 ... 103,E-3
Groesbeck• 3,373 ... 101,E-4
Groom 736 ... 97,G-2
Groves 17,090 ... 101,H-5
Groveton• 1,262 ... 101,G-4
Gruver 1,216 ... 97,F-1
Gunter 849 ... 101,E-1
Guthrie• ... 97,G-4
Hale Center 2,297 ... 97,F-3
Hallettsville• 2,865 ... 103,E-1
Hallsville 1,556 ... 101,G-2
Hamilton• 3,189 ... 100,D-3
Hamlin 3,248 ... 100,B-2
Happy 674 ... 97,F-3
Harker Heights 7,345 ... 100,D-4
Harlingen 43,543 ... 102,D-5
Haskell• 3,782 ... 100,B-2
Hawkins 1,302 ... 101,G-2
Hearne 5,418 ... 101,E-4
Hebbronville• ... 102,C-4
Hedley 380 ... 97,G-3
Hemphill• 1,353 ... 101,H-4
Hempstead• 3,456 ... 101,F-5
Henderson• 11,473 ... 101,G-3
Henrietta• 3,149 ... 100,D-1
Hereford• 15,853 ... 97,E-3
Hermleigh ... 97,G-5
Hico 1,375 ... 100,D-3
Hidalgo 2,288 ... 102,D-5
Higgins 702 ... 97,H-1
Highlands ... 103,G-1
Hillsboro• 7,397 ... 101,E-3
Hitchcock 6,655 ... 103,G-1
Holland 863 ... 100,D-4
Holliday 1,349 ... 100,C-1
Hondo• 6,057 ... 102,C-1
Honey Grove 1,973 ... 101,F-1
Hooks 2,507 ... 101,C-15
Houston• 1,594,086 ... 103,G-1
Howe 2,072 ... 101,E-1
Hubbard 1,676 ... 101,E-3
Hughes Springs 2,196 ... 101,G-2
Humble 6,729 ... 101,G-5
Huntington 1,672 ... 101,G-4
Huntsville• 23,936 ... 101,F-5
Hutto 659 ... 100,D-5
Idalou 2,348 ... 97,F-4
Ingleside 5,436 ... 103,E-3
Iowa Park 6,184 ... 100,C-1
Iraan 1,358 ... 99,F-2
Iredell 407 ... 100,D-3
Irving 109,943 ... 101,E-2
Italy 1,306 ... 101,E-3
Itasca 1,600 ... 101,E-3
Jacksboro• 4,000 ... 100,D-2
Jacksonville 12,264 ... 100,G-3
Jasper• 6,959 ... 101,H-4
Jayton• 638 ... 97,G-4
Jefferson• 2,643 ... 101,G-2
Jewett 597 ... 101,F-4
Joaquin 917 ... 101,H-3
Johnson City• 872 ... 100,C-5
Joshua 1,470 ... 100,D-3
Jourdanton• 2,743 ... 102,C-2
Junction• 2,593 ... 99,H-3
Justin 920 ... 100,D-2
Karnes City• 3,296 ... 102,D-2
Katy 5,600 ... 103,F-1
Kaufman• 4,658 ... 101,E-2
Keene 3,013 ... 100,D-3
Keller 4,143 ... 100,D-2
Kemp 1,035 ... 101,F-3
Kenedy 4,356 ... 102,D-2
Kennedale 2,594 ... 101,E-2
Kerens 1,582 ... 101,F-3
Kermit• 8,015 ... 98,D-1
Kerrville• 15,276 ... 102,C-1
Kilgore 10,968 ... 101,G-3
Killeen 46,296 ... 100,D-4
Kingsville• 28,808 ... 102,D-4
Kirbyville 1,972 ... 101,H-4
Knox City 1,546 ... 100,B-1
Kosse 484 ... 101,E-4
Kountze• 2,716 ... 101,H-5
Kyle 2,093 ... 102,D-1
La Feria 3,495 ... 102,D-5
La Grange• 3,768 ... 103,E-1
La Grulla 1,442 ... 102,C-5
La Joya 2,018 ... 102,C-5
La Marque 15,372 ... 103,G-1
La Porte 14,062 ... 103,G-1
La Villa ... 102,D-5
Lacy-Lakeview 2,752 ... 101,E-4
Ladonia 761 ... 101,F-1
Lake Jackson 19,102 ... 103,G-2
Lakeway 790 ... 100,D-5
Lamesa• 11,790 ... 97,F-5
Lampasas• 6,165 ... 100,D-4
Lancaster 14,807 ... 101,E-2
Laredo• 91,449 ... 102,B-4
Lawn 390 ... 100,B-3
League City 16,598 ... 103,G-1
Leakey• 468 ... 102,B-1
Lefors 829 ... 97,G-2
Leonard 1,421 ... 101,F-1
Levelland• 13,809 ... 97,E-4
Lewisville 24,273 ... 101,E-2
Lexington 1,065 ... 101,E-5
Liberty• 7,945 ... 101,G-5
Lindale 2,180 ... 101,E-2
Linden• 2,443 ... 101,G-2
Lipscomb• ... 97,G-1
Littlefield• 7,409 ... 97,E-4
Livingston• 4,928 ... 101,G-5
Llano• 3,071 ... 100,C-5
Lockhart• 7,953 ... 102,D-1
Lockney 2,334 ... 97,F-3
Lometa 666 ... 100,C-4
Lone Oak 467 ... 101,F-2
Longview• 62,762 ... 101,G-2
Loraine 929 ... 99,G-1
Lorenzo 1,394 ... 97,F-4
Los Fresnos 2,173 ... 102,D-5
Lott 865 ... 101,E-4
Lovelady 509 ... 101,F-4
Lubbock• 173,979 ... 97,F-4
Luckenbach ... 100,C-5
Lueders 420 ... 100,B-2
Lufkin• 28,562 ... 101,G-4
Luling 5,039 ... 102,D-1
Lyford 1,618 ... 102,D-5
Mabank 1,443 ... 101,F-3
Madisonville• 3,660 ... 101,F-4
Malakoff 2,082 ... 101,F-3
Malone 315 ... 101,E-3
Manor 1,044 ... 100,D-5
Mansfield 8,092 ... 101,E-2
Marble Falls 3,252 ... 100,D-5
Marfa• 2,466 ... 98,C-3
Marion 674 ... 102,D-1
Marlin• 7,099 ... 101,E-4
Marquez 231 ... 101,F-4
Marshall• 24,921 ... 101,G-2
Mart 2,324 ... 101,E-4
Mason• 2,153 ... 100,C-5
Matador• 1,052 ... 97,G-4
Mathis 5,667 ... 102,D-3
Maud 1,059 ... 101,G-1
Maypearl 626 ... 101,E-3
McAllen 67,042 ... 102,D-5
McCamey 2,436 ... 99,E-2
McGregor 4,513 ... 100,D-4
McKinney• 16,249 ... 101,E-2
McLean 1,160 ... 97,G-2
Meadow 591 ... 97,E-4
Megargel 381 ... 100,C-1
Melvin 202 ... 99,H-2
Memphis• 3,352 ... 97,G-3
Menard• 1,697 ... 99,H-2
Mentone• ... 98,D-1
Mercedes 11,851 ... 102,D-5
Meridian• 1,330 ... 100,D-3
Merkel 2,493 ... 100,B-3
Mertzon• 687 ... 99,G-2
Mesquite 67,053 ... 101,E-2
Mexia 7,094 ... 101,E-3
Miami• 813 ... 97,G-2
Midland• 70,525 ... 99,F-1
Midlothian 3,219 ... 101,E-3
Miles 720 ... 99,G-2
Milford 681 ... 101,E-3
Mineola 4,346 ... 101,F-2
Mineral Wells 14,468 ... 100,D-2
Mingus 212 ... 100,C-2
Mission 22,589 ... 102,D-5
Monahans• 8,397 ... 99,E-2
Montague• ... 100,D-1
Montgomery 258 ... 101,F-5
Moody 1,385 ... 100,D-4
Moran 344 ... 100,C-3
Morgan 485 ... 100,D-3
Morton• 2,674 ... 97,E-4
Moulton 1,009 ... 103,E-1
Mount Calm 393 ... 101,E-3
Mount Enterprise 485 ... 101,G-3
Mount Pleasant• 11,003 ... 101,G-2
Mount Vernon• 2,025 ... 101,G-2
Muenster 1,408 ... 100,D-1
Muleshoe 4,842 ... 97,E-3
Mullin 213 ... 100,C-4
Munday 1,738 ... 100,B-1
Nacogdoches• 27,149 ... 101,G-3
Naples 1,908 ... 101,G-2
Navasota• 5,971 ... 101,F-5
Nederland 16,855 ... 101,H-5
Needville 1,417 ... 103,F-1
New Boston 4,628 ... 101,G-1
New Braunfels• 22,402 ... 102,D-1
New Waverly 824 ... 101,F-5
Newcastle 688 ... 100,C-2
Newgulf ... 103,F-1
Newton• 1,620 ... 101,H-4
Nixon 2,008 ... 102,D-1
Nocona 2,992 ... 100,D-1
Nordheim 369 ... 102,D-2
Normangee 636 ... 101,F-4
Oakwood 606 ... 101,F-4
Odem 2,363 ... 102,D-3
Odessa• 90,027 ... 99,E-1
O'Donnell 1,200 ... 97,F-5
Olmos Park 2,069 ... 102,C-1
Olney 4,060 ... 100,C-2
Olton 2,235 ... 97,F-3
Omaha 960 ... 101,G-2
Orange• 23,628 ... 101,H-5
Orange Grove 1,212 ... 102,D-3
Overton 2,430 ... 101,G-3
Owentown ... 101,G-3
Ozona• ... 99,F-3
Paducah• 2,216 ... 97,G-4
Paint Rock• 256 ... 100,B-4
Palacios 4,667 ... 103,F-2
Palestine• 15,948 ... 101,F-3
Palmer 1,187 ... 101,E-3
Palo Pinto• ... 100,C-2
Pampa• 21,396 ... 97,G-2
Panhandle• 2,226 ... 97,F-2
Paris• 25,498 ... 101,F-1
Pasadena 112,560 ... 103,G-1
Pearsall• 7,383 ... 102,C-2
Pecan Gap 250 ... 101,F-1
Pecos• 12,855 ... 98,D-2
Perryton• 7,991 ... 97,G-1
Petersburg 1,633 ... 97,F-4
Petrolia 755 ... 100,C-1
Pharr 21,381 ... 102,D-5
Phillips ... 97,F-2
Pilot Point 2,211 ... 101,E-1
Pineland 1,111 ... 101,H-4
Pittsburg• 4,245 ... 101,G-2
Plains• 1,457 ... 97,E-4
Plainview• 22,187 ... 97,F-3
Plano 72,331 ... 101,E-2
Pleasanton 6,346 ... 102,C-2
Port Aransas 1,968 ... 103,E-3
Port Arthur 61,195 ... 101,H-5
Port Isabel 3,769 ... 103,E-5
Port Lavaca• 10,911 ... 103,E-2
Port Neches 13,944 ... 101,H-5
Portland 12,023 ... 103,E-3
Post• 3,961 ... 97,F-5
Poteet 3,086 ... 102,C-2
Poth 1,461 ... 102,D-2
Pottsboro 895 ... 101,E-1
Premont 2,984 ... 102,D-4
Presidio ... 98,C-4
Princeton 3,408 ... 101,E-2
Quanah• 3,890 ... 97,H-3
Queen City 1,748 ... 101,H-2
Quinlan 1,002 ... 101,F-2
Quitaque 696 ... 97,G-3
Quitman• 1,893 ... 101,F-2
Ralls 2,422 ... 97,F-4
Ranger 3,142 ... 100,C-3
Rankin• 1,216 ... 99,F-2
Raymondville• 9,493 ... 102,D-5
Redwater ... 101,G-1
Refugio• 3,898 ... 103,E-3
Rhome 478 ... 100,D-2
Rice 439 ... 101,E-3
Richland 260 ... 101,E-3
Richland Springs 420 ... 100,C-4
Richmond• 9,692 ... 103,F-1
Richwood 2,591 ... 103,G-2
Riesel 691 ... 101,E-4
Rio Grande City• ... 102,C-5
Rio Hondo 1,673 ... 102,D-5
Rising Star 1,204 ... 100,C-3
Roanoke 910 ... 101,E-2
Roaring Springs 315 ... 97,G-4
Robert Lee• 1,202 ... 99,G-1
Robstown 12,100 ... 102,D-3
Roby• 814 ... 97,G-5
Rochester 492 ... 100,B-2
Rockdale 5,611 ... 101,E-5
Rockport• 3,686 ... 103,E-3
Rocksprings• 1,317 ... 99,G-4
Rockwall• 5,939 ... 101,E-2
Rogers 1,242 ... 101,E-4
Roma-Los Saenz 3,384 ... 102,C-5
Ropesville 489 ... 97,E-4
Roscoe 1,628 ... 99,G-1
Rosebud 2,076 ... 101,E-4
Rosenberg 17,995 ... 103,F-1
Rotan 2,284 ... 97,G-5
Round Rock 11,812 ... 100,D-5
Royse City 1,566 ... 101,E-2
Rule 1,015 ... 100,B-2
Runge 1,244 ... 102,D-2
Rusk• 4,681 ... 101,G-3
Sabinal 1,827 ... 102,B-1
Sabine Pass ... 103,H-1
Saginaw 5,736 ... 100,D-2
Saint Jo 1,071 ... 100,D-1
San Angelo• 73,240 ... 99,G-2
San Antonio• 785,410 ... 102,C-1
San Augustine• 2,930 ... 101,H-4
San Benito 17,988 ... 102,D-5
San Diego• 5,225 ... 102,D-3
San Juan 7,608 ... 102,D-5
San Marcos• 23,420 ... 102,D-1
San Saba• 2,336 ... 100,C-4
Sanderson• ... 99,E-3
Sanger 2,574 ... 101,E-2
Santa Anna 1,535 ... 100,B-3
Santa Rosa 1,889 ... 102,D-5
Saratoga ... 101,G-5
Sarita• ... 102,D-4
Savoy 855 ... 101,E-1
Schulenburg 2,469 ... 103,E-1
Scroggins ... 101,G-2
Seadrift 1,277 ... 103,E-2
Seagoville 7,304 ... 101,E-2
Seagraves 2,596 ... 97,E-5
Sealy 3,875 ... 103,F-1
Seguin• 17,854 ... 102,D-1
Seminole• 6,080 ... 97,E-5
Seymour• 3,657 ... 100,B-1
Shafter ... 98,C-4
Shamrock 2,834 ... 97,G-2
Sherman• 30,413 ... 101,E-1
Shiner 2,213 ... 103,E-1
Sierra Blanca• ... 98,B-2
Silsbee 7,684 ... 101,H-5
Silverton• 918 ... 97,F-3
Sinton• 6,044 ... 102,D-3
Skidmore ... 102,D-3
Slaton 6,804 ... 97,F-4
Smiley 439 ... 102,D-1
Smithville 3,470 ... 103,E-1
Snyder• 12,705 ... 97,G-5
Somerville 1,814 ... 101,E-5
Sonora• 3,856 ... 99,G-3
Sour Lake 1,807 ... 101,H-5
South Houston 13,293 ... 103,G-1
Spearman• 3,413 ... 97,G-1
Spur 1,690 ... 97,G-4
Stafford 4,755 ... 103,F-1
Stamford 4,542 ... 100,B-2
Stanton• 2,314 ... 99,F-1
Stephenville• 11,881 ... 100,D-3
Sterling City• 915 ... 99,G-1
Stinnett• 2,222 ... 97,F-1
Stockdale 1,265 ... 102,D-2
Stratford• 1,917 ... 97,F-1
Strawn 694 ... 100,C-2
Streetman 415 ... 101,E-3
Sudan 1,091 ... 97,E-3
Sugar Land 8,826 ... 103,F-1
Sulphur Springs• 12,804 ... 101,F-2
Sundown 1,511 ... 97,E-4
Sunray 1,952 ... 97,F-1
Sunrise ... 101,E-4
Sweeny 3,538 ... 103,F-2
Sweetwater• 12,242 ... 97,G-5
Taft 3,686 ... 103,E-3
Tahoka• 3,262 ... 97,F-5
Talco 751 ... 101,G-1
Tascosa ... 97,E-2
Tatum 1,339 ... 101,G-3
Taylor 10,619 ... 100,D-5
Teague 3,390 ... 101,F-4
Tehuacana 265 ... 101,E-3
Temple 42,483 ... 100,D-4
Tenaha 1,005 ... 101,H-3
Terrell 13,225 ... 101,E-2
Terrell Hills 4,644 ... 102,C-1
Texarkana 31,271 ... 101,H-1
Texas City 41,403 ... 103,G-1
Texline 477 ... 97,E-1
Thorndale 1,300 ... 101,E-5
Thornton 498 ... 101,E-4
Thrall 573 ... 101,E-5
Three Rivers 2,133 ... 102,D-2
Throckmorton• 1,174 ... 100,C-2
Tilden• ... 102,C-2
Timpson 1,164 ... 101,G-3
Tioga 511 ... 101,E-1
Tolar 415 ... 100,D-3
Tomball 3,996 ... 101,F-5
Toyah 165 ... 98,D-2
Trenton 691 ... 101,E-1
Trinity 2,452 ... 101,G-4
Troup 1,911 ... 101,G-3
Tulia• 5,033 ... 97,F-3
Turkey 644 ... 97,G-3
Tuscola 660 ... 100,B-3
Tyler• 70,508 ... 101,F-3
Universal City 10,720 ... 102,D-1
University Park 22,254 ... 101,E-2
Uvalde• 14,178 ... 102,B-2
Valentine 328 ... 98,C-3
Valley Mills 1,236 ... 100,D-4
Van 1,881 ... 101,F-2
Van Alstyne 1,860 ... 101,E-1
Van Horn• 2,772 ... 98,C-2
Vega• 900 ... 97,E-2
Venus 518 ... 101,E-3
Vernon• 12,695 ... 100,B-1
Victoria• 50,695 ... 103,E-2
Vidor 12,117 ... 101,H-5
Waco• 101,261 ... 101,E-4
Waelder 942 ... 103,E-1
Waller 1,241 ... 101,F-5
Walnut Springs 613 ... 100,D-3
Waskom 1,821 ... 101,H-2
Waxahachie• 14,624 ... 101,E-3
Weatherford• 12,049 ... 100,D-2
Weimar 2,096 ... 103,E-1
Wellington• 3,043 ... 97,G-3
Wells 926 ... 101,G-4
Weslaco 19,331 ... 102,D-5
West 2,485 ... 101,E-3
West Columbia 4,109 ... 103,F-2
Wharton• 9,033 ... 103,F-1
Wheeler• 1,584 ... 97,G-2
White Deer 1,210 ... 97,G-2
Whiteface 463 ... 97,E-4
Whitesboro 3,197 ... 101,E-1
Whitewright 1,760 ... 101,E-1
Whitney 1,631 ... 100,D-3
Wichita Falls• 94,201 ... 100,C-1
Willis 1,674 ... 101,F-5
Wills Point 2,631 ... 101,F-2
Wilmer 2,367 ... 101,E-2
Wink 1,182 ... 98,D-1
Winnsboro 3,458 ... 101,F-2
Winters 3,061 ... 100,B-3
Wolfe City 1,594 ... 101,F-1
Woodsboro 1,974 ... 103,E-3
Woodville• 2,821 ... 101,H-4
Wortham 1,187 ... 101,E-3
Wylie 3,152 ... 101,E-2
Yoakum 6,148 ... 103,E-1
Yorktown 2,498 ... 102,D-2
Zapata• ... 102,C-4
Zavalla 762 ... 101,G-4

MZ-583-J-X1

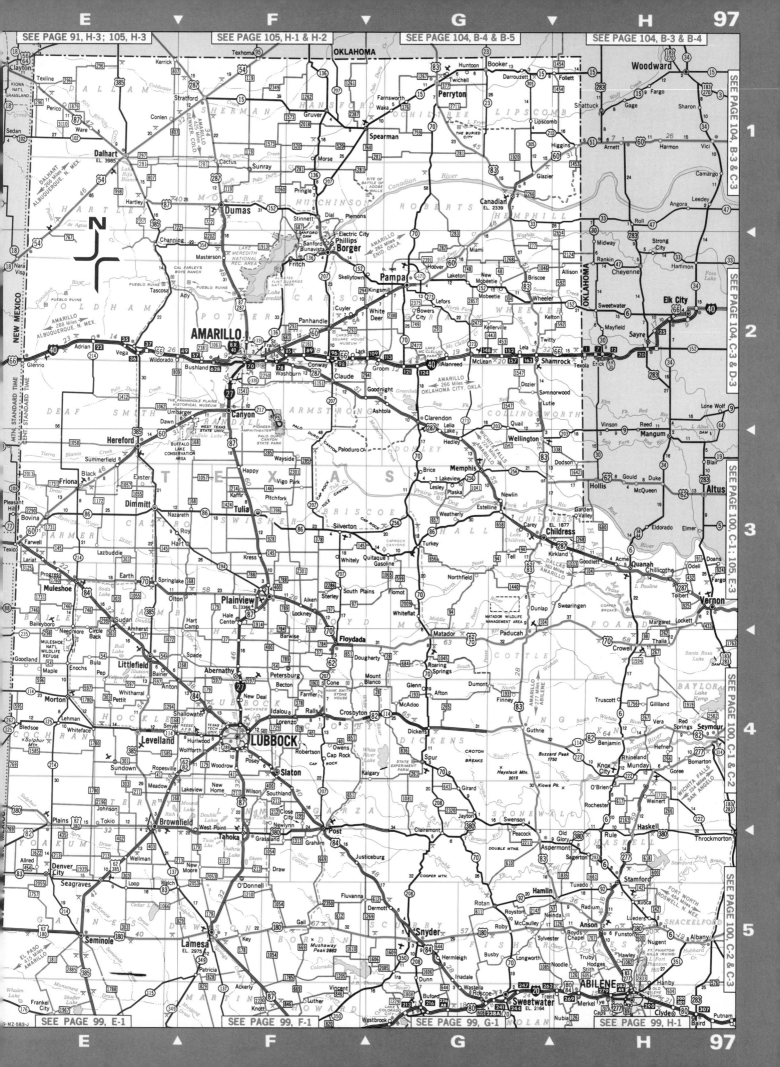

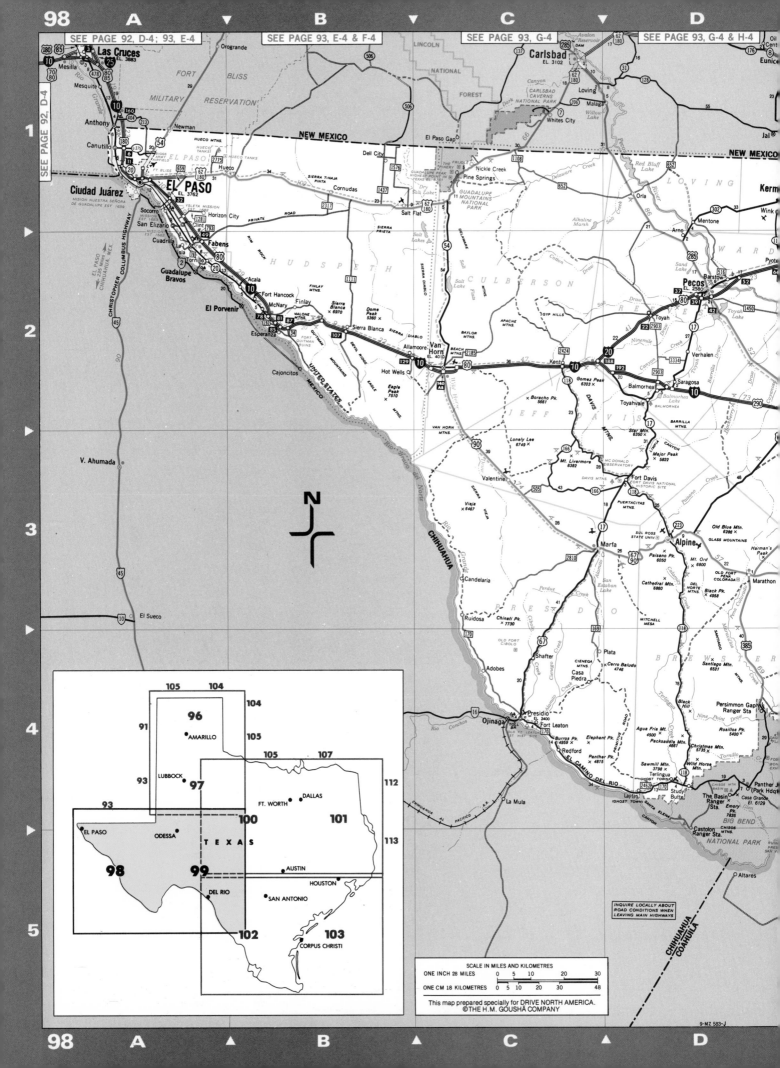

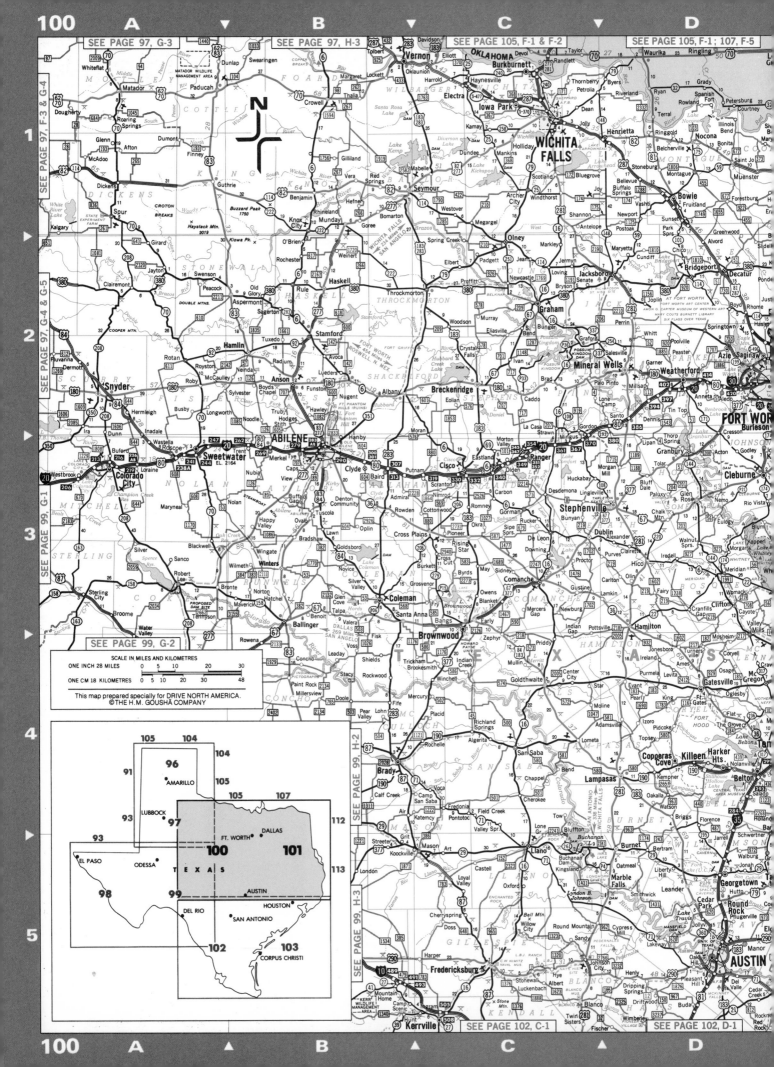

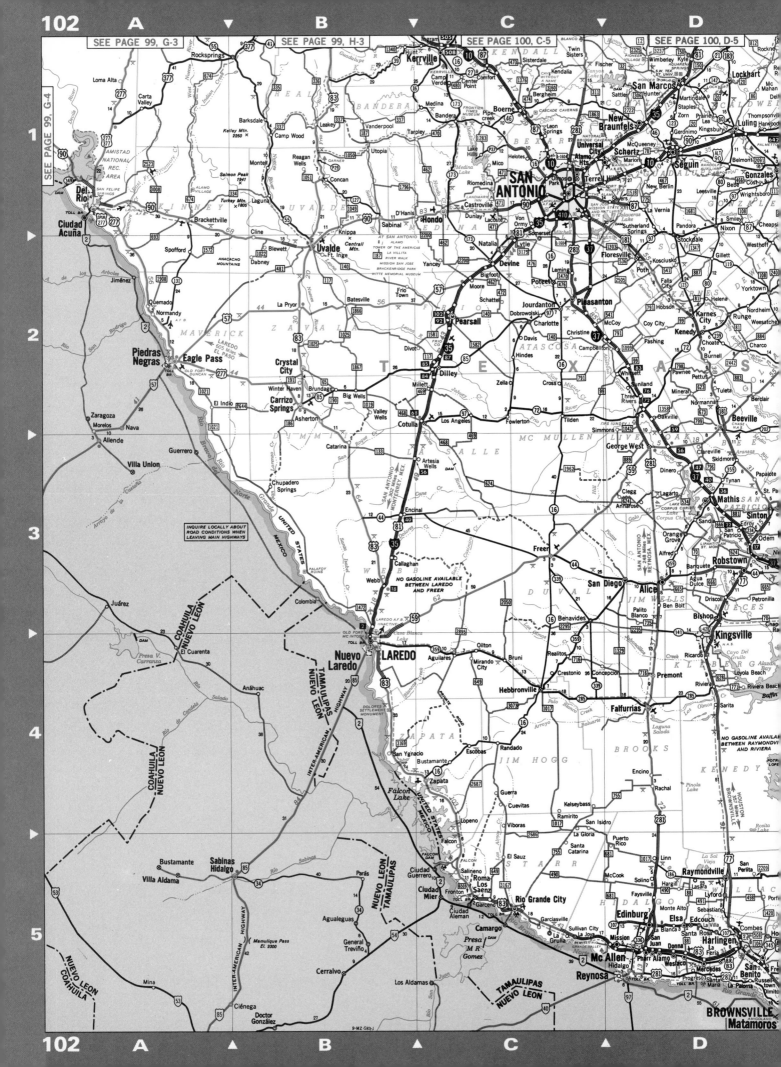

SEE PAGE 101, E-5   SEE PAGE 101, F-5   SEE PAGE 101, G-5   SEE PAGE 101, H-5

SEE PAGE 113, G-4

HOUSTON

Pasadena

Baytown

Texas City

GALVESTON

Victoria

Port Lavaca

CORPUS CHRISTI

GULF OF MEXICO

PADRE ISLAND NATIONAL SEASHORE

PADRE ISLAND NATIONAL SEASHORE

SCALE IN MILES AND KILOMETRES
ONE INCH 28 MILES   0 5 10   20   30
ONE CM 18 KILOMETRES   0 5 10 20 30   48

105   104
104

96

91   Amarillo   105

93   Lubbock
          97   107
                  105
93   112
          100   FT. WORTH DALLAS
El Paso   101
          Odessa   113
98   99   TEXAS
                  AUSTIN
          Del Rio   HOUSTON
          102   SAN ANTONIO   103
                  CORPUS CHRISTI

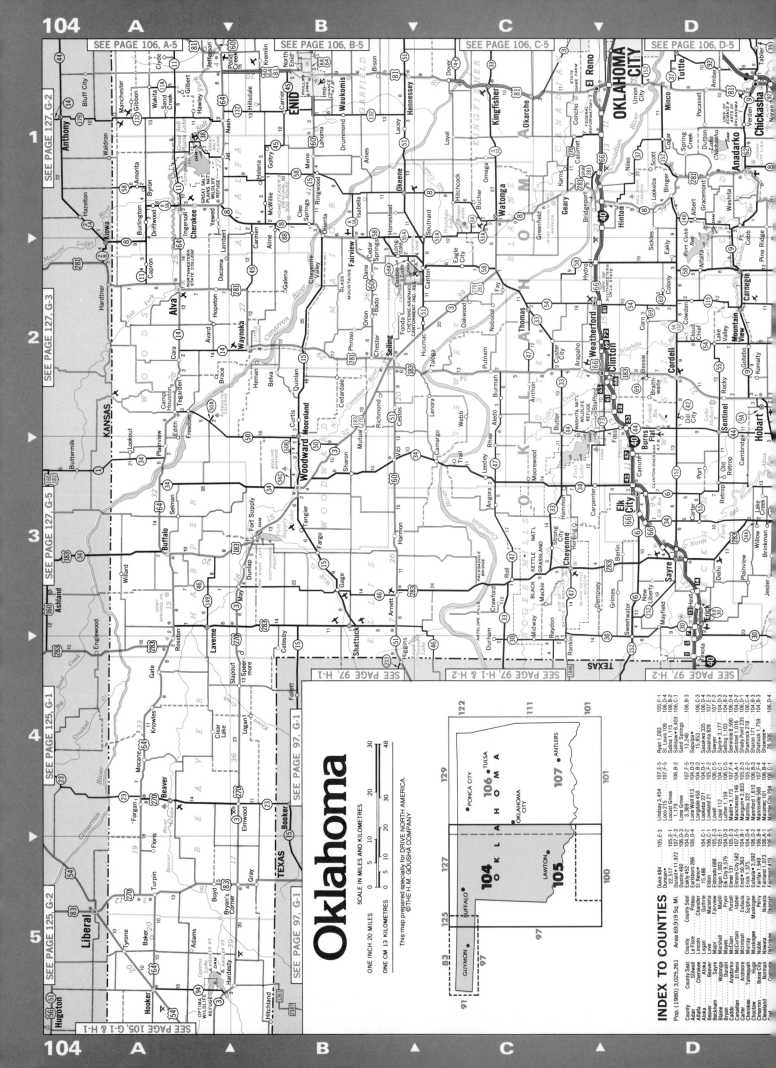

SEE PAGE 107, E-5   SEE PAGE 107, F-5   SEE PAGE 107, G-5   SEE PAGE 104, A-5   SEE PAGE 104, A-5

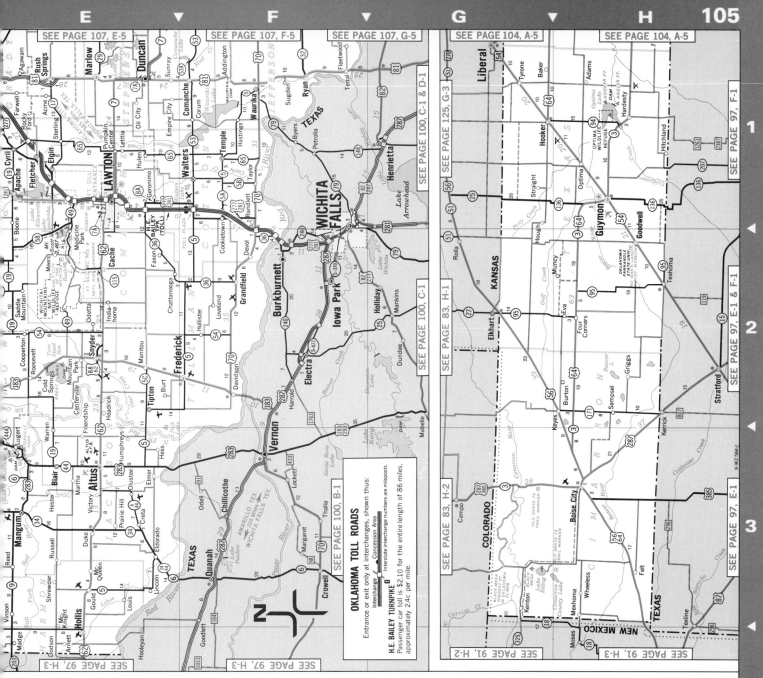

OKLAHOMA TOLL ROADS

Entrance or exit only at interchanges, shown thus: ▯
Interstate interchange numbers are mileposts.

■ Interchange   ▨ Concession Area

H.E. BAILEY TURNPIKE
Passenger car toll is $2.10 for the entire length of 86 miles, approximately 2.4¢ per mile.

SEE PAGE 100, C-1 & D-1
SEE PAGE 125, G-3
SEE PAGE 100, C-1
SEE PAGE 83, H-1
SEE PAGE 97, F-1
SEE PAGE 97, E-1 & F-1
SEE PAGE 100, B-1
SEE PAGE 83, H-2
SEE PAGE 97, E-1
SEE PAGE 91, H-3
SEE PAGE 97, H-3
SEE PAGE 91, H-2

PARTIAL LIST OF CITIES AND TOWNS

1980 Census
● County Seats

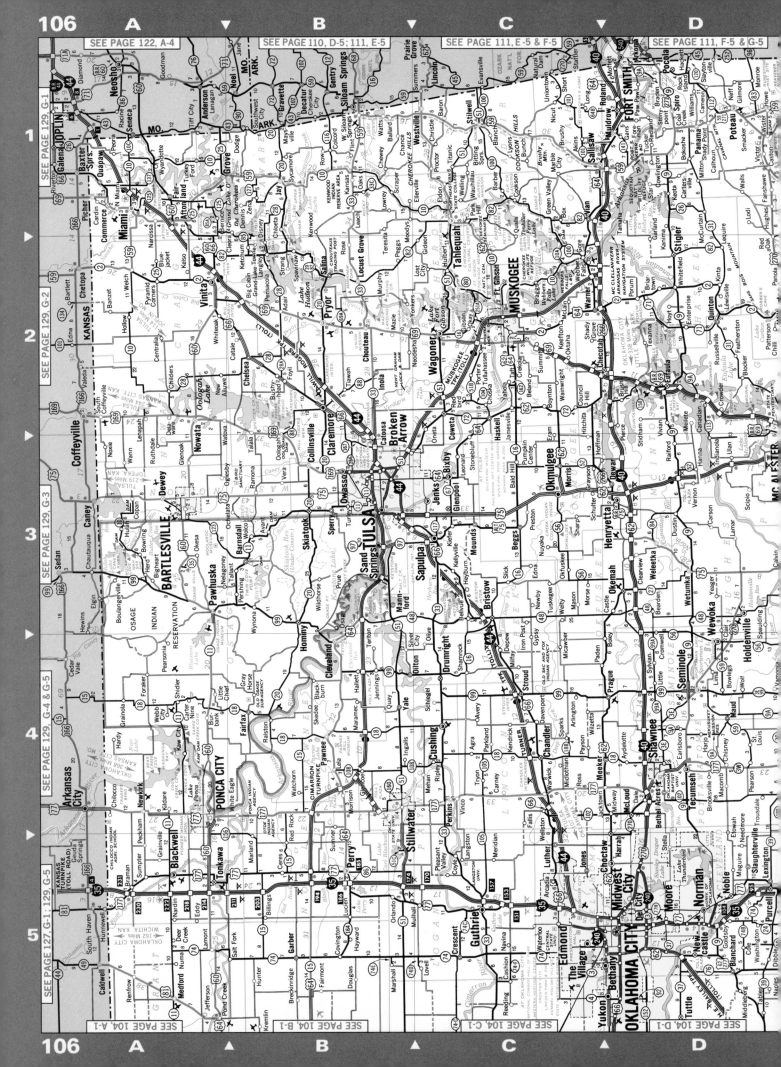

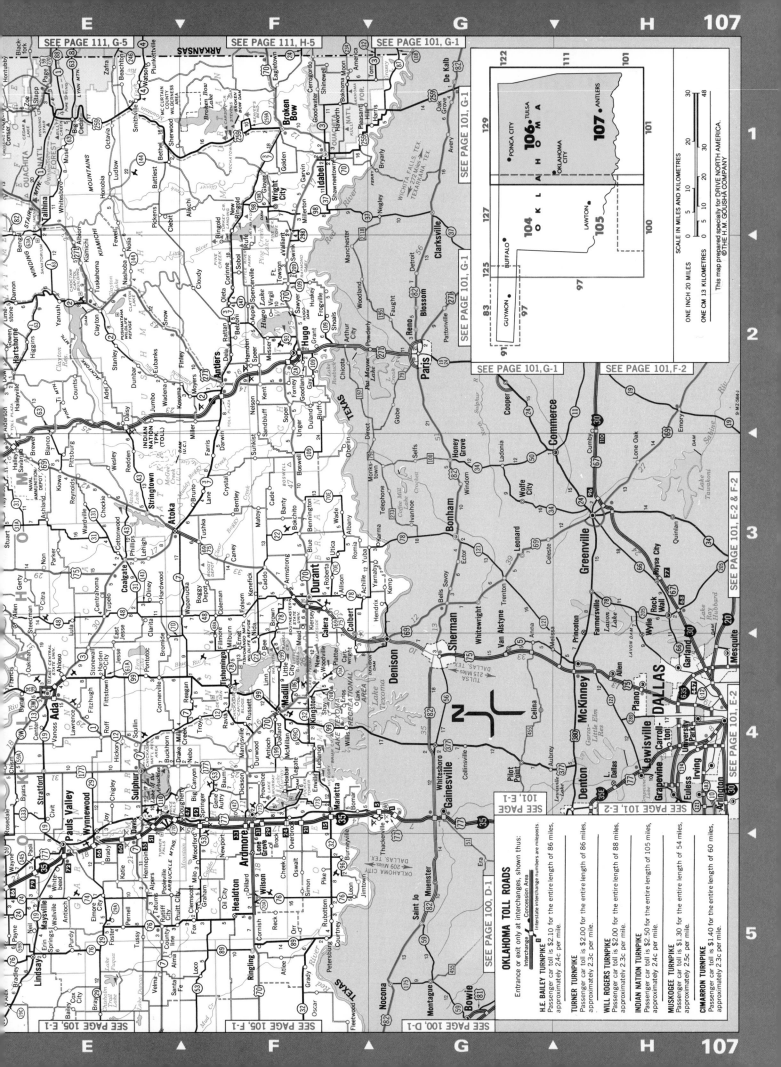

ARKANSAS

SEE PAGE 101, G-1

SEE PAGE 101, G-1

SEE PAGE 101, E-2 & F-2

SEE PAGE 101, G-1   SEE PAGE 101, F-2

SEE PAGE 101, E-2

SCALE IN MILES AND KILOMETRES

ONE INCH 20 MILES
ONE CM 13 KILOMETRES

This map prepared specially for DRIVE NORTH AMERICA.
©THE H.M. GOUSHA COMPANY

OKLAHOMA
TEXAS

OKLAHOMA TOLL ROADS

Entrance or exit only at interchanges, shown thus:
Interstate interchange numbers are mileposts.
☐ Interchange   Concession Area

H.E. BAILEY TURNPIKE
Passenger car toll is $2.10 for the entire length of 86 miles,
approximately 2.4c per mile.

TURNER TURNPIKE
Passenger car toll is $2.00 for the entire length of 86 miles,
approximately 2.3c per mile.

WILL ROGERS TURNPIKE
Passenger car toll is $2.00 for the entire length of 88 miles,
approximately 2.3c per mile.

INDIAN NATION TURNPIKE
Passenger car toll is $2.50 for the entire length of 105 miles,
approximately 2.4c per mile.

MUSKOGEE TURNPIKE
Passenger car toll is $1.30 for the entire length of 54 miles,
approximately 2.5c per mile.

CIMARRON TURNPIKE
Passenger car toll is $1.40 for the entire length of 60 miles,
approximately 2.3c per mile.

SEE PAGE 100, D-1

SEE PAGE 101, D-1

SEE PAGE 105, E-1   SEE PAGE 100, F-1   SEE PAGE 100, D-1

Back Roads and Bayous, Hot Springs and Cool Jazz

Arkansas/Louisiana/Mississippi

Arkansas' great stretches of forest-clad mountains to the west and bottomlands to the east give the state a beauty both wild and pastoral. In the heart of the rugged Ozarks is the Victorian town of **Eureka Springs (110, D-4),** a health resort built on a mountainside along a tangle of winding streets. The town is known for the performances of the Passion Play, which are staged in a 4,100-seat amphitheater throughout summer.

The stretch of Highway 7 between **Dogpatch (111, E-4)** and **Russellville (111, F-4)** is said to be one of the 10 most scenic drives in the country. It passes through the heavily forested Ozarks, descends to the Buffalo River through stands of sassafras, maple, oak and hickory, and climbs Judea ("Judy") Mountain for an expansive view of the Buffalo River Canyon.

Hot Springs (111, G-4), ringed by the wood-

Vestige of another century, a Mississippi paddle-wheeler plies the "Big Muddy."

ed Ouachita Mountains, is both city and national park. Two springs are kept open so visitors can see how the waters boil up; 45 others are sealed and their waters piped to bathhouses and fountains. Hiking and bridle paths lead through nearby woods.

The Crater of Diamonds, near the city of **Murfreesboro (111, H-4),** is the only diamond mine—actually, a field—in the United States. Amateur prospectors are allowed to keep whatever stones they find. Nearby Fort Smith National Historic Site was built in 1817 to keep peace among Indian tribes, white hunters and squatters in the frontier wilderness.

According to legend, **Little Rock (111, G-3),** the state capital, was named by French explorers who camped along the Arkansas River in 1722. Much of the atmosphere of the 19th century is retained in the city's historic Quapaw Quarter, where a number of stately homes have been preserved. The old state capitol, a lovely Greek Revival building, is now a museum.

Louisiana's—and the South's—most charismatic city is **New Orleans (117, F-3),** an enchanting blend of Mardi Gras festivity, Creole culture and cooking, Old South tradition and footloose jazz.

The historic French Quarter (Vieux Carré), where pirates and planters once roistered, retains a French-Spanish architectural flavor in lacy wrought-iron balconies, second-story verandas and lush, private courtyards. Banque de la Louisiane, built about 1826, and the 1857 Gallier residence are typical, although New Orleans' oldest building, the Ursuline Convent (1745), is pure French in character.

Jazz—an original American art form derived from African melodies mixed with hymns, blues, funeral marches, ragtime, even operatic arias—was born in New Orleans in the 1890s. Today traditional Dixieland jazz is best heard at Preservation Hall; jazz rhythms also travel the length of lively Bourbon Street.

New Orleans dons its most infectious, exciting colors during Mardi Gras—part of the Carnival season, which runs from January 6 until Lent. During this nonstop revelry decorated floats and costumed paraders celebrate the uninhibited spirit of the city.

West of New Orleans is bayou country, where dense forests of cypress, live oak and elm overhang lazy, winding creeks, and curtains of Spanish moss draped over nearly every branch create a dreamy, twilight atmosphere. **Lafayette (113, F-2),** a city of magnificent gardens, is an ideal starting point for exploring this corner of the state. To the east lies the Atchafalaya River, the last great swamp area of its kind in the Mississippi Valley. Birdlife is abundant and includes a number of tropical species; alligators are also plentiful.

French-speaking Acadians, expelled from Canada by the British, arrived in **St. Martinville (113, G-2)** in 1765 and established St. Martin de Tours Church. Near the church the graceful statue of Evangeline sits above the grave of Emmeline Labiche. Emmeline's search for her fiancé after the couple's exile from Nova Scotia inspired Longfellow's famous poem. A short trip from St. Martinville leads to Pine and Oak Alley, a mile-long drive lined by stately trees. Visitors can almost picture one night in 1850 when plantation owner Charles Durand sprayed the branches with cobwebs of gold and silver for the double wedding of his daughters.

Southwest of **New Iberia (113, G-2)** lie Avery and Jefferson islands, huge salt domes that rise abruptly from the surrounding marshland. Both islands have splendid gardens: Jefferson's are more formal in the English manner; Avery's Jungle Gardens contain species native to bayou country.

Baton Rouge (117, F-5) is Louisiana's capital, a major port, and a picturesque city of lakes and bayous. The commanding site and unusual Gothic Revival design of the Old State Capitol prompted Mark Twain to label it "the monstrosity of the Mississippi." The soaring new capitol is 34 stories high, the

A giant column, 65 feet tall, is one of the outstanding features of the underground Dripstone Trail through Blanchard Springs Caverns, Arkansas. At right, two faces of New Orleans: impromptu gospel on Bourbon Street; the magnificent Cathedral of St. Louis in the heart of the French Quarter.

tallest in the United States. South of Baton Rouge are such showpiece plantations as Nottaway (1859), with 64 rooms in almost perfect condition, and Houmas House, an 1840 Greek Revival mansion at **Burnside (117, F-4).**

The Golden Age of plantations reached its peak before the Civil War in **St. Francisville (113, F-1).** Here, profitable crops of cotton, sugarcane, indigo and tobacco made millionaires of planters such as Daniel Turnbull, who built Rosedown in 1835. Rosedown today is a faithful restoration with original Victorian, Empire and Federal-style furnishings. Oakley House (1799) was the home of pioneer naturalist and artist John James Audubon, whose first-edition prints from *Birds of America* hang throughout the house.

Antebellum architecture is also preserved in **Natchez (112, D-1),** Mississippi, the oldest city along the Mississippi River. Historically, the Briars is remembered as the home in which Confederate President Jefferson Davis wedded Varina Howell in 1845. It is a typical planter's home, built in 1812 on a bluff overlooking the Mississippi. Longwood, the country's largest octagonal house, was begun in

1858. Stanton Hall (1857) occupies a full city block; its parlor and music room alone are 70 feet in length.

From Natchez to Nashville, Tennessee, the Natchez Trace Parkway unrolls its romantic past. Beaten out by bison, the route was a highroad for Indians, explorers and settlers. Near Natchez the Trace skirts Emerald Mound, raised by a now-vanished Indian people, and Mount Locust Stand, a restored inn where travelers once slept three to a bed.

Vicksburg (116, C-4), rich in history, was the site of one of the Civil War's most decisive campaigns: a bloody, 47-day siege which ended in victory for the Union forces. Vicksburg National Military Park and Cemetery contains the remains of nine Confederate forts, 12 Union trenches, earthen parapets and gun emplacements. In the Old Court House tower is one of the oldest clocks still in use in the United States (1858); it went unscathed even during the long siege.

The proud Old Capitol (1840) in **Jackson (116, C-3)** once resounded to speeches by Andrew Jackson and Jefferson Davis, and here secession became law in 1861. Interior chambers have been restored and the old state offices now house a historical museum. The new state capitol, a dignified Renaissance structure complete with eagle-capped dome, was built in 1901–03.

Originally christened Possum Town, **Columbus (115, H-1)** was renamed in 1821. In the early 19th century its landed gentry built large homes, often in the then popular Greek Revival style, and settled down to a gracious life in town. More than 100 of these mansions remain, many owned by descendants of the original occupants. The impressive stately facades and gardens line broad streets in the historic center of town.

Magnolias, camelias, roses and crepe myrtles garland the resort town of **Biloxi (117, F-2),** also an important oyster and shrimp fishing port. Twelve years after the Civil War ended, Jefferson Davis came here for a visit. A year later he bought Beauvoir, a gracious mansion overlooking the Gulf of Mexico. In 1941 the house, outbuildings and 82 surrounding acres were restored. Much of the original furniture was found and returned, so that Beauvoir now looks as it did in the last century.

Cypress and Spanish moss shadow a dim Mississippi bayou (below).

The 1863 siege of Vicksburg (below) was a turning point of the Civil War.

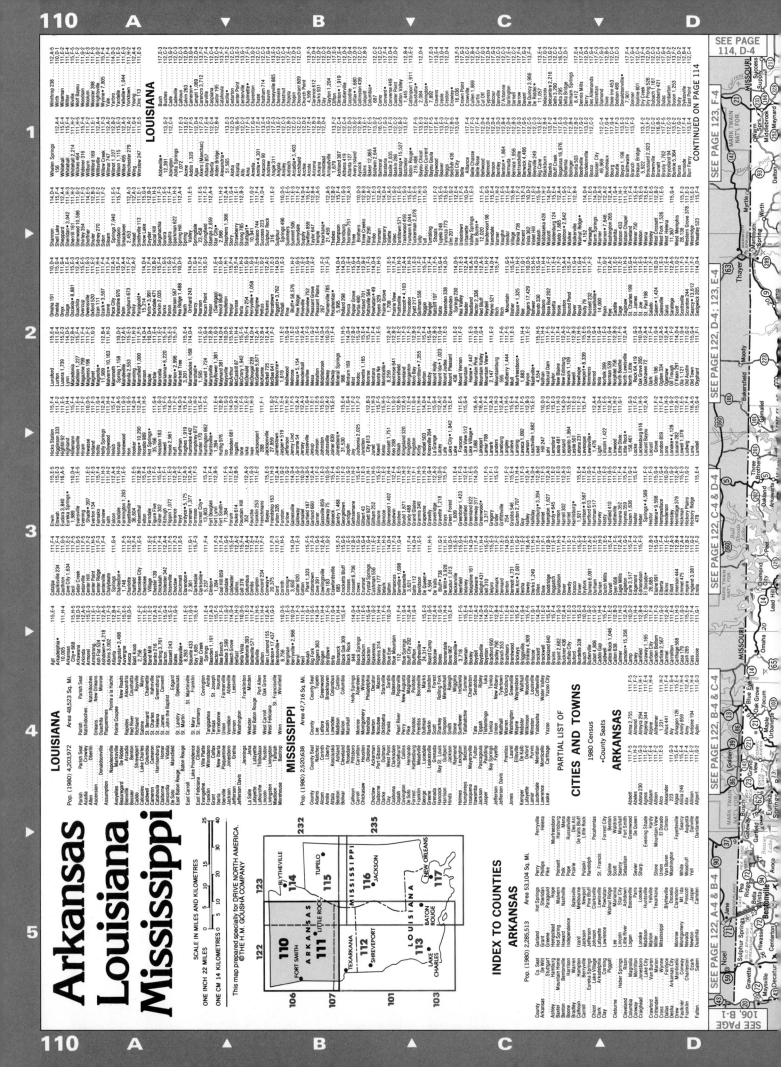

Arkansas Louisiana Mississippi

LOUISIANA
Pop. (1980) 4,203,972   Area 48,523 Sq. Mi.

MISSISSIPPI
Pop. (1980) 2,520,638   Area 47,716 Sq. Mi.

ARKANSAS
Pop. (1980) 2,285,513   Area 53,104 Sq. Mi.

SCALE IN MILES AND KILOMETRES
ONE INCH 22 MILES
ONE CM 14 KILOMETRES

This map prepared specially for DRIVE NORTH AMERICA.
© THE H. M. GOUSHA COMPANY

INDEX TO COUNTIES

PARTIAL LIST OF CITIES AND TOWNS

•County Seats

CONTINUED ON PAGE 114

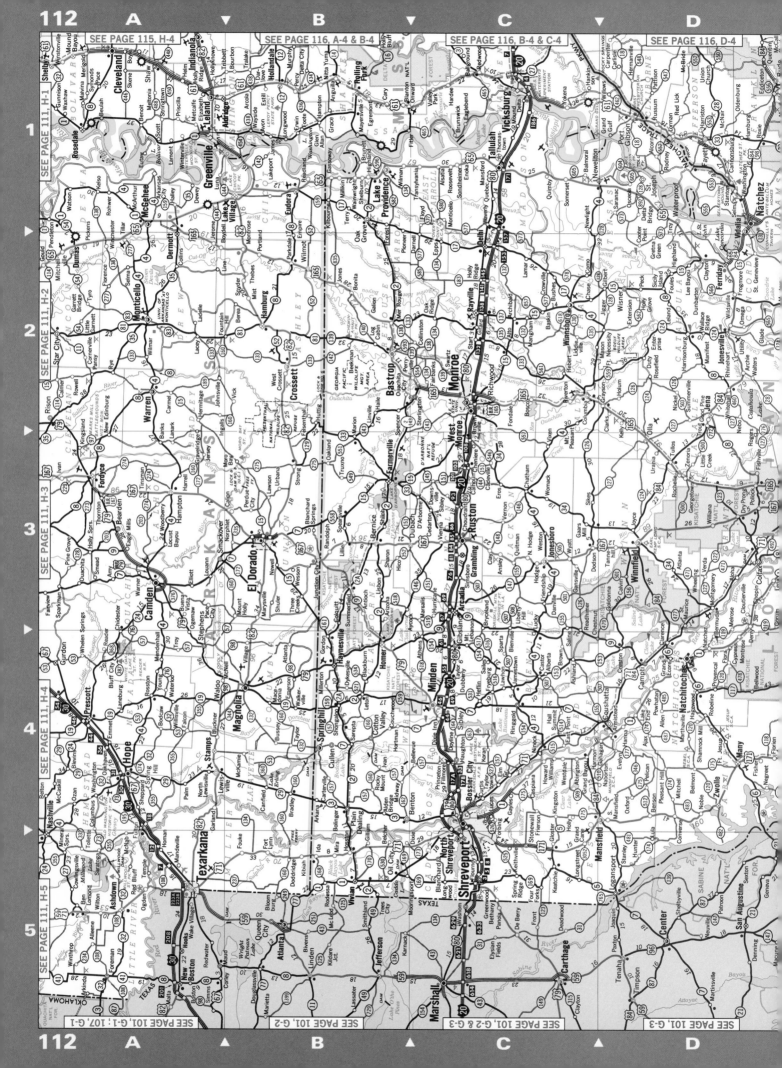

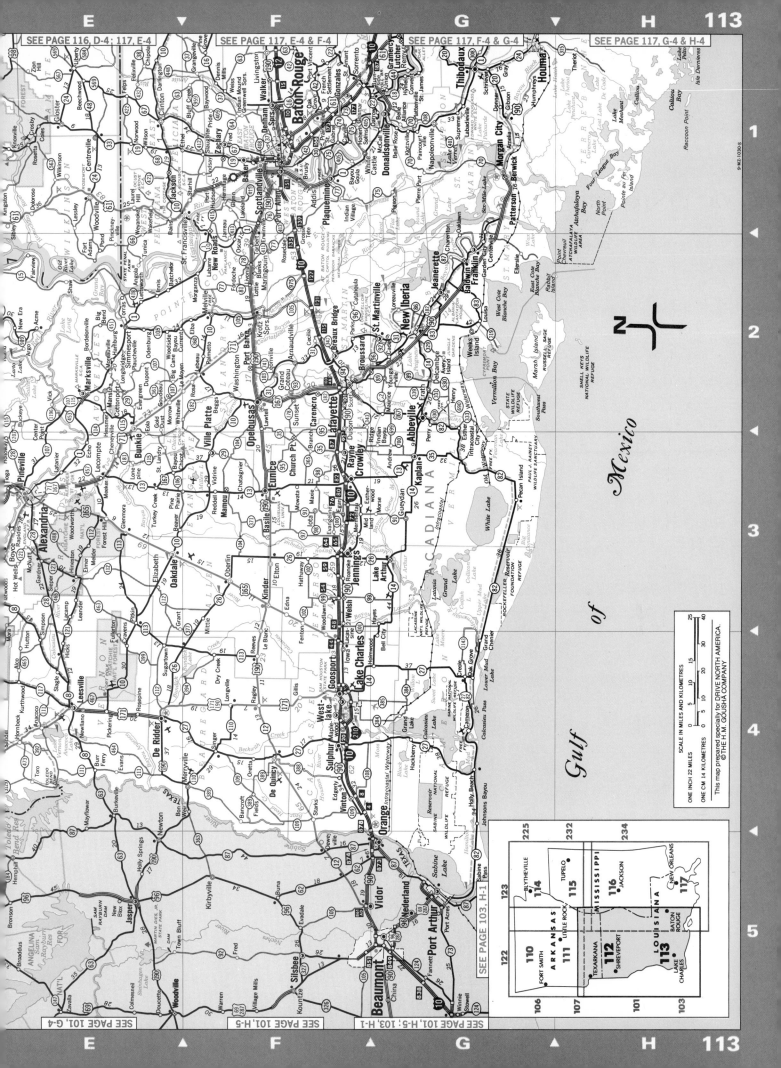

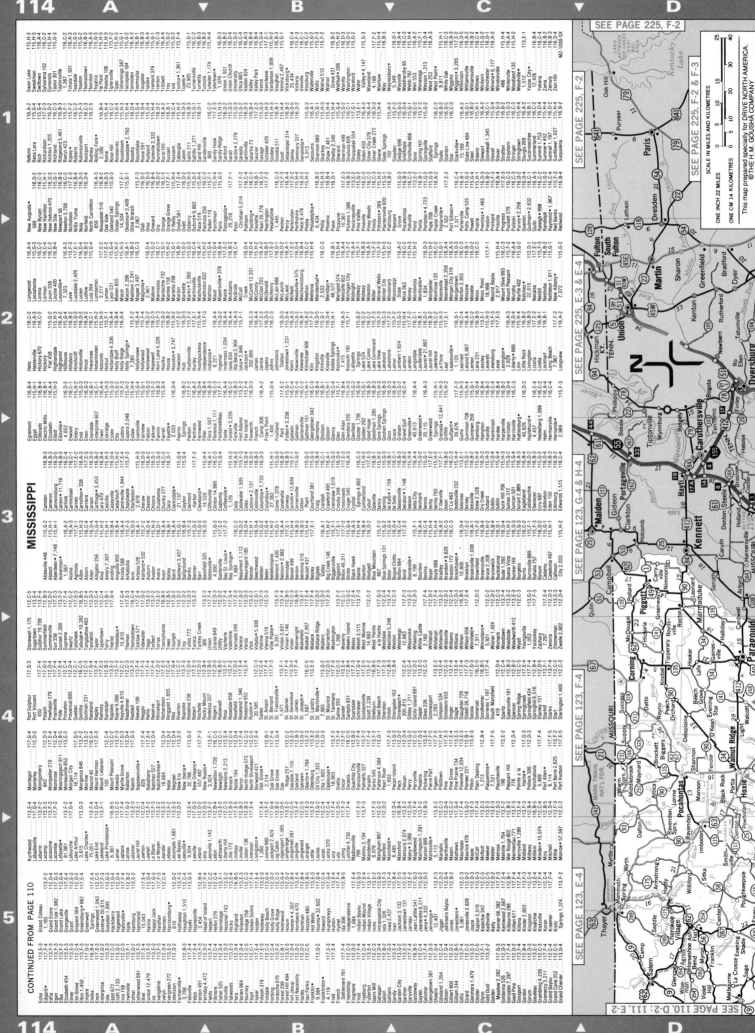

MISSISSIPPI

CONTINUED FROM PAGE 110

SEE PAGE 225, F-2
SEE PAGE 225, F-2 & F-3
SEE PAGE 225, E-3 & E-4
SEE PAGE 123, G-4 & H-4
SEE PAGE 123, F-4
SEE PAGE 123, E-4
SEE PAGE 110, D-2; 111, E-2

This map prepared specially for DRIVE NORTH AMERICA.
©THE H.M. GOUSHA COMPANY

SCALE IN MILES AND KILOMETRES
ONE INCH 22 MILES
ONE CM 14 KILOMETRES

MZ-1030-SX

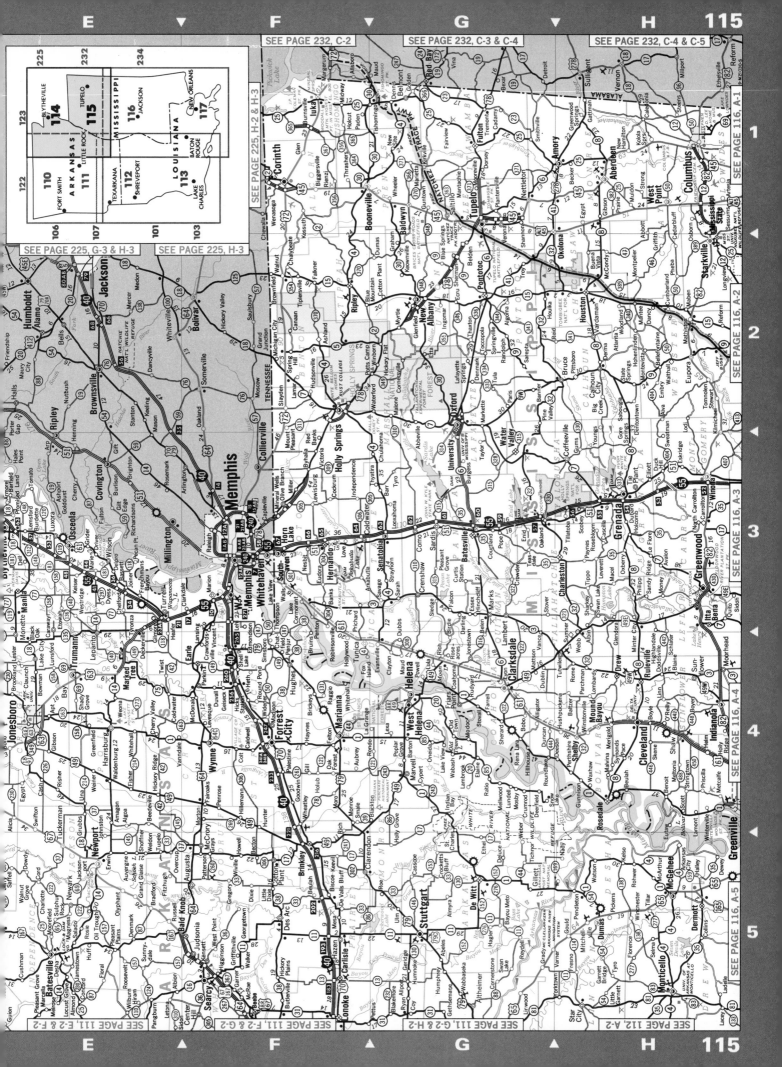

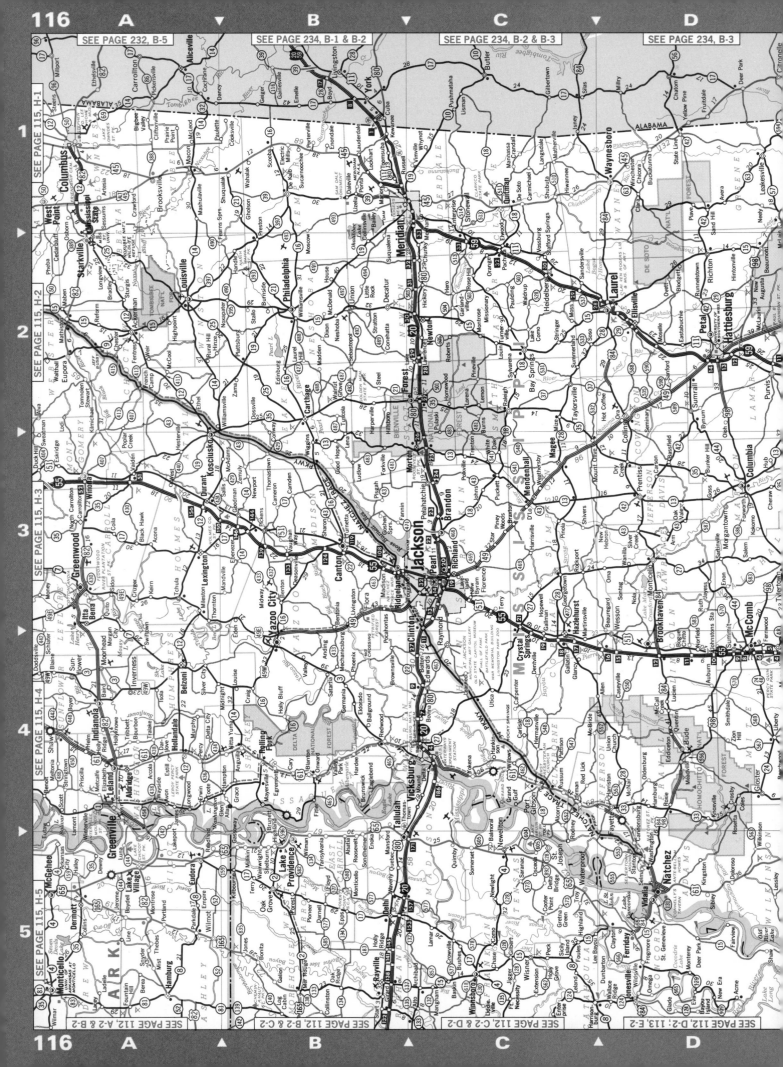

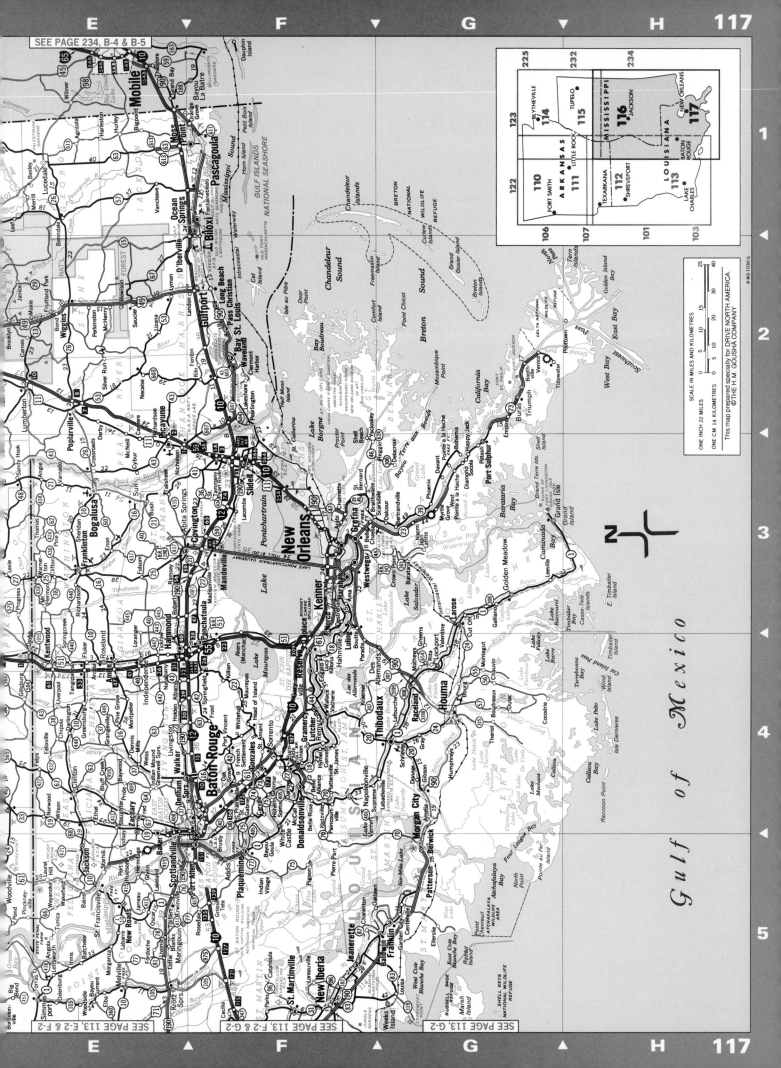

Memories of Tom and Huck, and 'Wicked' Dodge City

Missouri/Kansas/Nebraska/Iowa

Not just free land, but the promise of adventure and easy wealth lured Easterners to Missouri, Kansas, Nebraska and Iowa. Although many pressed on to the West Coast, those who stayed succeeded in transforming this vast heartland—known to pioneers as the "Great American Desert"—into a thriving agricultural and commercial region.

St. Louis (123, G-1), where the Missouri and Mississippi rivers meet, was a staging point for pioneers journeying to the Pacific. Today it is a splendid mix of old mansions and new skyscrapers. In the St. Louis Cathedral, religion has been well served by art. Mosaic images, depicting various saints and famous Missourians, tile the interior of its great central dome. Equally enchanting is the Missouri Botanical Garden, where visitors stroll among fragrant trees and shrubs, and through a rose garden with more than 2,000 blooms.

Interstate 44 sweeps like a broad ribbon across southeastern Missouri, giving no hint of the extraordinary country that lies to the south: a landscape of hills and hollows, of quiet streams and deep woods, of names like Jam Up Cave, Pulltite Spring and Jerktail Landing. This is Big Springs country, whose heart is the Current and Jacks Fork rivers. Some 130 square miles of these waters are now protected by the **Ozark National Scenic Riverways (123, F-4)**, a haven for canoeists, campers, fishermen and wildlife-watchers.

Missouri's river country was the setting for many books and stories penned by Samuel Clemens—better known as Mark Twain. The famous humorist spent part of his youth in a two-story clapboard house in **Hannibal (121, G-4)**. The house is now a museum; the fence made famous in *The Adventures of Tom Sawyer* stands beside it.

Independence (120, B-5) was home to Harry S. Truman, Missouri politician and 33rd President of the United States. A replica of his White House Office in the Truman Library and Museum displays many of his personal belongings; original documents on loan from the National Archives include the original United Nations Charter and Truman's V-E Day message.

A fur-trading post established in 1821 attracted the first permanent settlers to **Kansas City (120, B-5)**. Today Missouri's second largest city is a thriving industrial center. Visitors to the Country Club Plaza admire its Spanish-style architecture, red tile roofs, mosaics and Giralda Tower, modeled after the famous Moorish structure in Seville, Spain. Another city landmark, the Liberty Memorial, is dominated by a limestone shaft that soars 217 feet to an eternal flame. The Nelson Gallery of Art and Atkins Museum, which houses some 10,000 works of art, ranks among the finest American museums.

Before the completion of a telegraph system in 1861, almost 100 young men served as riders for the Pony Express between St. Joseph, Missouri, and Sacramento, California—a distance of 1,966 miles. The brick Pony Express Stables Museum in **St. Joseph (120, B-4)** was the starting point; it now exhibits saddles and weapons, and photographs, drawings and maps associated with the service. The four-story Patee House Museum, opened in 1858 as the "finest and largest hotel west of the Mississippi," features the main office of the Pony Express, located here in 1860.

The Pony Express and other travelers on the Oregon and Santa Fe trails depended on military posts for protection. **Fort Leavenworth (128, B-2)**, Kansas, founded in 1827 on bluffs above the Missouri River, was headquarters for the Army of the West in the Mexican War. The famed 7th Cavalry protected traffic on the Santa Fe Trail from **Fort Riley (128, C-4)**, built in 1853. Lt. Col. George A. Custer lived here in 1866–67, a decade before the Little Big Horn massacre.

Dodge City (127, E-5) is a reminder of the brawling, bawdy Wild West of legend. More than 50 bodies were buried in Boot Hill between 1872 and 1879, when this cattle town was known as "the wickedest little city in America." At the foot of the cemetery is a reconstruction of Dodge City's main street in the 1870s. Visitors can sidle up to the bar of the Long Branch Saloon to order sarsaparilla and admire portraits of Wyatt Earp, Doc Holliday, Bat Masterson and other gunslingers.

Kansas, generally considered one of the flattest states, actually slopes from more than 4,000 feet along the Colorado border to 700 feet on the Missouri line. At the bottom of the slope, in eastern Kansas, lie the Flint Hills, grass-covered escarpments rising 300 to 400 feet above the surrounding plateau. The town of **Eureka (129, E-4)**, east of Wichita, makes a good starting point for travel in this rugged country, where cowboys and cattle are often the only signs of man's presence.

One of the most colorful of frontier characters, William F. (Buffalo Bill) Cody, built a ranch in **North Platte (133, E-5)**, Nebraska, in 1886 when fortunes from his "Wild West Show" were running high. The 19-room building holds Victorian furniture, Indian relics, family photographs, and wallpaper depicting scenes from Cody's colorful life.

Weapons helped win the West—but plows, tractors and threshers helped it prosper. Two hundred pieces of farm equipment, including many steam-powered machines, fill the Stuhr Museum of the Prairie Pioneer near **Grand Island (133, E-1)**. The ultramodern museum building stands in striking contrast to the restored prairie buildings that surround it.

Omaha (134, D-2), in its infancy, watched two horse thieves dangle from the same rope in 1858. But with the coming of the railroad, the city shed its rough-and-ready image to become one of the farm belt's great commercial and industrial centers. The city's Joslyn Art Museum is one of the finest small muse-

St. Louis' Gateway Arch (above) is a soaring symbol of the Midwest. Nebraska's Chimney Rock (below) was a signpost to pioneers.

ums in the country. It has a large collection of European and American paintings which includes works by Rembrandt, El Greco, Renoir, Winslow Homer and Grant Wood, and objects representing 5,000 years of art from around the world.

Up to 1922, when ground was broken for Nebraska's Capitol in **Lincoln (135, E-3)**, most state houses were variations on the classical theme of the U.S. Capitol in Washington. But the 1920s marked the coming of age of the skyscraper, and bold horizontal and vertical forms were used here to successfully blend art and architecture.

The state capitol of neighboring Iowa in **Des Moines (139, E-3)** was completed in 1886. The monumental building is sometimes called the Golden Dome, after its central dome (275 feet high and 80 feet in diameter), the largest gold dome in the country. The Des Moines Art Center houses a substantial collection of graphics and 19th- and 20th-century American paintings. West of the city, the **Sheeder Prairie (139, E-4)** is one of

Hannibal, Missouri's monument to adventurous youth (right), consists of life-size statues of Mark Twain's immortal heroes, Tom Sawyer and Huckleberry Finn.

St. Louis old and new (left). The Renaissance dome of the stately Old Courthouse is mirrored in the facade of a high-rise building. The Courthouse has been the scene of many historic events, including the suits brought by the slave Dred Scott to win freedom for himself and his wife.

False-fronted stores and saloons line reconstructed Front Street in Dodge City, Kansas (below). Gamblers, gold-seekers and itchy-fingered gunmen on both sides of the law once made this the wildest cow town in the West. Today a variety show with cancan girls is presented nightly in summer; gunfights are staged each evening on the street outside.

only four areas of virgin prairie still in its natural state. A spring or summer walk through the fields blazing with wildflowers is a vivid reminder of prairie beauty.

Seven small villages—**Amana (141, E-4),** and East, Middle, High, West and South Amana and Homestead—were settled in 1855 by the Community of True Inspiration, a sect of religious refugees from Germany, France and Switzerland. The Amana Colonies, with woolen mills, meat-smoking plants, bakeries and crafts industries, became one of the most successful communities of its kind in America. Now the community also makes major appliances and furniture.

Once a thriving river town—the largest west of the Mississippi in the 1850s—**Bentonsport (141, H-4)** is now a museum of 19th-century homes, stores, churches and other buildings. The post office (1852) and a general store, its porch loaded with merchandise of 100 years ago, have been restored.

Dawn awakens an Iowa farm.

119

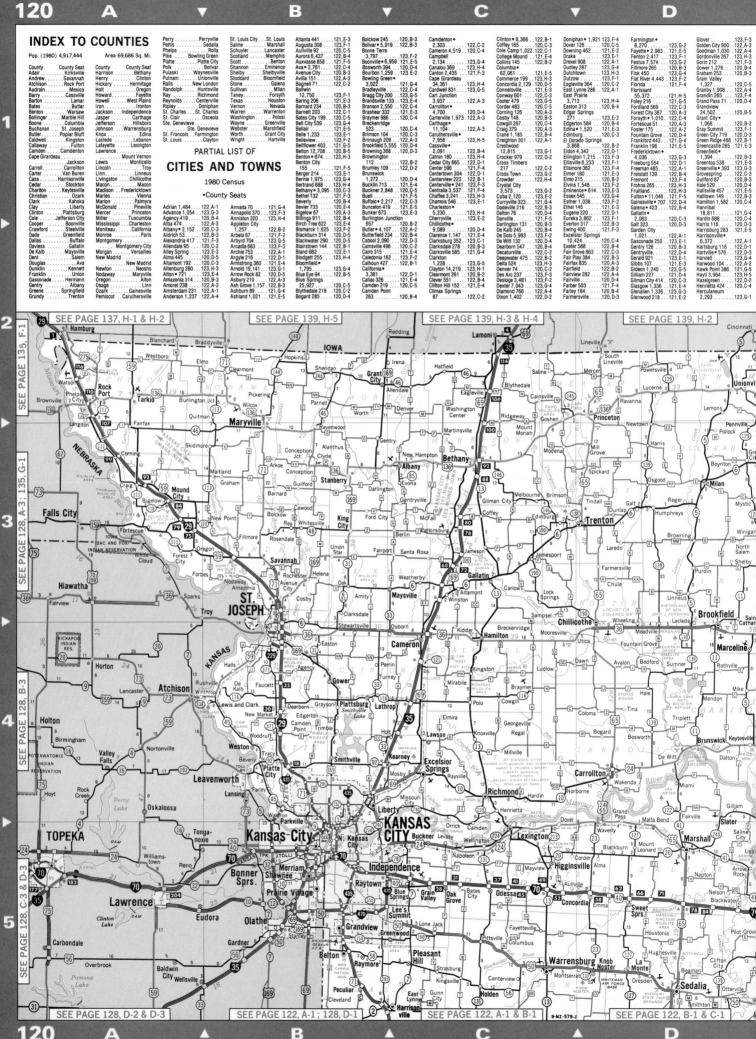

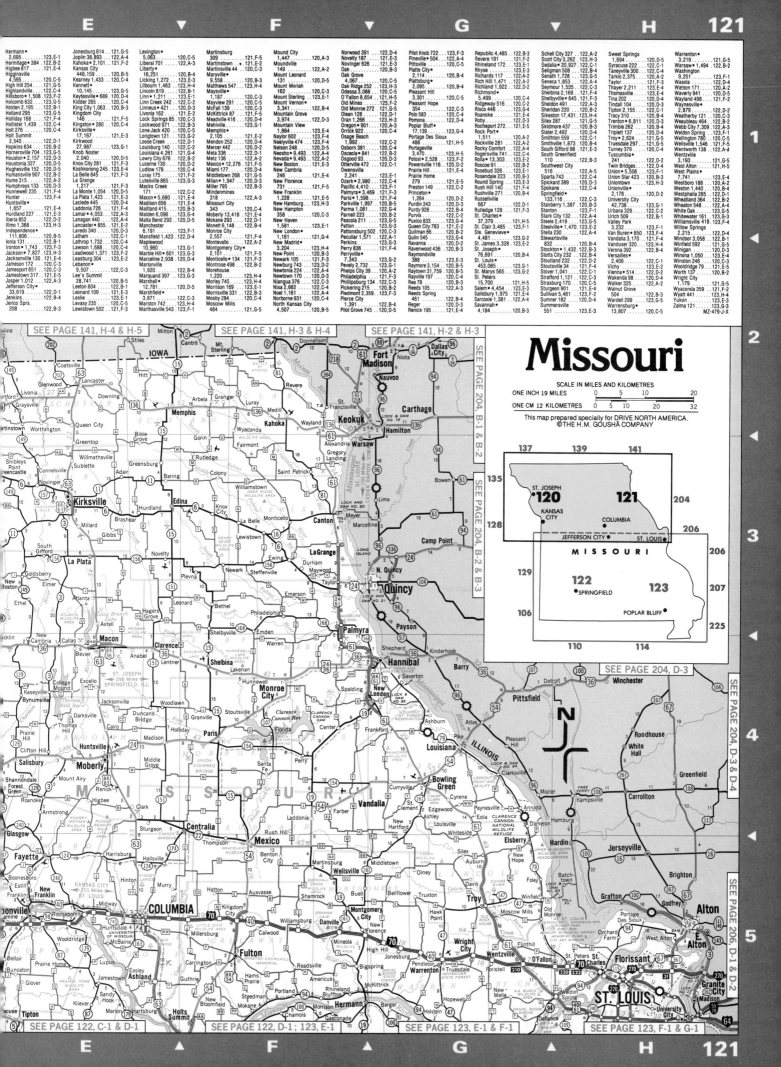

Hermann • ...123,E-1
Hermitage • 384 ...122,E-4
Higbee 817 ...121,E-4
Higginsville 4,595 ...120,C-5
Highland 1,176 ...123,G-5
Highlandville 910 ...122,A-4
Hillsboro • 1,508 ...123,F-2
Holcomb 632 ...123,G-4
Holden 2,195 ...122,B-1
Holland 295 ...123,G-5
Holliday 168 ...121,F-4
Hollister 1,439 ...122,C-4
Holt 276 ...120,C-5
Holt Summit 2,540 ...122,D-1
Hopkins 634 ...120,D-2
Hornersville 704 ...123,G-5
Houston • 2,157 ...122,D-3
Houstonia 327 ...120,D-5
Humphreys 133 ...120,D-3
Humansville 907 ...122,B-3
Hume 315 ...122,A-2
Hunnewell 235 ...121,F-4
Hunter • ...123,F-3
Huntsville • 1,657 ...121,E-4
Hurdland 227 ...121,E-3
Iberia 852 ...122,D-2
Independence • 111,806 ...120,B-5
Ionia 131 ...122,B-3
Ironton • 1,743 ...123,F-3
Jacksonville 130 ...121,E-4
Jameson 172 ...120,C-3
Jamesport 651 ...120,D-3
Jamestown 317 ...121,E-5
Jasper 1,012 ...122,A-3
Jefferson City • 33,619 ...122,D-1
Jenkins ...122,B-4
Jerico Sprs. 208 ...122,B-3

Jonesburg 614 ...121,G-5
Joplin 38,893 ...122,A-4
Kansas City 448,159 ...120,B-5
Kearney 1,433 ...120,C-4
Kennett • 10,145 ...123,G-5
Keytesville • 689 ...120,D-4
Kidder 265 ...120,C-4
King City 1,063 ...120,B-3
Kingdom City 146 ...121,F-5
Kingston • 280 ...120,C-4
Kirksville • 17,167 ...121,E-3
Kirkwood 27,987 ...123,G-1
Knob Noster 2,040 ...120,D-5
Knox City 281 ...121,E-3
Koshkonong 245 ...123,E-4
La Belle 645 ...121,F-3
La Grange 1,217 ...121,F-3
La Monte 1,054 ...120,D-5
La Plata 1,423 ...121,E-3
Laclede 445 ...120,D-4
Laddonia 726 ...121,F-4
Lamar • 4,053 ...122,A-3
Lanagan 440 ...122,A-4
Lancaster • 855 ...121,E-2
Laredo 340 ...120,D-3
Latham ...122,C-1
Lathrop 1,732 ...120,C-4
Lawson 1,688 ...120,C-4
Leadwood 1,371 ...123,F-2
Leasburg 304 ...123,E-2
Lebanon • 9,507 ...122,C-3
Lee's Summit 28,741 ...120,B-5
Leeton 604 ...120,C-5
Leonard 109 ...121,F-3
Leslie ...123,E-1
Levasy 235 ...120,C-5
Lewistown 502 ...121,F-3

Lexington • 5,063 ...120,C-5
Liberal 701 ...122,A-3
Liberty • 16,251 ...120,B-4
Licking 1,272 ...123,E-3
Lilbourn 1,463 ...123,H-4
Lincoln 819 ...122,B-1
Linn • 1,211 ...123,E-1
Linn Creek 242 ...122,C-2
Linneus • 421 ...120,D-3
Lock Springs 85 ...120,C-3
Lockwood 971 ...122,B-3
Lone Jack 420 ...120,C-5
Longtown 121 ...123,G-2
Loose Creek ...122,D-1
Louisburg ...122,C-2
Louisiana • 4,261 ...121,G-4
Lowry City 676 ...122,B-2
Lucerne 130 ...120,D-2
Ludlow 178 ...120,D-4
Luray 175 ...121,F-2
Lutesville 865 ...123,G-3
Macks Creek 171 ...122,C-2
Madison 580 ...121,E-4
Maitland 415 ...120,B-3
Malden 6,096 ...123,H-4
Malta Bend 292 ...120,D-5
Manchester 6,191 ...123,G-1
Mansfield 1,423 ...122,D-4
Maplewood 10,960 ...123,G-1
Marble Hill • 601 ...123,G-3
Marceline 2,938 ...120,D-4
Marionville 1,920 ...122,B-4
Marquand 397 ...123,G-3
Marshall • 12,781 ...120,D-5
Marshfield • 3,871 ...122,C-3
Marston 742 ...123,H-4
Marthasville 543 ...123,F-1

Martinsburg ...121,F-5
Martinstown • ...121,E-2
Maryville • 9,558 ...120,B-3
Matthews 547 ...123,H-4
Maysville • 1,187 ...120,C-3
Mayview 291 ...120,C-5
McFall 139 ...120,C-3
McKittrick 87 ...121,F-5
Meadville 416 ...120,D-4
Mehlville ...123,G-1
Memphis • 2,105 ...121,E-2
Mendon 252 ...120,D-4
Mercer 444 ...120,D-2
Meta 336 ...122,D-1
Metz 136 ...122,A-2
Mexico • 12,276 ...121,F-5
Miami 177 ...120,D-5
Middletown 268 ...121,G-5
Milan • 1,947 ...120,D-3
Miller 795 ...122,B-3
Mindenmines 318 ...122,A-3
Missouri City 343 ...120,C-4
Moberly 13,418 ...121,E-4
Mokane 293 ...122,D-1
Monett 6,148 ...122,B-4
Monroe City • 2,557 ...121,F-4
Montevallo 202 ...122,A-2
Montgomery City • 2,101 ...121,F-5
Monticello • 134 ...121,F-3
Montrose 498 ...122,B-2
Morehouse 1,220 ...123,H-4
Morley 745 ...123,H-4
Morrison 169 ...123,E-1
Morrisville 331 ...122,B-3
Mosby 284 ...120,C-4
Moscow Mills 484 ...121,G-5

Mound City 1,447 ...120,A-3
Moundville 143 ...122,A-2
Mount Leonard 131 ...120,D-5
Mount Moriah 162 ...120,D-2
Mount Sterling ...123,E-1
Mount Vernon • 3,341 ...122,B-4
Mountain Grove 3,974 ...123,E-4
Mountain View 1,664 ...123,E-4
Naylor 602 ...123,F-4
Neelyville 474 ...123,F-4
Nelson 248 ...120,D-5
Neosho • 9,493 ...122,A-4
Nevada • 9,493 ...122,A-2
New Boston ...121,E-3
New Cambria 246 ...121,E-4
New Florence 731 ...121,F-5
New Franklin 1,228 ...121,E-5
New Hamburg ...123,H-3
New Haven 358 ...120,C-3
New London • 1,161 ...121,G-4
New Madrid • 3,204 ...123,H-4
New Point ...120,B-3
Newark 105 ...121,F-3
Newburg 743 ...123,E-2
Newtonia 224 ...122,A-4
Newtown 170 ...120,D-3
Nixa 2,662 ...122,C-4
Noel 1,161 ...122,A-4
Norborne 931 ...120,C-4
North Kansas City 4,507 ...120,B-5

Norwood 391 ...122,D-4
Novelty 187 ...121,F-3
Novinger 626 ...121,E-3
Oak Grove 4,067 ...120,C-5
Oak Ridge 252 ...123,H-3
Odessa 3,088 ...120,C-5
O'Fallon 8,654 ...121,H-5
Old Mines ...123,F-2
Old Monroe 272 ...121,G-5
Olean 128 ...122,D-2
Oran 1,266 ...123,H-3
Oregon • 901 ...120,A-3
Orrick 922 ...120,C-5
Osage Beach 1,992 ...122,C-2
Osborn 381 ...120,C-4
Osceola • 841 ...122,B-2
Osgood 93 ...120,D-3
Otterville 472 ...122,C-1
Owensville 2,241 ...123,E-1
Ozark • 2,980 ...122,C-4
Pacific 4,410 ...123,F-1
Palmyra • 3,469 ...121,F-3
Paris • 1,598 ...121,F-4
Parma 1,061 ...123,H-4
Parnell 243 ...120,B-3
Pascola 211 ...123,H-4
Patton ...123,G-3
Pattonsburg 502 ...120,C-3
Peculiar 1,571 ...122,A-1
Perkins ...123,H-3
Perry 836 ...121,F-4
Perryville • ...123,G-2
Pevely 2,732 ...123,F-2
Phelps City 39 ...120,A-2
Philadelphia 166 ...121,F-4
Phillipsburg 134 ...122,C-3
Pickering 215 ...120,B-3
Piedmont 2,359 ...123,F-3
Pierce City 1,391 ...122,B-4
Pilot Grove 745 ...120,D-5

Pilot Knob 722 ...123,F-3
Pineville • 504 ...122,A-4
Pittsburg ...122,C-3
Platte City • 2,114 ...120,B-4
Plattsburg • 2,095 ...120,C-4
Pleasant Hill 3,301 ...120,C-5
Pleasant Hope 354 ...122,C-3
Polo 583 ...120,C-4
Pomona ...122,D-4
Poplar Bluff • 17,139 ...123,F-4
Portage Des Sioux 488 ...121,H-5
Portageville 3,470 ...123,H-5
Potosi • 2,528 ...123,F-2
Powersville 116 ...120,D-2
Prairie Hill ...121,E-4
Prairie Home 279 ...121,E-5
Preston 149 ...122,C-2
Princeton • 1,264 ...120,D-2
Purdin 243 ...120,D-3
Purdy 928 ...122,B-4
Purvis ...122,A-4
Puxico 833 ...123,G-4
Queen City 783 ...121,E-2
Quilin 545 ...123,G-4
Ravanna ...120,D-2
Ravenwood 436 ...120,B-3
Raymondville 388 ...123,E-3
Raymore 3,154 ...120,B-5
Raytown 31,759 ...120,B-5
Rayville 197 ...120,C-4
Rea 78 ...120,C-3
Reeds 105 ...122,A-3
Reeds Spring 461 ...122,C-4
Renick 195 ...121,E-4

Republic 4,485 ...122,B-3
Revere 191 ...121,F-2
Rhineland 172 ...121,F-5
Rich Hill 1,471 ...122,A-2
Richland 1,922 ...122,D-2
Richmond • 5,499 ...120,C-4
Ridgeway 516 ...120,D-2
Risco 446 ...123,H-4
Roach ...122,C-2
Rocheport 272 ...121,E-5
Rock Port • 1,511 ...120,A-2
Rockville 281 ...122,A-2
Rocky Comfort ...122,B-4
Rogersville 741 ...122,C-4
Rolla • 13,303 ...123,E-2
Roscoe 91 ...122,B-2
Rosebud 326 ...123,E-1
Rosendale 223 ...120,B-3
Round Spring ...123,E-3
Rush Hill 140 ...121,F-4
Rushville 271 ...120,B-4
Russellville 667 ...122,D-1
Rutledge 128 ...121,F-2
St. Charles • 37,379 ...121,H-5
St. Clair 3,485 ...123,F-1
Ste. Genevieve • 4,481 ...123,G-2
St. James • 3,328 ...123,E-2
St. Joseph • 76,691 ...120,B-4
St. Louis • 453,085 ...123,G-1
St. Marys 565 ...123,G-2
St. Peters 15,700 ...121,H-5
Salem • 4,454 ...123,E-3
Salisbury • 1,975 ...121,E-4
Sarcoxie 1,381 ...122,A-4
Savannah • 4,184 ...120,B-3

Schell City 327 ...122,A-2
Scott City 3,262 ...123,H-3
Sedalia • 20,927 ...122,C-1
Seligman 508 ...122,B-4
Senath 1,298 ...123,H-5
Seneca 1,853 ...122,A-4
Seymour 1,535 ...122,C-4
Shelbina 2,169 ...121,F-4
Shelbyville • 645 ...121,F-3
Sheldon 491 ...122,A-2
Sheridan 220 ...120,B-2
Sikeston 17,431 ...123,H-4
Silex 281 ...121,G-5
Skidmore 437 ...120,B-2
Slater 2,492 ...120,D-5
Smithton 559 ...122,C-1
Smithville 1,873 ...120,B-4
South Gifford 98 ...121,E-3
South Greenfield 110 ...122,B-3
Southwest City 516 ...122,A-4
Sparta 743 ...122,C-4
Spickard 389 ...120,D-3
Spokane ...122,C-4
Springfield • 133,116 ...122,C-4
Stanberry 1,387 ...120,B-3
Stanton ...123,F-1
Stark City 132 ...122,A-4
Steele 2,419 ...123,H-5
Steelville • 1,470 ...123,E-2
Stella 230 ...122,A-4
Stewartsville 832 ...120,B-4
Stockton • 1,432 ...122,B-3
Stotts City 232 ...122,B-4
Stoutland 232 ...122,D-2
Stoutsville 34 ...121,F-4
Stover 1,041 ...122,C-2
Strafford 1,121 ...122,C-4
Strasburg 170 ...120,C-5
Sturgeon 901 ...121,E-4
Sullivan 5,461 ...123,F-1
Sumner 182 ...120,D-4
Summersville 551 ...123,E-3

Sweet Springs 1,694 ...120,D-5
Syracuse 222 ...122,C-1
Tarkio 2,375 ...120,A-2
Taylor ...121,F-3
Thayer 2,211 ...123,E-4
Thomasville ...123,E-4
Tina 202 ...120,D-4
Tindall 104 ...120,D-3
Tipton 2,155 ...122,C-1
Tracy 310 ...120,B-4
Trenton • 6,811 ...120,D-3
Trimble 262 ...120,C-4
Troy • 2,624 ...121,G-5
Truesdale 379 ...121,G-5
Turney 379 ...120,C-4
Tuscumbia • 241 ...122,D-2
Twin Bridges ...122,D-4
Union • 5,506 ...123,F-1
Union Star 423 ...120,B-3
Uniontown ...123,G-2
Unionville • 2,178 ...120,D-2
University City 42,738 ...123,G-1
Urbana 329 ...122,C-3
Urich 509 ...122,B-1
Valley Park ...123,F-1
Van Buren • 850 ...123,F-3
Vandalia 3,170 ...121,F-4
Vanduser 320 ...123,H-4
Verona 392 ...122,B-4
Versailles • 2,406 ...122,C-1
Vichy ...123,E-2
Vienna • 514 ...122,D-2
Wakenda 88 ...120,D-4
Walker 325 ...122,A-2
Walnut Grove 504 ...122,B-3
Wardell 299 ...123,H-5
Warrensburg • 13,807 ...120,C-5

Warrenton • 3,219 ...121,G-5
Warsaw • 1,494 ...122,B-2
Washington 9,251 ...123,F-1
Wasola ...122,D-4
Watson 171 ...120,A-2
Waverly 941 ...120,D-5
Wayland 498 ...121,F-2
Waynesville • 2,879 ...122,D-2
Weatherby 121 ...120,C-3
Weaubleau 464 ...122,B-2
Webb City 7,309 ...122,A-4
Weldon Spring ...123,F-1
Wellington 780 ...120,C-5
Wellsville 1,546 ...121,F-5
Wentworth 138 ...122,A-4
Wentzville 3,193 ...121,G-5
West Alton ...121,H-5
West Plains • 7,741 ...123,E-4
Westboro 188 ...120,A-2
Weston 1,440 ...120,B-4
Westphalia 285 ...122,D-1
Wheatland 364 ...122,B-2
Wheaton 548 ...122,B-4
White Oak ...123,G-5
Whitewater 161 ...123,H-3
Williamsville 418 ...123,F-4
Willow Springs 2,215 ...123,E-4
Windsor 3,058 ...122,B-2
Winfield 592 ...121,G-5
Winigan ...120,D-3
Winona 1,050 ...123,E-4
Winston 246 ...120,C-3
Wooldridge 79 ...121,E-5
Worth 137 ...120,B-2
Wright City 1,179 ...121,G-5
Wyaconda 359 ...121,F-2
Wyatt 441 ...123,H-4
Yukon ...123,E-3
Zalma 121 ...123,G-3

MZ-479-J-X

Missouri

SCALE IN MILES AND KILOMETRES
ONE INCH 19 MILES
ONE CM 12 KILOMETRES

This map prepared specially for DRIVE NORTH AMERICA.
©THE H.M. GOUSHA COMPANY

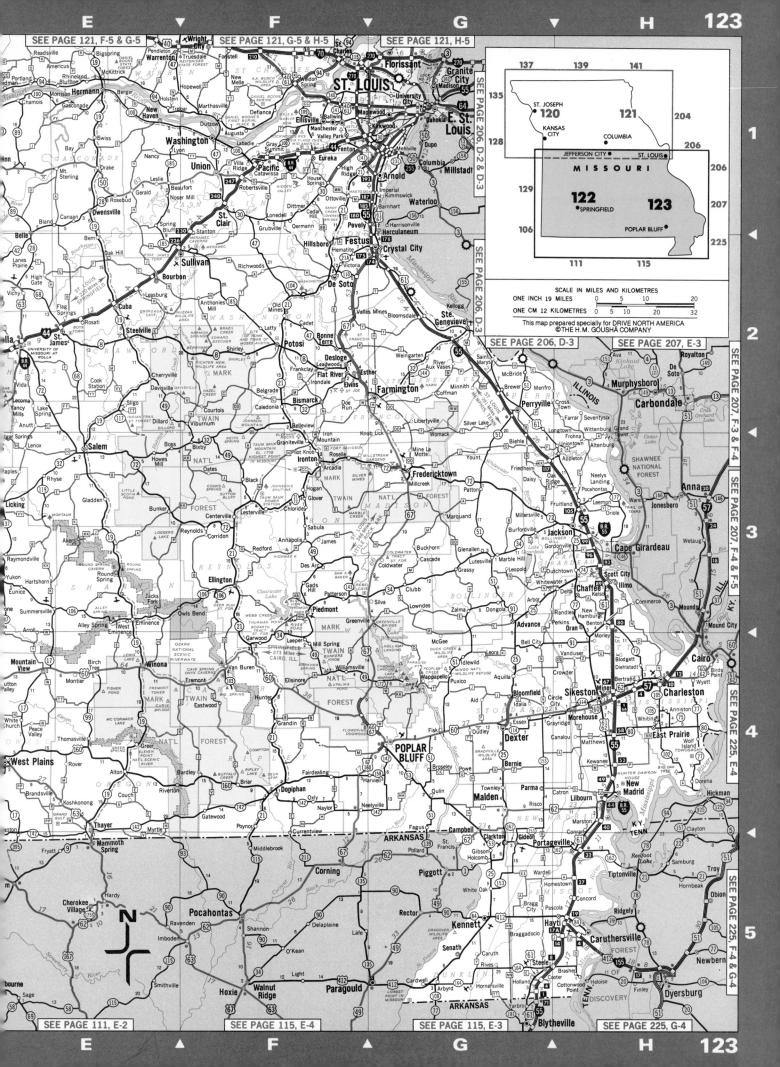

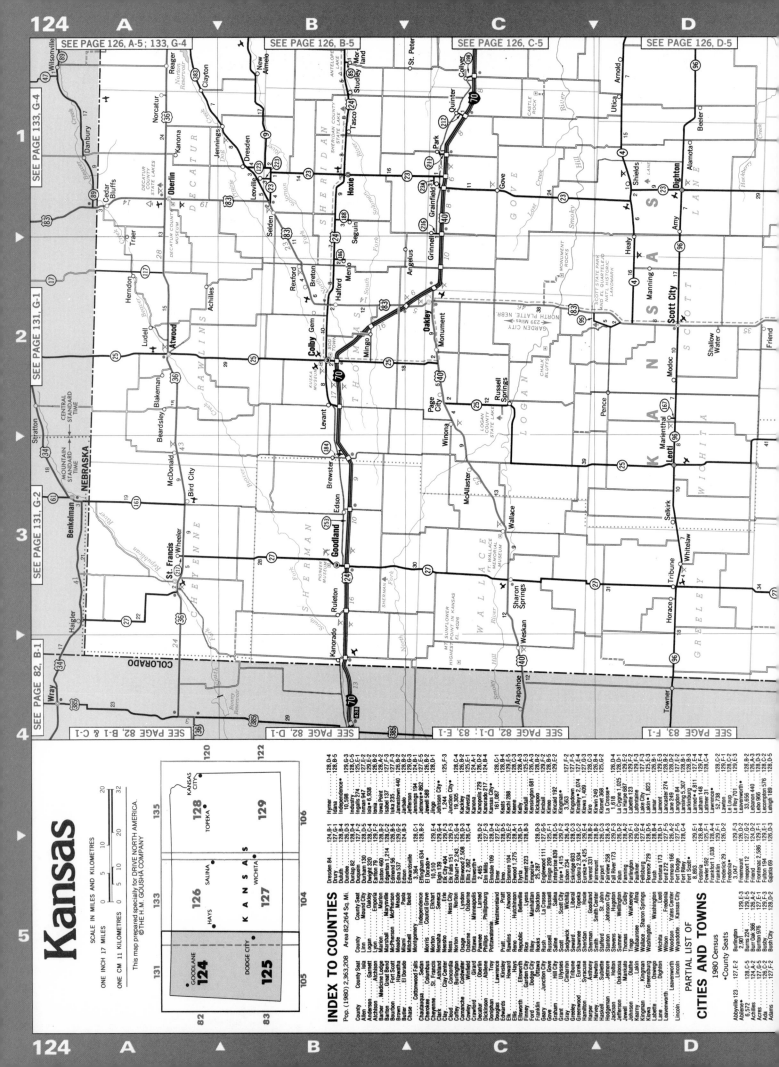

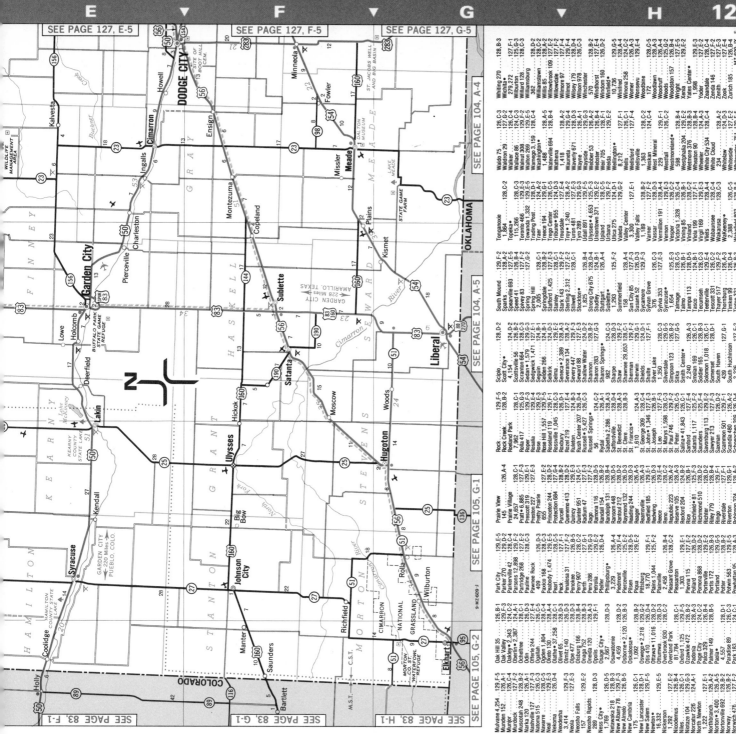

SEE PAGE 127, E-5 SEE PAGE 127, F-5 SEE PAGE 127, G-5
SEE PAGE 104, A-4
SEE PAGE 104, A-5
SEE PAGE 105, G-1
SEE PAGE 105, G-2
SEE PAGE 83, F-1 SEE PAGE 83, G-1 SEE PAGE 83, H-1

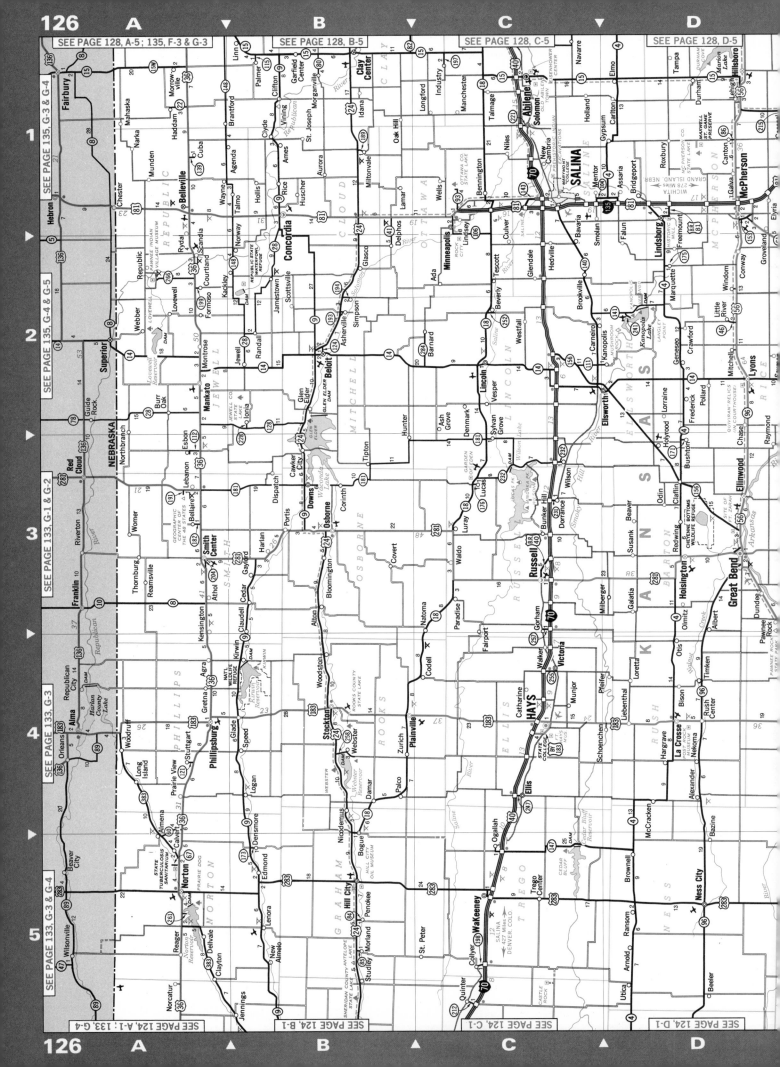

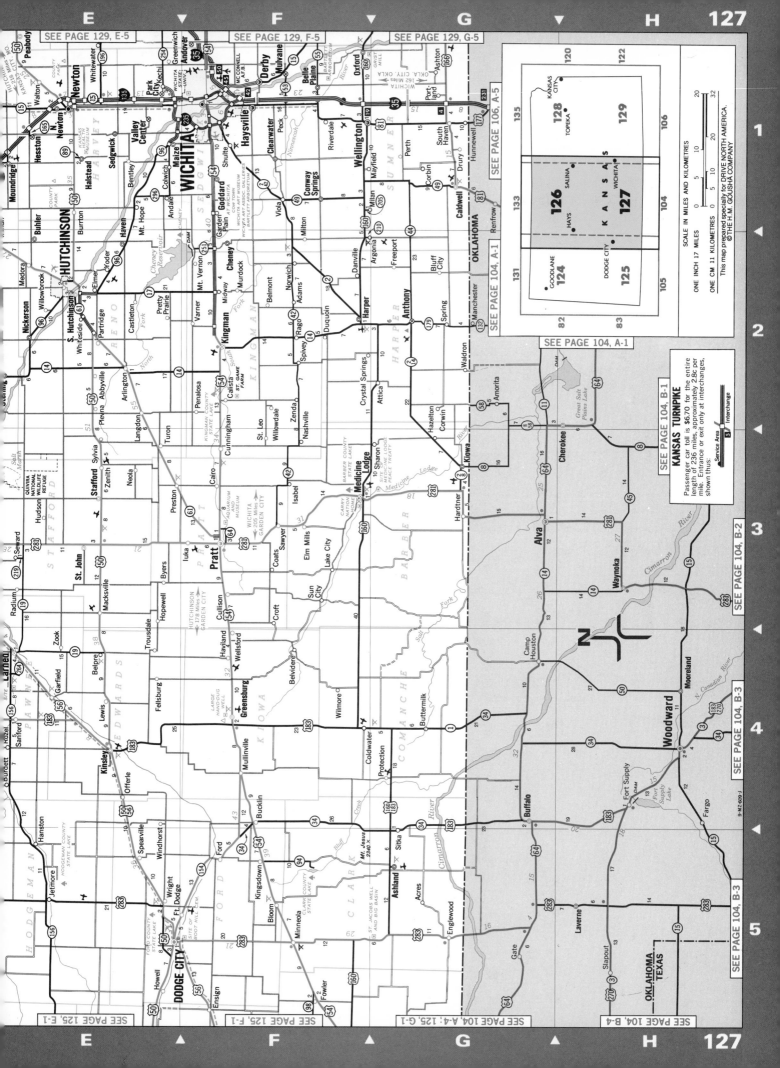

SEE PAGE 129, E-5   SEE PAGE 129, F-5   SEE PAGE 129, G-5

Peabody

Newton
Whitewater
Walton
Hesston
Moundridge
Sedgwick
Halstead
Burton

HUTCHINSON
Buhler
Nickerson
Willowbrook
Medora
S. Hutchinson
Partridge
Whiteside
Castleton
Arlington
Abbyville
Plevna
Langdon
Turon

Stafford
Sylvia
Zenith
Neola
Hudson
Seward

St. John
Macksville
Radium
Zook
Belpre

Larned
Garfield
Lewis
Sanford
Rozel

Kinsley
Offerle
Burdett
Hanston
Jetmore

DODGE CITY
Wright
Ford
Spearville
Windhorst
Howell
Ensign

WICHITA
Valley Center
Park City
Maize
Goddard
Garden Plain
Andale
Colwich
Bentley
Mt. Hope
Haven
Yoder
Elmer
Pretty Prairie
Cheney
Murdock
Cairo
Preston
Cunningham
St. Leo
Penalosa
Calista
Iuka
Byers

Pratt
Coats
Sawyer
Cullison
Hopewell
Haviland
Wellsford
Trousdale
Belpre

Greensburg
Fellsburg
Mullinville
Bucklin
Kingsdown
Minneola
Bloom
Fowler

Derby
Mulvane
Belle Plaine
Clearwater
Peck
Viola
Conway Springs
Milton
Norwich
Belmont
Adams
Zenda
Nashville
Willowdale
Isabel
Sun City
Croft
Belvidere
Wilmore
Coldwater
Protection
Sitka
Ashland
Acres
Englewood

Oxford
Wellington
Riverdale
Mayfield
Milan
Perth
Argonia
Freeport
Danville
Harper
Anthony
Spring
Manchester
Waldron
Corwin
Hazelton
Kiowa
Hardtner
Medicine Lodge
Sharon
Sun City
Buttermilk

South Haven
Corbin
Caldwell
Drury
Hunnewell
Renfrow
Bluff City
Amorita
Cherokee
Alva
Waynoka
Buffalo
Laverne
Gate
Slapout

OKLAHOMA
Woodward
Mooreland
Fort Supply
Fargo

SEE PAGE 106, A-5
SEE PAGE 104, A-1
SEE PAGE 104, B-1
SEE PAGE 104, B-2
SEE PAGE 104, B-3
SEE PAGE 104, A-4 · 125, G-1
SEE PAGE 104, B-4
SEE PAGE 125, E-1   SEE PAGE 125, F-1

OKLAHOMA
TEXAS

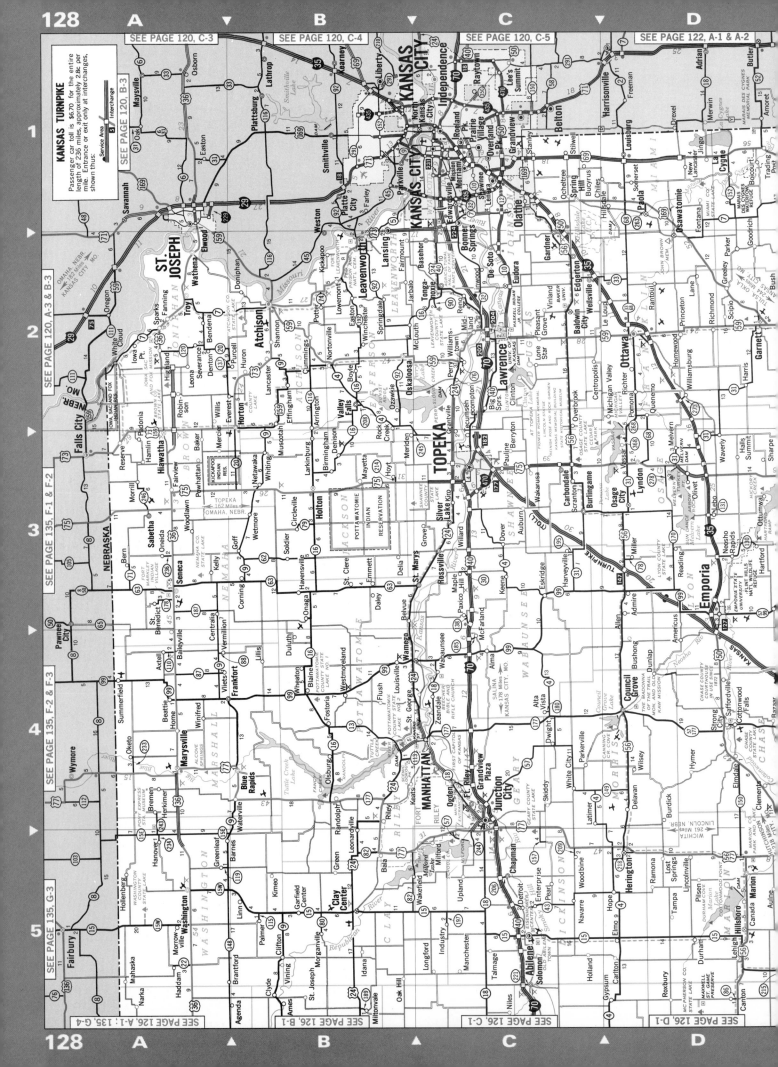

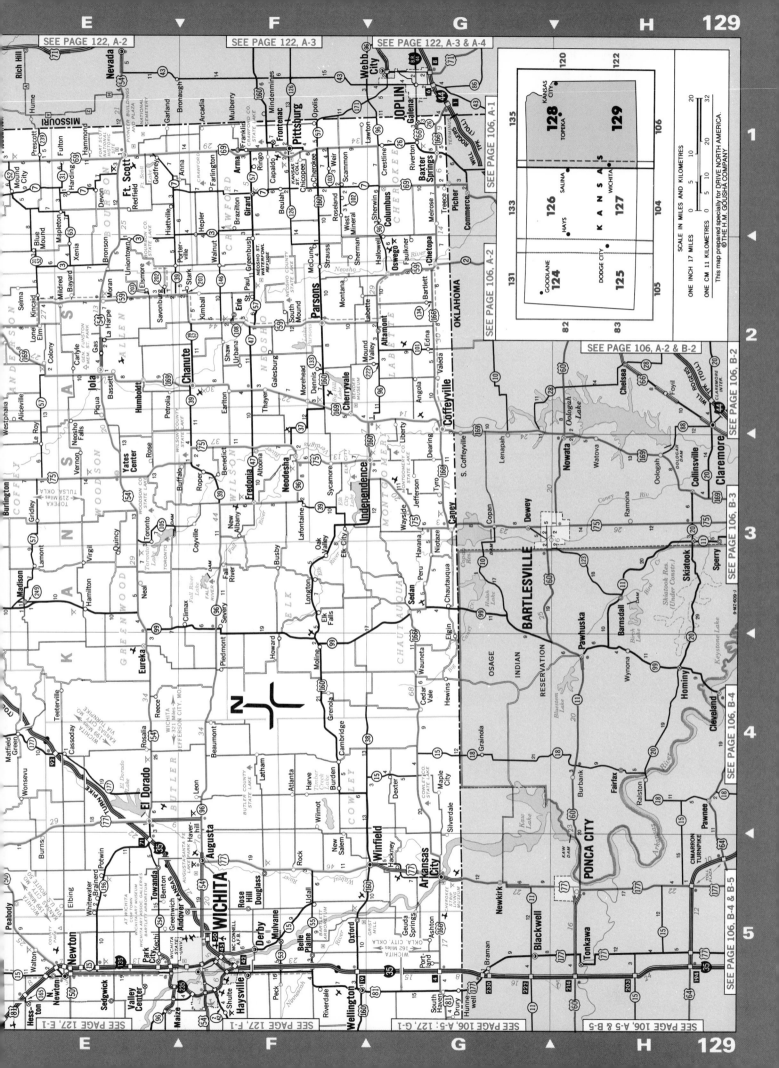

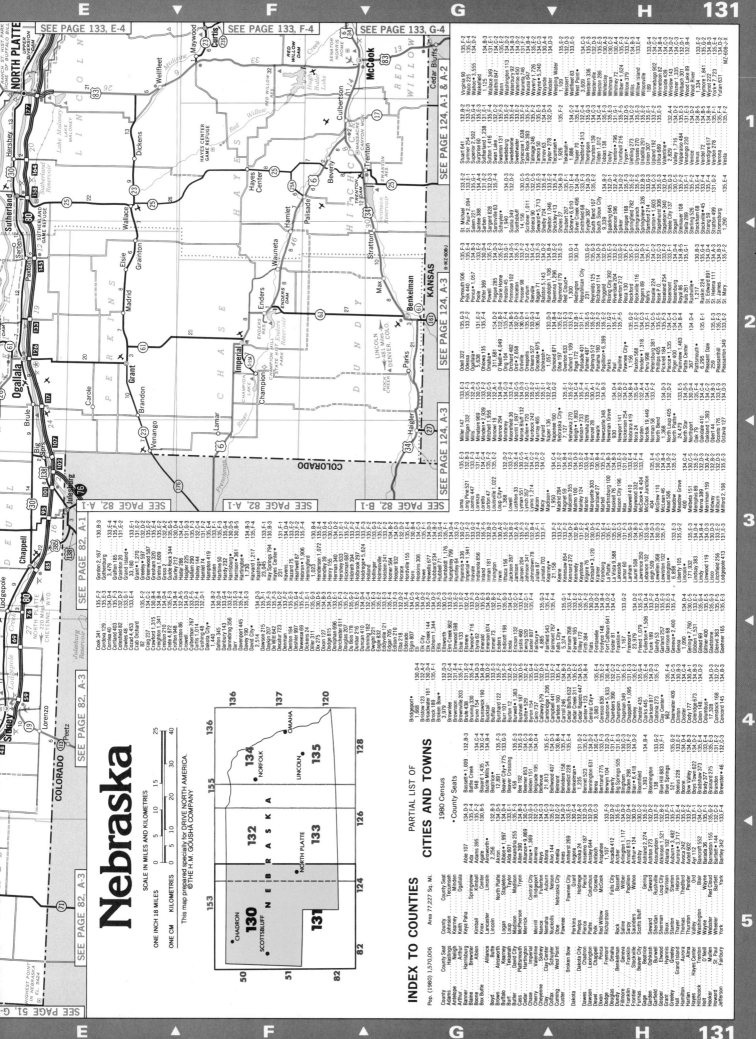

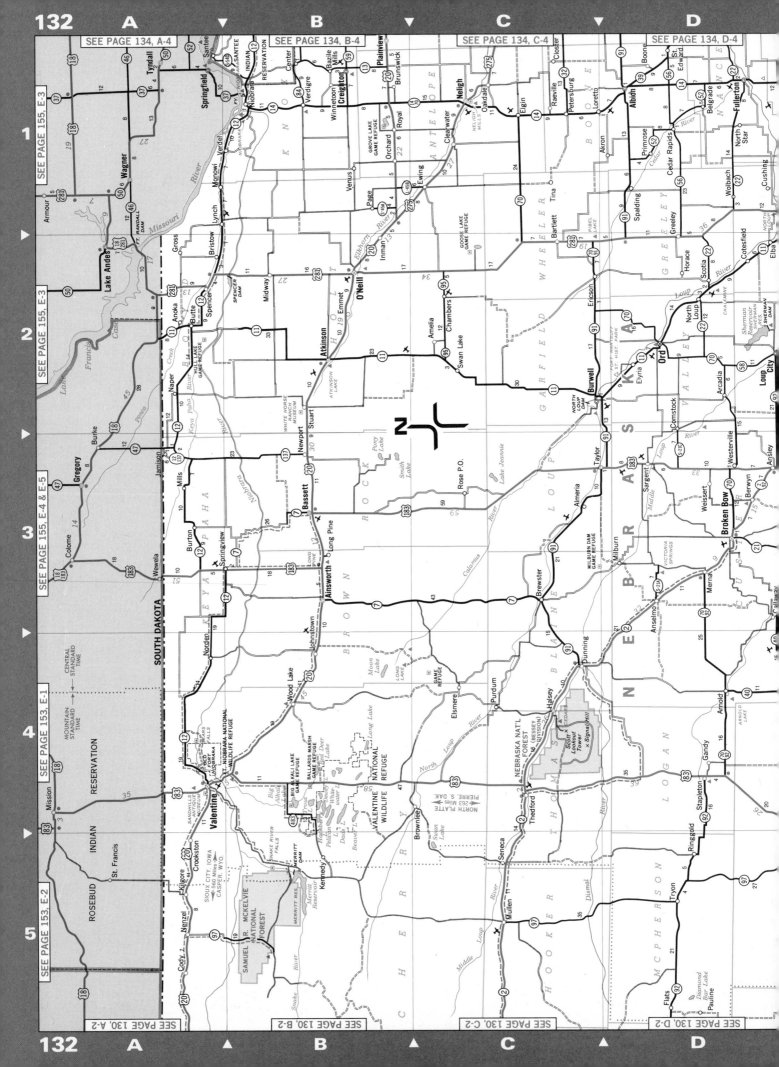

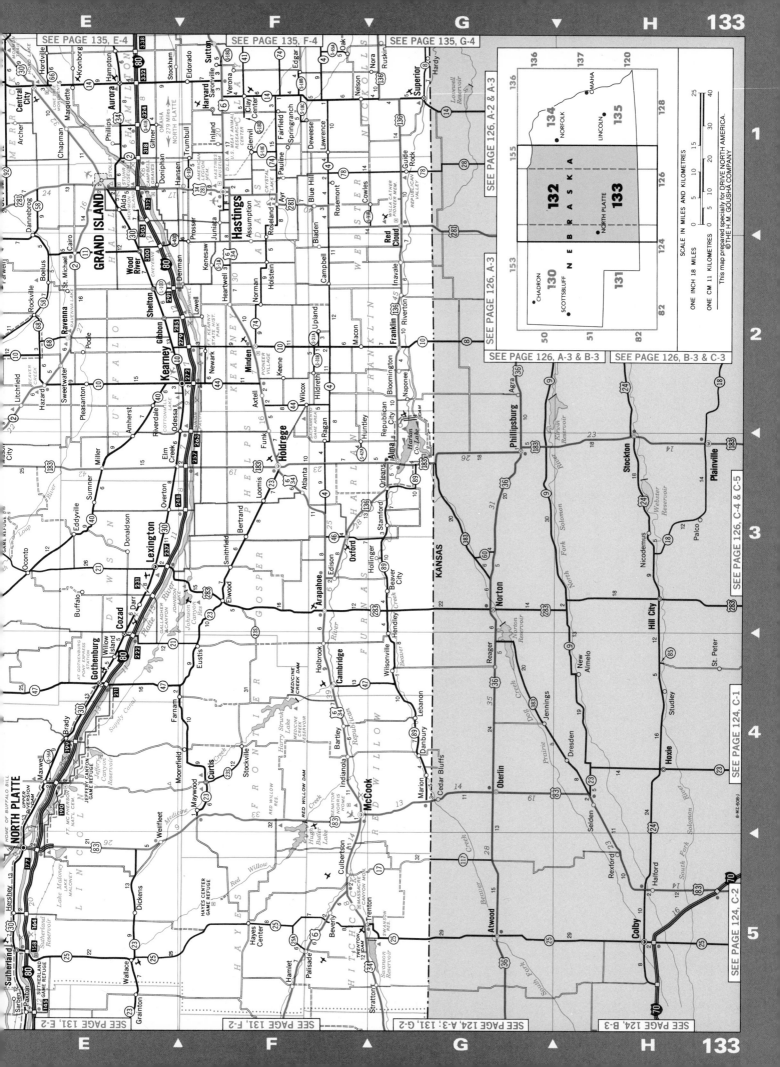

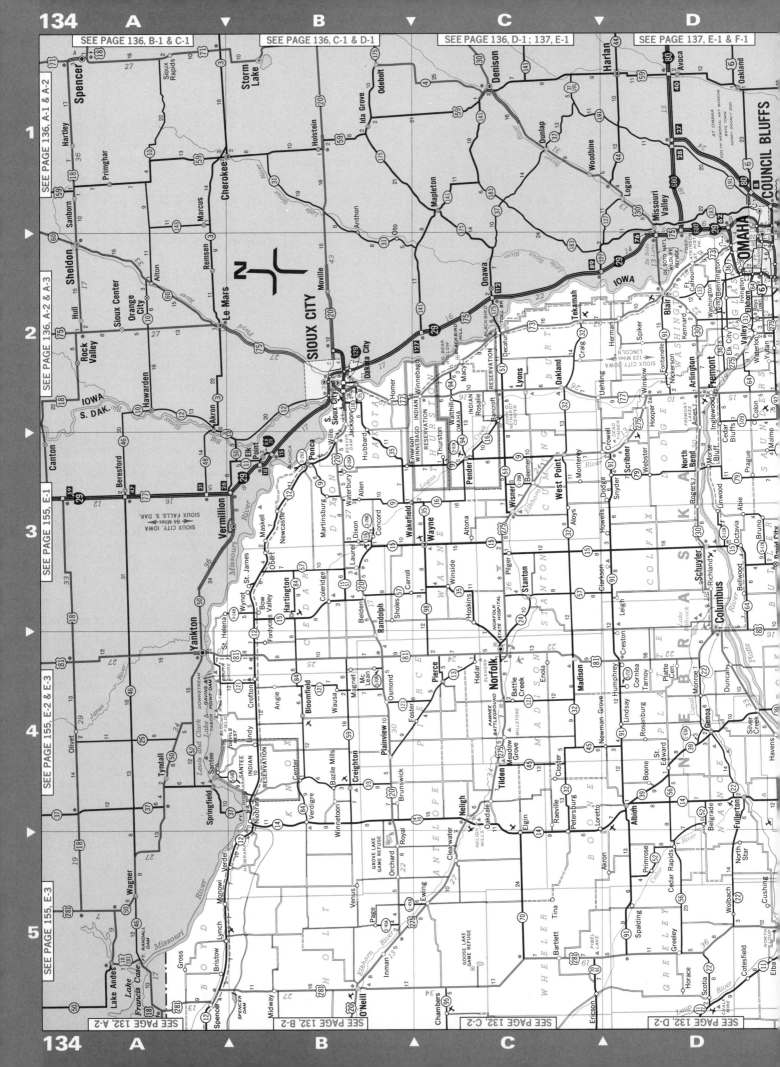

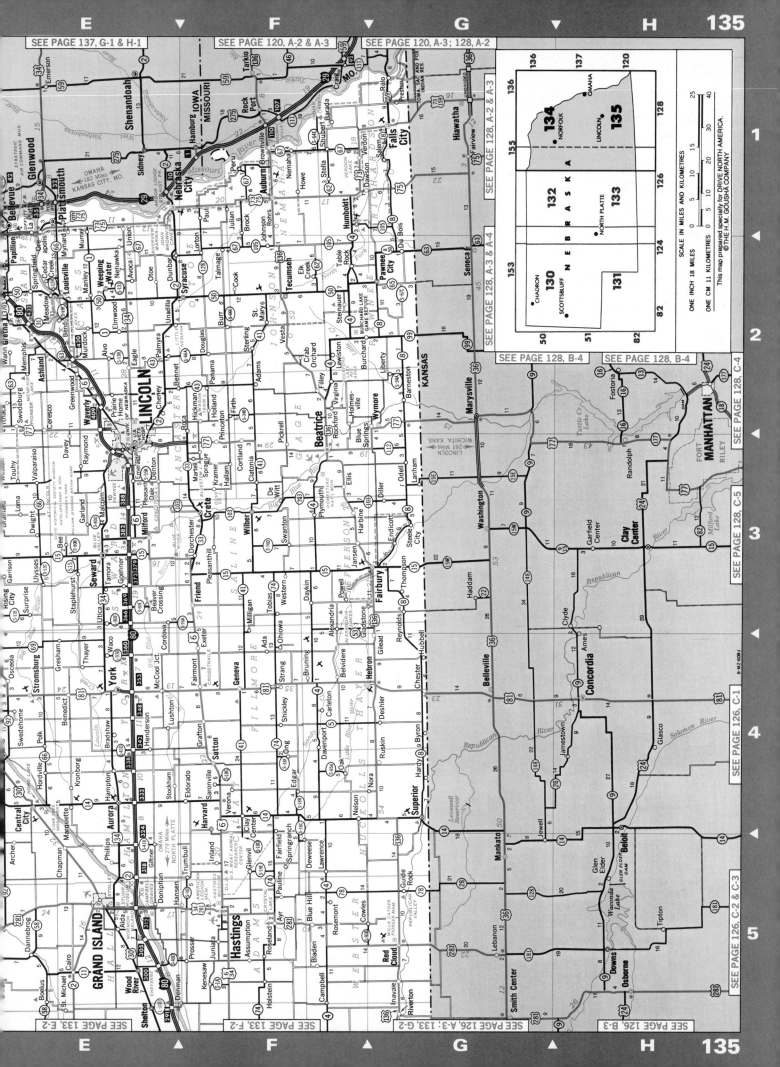

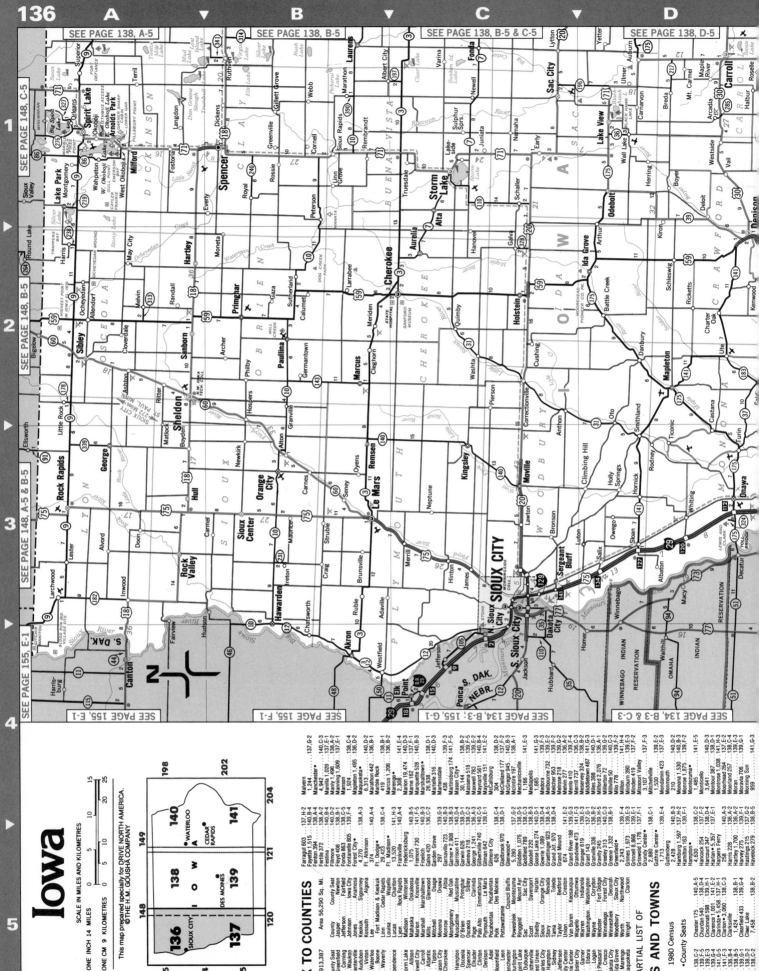

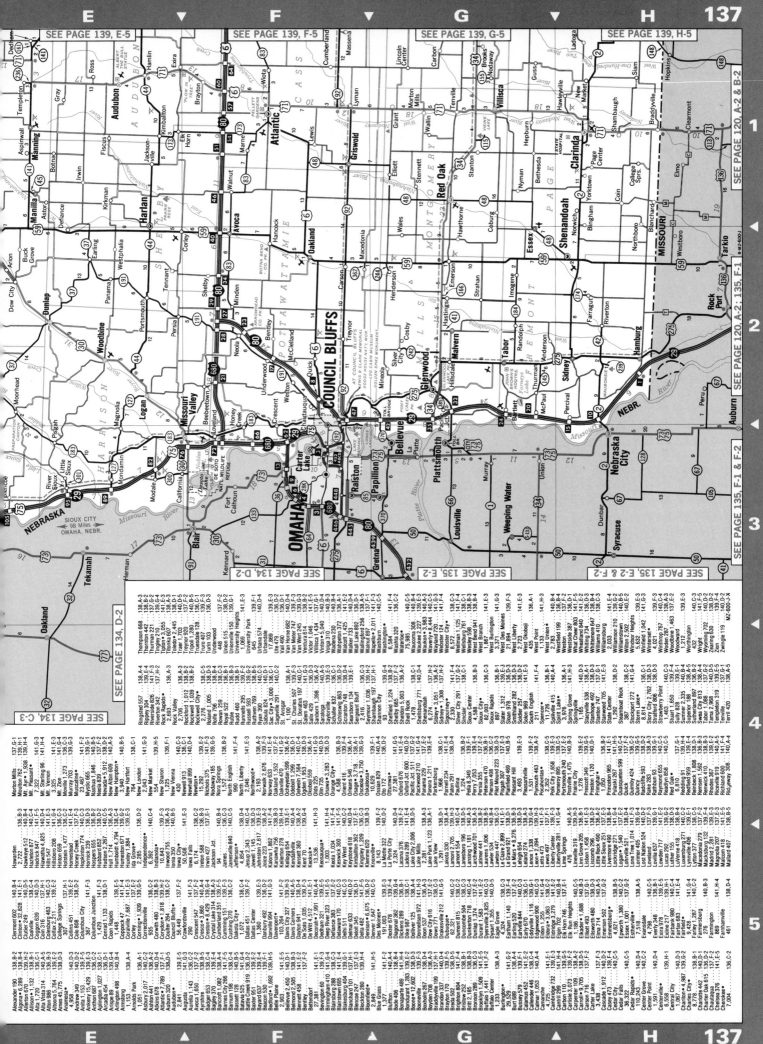

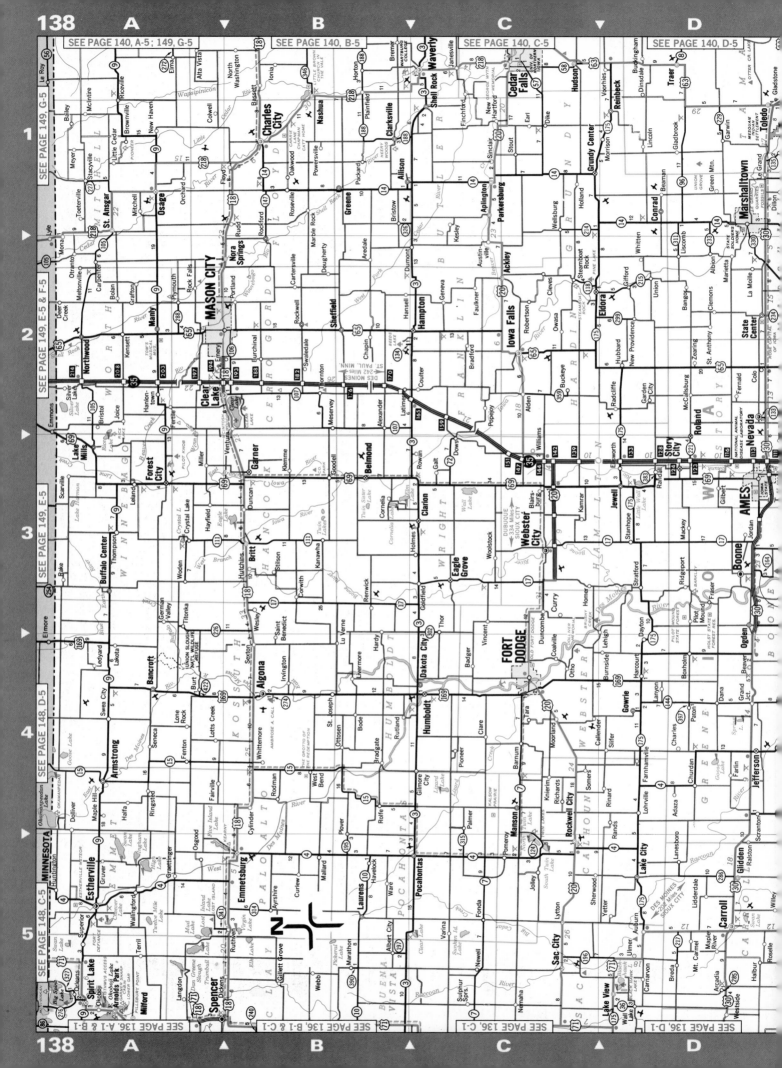

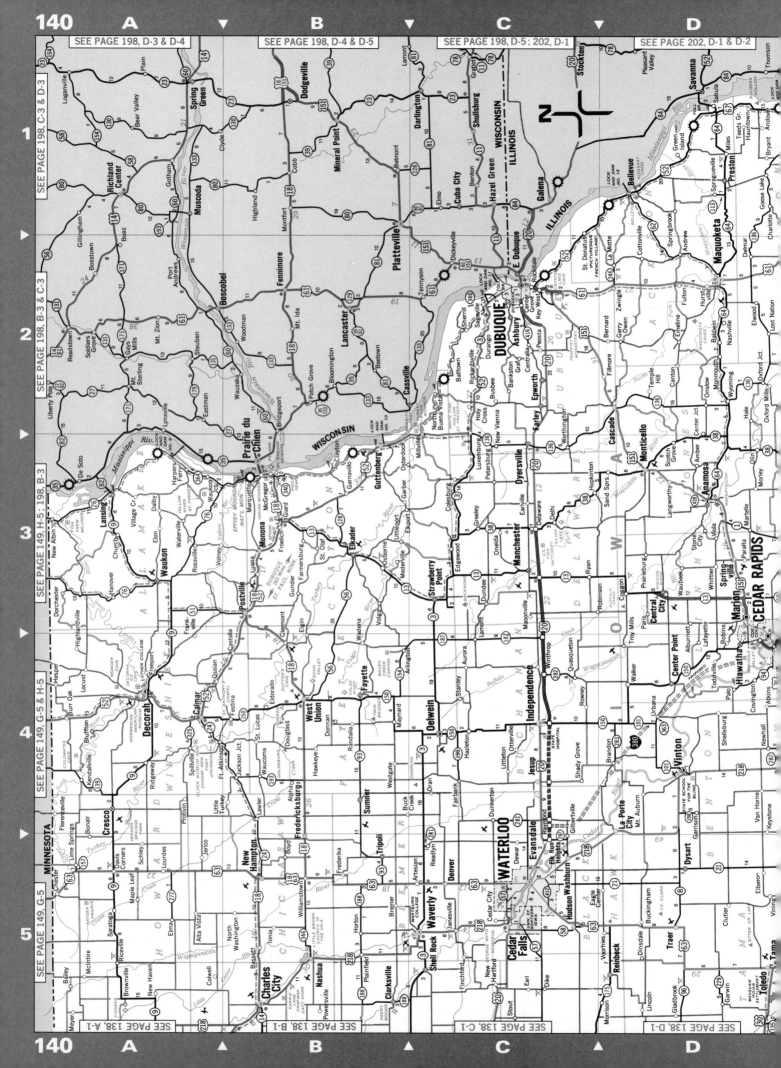

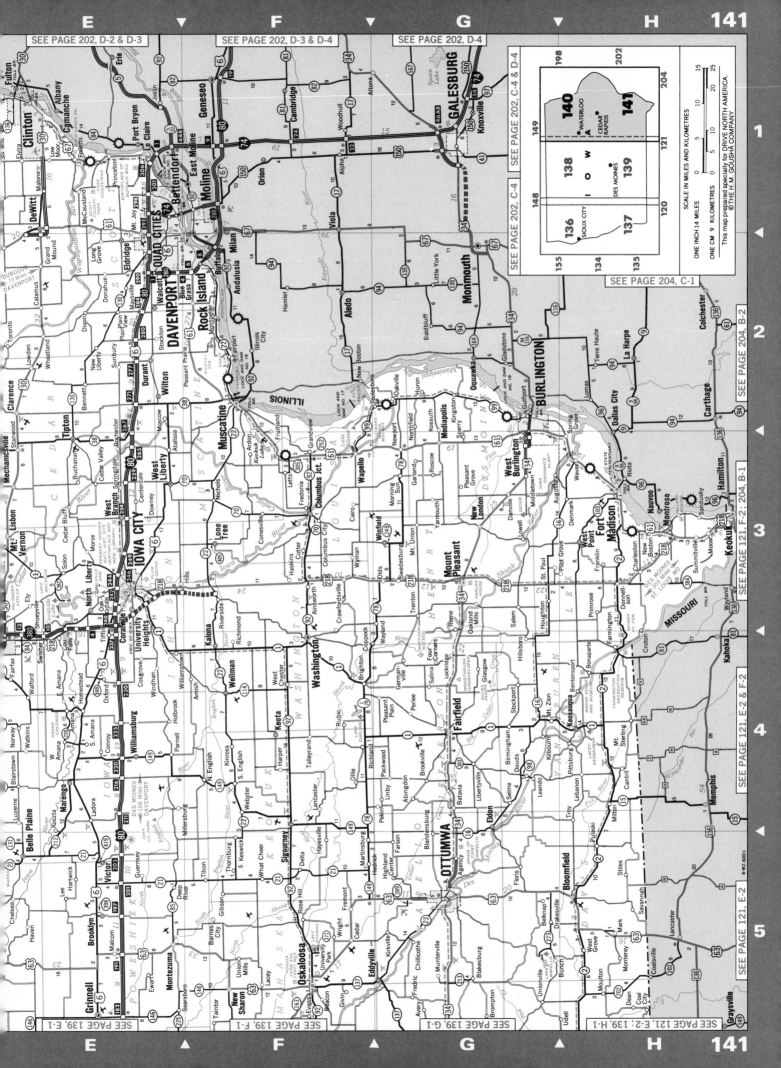

A Cultured, Colorful State of Tall Trees—and Taller Tales

Minnesota

Minnesota abounds with tall trees and even taller tales—of how the state's thousands of lakes were originally the hoofprints of Babe the Blue Ox, sidekick of legendary lumberjack Paul Bunyan. The true giants that shaped Minnesota's landscape, however, were the continental ice sheets that scraped and scoured the land.

Glaciers carved what Minnesotans call the Arrowhead, in the northeast corner of the state. At its tip is **Grand Portage National Monument (146, D-1).** The nine-mile Grand Portage Trail was a detour for fur traders bypassing the unnavigable falls of the Pigeon River. This area was the "great depot" of Montreal's North West Company, where voyageurs bartered trade goods from the East for furs from the Northwest.

Historic canoe routes wind through a maze of waterways in Superior National Forest's Boundary Waters Canoe Area, Voyageurs National Park, and Quetico Provincial Park in neighboring Ontario. In many areas of these riverine parks the only sounds to be heard are the dip of a paddle, the scream of an eagle or osprey, the murmur of distant rapids. In January, when the rivers and lakes are frozen, **Ely (146, D-3)** hosts the All-American Championship Sled Dog Races.

Iron mining has long been vital to the Arrowhead's economy. At **Chisholm (147, E-5),** a castle-like gateway leads to the Minnesota Museum of Mining with its replica of an iron mine and various mining memorabilia and exhibits. A short way along Route 169 is the Iron Range Interpretative Center, poised on the edge of a huge man-made canyon of the abandoned Glen Mine. Exhibits tell the story of iron mining and of the men who wrenched the red ore from the ground. At **Hibbing (147, E-5),** an observation platform overlooks the world's largest open-pit iron mine, the Hull-Rust-Mahoning Mine. Riding in an elevator cage that once carried miners into the state's deepest mine, visitors to **Tower Soudan State Park** descend nearly 2,400 feet below the surface in three minutes.

Much of Minnesota's mineral wealth is hauled by rail to Lake Superior, where it is loaded onto ships. In **Two Harbors (147, F-3),** visitors to the Lake County Historical and Railroad Museum can watch ore boats being loaded in Agate Bay. A picturesque lighthouse guards the harbor entrance.

Even more eye-catching is Split Rock Lighthouse, built in 1910 to keep ore-carrying vessels from coming to grief when their compasses were affected by the area's metallic rock formations. The lighthouse is being restored to its pre-1920 appearance, and is one of many historic and scenic points on the North Shore Drive along Lake Superior.

Duluth (147, G-4), at the south end of North Shore Drive, is among the nation's largest ports. The harbor and its aerial lift bridge can be viewed from Skyline Drive, which also passes through Hawk Ridge Na-

ture Preserve, one of the most rewarding spots in the world for hawk-watching. As many as 70,000 birds of prey have been recorded here between mid-August and December.

The Mississippi River separates the Twin Cities of **Minneapolis (149, F-3),** Minnesota's largest city, and **St. Paul** (once a frontier hamlet called "Pig's Eye"), the state's capital. More than 500 parks, lakes and lagoons occupy the metropolitan area of these two cities. Among the best is Minnehaha Park, a memorial to Henry Wadsworth Longfellow's epic poem "The Song of Hiawatha." Minneapolis Society of Fine Arts Park contains the Minneapolis Institute of Arts, a showplace of American art and furnished Early American rooms. A prize exhibit is a silver tea service crafted by Paul Revere.

Fort Snelling, carved from the wilderness in 1820, was the first permanent outpost in Minnesota. Restored to its 1820s appearance, the fort features such pioneer activities as blacksmithing, carpentry, baking and candle-making. At the Minnesota Zoological Garden, native wildlife roam throughout 500 landscaped acres. Animals from other parts of the world are also on view.

Twin Cities museums include the Gibbs Farm Museum, where pioneer arts and crafts are kept alive, and the American Swedish Institute, a 33-room castle with displays of Swedish glass, textiles and 17th- and 18th-century antiques. The Science Museum of Minnesota looks toward the future with space programs shown on a domed overhead screen. The state capitol contains many sculptures beneath the world's largest self-supporting marble dome. St. Paul's City Hall and Court House embraces a three-story, white onyx statue of the Indian God of Peace.

In **Brainerd (145, G-2),** the name of Paul Bunyan has been given to an area devoted to producing trees rather than consuming them. The Paul Bunyan Arboretum also has nature trails, wildflower display areas and wildlife feeding stations. A 50-foot statue of Paul, accompanied by a bigger-than-life replica of Babe the Blue Ox, greets visitors to the Paul Bunyan Amusement Center.

Salvaged old buildings have been assembled at Lumbertown, U.S.A., in **Gull Lake (145, G-2)** to portray life on the Minnesota frontier. A riverboat cruises past an old-time lumberyard and the lodge of the state's first lumberjack, the beaver. A maple sugar factory, an undertaker's parlor, a railroad depot and a livery stable are among the 26 restorations.

As well as the legendary Paul Bunyan, Minnesota has produced some real-life notables. Charles Lindbergh, the "Lone Eagle," who was the first to fly alone across the Atlantic, spent his boyhood in **Little Falls (145, H-2).** His home and an interpretive center are in a state park. Nobel Prize-winning author Sinclair Lewis tarnished the image of small-town America in *Main Street*, based on his

White water, quiet water: the lure of Boundary Waters Canoe Area.

Toboggans and Turkey Parades

Minnesotans revel in fairs and festivals, parades and pageantry. The St. Paul Winter Carnival—two weeks of ski races (*right*), bonspiels, ice fishing competitions, tobogganing, even a moustache contest (*bottom right*)—bills itself as the largest winter carnival in the United States. Not to be outdone, Minneapolis makes a big splash each summer with its 240-event Aquatennial, which it claims to be the biggest *summer* festival.

Other events celebrate the state's ethnic diversity. Thousands of Minnesotans of Swedish ancestry gather in Minneapolis each June for Svenskarnas Dag festivities. The town of Pipestone stages the Song of Hiawatha Pageant on three consecutive weekends in July and August. New Ulm pays tribute to its Teutonic heritage with a lively Heritagefest every July.

History or weather have little to do with Worthington's Turkey Days in September, when gobblers parade down the town's main street (*below*), unaware that trail's end will be a soup factory.

Minneapolis' IDS Center, one of the Midwest's tallest buildings, looms above the skyline. Glass-enclosed skyways link the 57-story monolith with other city blocks.

Segal's The Diner *and Oldenburg's* Falling Shoestring Potatoes *are among many outstanding examples of 20th-century sculpture emphasized in Minneapolis' Walker Art Center. Also featured are contemporary paintings by American and European artists; one of the holdings is a bigger-than-life self-portrait (below) by Washington artist Chuck Close.*

boyhood years in **Sauk Centre (148, C-1).** But the town seems to hold no grudges, having renamed its central thoroughfare "Original Main Street." The writer's former home stands on Sinclair Lewis Avenue; his manuscripts, photographs and letters are on view at an interpretive center nearby.

Did Vikings explore Minnesota 130 years before Columbus reached America? The inscription on a 200-pound stone in **Alexandria (145, H-3),** discovered by a farmer in 1898, says they did. In the runic writing of ancient northern Europe, the Kensington Runestone tells of Viking experiences in the area and is dated 1362.

Cutting through sandstone bluffs along the Mississippi, Memorial Skyline Drive in **Red Wing (149, G-3)** provides superb views of the river valley. On the river itself, at **Winona (149, H-4),** is the Wilkie Steamboat Center, housing a unique collection of riverboat photographs, documents and artifacts.

New Ulm (148, D-4), attacked twice by the Sioux in 1862, was temporarily abandoned. But settlers returned, establishing a pocket of old Germany on the plains. Hermann's Monument, a 102-foot-high monument to freedom, unity and self-government, commands a panoramic view of the countryside. New Ulm's architectural highlight, however, is its post office. Built in 1910, it is a delightful Victorian structure of red brick, horizontally striped from rooftop to basement with white stone.

Tamarac National Wildlife Refuge (145, F-3) is a splendid mix of conifers to the north, hardwoods to the south, and tallgrass prairie to the west. Along 35 miles of roads, historical markers indicate old thoroughfares, a Chippewa burial ground, Indian mounds and the remains of a logging operation. Nearby is **Itasca State Park (145, F-3),** headwaters of the Mississippi River. From the visitor center, a short path leads to a small footbridge spanning the continent's mightiest river—here only a brook.

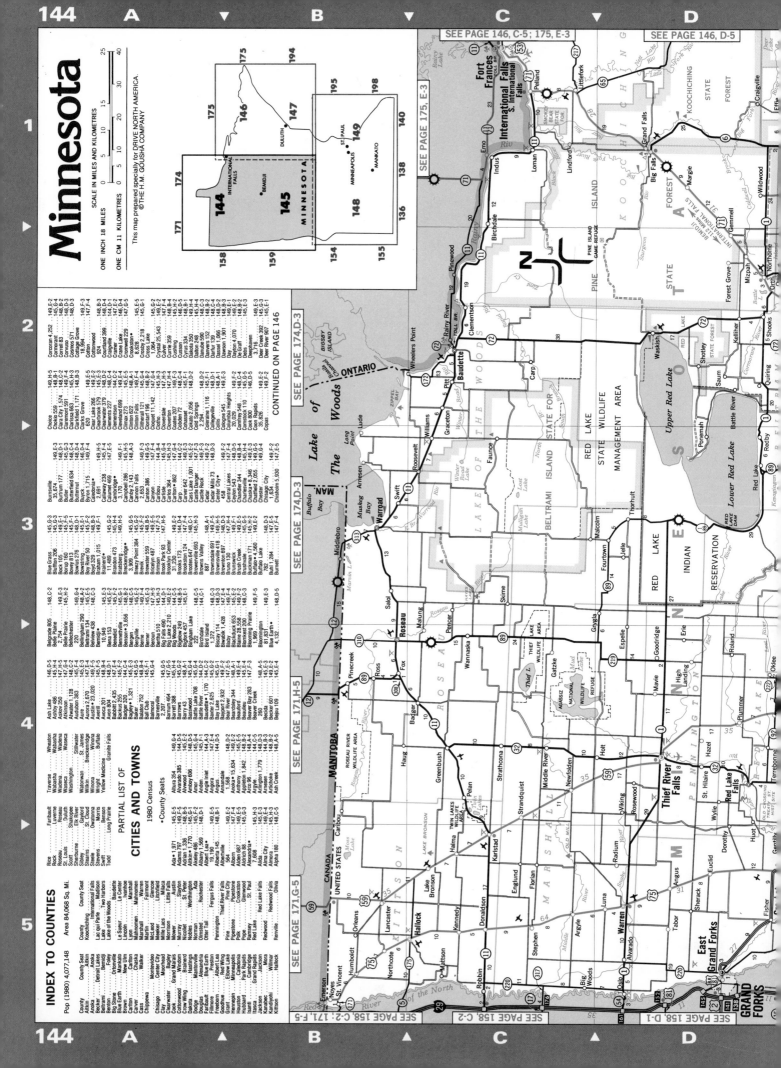

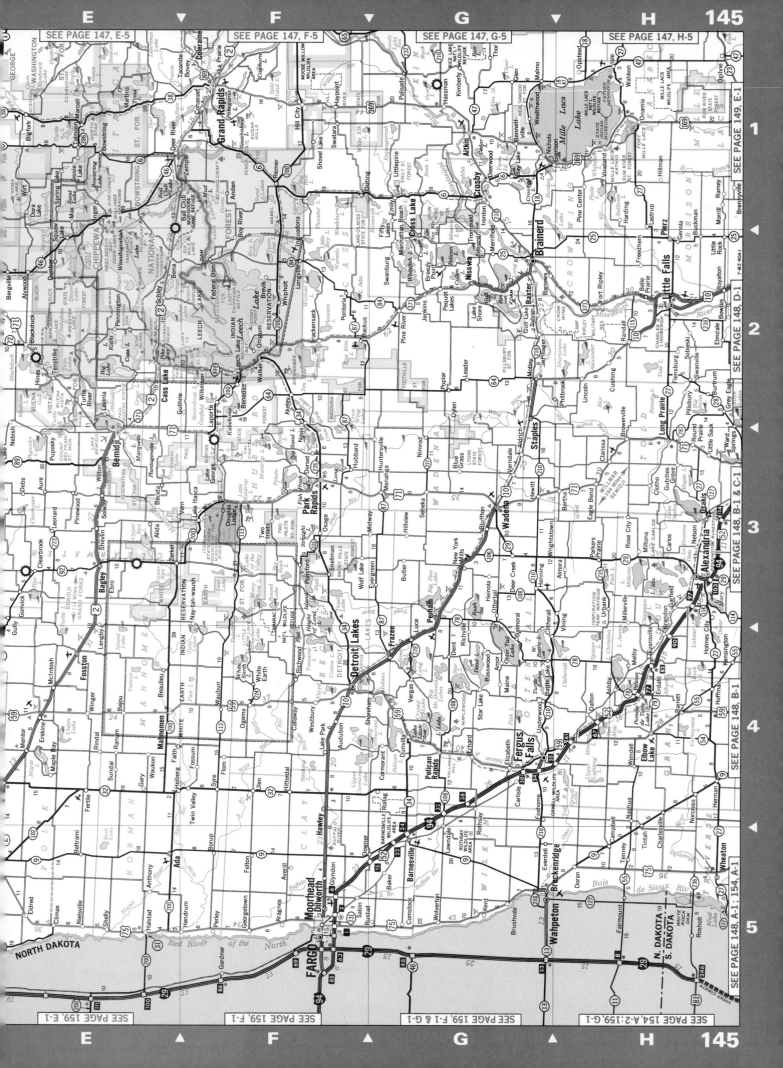

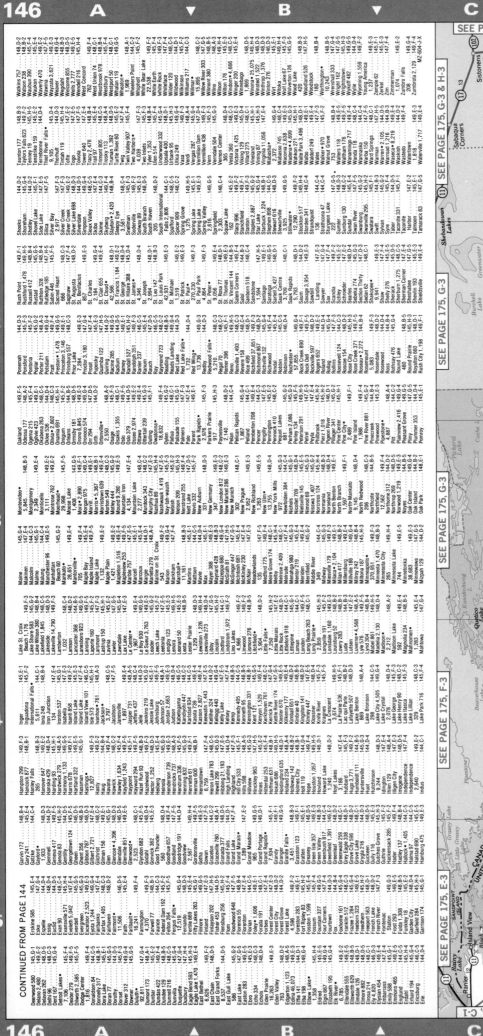

CONTINUED FROM PAGE 144

SEE PAGE 175, H-4

SEE PAGE 175, H-4

SEE PAGE 175, G-3 & H-3

SEE PAGE 175, G-3

SEE PAGE 175, G-3

SEE PAGE 175, F-3

SEE PAGE 175, E-3

SEE PAGE 144, C-1

SEE PAGE 144, D-1

EASTERN STANDARD TIME
CENTRAL STANDARD TIME

ONTARIO

QUETICO PROVINCIAL PARK

VOYAGEURS NATIONAL PARK

KABETOGAMA STATE FOREST

CANADA
UNITED STATES

DULUTH 164 Miles

Grand Portage

Grand Marais

Ely

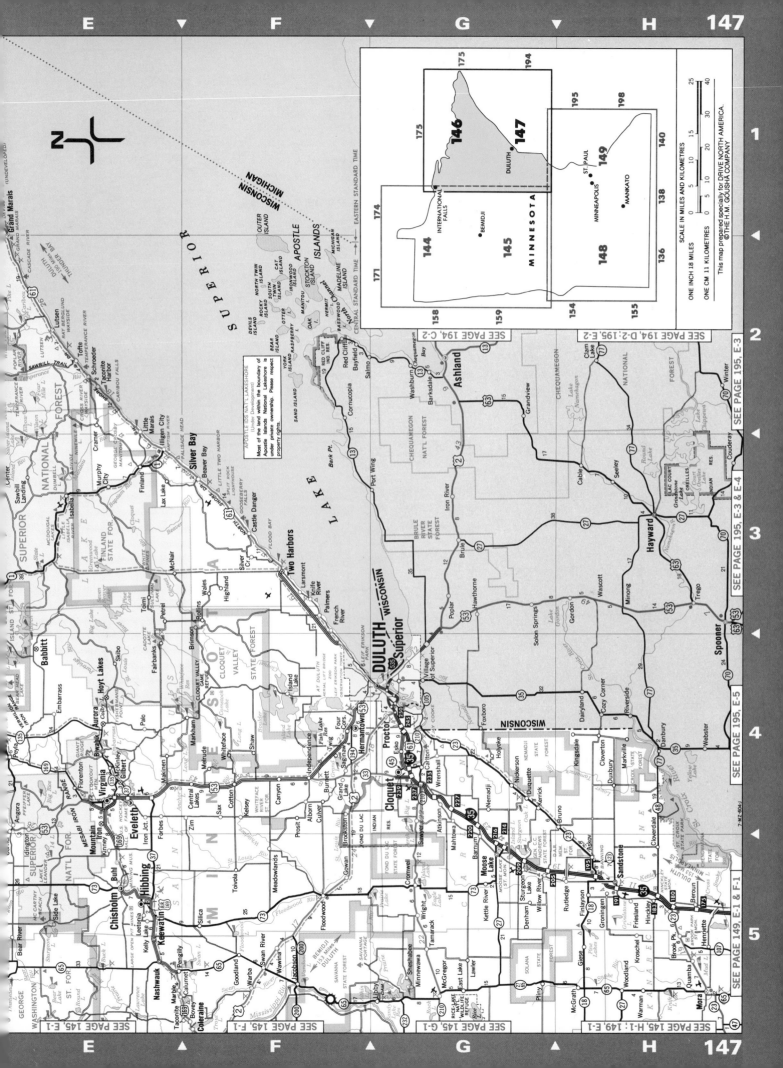

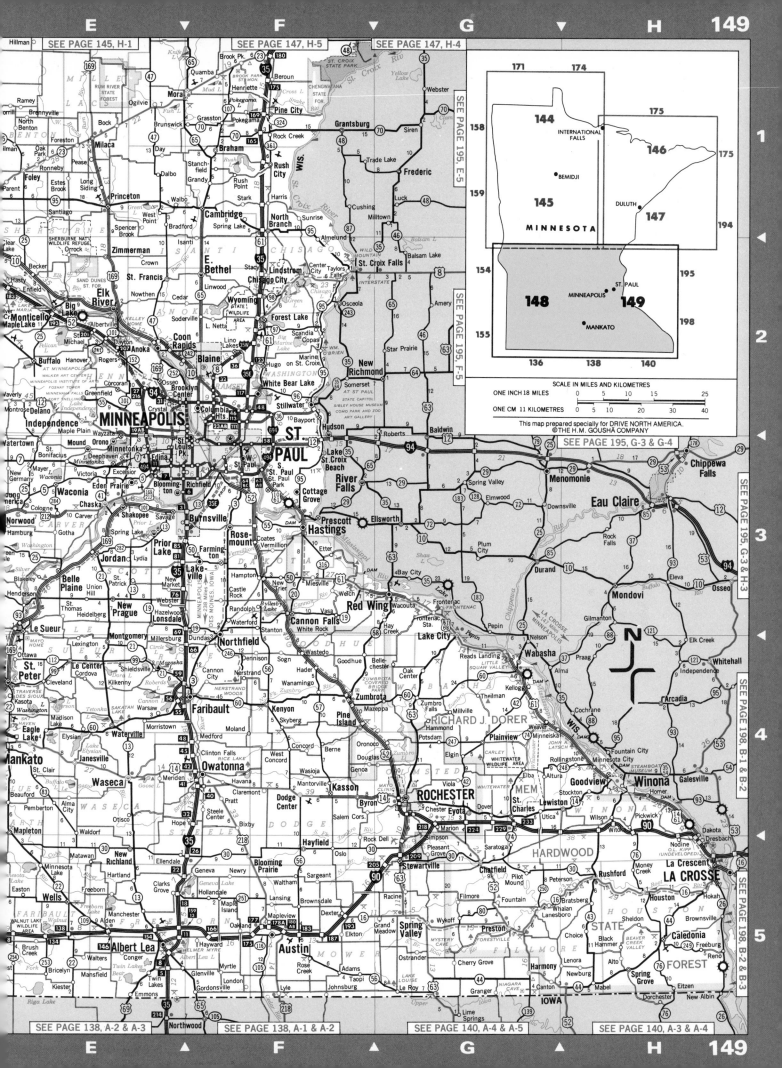

Rushmore's Famous Faces, Laura's 'Little House on the Prairie'

North and South Dakota

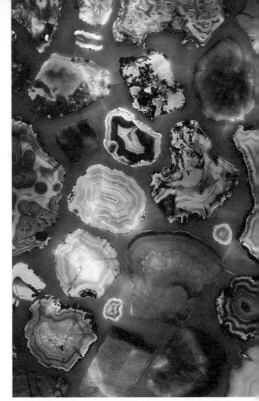

North Dakota, the "Peace Garden State," shares the **International Peace Garden (158, B-5)** with neighboring Manitoba. The gateway to this unique park stands between the United States and Canada, on the world's longest undefended border. Scenic drives wind through both countries, circling forest-fringed lakes where waterfowl are common.

Historic **Fort Totten (158, D-4)** remains the best preserved post from the days of the Plains Indian wars. Officers' houses, enlisted men's barracks, the quartermaster's storehouse, and quarters for the commanding officer, surgeon and chaplain surround the parade ground.

In the 1870s, land in North Dakota was bought in huge blocks of 7,000 to 75,000 acres. As many as 1,000 men might work one farm. In Bonanzaville, U.S.A. in **West Fargo (159, F-1)**, 25 furnished buildings re-create a village typical of the Red River Valley in the days of bonanza farming.

A string of forts along the Missouri established the river as the Plains Indian frontier in the 1860s and 1870s. Fort Lincoln State Park near **Mandan (157, G-2)** preserves a reconstructed Mandan Indian village and a rebuilt blockhouse of Fort McKeen, established in 1872. Renamed for Abraham Lincoln, the fort was the base for Col. George A. Custer and the 7th Cavalry until their fatal encounter at the Little Bighorn.

Statues on the state capitol grounds in **Bismarck (157, G-1)** commemorate pioneer families and Sakakawea, a Shoshone woman who acted as guide for the historic Lewis and Clark expedition across North America (1803–06). The expedition's 1804–05 winter camp, palisaded with cottonwood logs, has been reconstructed on its original site near **Washburn (157, F-2)**.

More than 300 operational antique farm machines, tractors and trucks fill the Makoti Threshing Association Museum in **Makoti (157, E-3)**. Gigantic tractors of the early 1900s trace the beginnings of modern agriculture. The 1909 gas-driven Hart Parr weighs ten tons; the drive wheels of the 1914 Big Four are more than eight feet high.

In the 1880s, the little cow town of **Medora (157, F-5)** began to bill itself as a hunting center for easterners who longed to visit the vanishing frontier. (One of these hunters was Theodore Roosevelt, who became part owner of a ranch nearby.) Much of Medora has been restored to its 1880s appearance, when it was founded by the Marquis de Mores, a French adventurer. De Mores named the town for his bride and built a lavish, 26-room chateau, now a state historic site.

Theodore Roosevelt National Park (157, F-5) preserves the President's beloved Badlands. In the South Unit are petrified trees, veins of lignite coal and several scenic overlooks. The cabin that served as headquarters for Roosevelt's Maltese Cross Ranch is adjacent to the Visitor Center.

South Dakota is best known for its Black Hills, which rise dramatically in the western part of the state. A thick evergreen covering gives a shadowy appearance to the hills, and provides habitat for pronghorn antelope, wild burros and one of the country's largest remaining bison herds. In **Custer State Park (153, E-5)**, the Wildlife Loop Road winds southeast through deer country, then north, where bison are within easy view. The Needles Highway passes a jagged range of erosion-carved spires for 14 spectacular miles.

Jewel Cave National Monument (153, E-5), the fourth largest cave system in the world, lies beneath the Black Hills. Sixty miles of explored passages sparkle with brilliant clusters of aragonite, and calcite and gypsum flowers. **Wind Cave National Park** is most noted for its delicate calcite boxwork formations, resembling honeycombs.

Two of the outstanding features of this

Agate slabs serve as windowpanes (above) at the Paul Broste Rock Museum in Parshall, N.D.

At Wounded Knee Battlefield (above) rest Big Foot and 129 of his followers.

realm of scenic wonders are man-made. The massive granite heads of George Washington, Thomas Jefferson, Theodore Roosevelt and Abraham Lincoln atop **Mount Rushmore National Monument (152, D-5)** commemorate these men's contribution to American democracy. The gigantic figure of Crazy Horse near **Custer** is the singlehanded creation of sculptor Korczak Ziolkowski. Upon completion, an estimated 10 million tons of granite will have been blasted from Thunderhead Mountain.

More gold has come from the Homestake Gold Mine in **Lead (152, C-5)** than from any other mine in North America. The Homestake was opened in 1876 by miners responding to Custer's report that the Black Hills contained "gold from the grass roots down." There are tours of the mine's surface operations. Down the canyon from Lead is **Deadwood,** once one of the rowdiest of wild West towns. Such frontier notables as Wild Bill Hickok and Calamity Jane rest in Mount Moriah Cemetery. Exhibits in the Adams Memorial Museum tell the colorful story of settlement in the Black Hills.

One of the most tragic events in Western history is commemorated at **Wounded Knee Battlefield (153, F-3)**. On December 28, 1890, more than 400 Sioux led by Chief Big Foot

The different layers of rock in the Badlands buttes are clearly highlighted in this dramatic view of Cedar Pass (above). Designed to be seen from below, the 60-foot faces of Mount Rushmore National Monument (left) appear lofty and dignified.

A Palace with a Difference

Since prehistoric times man has celebrated the harvesting of his crops. The way they do it in Mitchell, South Dakota, is to decorate the minareted, brick Corn Palace convention hall with thousands of bushels of locally grown corn and grasses. Each year a different theme is chosen for the murals, often including a familiar state landmark (*below*). Then, for a week in September, Mitchell holds a festival of agricultural displays, a carnival, parades and big band shows at the Palace.

The idea originated in 1892 with two local businessmen who wanted a new way to celebrate an old tradition. For the past 30 years South Dakota Indian artist Oscar Howe has designed the varicolored corn murals.

were apprehended by the 7th Cavalry. During a weapons search the following day, a shot rang out. What followed was a storm of gunfire that killed about 200 Indian men, women and children. The event was the last full-scale encounter between the northern Plains Indians and the Army.

Rapid City (152, D-4) is a gateway to the Black Hills to the west and the Badlands to the east. The Museum of Geology at South Dakota School of Mines and Technology contains minerals, fossils and meteorites found in the area, along with samples of gold and a reconstructed dinosaur skeleton. The past and present arts of the Sioux are recorded in the Sioux Indian Museum and Crafts Center.

Just below Interstate 90, the rolling flow of South Dakota's grasslands erupts in a jagged row of sawtooth peaks. They serve as signposts to the wilderness of water-carved rock and gutted canyons that sprawl southward to form **Badlands National Park (153, E-3)**— one of the most forbidding landscapes on earth. Within the eroded, seemingly barren canyons roam mule deer, coyotes, buffalo and antelope. A visitor center offers naturalist-conducted hikes from early June through September.

The South Dakota State Capitol in **Pierre (152, D-1)** is set in wooded grounds beside a 10-acre lake. An artesian well that feeds the lake contains so much natural gas that it flames up in a perpetually burning fountain, especially spectacular at night. In the Robinson Museum is a small lead tablet that was placed on a hill overlooking the Missouri River in 1743 by French explorers searching for a route to the Pacific. Downstream, bald eagles—the largest such concentration in the lower 48 states—soar above the ruins of Fort Randall and Lake Francis Case each winter.

North of Pierre, the Klein Museum in **Mobridge (152, B-1)** holds a fine collection of artifacts relating to the Sioux and their great leader, Sitting Bull. Photographs of famous Plains Indian chiefs, a superb gun collection, wampum, warbonnets and a rare Ghost Dance shirt are preserved in the Pettigrew Museum in **Sioux Falls (155, E-1)**. Set amid century-old farms outside the city is EROS, the Earth Resources Observation System Data Center. After a tour of the complex, which processes high-altitude photographs, visitors can order a satellite shot of their hometown.

Most of the 40 buildings of Prairie Village west of **Madison (154, D-2)** were moved here from other towns, but the flavor of an authentic pioneer community has been preserved. To the northwest is **De Smet,** the prairie town made famous in Laura Ingalls Wilder's *Little House on the Prairie* books. Guided tours of sites portrayed in the stories are available in summer, beginning at the Surveyor's House, the white frame building that seemed so magnificent to the little girl who moved here in 1879 from an unpainted shack on the open prairie.

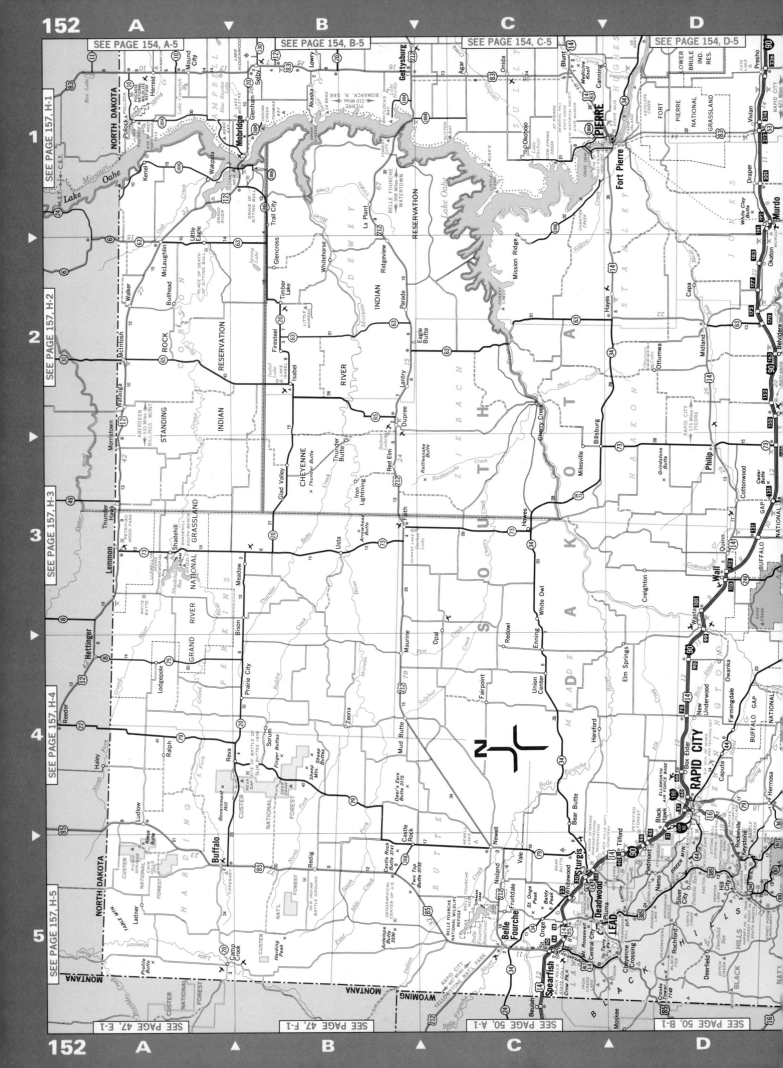

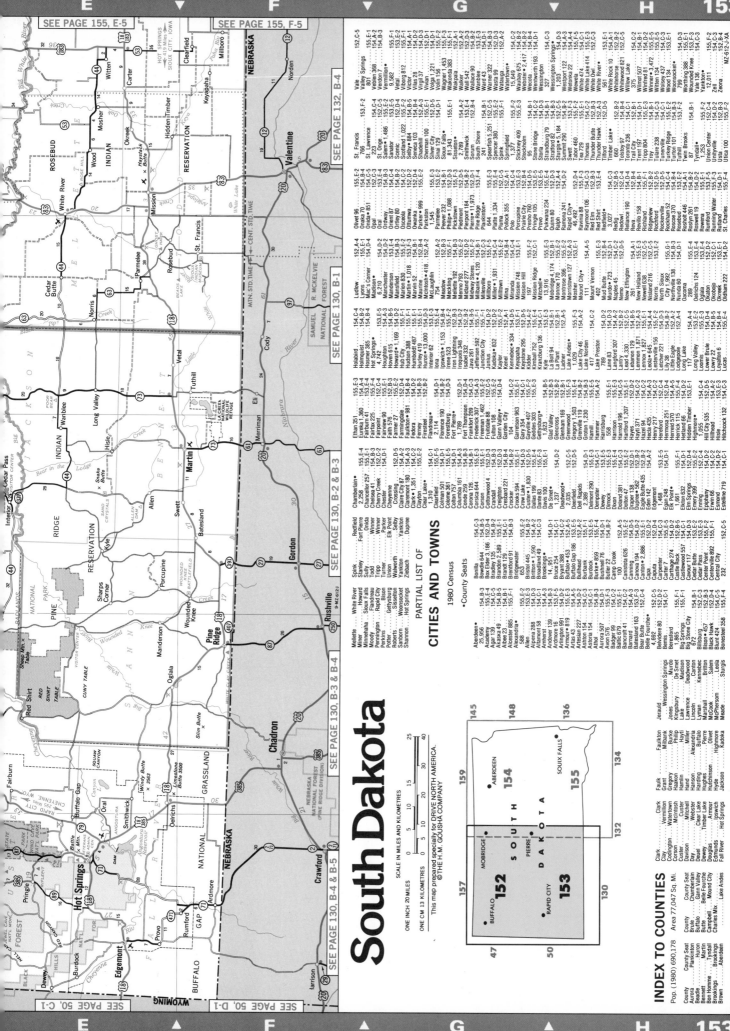
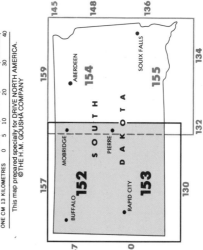

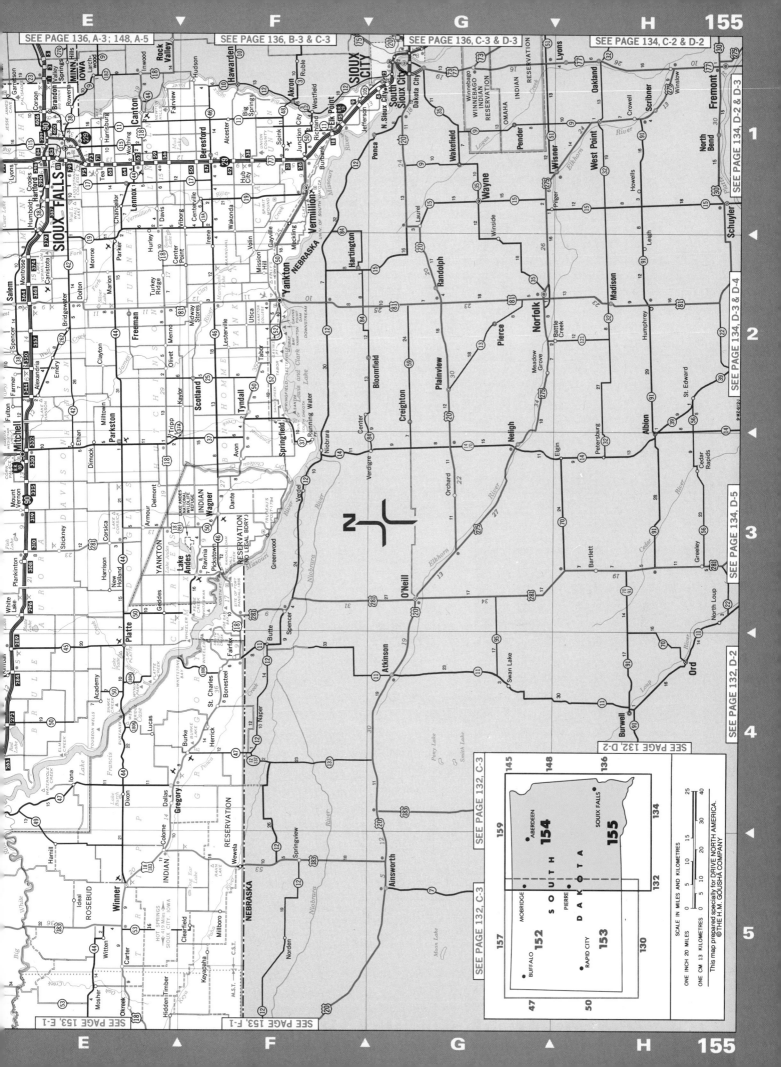

SIOUX FALLS

SIOUX CITY

South Sioux City

Yankton

Vermillion

Norfolk

O'Neill

Mitchell

Winner

NEBRASKA

SOUTH DAKOTA

SEE PAGE 132, C-3
SEE PAGE 132, D-2
SEE PAGE 134, D-5
SEE PAGE 134, D-3 & D-4
SEE PAGE 134, D-2 & D-3
SEE PAGE 134, D-3

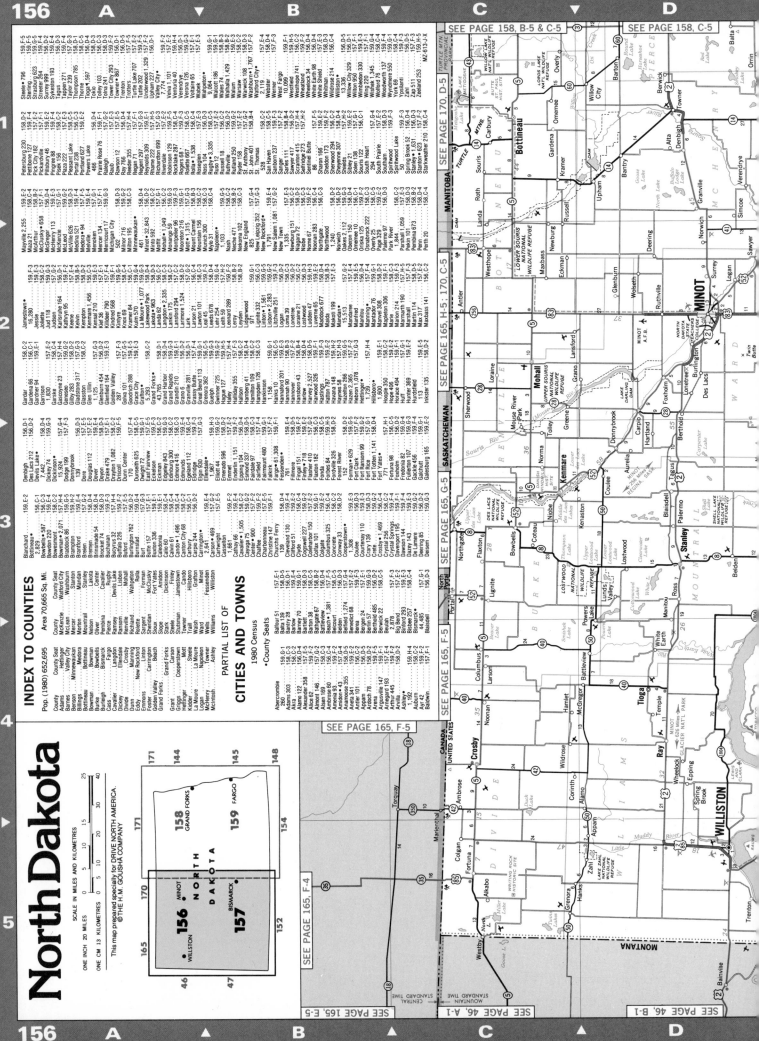

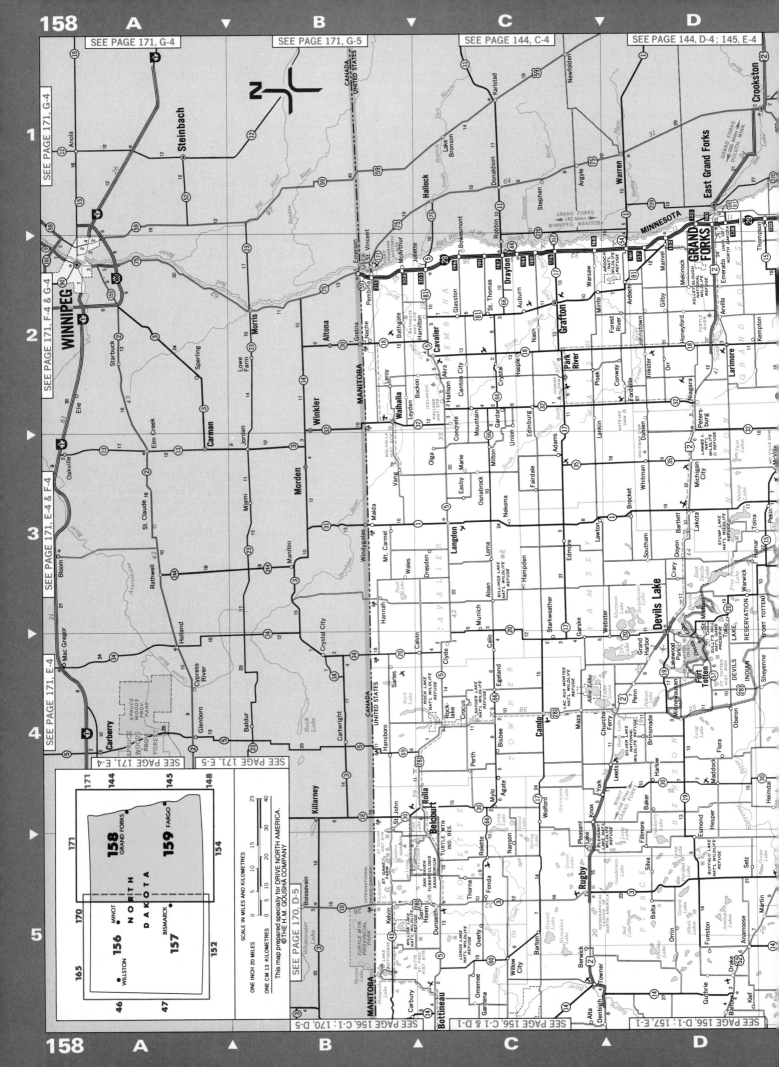

Riel's Capital, Grey Owl's Cabin, and the 'Queen City of the Prairies'

Saskatchewan

At harvesttime, Saskatchewan's wheat fields shimmer like burnished gold flowing over a wide horizon punctuated only by the occasional silhouette of a grain elevator. Yet more than half of this prairie province is forest, and there are scenic gems to surprise those who expect uninterrupted flatlands—the lush greenery of the Cypress Hills and the Sahara-like dunes of the South Saskatchewan River Valley, the badlands of the south and the lakes, rivers and towering conifers of the north.

The Cypress Hills straddle the Saskatchewan–Alberta border. Surrounded by semiarid plains, this cool, moist upland is brightened by silvery lupine, shooting star and bunchberry, wildflowers usually found in the Rockies farther west. Dividing **Cypress Hills Provincial Park (164, A-4)** is The Gap, a narrow valley littered with glacial knobs (rock and earth mounds) and kettles (meltwater lakes). The Rock Pile, about 100 huge stones laid out as though once part of a wall, has been variously attributed to Mayans or Aztecs.

Pronghorn antelope, mule deer and sharptailed grouse abound in the Great Sand Hills, 15,500 square kilometres of wind-rippled dunes. The hills extend 110 kilometres from just north of **Maple Creek (164, A-4)** to the South Saskatchewan River.

Visitors to **Swift Current (164, B-3)** can relive Saskatchewan's yesterdays each July during Frontier Days, the province's biggest rodeo—a wild West pageant of parades, street dancing and a fair.

Rustlers once hid from the law in the Big Muddy Badlands, a rugged valley of scarred earth and eroded sandstone between Willow Bunch and Big Muddy Lake. Guided tours starting at **Big Beaver (165, E-5)** are offered in July. The route passes weirdly shaped badland formations, the cave hideout of outlaw Sam Kelly, the site of a 1902 North West Mounted Police post, and prehistoric Indian effigies (outlines made of stones) depicting bison and turtles. Rising like a fortress above the prairie, a 60-metre-high mound of compressed clay called Castle Butte marks the northern extent of the Badlands.

Footprints, hoofprints, hands and faces are among 40 ancient Indian symbols preserved atop a sandstone outcrop in **St. Victor Petroglyphs Historic Park (164, D-5)**. North on Highway 2, the Prairie Pioneer Village brings to life a Saskatchewan town of the late 19th century. Its restored buildings include a church, fire hall, barbershop and smithy, all gathered from the surrounding countryside. The Western Development Museum in **Moose Jaw (164, D-3)** traces the history of transportation in the province with cars, locomotives and aircraft, including a 1927 Red Pheasant biplane that once flew sightseers for a fee of one cent per pound of body weight.

Regina (165, E-3), the provincial capital, celebrates its prairie roots in July with Buffalo Days, which features horse racing, a mid-

way, a rodeo and grandstand entertainment. In the heart of the "Queen City of the Prairies" lies Wascana Centre, a lovely park with cycling and walking paths, scenic drives and a man-made lake. Portraits of prominent historical figures hang in three galleries in the Legislative Building, a Gothic edifice set off by fountains and formal gardens. The Saskatchewan Museum of Natural History contains dinosaur fossils, prehistoric Indian artifacts and mounted animals in 24 life-size dioramas. The restored boyhood home of John Diefenbaker has been moved to Wascana Centre from the town of Borden.

North of Regina, the tranquil Qu'Appelle River meanders across southern Saskatchewan through a broad valley furrowed by ravines. Dense stands of trembling aspen and clumps of buffalo berry thrive on the moist, north-facing slopes. Western red lilies and goldenrods grow on the dry, south-facing slopes. At **Fort Qu'Appelle (165, F-3)**, a cabin used by Maj. Gen. Frederick Middleton during the 1885 Northwest Rebellion is now part of the Fort Qu'Appelle Museum. Visitors to the Hansen-Ross Pottery can watch craftsmen shape Cypress Hills clay into distinctive stoneware and ceramics.

Horse racing, cricket, billiards and fox hunting were favorite pastimes at Cannington Manor, an enclave of English aristocrats established in the 1880s near present-day **Manor (165, G-4)**. All that remains of this "Little England on the Prairies" are a carpenter's shop, a bachelor's cabin, the Maltby and Hewlett houses and a restored log church.

Saskatoon (164, C-1), once a temperance colony, is now the province's second largest city. Part of its history is related at the Ukrainian Museum of Arts and Crafts, with displays of traditional costumes, tapestries and wood-inlaid objects. The Western Development Museum features collections of agricultural machinery, antique automobiles, and 26 refurbished buildings in a pioneer village setting. Mount Blackstrap, at 90 metres, is no Matterhorn, but the man-made hill does provide downhill skiing in winter and scenic views in summer.

Botanical gardens and paintings by Emily Carr, Lawren Harris and A. Y. Jackson highlight the Mendel Art Gallery and Civic Conservatory. During the Saskatchewan Exposition, a week-long fair and pageant each July, Saskatoon residents don turn-of-the-century garb and celebrate with such events as livestock and agricultural shows, demonstrations of steam and gas tractors, and Louis Riel Day—a commemoration of the Métis leader who sought independence for his people.

Batoche National Historic Site (163, E-5) marks the battlefield where Canadian militia used the multi-barreled Gatling gun to crush the Northwest Rebellion in 1815. The nearby Church of Saint-Antoine-de-Padoue and its bullet-scarred rectory are the only remains of the Métis "capital." A museum contains some

Abe Farwell's Trading Post, near Fort Walsh, is stocked with furs and whiskey kegs.

The Cypress Hills (left) are 2,500 square kilometres of undulating forests, lakes and rivers ringed by semi-arid plains. French explorers mistook the lodgepole pine that thrives at the highest elevations for jack pine (cyprès) and called the hills Montagne du Cyprès. This was roughly translated into Cypress Hills, although no cypress trees grow here.

Most of Saskatchewan's wheat is trucked to grain elevators (right), where it is weighed and graded. From there it travels by rail to West Coast ports; to Churchill, Manitoba; or to Thunder Bay, Ontario, for shipment to faraway ports.

The RCMP Story, Past and Present

Visitors to the Depot Division of the RCMP in Regina are likely to find recruits trained to handle high-powered police cruisers rather than mettlesome horses. Early weapons, uniforms, and the crucifix that Louis Riel carried to the scaffold are displayed in the RCMP Museum. The Little Chapel on the Square, Regina's oldest building, was built as a mess hall in 1883 and converted to a chapel 14 years later. Beyond the square is a cemetery almost as old as the force.

In 1905, Regina city fathers decided to make the desolate prairie city bloom. The result, Wascana Centre (below), is an attractive oasis of greenery.

of Riel's personal effects and the .44 revolver of Gabriel Dumont, his commander-in-chief.

Within the palisades of **Fort Carlton (163, E-5)**, once the most important fur-trade fort between the Red River and the Rockies, are officers' quarters, a storehouse, a guardroom and a dispensary. The reconstructed 1810 Hudson's Bay Company post, now a historic park, stands on the forested banks of the North Saskatchewan River.

Traces of the province's proud, often violent past remain also at **Fort Battleford (162, C-5)**, where much of the Northwest Rebellion was fought in 1885. The fort, founded in 1876, was district headquarters for the North West Mounted Police. Cree Chief Poundmaker's war club and Winchester rifle and a 10-barrel Gatling gun used to suppress the Métis rebellion are in an interpretive center. At a branch of the Western Development Museum in North Battleford, a Battleford Rifle Company building (1879), a turn-of-the-century NWMP post, four churches, a barbershop and a fire hall line the plank streets of a re-created prairie village.

With the end of the Northwest Rebellion, and the completion of the Canadian Pacific Railway settlers flooded into the province—Ukrainians, Britons, Germans, Scandinavians, and Americans whose own West was filling up. This cultural heritage is perhaps most evident in east-central Saskatchewan. In **Kamsack (165, G-2)**, a Russian-style meeting hall and the gleaming domes of Ukrainian Orthodox and Roman Catholic churches reflect the town's ethnic past. One of the finest religious frescoes in North America decorates St. Mary's Ukrainian Catholic Church in **Yorkton (165, G-2)**. The painting, 19 metres across, depicts the crowning of the Virgin Mary in heaven. A Ukrainian kitchen, an English parlor and a German dining room are furnished in pioneer style at the Western Development Museum.

Deep in **Prince Albert National Park (163, E-3)** are the cabin and grave of Grey Owl (Archibald Stansfeld Belaney), woodsman, author and conservationist who penned such nature classics as The Adventures of Sajo and her Beaver People and Tales of an Empty Cabin. Three distinct vegetation zones meet in the park. Badgers inhabit a prairie region where meadow rue and woolly yarrow thrive; wapiti roam aspen parkland; and gray wolves range boreal forests of white spruce and tamarack.

161

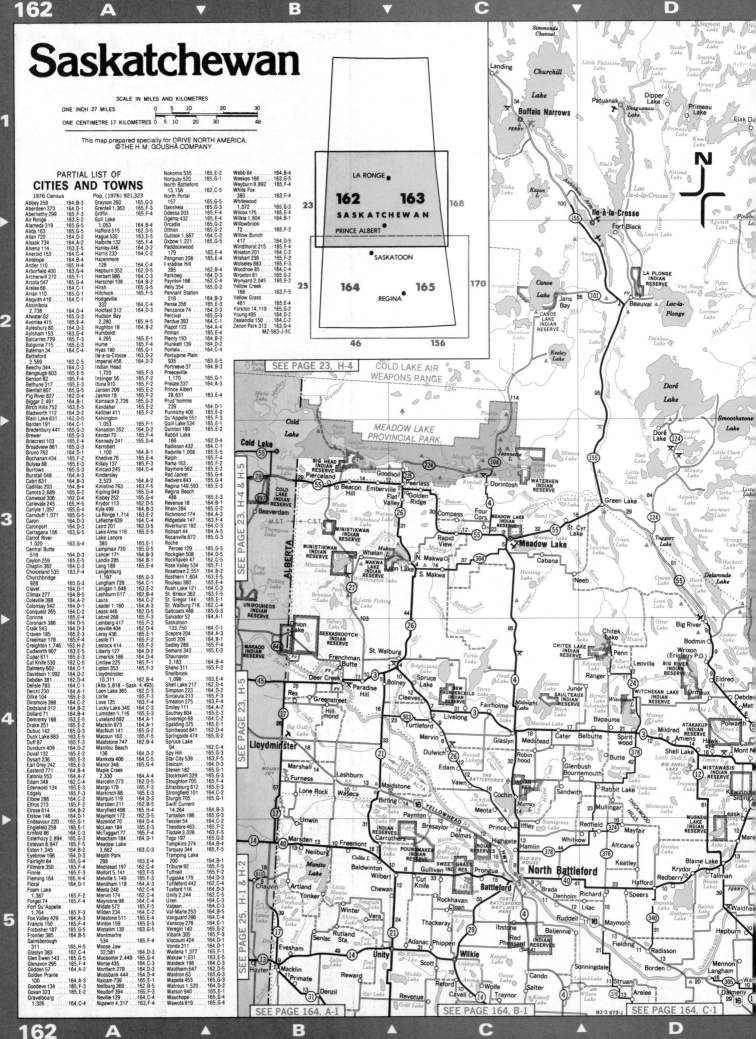

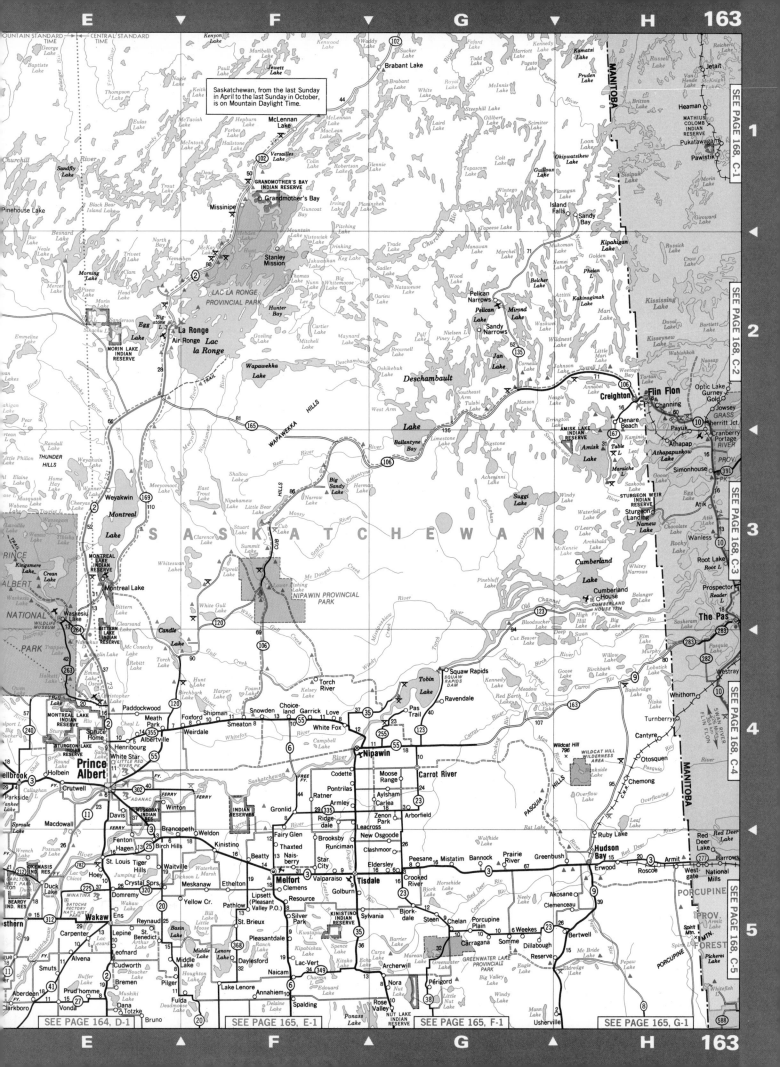

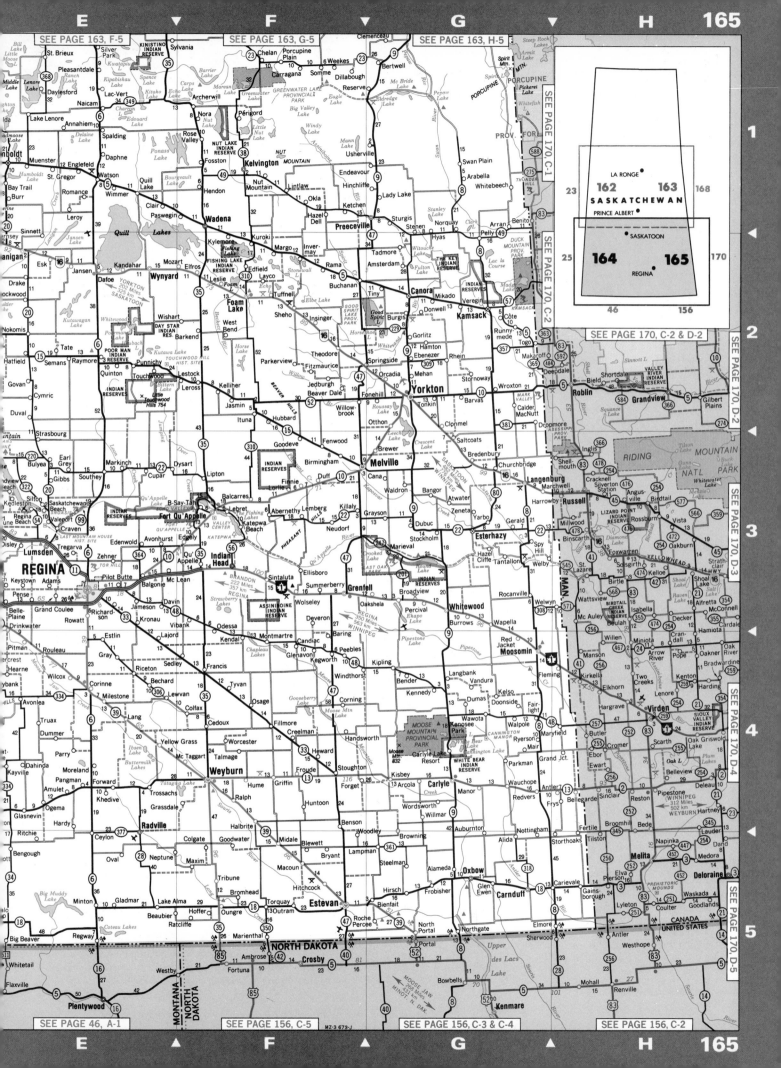

A Rich, Prairie Heartland
Where Fairs and Festivals Flourish

Manitoba

Some 580,000 people, more than half of Manitoba's population, live in **Winnipeg (171, G-4)**, a provincial capital of elegant churches, beautiful parks and wide, wind-swept avenues. Famed for its wealth of artistic attractions—including the world-renowned Royal Winnipeg Ballet—this prairie city enjoys a sizable reputation as the cultural capital of the Canadian West.

The scene for much of Winnipeg's artistic activity is the Centennial Centre, home to ballet, opera and symphony. The complex also contains the Museum of Man and Nature, where a 16-metre, oak-hulled replica of the Hudson's Bay Company ship *Nonsuch* sits alongside a replica of London's Deptford Dock. At the Centre's planetarium, visitors witness remarkable special effects—from flying saucers to the death of a star.

The Winnipeg Art Gallery, distinctive for its wedge-shaped design, has the world's largest collection of Inuit art. Visitors can view sculpture in a fourth-floor rooftop gallery. On the outskirts of the city, a dramatic glass-and-metal half-pyramid houses a branch of the Royal Canadian Mint.

Fountains and flower gardens form a colorful setting for the Manitoba Legislative Building. The sculpture *Golden Boy* crowns its dome; bronze bison guard the lobby. On nearby Carlton Street, guides in period dress conduct tours of Dalnavert, a gracious Victorian home with oak ceilings, a magnificent stained glass window and a wide, gingerbread-trimmed veranda. The mansion was built for Sir John Hugh Macdonald, Manitoba's eighth premier and son of Sir John A. Macdonald, Canada's first prime minister.

Snow leopards, Siberian tigers and Père David's deer (now extinct in the wild) are part of a unique collection of rare and endangered species at the Assiniboine Park Zoo. Across town, the Living Prairie Museum preserves a patch of land untouched by the plow—a remnant of the tallgrass prairie that once covered much of North America.

St. Boniface, now part of Winnipeg, is the largest French-speaking community in Canada outside Quebec. The starkly modern St. Boniface Basilica was built behind the facade of the original structure (1908); the earlier building was ravaged by fire in 1968. In the shadow of the cathedral, a simple granite column marks the grave of rebel Métis leader Louis Riel

Manitoba's smaller towns have a well-deserved reputation for charm, beauty and hospitality. Ranchers in **Morris (171, F-5)** don chaps and Stetsons and whoop it up each July during the five-day Manitoba Stampede, Canada's second largest rodeo (after the Calgary Stampede). Antique farm equipment from the Threshermen's Museum in **Winkler (171, F-5)** is put to work each September during the Threshermen's Reunion. More unusual sport leaps to life during the Canadian frog jumping championships each August in **St. Pierre-Jolys (171, G-1)**.

Despite floods, droughts and plagues of grasshoppers, Winnipeg (above) prospered.

Giant steam tractors (left) snort to life each fall at threshermen's reunions.

A sea of sunflowers (below), a major prairie crop, ripens near Altona.

Southwestern Manitoba's secluded river valleys and wooded Pembina Hills provide splendid contrast to the flatlands of the prairies. The International Peace Garden, part of **Turtle Mountain Provincial Park (170, D-5)**, sits astride the Canada–U.S. border midway between the Atlantic and the Pacific and only 72 kilometres from the geographic center of North America (Rugby, North Dakota). The provincial park itself, dotted with sloughs and small lakes, is a stopover for some 250 species of migratory birds.

Brandon (170, D-4), Manitoba's second largest city, occupies a scenic setting in the broad valley of the Assiniboine River. The Provincial Exhibition of Manitoba in July includes livestock and horticultural exhibits, a midway and a rodeo. The Royal Manitoba Winter Fair features horse shows and livestock and industrial displays.

In the heart of southern Manitoba's fertile farmlands rise the Carberry Sandhills, a wild mix of evergreen stands, deciduous forests, grassy plains and a 40-square-kilometre expanse of sand dunes. The dunes straddle

Its cluster of ornate Byzantine-style cupolas distinguishes the Grotto-Church of the Immaculate Conception near Winnipeg.

Successor to York boats and stern-wheelers, the Lord Selkirk II *cruises Lake Winnipeg.*

An Ethnic Mosaic of Tradition and Change

Manitobans are not one people, but many. In Dauphin, cossack riders parade through the streets to the sound of balalaikas, and townsfolk in Ukrainian costume feast on *pirogi*, *Holupchi* and other Slavic delicacies during the National Ukrainian Festival in August.

The first large group of Mennonites to homestead in western Canada came to Manitoba in 1874. Some of their buildings, including a cheese factory, a smithy and a thatched-roof cabin, have been reconstructed in the Mennonite Village Museum at Steinbach.

Descendents of the Icelanders who settled Gimli celebrate their heritage with parades, songs and dances during the midsummer *Islendingadagurinn* (Icelandic Festival.) An Icelandic fishing village has been re-created in nearby Hecla Provincial Park.

Nowhere is Manitoba's ethnic diversity richer than in Winnipeg, which celebrates its roots with Folklorama. During the lively summer carnival each of the city's 30 cultural groups hosts a pavilion featuring costumes and customs, food and drink.

Two faces of Manitoba: A Mennonite woman preparing bread at Steinbach; Japanese-Canadian children in Winnipeg.

Spruce Woods Provincial Park (171, E-4) and the adjoining provincial forest, and can be toured along the self-guided Spirit Hills Interpretive Trail.

Much of Manitoba's first, largest and perhaps most popular provincial park—Whiteshell (171, H-4)—is still wilderness, accessible only by boat or plane. In summer, visitors flock to the town of Falcon Lake, gateway to the park, for boating, waterskiing, swimming and fishing. A trail near Betula Lake leads to boulder outlines of birds, turtles, fish and snakes made nearly 1,000 years ago by Ojibwa Indians.

Some of Lake Winnipeg's finest shoreline curves through Grand Beach Provincial Park (171, G-3), where waves lap clear stretches of white sand. A self-guided nature trail ascends a hill terraced by three shorelines—5,000, 7,500 and 10,000 years old. Elk Island, a wilderness section of this popular park, can be reached by wading or boating across a narrow strait.

Manitoba's only national park, Riding Mountain (170, D-3), occupies part of the Manitoba Escarpment, which extends into Saskatchewan. The park's northern and eastern boundaries rise some 450 metres above the surrounding farmlands. Park roads and more than 160 kilometres of backpacking, riding and nature trails crisscross the reserve. Naturalists conduct elk-bugling sessions during the fall mating season, and are often met with authentic responses.

The Minnedosa River has carved a wide valley south of Riding Mountain. This gives a superb setting to Minnedosa (170, D-4), one of Manitoba's prettiest towns. A dam on the river forms a lake that attracts swimmers and waterskiers. The Minnedosa and District Cooperative Museum displays artifacts of homestead life.

A sweeping valley with a checkerboard of farms separates the low, blue ridge of Riding Mountain from the striking outline of Duck Mountain. Herds of wapiti and mule deer roam Duck Mountain Provincial Park (170, D-2), also a nesting ground for great blue herons, turkey vultures and white pelicans. Manitoba's highest point, 831-metre Baldy Mountain, throws its shadow across the park's southeast corner.

Farther north are dense coniferous forests and myriad lakes, the preserve of wilderness campers, canoeists and fishermen. In February, muskrat skinning, moose calling and a 340-kilometre dog derby highlight the four-day Northern Manitoba Trappers' Festival at The Pas (168, C-4). Native dances and hatchet- and spear-throwing contests enliven Opasquia Indian Days in August. Christ Church (1840) contains furnishings made in 1848 by a rescue party en route to the Arctic in search of explorer Sir John Franklin. The Little Northern Museum displays Inuit miniature ivory carvings, a copy of *The Origin of Species* signed by Charles Darwin, and a letterpress and bookbinder from the Hudson's Bay Company post at York Factory.

Prize catches in the July Trout Festival in Flin Flon (168, C-2) weigh as much as 18 kilograms. The lifeblood of the region, however, is not fish but minerals. Visitors can tour the Hudson Bay Mining and Smelting Company plant, which refines gold and silver. Flin Flon derives its fanciful name from Josiah Flintabbatey Flonatin, the fictional hero of the 1905 novel *The Sunless City*.

167

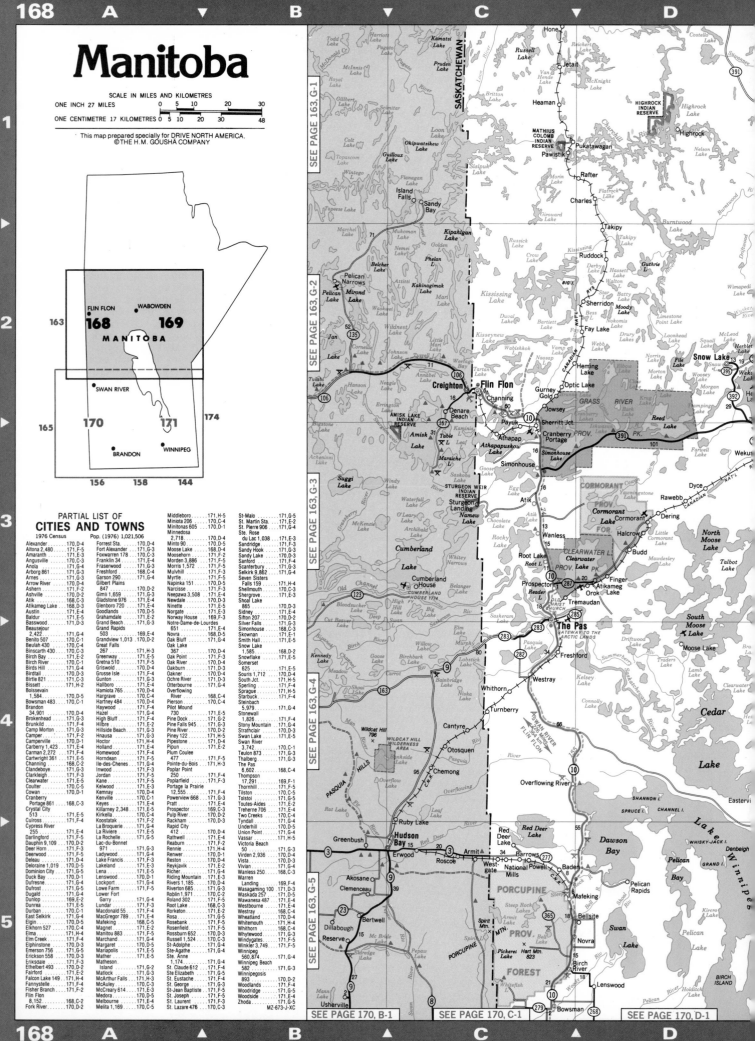

Manitoba

SCALE IN MILES AND KILOMETRES

ONE INCH 27 MILES

ONE CENTIMETRE 17 KILOMETRES

This map prepared specially for DRIVE NORTH AMERICA.
©THE H.M. GOUSHA COMPANY

163 — 168 169 — MANITOBA — 174

165 — 170 171 — 156 158 144

PARTIAL LIST OF CITIES AND TOWNS

1976 Census   Pop. (1976) 1,021,506

Name	Page,Grid
Alexander	170,D-4
Altona 2,480	171,H-5
Amaranth	171,E-3
Angusville	170,C-3
Anola	171,G-4
Arborg 861	171,G-3
Arnes	171,G-3
Arrow River	170,D-4
Ashern	171,F-2
Ashville	170,D-2
Atik	168,C-3
Atikameg Lake	168,D-3
Austin	171,E-4
Baldur	171,E-5
Basswood	171,D-3
Beausejour 2,422	171,G-4
Benito 507	170,C-1
Beulah 430	170,C-4
Binscarth 430	170,C-3
Birch Bay	171,E-2
Birch River	170,C-1
Birds Hill	171,G-4
Birdtail	170,D-3
Birtle 821	171,C-3
Bissett	171,H-2
Boissevain 1,584	170,D-5
Bowsman 483	170,C-1
Brandon 34,901	170,D-4
Brokenhead	171,G-3
Brunkild	171,F-4
Camp Morton	171,G-3
Camper	171,E-2
Camperville	170,D-1
Carberry 1,423	171,E-4
Carman 2,272	171,F-4
Cartwright 361	171,E-5
Channing	168,C-2
Clandeboye	171,G-3
Clarkleigh	171,F-3
Clearwater	171,E-5
Coulter	170,C-5
Cowan	170,D-1
Cranberry Portage 861	168,C-3
Crystal City 513	171,E-5
Culross	171,F-4
Cypress River 255	171,E-4
Darlingford	171,F-5
Dauphin 9,109	170,D-2
Deer Horn	170,D-3
Deerwood	171,F-5
Delau	170,D-2
Deloraine 1,019	170,D-5
Dominion City	171,G-5
Duck Bay	170,D-1
Dufresne	171,G-4
Dufrost	171,G-5
Dugald	171,G-4
Dunlop	169,E-2
Dunrea	170,D-4
Durban	170,C-1
East Selkirk	171,G-4
Elgin	170,D-5
Elkhorn 527	170,C-4
Elma	171,H-4
Elm Creek	171,F-4
Elphinstone	170,D-3
Emerson 756	171,G-5
Erickson 558	170,D-3
Eriksdale	171,F-3
Ethelbert 493	170,D-2
Fairford	171,F-2
Falcon Lake 149	171,H-4
Fannystelle	171,F-4
Fisher Branch	171,F-2
Flin Flon 8,152	168,C-2
Fork River	170,D-2

Name	Page,Grid
Forrest Sta.	170,D-4
Fort Alexander	171,G-3
Foxwarren 178	170,C-3
Franklin 34	171,E-4
Fraserwood	171,G-3
Freshford	168,C-4
Garson 290	171,G-4
Gilbert Plains 847	170,D-2
Gimli 1,659	171,G-3
Gladstone 976	171,E-4
Glenboro 720	171,E-4
Goodlands	170,D-5
Grahamdale	171,F-2
Grand Beach	171,G-3
Grand Rapids 503	169,E-4
Grandview 1,013	170,D-2
Great Falls 267	171,H-3
Greenway	171,E-5
Gretna 510	171,F-5
Griswold	170,D-4
Grosse Isle	171,F-4
Gunton	171,G-3
Hallboro	171,E-4
Hamiota 765	170,D-4
Hargrave	170,C-4
Hartney 484	170,D-4
Haywood	171,F-4
Hazel	171,E-5
High Bluff	171,F-4
Hilbre	171,E-2
Hillside Beach	171,G-3
Hnausa	171,G-3
Hoctor	171,H-4
Holland	171,E-4
Homewood	171,F-4
Horndean	171,F-5
Ile-des-Chenes	171,G-4
Inwood	171,F-3
Jordan	171,F-4
Kane	171,F-5
Kelwood	171,E-3
Kemnay	170,D-4
Kenville	170,C-1
Keyes	171,E-4
Killarney 2,348	171,E-5
Kirkella	170,C-4
Koostatak	171,F-2
La Broquerie	171,G-4
La Riviere	171,E-5
La Rochelle	171,G-5
Lac-du-Bonnet 971	171,G-4
Ladywood	171,G-4
Lake Francis	171,F-3
Lakeland	171,E-3
Lena	170,D-5
Lenswood	170,D-1
Lockport	171,G-4
Lowe Farm	171,F-5
Lower Fort Garry	171,G-4
Lundar	171,F-3
Macdonald 55	171,F-4
MacGregor 789	171,E-4
Mafeking	168,C-5
Magnet	171,E-2
Manitou 883	171,F-5
Marchand	171,G-5
Margaret	170,D-5
Mariapolis	171,E-5
Mather	171,E-5
Matheson Island	171,G-2
Matlock	171,G-3
McArthur Falls	171,H-3
McAuley	170,C-3
McCreary 614	170,E-3
Medora	170,D-5
Melbourne	171,E-4
Melita 1,169	170,C-5

Name	Page,Grid
Middleboro	171,H-5
Miniota 206	170,C-4
Minitonas 605	170,D-1
Minnedosa 2,718	170,D-4
Minto 90	170,D-5
Moose Lake	168,D-4
Moosehorn	171,F-2
Morden 3,886	171,F-5
Morris 1,572	171,F-5
Mulvihill	171,F-3
Myrtle	171,F-5
Napinka 151	170,D-5
Narcisse	171,F-3
Neepawa 3,508	171,E-4
Newdale	170,D-3
Ninette	171,E-5
Norgate	171,E-3
Norway House	169,F-3
Notre-Dame-de-Lourdes 651	171,E-4
Novra	168,D-5
Oak Bluff	171,G-4
Oak Lake 367	170,D-4
Oak Point	171,F-3
Oak River	170,D-4
Oakburn	171,D-3
Oakner	170,D-4
Ochre River	170,D-3
Otterburne	171,G-4
Overflowing River	168,C-4
Pierson	170,C-4
Pilot Mound 730	171,E-5
Pine Dock	171,G-2
Pine Falls 945	171,G-3
Pine River	170,D-2
Piney 122	171,H-5
Pipestone	171,D-4
Pipun	171,E-2
Plum Coulee 477	171,F-5
Pointe-du-Bois	171,H-3
Poplar Point 250	171,F-4
Poplarfield	171,F-3
Portage la Prairie 12,555	171,F-4
Powerview 668	171,G-3
Pratt	171,E-4
Prospector	169,C-3
Pulp River	170,D-2
Rackham	170,D-3
Rapid City 412	170,D-4
Rathwell	171,E-4
Reaburn	171,F-2
Rennie	171,H-4
Renwer	170,D-1
Reston	170,D-4
Reykjavik	171,E-2
Richer	171,G-4
Riding Mountain	171,E-3
Rivers 1,185	170,D-4
Riverton 685	171,G-3
Roblin 1,971	170,C-2
Roland 302	171,F-5
Root Lake	168,C-3
Rorketon	171,E-2
Rosa	171,G-5
Rosebank	171,F-5
Rosenfield	171,F-5
Rossburn 652	170,D-3
Russell 1,524	170,C-3
St-Adolphe	171,G-4
St-Agathe	171,G-4
Ste. Anne 1,174	171,G-4
St. Claude 612	171,F-4
Ste Elizabeth	171,G-5
St. Eustache	171,F-4
St. George	171,G-3
St-Jean Baptiste	171,G-5
St. Joseph	171,F-5
St. Laurent	171,F-3
St. Lazare 476	171,C-3

Name	Page,Grid
St-Malo	171,G-5
St. Martin Sta.	171,E-2
St. Pierre 906	171,G-4
Ste. Rose du Lac 1,038	171,E-3
Sandridge	171,F-3
Sandy Hook	171,G-3
Sandy Lake	170,D-3
Sanford	171,F-4
Scanterbury	171,G-3
Selkirk 9,862	171,G-4
Seven Sisters Falls 159	171,H-4
Shellmouth	170,C-3
Shergrove	171,E-3
Shoal Lake 865	170,D-3
Sidney	171,E-4
Sifton 207	170,D-2
Silver Falls	171,H-3
Simonhouse	168,C-3
Skownan	171,E-1
Smith Hall	171,E-5
Snow Lake 1,585	168,D-2
Somerset 625	171,E-5
Souris 1,712	170,D-4
South Jct.	171,H-5
Sperling	171,F-4
Sprague	171,H-5
Starbuck	171,F-4
Steinbach 5,979	171,G-4
Stonewall 1,826	171,F-4
Stony Mountain	171,F-4
Strathclair	170,D-3
Swan Lake	171,E-5
Swan River 3,742	170,C-1
Teulon 873	171,G-3
Thalberg	171,G-3
The Pas 6,602	168,C-4
Thompson 17,291	169,F-1
Thornhill	171,F-5
Tilston	170,C-5
Tolstoi	171,G-5
Toutes-Aides	171,E-2
Treherne 706	171,E-4
Two Creeks	170,C-4
Tyndall	171,G-4
Underhill	170,D-5
Union Point	171,G-4
Vassar	171,H-5
Victoria Beach 50	171,G-3
Virden 2,936	170,D-4
Vista	170,D-3
Vivian	171,G-4
Wanless 250	168,C-3
Warren Landing	169,F-4
Wasagaming 100	171,D-3
Waskada 257	170,D-5
Wawanesa 487	171,E-4
Westbourne	171,E-4
Westray	168,C-4
Westway	170,D-4
Whitemouth	171,H-4
Whithorn	168,C-4
Whytewood	171,G-3
Windygates	171,F-5
Winkler 3,749	171,F-5
Winnipeg 560,874	171,G-4
Winnipeg Beach 582	171,G-3
Winnipegosis 893	170,D-2
Woodlands	171,F-4
Woodridge	171,G-4
Woodside	171,E-4
Zhoda	171,G-5

MZ-673-J-XC

SEE PAGE 163, G-1
SEE PAGE 163, G-2
SEE PAGE 163, G-3
SEE PAGE 163, G-4
SEE PAGE 163, G-5

SEE PAGE 170, B-1   SEE PAGE 170, C-1   SEE PAGE 170, D-1

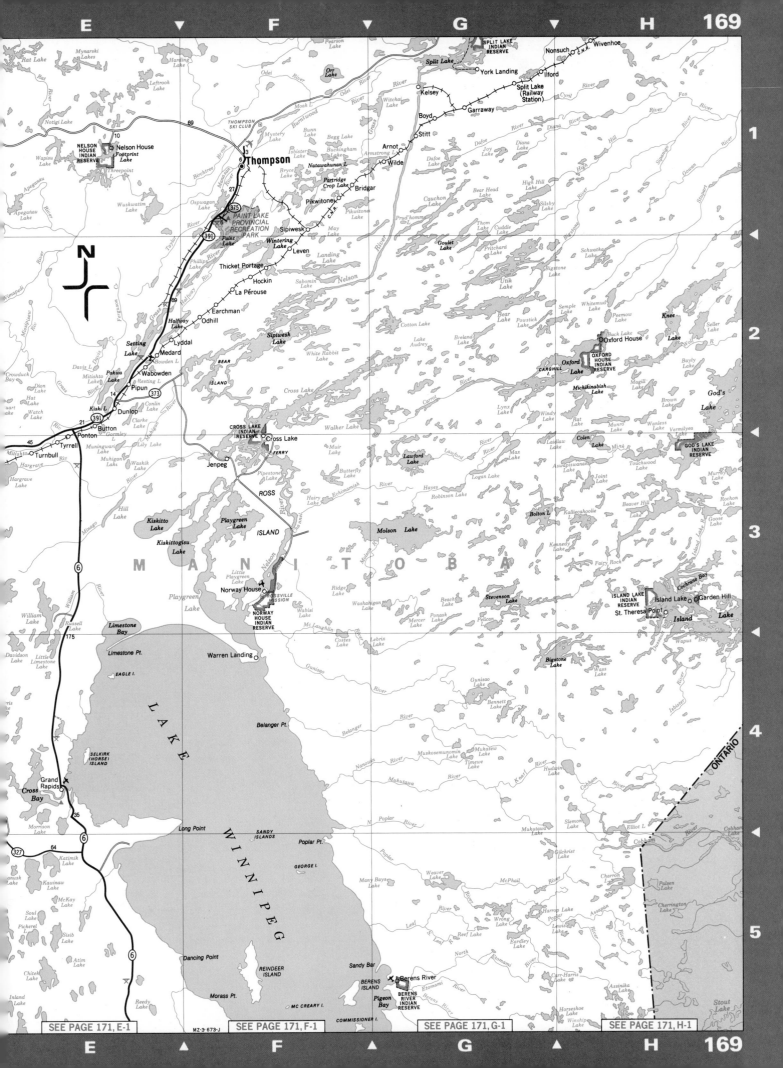

Eternal Niagara, Modern Toronto, Indian Tales and Storybook Charm

Ontario

Canada's commercial heartland, Ontario, is home to almost a third of the nation's people. Yet within scant driving hours of its busy towns and cities, the pace of modern life slows to mark time with the gentler rhythms of a countryside both varied and inviting.

Kenora (175, E-2), in the north, is a popular starting point for sportsmen entering the Lake of the Woods, a superb summer recreation area dotted with more than 14,000 islands. The lake sprawls across parts of Ontario, Manitoba and Minnesota, and was once the exclusive domain of Cree, Ojibwa and Sioux Indians, whose paintings and rock carvings survive at more than 15 sites.

With a stroke of a paddle, canoeists can slip into the past on the 525-kilometre Boundary Waters Fur Trade Canoe Route between Pigeon River and **Thunder Bay (175, H-4)**. Part of the route skirts **Quetico Provincial Park (175, F-4)**, a wilderness of cobalt lakes and 200-year-old pines. In **Ouimet Canyon Provincial Park (176, A-3)**, sheer cliffs plunge 100 metres to a rock-strewn canyon floor where ice lingers into summer.

For seekers of more far-flung wilderness, the Polar Bear Express travels between **Cochrane (177, G-2)** and Moosonee, near the shores of James Bay. Southeast of Cochrane is **Cobalt (177, H-4)**, where the world's richest vein of silver was discovered in 1903 (samples are exhibited in the Northern Ontario Mining Museum).

Manitoulin Island, the world's largest freshwater island, separates Lake Huron and the blue waters of Georgian Bay. The island abounds in Indian legends and storybook charm, fine beaches and picturesque towns. On the mainland, **Killarney Provincial Park (178, D-2)** preserves ancient maple and birch trees, and water so clear that objects can be seen to depths of 20 metres. Ontario's oldest (1893) provincial park, **Algonquin (182, A-2)**, lies to the east. A forested wilderness of 1,500 lakes, it is best explored by canoe or on foot.

On the Bruce Peninsula the famous 133-kilometre Bruce Trail passes ravines, caves, beaches, forests and rare wildflowers. Along its northern stretches, the trail offers splendid views of Georgian Bay, graveyard of ships (many littering the lakebed in Fathom Five Provincial Park). In **Georgian Bay Islands National Park (178, C-3)** is Flowerpot Island and its distinctive pillars of rock—former headlands sawed off by the sea.

Palisaded Sainte-Marie among the Hurons near **Midland (179, F-5)** re-creates the first European settlement (1639) in Ontario. On the grounds are the re-created Church of St. Joseph—the oldest (1642) Christian shrine in Ontario—and the grave of Saint Jean de Brébeuf, martyred near here.

A Mohawk Indian chief (Joseph Brant) gave **Brantford (181, E-3)** its name, and a Scottish inventor (Alexander Graham Bell) brought it world attention as the birthplace of the telephone. The Bell Homestead, where the idea of the telephone was conceived in 1874, displays replicas of early telephones; nearby, visitors can examine one of Canada's first switchboards (1880).

Canada's first Shakespearian Festival was staged at **Stratford (180, D-3)** in 1953 inside a rented tent. Today hundreds of thousands of theatergoers flock here every summer to enjoy performances not only of Shakespeare's works, but also of plays by such dramatists as Molière, Checkov and Ibsen.

Point Pelee, an 18-kilometre sandspit in Lake Erie, is Canada's southernmost mainland point. Two major flyways intersect above **Point Pelee National Park (180, A-5)**, and more than 300 bird species have been spotted here. A long, frost-free growing season fosters unusual plant life: sassafras, swamp rose mallow and cactus.

Museums, parks and historical sites in the Niagara region attract millions of visitors each year—but such works of man are dwarfed by **Niagara Falls (181, G-4)**. The 54-metre-high Horseshoe Falls and the 56-metre-high American Falls have inspired centuries of wonder, and such death-defying theatrics as Blondin's 1859 tightrope crossing. The *Maid of the Mist* cruises to the foot of Horseshoe Falls, and an aero car glides 37 metres above the whirlpools of Niagara Gorge.

The scenic Niagara Parkway along the Niagara River leads to **Niagara-on-the-Lake (181, G-3)**, site of the Shaw Festival, an internationally acclaimed theater program based largely on the works of George Bernard Shaw. Broad lawns and lovingly restored buildings make this 19th-century town one of Canada's most charming. On a clear day shoreline vantage points provide fine views of Toronto's CN Tower (the world's tallest free-standing structure), rising 553 metres above the blue of Lake Ontario.

Almost one in three Ontarians lives in **Toronto (181, F-3)**, appropriately named after a Huron word for "a place of meeting." Toronto's wealth and dynamism is reflected in its soaring architecture and the futuristic, curved, twin towers of its city hall.

In less than a century Toronto has evolved from "Muddy York" to one of the most civilized cities in North America, and its attractions are many. An outstanding collection of Canadian and European paintings and sculptures by Picasso and Henry Moore is displayed in the Art Gallery of Ontario. The Royal Ontario Museum, Canada's largest museum, houses some five million artifacts and specimens, including one of the finest presentations of Chinese art in the Western world. In the stone and rough-hewn galleries of the McMichael Canadian Collection in suburban **Kleinburg (181, F-2)** hang many of the finest artworks by the Group of Seven.

Strange scents and exotic languages fill Toronto's Kensington Market, a European-style street market between Dundas and College streets. A quieter retreat is Toronto Island Park and its beaches, lagoons and wildlife preserve. Ontario Place, a popular

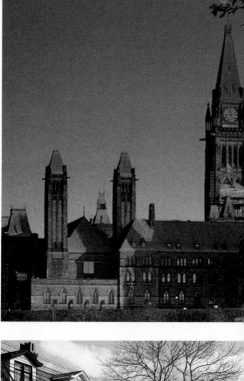

*Toronto's Markham Village (*above)*, alive with shops and galleries, retains a turn-of-the-century architectural flavor. A skein of fiberglass geese (*right) *soars over shoppers in the Eaton Centre.*

recreation complex on three man-made islands, beckons with concerts, a children's village and a six-story movie screen. At the Ontario Science Centre a laser beam cuts through bricks, computers play tic-tac-toe and a demonstration of static electricity leaves visitors' hair literally standing on end. More than 3,500 animals roam the paddocks of Metro Toronto Zoo, which are landscaped to simulate natural habitats.

At Fort York, built by the British in 1814-1816, scarlet-jacketed militia march to the cadence of fife and drum. Casa Loma, North America's largest castle, is a lavish monument to Bay Street financier Sir Henry Pellatt and the affluent early 1900s. Suburban North York preserves Ontario's past at Black Creek Pioneer Village, where 19th-century houses, farm buildings and shops have been relocated from surrounding communities.

Kingston (182, F-5) was, in turn, an Indian village, a French fortress, a British stronghold and—briefly—Canada's capital. Red-coated guards execute a smart Changing of the Guard at Old Fort Henry (1832–36), once Canada's mightiest fortress. Nearby Bellevue House, an 1840 Tuscan-style villa furnished in period style, was the home of Prime Minister Sir John A. Macdonald.

Boats from Kingston—including the paddle-wheeler *Island Queen*—cruise through

Flower-lined parks and drives complement the quiet dignity of Ottawa's Parliament Hill (above).

More than three million blossoming tulips (above) transform the nation's capital into a riot of Maytime color.

Light unfolds eerily in Algonquin Provincial Park—a realm of lakes, streams, spruce bogs, forests and magnificent solitude.

Kingston's Old Fort Henry was raised "as a bulwark against American aggression." Cannon (above) still blast salutes.

the enchanting Thousand Islands (there are actually more than 1,800 islands), passing the fairy-tale spires of Boldt Castle.

Echoes of Old Canada reverberate in Upper Canada Village, a re-created pre-Confederation era village near **Morrisburg (183, F-4)**. Costumed staff tread corduroy streets and demonstrate pioneer skills at a sawmill, a smithy and 32 other historical buildings.

Ottawa (183, E-2), the nation's capital, lies north. In a blaze of scarlet, the Changing of the Guard lends pomp to Parliament Hill, where three imposing Gothic buildings and the 89-metre Peace Tower dominate. In summer the Rideau Canal becomes a magnet for strollers; winter transforms the canal into the world's largest skating rink. On the west bank, the three theaters of the National Arts Centre host entertainment ranging from

Strauss to Shakespeare. The National Gallery, Canada's most extensive art collection, contains Canadian and foreign works, including masterpieces by Rubens, Rembrandt and Cézanne. The evolution of man and the culture of Canada are explored through artifacts and dioramas at the National Museum of Man. In the adjoining National Museum of Natural Science, exhibits of minerals, plants and animals trace the geological and natural history of the earth.

Visitors to Ottawa can also tour several stately government residences, including Rideau Hall (1838), the Governor General's home; Earnscliffe, Sir John A. Macdonald's home; and Laurier House (1878), filled with the belongings of Sir Wilfrid Laurier and William Lyon Mackenzie King, the prime ministers who lived there.

173

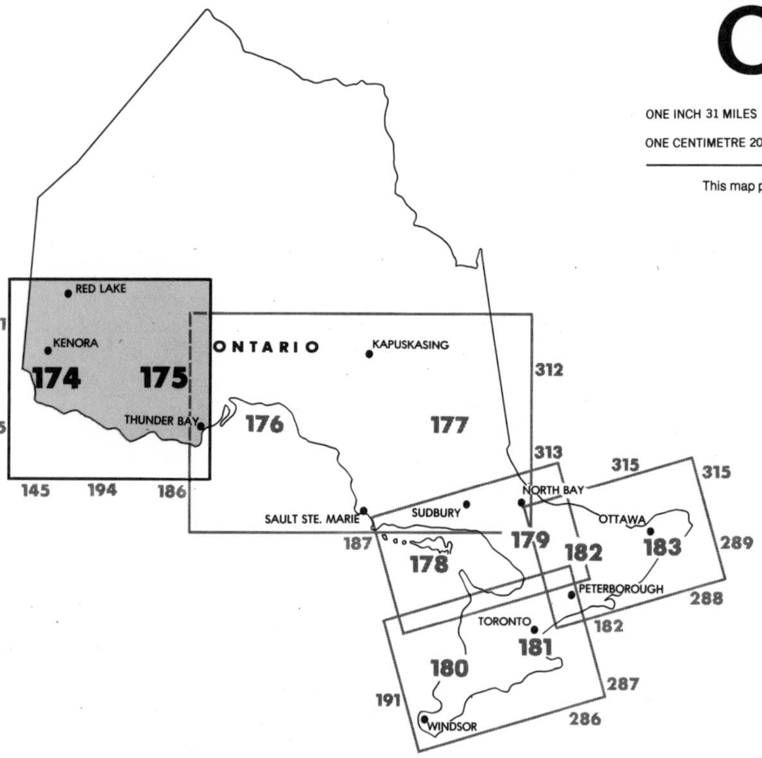

RED LAKE
KENORA
174
175
THUNDER BAY
ONTARIO
KAPUSKASING
176
177
171
145
194
186
312
313
315
SAULT STE. MARIE
SUDBURY
NORTH BAY
OTTAWA
187
178
179
182
183
289
288
PETERBOROUGH
TORONTO
181
180
191
WINDSOR
286
287

Ontario

SCALE IN MILES AND KILOMETRES
ONE INCH 31 MILES 0 5 10 20 30 40
ONE CENTIMETRE 20 KILOMETRES 0 5 10 20 30 40 64

This map prepared specially for DRIVE NORTH AMERICA.
©THE H.M. GOUSHĀ COMPANY

PARTIAL LIST OF

CITIES AND TOWNS

1976 Census

•County Seats

Pop.(1976) 8,264,465

Actinolite 80 ... 182,C-4
Acton ... 181,E-3
Addison 98 ... 183,E-4
Agawa Bay 20 ... 176,D-4
Ahmic Harbour 61 ... 179,F-3
Ailsa Craig 701 ... 180,C-3
Ajax 20,774 ... 181,G-2
Alexandria 3,498 ... 183,G-3
Alfred 1,105 ... 183,G-2
Allanburg ... 181,G-4
Allanwater 35 ... 175,H-2
Allenford 250 ... 178,D-5
Alliston 4,155 ... 181,F-2
Almonte 3,693 ... 183,E-3
Alvinston 672 ... 180,C-4
Amberley ... 180,C-2
Amherstburg 5,566 ... 180,A-5
Ardbeg 38 ... 179,F-3
Ardtrea 31 ... 179,G-5
Arkona 458 ... 180,C-3
Armstrong 1,444 ... 176,A-1
Arnprior 6,111 ... 182,D-2
Arnstein 90 ... 179,F-2
Aroland ... 176,B-1
Arthur 1,660 ... 181,E-2
Ashburn ... 181,G-2
Athens 1,054 ... 183,E-4
Atherley 367 ... 179,G-5
Atikokan 5,803 ... 175,G-3
Aurora 14,249 ... 181,F-2
Aylmer 5,125 ... 180,D-4
Ayr 1,331 ... 181,E-3
Bala 536 ... 179,F-4
Balmertown 1,253 ... 175,E-1
Bancroft 2,332 ... 182,B-3
Bankfield ... 176,B-2
Bar River 42 ... 177,E-5
Barrie• 34,389 ... 181,F-1
Barriefield 220 ... 182,D-5
Barry's Bay 1,266 ... 182,C-2
Barwick 60 ... 175,E-3
Batchawana Bay 141 ... 175,D-5
Bath 762 ... 182,D-5
Baysville 240 ... 179,G-4
Beamsville ... 181,F-4
Bear Lake ... 179,F-3
Beardmore 659 ... 176,B-2
Bearverton 1,737 ... 181,G-1
Beaumaris 47 ... 179,F-4
Beeton 1,604 ... 181,F-2
Belle River 3,254 ... 180,A-5
Belleville• 35,311 ... 182,C-5
Bigwood ... 179,E-2
Birkendale ... 179,G-4
Bismark 64 ... 181,F-4
Black Hawk ... 175,E-3
Blackstock ... 181,G-2
Blenheim 3,804 ... 180,B-5
Blind River 3,142 ... 178,B-1
Bloomfield 756 ... 182.C-5
Blythe 866 ... 180,C-2
Bobcaygeon 1,562 ... 181,H-1
Bolton ... 181,F-2
Bond Head 562 ... 181,F-2
Bothwell 899 ... 180,C-4
Bowmanville ... 181,G-2
Bracebridge• 8,428 ... 179,G-4
Bradford 5,080 ... 181,F-2
Braeside 538 ... 182,D-2
Brampton 103,459 ... 181,F-2
Brantford 66,950 ... 181,E-3
Brechin 255 ... 179,G-5
Brewers Mills ... 182,D-4
Bright 324 ... 180,D-3
Brighton 3,199 ... 182,B-5
Britt 468 ... 179,E-2
Brockville• 19,903 ... 183,E-4
Brooklin ... 181,G-2
Brownsville 310 ... 180,D-4
Bruce Lake ... 175,E-1
Bruce Mines 517 ... 178,A-1
Brucedale 36 ... 181,E-2
Brussels 1,043 ... 180,D-2
Burgessville 289 ... 180,D-4
Burk's Falls 871 ... 179,G-3
Burlington 104,314 ... 181,F-3
Burriss ... 175,E-3
Cache Bay 691 ... 179,F-1
Calabogie 289 ... 182,D-3
Caledon 22,434 ... 181,F-2
Caledonia 1,312 ... 181,E-4
Callander 1,058 ... 179,G-2
Camilla 29 ... 181,E-2
Campbellford 3,487 ... 182,B-4
Campbellville ... 181,E-3
Canboro ... 181,F-4
Cane ... 177,H-4
Cannington 1,419 ... 181,G-1
Capreol 4,089 ... 177,G-5
Caramat 382 ... 176,C-2
Cardiff 496 ... 183,B-3
Cardinal 1,867 ... 183,F-4
Carleton Pl 5,256 ... 183,E-3
Carlsruhe 90 ... 181,D-1
Carp 691 ... 183,E-3
Cartier 673 ... 177,G-5
Casselman 1,422 ... 183,F-3
Castleton 326 ... 182,B-5
Cataraqui ... 182,D-5
Cathcart 133 ... 181,E-4
Cavers 1 ... 176,B-3
Cayuga• ... 181,F-4
Cecebe 22 ... 179,G-3
Cedar Springs 281 ... 180,B-5
Centralia ... 180,C-3
Chalk River 1,095 ... 182,C-1
Chambers Corners 62 ... 181,F-4
Chapleau 3,294 ... 177,E-4
Chapman 392 ... 182,C-4
Charleston 130 ... 183,E-4
Charlton 189 ... 177,H-4
Chatham• 38,685 ... 180,B-5
Chatsworth 394 ... 178,D-5
Chesley 1,839 ... 180,D-1
Chesterville 1,324 ... 183,F-3
Chippawa ... 181,G-4
Chippawa Hill ... 178,D-5
City View ... 183,E-3
Clandeboye 152 ... 180,C-3
Clarksburg 481 ... 179,E-5
Clifford 641 ... 181,D-2
Clinton 3,151 ... 180,C-2
Cloyne 138 ... 182,C-4
Cobalt 2,056 ... 177,H-4
Cobden 1,025 ... 182,D-2
Coboconk 377 ... 179,G-5
Cobourg• 11,421 ... 182,B-5
Cochenour 624 ... 175,E-1
Cochrane• 4,974 ... 177,G-2
Colborne 1,724 ... 182,B-5
Colchester 930 ... 180,A-5
Cold Springs 92 ... 182,B-5
Coldwater 803 ... 179,F-5
Collingwood 11,114 ... 179,E-5
Collins 102 ... 175,H-2
Commanda 27 ... 179,G-2
Coniston ... 177,G-5
Consecon 363 ... 182,C-5
Coopers Falls 30 ... 179,G-5
Copetown 147 ... 181,E-3
Coppell 77 ... 177,E-2
Copper Cliff ... 177,G-5
Corbeil 79 ... 179,G-2
Corbetton 90 ... 181,E-2
Cormac 51 ... 182,C-2
Cornwall• 46,121 ... 183,G-3
Courtland 602 ... 180,D-4
Courtright ... 180,B-4
Craigleith 131 ... 179,E-5
Crediton 439 ... 180,C-3
Creemore 1,089 ... 181,E-1
Cromarty 44 ... 180,C-3
Crosby 27 ... 182,D-4
Crosshill 69 ... 180,D-3
Crow Lake 46 ... 182,D-4
Crysler 490 ... 183,F-3
Crystal Beach 106 ... 181,G-4
Crystal Falls 96 ... 179,F-1
Cumberland 550 ... 183,F-2
Cumberland Beach 686 ... 179,G-5
Curve Lake ... 182,A-4
Dacre 79 ... 182,D-2
Dalrymple 55 ... 179,G-5
Dane 59 ... 177,H-4
Deep River 5,565 ... 182,C-1
Delhi 3,929 ... 181,E-4
Deloro 238 ... 182,B-4
Desbarats 252 ... 177,E-5
Deseronto 1,893 ... 182,C-5
Devlin 93 ... 175,E-3
Dinorwic 68 ... 175,F-2
Dorion ... 176,A-3
Dornoch ... 180,D-1
Dorset ... 179,G-4
Drayton 801 ... 181,E-2
Dresden 2,484 ... 180,B-4
Dryden 6,799 ... 175,F-2
Dunchurch 150 ... 179,F-3
Dundalk 1,165 ... 181,E-1
Dundas 19,179 ... 181,E-3
Dunnville 11,642 ... 181,F-4
Dunrobin 50 ... 183,E-2
Duntroon 109 ... 181,E-1
Durham ... 180,D-1
Dutton 1,036 ... 180,C-4
Dwight 96 ... 179,G-4
Dyment 95 ... 175,F-2
Eagle 132 ... 180,C-4
Eagle River 146 ... 175,E-2
Ear Falls 1,717 ... 175,F-1
Earlton 1,008 ... 177,H-4
East York 106,950 ... 181,F-2
Echo Bay 745 ... 177,E-5
Eganville 1,328 ... 182,C-2
Elgin 521 ... 183,E-4
Elginfield 115 ... 180,C-3
Elk Lake 564 ... 177,G-4
Elliot Lake 8,849 ... 177,F-5
Elma 59 ... 183,F-3
Elmira 7,034 ... 181,E-3
Elmvale 1,176 ... 179,F-5
Elmwood 423 ... 180,D-1
Elora 2,589 ... 181,E-2
Embro 800 ... 180,D-3
Emo 792 ... 175,E-3
Emsdale 110 ... 179,G-3
Englehart 1,767 ... 177,H-4
English River 20 ... 175,G-3
Erie Beach 254 ... 180,B-5
Erieau 453 ... 180,B-5
Erin 2,007 ... 181,E-2
Espanola 5,926 ... 178,D-1
Essex 5,577 ... 180,A-5
Estaire 212 ... 179,E-1
Etobicoke 297,109 ... 181,F-2
Exeter 3,494 ... 180,C-3
Fairground 88 ... 180,D-4
Fairholme ... 179,F-3
Fauquier 620 ... 177,F-2
Fenelon Falls 1,637 ... 181,G-1
Fergus 6,001 ... 181,E-2
Feronia ... 179,G-2
Field 568 ... 177,H-5
Finch 407 ... 183,F-3
Flesherton 568 ... 181,E-1
Foleyet 538 ... 177,F-3
Fonthill ... 181,F-4
Footes Bay 48 ... 179,F-4
Forest 2,557 ... 180,B-3
Forest Mills ... 182,C-4
Fort Erie 24,031 ... 181,G-4
Fort Frances• 9,325 ... 175,E-3
Fowlers Corners ... 182,A-4
Foxboro ... 182,C-5
Frankford 1,851 ... 182,B-5
Franz 39 ... 176,D-3
Fryatt ... 177,E-2
Gads Hill 109 ... 180,D-3
Gananoque 5,103 ... 183,E-5
Gasline ... 181,G-4
Georgetown ... 181,F-3
Geraldton 3,127 ... 176,B-2
Gesto 100 ... 180,A-5
Glen Alda ... 182,B-3
Glen Orchard 52 ... 179,F-4
Glencairn 110 ... 181,F-1
Glencoe 1,818 ... 180,C-4
Goderich• 7,385 ... 180,C-2
Gogama 702 ... 177,F-4
Golden Lake 229 ... 182,C-2
Golden Valley 96 ... 179,F-2
Gooderham 182 ... 182,A-3
Gordon Bay ... 179,F-4
Gore Bay• 767 ... 178,B-2
Goulais 96 ... 176,D-5
Grafton 402 ... 182,B-5
Graham 60 ... 175,G-3
Grand Bend 750 ... 180,C-3
Grand Valley 1,096 ... 181,E-2
Grassmere ... 179,G-3
Gravenhurst 7,986 ... 179,G-4
Greenbush 61 ... 183,E-4
Griffith 119 ... 182,C-3
Grimsby 15,567 ... 181,F-3
Guelph• 67,538 ... 181,E-3
Hagar 1,079 ... 177,G-5
Hagarsville ... 181,E-4
Haileybury• 4,939 ... 177,H-4
Hallebourg 191 ... 177,E-2
Hamilton• 312,003 ... 181,F-3
Hanover 5,691 ... 180,D-1
Harris Hill ... 174,D-3
Harriston 1,872 ... 180,D-2
Harrow 1,936 ... 180,A-5
Harrowsmith 533 ... 183,D-4
Harty 251 ... 177,F-2
Hastings 990 ... 182,B-4
Havelock 1,280 ... 182,B-4
Hawk Junction 363 ... 176,D-4
Hawkesbury 9,789 ... 183,G-2
Head Lake 2 ... 179,G-5
Hearst 5,195 ... 177,E-2
Heaslip 27 ... 177,H-4
Hemlo ... 176,C-3
Henderson 48 ... 182,C-4
Hensall 993 ... 180,C-3
Hepworth 377 ... 178,D-5
Hespeler ... 181,E-3
Highgate 418 ... 180,C-4
Hillsdale 274 ... 179,F-5
Hillside 63 ... 179,G-3
Hilton 126 ... 182,B-1
Hilton Beach 222 ... 178,A-1
Holmesville 34 ... 180,C-2
Hornepayne 1,694 ... 176,D-2
Hudson 565 ... 175,F-2
Humphrey ... 179,F-4
Huntsville 11,123 ... 179,G-4
Hurkett 35 ... 176,A-3
Hyndfold 101 ... 183,D-2
Ida 54 ... 181,H-2
Ingersoll 8,198 ... 180,D-4
Ingleside 1,106 ... 183,F-3
Inkerman 107 ... 183,F-3
Innerkip 655 ... 180,D-3
Inverary 252 ... 183,D-4
Inwood 243 ... 180,B-4
Iona 120 ... 180,C-4
Iron Bridge 790 ... 178,B-1
Irondale ... 182,A-3
Iroquois 1,278 ... 183,F-4
Iroquis Falls 6,887 ... 177,G-3
Island Lake 160 ... 177,E-5
Ivanhoe 45 ... 182,C-4
Janetville 296 ... 181,G-2
Jarvis ... 181,E-4
Jasper 374 ... 183,E-4
Jellicoe 163 ... 176,B-2
Johnstown 560 ... 183,F-4
Jones Falls 44 ... 182,D-4
Joyceville ... 182,D-4
Kagawong 141 ... 178,C-2
Kakabeka Falls 367 ... 175,H-4
Kaladar 262 ... 183,C-4
Kapuskasing 12,676 ... 177,F-2
Kashabowie 71 ... 175,G-3
Kawene ... 175,G-3
Kearney 285 ... 179,G-3
Keene 275 ... 182,B-5
Keewatin 1,954 ... 174,D-2
Kemptville 2,544 ... 183,E-3
Kenabeck 34 ... 177,H-4
Kenilworth 105 ... 181,E-2
Kenora• 10,565 ... 175,E-2
Killaloe Sta. 699 ... 182,C-2
Killarney 445 ... 178,D-2
Kincardine 4,182 ... 180,C-1
King Kirkland 355 ... 177,H-3
Kingston• 56,032 ... 182,D-5
Kingsville 4,692 ... 180,A-5
Kinmount 270 ... 179,H-5
Kirkfield 200 ... 179,G-5
Kirkland Lake 13,567 ... 177,H-3
Kitchener• • 131,870 ... 181,E-3
Lac Ste. Therese ... 177,E-2
Lafontaine 230 ... 179,F-5
Lakefield 2,240 ... 182,B-4
Lanark 803 ... 182,D-3
Lancaster 540 ... 183,G-3
Larder Lake 1,238 ... 177,H-3
Latchford 457 ... 177,H-4
Latta ... 182,C-5
Lavigne ... 179,F-1
Leamington 11,169 ... 180,A-5
Lefroy 534 ... 181,F-1
Lepage ... 177,F-2
Limoges 616 ... 183,F-3
Lindsay• 13,062 ... 181,G-1
Lions' Head 500 ... 178,D-4
Listowel 5,126 ... 180,D-2
Little Current 1,476 ... 178,C-2
Lively ... 177,G-5
London• 240,392 ... 180,D-4
Longlac 1,934 ... 176,C-2
L'Orignal• 1,380 ... 183,G-2
Loring 183 ... 179,F-2
Lowther ... 177,E-2
Lucan 1,377 ... 180,C-3
Lucknow 1,127 ... 180,C-2
Lutterworth 488 ... 179,H-4
Mackey ... 182,B-1
MacTier 690 ... 179,F-4
Madoc 1,538 ... 182,C-4
Madsen 391 ... 175,E-1
Maidstone 59 ... 180,A-5
Mallorytown 290 ... 183,E-4
Manchester 70 ... 181,G-2
Manitouwadge 3,507 ... 176,C-2
Manitowaning 378 ... 178,C-2
Manotick Station 88 ... 183,E-3
Maple ... 181,F-2
Maple Island 11 ... 179,F-3
Maple Leaf 92 ... 182,B-3
Mar ... 178,D-4
Marathon 2,258 ... 176,C-3
Markdale 1,361 ... 181,E-1
Markham 56,206 ... 181,G-2
Markstay 521 ... 177,G-5
Marmora 1,326 ... 182,B-4
Marten River 25 ... 177,H-5
Marysville 33 ... 180,B-4
Massey 1,345 ... 178,C-1
Matachewan 613 ... 177,G-4
Matheson 703 ... 177,G-3
Mattawa ... 179,H-2
Mattice 816 ... 177,E-2
Maxville 852 ... 183,G-3
Maynooth 281 ... 182,B-3
McArthur's Mills 51 ... 182,C-3
McGregor 810 ... 180,A-5
McIntosh ... 175,E-2
McKellar 209 ... 179,F-3
McKerrow 323 ... 178,D-1
Meaford 4,319 ... 179,E-5
Merlin 722 ... 180,B-5
Merrickville 932 ... 183,E-3
Michipicoten Harbour 82 ... 176,D-4
Michipicoten River 190 ... 176,D-4
Middleville 110 ... 183,D-3
Midland 11,568 ... 179,F-5
Mildmay 990 ... 180,D-2
Milford Bay 320 ... 179,F-4
Millbrook 898 ... 182,A-5
Milton• 20,756 ... 181,F-3
Milverton 1,393 ... 180,D-3
Mindemoya 407 ... 178,C-2
Mine Centre 88 ... 175,F-3
Miners Bay ... 179,G-5
Minett 50 ... 179,F-4
Missanabie 242 ... 177,E-3
Mississauga 250,017 ... 181,F-3
Mitchell 2,742 ... 180,D-3
Moffat 379 ... 181,E-3
Monkton 550 ... 180,D-2
Montreal River Harbour 46 ... 176,D-4
Moonbeam 925 ... 177,F-2
Morpeth 305 ... 180,C-5
Morrisburg 2,188 ... 183,F-4
Morton 76 ... 183,E-4
Moscow 71 ... 182,D-4
Mt. Albert 909 ... 181,G-2
Mt. Brydges 1,573 ... 180,C-4
Mt. Elgin 289 ... 180,D-4
Mt. Forest 3,376 ... 180,D-2
Mt. Hope 687 ... 181,F-3
Mt. Julian ... 182,B-4
Muirkirk 48 ... 180,C-4
Myers Cave ... 183,C-3
Myrtle ... 181,G-2
Nairn 457 ... 178,D-1
Nairn 491 ... 180,C-3
Nakina 602 ... 176,C-1
Napanee• 4,844 ... 182,C-5
Naughton ... 178,D-1
Nellie Lake ... 177,G-3
Nestleton Station 137 ... 181,G-2
Nestor Falls ... 175,E-3
Neustadt 543 ... 180,D-2
New Dundee 741 ... 181,E-3
New Glasgow 49 ... 180,C-4
New Hamburg 3,628 ... 180,D-3
New Liskeard 5,601 ... 177,H-4
New Lowell 257 ... 181,F-1
New Sarum ... 180,D-4
Newboro 259 ... 182,D-4
Newburgh 628 ... 182,D-5
Newbury 388 ... 180,C-4
Newcastle 31,928 ... 181,H-2
Newmarket 24,795 ... 181,F-2
Niagara Falls 69,423 ... 181,G-4
Niagara on-the-Lake 12,485 ... 181,G-3
Nipigon 2,224 ... 176,B-3
Nipissing 1,195 ... 179,G-2
Nobel 291 ... 179,F-3
Noelville 665 ... 179,E-2
Norham 97 ... 182,B-5
Norland 203 ... 179,G-5
Normandale 138 ... 181,E-4
North Bay• 51,639 ... 179,G-2
North Bruce 53 ... 181,D-1
North Gower 625 ... 183,E-3
North Lancaster 174 ... 183,G-3
North York 558,398 ... 181,F-2
Norwich 1,891 ... 180,D-4
Norwood 1,243 ... 182,B-4
Novar 176 ... 179,G-3
Oak Lake 367 ... 182,B-4
Oakville 68,950 ... 181,F-3
Oakwood 382 ... 181,G-1
Oba 60 ... 177,E-2
Odessa 877 ... 182,D-5
Ohsweken ... 181,E-4
Oil Springs 618 ... 180,B-4
Oliphant 37 ... 178,D-4
Omemee 790 ... 181,H-1
Onondaga 1,345 ... 181,E-4
Opasatika 798 ... 177,E-2
Ophir ... 177,E-5
Orangeville• 12,021 ... 181,E-2
Orient Bay 13 ... 176,B-2
Orillia 24,412 ... 179,G-5
Orr Lake 249 ... 179,F-5
Orton 109 ... 181,E-2
Oshawa 107,023 ... 181,G-2
Ospringe 54 ... 181,E-2
Ottawa• 304,462 ... 183,E-2
Owen Sound• 19,525 ... 179,D-5
Oxdrift ... 175,F-2
Oxtongue Lake 42 ... 179,G-3
Paincourt 403 ... 180,B-5
Paisley 1,033 ... 180,D-1
Pakesley ... 179,E-2
Palmerston 1,961 ... 180,D-2
Paris 6,713 ... 181,E-3
Parkhill 1,300 ... 180,C-3
Parry Sound• 5,501 ... 179,F-3
Parthia ... 177,E-2
Pass Lake ... 176,A-3
Pearceley 16 ... 179,G-3
Pearl ... 176,A-3
Pembroke• 14,927 ... 182,C-2
Penetanguishene 5,460 ... 179,F-5
Perkinsfield 342 ... 179,F-5
Perth• 5,675 ... 183,E-3
Perrault Falls ... 175,F-1
Petawawa 5,815 ... 182,C-1
Peterborough• 59,683 ... 182,A-4
Petrolia 4,393 ... 180,B-4
Pickering 27,879 ... 181,G-2
Picton• 4,649 ... 182,C-5
Pinewood 92 ... 175,E-3
Plainfield 90 ... 182,C-5
Pt. Edward 2,524 ... 180,B-3
Pointe au Baril Station 197 ... 179,E-3
Poole 37 ... 180,D-3
Poplar Dale 29 ... 177,E-5
Porquis Junction ... 177,G-3
Port Bruce 146 ... 180,D-4
Port Burwell 726 ... 180,D-4
Port Carling 628 ... 179,F-4
Port Cármen 14 ... 179,F-3
Port Colborne 20,536 ... 181,F-4
Port Dover ... 181,E-4
Port Elgin 492 ... 178,D-5
Port Franks 170 ... 180,C-3
Port Hope 9,788 ... 182,A-5
Port Loring 162 ... 179,F-2
Port McNicoll 1,522 ... 179,F-5
Port Perry 3,917 ... 181,G-2
Port Rowan 806 ... 181,E-4
Port Severn 171 ... 179,F-4
Port Stanley 1,707 ... 180,D-4
Port Sydeny ... 179,G-4
Portland ... 183,E-4
Potter ... 177,G-3
Powassan 1,238 ... 179,G-2
Prescott 4,975 ... 183,F-4
Primrose 27 ... 181,E-2
Prospect 40 ... 183,E-3
Putnam 77 ... 180,D-4
Quadeville 144 ... 182,C-3
Queensborough 64 ... 182,C-4
Queenston ... 181,G-4
Queensville 327 ... 181,F-2
Rainy River 1,092 ... 174,D-3
Raith ... 175,H-3
Ramore ... 177,G-3
Ranger Lake ... 177,E-5
Reaboro 71 ... 181,H-1
Red Lake 2,256 ... 175,E-1
Red Rock 1,244 ... 176,B-3
Redditt ... 175,E-2
Reesor ... 177,E-2
Renfrew 8,617 ... 182,D-2
Richmond 2,667 ... 183,E-3
Richmond Hill 34,716 ... 181,F-2
Ridgetown 3,100 ... 180,B-5
Ripley 577 ... 180,C-1
River Valley 239 ... 177,H-5
Roblin 84 ... 182,C-4
Rockland 3,930 ... 183,F-2
Rockwood 959 ... 181,E-3
Rocky Bay ... 176,B-2
Rodney 983 ... 180,C-4
Roslin 161 ... 182,C-4
Rosseau 260 ... 179,F-4
Rossport 96 ... 176,B-3
Rothsay 78 ... 181,E-2
Round Lake Centre ... 182,C-2
Russeldale 33 ... 180,D-3
Rutherglen 85 ... 179,G-2
Ruthven 384 ... 180,A-5
Rutter 32 ... 179,E-2
St. Agatha 517 ... 181,E-3
St. Catharines• 123,351 ... 181,F-4
St. Charles 347 ... 179,E-1
St. Clair Beach 1,953 ... 180,A-5
St-Eugene 493 ... 183,G-2
St. Helen 41 ... 180,C-2
St. Jacobs 852 ... 181,E-3
St. Joseph 983 ... 180,C-3
St. Mary's 4,843 ... 180,D-3
St. Ola 40 ... 182,C-3
St. Thomas• 27,206 ... 180,D-4
Salford 153 ... 180,D-4
Sand Lake ... 179,G-3
Sapawe 34 ... 175,G-3
Sarnia• 55,576 ... 180,B-3
Sault Ste. Marie• 81,048 ... 176,D-5
Savanne ... 175,H-3
Scarborough 387,149 ... 181,G-2
Schreiber 1,982 ... 176,B-3
Scotia 26 ... 179,G-3
Seaforth 2,084 ... 180,C-2
Searchmont 390 ... 177,E-5
Sebright 38 ... 179,G-5
Seelys Bay 452 ... 183,E-4
Selby 131 ... 182,C-5
Selwyn ... 182,A-4
Shabaqua Corners ... 175,H-3
Shallow Lake 411 ... 178,D-5
Shanly 33 ... 183,F-4
Shannonville 299 ... 182,C-5
Sharbot Lake 296 ... 183,D-4
Sharon 979 ... 181,F-2
Shebandowan ... 175,H-3
hedden 346 ... 180,C-4
Sheguiandah 57 ... 178,C-2
Shelburne 2,928 ... 181,E-2
Shillington 56 ... 177,G-3
Shrewsbury 97 ... 180,B-5
Simcoe• 14,189 ... 181,E-4
Singhampton 238 ... 181,E-1
Sioux Lookout 3,108 ... 175,F-2
Sioux Narrows 5 ... 175,E-2
Sistonens Corners ... 175,H-4
Smiths Falls 9,279 ... 183,E-3
Smooth Rock Falls 2,446 ... 177,F-2
Sombra 4,277 ... 180,B-4
South Baymoor 74 ... 178,C-3
South River 1,094 ... 179,G-3
South Woodslee 241 ... 180,A-5
Southampton 2,734 ... 178,D-5
Southwold 4,562 ... 180,C-4
Sowerby 50 ... 178,A-1
Spanish 1,082 ... 178,C-1
Spragge 97 ... 178,B-1
Springfield 522 ... 180,D-4
Springford 279 ... 180,D-4
Sprucedale 214 ... 179,G-3
Staples 117 ... 180,A-5
Starratt-Olsen 41 ... 175,E-1
Stayner 2,454 ... 181,F-1
Stella 83 ... 182,D-5
Stirling 1,571 ... 182,C-4
Stittsville 2,703 ... 183,E-3
Stokes Bay 123 ... 178,D-4
Stoney Creek 30,294 ... 181,F-3
Stouffville, ... 181,G-2
Stratford• 25,657 ... 180,D-3
Strathroy 7,769 ... 180,C-4
Stratton 100 ... 175,E-3
Streetsville ... 181,F-3
Strickland ... 177,F-2
Sturgeon Falls 6,400 ... 179,F-1
Sudbury• 97,604 ... 177,G-5
Sultan 274 ... 177,F-4
Summerstown 175 ... 183,G-3
Sunridge 692 ... 179,G-3
Sutton 3,655 ... 181,G-1
Tara 717 ... 178,D-5
Tavistock 1,783 ... 180,D-3
Tecumseh 5,326 ... 180,A-5
Teeswater 988 ... 180,D-2
Terrace Bay 2,088 ... 176,B-3
Teviotdale 25 ... 180,D-2
Thamesville 1,003 ... 180,B-4
Thedford 715 ... 180,C-3
Thessalon 1,824 ... 178,A-1
Thornbury 1,326 ... 179,E-5
Thornloe 151 ... 177,H-4
Thorold 14,944 ... 181,G-4
Thunder Bay 111,476 ... 176,A-3
Tichborne 168 ... 183,D-4
Tilbury 4,248 ... 180,B-5
Tillsonburg 9,404 ... 180,D-4
Timmins 44,747 ... 177,G-3
Tiverton 825 ... 180,C-1
Tobermory 317 ... 178,C-3
Toronto• 633,318 ... 181,F-3
Torrance 210 ... 179,F-4
Tottenham 2,747 ... 181,F-2
Treadwell 47 ... 183,F-2
Trent River 201 ... 182,B-4
Trenton 15,465 ... 182,B-5
Trout Creek 623 ... 179,G-2
Troy 145 ... 181,E-3
Turkey Point 369 ... 181,E-4
Tweed 1,654 ... 182,C-4
Tycronnel 40 ... 180,C-4
Udora 310 ... 181,G-1
Ufford ... 179,G-4
Ullswater ... 179,F-4
Union 462 ... 180,D-4
Union Creek ... 179,H-5
Uno Park ... 177,H-4
Uphill 26 ... 179,G-5
Upsala ... 175,G-3
Uxbridge 4,354 ... 181,G-2
Val Rita 728 ... 177,F-2
Vanier 19,812 ... 183,E-2
Vankleek Hill 1,568 ... 183,G-2
Varney 87 ... 180,D-1
Vasey 51 ... 179,F-5
Vermillion Bay 570 ... 175,E-2
Verner 1,055 ... 179,F-1
Vernonville ... 182,B-5
Verschoyle 67 ... 180,D-4
Victoria Harbour 1,310 ... 179,F-5
Vienna 398 ... 180,D-4
Virgil ... 181,G-3
Waba 51 ... 182,D-3
Wabigoon 362 ... 175,F-2
Walkerton 4,626 ... 180,D-1
Wallaceburg 11,132 ... 180,B-4
Wardsville 448 ... 180,C-4
Warren 612 ... 179,E-1
Wasaga Beach 4,985 ... 179,F-5
Washago 442 ... 179,G-5
Waterdown 2,737 ... 181,F-3
Waterford ... 181,E-4
Waterloo 46,623 ... 181,E-3
Watford 1,365 ... 180,C-4
Waubamik 35 ... 179,F-3
Waupoos 92 ... 182,C-5
Wawa 4,272 ... 176,D-4
Webbwood 464 ... 178,C-1
Welland• 45,047 ... 181,F-4
Wellesley 842 ... 180,D-3
Wellington 1,057 ... 182,C-5
Wendover 362 ... 183,F-2
West Bay ... 178,C-2
West Lorne 1,171 ... 180,C-4
Westbrook ... 182,D-5
Westport 644 ... 183,D-4
Westree ... 177,G-4
Wheatley 1,637 ... 180,B-5
Whitby• 28,173 ... 181,G-2
White River 754 ... 176,D-3
Whitefish ... 178,D-1
Whitefish Falls 161 ... 178,D-2
Whitestone 37 ... 179,F-3
Whitney 767 ... 182,B-2
Wiarton 2,144 ... 178,D-4
Wikwemikong 941 ... 178,D-2
Wilfrid 85 ... 181,G-1
Williamsburg 407 ... 183,F-3
Williamsford 264 ... 180,D-1
Wilno 164 ... 182,C-2
Winchester 1,745 ... 183,F-3
Windermere 110 ... 179,F-4
Windsor• 196,526 ... 180,A-5
Wingham 2,871 ... 180,D-2
Woodbridge ... 181,F-2
Woodford 54 ... 179,E-5
Woodham 100 ... 180,C-3
Woodstock• 26,779 ... 180,D-3
Woodville 573 ... 181,G-1
Worthington 107 ... 178,D-1
Wyoming 1,646 ... 180,B-4
Yarker 365 ... 183,D-4
Yonge Mills 97 ... 183,E-4
York 141,367 ... 181,F-2
York 115 ... 181,F-4
Youngs Point 202 ... 182,B-4
Zephyr 201 ... 181,G-2

MZ-675-J-XC

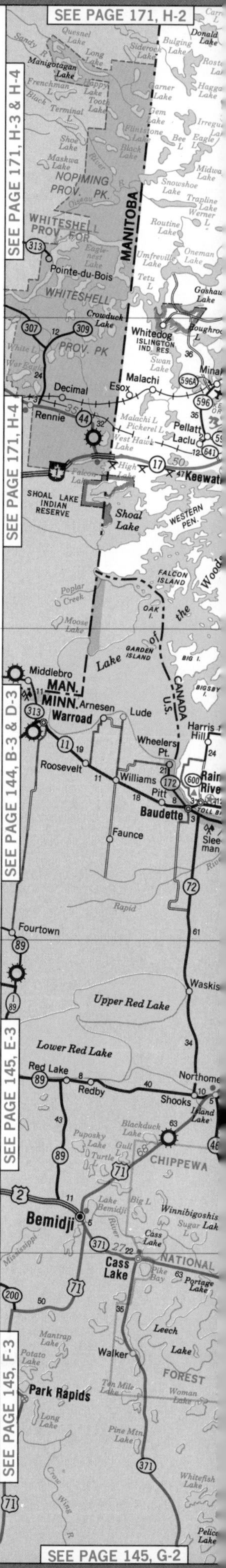

SEE PAGE 171, H-2
SEE PAGE 171, H-3 & H-4
SEE PAGE 171, H-4
SEE PAGE 144, B-3 & D-3
SEE PAGE 145, E-3
SEE PAGE 145, F-3
SEE PAGE 145, G-2
MANITOBA
NOPIMING PROV. PK.
WHITESHELL PROV. FOR.
WHITESHELL PROV. PK.
Pointe-du-Bois
Whitedog
Malachi
Decimal
Rennie
Pellatt
Keewatin
SHOAL LAKE INDIAN RESERVE
Shoal Lake
Middlebro
MAN.
MINN.
Arnesen
Lude
Warroad
Roosevelt
Williams
Baudette
Faunce
Fourtown
Upper Red Lake
Lower Red Lake
Red Lake
Redby
Shooks
Northome
CHIPPEWA
Bemidji
NATIONAL
Cass Lake
Walker
FOREST
Park Rapids
Leech Lake

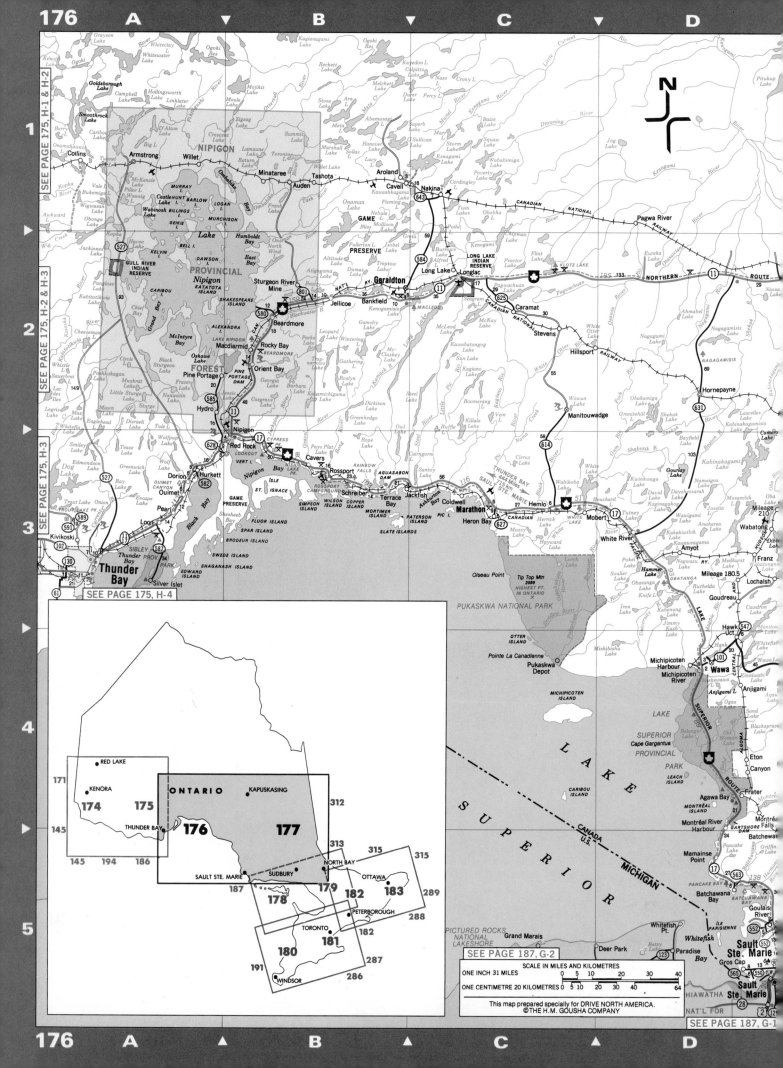

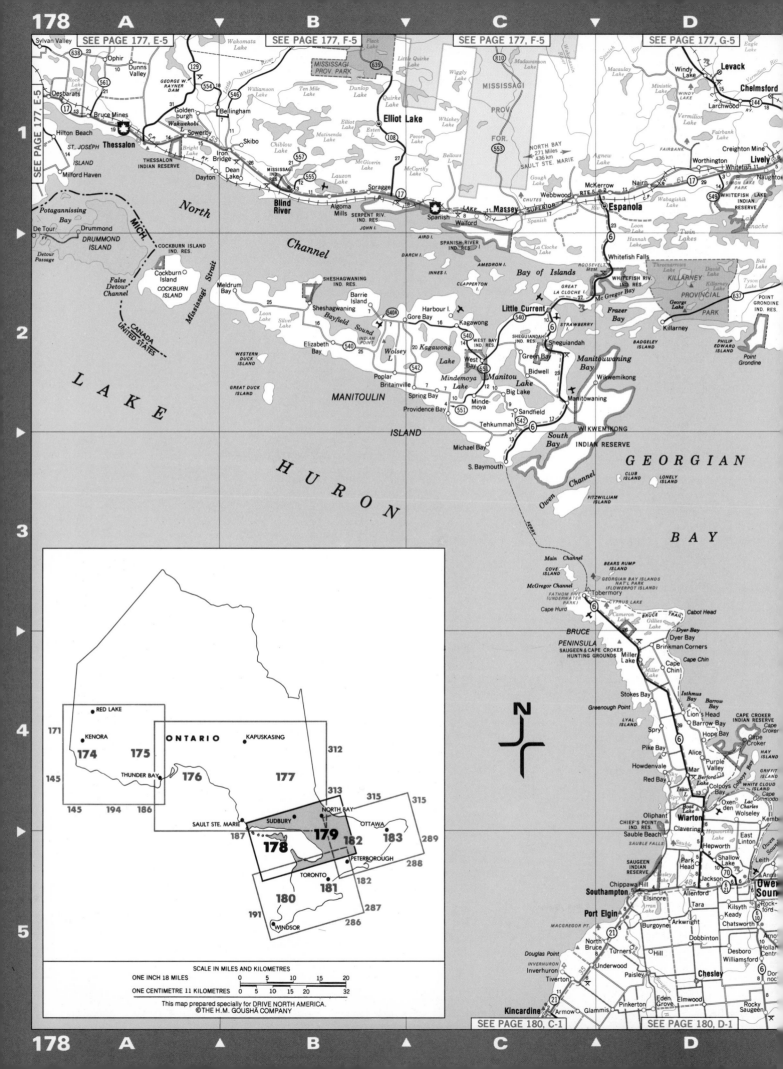

SEE PAGE 177, G-5   SEE PAGE 177, H-5   SEE PAGE 313, E-4   SEE PAGE 313, E-3 & E-4

SEE PAGE 313, E-3

SEE PAGE 182, B-1

SEE PAGE 182, B-2

SEE PAGE 182, B-3

SEE PAGE 182, B-3 & B-4

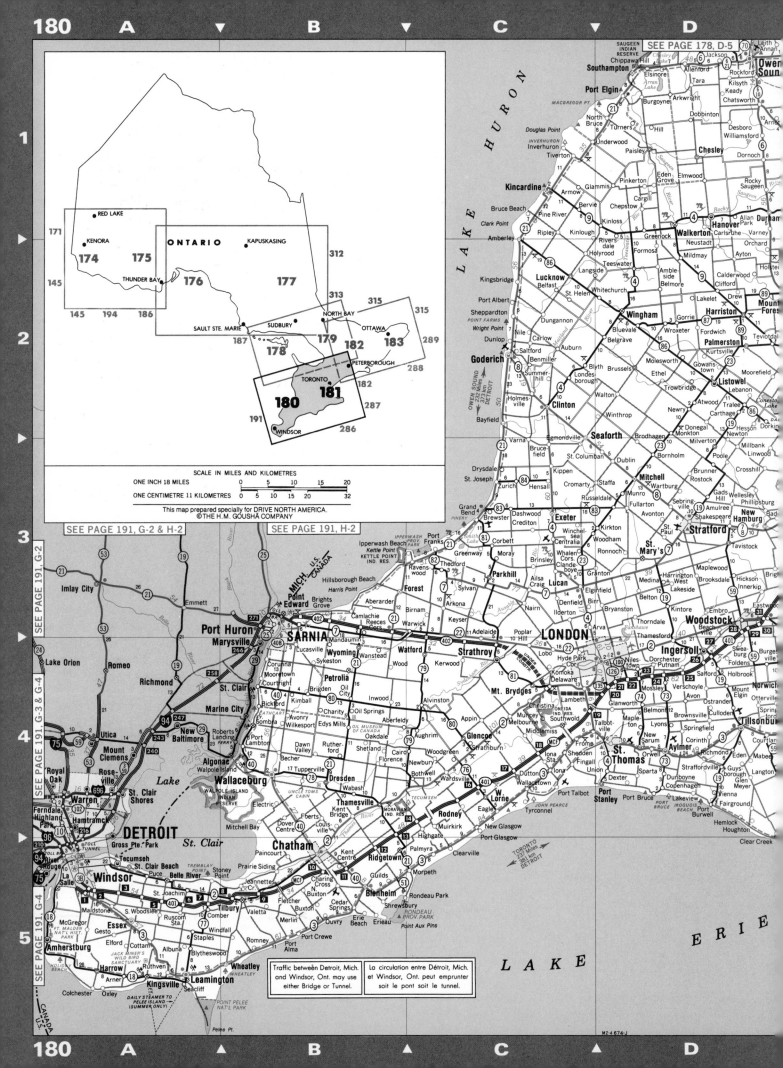

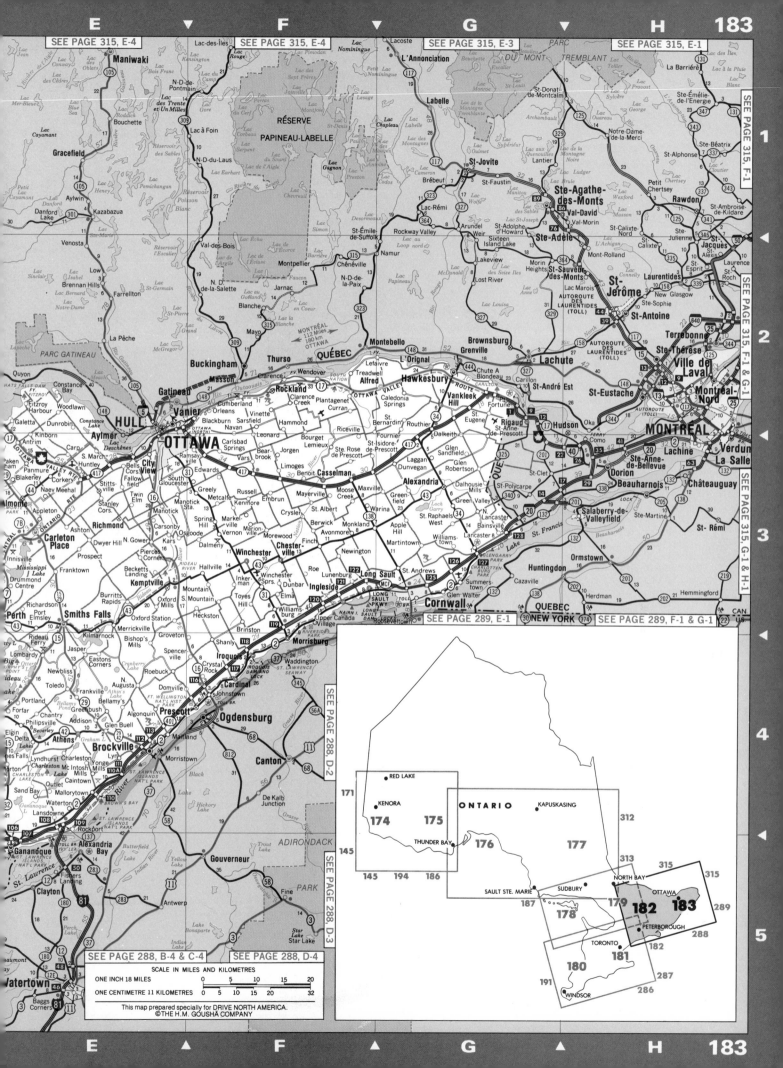

The Upper and Lower Peninsulas: a Tale of Two Michigans

Michigan

Water is never far on the Upper and Lower peninsulas, the geographic thumb and forefinger that comprise Michigan. Fringed by four of the Great Lakes, the state has 11,000 smaller lakes, some 36,000 miles of rivers and streams, and the longest freshwater shoreline of any state.

Detroit (191, H-4), the city that put America on wheels, dominates the Lower Peninsula. Established by the French in 1701, America's sixth largest city hurtled to the industrial forefront in 1913, when Henry Ford's Model T first rolled off the original assembly line.

The Detroit Institute of Arts, the largest city-owned museum in the country, displays paintings by van Gogh, Cézanne, Degas, Rembrandt, Brueghel, Rubens and Gainsborough. Such American artists as Whistler, Seth Eastman and Thomas Eakins are also represented.

A U.S. $10,000 bill, a rare four-dollar gold piece and crude Lydian coins dating from 640 B.C. are among 11,000 samples of ancient and modern currency in the National Bank of Detroit's Money Museum. Objects used for barter—some more than 4,000 years old—include cowrie shells, a Japanese money tree and a Mexican leather token.

Polar bears—one of the largest groups in captivity—inhabit caves and terraces at the Detroit Zoological Park. Gazelles, flamingos and cranes roam a realistically re-created African swamp.

Cranbrook is a remarkable complex of museums, libraries and gardens in suburban Bloomfield Hills. Works by modern sculptor Carl Milles highlight the Cranbrook Academy of Art. Innovative "hands-on" exhibits in the Institute of Science encourage visitors to learn about the world around them. Pine-edged walks wind past water cascades, statues, a 400-seat theater, and through floral displays in the Cranbrook House Gardens.

North of Detroit, at **Flint (191, F-2)**, the Alfred P. Sloan Jr. Museum displays more than 60 vintage automobiles and carriages, many in working order. Rare antique paperweights and Renaissance tapestries grace the Dewaters Art Center. Crossroads Village, a restored 19th-century community, is served by a steam-powered locomotive and train that chugs along a narrow-gauge track.

Old World charm permeates **Frankenmuth (191, F-2)**, founded in 1845 by Bavarian pioneers as a religious mission. A replica of a 19th-century covered bridge spans the Cass River. Wooden miniatures depicting the Pied Piper legend emerge from the clock face of the Glockenspiel Tower to the melody of a 35-bell carillon. In June, Frankenmuth comes alive with the revelry of the Bavarian Festival.

West of Detroit is **Jackson (191, E-4)**, site of the Michigan Space Center. The gold-hued, geodesic museum building contains the Apollo 9 command module, a lunar surveyor, spacesuits, satellites, specimens of moon rock and an 85-foot Redstone rocket.

Battle Creek (190, D-4), the "Breakfast Food Capital of America," is where the Kellogg brothers created corn flakes in 1898. Today visitors can tour the Kellogg Company plant. Exhibits in the Kingman Museum of Natural History—an "environmental observatory" housed in the Leila Arboretum—explore the role of man in the universe.

Michigan's second largest city is **Grand Rapids (190, C-3)**. Founded as a fur-trade post in 1826, it prospered from furniture manufacturing. The extravagant life-style of its leading families is glimpsed on Heritage Hill, a fashionable 19th-century neighborhood embracing 70 architectural styles. The Grand Rapids Art Museum has seven galleries devoted to the fine arts, with particular focus on German Expressionism. In the Grand Rapids Public Museum, Gaslight Village recalls the "good old days" along a street paved with cedar blocks and lined with re-created shops.

The town of **Holland (190, B-3)**, ablaze with color during the May Tulip Time Festival, bears the stamp of Dutch pioneers who settled here in 1847. The sails of a windmill catch the breeze on downtown Windmill Island, site of tulip gardens, canals and a working drawbridge. A detailed history of furniture design- from English Regency to modern American—is presented in the Baker Furniture Museum. North of Holland, on the Lake Michigan coast, the "singing sands" of **Grand Haven (190, B-2)** emit a curious whistling sound—a phenomenon that occurs in few other places in the world.

At the base of Leelanau Peninsula rises **Sleeping Bear Dunes National Lakeshore (188, B-3)**—"America's biggest sandpile." This legacy of unspoiled Great Lakes scenery is one of the most striking sights on Lake Michigan. Steep, rugged slopes tower from broad stretches of flat white beach to a height of 460 feet above the sparkling waters of the lake. The dunes are among the biggest in the world, exceeded only by some in Colorado, the Sahara and Saudi Arabia.

Jutting into Grand Traverse Bay is Old Mission Peninsula, its treacherous coast guarded by the Old Mission Lighthouse (1870). Each fall the fertile vineyards and orchards surrounding **Traverse City (188, C-3)** produce prize-winning wines and millions of pounds of cherries.

In 1715 French troops built palisaded Fort Michilimackinac near present-day Mackinaw City, overlooking the strategic straits that separate Lake Huron and Lake Michigan. The eight buildings surrounded by a log palisade are reconstructions based on historic records. Dioramas dramatize the 1763 massacre of British troops at the fort by Chippewa Indians during Pontiac's Rebellion. Today the straits are spanned by "Mighty Mac," a five-mile bridge linking the Upper and Lower peninsulas.

Mackinac Island (189, E-1), where cannons still boom and horse-drawn buggies clatter, is a pristine refuge from modern Michigan. The stately Grand Hotel, where guests stroll along the country's longest veranda, is one of many charming island inns. High on a bluff overlooking the city of Mackinac Island are the gleaming white buildings of Fort Mackinac. Blockhouses, barracks and officers' quarters contain exhibits and period settings with costumed figures that illuminate the fort's colorful history. Thick stone walls notched with gunports surround the 14 origi-

Lake Superior's Pictured Rocks include the fancifully named Lover's Leap, Miners Castle, Indian Head and Chapel Rock (above).

nal buildings. Staff in military garb fire cannons and muskets during summer drills.

The St. Marys Falls Canal (better known as the Soo Locks) of **Sault Ste. Marie (187, G-1)** is the only water link for ships between Lake Superior and Lake Huron. Visitors can watch the vessels inching through the five locks, the largest of which accommodates freighters up to 1,100 feet long and 105 feet wide. A guided tour of the museum ship *Valley Camp* reveals the ship's three gigantic holds, ballast tanks, pilothouse, captain's quarters, engine room, galley and seamen's quarters.

Soo Junction (187, H-3) is the departure point for the Toonerville Trolley and Boat Trip. Visitors ride a narrow-gauge railroad through dense stands of spruce and pine, then transfer to boats which cruise past the broad curtain of 190-foot-wide Tahquamenon Upper Falls.

Fayette State Park (187, F-4), a restored ghost town, re-creates a time when Fayette

Visitors to Mackinac Island return year after year. But only after they have sampled the delicious product of one of the many fudge shops on Huron Street (below) are they considered to be true "fudgies," as the islanders call visitors.

Detroit's seven-tower Renaissance Center (left).

Of Horseless Carriages and Historic Light Bulbs

From log cabins to sophisticated mechanical exhibitions, Dearborn's Edison Institute presents an amazing record of daily American life. The enormous complex includes Greenfield Village, a collection of historic homes, shops, laboratories, mills and factories from different periods; the Henry Ford Museum of mechanical and decorative arts; a research library; and the Ford Archives.

The museum's transportation exhibit is the world's largest, with displays ranging from birchbark canoes to the single-engine *Spirit of St. Louis* (*left*), in which Charles Lindbergh crossed the Atlantic in 1927. When the newly formed Ford Motor Company opened its first factory (*right*) in 1903, parts were hauled to the building by horses. Assembling 15 cars a day was the company's ambitious production goal.

Completed in 1933, Diego Rivera's bold frescoes in the Institute of Arts depict industrial Detroit.

was a bustling iron-smelting center. Rebuilt charcoal and lime kilns and partially restored blast ovens illustrate early smelting methods.

Metallic ores add the color to **Pictured Rocks National Lakeshore (187, F-3)**, a 15-mile stretch of richly hued sandstone cliffs carved by wind and water into caves, columns, arches and headlands. The cliffs rise abruptly from Lake Superior up to 200 feet above the water. Tour boats leave daily in summer from Munising.

When night settles over **Isle Royale National Park (186, B-1)**, visitors may hear the most chilling sound in the North American wilderness: the howling of wolves. The island is home to about 14 timber wolves, which prey on the 700 or so moose that browse in the shallow lakes. There is excellent fishing in the park's multitude of lakes and fjord-like inlets, and hiking through a roadless wilderness of hardwood and evergreen forests.

SEE PAGE 175, H-4

ISLE ROYALE NATIONAL PARK
SCALE: SAME AS MAIN MAP

CENTRAL STANDARD TIME → EASTERN STANDARD TIME

SEE PAGE 175, H-4
SEE PAGE 194, C-1
SEE PAGE 194, D-1; 196, D-5
SEE PAGE 197, E-5
SEE PAGE 197, E-4
SEE PAGE 197, E-3
SEE PAGE 197, E-2
SEE PAGE 197, F-2

Michigan

SCALE IN MILES AND KILOMETRES
ONE INCH 16 MILES
ONE CM 10 KILOMETRES

This map prepared specially for DRIVE NORTH AMERICA.
©THE H.M. GOUSHA COMPANY

INDEX TO COUNTIES

Pop. (1980) 9,258,344   Area 58,216 Sq. Mi.

County	County Seat
Alcona	Harrisville
Alger	Munising
Allegan	Allegan
Alpena	Alpena
Antrim	Bellaire
Arenac	Standish
Baraga	L'Anse
Barry	Hastings
Bay	Bay City
Benzie	Beulah
Berrien	St. Joseph
Branch	Coldwater
Calhoun	Marshall
Cass	Cassopolis
Charlevoix	Charlevoix
Cheboygan	Cheboygan
Chippewa	Sault Ste. Marie
Clare	Harrison
Clinton	St. Johns
Crawford	Grayling
Delta	Escanaba
Dickinson	Iron Mountain
Eaton	Charlotte
Emmet	Petoskey
Genesee	Flint
Gladwin	Gladwin
Gogebic	Bessemer

County	County Seat
Grand Traverse	Traverse City
Gratiot	Ithaca
Hillsdale	Hillsdale
Houghton	Houghton
Huron	Bad Axe
Ingham	Mason
Ionia	Ionia
Iosco	Tawas City
Iron	Crystal Falls
Isabella	Mt. Pleasant
Jackson	Jackson
Kalamazoo	Kalamazoo
Kalkaska	Kalkaska
Kent	Grand Rapids
Keweenaw	Eagle River
Lake	Baldwin
Lapeer	Lapeer
Leelanau	Leland
Lenawee	Adrian
Livingston	Howell
Luce	Newberry
Mackinac	St. Ignace
Macomb	Mt. Clemens
Manistee	Manistee
Marquette	Marquette
Mason	Ludington
Mecosta	Big Rapids
Menominee	Menominee

County	County Seat
Midland	Midland
Missaukee	Lake City
Monroe	Monroe
Montcalm	Stanton
Montmorency	Atlanta
Muskegon	Muskegon
Newaygo	White Cloud
Oakland	Pontiac
Oceana	Hart
Ogemaw	West Branch
Ontonagon	Ontonagon
Osceola	Reed City
Oscoda	Mio
Otsego	Gaylord
Ottawa	Grand Haven
Presque Isle	Rogers City
Roscommon	Roscommon
Saginaw	Saginaw
St. Clair	Port Huron
St. Joseph	Centreville
Sanilac	Sandusky
Schoolcraft	Manistique
Shiawassee	Corunna
Tuscola	Caro
Van Buren	Paw Paw
Washtenaw	Ann Arbor
Wayne	Detroit
Wexford	Cadillac

PARTIAL LIST OF

CITIES AND TOWNS

1980 Census   •County Seats

Place	Pop	Grid
Acme		188,C-3
Addison 655		191,E-5
Adrian	21,186	191,F-5
Akron 538		191,F-1
Alanson 508		188,D-2
Albion 11,059		190,D-4
Algonac 4,412		191,H-3
Allegan 4,576		190,B-3
Allen 266		190,D-5
Allen Park	34,196	191,G-4
Allouez		186,D-1
Alma 9,652		190,D-2
Almont 1,857		191,G-3
Alpena• 12,214		189,F-2
Alpha 229		186,C-4
Amasa		186,C-3
Anchorville		191,H-3
Ann Arbor• 107,316		191,F-4
Applegate 257		191,H-2
Armada 1,392		191,H-3
Ashley 570		190,D-2
Athens 960		190,D-5
Atlanta•		189,E-3

Place	Pop	Grid
Atlantic Mine		186,C-1
Au Gres 768		189,F-5
Auburn 1,921		191,F-1
Auburn Heights		191,G-3
Augusta 913		190,C-4
Austin		187,E-3
Avoca		191,H-2
Bad Axe• 3,184		189,G-5
Baldwin• 674		188,B-5
Bancroft 618		191,F-3
Bangor 2,001		190,B-4
Baraga 1,055		186,C-2
Bark River		187,E-4
Barryton 422		190,C-1
Battle Creek 35,724		190,D-4
Bay City• 41,593		191,F-1
Bay Port		189,G-5
Bear Lake 388		188,B-2
Beaverton 1,025		189,F-5
Bedford		190,D-4
Belding 5,634		190,D-2
Bellaire• 1,063		188,D-3
Belleville 3,366		191,G-4
Bellevue 1,289		190,D-4
Benton Harbor 14,707		190,A-4
Benton Heights		190,A-4
Berkley 18,637		191,G-4
Berrien Springs 2,042		190,B-5
Bessemer• 2,553		186,A-3
Beulah• 454		188,B-3
Big Rapids• 14,361		190,C-1
Birch Run 1,196		191,F-2
Birmingham 21,689		191,G-4
Blissfield 3,107		191,F-5
Bloomfield Hill 3,985		191,G-3
Bloomingdale 537		190,B-4
Boyne City 3,348		188,D-2
Boyne Falls 378		188,D-2
Breckenridge 1,495		190,D-2
Breedsville 244		190,B-4
Bridgman 2,235		190,A-5
Brighton 4,268		191,F-4
Britton 693		191,F-5
Bronson 2,271		190,D-5

Place	Pop	Grid
Brooklyn 1,110		191,E-4
Brown City 1,163		191,G-2
Bruce Crossing		186,B-2
Buchanan 5,142		190,B-5
Buckley 357		188,C-4
Bullock Creek		191,E-1
Burnside		191,G-2
Burr Oak 853		190,C-5
Burton 29,976		191,F-2
Byron 689		191,F-3
Byron Center		190,C-3
Cadillac• 10,199		188,C-4
Calumet 1,013		186,C-1
Cambridge Jct.		191,E-5
Camden 420		190,D-5
Capac 1,377		191,H-2
Carleton 2,786		191,G-5
Carney		187,E-5
Caro• 4,317		191,G-1
Carrollton		191,F-1
Carson City 1,229		190,D-2
Carsonville 622		191,H-1
Cascade		190,C-3
Caseville 851		189,G-5
Casnovia 348		190,C-2
Caspian 1,038		186,C-3
Cass City 2,258		191,G-1
Cassopolis• 1,933		190,B-5
Cedar Springs 2,615		190,C-2
Cedarville 244		187,G-2
Center Line 9,293		191,G-4

Place	Pop	Grid
Central Lake 895		188,C-2
Centreville• 1,202		190,C-5
Champion		186,D-3
Channing		186,D-3
Charleston		191,H-1
Charlevoix• 3,296		188,D-2
Charlotte• 8,251		190,D-3
Chassell		186,C-1
Chatham 315		187,F-3
Cheboygan• 5,106		189,E-1
Chelsea 3,816		191,F-4
Chesaning 2,656		191,E-2
Chippewa Lake		190,C-1
Clare 3,300		188,D-5
Clarklake		191,E-4
Clarkston 968		191,G-3
Clarksville 348		190,D-3
Clawson 15,103		191,G-4
Clayton 396		191,E-5
Clifford 406		191,G-2
Climax 619		190,C-4
Clinton 2,342		191,F-5
Clio 2,669		191,F-2
Coldwater• 9,461		190,D-5
Coleman 1,429		191,E-1
Coloma 1,833		190,B-4
Colon 1,190		190,C-5
Columbiaville 953		191,G-2
Comstock		191,G-2
Concord 900		191,E-4
Constantine 1,680		190,C-5

CONTINUED ON PAGE 189

8-MZ-529-J

SEE PAGE 176, D-5
SEE PAGE 177, E-5
SEE MAIN MAP BELOW
SEE PAGE 177, E-5
SEE PAGE 188, D-1
SEE PAGE 188, D-1
SEE INSET ABOVE
SEE PAGE 188, D-1
SEE PAGE 188, D-1 & D-2
SEE PAGE 197, F-1 & F-2
SEE PAGE 188, C-2 & D-2

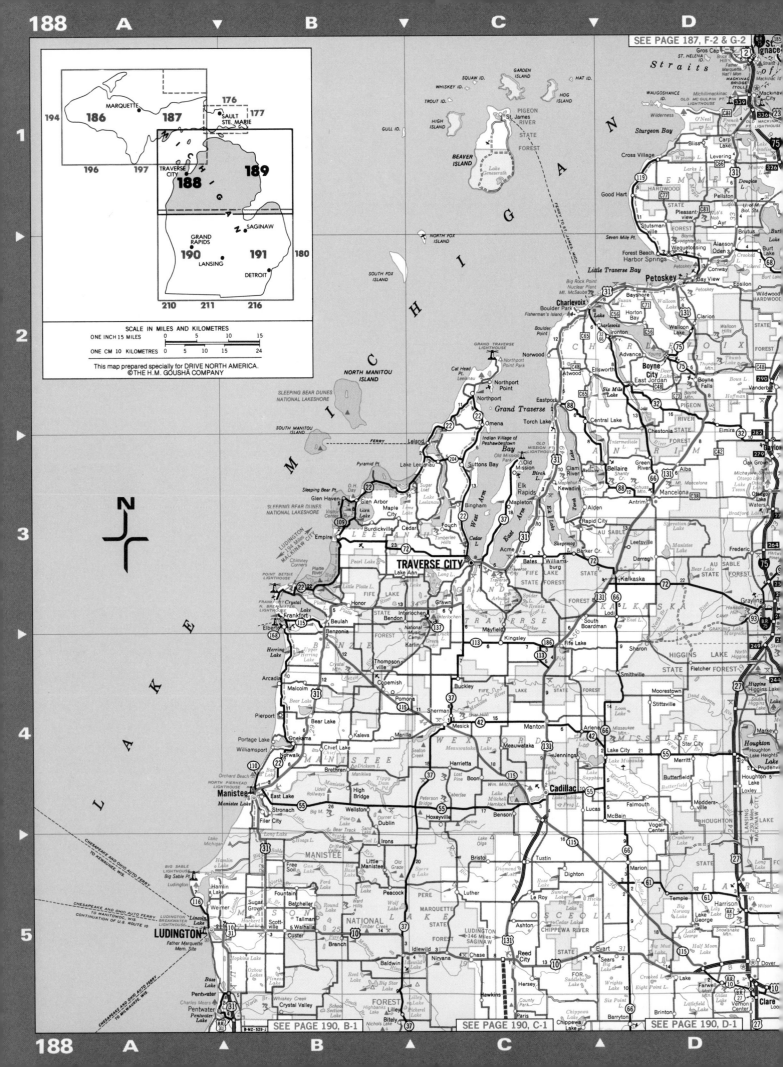

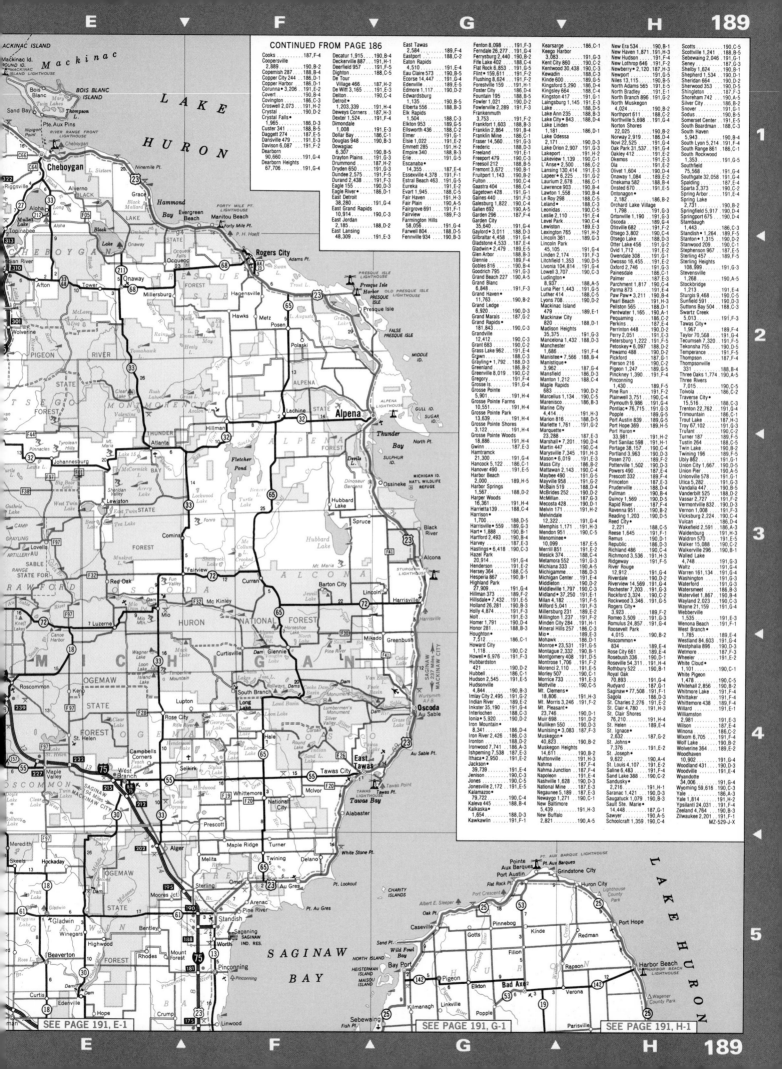

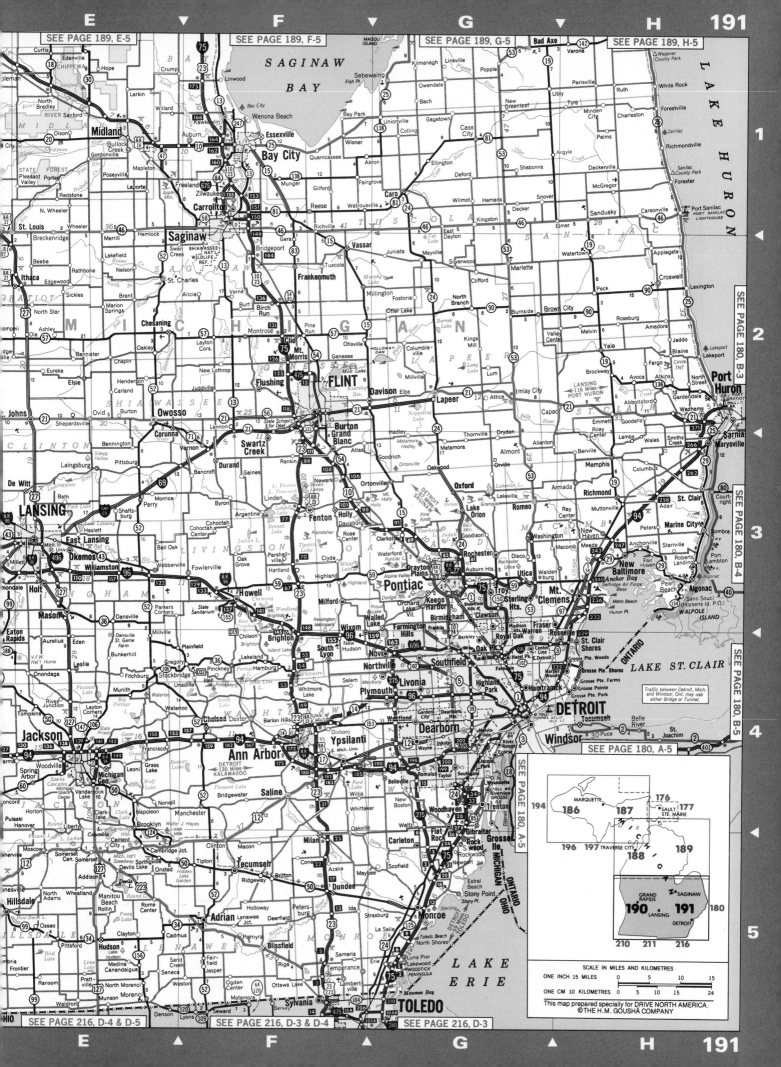

Rooftop Dragons, Gaslit Streets, Sands that 'Sing' Underfoot

Wisconsin

Spectators at the Milwaukee Public Museum almost feel themselves part of The Bison Hunt.

Art meets agriculture on a Wisconsin farm near Rhinelander (above).

Wisconsin's role as the leading producer of milk, butter and cheese in the United States has earned it the nickname America's Dairyland. But visitors can see more than contented cows in this varied state. Its rolling farmland is dappled by nearly 15,000 lakes and threaded by 7,400 rivers and streams, a recreational paradise for fishermen, boaters and campers. There are also spectacular highways that skirt the rugged bluffs of Lake Superior, and tranquil drives past the picturesque coves and inlets of the Bayfield Peninsula and the Lake Michigan shore.

Wild Wisconsin is best savored among Lake Superior's Apostle Islands, 22 wind- and water-sculpted retreats for campers, hikers, sailors and fishermen. Twenty of the islands are protected as national lakeshore. Boats from the village of **Bayfield (194, B-2)** tour the archipelago, a red sandstone masterpiece of cliffs, pillars, arches, inlets and bays. Cruise boats ply the lake, between the village and Stockton Island, where the sands of one of the most attractive beaches on the Great Lakes "sing" underfoot. Madeline Island, largest of the Apostles, is serviced hourly in summer by car ferries. An Indian burial ground south of the La Pointe ferry dock contains wooden structures built to house the spirits of the dead. More than 45 miles of roads weave and dip along the shoreline.

One of the great unspoiled rivers in the United States, the St. Croix, flows from Upper St. Croix Lake near **Solon Springs (194, C-4)** south to the Mississippi. Along its course are riverbed holes up to 60 feet deep and 7 miles of white water that sluices over glacial boulders and ledges at Kettle Rapids.

The Wisconsin River also provides spectacular scenery where it flows through the Dells, a 16-mile stretch of sandstone formations fashioned by glacial meltwater at the end of the last ice age. Sightseeing boats take visitors past grottos, towering cliffs and monoliths, and through a deep, narrow valley.

Farther downstream on the Wisconsin,

near the town of **Spring Green (198, D-4)**, Madison sculptor Alex Jordan designed the House on the Rock—a multilevel sandstone home built around and through a 59-foot-high chimney rock overlooking the Wyoming Valley. Also on the grounds are the Mill House with its 16-foot waterwheel and the world's biggest fireplace; a large collection of mechanical music makers; and the "Streets of Yesterday," where shops recall the gaslit era of the 1880s.

South of Spring Green stands Taliesin, the home and studio of American architect Frank Lloyd Wright. Students study architecture at the Frank Lloyd Wright Foundation school, set on rolling farmland that is said to have influenced his "prairie school" of design.

Wright also left his mark on **Madison (199, E-4)**, the state capital. He designed the Unitarian Church (1951), whose striking prow-like roof, covered with green copper strips, incorporates chapel, spire and parish hall. Another dramatic architectural landmark in Madison is the Wisconsin State Capitol, built in Roman Renaissance style and topped by a gleaming white granite dome only a few inches lower than that of the U.S. Capitol.

Traditional domestic architecture graces Villa Louis, a Victorian mansion built at **Prairie du Chien (198, B-4)** in 1843 on the remains of a 2,000-year-old Indian burial mound. Waterford crystal chandeliers illuminate elegant 19th-century furnishings; the library contains more than 3,000 books printed before 1890.

Near **Blue Mounds (198, D-4)**, in the fancifully named Valley of the Elves, is Little Norway—a dozen restored Norwegian-style log buildings erected in 1856 by homesteader Osten Olson Haugen and containing a superb collection of Early American and Scandinavian antiques. The Norway Building, an 1885 replica of a 12th-century stave church of hewn oak, is protected from evil spirits by

Visitors to two of Milwaukee's major breweries, both listed on the National Register of Historic Places, can learn about brewing and enjoy a glass of frothy refreshment.

Mainsheets taut and sails full, sailboats round a buoy during a Lake Michigan regatta. Clear water and steady breezes mean good sailing on Wisconsin's two Great Lakes and thousands of inland bodies of water. Beneath the surface lurk many of North America's finest game fish: northern pike, smallmouth bass, walleye, muskellunge and lake trout.

fire-breathing rooftop dragons. The rustic structure was carved in Norway and reassembled at the 1893 World's Columbian Exposition in Chicago. East, at Cave of the Mounds, visitors can examine a dozen dramatically lighted chambers in a vast limestone cavern.

At **Mineral Point (198, D-5),** six restored Cornish houses on Shake Rag Street display tools, furniture and equipment used by Cornish miners who came here to work the area's lead deposits in the 1820s. Houses built by the miners into the sides of mudbanks gave Wisconsin another nickname—the Badger State.

Yodels echo through the hills near **New Glarus (199, E-5)** each summer as the town celebrates its founding (in 1845, by Swiss settlers) with the Heidi Festival, the Volksfest and the Wilhelm Tell Pageant. Buildings in the Swiss Historical Village include a church, a cabin, a schoolhouse, a cheese factory and a firehouse.

Milwaukee (199, H-4) attracted thousands of German immigrants in the mid-19th century, and the state's largest city still maintains a strong German flavor—as does its beer. Visitors can tour the Pabst and Miller breweries. Although beer made Milwaukee famous, the city is also known for its many cultural attractions. The Milwaukee Art Center contains a fine collection of 20th-century works, and pieces by European old masters (among them Zurbarán's superb *St. Francis*). A branch museum for the decorative arts is north of the Center in Villa Terrace, a Mediterranean-style mansion.

In the Milwaukee Public Museum, life-size dioramas provide cultural and ecological tours of the world. Visitors can stroll past replicas of a Melanesian ceremonial house, an Ikona village, and a Guatemalan marketplace, marvel at the danger of a bison hunt, and even walk into an igloo. A dry goods store, an optometrist's office and an apothecary shop line gaslit brick roads and wooden sidewalks in the "Streets of Old Milwaukee" display. In suburban **Franklin,** a German Stuka, a Japanese Nakajima and a 1911 Curtiss A-1 (the oldest licensed fighter plane in the United States) are among 200 aircraft in the EAA Air Museum.

Three centuries of English domestic interiors are represented in a rambling Tudor mansion built for lumber baron Nathan Paine in **Oshkosh (199, F-2),** once known as Sawdust City for its sawmills. Now the Paine Art Center and Arboretum, the house is furnished with Paine's collection of antique Persian rugs, paintings and sculptures. Self-guided walks lead through an arboretum and formal gardens.

Green Bay (197, H-2) is Wisconsin's oldest city—a trading center as early as 1669. Classic examples of 19th-century architecture in Heritage Hill State Park include the Greek Revival Cotton House, constructed in the early 1840s. Visitors to Rail America can ride an 1890 passenger car and view a railroad collection that features a Pullman parlor car used by Sir Winston Churchill, the largest steam engine ever built, and Dwight Eisenhower's locomotive, command car and staff car from the Second World War.

Northeast of Green Bay lies the "Cape Cod of the Midwest," a region of summer resorts, quaint fishing villages and scenic coastal routes on the Door County Peninsula. One of the oldest Icelandic communities in the United States was established in 1869 on **Washington Island (197, F-1),** separated from the peninsula by a treacherous strait called "Death's Door."

To the west on the mainland is a lakeland that was once heavily forested. Huge tracts have been logged and forestry has declined, but traces of the area's lumbering past remain. At **Rhinelander (197, E-5),** born as a lumber town in the 1880s, Pioneer Park's Logging Museum contains a reconstructed logging camp with living quarters, smithy, 1879 railroad engine and cook's hut. A more fanciful attraction is a replica of the Hodag, a shaggy-haired, horn-backed mythical creature that is part of Wisconsin lore.

In the town of **Hayward (194, D-3),** visitors can stand in the world's only four-story fish. The concrete, steel and fiberglass version of a muskellunge (the state fish) is a major attraction at the National Fresh Water Fishing Hall of Fame. The fish houses a museum and an observation deck in its gaping mouth.

Historyland, just east of Hayward, hosts the All-Tribes Powwow, a Fourth of July celebration of traditional dance and music that attracts Indians from all over the United States. Later in the month, woodsmen gather here for the World Lumberjack Championships, with such skill-testing events as logrolling, chopping and tree-climbing. The paddle-wheeler *Namekagon Queen* leaves Historyland hourly for cruises on the Namekagon River.

Sawdust and Greasepaint Under the Big Top

Pleasant memories from the days of traveling circuses are awakened at Baraboo's Circus World Museum, located in the original winter quarters of Ringling Brothers Circus. More than 100 ornately carved and painted circus wagons have been restored and are displayed in the huge Circus Parade Pavilion. Six- and eight-member teams of Percherons (draft horses) pull some of the wagons and help unload the circus trains. Visitors can see a re-creation of P. T. Barnum's fabulous 19th-century sideshow

and a one-ring presentation of trained animal and aerial acts. Children enjoy an antique merry-go-round, goat- and pony-cart rides, a petting menagerie, and the animated, 3,000-piece miniature circus. A remarkable library and research center devoted to circus history contains more than 5,000 original posters.

Circus World houses one-third of the world's operating calliopes (pronounced "cally-ope" by circus people), which play in almost continuous concert.

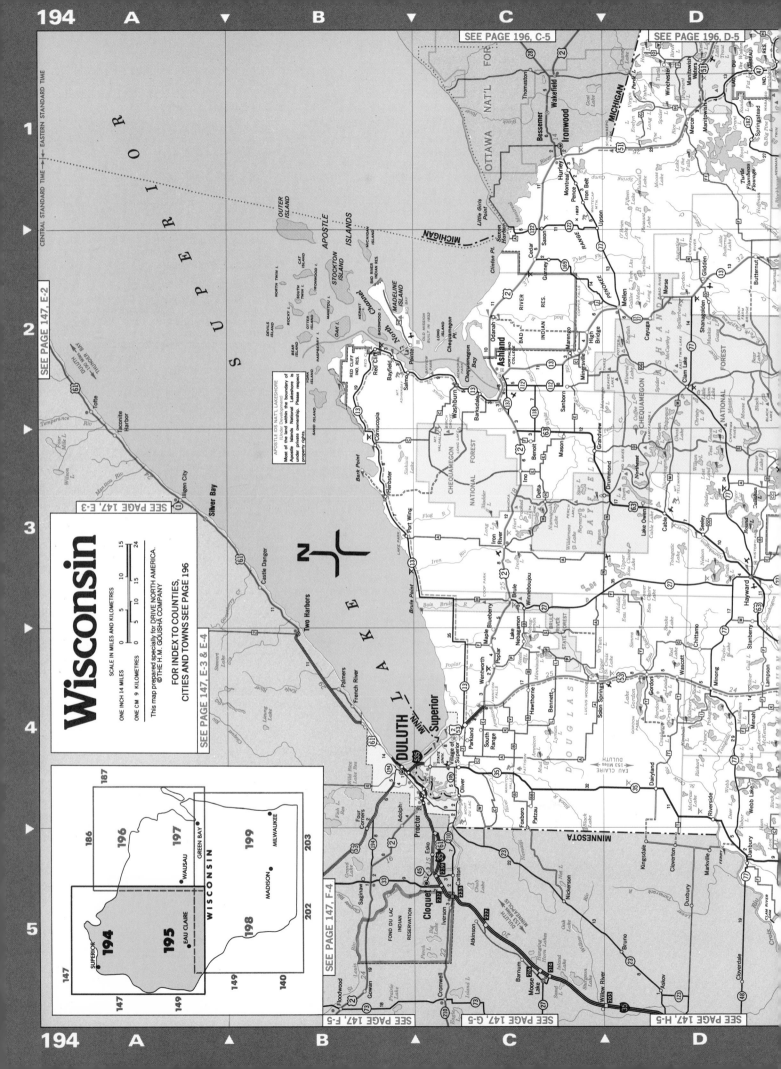

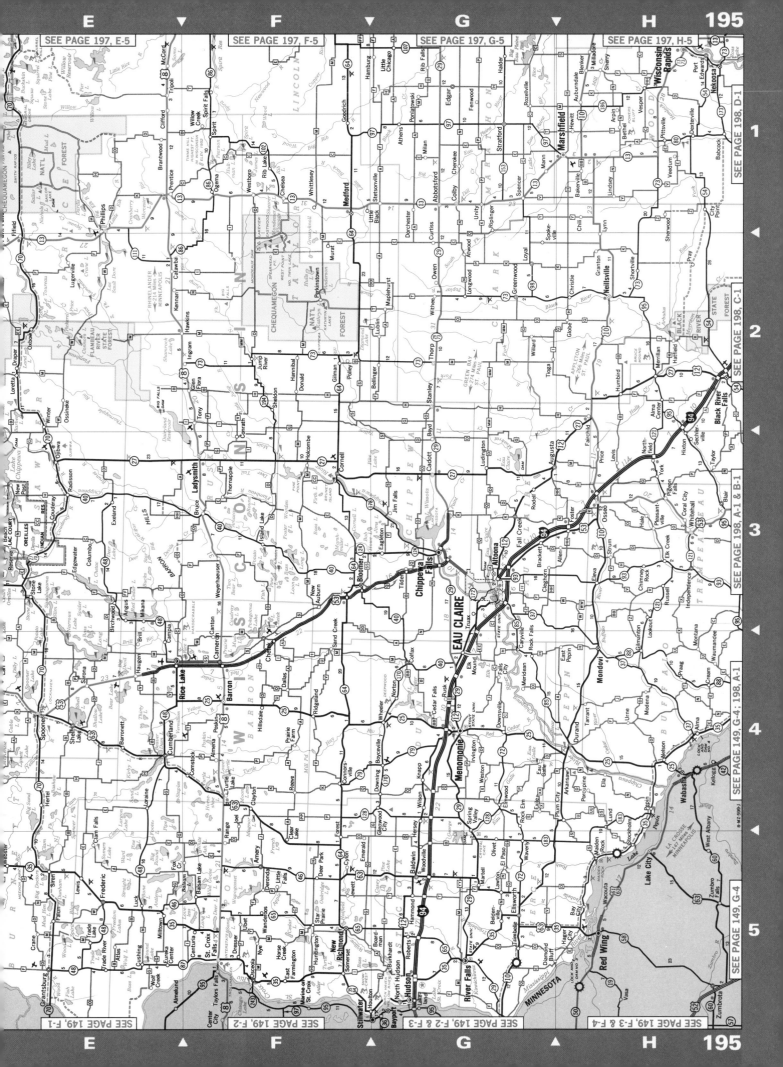

INDEX TO COUNTIES

Pop. (1980) 4,705,335   Area 56,154 Sq. Mi.

County	County Seat

(Index to Counties listing with county names and county-seat references, followed by the alphabetical grid-reference index of Wisconsin cities and towns. Entries are arranged in multiple narrow columns across the page with map grid references such as 195-F-2, 199-F-3, etc.)

PARTIAL LIST OF CITIES AND TOWNS

1980 Census

• County Seats

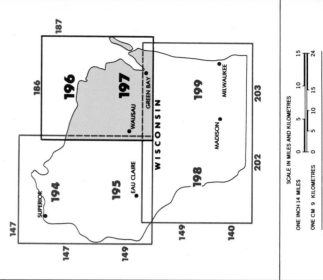

(Locator map of Wisconsin showing adjacent page numbers: 186, 187, 196, 197, 199, 203, 194, 195, 198, 202, 147, 149, 140. Cities shown: SUPERIOR, EAU CLAIRE, WAUSAU, GREEN BAY, MILWAUKEE, MADISON.)

SCALE IN MILES AND KILOMETRES

ONE INCH 14 MILES
ONE CM 9 KILOMETRES

This map prepared specially for DRIVE NORTH AMERICA.

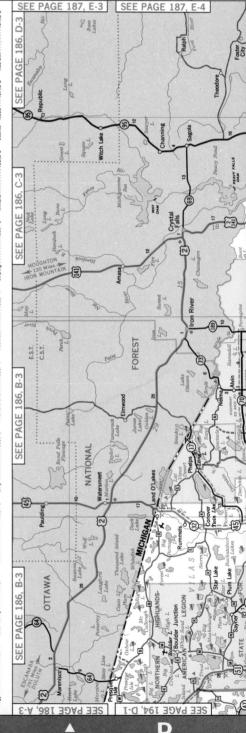

SEE PAGE 187, E-3   SEE PAGE 187, E-4

SEE PAGE 186, D-3

SEE PAGE 186, C-3

SEE PAGE 186, B-3

SEE PAGE 186, B-3

SEE PAGE 194, D-1

SEE PAGE 194, A-3

(Map of northern Wisconsin / Upper Michigan border region showing FOREST county, NATIONAL FOREST, MICHIGAN, OTTAWA, places including Republic, Channing, Sagola, Crystal Falls, Iron River, Amasa, Watersmeet, Land O'Lakes, Phelps, Conover, Twin Lakes, Paulding, Marenisco, Sayner, and numerous lakes.)

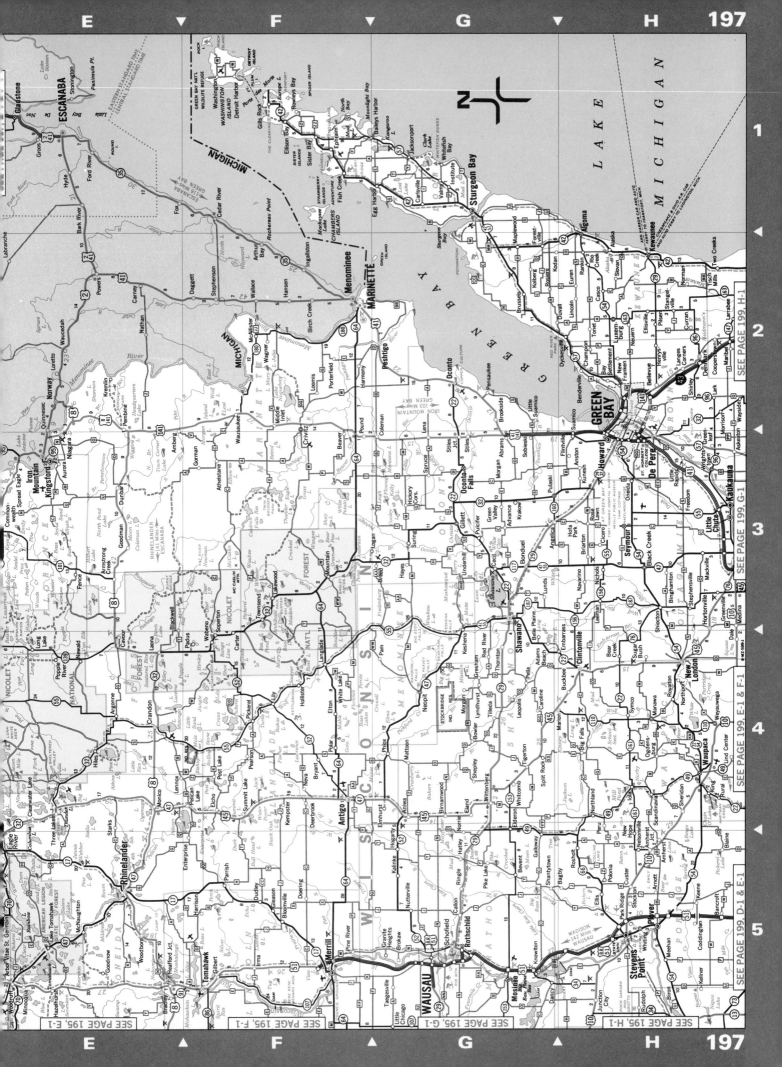

SEE PAGE 199, H-1
SEE PAGE 199, G-1
SEE PAGE 199, E-1 & F-1
SEE PAGE 199, D-1 & E-1
SEE PAGE 195, E-1
SEE PAGE 195, F-1
SEE PAGE 195, G-1
SEE PAGE 195, H-1

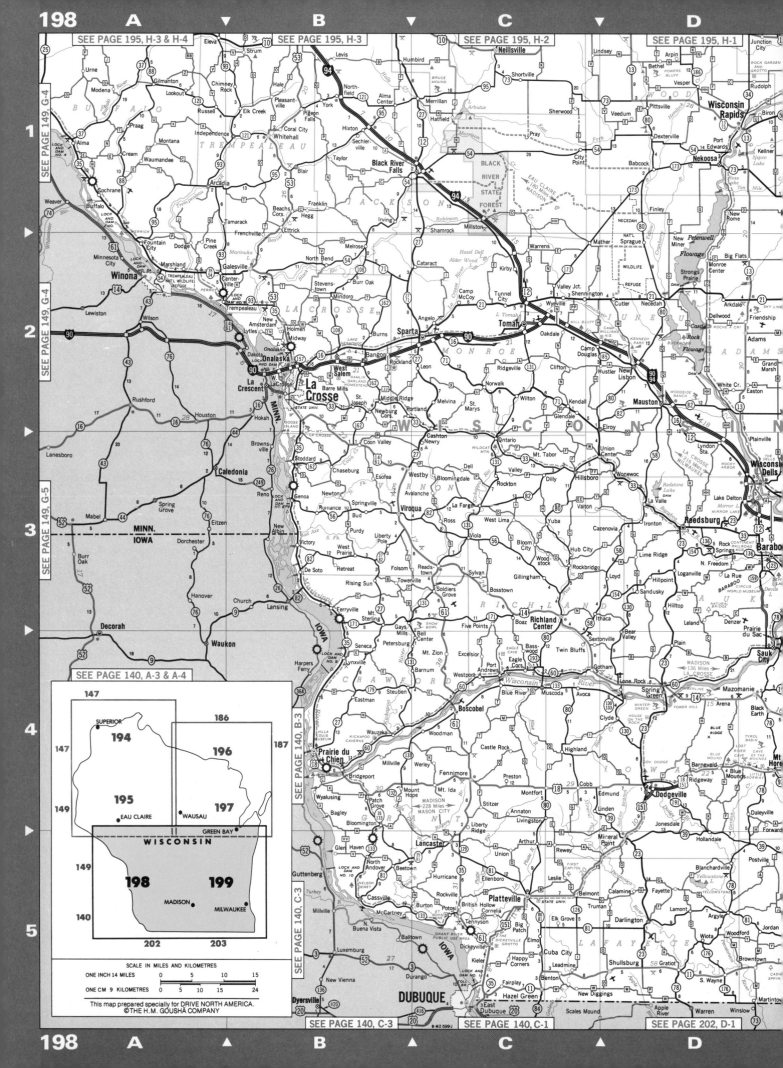

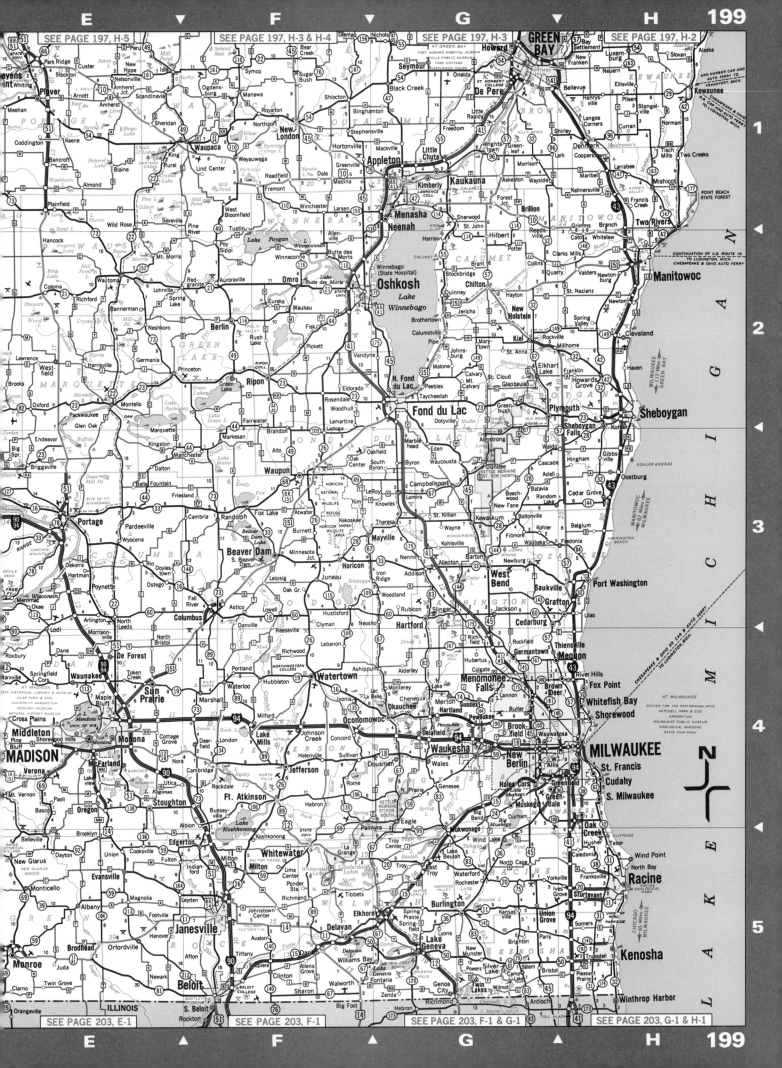

Gardens and Great Buildings in the Land of Lincoln

Illinois

Illinois is the Prairie State—anvil-flat, rich with corn, wheat and livestock, and dotted by weathered barns and silos. Yet it is not this agricultural wealth that captures the imagination of most visitors to the state; it is the soaring steel-and-concrete skyline of the Midwest's largest city, **Chicago (203, H-2).**

This "City of the Big Shoulders," as Illinois-born poet Carl Sandburg described it, stands at the meeting of prairie and river, on the shores of Lake Michigan. It is the nation's second largest metropolis, a manufacturing and transportation hub. It is also the home of the world's biggest grain exchange, of the busiest airport in the United States, and of an internationally renowned symphony orchestra. (The orchestra gives summer concerts at suburban Highland Park, during the Ravinia Festival.)

The Great Fire of 1871 destroyed many of the city's historic buildings—but it also sparked a renaissance that has endowed Chicago with some of the country's most innovative architecture. Birthplace (in the 1880s) of the skyscraper, Chicago now boasts the world's tallest building—the 110-story Sears Tower—and the 100-story glass-and-steel John Hancock Center, whose 94th-floor observatory overlooks four states.

The influence of the turn-of-the-century Chicago School of Architecture can be seen in the cast iron and terra-cotta ornamentation that frames the show windows of the Carson Pirie Scott Building. The structure was designed by Louis Sullivan, who built some of the country's first skyscrapers. Colored marble, carved wood and Tiffany mosaics and lamps lend gentle splendor to the interior of the Chicago Public Library (1897). Gaslit cobblestone streets help to re-create the glamor of the Gay Nineties in the Prairie Avenue Historic District, once a neighborhood of millionaires. The granite Glessner House (1886), a Romanesque mansion built around an open courtyard, is the last surviving work in Chicago by Henry Hobson Richardson, who greatly influenced the founders of the Chicago School. Other architectural masterpieces include Marshall Field & Co., a department store with a Tiffany dome; and the Chicago Water Tower (1869), a castellated Gothic survivor of the 1871 fire.

The great American architect Frank Lloyd Wright designed 25 homes in suburban **Oak Park,** where he lived and worked for more than 20 years. Wright's home and studio can be toured. Skylights above glass ceilings illuminate the interior of the flat-roofed Unity Temple (1908), the first public building designed by Wright.

Paintings in the Art Institute of Chicago date from the 13th century, and include *Assumption of the Virgin* by El Greco, Seurat's *Sunday Afternoon on the Island of La Grande Jatte* and the Grant Wood classic *American Gothic.* The University of Chicago's Oriental

Memories of a Favorite Son: from Railsplitter to Beloved President

"To this place, and the kindness of these people, I owe everything." So said Abraham Lincoln as he left Springfield for the White House some 120 years ago. The mark of Lincoln is still on his adopted state, where his body is entombed in Springfield's Oak Ridge Cemetery. Lincoln was a gangling youth when he came to New Salem in 1831. In six years there he was a storekeeper, a surveyor, a woodchopper and a postmaster. Today visitors can wander the dirt streets of the restored town much as Lincoln did. Also preserved is Lincoln's clapboard home in Springfield (*above*), the only house he ever owned. Lincoln was notified of his nomination for the presidency in the north parlor.

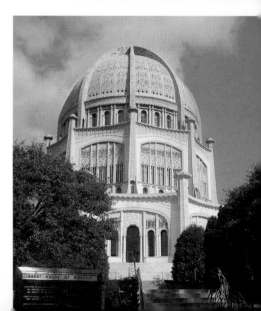

Institute Museum houses one of the world's most extensive collections of ancient Near Eastern art and archeology. Artifacts in the Field Museum of Natural History trace the development of Stone Age man, and of later primitive peoples and Asian, African and American Indian cultures.

The Museum of Science and Industry, the world's largest science museum, is an adventure for the mind. There are displays demonstrating the laws of magnetism and electricity; exhibits on the discoveries of Newton and Galileo; replicas of a coal mine and a large Midwestern farm; a miniature circus that re-creates life under the big top; and a "Fairy Castle" containing such fanciful items as Cinderella's glass slippers and King Arthur's Round Table.

The dramatic thrust of Chicago's skyscrapers is softened by the beauty of the city's parks and gardens. More than 8,000 plants grow in a vast rose garden at Grant Park—often called the city's front yard. At Lincoln Park, magnificent floral displays abound in a formal garden, a rock garden and a "Grandmother's Garden." The park's conservatory houses plants from around the world. More than 2,000 mammals, birds and reptiles inhabit the Lincoln Park Zoo. Orangutans, chimpanzees and gorillas form what is considered one of the world's finest collections of great apes.

Springfield (205, E-3), on the Sangamon River in central Illinois, was selected as the state capital through the efforts of Abraham Lincoln, the city's most famous adopted son. For a short time, Lincoln was closely associated with the Old Illinois State Capitol (1839): he served in the 12th General Assembly

Horse? Dog? Friendly prehistoric monster? Passersby at the grand plaza of Chicago's Daley Plaza (above) decide for themselves. Picasso donated the design of the 50-foot-high sculpture—now a city landmark—with no title attached.

Lakefront Park (left) is the centerpiece of Chicago's 29-mile lakefront, where pleasure boats bob inside sheltered breakwaters.

(1840–1841), researched cases in its law library, and delivered his famous "House Divided" speech here. After his assassination in 1865 his body lay in state here the night before his entombment in nearby Oak Ridge Cemetery. The present state capitol, begun in 1868 and completed 20 years later, has been in use since 1876. Tiers of columns, arches and curved windows cover its limestone facing. Outside are statues of Lincoln and his political rival, Stephen Douglas.

In **Galesburg (202, C-4),** the ashes of Illinois poet Carl Sandburg are buried behind the three-room cottage in which he was born in 1878. At nearby Bishop Hill State Historic Site, 13 buildings constructed by Swedish immigrants who settled here in 1846 include a smithy, the gambrel-roofed colony church and the Bjorkland Hotel, once an important stagecoach stop.

Nauvoo (204, B-1), on the banks of the Mississippi, became the state's largest community in 1839 as the national center for the Mormon religion. Seven years later, the Mormons abandoned Nauvoo to follow Brigham Young to Utah. Among more than 30 historic buildings in town are the two-story brick house built in 1844 by Brigham Young, and the restored homestead (begun in 1803) and gray-shuttered home (1842) of Joseph Smith, a Mormon prophet.

The stately homes of **Galena (202, C-1)** recall the town's mid-19th century heyday as a lead-mining town and Mississippi River port. The oldest dwelling is a two-story stone residence built by pioneer John Dowling in 1826. A modest brick house was given by Galena to Ulysses S. Grant when the hometown hero returned after the Civil War. The dining room table is set with china used by the Grants in the White House. At the Stockade, a refuge for settlers during the 1832 Black Hawk War, Indian relics are displayed in the original log house and underground rooms.

Although much of Illinois' rolling landscape has been farmed or settled, vast areas have been set aside as parks and preserves. More than 100,000 ducks and 40,000 Canada geese stop at Chautauqua National Wildlife Refuge southwest of **Peoria (203, E-5)** during fall and spring migrations. Steep limestone palisades flank the Mississippi River near **Savanna (202, D-2),** offering views of wooded islands and the broad lowlands of Iowa.

Shawnee National Forest (207, E-4), near the confluence of the Ohio and Mississippi rivers, is populated by 500 species of wildlife and crisscrossed by hiking trails. Giant City State Park, located in the forest, is dotted with immense sandstone blocks. A road north of Wolf Lake leads to a high bluff overlooking the rugged Illinois Ozarks, then winds to shallow Horseshoe Lake, a wintering site for bald eagles and Canada geese. In the Garden of the Gods to the northeast are weirdly shaped sandstone towers, overhangs and balanced boulders. Nearby Tower Rock stands majestically above the muddy waters of the Ohio River, providing a view of the distant Kentucky floodplains.

Just outside the forest is Cave-in-Rock, a cavern 300 feet long and 40 feet high that once sheltered river pirates and highwaymen. Old Shawneetown to the north is a virtual ghost town which, despite some restoration, still bears the ravages of the 1937 flood of the Ohio River that all but destroyed the city.

Architect-designer Alexander Girard's 180-foot-long collage (above) dominates the Deere and Company Administrative Center in Moline. The mural is a nostalgic collection of 2,000 objects—memorabilia reflecting rural America in the 19th and early 20th centuries

Walkways lead to the nine entrances of the Bahá'í House of Worship in Wilmette (left), a stunning architectural symbol of Bahá'í faith in the oneness of God, religion and mankind.

Giant teeth "talk" to visitors (right) in Chicago's imaginative Museum of Science and Industry.

Illinois

SCALE IN MILES AND KILOMETRES

ONE INCH 15 MILES
ONE CM 10 KILOMETRES

0 5 10 15
0 5 10 15 24

This map prepared specially for DRIVE NORTH AMERICA
©THE H.M. GOUSHA COMPANY

INDEX TO COUNTIES

Pop. (1980) 11,418,461   Area 56,400 Sq. Mi.

County	County Seat
Adams	Quincy
Alexander	Cairo
Bond	Greenville
Boone	Belvidere
Brown	Mount Sterling
Bureau	Princeton
Calhoun	Hardin
Carroll	Mount Carroll
Cass	Virginia
Champaign	Urbana
Christian	Taylorville
Clark	Marshall
Clay	Louisville
Clinton	Carlyle
Coles	Charleston
Cook	Chicago
Crawford	Robinson
Cumberland	Toledo
De Kalb	Sycamore
De Witt	Clinton
Douglas	Tuscola
Du Page	Wheaton
Edgar	Paris
Edwards	Albion
Effingham	Effingham
Fayette	Vandalia
Ford	Paxton
Franklin	Benton
Fulton	Lewistown
Gallatin	Shawneetown
Greene	Carrollton
Grundy	Morris
Hamilton	McLeansboro
Hancock	Carthage
Hardin	Elizabethtown
Henderson	Oquawka
Henry	Cambridge
Iroquois	Watseka
Jackson	Murphysboro
Jasper	Newton
Jefferson	Mount Vernon
Jersey	Jerseyville
Jo Daviess	Galena
Johnson	Vienna
Kane	Geneva
Kankakee	Kankakee
Kendall	Yorkville
Knox	Galesburg
La Salle	Ottawa
Lake	Waukegan
Lawrence	Lawrenceville
Lee	Dixon
Livingston	Pontiac
Logan	Lincoln
Macon	Decatur
Macoupin	Carlinville
Madison	Edwardsville
Marion	Salem
Marshall	Lacon
Mason	Havana
Massac	Metropolis
McDonough	Macomb
McHenry	Woodstock
McLean	Bloomington
Menard	Petersburg
Mercer	Aledo
Monroe	Waterloo
Montgomery	Hillsboro
Morgan	Jacksonville
Moultrie	Sullivan
Ogle	Oregon
Peoria	Peoria
Perry	Pinckneyville
Piatt	Monticello
Pike	Pittsfield
Pope	Golconda
Pulaski	Mound City
Putnam	Hennepin
Randolph	Chester
Richland	Olney
Rock Island	Rock Island
St. Clair	Belleville
Saline	Harrisburg
Sangamon	Springfield
Schuyler	Rushville
Scott	Winchester
Shelby	Shelbyville
Stark	Toulon
Stephenson	Freeport
Tazewell	Pekin
Union	Jonesboro
Vermilion	Danville
Wabash	Mount Carmel
Warren	Monmouth
Washington	Nashville
Wayne	Fairfield
White	Carmi
Whiteside	Morrison
Will	Joliet
Williamson	Marion
Winnebago	Rockford
Woodford	Eureka

PARTIAL LIST OF
CITIES AND TOWNS

1980 Census
•County Seats

Abingdon 4,210 ...202,C-4	Avon 1,019 ...202,C-5	Braidwood 3,429 ...203,G-3
Adair ...204,C-2	Baldhill ...202,B-4	Breckenridge ...205,E-3
Addieville ...207,E-2	Banner ...204,D-1	Breese 3,516 ...207,E-2
Albany 1,014 ...202,D-2	Barrington 9,029 ...203,G-1	Bridgeport 2,281 ...207,H-2
Albion • 2,285 ...207,G-2	Barry 1,487 ...204,B-3	Brighton 2,364 ...204,D-5
Alden ...203,F-1	Bartonville ...204,D-1	Brimfield 890 ...202,D-4
Aledo • 3,881 ...202,C-4	Batavia 12,574 ...203,G-2	Brooklyn 1,233 ...204,C-2
Alexis 1,076 ...202,C-4	Beardstown 6,338 ...204,C-2	Brookport 1,128 ...207,F-5
Algonquin 5,834 ...203,G-1	Beaucoup ...207,E-2	Brownsville ...207,G-3
Allen ...205,E-2	Beckemeyer 1,119 ...207,E-2	Buckingham ...203,G-4
Allendale ...207,H-2	Beecher 2,024 ...203,H-3	Buckner 520 ...207,F-3
Alhambra ...206,D-1	Beecher City 888 ...205,G-4	Buda 668 ...202,D-3
Alpha 815 ...202,C-4	Beecreek ...204,C-4	Budd ...203,F-4
Alsey ...204,C-3	Belle Prairie City 58 ...207,F-3	Bunker Hill 1,700 ...204,D-5
Alta ...203,E-4	Belleville • 42,150 ...206,D-2	Bushnell 3,811 ...204,C-1
Altamont 2,389 ...205,F-4	Bellevue 2,045 ...202,D-5	Butler ...205,E-4
Alton 34,171 ...206,D-1	Belvidere • 15,176 ...203,G-1	Byron 2,035 ...203,E-2
Altona ...202,D-4	Bement 1,770 ...205,F-2	Cabery ...203,G-4
Amboy 2,377 ...203,E-2	Benld 1,638 ...204,D-4	Cache ...207,E-5
Andalusia 1,238 ...202,C-3	Benson ...203,E-4	Cahokia 18,904 ...206,D-2
Andres ...203,H-3	Benton • 7,778 ...207,F-3	Cairo • 5,931 ...207,E-5
Anna 5,408 ...207,E-4	Bethalto 8,630 ...206,D-1	Caledonia ...203,F-1
Annawan 908 ...202,D-3	Bethany 1,550 ...205,F-3	Camargo ...205,G-3
Antioch 4,419 ...203,G-1	Big Rock ...203,F-2	Cambridge • 2,217 ...202,D-3
Arcola 2,714 ...205,G-3	Blandinsville ...204,B-2	Camden ...204,C-2
Arenzville 495 ...204,C-3	886 ...204,B-1	Camp Point 1,285 ...204,B-2
Argenta 994 ...205,F-2	Bloomfield ...205,H-3	Canton 14,626 ...204,D-1
Arlington ...203,E-3	Bloomfield ...204,D-4	Capron 678 ...203,F-1
Arlington Heights 66,116 ...203,G-2	Bloomington • 44,189 ...205,F-1	Carbondale 27,194 ...207,E-4
Armstrong ...205,H-2	Blue Island 21,855 ...203,H-3	Carlinville • 5,439 ...204,D-4
Arthur 2,122 ...205,G-3	Blue Mound 1,338 ...205,E-3	Carlock 410 ...205,E-1
Ashkum 908 ...203,G-4	Bluff Springs ...204,C-2	Carlyle • 3,388 ...207,E-2
Ashland 1,351 ...204,D-3	Bluffs 821 ...204,C-3	Carmi • 6,264 ...207,G-3
Ashley 658 ...207,E-3	Blyton ...204,C-1	Carpentersville 23,272 ...203,G-2
Ashmore ...205,H-3	Boden ...207,F-4	Carrier Mills 2,268 ...207,F-4
Ashton 1,140 ...203,E-2	Bolingbrook 37,261 ...203,G-2	Carrollton • 2,816 ...204,C-4
Assumption 1,283 ...205,F-4	Bourbonnais 13,280 ...203,H-4	Cartersville 3,445 ...207,F-4
Astoria 1,370 ...204,C-2	Bowen 525 ...204,B-2	Carthage • 2,978 ...204,B-2
Athens 1,371 ...204,D-3	Boyleston ...207,G-2	Cary 6,640 ...203,G-1
Atkinson 1,138 ...202,D-3	Bradford 924 ...203,E-4	Casey 3,026 ...205,G-4
Atlanta 1,807 ...205,E-2	Bradley 11,008 ...203,H-4	
Atlas ...204,B-3		
Atterberry ...204,D-2		
Atwood 1,464 ...205,G-3		
Auburn 3,616 ...204,D-3		
Augusta 764 ...204,B-2		
Aurora 81,293 ...203,G-2		
Ava 811 ...207,E-3		
Aviston 846 ...207,E-2		

CONTINUED ON PAGE 206

ILLINOIS TOLL ROADS

EAST - WEST TOLLWAY Speed limit is as posted. Passenger car toll is $1.90 for the entire length of 97.7 miles, approximately 1.9c per mile.

NORTHWEST TOLLWAY Speed limit is as posted. Passenger car toll is $1.50 for the entire length of 76.2 miles, approximately 2c per mile.

TRI - STATE TOLLWAY Speed limit is as posted. Passenger car toll is $1.80 for the entire length of 77.1 miles, approximately 2.3c per mile.

CHICAGO SKYWAY Speed limit is as posted. Passenger car toll is .90c for the entire length of 7.8 miles.

TOLL HIGHWAY INTERCHANGES

Access is limited as indicated below.

- **A** On and Off in all Directions
- **B** Eastbound Off-Westbound On
- **C** Eastbound On-Westbound Off
- **D** Northbound Off-Southbound On
- **E** Northbound On-Southbound Off
- **F** Westbound Off
- **G** Northbound Off & On-Southbound Off
- **H** Eastbound On and Off
- **Z** Toll Road to Toll Road Only

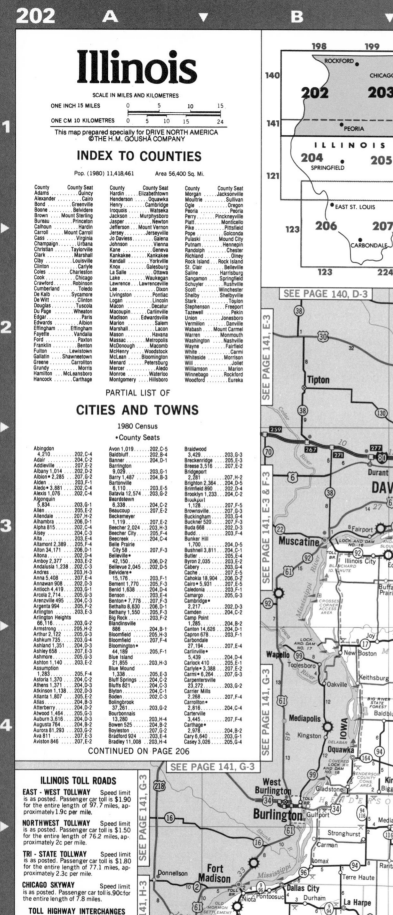

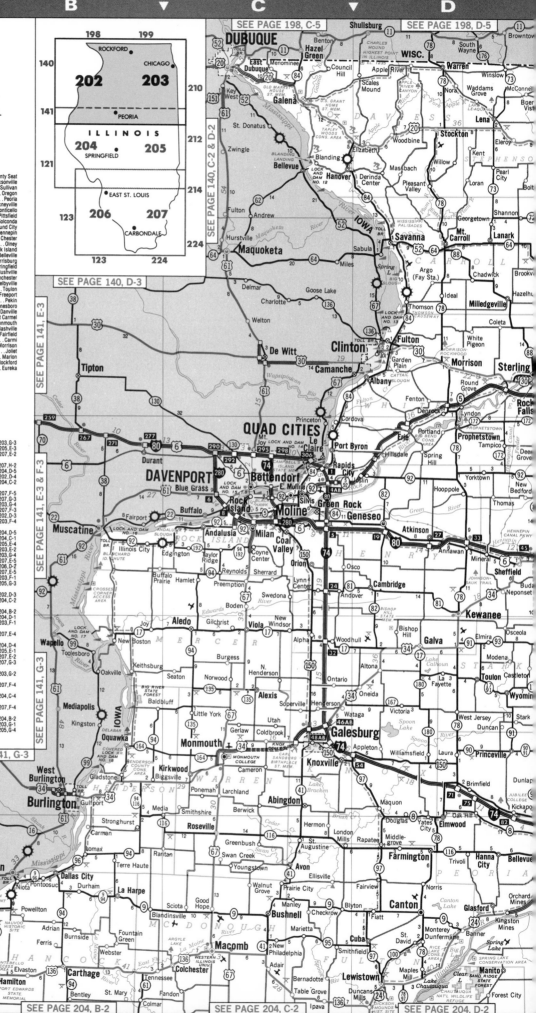

SEE PAGE 198, C-5
SEE PAGE 198, D-5
SEE PAGE 140, C-2 & D-2
SEE PAGE 140, D-3
SEE PAGE 141, E-3
SEE PAGE 141, E-3 & F-3
SEE PAGE 141, G-3
SEE PAGE 141, G-3
SEE PAGE 121, F-2; 141, H-3
SEE PAGE 204, B-2
SEE PAGE 204, C-2
SEE PAGE 204, D-2

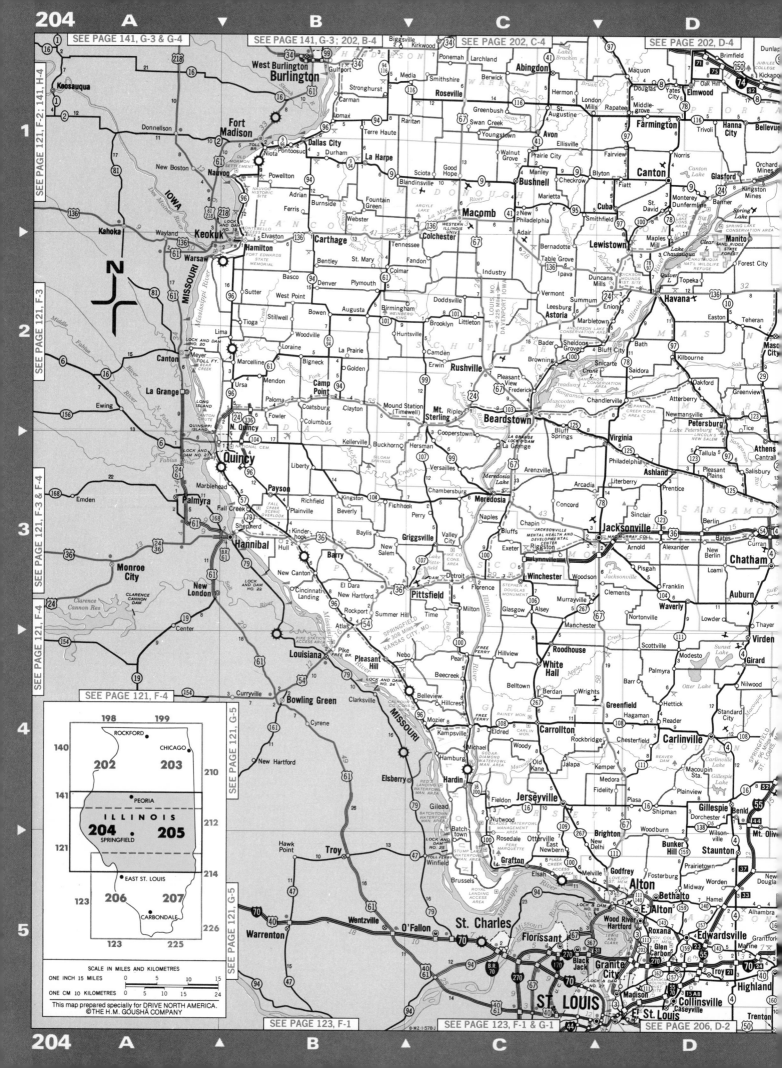

CONTINUED FROM PAGE 202

Caseyville 4,308 ... 206,D-2
Castleton ... 202,D-4
Catlin 2,226 ... 205,H-2
Cazenovia ... 203,E-4
Cedarville ... 203,E-1
Central ... 203,G-3
Central City 1,505 ... 207,E-2
Centralia 15,126 ... 207,E-2
Cerro Gordo 1,553 ... 205,F-3
Chadwick 631 ... 202,D-2
Chambersburg ... 204,C-3
Champaign 58,133 ... 205,G-2
Chandlerville 842 ... 204,D-2
Channahon 3,734 ... 203,G-3
Chapin ... 204,C-3
Charleston• 19,355 ... 205,G-4
Chatham 5,597 ... 204,D-3
Chatsworth 1,187 ... 203,G-5
Chebanse 1,191 ... 203,G-4
Chemung ... 203,F-1
Chenoa 1,847 ... 203,F-5
Cherry ... 203,E-3
Cherry Valley 946 ... 203,F-1
Chester• 8,027 ... 206,D-3
Chesterfield ... 204,D-4
Chesterville ... 205,G-3
Chicago• 3,005,072 ... 203,H-2
Chicago Heights 37,026 ... 203,H-3
Chillicothe 6,176 ... 203,E-4
Chrisman 1,413 ... 205,H-3
Christopher 3,086 ... 207,F-3
Cisne 705 ... 207,G-2
Cissna Park 825 ... 205,H-1
Clark Center ... 205,H-4
Clarksdale ... 205,E-4
Clay City 1,038 ... 207,G-2
Clayton 889 ... 204,B-2
Clifton 1,390 ... 203,G-4
Clinton• 8,014 ... 205,F-2
Coal City 3,028 ... 203,G-3
Coal Valley 3,800 ... 202,C-3
Coatsburg ... 204,B-2
Cobden 571 ... 207,E-4
Colchester 1,729 ... 204,C-1
Colfax 920 ... 205,F-1
Collinsville 19,613 ... 206,D-2
Columbia 4,269 ... 206,D-2
Cornell 1,118 ... 203,F-4
Coulterville ... 207,E-3
Cowden ... 205,F-4
Cowling ... 207,H-3
Crab Orchard ... 207,F-4
Creal Springs 845 ... 207,F-4
Crete 5,417 ... 203,H-3
Creve Coeur 6,851 ... 203,E-5
Crossville 944 ... 207,G-3
Crystal Lake 18,590 ... 203,G-1
Cuba 1,648 ... 204,D-1
Cypress 271 ... 207,F-5
Dakota ... 203,E-1
Dallas City 1,408 ... 202,B-5
Dana ... 203,F-4
Danforth ... 203,G-4
Danvers 921 ... 205,E-1
Danville• 38,985 ... 205,H-2
Davis ... 203,E-1
De Kalb 33,099 ... 203,F-2
De Pue 1,873 ... 203,E-3
De Soto 1,589 ... 207,E-4
Decatur• 94,081 ... 205,F-3
Deer Grove ... 202,D-3
Delavan 1,973 ... 205,E-2
Des Plaines 53,568 ... 203,G-2
Detroit ... 204,C-3
Diamond ... 203,G-3
Dieterich ... 205,G-4
Dillsburg ... 205,G-2
Diona ... 205,G-4
Dixon• 15,659 ... 203,E-2
Dolton 24,766 ... 203,H-3
Dongola 611 ... 207,E-5
Donovan ... 203,H-4
Du Quoin 6,594 ... 207,E-3
Duncans Mills ... 204,D-2
Dundas ... 207,G-1
Dupo 3,039 ... 206,D-2
Durand ... 203,E-1
Dwight 4,146 ... 203,G-4
Earlville 1,382 ... 203,F-3
East Alton 7,123 ... 206,D-1
East Dubuque 2,194 ... 202,C-1
East Dundee 2,618 ... 203,G-1
East Moline 20,907 ... 202,C-3
East Peoria 22,385 ... 203,E-5
East St. Louis 55,200 ... 206,D-2
Edgington ... 202,C-3
Edinburg 1,231 ... 205,E-3
Edwardsville• 12,460 ... 206,D-1
Effingham• 11,270 ... 205,F-4
El Paso 2,676 ... 203,F-5
Elburn 1,224 ... 203,G-2
Eldorado 5,198 ... 207,G-4
Eldred ... 204,C-4
Eleroy ... 202,D-1
Elgin 63,798 ... 203,G-2
Elizabeth 772 ... 202,D-1
Elizabethtown• 478 ... 207,G-4
Elk Grove Village 28,907 ... 203,G-2
Elkville 973 ... 207,E-3
Ellis Grove ... 206,D-3
Elmira ... 202,D-4
Elmwood 2,117 ... 202,D-5
Elvaston ... 204,B-2
Elwin ... 205,F-3
Elwood 814 ... 203,G-3
Enfield 890 ... 207,G-3
Erie 1,725 ... 202,D-3
Ernst ... 205,H-4
Eureka• 4,306 ... 203,E-5
Evanston 73,706 ... 203,H-2
Evansville 863 ... 206,D-3
Fairbury 3,544 ... 203,F-5
Fairfield• 5,954 ... 207,G-2
Fairman ... 207,E-2
Fairmount 851 ... 205,H-2
Fairview Heights 12,414 ... 206,D-2
Farmer City 2,252 ... 205,F-2
Farmington 3,118 ... 202,D-5
Fayetteville ... 206,D-2
Fiatt ... 204,D-1
Fisher 1,572 ... 205,G-2
Flanagan ... 203,F-4
Flora 5,379 ... 207,G-2
Florence ... 204,C-3
Forrest 1,246 ... 203,G-5
Forreston 1,384 ... 203,E-2
Fowler ... 204,B-2
Fox Lake 6,381 ... 203,G-1
Fox River Grove 2,515 ... 203,G-1
Frankfort 4,357 ... 203,H-3
Franklin Grove 965 ... 203,E-2
Freeburg 2,989 ... 206,D-2
Freeport• 26,406 ... 203,E-1
Fulton 3,936 ... 202,D-2
Galatia 1,042 ... 207,F-4
Galena• 3,876 ... 202,C-1
Galesburg• 35,305 ... 202,C-4
Galva 3,185 ... 202,D-4
Garber ... 205,G-1
Garden Prairie ... 203,F-1
Gardner 1,322 ... 203,G-4
Garfield ... 203,F-4
Garrett ... 205,G-3
Gays ... 205,G-4
Geff ... 207,G-2
Geneseo 6,373 ... 202,D-3
Geneva• 9,881 ... 203,G-2
Genoa 3,276 ... 203,F-2
Georgetown 4,220 ... 205,H-2
Germantown 1,191 ... 207,E-2
Gibson City 3,498 ... 205,G-1
Gifford ... 205,G-2
Gilchrist ... 202,C-4
Gillespie 3,740 ... 204,D-4
Gilman 1,913 ... 203,G-5
Girard 2,246 ... 204,D-4
Glasford 1,201 ... 204,D-1
Glen Carbon 5,197 ... 206,D-2
Glencoe 9,200 ... 203,H-1
Glenn ... 207,E-4
Godfrey ... 204,D-5
Golconda• 960 ... 207,G-5
Good Hope ... 204,C-1
Goodfield 500 ... 203,E-5
Gordon ... 205,H-5
Grafton 1,024 ... 204,C-5
Grand Chain ... 207,F-5
Grand Ridge 684 ... 203,F-3
Grand Tower 748 ... 207,E-4
Granite City 36,815 ... 206,D-2
Grant Park 1,038 ... 203,H-3
Granville 1,537 ... 203,E-3
Graymont ... 203,F-4
Grayslake 5,260 ... 203,G-1
Grayville 2,313 ... 207,G-3
Green Rock 3,324 ... 202,C-3
Greenfield 1,090 ... 204,D-4
Greenup 1,655 ... 205,G-4
Greenview 830 ... 204,D-2
Greenville• 5,271 ... 207,E-1
Gridley 1,246 ... 203,F-5
Griggsville 1,301 ... 204,C-3
Gulfport ... 202,B-4
Hagaman ... 204,D-4
Hamel 537 ... 206,D-1
Hamilton 3,509 ... 204,B-2
Hammond ... 205,F-3
Hampshire 1,735 ... 203,F-2
Hanna City 1,361 ... 202,D-5
Hanover 1,069 ... 202,C-1
Hardin• 1,107 ... 204,C-4
Harmony ... 203,F-1
Harrisburg• 9,322 ... 207,F-4
Harrison ... 203,E-1
Hartford 1,887 ... 206,D-1
Hartsburg ... 205,E-2
Harvard• 5,126 ... 203,F-1
Harvel ... 205,E-4
Havana• 2,682 ... 204,D-2
Hebron 786 ... 203,G-1
Hecker ... 206,D-3
Hennepin• 716 ... 203,E-3
Henning ... 205,H-2
Henry 2,740 ... 203,E-4
Herborn ... 205,F-4
Herrin 10,040 ... 207,F-4
Herscher ... 203,G-4
Hettick ... 204,D-4
Heyworth 1,598 ... 205,F-2
Hidalgo ... 205,G-4
Highland 7,122 ... 206,D-2
Highland Park 30,611 ... 203,H-1
Hillcrest ... 203,F-2
Hillsboro• 4,408 ... 205,E-4
Hillsdale 731 ... 202,D-3
Hinckley 1,447 ... 203,F-2
Hindsboro ... 205,G-3
Hoffman Estates 38,258 ... 203,G-2
Homer 1,279 ... 205,G-2
Hoopeston 6,411 ... 205,H-1
Hord ... 207,F-1
Huey ... 207,E-2
Hull ... 204,B-3
Hume ... 205,H-3
Huntley 1,646 ... 203,G-1
Illinois City ... 202,B-3
Illiopolis 1,118 ... 205,E-3
Industry ... 204,C-2
Ipava 661 ... 204,C-2
Iroquois ... 203,H-4
Irving ... 205,E-4
Irwin ... 203,G-4
Jacksonville• 20,284 ... 204,D-3
Jerseyville• 7,506 ... 204,C-4
Jewett ... 205,G-4
Johnston City 3,873 ... 207,F-4
Joliet• 77,956 ... 203,G-3
Jonesboro• 1,842 ... 207,E-4
Kankakee• 30,141 ... 203,H-4
Kansas 791 ... 205,H-3
Karnak 646 ... 207,F-5
Keensburg ... 207,H-2
Keithsburg 936 ... 202,B-4
Kemper ... 204,D-4
Keptown ... 205,F-4
Kewanee 14,508 ... 202,D-3
Kincaid 1,591 ... 205,E-3
Kinmundy 945 ... 207,F-2
Kinderhook 259 ... 204,B-3
Kirkland 1,155 ... 203,F-2
Kirkwood 1,008 ... 202,C-4
Knoxville 3,432 ... 202,C-4
Lacon• 2,135 ... 203,E-4
La Fayette ... 202,D-4
La Grange 15,681 ... 203,H-2
La Harpe 1,471 ... 204,B-1
La Moille 734 ... 203,E-3
La Place ... 205,F-3
La Rose ... 203,E-4
La Salle 10,347 ... 203,E-3
Ladd 1,337 ... 203,E-3
Lake Forest 15,245 ... 203,H-1
Lake Zurich 8,225 ... 203,G-1
Lanark 1,483 ... 202,D-2
Laura ... 202,D-4
Lawrenceville• 5,652 ... 207,H-2
Le Roy 2,870 ... 205,F-2
Leaf River ... 203,E-2
Lebanon 3,245 ... 206,D-2
Lena 2,295 ... 202,D-1
Lewistown• 2,758 ... 204,D-2
Lexington 1,806 ... 203,F-5
Liberty 16,327 ... 204,B-3
Lincoln• ... 205,E-2
Lindenhurst ... 203,G-1
Lis ... 205,G-5
Lisle 13,625 ... 203,G-2
Litchfield 7,204 ... 205,E-4
Littleton ... 204,C-2
Livingston ... 205,H-4
Lockport 9,017 ... 203,G-3
Lomax ... 202,B-5
Long Creek ... 205,F-3
Lostant ... 203,F-4
Louisville• 1,166 ... 207,G-2
Loves Park 13,192 ... 203,F-1
Lovington 1,313 ... 205,F-3
Low Point ... 203,E-4
Lyndon 777 ... 202,D-2
Mackinaw 1,354 ... 205,E-1
Macomb• 19,632 ... 204,C-1
Macon 1,300 ... 205,F-3
Madison 5,915 ... 206,D-2
Magnolia ... 203,E-4
Mahomet 1,986 ... 205,G-2
Manchester ... 204,C-3
Manhattan 1,944 ... 203,G-3
Manito 1,869 ... 204,D-2
Manley ... 204,C-1
Mansfield 921 ... 205,F-2
Manteno 3,155 ... 203,H-3
Maples Mill ... 204,D-2
Maquon ... 202,D-4
Marblehead ... 204,B-3
Marengo 4,361 ... 203,F-1
Marietta ... 204,C-1
Marion• 14,031 ... 207,F-4
Marissa 2,568 ... 206,D-3
Maroa 1,760 ... 205,F-2
Marquette Heights 3,386 ... 203,E-5
Marseilles 4,766 ... 203,F-3
Marshall• 3,655 ... 205,H-4
Martinsville 1,298 ... 205,H-4
Martinton ... 203,H-4
Mascoutah 4,962 ... 206,D-2
Mason City 2,719 ... 204,D-2
Mattoon 19,787 ... 205,G-4
Mazon ... 203,G-3
McClure ... 207,E-5
McHenry 10,908 ... 203,G-1
McLean 836 ... 205,E-2
McLeansboro• 2,960 ... 207,F-3
Medora ... 204,D-4
Mendon 979 ... 204,B-2
Mendota 7,134 ... 203,E-3
Meredosia 1,272 ... 204,C-3
Meriden ... 203,F-3
Metamora 2,482 ... 203,E-4
Metcalf ... 205,H-3
Metropolis• 7,171 ... 207,F-5
Middlegrove ... 202,D-5
Milan 6,264 ... 202,C-3
Milford 1,716 ... 203,H-5
Mill Creek ... 207,E-5
Mill Shoals ... 207,G-3
Milledgeville 1,209 ... 202,D-2
Millersville ... 205,E-4
Millstadt 2,736 ... 206,D-2
Milton ... 204,C-3
Minier 1,261 ... 205,E-1
Minonk 2,039 ... 203,F-4
Modesto ... 204,D-4
Moline 45,709 ... 202,C-3
Momence 3,297 ... 203,H-4
Monee ... 203,H-3
Monmouth• 10,706 ... 202,C-4
Monterey ... 204,D-1
Monticello• 4,753 ... 205,F-2
Montrose 8,833 ... 205,G-4
Morris• ... 203,G-3
Morrison• 4,605 ... 202,D-2
Morrisonville 1,208 ... 205,E-4
Morton 14,178 ... 205,E-1
Mound City• 1,102 ... 207,E-5
Mounds 1,669 ... 207,E-5
Mt. Carmel• 8,908 ... 207,H-2
Mt. Carroll• 1,936 ... 202,D-2
Mt. Morris 2,989 ... 203,E-2
Mt. Olive 2,357 ... 204,D-4
Mt. Pulaski 1,783 ... 205,E-2
Mt. Sterling• 2,186 ... 204,C-2
Mt. Vernon• 16,995 ... 207,F-3
Moweaqua 1,922 ... 205,F-3
Mozier ... 204,C-4
Mulberry Grove 707 ... 205,E-5
Mundelein 17,053 ... 203,G-1
Murphysboro• 9,866 ... 207,E-4
Murrayville ... 204,C-3
Naperville 42,330 ... 203,G-2
Nashville• 3,186 ... 207,E-2
Nauvoo 1,133 ... 204,B-1
Neoga 1,736 ... 205,G-4
Neponset ... 202,D-3
New Athens 1,937 ... 206,D-3
New Baden 2,476 ... 206,D-2
New Boston 731 ... 202,B-4
New Burnside 276 ... 207,F-4
New Delhi ... 204,C-5
New Hanover Station ... 206,D-2
New Hartford ... 204,B-3
New Haven 559 ... 207,G-3
New Lenox 5,792 ... 203,G-3
New Memphis ... 206,D-2
New Philadelphia ... 204,C-1
New Windsor ... 202,C-4
Newman 1,079 ... 205,G-3
Newton• ... 205,G-5
Nokomis 2,656 ... 205,E-4
Normal 35,672 ... 205,F-1
Normandy ... 203,E-3
Norris City 1,515 ... 207,G-3
North Aurora 5,205 ... 203,G-2
North Chicago 38,774 ... 203,H-1
North Pekin 1,824 ... 205,E-1
N. Quincy ... 204,B-2
Northbrook 30,735 ... 203,H-2
Oak Lawn 60,590 ... 203,H-2
Oak Park 54,887 ... 203,H-2
Oakford 1,035 ... 204,D-2
Oakland ... 205,G-3
Oblong 1,840 ... 205,H-5
Oconee ... 205,E-4
Odell 1,083 ... 203,F-4
Odin 1,285 ... 207,F-2
O'Fallon 10,217 ... 206,D-2
Oglesby 3,979 ... 203,F-3
Ohio ... 203,E-3
Ohlman ... 205,E-4
Oilfield ... 205,G-4
Okawville 1,337 ... 207,E-2
Old Kane ... 204,C-2
Old Ripley ... 207,E-1
Olive Branch ... 207,E-5
Oliver ... 205,H-4
Olney• 9,026 ... 207,G-2
Omaha ... 207,G-3
Onarga 1,269 ... 203,E-1
Oneco ... 203,E-1
Oquawka• 1,533 ... 202,B-4
Orangeville ... 203,E-1
Oreana ... 205,F-3
Oregon• 3,559 ... 203,E-2
Orion 2,013 ... 202,C-3
Ospur ... 205,F-2
Oswego 3,021 ... 203,G-3
Ottawa• 18,166 ... 203,F-3
Owaneco ... 205,E-4
Palatine 32,166 ... 203,G-2
Palestine 1,718 ... 205,H-5
Palmer ... 205,E-4
Palmyra ... 204,D-4
Paloma ... 204,B-2
Pana 6,040 ... 205,F-4
Paris• 9,885 ... 205,H-3
Park Forest 26,222 ... 203,H-3
Park Ridge 38,704 ... 203,H-2
Parkersburg ... 207,G-2
Patton ... 207,H-2
Paw Paw 839 ... 203,F-3
Pawnee 2,577 ... 205,E-3
Paxton• 4,258 ... 205,G-1
Pearl 661 ... 204,C-4
Pearl City ... 202,D-1
Pecatonica 1,732 ... 203,E-1
Pekin• 33,967 ... 205,E-1
Peoria• 124,160 ... 203,E-5
Peoria Heights 7,453 ... 203,E-5
Peotone 2,832 ... 203,H-3
Percy 1,053 ... 207,E-3
Peru 10,886 ... 203,E-3
Petersburg• 2,419 ... 204,D-2
Philadelphia ... 204,D-3
Piasa ... 204,D-4
Pike ... 204,B-4
Pinckneyville• 3,319 ... 207,E-3
Piper City 905 ... 203,G-5
Pisgah ... 204,D-3
Pittsfield• 4,170 ... 204,C-3
Plainfield 4,485 ... 203,G-3
Plano 4,875 ... 203,F-3
Pleasant Hill 1,112 ... 204,B-4
Pleasant Valley ... 202,D-1
Plum Hill ... 207,E-2
Plymouth 649 ... 204,B-2
Pocahontas 866 ... 207,E-1
Polo 2,043 ... 203,E-2
Pontiac• 11,227 ... 203,F-4
Pontoosuc ... 202,B-5
Poplar Grove ... 203,F-1
Port Byron 1,289 ... 202,C-3
Potomac 909 ... 205,H-2
Prairie Center ... 203,F-3
Preemption ... 202,C-3
Princeton• 7,342 ... 203,E-3
Princeville 1,712 ... 202,D-4
Prophetstown 2,141 ... 202,D-3
Pulaski ... 207,E-5
Quincy• 42,352 ... 204,A-3
Radford ... 205,F-3
Ramsey 1,058 ... 205,E-4
Rankin 727 ... 205,H-1
Ransom ... 203,F-4
Rantoul 20,161 ... 205,G-2
Rapatee ... 202,D-5
Rapids City ... 202,C-3
Raymond 957 ... 205,E-4
Reader ... 204,D-4
Reading ... 203,F-4
Red Bud 2,850 ... 206,D-3
Reddick ... 203,G-4
Reynolds ... 202,C-3
Richmond 1,068 ... 203,G-1
Richview ... 207,E-2
Ridge Farm 1,096 ... 205,H-3
Ridgway 1,245 ... 207,G-4
Risk ... 203,G-5
Riverton 2,783 ... 205,E-3
Roanoke 2,001 ... 203,E-4
Robinson• 7,285 ... 205,H-5
Rochelle 8,982 ... 203,F-2
Rochester 2,488 ... 205,E-3
Rock City ... 203,E-1
Rock Falls 10,624 ... 202,D-2
Rock Island• 47,036 ... 202,C-3
Rockbridge ... 204,D-4
Rockford• 139,712 ... 203,E-1
Rockton 2,313 ... 203,F-1
Rockwood ... 206,D-4
Rome ... 203,E-4
Romeoville 15,519 ... 203,G-3
Roodhouse 2,364 ... 204,C-4
Rosamond ... 205,E-4
Roselle 16,948 ... 203,G-2
Roseville 1,254 ... 202,C-5
Rosiclare 1,441 ... 207,G-4
Rossville 1,363 ... 205,H-2
Roxana 1,587 ... 206,D-1
Royalton 1,320 ... 207,E-4
Ruma 254 ... 206,D-3
Rushville• 3,348 ... 204,C-2
St. Anne 1,421 ... 203,H-4
St. Augustine ... 202,C-5
St. Charles 17,492 ... 203,G-2
St. David 786 ... 204,D-1
St. Elmo 1,611 ... 205,F-5
St. Francisville 1,040 ... 207,H-2
St. Joseph 1,900 ... 205,G-2
St. Libory ... 206,D-2
St. Peter ... 207,F-1
Salem• 7,813 ... 207,F-2
Salisbury ... 204,D-3
Samsville ... 207,G-2
San Jose 784 ... 205,E-2
Sandoval 1,734 ... 207,E-2
Sandwich 3,675 ... 203,F-3
Saunemin ... 203,G-4
Savanna 4,529 ... 202,D-2
Saybrook 882 ... 205,F-2
Schram City 708 ... 205,E-4
Seneca 2,098 ... 203,F-3
Serena ... 203,F-3
Sesser 2,238 ... 207,F-3
Shabbona ... 203,F-2
Sharpsburg ... 205,E-3
Shattuc ... 207,E-2
Shawneetown• 1,841 ... 207,G-4
Sheffield 1,130 ... 202,D-3
Shelbyville• 5,259 ... 205,F-4
Sheldon 1,215 ... 203,H-5
Shepherd ... 204,B-3
Sheridan 719 ... 203,F-3
Shipman ... 204,D-4
Shobonier ... 207,F-1
Sibley ... 205,G-1
Sigel ... 205,G-4
Silvis 7,130 ... 202,C-3
Smithton ... 206,D-2
Somonauk ... 203,F-3
Sorento 677 ... 205,E-5
South Beloit 4,088 ... 203,F-1
South Elgin 6,218 ... 203,G-2
South Holland 24,977 ... 203,H-3
South Pekin 1,243 ... 205,E-1
Southern View 1,306 ... 205,E-3
Sparland ... 203,E-4
Sparta 4,957 ... 206,D-3
Speer ... 203,E-4
Spring Bay ... 203,E-4
Spring Valley 5,822 ... 203,E-3
Springerton ... 207,G-3
Springfield• 99,637 ... 205,E-3
Staunton 4,744 ... 204,D-5
Steeleville 2,240 ... 206,D-3
Steger 9,269 ... 203,H-3
Sterling 16,273 ... 202,D-2
Stewardson ... 205,F-4
Stillman Valley ... 203,E-2
Stockton 1,872 ... 202,D-1
Stonefort ... 207,F-4
Stonington 1,184 ... 205,E-3
Strasburg ... 205,F-4
Strawn ... 203,G-5
Streator 14,769 ... 203,F-4
Stronghurst 865 ... 202,B-5
Sublette ... 203,E-3
Sullivan• 4,526 ... 205,F-3
Summer Hill ... 204,B-3
Summerfield ... 206,D-2
Summum ... 204,C-2
Sumner 1,238 ... 207,H-2
Swansea 5,347 ... 206,D-2
Sycamore• 9,219 ... 203,F-2
Table Grove ... 204,C-2
Tamalco ... 207,E-2
Tamaroa 885 ... 207,E-3
Tamms ... 207,E-5
Taylor Ridge ... 202,C-3
Taylorville• 11,386 ... 205,E-3
Tennessee ... 204,B-2
Terre Haute ... 202,B-5
Teutopolis 1,414 ... 205,G-4
Thayer 759 ... 204,D-3
Thebes ... 207,E-5
Tilden 1,025 ... 206,D-3
Tilton ... 205,H-2
Timewell ... 204,B-2
Tiskilwa 990 ... 203,E-3
Toledo• 1,284 ... 205,G-4
Tolono 2,434 ... 205,G-2
Toluca 1,471 ... 203,E-4
Tonica 695 ... 203,F-4
Toulon• 1,390 ... 202,D-4
Tower Hill ... 205,F-4
Tremont 2,096 ... 205,E-1
Trenton 2,504 ... 206,D-2
Trimble ... 205,H-4
Trivoli ... 202,D-5
Troy 3,772 ... 206,D-2
Tuscola• 3,839 ... 205,G-3
Ullin ... 207,E-5
Union ... 203,F-1
Union Hill ... 203,G-4
Urbana• 35,978 ... 205,G-2
Vandalia• 5,338 ... 205,E-5
Varna ... 203,E-4
Velma ... 205,E-4
Vermont 885 ... 204,C-2
Vernon ... 207,F-1
Vevay Park ... 205,G-4
Victoria ... 202,D-4
Vienna• 1,420 ... 207,F-5
Villa Grove 2,707 ... 205,G-3
Viola 1,144 ... 202,C-4
Virden 3,899 ... 204,D-4
Virgil ... 203,F-2
Virginia• 1,825 ... 204,D-3
Walnut 1,513 ... 203,E-3
Waltonville ... 207,F-3
Wamac 1,665 ... 207,E-2
Wapella ... 205,F-2
Ware ... 207,E-4
Warren 1,595 ... 202,D-1
Warrensburg 1,372 ... 205,F-3
Warsaw 1,842 ... 204,A-2
Washburn 1,206 ... 203,E-4
Washington 10,364 ... 203,E-5
Waterloo• 4,646 ... 206,D-2
Watseka• 5,543 ... 203,H-4
Watson ... 205,F-5
Wauconda 5,688 ... 203,G-1
Waukegan• 67,653 ... 203,H-1
Waverly 1,537 ... 204,D-3
Wayne City 1,132 ... 207,F-2
Wenona 1,025 ... 203,F-4
W. Chicago 12,550 ... 203,G-2
West Frankfort 9,437 ... 207,F-3
West Jersey ... 202,D-4
West Salem 1,145 ... 207,G-2
West Union ... 205,H-4
West Vienna ... 207,F-4
Westville 3,573 ... 205,H-2
Wetaug ... 207,E-5
Wheaton• 43,043 ... 203,G-2
Wheeler ... 205,G-5
White Hall 2,935 ... 204,C-4
White Heath ... 205,G-2
Whitehill ... 207,F-5
Williamsfield ... 202,D-4
Wilmington 4,424 ... 203,G-3
Wilsonville 608 ... 204,D-4
Wilton Center ... 203,G-3
Winchester• 1,716 ... 204,C-3
Windsor 1,228 ... 205,F-4
Winnebago 1,644 ... 203,E-1
Winnetka 12,772 ... 203,H-2
Winthrop Harbor 5,438 ... 203,H-1
Witt 1,205 ... 205,E-4
Wolf Lake ... 207,E-4
Wood River 12,449 ... 206,D-1
Woodbine ... 202,D-1
Woodbury ... 205,G-4
Woodstock• 11,725 ... 203,G-1
Woosung ... 203,E-2
Worden 953 ... 204,D-5
Wyanet 1,069 ... 203,E-3
Wyoming 1,614 ... 202,D-4
Xenia ... 207,F-2
Yorktown ... 202,D-3
Yorkville• 3,422 ... 203,G-3
Zeigler 1,858 ... 207,F-3
Zion 17,861 ... 203,H-1

MZ-578-J-X1

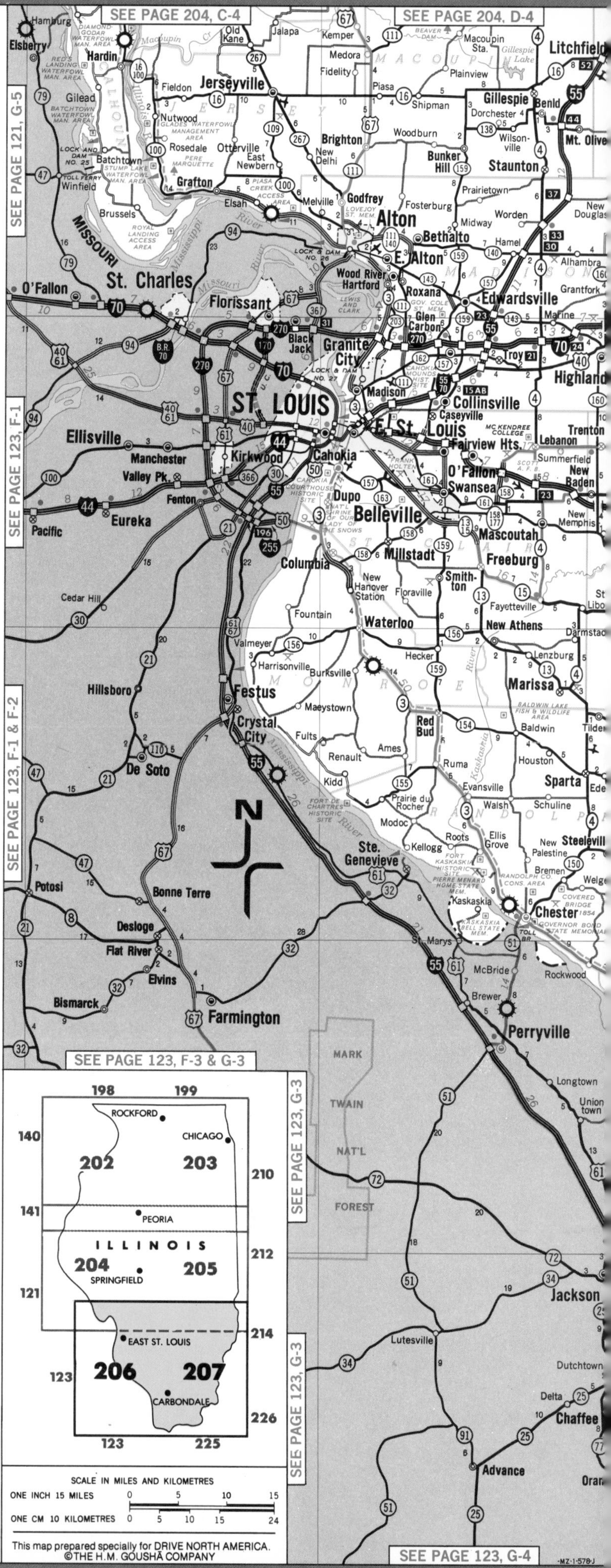

SEE PAGE 204, C-4
SEE PAGE 204, D-4
SEE PAGE 121, G-5
SEE PAGE 123, F-1
SEE PAGE 123, F-1 & F-2
SEE PAGE 123, F-3 & G-3
SEE PAGE 123, G-3
SEE PAGE 123, G-4
Hamburg
Hardin
Jerseyville
Litchfield
Gillespie
Staunton
Grafton
Alton
Godfrey
St. Charles
Florissant
O'Fallon
Edwardsville
Granite City
ST. LOUIS
E. St. Louis
Collinsville
Ellisville
Manchester
Kirkwood
Cahokia
Belleville
Eureka
Pacific
Columbia
Waterloo
Mascoutah
Freeburg
Festus
Crystal City
Hillsboro
De Soto
Red Bud
Sparta
Ste. Genevieve
Chester
Bonne Terre
Flat River
Farmington
Potosi
Perryville
Jackson
Chaffee
Advance
MISSOURI
ILLINOIS
ROCKFORD
CHICAGO
PEORIA
SPRINGFIELD
EAST ST. LOUIS
CARBONDALE
202
203
204
205
206
207
SCALE IN MILES AND KILOMETRES
ONE INCH 15 MILES
ONE CM 10 KILOMETRES

This map prepared specially for DRIVE NORTH AMERICA.
©THE H.M. GOUSHA COMPANY

MZ-1-578-J

Pioneers, Modern Architects and Mysterious Mound Builders

Indiana/Ohio

Old ways endure among the Amish of Indiana and Ohio.

Though geographically east of center, Indiana and Ohio are where Middle America begins. Long a prosperous agricultural and industrial heartland, this region now manifests much of its wealth in its large cities. The simpler riches of the countryside—small-town churches, wooden farmhouses and silos, one-room schools—are reminders of the rural past.

At the heart of Indiana is its capital, **Indianapolis (213, E-4)**, host of the world-famous Indianapolis 500 auto race each May. One of the city's cultural treasures is the Indianapolis Museum of Art, a complex of buildings that embraces 4,000 years of art. Among the museum's prizes are works by Titian, Rembrandt and El Greco; some of the finest French Impressionist paintings in the United States; and a collection of American art that includes two major Edward Hopper paintings and Robert Indiana's famous painting *Love*. The Children's Museum of Indianapolis displays American Indian artifacts, a 2,500-year-old mummy, an Indianapolis 500 racing car, and miniature electric trains that chuff around a landscaped layout.

At **Fort Wayne (211, G-4)**, the Louis A. Warren Lincoln Library and Museum has objects owned by the President, and one of the largest collections of printed matter pertaining to him. Among some 16,000 items are 85 documents in his handwriting. Nearby, staff in period dress enliven Historic Fort Wayne, 11 low buildings reconstructed from the original plans of a fort built here in 1816.

South of Fort Wayne is Amish country, settled in the 1850s by Amish immigrants fleeing religious persecution in Europe. **Berne (213, H-1)** contains Amishville, U.S.A., where wagons and buggies tour an authentic Amish farm maintained in old-fashioned style and incorporating the Grossdawdy House (the granddaddy house), a smokehouse and a kettlehouse.

The mid-1800s come back to life near **Mitchell (214, D-3)** among the restored shops

and mills of Spring Mill Village, once a frontier trading post. An 1828 general store is provisioned with period goods; an apothecary shop displays patent medicines, surgical instruments and a dentist's chair; and craftsmen fashion leather goods in the Munson House. There is also a working whiskey distillery and the three-story Hamer Grist Mill (1817). Power generated by its 24-foot wheel is used to grind corn.

Farther south, near **Corydon (215, E-4)**, is Wyandotte Cave, one of the largest in the country. Incorporating 25 miles of charted passageways, the cave contains one of the world's biggest subterranean chambers—roughly 2,600 feet around and 200 feet high—and 141-foot-high Monument Mountain, the largest known underground mountain.

When Abraham Lincoln was seven years old, his family moved to the site of the Lincoln Boyhood National Memorial near **Boonville (214, B-5)**, where they worked a frontier farm from 1816 to 1830. The memorial building of Indiana limestone is rich with Lincoln memorabilia and period pieces. Livestock and crops are exhibited along with farm implements and tools in the Lincoln Living Historical Farm.

New Harmony (214, A-4) is the site of two unsuccessful experiments to create a utopian community—first by a group of German artisans (the Harmonists) in 1814, and subsequently by an 1825 colony led by British reformer Robert Owen. Restored buildings include an opera house; the Old Fauntleroy Home, headquarters for the Minerva Society (an early women's club); and the Workingman's Institute, founded in 1838 to educate those "who work with their hands."

How did the Indians of Ohio live during the 16th century? Some of the answers are on view at the Angel Mound State Memorial near **Evansville (214, B-5)**. Much of the site has been carefully reconstructed to look as it did when some 1,000 Indians lived here, from about 1300 to 1500.

In the small Indiana town of **Columbus (215, F-1)** there are more excellent examples of modern architecture than in any other place of its size in the world. Among 47 outstanding buildings built since 1957 are the Cleo Rogers Memorial Library, designed by I. M. Pei and graced by Henry Moore's sculpture *Large Arch*; and the North Christian Church, designed by Eero Saarinen so that the 192-foot-high spire, copper-sheathed ribs and slate roof appear the same from all angles.

Once the busiest inland port in the United States, **Cincinnati (220, A-3)**, Ohio, was also the gateway to the South for river traffic plying the Ohio River. Henry Wadsworth Longfellow and Winston Churchill hailed the city's attractive location. At Cincinnati's Art Museum, 100 galleries display one of the foremost collections of musical instruments in the United States. The Taft Museum is a Federal-style mansion (1820) where William Taft accepted the 1908 Republican presidential nomination. Lavishly furnished rooms are hung with a splendid collection of French Renaissance painted enamel portraits.

Dayton (220, B-2), at the meeting of four streams, hosts a barnstorming air show in July. At the U.S. Air Force Museum, the world's oldest and largest military aviation museum, 200 aircraft, missiles and space capsules trace the development of flight. Nearby Huffman Field is the world's first airport and the site of experimental flights by Wilbur and Orville Wright. In Carillon Park are the Wright brothers' second airplane and the two-story Newcom Tavern, Dayton's oldest building (1796). Art from all periods is represented at the Dayton Art Institute. Exhibits include a Chinese burial urn (c. 2200 B.C.), a ninth-century Mayan vase and Rubens' *Study Head of an Old Man.*

The Ohio State Capitol (1861) at **Columbus (220, D-1)** is considered to be the finest example of Doric architecture in the United States. The 120-foot-high dome bears plaques com-

Drivers, mechanics and spectators crowd the Indianapolis Motor Speedway (left), where the Indianapolis 500 has been run every Memorial Day since 1911. Balloon tires, ethyl gasoline and the rearview mirror are among the automotive improvements introduced in past races.

Ohio's University of Miami at Oxford preserves a large collection of William Holmes McGuffey's Eclectic Readers *(right)—a major source of learning in the 1800s.*

A 132-foot mosaic mural of Christ (below) rises above the library entrance of Notre Dame University in South Bend, Indiana.

The Hopewell Legacy: A Serpent of Earth and Stone

The mysterious effigy of a giant snake curves along a hillside in Serpent Mound State Memorial, near Locust Grove, Ohio, for almost a quarter of a mile. The prehistoric Hopewell Indians probably constructed the serpent between 1000 B.C. and A.D. 700. Excavations have established that the mystical design was first laid out with stones and clay and covered with soil.

memorating the eight Ohio-born Presidents. In the Columbus Museum of Art are works by Picasso and Matisse, and Boucher's *Earth: Vertumnus and Pomona.*

The Museum of Art in **Toledo (216, D-3)** is also a cultural treasure house. A medieval cloister, classical and Oriental art, antique glass, paintings by old masters and 20th-century Americans and prized sculptures by Rodin and Moore are displayed.

Founded in 1796 by General Moses Cleaveland, the pioneer surveyor of northern Ohio, **Cleveland (218, B-3)** grew slowly at first. Only when water routes opened south to the Ohio River and along the Great Lakes did this great city on Lake Erie mushroom commercially. Today it is distinguished as the home of one of the country's first professional resident theaters and a world-famous symphony orchestra. The Cleveland Museum of Art is not only among the country's finest in terms of quality and range of its collections, it is also one of the most beautifully situated. Although the emphasis in the Western Re-

serve Historical Society Museum is on Ohio's history, exhibits range from an 1890 dollhouse to the 13½-foot sloop *Tinkerbelle* in which Robert Manry sailed across the Atlantic.

The history and lore of American football are enshrined in the Pro Football Hall of Fame in **Canton (218, D-2)**. The museum building, capped by a football-shaped dome, is filled with busts of football's greatest players, films of past Superbowls, and equipment used in scoring some of the game's most famous touchdowns.

At **Zoar Village State Memorial (219, E-2)**, a dozen original buildings remain of a settlement established in 1817 by 300 Zoarites, religious separatists from Germany. In 1772, another religious sect built Ohio's first village, school and church on a site near **New Philadelphia (219, E-2)**, now preserved in Schoenbrunn Village State Memorial. The church, school and several log cabins have been restored and furnished to appear much as they did more than 200 years ago.

209

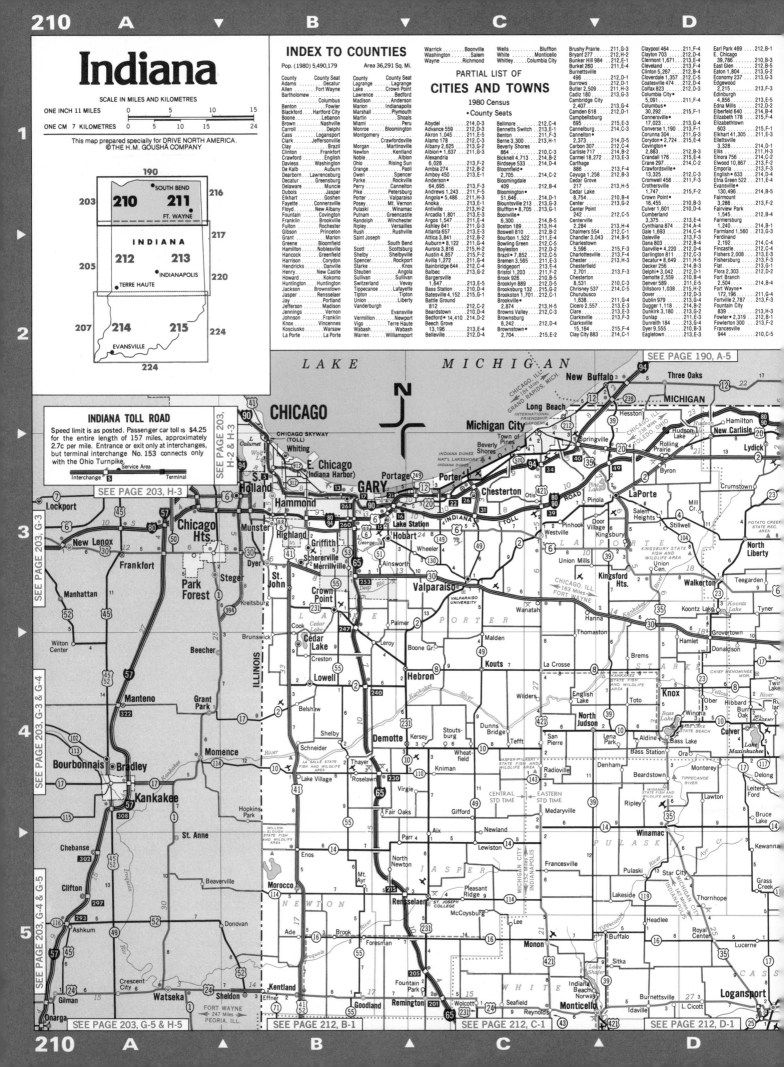

Indiana

SCALE IN MILES AND KILOMETRES

ONE INCH 11 MILES

ONE CM 7 KILOMETRES

0 5 10 15

0 5 10 15 24

This map prepared specially for DRIVE NORTH AMERICA.
©THE H.M. GOUSHA COMPANY

190

SOUTH BEND

203 210 211 216

FT. WAYNE

INDIANA 217

205 212 213 220

INDIANAPOLIS

TERRE HAUTE

207 214 215 224

EVANSVILLE

224

INDEX TO COUNTIES

Pop. (1980) 5,490,179   Area 36,291 Sq. Mi.

County	County Seat
Adams	Decatur
Allen	Fort Wayne
Bartholomew	Columbus
Benton	Fowler
Blackford	Hartford City
Boone	Lebanon
Brown	Nashville
Carroll	Delphi
Cass	Logansport
Clark	Jeffersonville
Clay	Brazil
Clinton	Frankfort
Crawford	English
Daviess	Washington
De Kalb	Auburn
Dearborn	Lawrenceburg
Decatur	Greensburg
Delaware	Muncie
Dubois	Jasper
Elkhart	Goshen
Fayette	Connersville
Floyd	New Albany
Fountain	Covington
Franklin	Brookville
Fulton	Rochester
Gibson	Princeton
Grant	Marion
Greene	Bloomfield
Hamilton	Noblesville
Hancock	Greenfield
Harrison	Corydon
Hendricks	Danville
Henry	New Castle
Howard	Kokomo
Huntington	Huntington
Jackson	Brownstown
Jasper	Rensselaer
Jay	Portland
Jefferson	Madison
Jennings	Vernon
Johnson	Franklin
Knox	Vincennes
Kosciusko	Warsaw
La Porte	La Porte

County	County Seat
Lagrange	Lagrange
Lake	Crown Point
Lawrence	Bedford
Madison	Anderson
Marion	Indianapolis
Marshall	Plymouth
Martin	Shoals
Miami	Peru
Monroe	Bloomington
Montgomery	Crawfordsville
Morgan	Martinsville
Newton	Kentland
Noble	Albion
Ohio	Rising Sun
Orange	Paoli
Owen	Spencer
Parke	Rockville
Perry	Cannelton
Pike	Petersburg
Porter	Valparaiso
Posey	Mt. Vernon
Pulaski	Winamac
Putnam	Greencastle
Randolph	Winchester
Ripley	Versailles
Rush	Rushville
St. Joseph	South Bend
Scott	Scottsburg
Shelby	Shelbyville
Spencer	Rockport
Starke	Knox
Steuben	Angola
Sullivan	Sullivan
Switzerland	Vevay
Tippecanoe	Lafayette
Tipton	Tipton
Union	Liberty
Vanderburgh	Evansville
Vermillion	Newport
Vigo	Terre Haute
Wabash	Wabash
Warren	Williamsport

County	County Seat
Warrick	Boonville
Washington	Salem
Wayne	Richmond
Wells	Bluffton
White	Monticello
Whitley	Columbia City

PARTIAL LIST OF CITIES AND TOWNS

1980 Census

• County Seats

Abydel	214,D-3
Advance 559	212,D-3
Akron 1,045	211,E-5
Alamo 178	212,C-5
Albany 2,625	213,G-4
Albion • 1,637	211,G-3
Alexandria 6,028	213,F-2
Ambia 274	212,B-2
Amboy 450	213,E-1
Anderson • 64,695	213,F-2
Andrews 1,243	211,F-5
Angola • 5,486	211,H-3
Anoka	213,E-1
Antiville	213,H-2
Arcadia 1,801	213,E-1
Argos 1,547	211,E-4
Ashley 841	211,G-3
Atlanta 657	213,E-3
Attica 3,841	212,C-2
Auburn • 8,122	211,G-4
Aurora 3,816	215,H-2
Austin 4,857	215,F-2
Avila 1,272	211,G-4
Bainbridge 644	212,C-4
Balbec	213,G-2
Bargersville	
1,647	213,E-5
Bass Station	210,D-4
Batesville 4,152	215,G-1
Battle Ground 812	212,C-2
Beardstown	210,D-4
Bedford • 14,410	214,D-2
Beech Grove	
13,196	213,E-4
Belleville	212,D-4

Bellmore	212,C-4
Bennetts Switch	213,E-1
Benton	211,F-3
Berne 3,300	213,H-1
Beverly Shores	
864	210,C-3
Bicknell 4,713	214,B-2
Birdseye 533	214,D-4
Bloomingdale	
409	212,B-4
Bloomington •	
51,646	214,D-1
Blountsville 213	213,G-3
Bluffton • 8,705	213,G-1
Boonville • 6,300	214,B-5
Boston 189	213,H-4
Boswell 810	212,B-2
Bourbon 1,522	211,E-4
Bowling Green	212,C-5
Boylestown	212,D-2
Brazil • 7,852	212,C-5
Bremen 3,565	211,E-3
Bridgeport	212,D-4
Bristol 1,203	211,F-2
Brook 926	210,B-5
Brooklyn 889	212,D-5
Brooksburg 132	215,G-2
Brookston 1,701	212,C-1
Brookville •	
2,874	213,H-5
Browns Valley	212,C-3
Brownsburg	
6,242	212,D-4
Brownstown •	
2,704	215,E-2

Brushy Prairie	211,G-3
Bryant 277	213,H-2
Bunker Hill 984	212,E-1
Burket 260	211,E-4
Burnettsville	
496	212,D-1
Burrows	212,D-1
Butler 2,509	211,H-3
Cadiz 180	213,G-3
Cambridge City	
2,407	213,G-4
Camden 618	212,D-1
Campbellsburg	
695	215,E-3
Cannelburg	214,C-3
Cannelton •	214,D-5
Carbon 307	212,C-5
Carlisle 717	214,B-2
Carmel 18,272	213,E-3
Carthage	213,F-4
Cayuga 1,258	212,B-3
Cedar Grove	213,H-5
Cedar Lake	
8,754	210,B-3
Center	213,G-2
Center Point	
242	212,C-5
Centerville	
2,284	213,H-4
Cynthiana 874	214,A-4
Chalmers 554	212,C-1
Chandler 3,043	214,B-5
Charlestown •	
5,596	215,F-3
Charlottesville	213,F-4
Chester	213,H-3
Chesterfield	
2,701	213,F-3
Chesterton	
8,531	210,C-3
Chrisney 537	214,C-5
Churubusco	
1,638	211,G-4
Cicero 2,557	213,E-3
Clare	213,E-3
Clarksville	
15,164	215,F-4
Clay City 883	214,C-1

Claypool 464	211,F-4
Clayton 703	212,D-4
Clermont 1,671	213,E-4
Cleveland	213,F-4
Clinton 5,267	212,B-4
Cloverdale 1,357	212,C-5
Coatesville 474	212,D-4
Colfax 823	212,D-3
Columbia City •	
5,091	211,F,H-4
Columbus •	
30,292	215,F-1
Connersville •	
17,023	213,G-4
Converse 1,190	213,F-1
Corunna 304	211,G-3
Corydon • 2,724	215,E-4
Covington •	
2,883	212,B-3
Crandall 176	215,E-4
Crane 297	214,C-2
Crawfordsville •	
13,325	212,C-3
Cromwell 458	211,F-3
Crothersville	
1,747	215,F-2
Crown Point •	
16,455	210,B-3
Culver 1,601	210,D-4
Cumberland	
3,375	213,E-4
Dale 1,693	214,C-4
Daleville	213,F-3
Dana 803	212,B-4
Danville • 4,220	212,B-4
Darlington 811	212,C-3
Decatur • 8,649	211,H-5
Decker 256	214,B-3
Delphi • 3,042	212,D-1
Demotte 2,559	210,B-4
Denver 589	211,E-5
Dillsboro 1,038	215,H-2
Dover	213,G-4
Dublin 979	213,G-4
Dugger 1,118	214,B-2
Dunkirk 3,180	213,G-2
Dunlap	211,E-3
Dunreith 184	213,G-4
Dyer 9,555	210,B-3

Earl Park 469	212,B-1
E. Chicago	
39,786	210,B-3
East Glen	212,B-5
Eaton 1,804	213,G-2
Economy 237	213,G-3
Edgewood	
2,215	213,F-2
Edinburgh	
4,856	213,E-5
Edna Mills	212,D-1
Elberfeld 640	214,B-4
Elizabeth 178	215,F-5
Elizabethtown	
603	215,F-1
Elkhart 41,305	211,F-3
Ellettsville	
3,328	214,C-1
Ellis	213,H-1
Elnora 756	214,C-2
Elwood 10,867	213,F-2
Emporia	213,F-2
English • 633	214,D-4
Etna Green 522	211,E-4
Evansville •	
130,496	214,B-5
Fairmount	
3,286	213,F-2
Fairview Park	
1,545	212,B-4
Farmersburg	
1,240	214,B-1
Farmland 1,560	213,G-3
Ferdinand	
2,192	214,C-4
Fincastle	212,C-4
Fishers 2,008	213,E-3
Fishersburg	213,F-3
Fiat	213,E-3
Flora 2,303	212,D-2
Fort Branch	
2,504	214,B-4
Fort Wayne •	
172,196	211,G-4
Fortville 2,787	213,F-3
Fountain City	
839	213,H-3
Fowler • 2,319	212,B-1
Fowlerton 300	213,F-2
Francesville	
944	210,C-5

SEE PAGE 190, A-5
SEE PAGE 203, H-2 & H-3
SEE PAGE 203, H-3
SEE PAGE 203; G-3
SEE PAGE 203; G-3 & G-4
SEE PAGE 203; G-4 & G-5
SEE PAGE 203, G-5 & H-5
SEE PAGE 212, B-1
SEE PAGE 212, C-1
SEE PAGE 212, D-1

INDIANA TOLL ROAD

Speed limit is as posted. Passenger car toll is $4.25 for the entire length of 157 miles, approximately 2.7¢ per mile. Entrance or exit only at interchanges, but terminal interchange No. 153 connects only with the Ohio Turnpike.

Service Area

Interchange Terminal

MZ-593-J-X

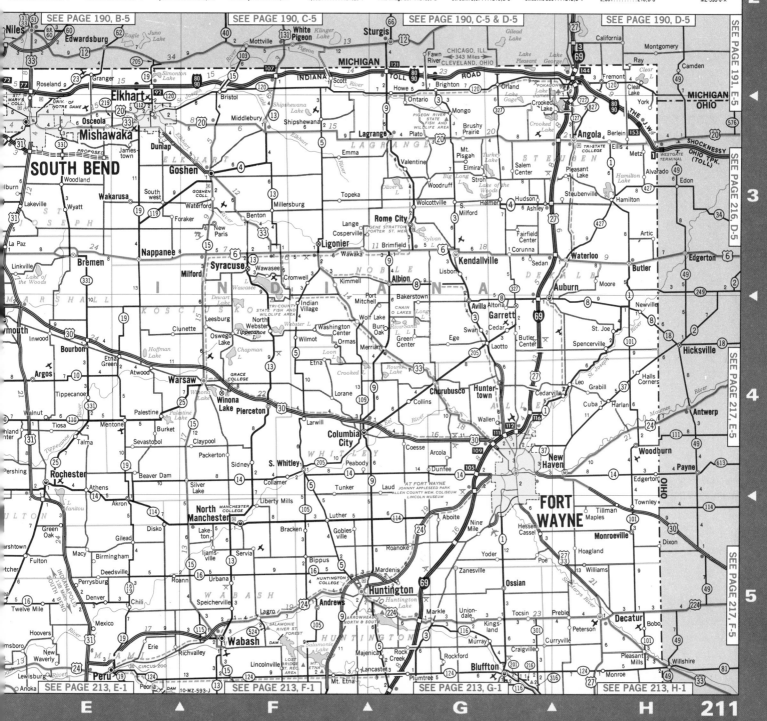

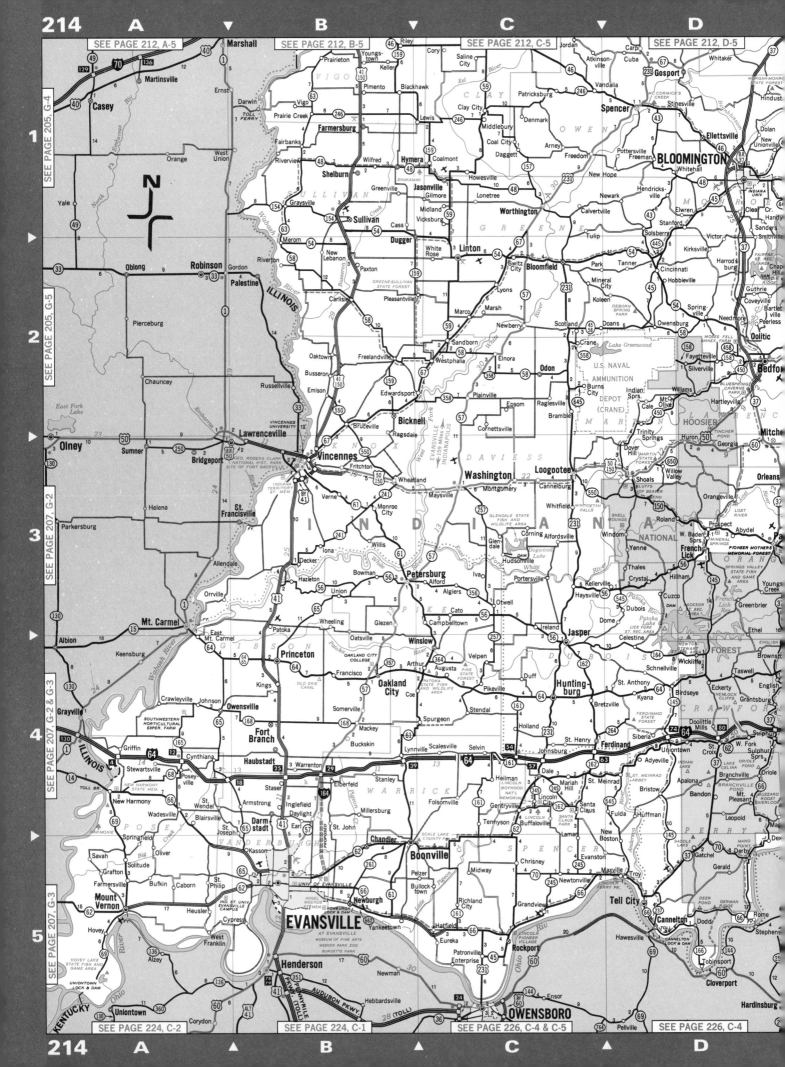

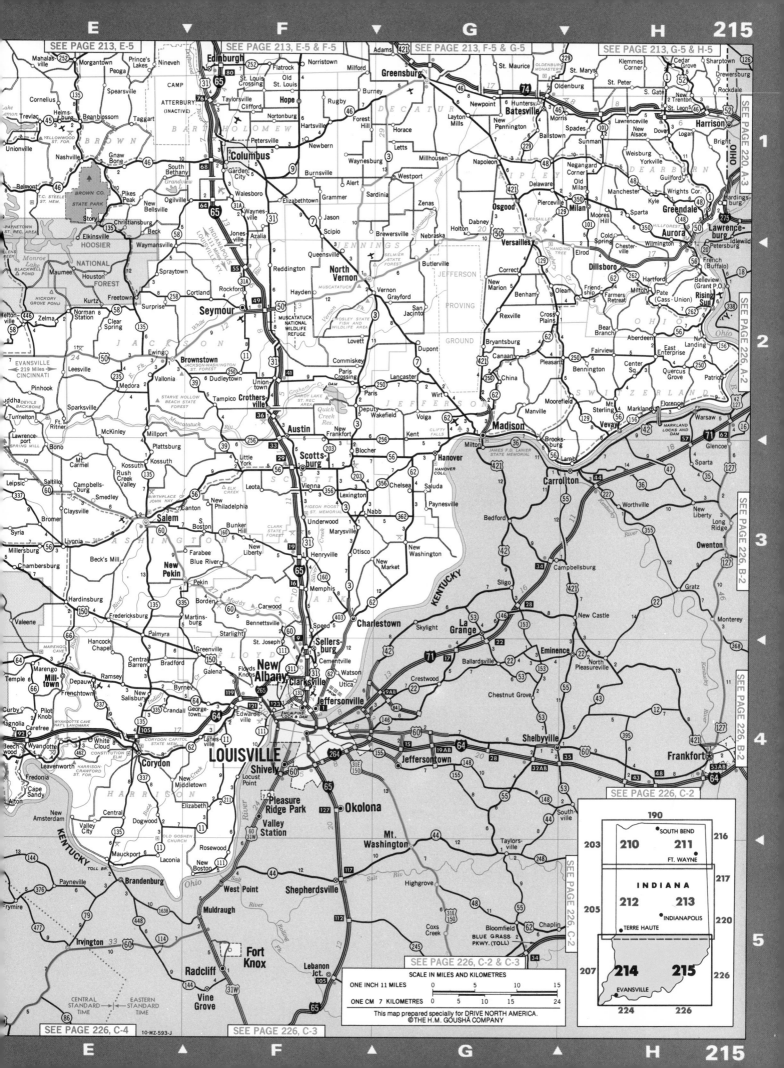

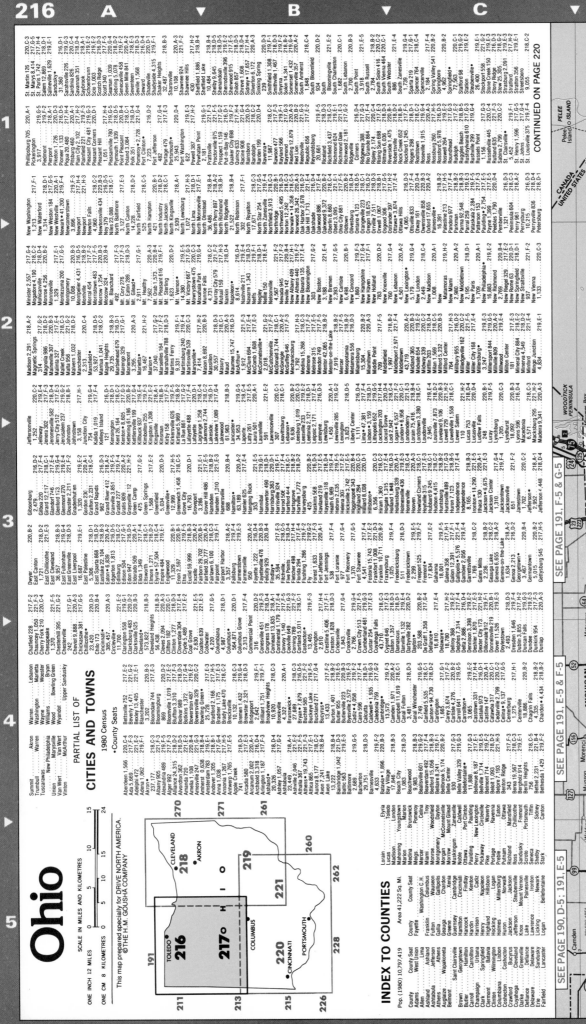

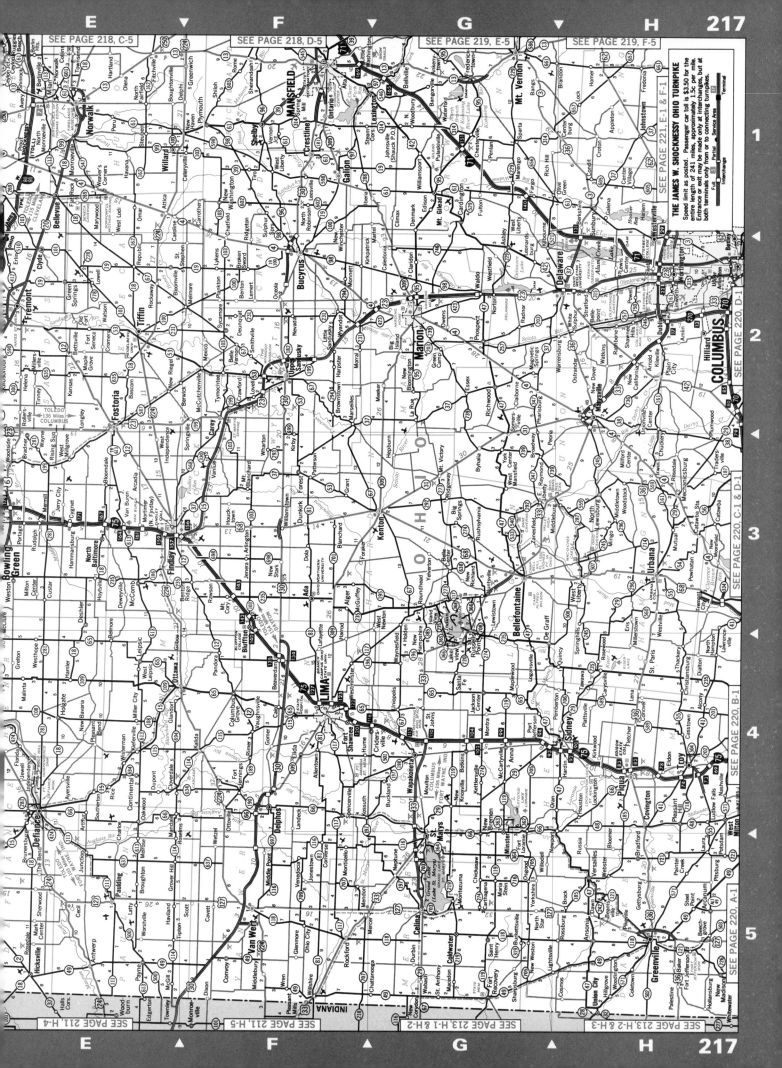

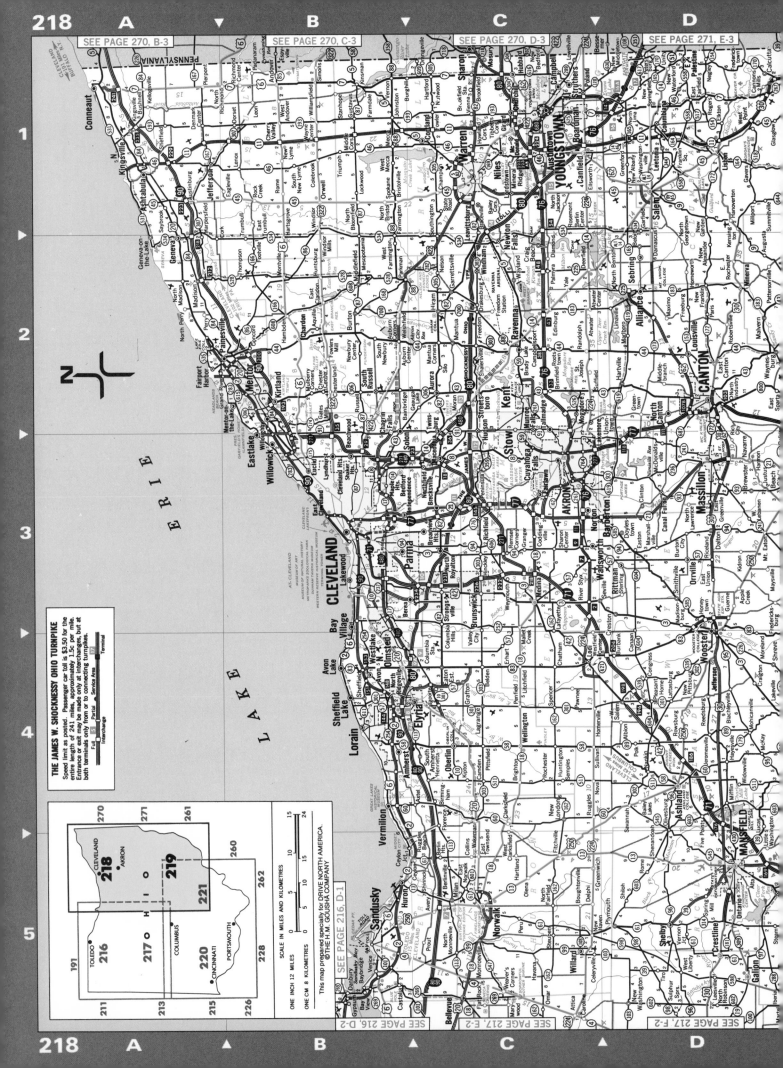

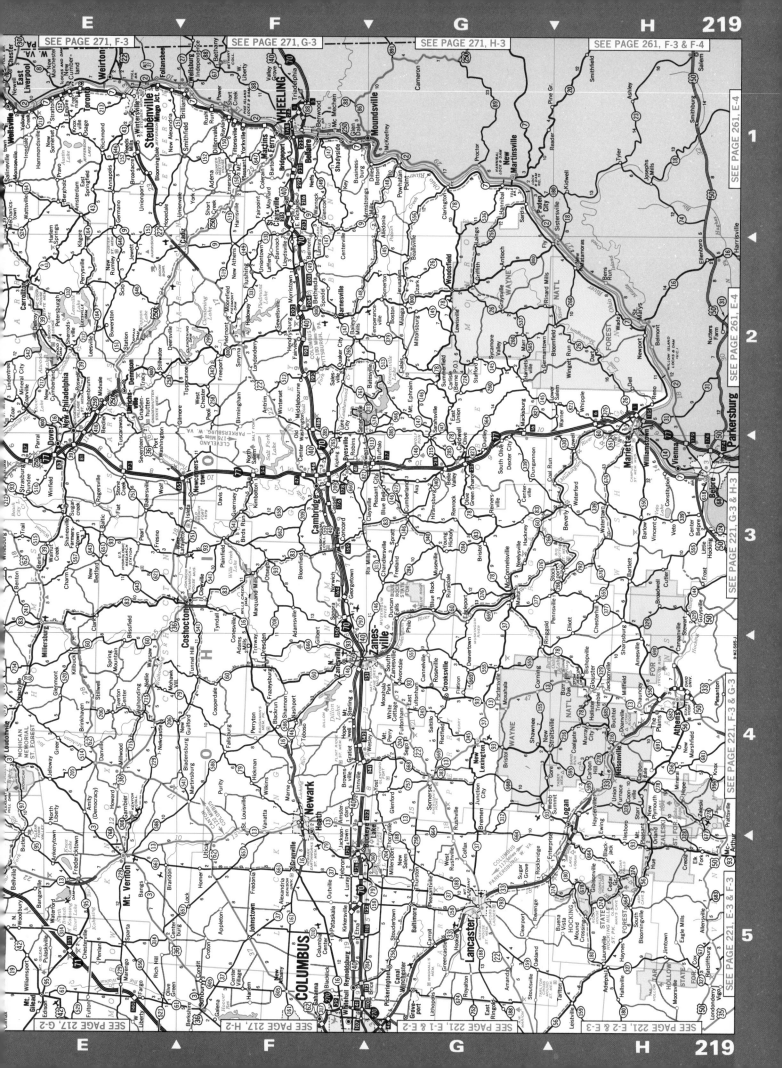

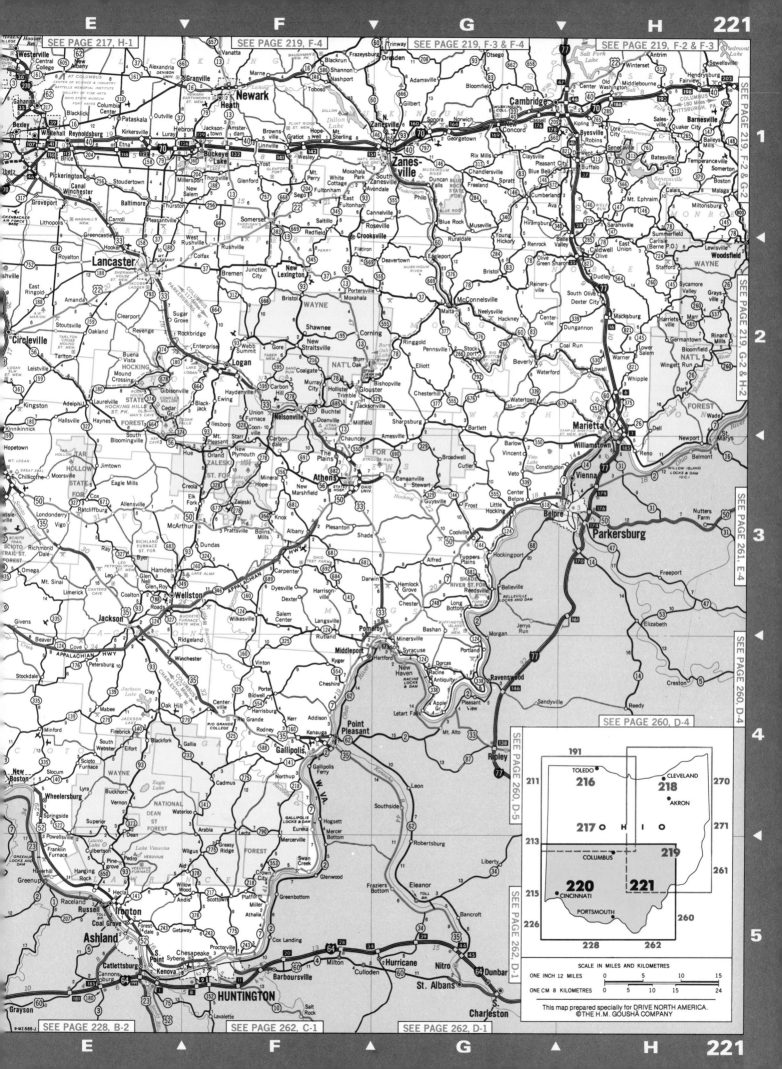

Fabled Racehorses, Country Music and a Battle Above the Clouds

Kentucky/Tennessee

Kentucky and Tennessee display a splendid blend of Southern charm and Yankee spirit. But though both states commemorate the events of the Civil War, behind battlefields and antebellum mansions rise the vigorous cities of today.

Lexington (228, C-5) was home to Henry Clay, the "Great Pacificator," whose diplomacy helped delay the start of the Civil War. Ashland, his residence for 40 years until his death in 1852, contains four generations of Clay family possessions. Other restored Lexington houses include the girlhood home of Mary Todd Lincoln, the 1814 Hunt-Morgan House, and Waveland State Shrine, a restored mansion and plantation village.

Lexington is the heart of the Bluegrass country, source of Kentucky's renowned race horses. A guided walking tour of Kentucky Horse Park, located on 1,032 white-fenced acres, leads visitors past farriers fitting horseshoes and grooms tending various breeds of horses. (Other thoroughbred farms are in the area; visiting hours are posted at their gates.)

In **Harrodsburg (226, C-2)**, in 1774, James Harrod and his party founded the first permanent settlement west of the Alleghenies. Old Fort Harrod State Park maintains a reproduction of the fort they built, its blockhouses and cabins. A cemetery with the graves of 500 early settlers, a log cabin where Abraham Lincoln's parents were married, and a museum of Kentucky history are also on the grounds.

Northeast of here, Shaker Village reflects the life-style of a communal sect whose industry and inventiveness created the clothespin, the circular saw and a form of washing machine. The 27 meticulously restored frame and brick buildings stand in the midst of 2,250 acres of original Shaker farmland.

The Stephen Foster Story, a summer pageant featuring 50 of the composer's most familiar songs, is staged at My Old Kentucky Home State Park in **Bardstown (226, C-2)**. Federal Hill is the dignified 1818 brick mansion that inspired Foster's ballad "My Old Kentucky Home," today the State song.

Abraham Lincoln Birthplace National Historic Site at **Hogdenville (226, D-3)** is a granite and marble building enclosing the log cabin believed to have been Lincoln's birthplace in 1809. Less than three years later, Lincoln's father moved the family some 10 miles away to **Knob Creek,** where a replica of Lincoln's boyhood home now stands.

The Old Capitol Building in **Frankfort (226, B-3),** with its elegant rotunda and sweeping staircase, is among the finest Greek Revival buildings in the country. Completed in 1829, it now houses the Kentucky Historical Society and a museum that contains Daniel Boone's faithful companion—a flintlock rifle inscribed "Boon's Best Fren." The imposing brick Liberty Hall was built around 1796 for John Brown, one of the two first senators to represent Kentucky.

The J. B. Speed Art Museum in **Louisville (226, B-3)** houses exhibits that range from 3,000 B.C. to the present, including the bronze *Horse and Rider*—believed to have been cast by Leonardo da Vinci. Revolutionary War hero George Rogers Clark spent his last years at Locust Grove, a restored Georgian house built around 1790. The stern-wheeler *Belle of Louisville* carries passengers back into the past on cruises of the Ohio River.

Daniel Boone—and the pioneers who followed him—crossed the Appalachian Mountains through **Cumberland Gap (229, E-3)**. Pinnacle Road now traverses the ridge and provides sweeping views of several states. At Cumberland Falls State Resort near **Corbin (229, E-4)**, the Cumberland River roars over a cliff in a 150-foot wide curtain of water in the heart of Daniel Boone National Forest.

The astonishing thing about **Mammoth Cave National Park (226, D-3)** is the extent of its labyrinthine depths. Both the world's longest and third longest cave systems are here—in all, 200 miles of explored passages, and hundreds of miles of unexplored ones. Guided cave tours pass Frozen Niagara, Mammoth Dome and the Snowball Room, whose ceiling is covered with gypsum flowers.

The Mississippi River port of **Memphis (225, H-5)** is Tennessee's largest city. Jazz musician W. C. Handy is commemorated by a statue on Beale Street, where he composed his "Memphis Blues." Elvis Presley's gold and platinum records, gun and guitar collections, and his pink 1955 Cadillac are enshrined at Graceland, the singer's former mansion.

Nine of Memphis' oldest residences and four carriage houses, a dollhouse and a playhouse stand in the Victorian Village Historic District. At Brooks Memorial Art Gallery, 10 galleries house Renaissance masterpieces, English landscapes, American works of the 18th and 19th centuries, and priceless examples of porcelain and glass. South of Memphis, Choctaw Indians demonstrate centuries-old crafts and conduct tours of Chucalissa Indian Village.

As the ballad says, railroad hero Casey Jones drove Engine No. 382—a ten-wheeled steam locomotive—to his death in 1900. A sister engine stands on the grounds of Jones' home in **Jackson (225, G-3)**. Another adopted son, eleventh President James Knox Polk spent much of his boyhood in an elegant house in **Columbia (227, G-5)**, built by his father in 1816.

Nashville (227, F-4) is the lively capital of Tennessee—and of country music. The Country Music Hall of Fame is filled with rare films and recordings, musical instruments, costumes, and exhibits ranging from Roy Rogers' cowboy boots to Rex Allen's Colt .45. The Grand Ole Opry, which has broadcast every week since 1925, is the oldest continuous radio program in the country.

Bronze doors—thought to be the world's largest—lead into the Nashville Parthenon, a re-creation of the original temple in Athens.

On a rise in downtown Nashville stands another Greek-inspired building, the Tennessee State Capitol (1859). Belle Meade, completed in 1853, was the focal point of America's first horse farm. The portico of this graceful Greek Revival mansion bears bullet nicks from the Battle of Nashville. The Hermitage, also meticulously restored and maintained, was for 40 years the home of Andrew Jackson, seventh President of the United States.

Chattanooga (227, H-2) owes much of its fame to the popular song "Chattanooga Choo Choo." The song's namesake is part of a landscaped complex of hotels, restaurants and shops. The white, colonnaded Hunter Museum of Art, on a bluff above the Tennessee River, commands a striking setting for its collection of 18th- to 20th-century American art.

An incline railway climbs to the top of Lookout Mountain and a breathtaking view of seven states. Lookout Mountain Museum is beside the site of the Battle Above the Clouds, one of the most bitterly contested vantage points of the Civil War. To the north, Signal Mountain overlooks the "Grand Canyon" of the Tennessee River.

Knoxville (229, G-4), once a repair and

supply stop for westbound wagon trains, is the commercial center of the rich East Tennessee Valley. The Blount Mansion was built in 1792 for William Blount, whom George Washington appointed governor of the Territory South of the Ohio River. Furnishings in the house include a tin and sweet gum chandelier and a Hepplewhite table. Antique furniture also graces the marble and limestone Ramsey House (1797), and the elegant Craighead-Jackson House (1818).

Gatlinburg (229, G-3) is a center for southern mountain crafts and the gateway to Great Smoky Mountains National Park—800 square miles of forest, wild and intact, astride the Tennessee–North Carolina border. Vegetation here is so lush that the vapor it gives off, cooling and condensing on its way up the mountain, spreads a blue veil over the land—the "smoke" of the Smokies.

Heels click and petticoats whirl during a broadcast of Memphis' Grand Ole Opry (above), premier showcase of country music.

America's finest thoroughbreds have thundered around the track at Churchill Downs in Louisville (below) since 1875.

Spruce, fir and hemlock reach toward the sky in Great Smoky Mountains National Park (above) with a majesty equalled only by California's redwoods. Some trees here predate the discovery of America—giants with trunks measuring 25 feet in diameter.

Members of the Shaker sect often went into trembling ecstasies during religious services. But the society's way of life— re-created near Harrodsburg, Kentucky (below)—was as ascetic as its mode of worship was passionate.

With a welcoming wave and drawled "Howdy," one of Memphis' more colorful residents greets a group of out-of-towners.

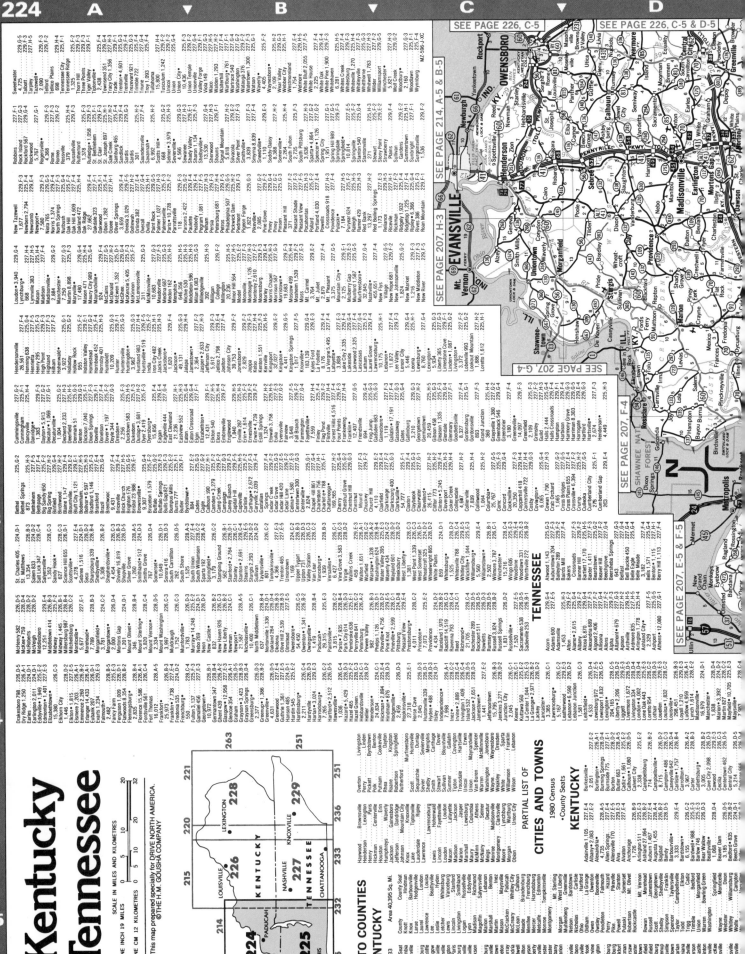

Kentucky
Tennessee

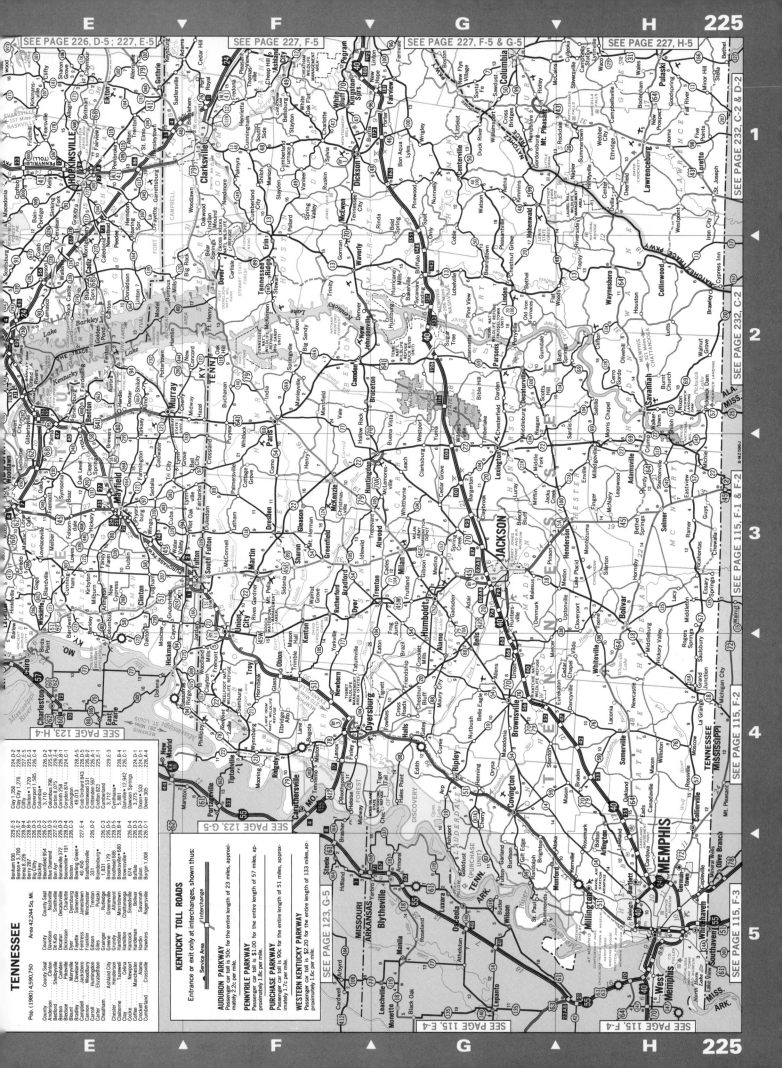

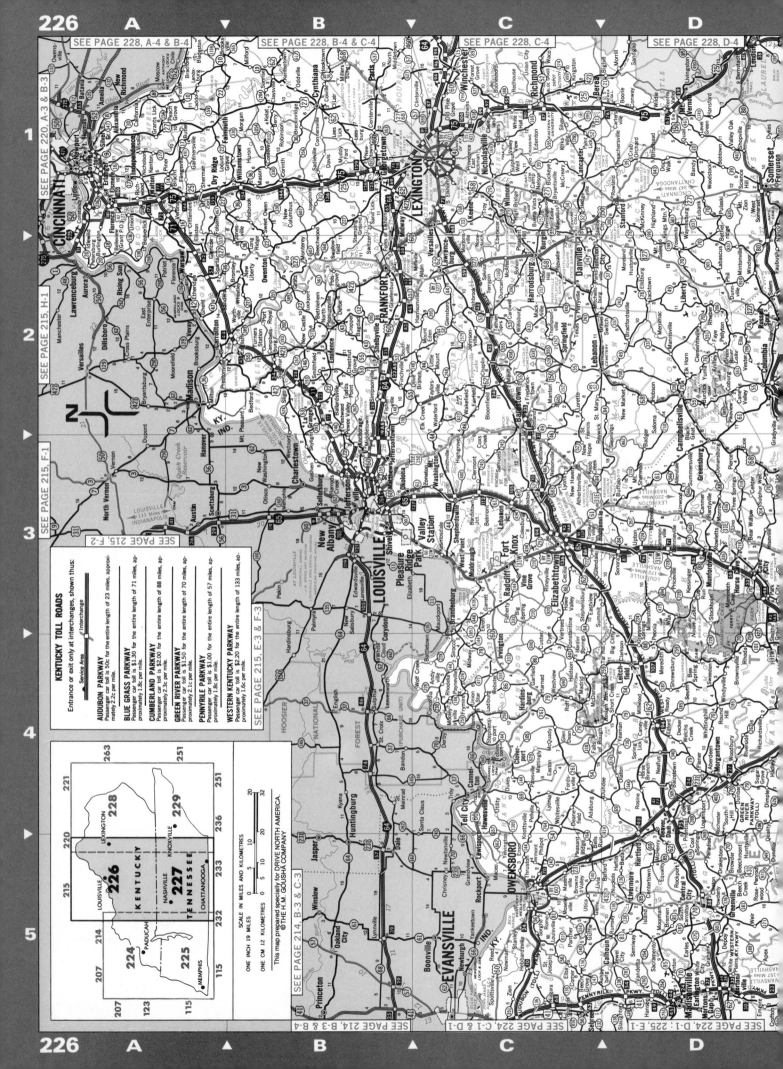

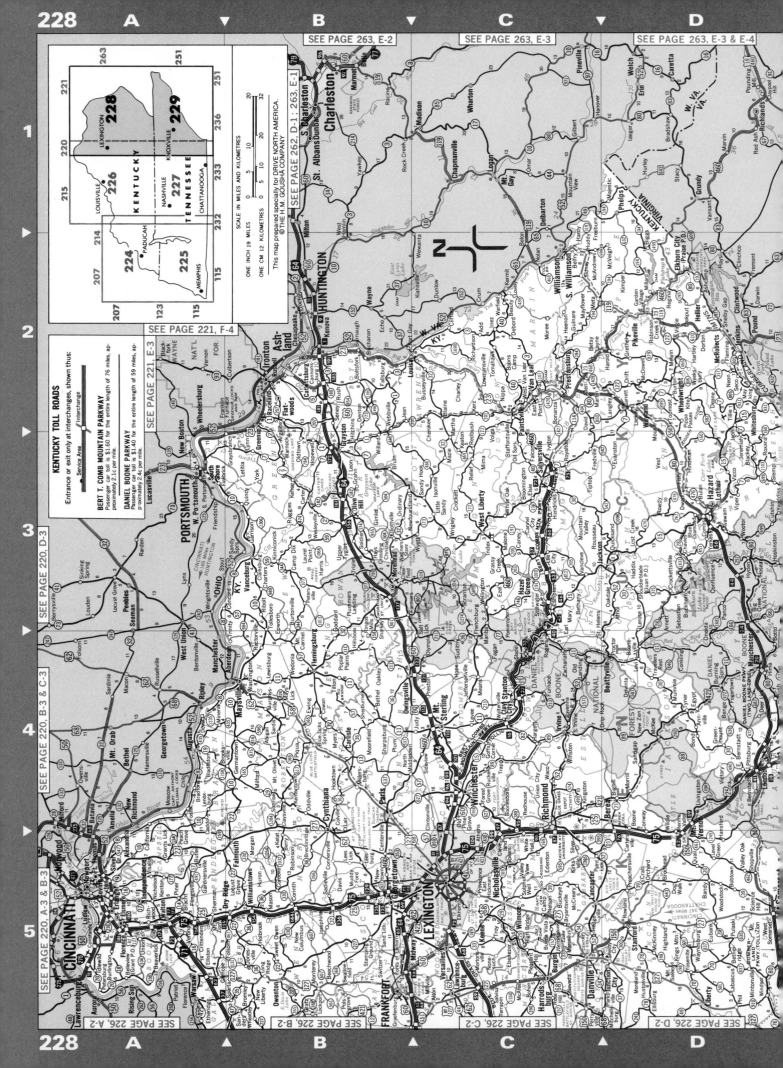

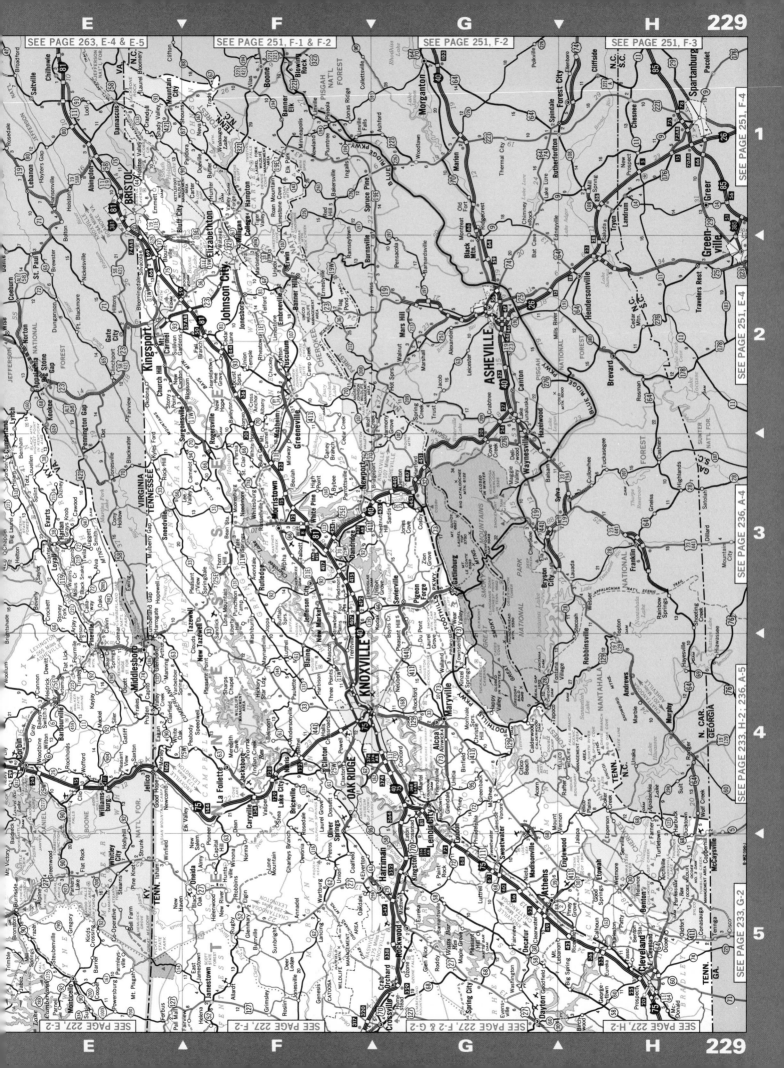

In the Heart of the New South, Golden Isles and a Parade in Stone

Alabama/Georgia

The U.S.S. *Alabama* carried that state's name proudly into battle during World War II. Grateful residents saved the battleship from being scrapped in 1962, and gave it a final resting place in **Mobile (234, B-5)**, Alabama's only seaport. Oakleigh mansion (1833), sited serenely in the grove for which is was named, is furnished with Empire, Regency and early Victorian pieces. Other reminders of antebellum Mobile are preserved in the Church Street Historic District.

Montgomery (235, E-2), Alabama's capital, was also the first capital of the Confederacy. In the State Capitol the South's first congress convened in 1861, adopted a constitution and chose a president—Jefferson Davis. For three months the President and his family lived in an 1835 clapboard building, now called the White House of the Confederacy.

A bronze figure of Booker T. Washington removing the veil of ignorance from a black man commemorates the great educator and founder of the **Tuskegee Institute (235, F-2)**. His home, The Oaks, is a rambling house of handmade bricks from the Institute's yard. In 1896, George Washington Carver began research here that resulted in hundreds of new uses for peanuts, sweet potatoes, and even the clay in which they grew. Examples of his achievements are displayed in the George Washington Carver Museum.

A 55-foot figure of Vulcan, Roman god of fire, overlooks **Birmingham (232, D-5)**, symbolizing the iron and steel industry that forged this city's growth. Visitors to the Birmingham Botanical Gardens enjoy seasonal displays as well as seven acres of Japanese gardens. The Birmingham Museum of Art exhibits nearly 7,000 objects, ranging from ancient Egyptian artifacts to a gleaming collection of English and American silver. Visitors to DeSoto Caverns, six miles from **Childersburg (233, E-5)**, enter a lofty chamber known as Kymulga Cave. The onyx-lined walls glow with rich colors.

Huntsville (233, E-3), fueled by the aerospace industry, bills itself as the "Space Capital of the Universe." Lending strength to this claim is the Alabama Space and Rocket Center's fascinating collection: an Apollo command module with its charred heat shield, a lunar landing vehicle and the training version of the lunar rover left on the moon.

The inspiring story of Helen Keller lives on at Ivy Green, her birthplace in **Tuscumbia (232, C-3)**. The tiny cottage where Miss Keller lived and studied as a child is beside the main house. The grounds include the pump where she first learned the meaning of words, when water was splashed on her hand as her teacher Anne Sullivan tapped out the letters for the word "water."

Georgia's capital, **Atlanta (233, H-4)**, has chosen as its symbol the phoenix, the mythical bird that rose from its own ashes. In 1864, this supply center for the Confederacy was razed by Union troops under General William Sherman. (The burning of Atlanta is depicted in a 400-foot-long painting at Grant Park.) Sweeping steps flanking a tiered fountain lead to Swan House (1928), set amid 23 acres of terraced lawns and formal gardens. Uncle Remus, Br'er Rabbit and the other "critters" came to life in the home of their creator, Joel Chandler Harris. In the churchyard of the Ebenezer Baptist Church lies civil rights leader Martin Luther King, Jr.

The gold-plated dome of the Georgia State Capitol (1889) shares Atlanta's skyline with the Peachtree Plaza, a four-tower complex of hotels, offices, shops and restaurants. The nearby Atlanta Memorial Arts Center houses the Atlanta School of Art, the Atlanta Symphony Orchestra and the High Museum of Art. West of Atlanta, Six Flags Over Georgia portrays the colorful history of Georgia and the South under the rule of Spain, France, England, the Republic of Georgia, the Confederacy and the United States.

The restoration of New Echota, east of **Calhoun (233, G-3)**, is a poignant reminder of the expulsion of the Cherokee Indians from their homeland. New Echota was the capital of the Cherokee Nation from 1825 to 1838, when the tribe was forced west into what is now Oklahoma. The first Indian newspaper, the *Cherokee Phoenix* (1828), was published in the Print Shop, now reconstructed.

From the 1870s to the 1920s, most well-known actors, lecturers and singers touring the South stopped in **Columbus (235, G-2)** to play the Springer Opera House. Edwin Booth, Oscar Wilde, William Jennings Bryan and the Barrymores are remembered in the theater's museum. Attracted to nearby **Warm Springs (235, G-1)** by the healing properties of its waters, the polio-afflicted Franklin D. Roosevelt built an unpretentious clapboard cottage here in 1932. He died 13 years later in this "Little White House."

Andersonville National Historic Site (235, H-2) marks the location of an infamous prison where about 13,000 Union soldiers died in 1864–65. As many as 33,000 men were held behind the 15-foot stockade, now reconstructed. Westville Village in **Lumpkin (235, G-2)** recalls a gentler time with its faithful recreation of an 1850 community.

Athens (236, B-4), famous for its pre-Civil War mansions with their boxwood hedges, has been called the Classic City of the South. An "Athens of Old" walking tour passes a number of these Greek Revival homes, including the Taylor-Grady House (1839), handsomely furnished with period pieces.

Tobacco, cotton and Georgia red brick built **Augusta (236, C-2)**; the Masters Golf Tournament has made it a familiar name. The Gertrude Herbert Memorial Institute of Art is housed in an 1818 frame residence. The Mackay House (1760) is Augusta's oldest home and one of the South's most important Colonial buildings. During the American Revolution, 13 American rebels were hanged from the exterior staircase.

In 1851, William Butler Johnston returned

The massive columns of Sturdivant Hall Museum in Selma, Alabama, frame a modern-day Scarlett O'Hara.

to **Macon (236, D-5)** from Italy determined to reproduce an Italian villa. His red brick 24-room mansion, now the Hay House, took seven years to build and displays the craftsmanship typical of the Italian Renaissance. The splendidly restored Grand Opera House contains a stage so large that the chariot race scene from *Ben Hur* was once performed here with live horses.

One of the first planned cities in the United States and, for that reason, one of the loveliest today, **Savannah (237, F-1)** was laid out in parks and squares in 1733. More than 1,100 19th-century homes and commercial buildings constitute its historic district, the largest in the United States. The cobbled streets of Factor's Walk once echoed the footsteps of wealthy cotton merchants. The spirited founder of the Girl Scouts of the U.S.A. was born in the Juliette Gordon Low House in 1860, now the national center of the Girl Scouts. Antique furniture, paintings and

Ghostly stands of moss-draped cypress loom above the tea-colored waters of Georgia's Okefenokee Swamp.

A Monument to the Confederacy

At Stone Mountain Park near Atlanta is the largest granite monolith east of the Mississippi. Carved into the mountain's great gray face are the figures of three Confederate heroes of the Civil War: President Jefferson Davis and Generals Robert E. Lee and Stonewall Jackson, riding their mounts as if before a military review. Cable cars whisk sightseers to the 825-foot summit, also reached by a steep, 1½-mile trail.

In the center of the 3,200-acre park, Memorial Hall recounts the great battles of the Civil War and the monumental carving of the memorial. The reconstructed Ante-Bellum Plantation gives visitors a glimpse of the Old South, while picnic areas, nature trails, swimming, fishing, boating and stern-wheeler cruises enable them to enjoy the present one.

The Old and New South: Savannah's 1724 Herb House (above), now a restaurant; the soaring atrium of Atlanta's Hyatt Regency Hotel (left) in the Peachtree Plaza.

decorative arts delight visitors to the Telfair Academy of Arts and Sciences (1818).

Georgia's Golden Isles—**Jekyll (237, G-1), St. Simons** and **Sea Island**—reflect both the frustrated hopes of Spanish treasure seekers and the beauty of the islands' marshes. The Jekyll Island Club, whose members reputedly controlled one-sixth of the world's wealth, was a playground of the very rich. A chapel and seven lavish vacation "cottages" in Millionaire's Village are now part of a state park. **Cumberland Island National Seashore (237, H-1)** protects one of the largest and loveliest of Georgia's barrier islands.

In southern Georgia and northern Florida lies the 681-square-mile **Okefenokee National Wildlife Refuge (237, H-3)**. In places, it is a dim world of tannin-stained water at the base of giant bald cypress trees. Other parts are dazzling with subtropical sunlight. Naturalists conduct nature tours along a boardwalk. At the Okefenokee Swamp Park, natural and human history is interpreted in the Ecology Center, the Serpentarium and the Pioneer Island Museum.

231

Alabama Georgia

SCALE IN MILES AND KILOMETRES

ONE INCH 19 MILES 0 5 10 20

ONE CM 12 KILOMETRES 0 5 10 20 32

This map prepared specially for DRIVE NORTH AMERICA.

©THE H.M. GOUSHĀ COMPANY

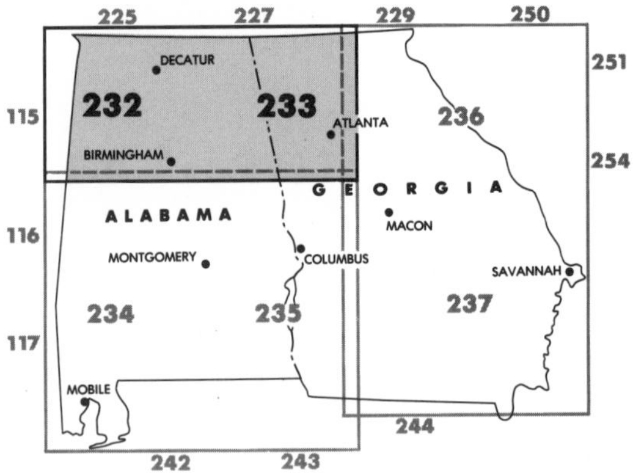

INDEX TO COUNTIES

ALABAMA

Pop. (1980) 3,890,061 Area 51,609 Sq. Mi.

County	County Seat	County	County Seat
Autauga	Prattville	Jackson	Scottsboro
Baldwin	Bay Minette	Jefferson	Birmingham
Barbour	Clayton	Lamar	Vernon
Bibb	Centreville	Lauderdale	Florence
Blount	Oneonta	Lawrence	Moulton
Bullock	Union Springs	Lee	Opelika
Butler	Greenville	Limestone	Athens
Calhoun	Anniston	Lowndes	Hayneville
Chambers	Lafayette	Macon	Tuskegee
Cherokee	Centre	Madison	Huntsville
Chilton	Clanton	Marengo	Linden
Choctaw	Butler	Marion	Hamilton
Clarke	Grove Hill	Marshall	Guntersville
Clay	Ashland	Mobile	Mobile
Cleburne	Heflin	Monroe	Monroeville
Coffee	Elba	Montgomery	Montgomery
Colbert	Tuscumbia	Morgan	Decatur
Conecuh	Evergreen	Perry	Marion
Coosa	Rockford	Pickens	Carrollton
Covington	Andalusia	Pike	Troy
Crenshaw	Luverne	Randolph	Wedowee
Cullman	Cullman	Russell	Phenix City
Dale	Ozark	Saint Clair	Pell City
Dallas	Selma	Shelby	Columbiana
De Kalb	Fort Payne	Sumter	Livingston
Elmore	Wetumpka	Talladega	Talladega
Escambia	Brewton	Tallapoosa	Dadeville
Etowah	Gadsden	Tuscaloosa	Tuscaloosa
Fayette	Fayette	Walker	Jasper
Franklin	Russellville	Washington	Chatom
Geneva	Geneva	Wilcox	Camden
Greene	Eutaw	Winston	Double Springs
Hale	Greensboro		
Henry	Abbeville		
Houston	Dothan		

GEORGIA

Pop. (1980) 5,464,265 Area 58,876 Sq. Mi.

County	County Seat	County	County Seat
Appling	Baxley	Elbert	Elberton
Atkinson	Pearson	Emanuel	Swainsboro
Bacon	Alma	Evans	Claxton
Baker	Newton	Fannin	Blue Ridge
Baldwin	Milledgeville	Fayette	Fayetteville
Banks	Homer	Floyd	Rome
Barrow	Winder	Forsyth	Cumming
Bartow	Cartersville	Franklin	Carnesville
Ben Hill	Fitzgerald	Fulton	Atlanta
Berrien	Nashville	Gilmer	Ellijay
Bibb	Macon	Glascock	Gibson
Bleckley	Cochran	Glynn	Brunswick
Brantley	Nahunta	Gordon	Calhoun
Brooks	Quitman	Grady	Cairo
Bryan	Pembroke	Greene	Greensboro
Bulloch	Statesboro	Gwinnett	Lawrenceville
Burke	Waynesboro	Habersham	Clarkesville
Butts	Jackson	Hall	Gainesville
Calhoun	Morgan	Hancock	Sparta
Camden	Woodbine	Haralson	Buchanan
Candler	Metter	Harris	Hamilton
Carroll	Carrollton	Hart	Hartwell
Catoosa	Ringgold	Heard	Franklin
Charlton	Folkston	Henry	McDonough
Chatham	Savannah	Houston	Perry
Chattahoochee	Cusseta	Irwin	Ocilla
Chattooga	Summerville	Jackson	Jefferson
Cherokee	Canton	Jasper	Monticello
Clarke	Athens	Jeff Davis	Hazlehurst
Clay	Fort Gaines	Jefferson	Louisville
Clayton	Jonesboro	Jenkins	Millen
Clinch	Homerville	Johnson	Wrightsville
Cobb	Marietta	Jones	Gray
Coffee	Douglas	Lamar	Barnesville
Colquitt	Moultrie	Lanier	Lakeland
Columbia	Appling	Laurens	Dublin
Cook	Adel	Lee	Leesburg
Coweta	Newnan	Liberty	Hinesville
Crawford	Knoxville	Lincoln	Lincolnton
Crisp	Cordele	Long	Ludowici
Dade	Trenton	Lowndes	Valdosta
Dawson	Dawsonville	Lumpkin	Dahlonega
Decatur	Bainbridge	Macon	Oglethorpe
De Kalb	Decatur	Madison	Danielsville
Dodge	Eastman	Marion	Buena Vista
Dooly	Vienna	McDuffie	Thomson
Dougherty	Albany	McIntosh	Darien
Douglas	Douglasville	Meriwether	Greenville
Early	Blakely	Miller	Colquitt
Echols	Statenville	Mitchell	Camilla
Effingham	Springfield	Monroe	Forsyth
		Montgomery	Mt. Vernon

County	County Seat	County	County Seat
Morgan	Madison	Tattnall	Reidsville
Murray	Chatsworth	Taylor	Butler
Muscogee	Columbus	Telfair	McRae
Newton	Covington	Terrell	Dawson
Oconee	Watkinsville	Thomas	Thomasville
Oglethorpe	Lexington	Tift	Tifton
Paulding	Dallas	Toombs	Lyons
Peach	Fort Valley	Towns	Hiawassee
Pickens	Jasper	Treutlen	Soperton
Pierce	Blackshear	Troup	La Grange
Pike	Zebulon	Turner	Ashburn
Polk	Cedartown	Twiggs	Jeffersonville
Pulaski	Hawkinsville	Union	Blairsville
Putnam	Eatonton	Upson	Thomaston
Quitman	Georgetown	Walker	LaFayette
Rabun	Clayton	Walton	Monroe
Randolph	Cuthbert	Ware	Waycross
Richmond	Augusta	Warren	Warrenton
Rockdale	Conyers	Washington	Sandersville
Schley	Ellaville	Wayne	Jesup
Screven	Sylvania	Webster	Preston
Seminole	Donalsonville	Wheeler	Alamo
Spalding	Griffin	White	Cleveland
Stephens	Toccoa	Whitfield	Dalton
Stewart	Lumpkin	Wilcox	Abbeville
Sumter	Americus	Wilkes	Washington
Talbot	Talbotton	Wilkinson	Irwinton
Taliaferro	Crawfordville	Worth	Sylvester

PARTIAL LIST OF

CITIES AND TOWNS

1980 Census

• County Seats

ALABAMA

Abanda 233,F-5
Abbeville• 3,155 235,G-3
Aberfoil 235,F-2
Abernant 232,D-5
Ada 235,E-2
Adamsville 2,498 232,D-5
Addison 746 232,D-3
Akron 604 234,C-1
Alabaster 7,079 232,D-5
Alberta 234,C-2
Albertville 12,039 233,E-3
Alexander City 13,807 235,F-1
Aliceville 3,207 232,B-5
Allgood 387 233,E-4
Allsboro 232,B-3
Andalusia• 10,415 235,E-4
Anderson 405 232,D-2
Annemanie 234,C-2
Anniston• 29,523 233,F-4
Arab 5,967 233,E-3
Ardmore 1,096 232,D-2
Argo 233,E-4
Ariton 844 235,F-3
Ashford 2,165 235,G-4
Ashland• 2,052 233,F-5
Ashville 1,489 233,E-4
Athens• 14,558 232,D-2
Atmore 8,789 234,C-4
Attalla 7,737 233,E-4
Auburn 28,471 235,F-1
Autaugaville 843 234,D-2
Awin 234,D-3
Axis 234,B-4
Baileyton 396 233,E-3
Banks 160 235,F-3
Bankston 232,C-4
Barfield 233,F-5
Barrytown 234,B-3
Barton 232,C-3
Bay Minette• 7,455 234,C-4
Bayou La Batre 2,055 234,B-5
Bear Creek 353 232,C-3
Beatrice 558 234,D-3
Beaverton 360 232,C-4
Belgreen 232,C-3
Belk 308 232,C-4
Belle Mina 232,D-3
Belleville 234,D-3
Benton 74 234,D-2
Bessemer 31,729 232,D-5
Bexar 232,B-3
Birmingham• 284,413 232,D-5
Black 156 235,F-4
Blacksher 234,C-4
Bladon Springs 234,B-3
Bleecker 235,G-1
Blount Springs 232,D-4
Blountsville 1,509 233,E-4
Blue Mountain 284 233,F-4
Blue Springs 112 235,F-3
Boaz 7,151 233,E-4
Boligee 164 234,B-1
Bolinger 234,B-3
Bon Air 118 233,E-5
Boothton 232,D-5
Boyd 234,B-1
Braggs 234,D-2
Branchville 365 233,E-4
Brantley 234,D-2
Brantley 1,151 235,E-3
Bremen 232,D-4
Brent 2,862 234,D-1
Brewton• 6,680 234,D-4
Bridgeport 2,974 233,F-2
Brighton 5,308 232,D-5
Brooksville 233,E-4
Brookwood 492 232,D-5
Browns 234,C-2
Brundidge 3,213 235,F-3
Bucks 234,B-4
Buhl 232,C-5
Burkville 235,E-2
Burnsville 234,D-2
Butler• 1,882 234,B-2
Cahaba 234,D-2
Calera 2,035 232,D-5
Calvert 234,B-4
Camden• 2,406 234,D-2
Camp Hill 1,628 235,F-1
Campbell 234,B-3
Carbon Hill 2,452 232,C-4
Carrollton• 1,104 232,B-5
Carrville 820 235,F-2
Castleberry 847 234,D-4
Catherine 234,C-2
Cecil 235,E-2
Cedar Bluff 1,129 233,F-3
Cedarville 234,C-1
Center Star 232,C-2
Central 235,E-1
Centre• 2,351 233,F-4
Centreville• 2,504 234,D-1
Chancellor 235,F-4
Chandler Springs 233,E-5
Chastang 234,B-4
Chatom• 1,122 234,B-3
Chelsea 233,E-5
Cherokee 1,589 232,C-3
Chickasaw 7,402 234,B-4
Childersburg 5,084 233,E-5
Chrysler 234,C-4
Chunchula 234,B-4
Citronelle 2,841 234,B-4
Clanton• 5,832 235,E-1
Claud 235,E-1
Clayhatchee 560 235,F-4
Clayton• 1,589 235,F-3
Cleveland 487 233,E-4
Cleveland Crossroads 233,E-5
Clinton 234,C-1
Clio 1,224 235,F-3
Clopton 235,F-3
Coal Fire 232,B-5
Coatopa 234,B-2
Cochrane 234,B-1
Coffeeville 448 234,B-3
Coker 232,C-5
Collbran 233,F-3
Collinsville 1,383 233,F-3
Columbiana• 2,655 233,E-5
Columbus City 233,E-3
Consul 234,C-2
Cooper 235,E-1
Cordova 3,123 232,D-4
Cottondale 232,C-5
Cottonton 235,G-2
Cottonwood 1,352 235,F-4
Courtland 456 232,D-3
Covin 232,C-4
Coxey 232,D-2
Crane Hill 232,D-4
Crawford 235,G-2
Creola 673 234,B-4
Crossville 1,222 233,F-3
Cuba 486 234,B-2
Cullman• 13,084 232,D-4
Dadeville• 3,263 235,F-1
Daleville 4,250 235,F-4
Dancy 234,B-1
Danville 232,D-3
Daphne 3,406 234,C-5
Dauphin Island 234,B-5
Daviston 334 235,F-1
Davisville 235,F-2
Dawes 234,B-5
Deatsville 235,E-1
Decatur• 42,002 232,D-3
Deer Park 234,B-4
Delta 233,F-5
Demopolis 7,678 234,C-2
Detroit 326 232,B-4
Devenport 235,E-2
Dixiana 232,D-4
Dixie 234,D-4
Dixons Mills 234,C-2
Dora 2,327 232,D-4
Dothan• 48,750 235,F-4
Double Springs• 1,057 232,C-4
Douglas 116 233,E-4
Dozier 494 235,E-3
Dry Forks 234,C-3
Duncanville 232,C-5
Dutton 276 233,F-3
East Brewton 2,964 234,D-4
Eclectic 1,124 235,E-1
Edwin 235,F-3
Elba• 4,355 235,E-3
Elberta 491 234,C-5
Eldridge 230 232,C-4
Elgin 232,C-2
Elmore 235,E-2
Emelle 234,B-1
Enterprise 18,033 235,F-4
Eoline 234,D-1
Epes 399 234,B-1
Equality 235,E-1
Ethelsville 95 232,B-5
Eufaula 12,097 235,G-3
Eunola 169 235,F-4
Eutaw• 2,444 234,C-1
Evergreen• 4,171 234,D-3
Fairfax 235,G-1
Fairfield 13,040 232,D-5
Fairford 234,B-4
Fairhope 7,286 234,C-5
Falkville 1,310 232,D-3
Faunsdale 174 234,C-2
Fayette• 5,287 232,C-4
Fisk 233,E-2
Fitzpatrick 235,F-2
Five Points 197 235,F-1
Flat Creek 232,D-4
Flat Rock 233,F-3
Flint 673 232,D-3
Flomaton 1,882 234,D-4
Florala 2,165 235,E-4
Florence• 37,029 232,C-2
Foley 4,003 234,C-5
Forkland 429 234,C-1
Forney 233,F-4
Fort Davis 235,F-2
Fort Deposit 1,519 235,E-2
Fort Mitchell 235,G-2
Fort Payne• 11,485 233,F-3
Fosters 232,C-5
Fountain 234,C-3
Francisco 233,E-2
Franklin 133 234,C-3
Fredonia 235,G-1
Frisco City 1,424 234,C-3
Fruitdale 234,B-4
Fruithurst 239 233,F-4
Fultondale 6,217 232,D-4
Furman 234,D-2
Fyffe 1,305 233,F-3
Gadsden• 47,565 233,E-4
Gantt 314 235,E-3
Garden City 655 232,D-4
Gardendale 7,928 232,D-4
Gaylesville 192 233,F-3
Geiger 200 234,B-1
Geneva• 4,866 235,F-4
Georgiana 1,993 234,D-3
Geraldine 911 233,E-3
Gilbertown 218 234,B-3
Glen Allen 312 232,C-4
Glencoe 4,648 233,F-4
Goodwater 1,895 235,E-1
Gordo 2,112 232,C-5
Gordon 362 235,G-4
Gosport 234,C-3
Graball 235,G-3
Graham 233,F-5
Grand Bay 234,B-5
Grangeburg 235,G-4
Graysville 2,642 232,D-4
Green Hill 232,C-2
Greensboro• 3,248 234,C-1
Greenville• 7,807 234,D-3
Grove Hill• 1,912 234,C-3
Guin 2,418 232,C-4
Gulf Shores 1,233 234,C-5
Guntersville• 7,041 233,E-3
Gurley 735 233,E-3
Hackleburg 883 232,C-3
Hagler 234,C-1
Haleburg 106 235,G-3
Haleyville 5,306 232,C-3
Hamilton• 4,792 232,C-4
Hammondville 369 233,F-3
Hanceville 2,220 232,D-4
Hanover 235,E-1
Harpersville 934 233,E-5
Harrisburg 234,D-1
Hartford 2,647 235,F-4
Hartselle 8,858 232,D-3
Hatchechubbee 235,G-2
Havana 234,C-1
Hayneville• 592 235,E-2
Hazel Green 233,E-2
Hazen 234,D-2
Headland 3,327 235,F-4
Heath 354 235,E-4
Heflin• 3,014 233,F-4
Heiberger 234,D-1
Helena 2,130 232,D-5
Herbert 234,D-3
Highland Home 235,E-3
Hissop 235,E-1
Hodges 250 232,C-3
Hokes Bluff 3,216 233,F-4
Hollins 233,E-5
Holly Pond 493 233,E-4
Hollywood 1,110 233,F-3
Homewood 21,271 232,D-5
Hope Hull 235,E-2
Hueytown 13,309 232,D-5
Hugo 234,C-2
Huntsville• 142,513 233,E-3
Hurtsboro 752 235,F-2
Huxford 234,C-4
Ider 698 233,F-3
Intercourse 234,B-2
Irondale 6,521 232,D-5
Irvington 234,B-5
Isbell 232,C-3
Isney 234,B-3
Jachin 234,B-2
Jackson 6,073 234,C-3
Jacksonville 9,735 233,F-4
Jamestown 233,F-3
Jasper• 11,894 232,D-4
Jefferson 234,C-2
Jemison 1,828 234,D-1
Johns 232,D-5
Jones Chapel 232,D-3
Kansas 267 232,C-4
Keener 233,F-4
Kelly's Crossroads 235,E-1
Kellyton 235,E-1
Kennedy 604 232,C-4
Killen 747 232,C-2
Kilpatrick 233,E-3
Kimbrough 234,C-2
Kinsey 1,239 235,F-4
Kinston 604 235,E-4
Knoxville 234,C-1
Laceys Spring 233,E-3
Lacon 232,D-3
Ladonia 235,G-2
Lafayette• 3,647 235,F-1
Lamison 234,C-2
Landersville 232,C-3
Lanett 6,897 235,G-1
Laneville 234,C-2
Langdale 235,G-1
Langston 233,E-3
Larkinsville 233,E-3
Lawrenceville 235,G-3
Leeds 8,638 233,E-5
Leesburg 116 233,F-4
Leighton 1,218 232,C-3
Letohatchee 235,E-2
Lewiston 234,B-1
Lexington 884 232,D-2
Liberty 234,D-3
Lillian 234,C-5
Lincoln 2,081 233,E-5
Linden• 2,773 234,C-2
Lineville 2,257 233,F-5
Lipscomb 3,741 232,D-5
Lisman 401 234,B-2
Littleville 1,262 232,C-3
Livingston• 3,187 234,B-1
Loachapoka 335 235,F-1
Lockhart 547 235,E-4
Locust Fork 488 233,E-4
London 233,E-5
Louisville 791 235,F-3
Lowndesboro 207 235,E-2
Loxley 804 234,C-5
Lugo 235,G-3
Luverne• 2,639 235,E-3
Lynn 554 232,C-4
Madison 4,057 232,D-3
Madrid 172 235,F-4
Magnolia Springs 234,C-5
Malcolm 234,B-4
Malvern 558 235,F-4
Mantua 232,C-5
Maplesville 754 234,D-1
Margerum 232,B-2
Marion• 4,467 234,D-1
Marvyn 235,F-2
Maysville 233,E-3
McCalla 232,D-5
McIntosh 319 234,B-4
McKenzie 605 234,D-3
Megargel 234,C-3
Mellow Valley 233,F-5
Mentone 476 233,F-3
Meridianville 233,E-2
Mexia 234,C-3
Midland City 1,903 235,F-4
Midway 234,D-3
Midway 593 235,F-2
Mignon 233,E-5
Millerville 233,F-5
Millport 1,287 232,B-5

Milltry 956 ....234,B-3
Millstead 235,F-2
Mobile
200, 452 ....234,B-5
Monroeville
5,674 ....234,C-3
Montevallo
3,965 ....234,C-3
Montgomery
178,157 ....235,F-3
Monticello 235,F-3
Montrose 234,C-5
Moody 1,840 ....235,E-3
Moores Bridge 234,B-2
Mooresville 58 ....234,C-1
Morgan City 233,E-3
Morris 623 ....232,D-4
Morvin 234,C-4
Moulton 3,197 ....232,D-3
Moundville 1,310 ....234,C-1
Mount Vernon
1,038 ....234,D-2
Mount Willing 234,D-2
Mountain Brook
17,400 ....232,D-3
Mountain Creek 235,E-1
Mountainboro
266 ....235,E-4
Munford 233,F-5
Muscadine 233,F-4
Muscle Shoals
8,911 ....232,C-2
Myrtlewood 252 ....234,C-2
Nanafalia 234,C-3
Natural Bridge 232,C-4
Nauvoo 259 ....232,C-4
Needham 234,B-2
New Brockton
1,392 ....235,F-4
New Hope 1,546 ....233,E-3
New Lexington 232,C-5
New Site 340 ....235,F-1
Newburg 232,C-2
Newton 1,540 ....235,F-4
Newtonville 232,C-5
Newville 814 ....235,F-3

Nixon Chapel 233,E-3
Normal 235,F-2
Northport 14,291 ....232,C-5
Notasulga 876 ....235,F-2
Oakman 770 ....232,C-5
Odenville 724 ....233,E-4
Oleander 233,E-3
Oneonta 4,824 ....233,E-4
Opelika 21,896 ....235,F-1
Opp 7,204 ....235,F-4
Orange Beach 234,C-5
Orrville 349 ....234,D-2
Owens Cross Road
804 ....235,E-2
Oxford 8,939 ....233,F-5
Ozark 13,188 ....235,F-4
Paint Rock 221 ....233,E-2
Palmerdale 235,E-3
Palmetto 232,C-5
Pansey 235,G-4
Parkdale 235,E-4
Parrish 1,583 ....232,D-4
Pell City 6,616 ....233,E-4
Penton 235,E-1
Pepperell 235,F-1
Perdido 234,C-4
Perdue Hill 234,C-3
Peterson 232,C-5
Petersville 232,C-2
Phenix City • 235,G-2
Phil Campbell
1,549 ....232,C-3
Pickensville 132 ....232,B-3
Piedmont 5,544 ....233,F-4
Pike Road 235,F-2
Pinckard 771 ....235,F-4
Pine Apple 298 ....234,D-3
Pine Hill 510 ....234,C-2
Pine Level 235,F-2
Pine Level 235,F-2
Pinson 232,D-4
Pittsview 235,G-2

Point Clear 234,C-5
Poplar Springs 232,C-4
Port
Birmingham 232,D-5
Prairieville 234,C-2
Prattville
18,647 ....235,E-2
Prichard 39,541 ....234,B-5
Princeton 233,E-2
Providence 363 ....234,D-2
Ragland 1,860 ....233,E-4
Rainbow City
6,299 ....233,E-4
Rainsville 3,907 ....233,E-3
Ralph 234,C-1
Ramer 235,F-2
Ranburne 417 ....233,F-4
Range 234,D-4
Red Bay 3,232 ....232,B-3
Red Level 504 ....235,E-3
Reece City 718 ....233,E-3
Reeltown 235,F-1
Reform 2,245 ....232,C-5
Remlap 233,E-4
Repton 313 ....234,D-3
River Falls 669 ....235,G-1
River View 235,G-1
Riverside 849 ....233,E-4
Roanoke 5,896 ....233,F-5
Robertsdale
2,306 ....234,C-5
Robinson
Springs 235,E-2
Rock Mills 233,G-5
Rockford 494 ....235,E-1
Rogersville 1,224 ....232,D-2
Rome 234,D-4
Rosebud 234,D-3
Russell 234,B-4
Russellville •
8,195 ....232,C-3
Rutledge 496 ....235,E-3
Safford 234,C-2
Saginaw 232,D-5
St. Clair
Springs 233,E-4

St. Elmo 234,B-5
St. Stephens 234,B-3
Salem 235,F-1
Salem 232,C-5
Samson 2,402 ....235,E-4
Santuck 235,E-1
Saraland 9,833 ....234,B-4
Sardis 232,B-4
Satsuma 3,791 ....234,B-4
Sayerville 234,C-1
Scottsboro •
14,758 ....233,E-3
Seale 235,G-2
Section 821 ....233,E-3
Sellers 235,E-3
Selma • 26,684 ....234,D-2
Semmes 234,B-5
Sheffield
11,903 ....232,C-3
Shopton 235,F-2
Shorter 235,F-2
Silas 341 ....234,B-3
Silverhill 624 ....234,C-5
Slocomb 2,153 ....235,F-4
Snead 667 ....233,E-4
Snowdoun 235,F-2
Somerville 140 ....232,D-3
Southside 4,848 ....233,E-4
Spring Hill 235,F-3
Springville
1,476 ....233,E-4
Sprott 234,D-1
Spruce Pine 232,C-3
Stanton 234,D-1
Stapleton 234,C-5
Steele 795 ....233,E-4
Sterrett 233,E-5
Stevenson
2,568 ....233,F-2
Stewartville 235,E-1
Stockton 234,C-4
Sulligent 2,130 ....234,B-4

Sumiton 2,815 ....232,D-4
Summerdale
546 ....234,C-5
Summit 233,E-3
Suttle 234,D-2
Swaim 233,E-2
Sweet Water 253 ....234,C-2
Sylacauga
12,708 ....233,E-5
Talladega •
19,128 ....233,E-5
Tallassee
4,763 ....235,F-2
Taylor 1,003 ....235,F-4
Taylorville 232,C-4
Tensaw 234,C-4
Terese 235,G-3
Texasville 234,F-5
The Bottle 235,G-1
Theodore 234,B-5
Thomaston 679 ....234,D-1
Thomasville
4,387 ....234,C-3
Thorsby 1,422 ....234,D-1
Three Notch 235,F-2
Tibbie 234,B-3
Toney 232,D-2
Town Creek
1,201 ....232,D-3
Townley 232,C-4
Toxey 265 ....234,B-3
Trafford 673 ....232,D-4
Troy • 12,587 ....235,F-3
Trussville 3,507 ....233,E-4
Tunnel Springs 234,D-3
Tuscaloosa •
75,143 ....232,C-5
Tuscumbia •
9,137 ....232,C-3
Tuskegee •
12,716 ....235,F-1
Union Springs •
4,431 ....235,F-2
Uniontown
2,112 ....234,C-2

Uriah 234,C-4
Valhermoso
Springs 232,D-3
Valley Head
609 ....233,E-2
Vance 254 ....232,D-5
Verbena 235,E-1
Vernon • 2,609 ....232,B-4
Victoria 235,F-3
Vidette 235,E-4
Village Springs 233,E-4
Vina 380 ....232,B-3
Vincent 1,652 ....233,E-5
Vineland 234,C-2
Vinemont 615 ....232,D-3
Vredenburgh
433 ....234,C-3
Wadley 532 ....233,F-5
Wagarville 234,B-4
Walnut Grove
510 ....233,E-4
Walnut Hill 234,F-5
Warrior 232,D-4
Waterloo 232,C-2
Waverly 228 ....233,F-1
Weaver 2,765 ....233,F-4
Webb 448 ....235,G-4
Wedgeworth 234,C-1
Wedowee 908 ....233,F-5
Welch 235,F-1
West Blocton
1,147 ....232,D-5
Wetumpka •
4,341 ....235,E-2
Whatley 234,C-3
Wheeler 232,D-2
White Plains 233,F-4
White Plains 235,F-1
Whiteside 232,D-3
Whitney 235,F-1
Wicksburg 235,G-4
Wilmer 581 ....234,B-4
Wilsonville
914 ....233,E-5
Wilton 642 ....234,D-1

Winfield 3,781 ....232,C-4
Winterboro 233,E-5
Woodland 192 ....233,F-5
Woodstock 232,D-5

GEORGIA

Abbeville • 985 ....237,F-4
Acworth 3,648 ....233,G-4
Adairsville 1,739 ....233,G-3
Adel • 5,592 ....237,G-2
Adrian 756 ....237,F-2
Ailey 579 ....237,F-3
Aldora 139 ....235,H-1
Allentown 321 ....237,F-2
Alma • 3,819 ....237,G-3
Alpharetta
3,128 ....233,G-4
Alvaton 91 ....237,H-5
Ambrose 360 ....237,G-4
Americus •
16,120 ....237,F-5
Andersonville
267 ....235,H-5
Apalachee 236,C-4
Arabi 376 ....237,F-5
Aragon 855 ....233,G-4
Argyle 237,G-3
Arlington 1,572 ....235,G-3
Armuchee 233,G-3
Ashburn • 4,766 ....237,F-5
Atco 233,G-4
Athens • 42,549 ....236,D-4
Atkinson 237,G-2
Attapulgus 623 ....235,H-4
Augusta •
47,532 ....236,C-2
Austell 3,939 ....233,G-4
Avera 248 ....236,B-3

Woodville 609 ....233,E-3
Wren 232,D-3
Yellow Pine 234,B-3
York 3,392 ....234,B-2

Axson 237,G-3
Baconton 763 ....237,F-5
Baingbridge •
10,553 ....235,H-4
Baldwin 1,380 ....236,A-3
Ball Ground 640 ....233,G-4
Barnesville •
4,887 ....235,H-1
Barretts 237,H-4
Bartow 357 ....236,D-3
Baxley • 3,586 ....237,F-5
Beachton 235,H-5
Bellville 173 ....237,F-5
Benevolence 138 ....235,G-5
Berlin 538 ....237,G-5
Berner 235,H-1
Bethlehem 281 ....236,C-4
Bishop 172 ....236,C-4
Blackshear •
3,222 ....237,G-3
Blairsville • 530 ....236,A-3
Blakely • 5,880 ....235,G-4
Biltolton 237,E-1
Bloomingdale
1,855 ....237,F-1
Blue Ridge •
1,376 ....233,G-2
Bluffton 132 ....235,G-4
Bogart 819 ....236,B-5
Bolingbroke 235,H-1
Bonaire 237,E-5
Boston 1,424 ....237,H-5
Barwick 357 ....236,C-4
Bowdon 1,743 ....233,G-4
Bowens Mill 318 ....237,F-4
Bowersville 318 ....236,B-4
Bowman 890 ....236,B-4
Boykin 235,G-4
Braganza 237,G-3

Bremen 4,579 ....233,G-4
Brewton 237,E-3
Brinson 274 ....235,G-4
Bristol 237,G-2
Broadhurst 237,G-2
Bronwood 524 ....235,H-3
Brookfield 237,E-2
Brooklet 1,035 ....237,E-2
Broxton 1,117 ....237,F-4
Brunswick •
17,605 ....237,G-1
Buchanan •
1,019 ....233,G-4
Buckhead 219 ....236,C-4
Buena Vista •
1,544 ....235,H-2
Buford 6,697 ....236,B-5
Butler • 1,959 ....235,H-2
Byron 1,661 ....237,E-5
Cadley 237,H-4
Cadwell 353 ....237,E-4
Cairo • 8,777 ....235,H-4
Calhoun • 5,335 ....233,G-3
Calvary 235,H-5
Camak 283 ....236,C-3
Camilla • 5,414 ....235,H-4
Canon 704 ....236,B-4
Canton 3,601 ....233,G-4
Carlton 291 ....236,B-4
Carnegie 235,G-3
Carnesville • 465 ....236,B-4
Carrollton •
14,078 ....233,G-5
Cataula 233,H-2
Cave Spring
883 ....233,G-3
Cecil 280 ....237,G-2
Cedartown •
8,619 ....233,G-4
Centerville
2,622 ....237,E-5
Chamblee 7,137 ....233,H-4
Charing 235,H-2

Chatsworth •
2,493 ....233,G-3
Chauncey 350 ....237,F-4
Chester 237,F-3
Chickamauga
2,232 ....233,G-3
Claxton • 2,694 ....237,F-2
Clayton • 1,838 ....236,A-4
Clermont 300 ....236,A-5
Cleveland •
1,578 ....235,H-4
Clinton 236,D-5
Cloudland 233,G-3
Coal Mountain 236,B-4
Cobbtown 494 ....237,F-2
Cochran • 5,121 ....237,F-4
Colbert 498 ....236,B-4
College Park
24,632 ....233,H-4
Collins 639 ....237,F-2
Colquitt • 2,065 ....235,G-4
Columbus •
169,441 ....235,G-2
Comer 930 ....236,B-4
Commerce
4,092 ....236,B-4
Concord 317 ....235,H-1
Conyers •
6,567 ....236,C-5
Coolidge 736 ....237,G-5
Coosa 233,G-3
Cordele •
10,914 ....237,F-5
Cornelia 3,203 ....236,A-5
Coverdale 237,F-5
Covington •
10,586 ....236,C-5
Crandall 233,G-2
Crawfordville
594 ....236,C-4

Crosland 237,G-5
Culloden 281 ....235,H-1
Cumming •
2,094 ....233,H-4
Cusseta • 1,218 ....235,H-2
Cuthbert •
1,348 ....235,G-3
Dacula 1,577 ....236,B-5
Dahlonega •
342 ....233,H-4
De Soto 248 ....237,F-5
Dearing 539 ....236,C-3
Decatur •
18,404 ....233,H-4
Demorest 1,130 ....236,A-5
Denton 286 ....237,F-3
Dexter 527 ....237,F-3
Dillard 258 ....236,A-4
Dock Junction
7,641 ....237,G-1
Doerun 1,062 ....237,F-5
Doles 237,F-5
Donalsonville •
2,844 ....235,G-4
Douglas •
10,980 ....237,G-3
Douglasville •
8,483 ....233,G-4
Du Pont 167 ....237,G-2
Dublin • 16,083 ....237,F-3
Dudley 425 ....237,F-3
Duluth 2,956 ....233,H-4
Durand 206 ....235,H-2

CONTINUED ON PAGE 234

SEE PAGE 227, H-4 | SEE PAGE 227, H-3 | SEE PAGE 227, H-1 & H-2 | SEE PAGE 229, H-4 & H-5

SEE PAGE 236, A-5 | SEE PAGE 236, A-5 & B-5 | SEE PAGE 236, B-5 & C-5 | SEE PAGE 236, C-5 & D-5

SEE PAGE 235, E-1 | SEE PAGE 235, F-1 | SEE PAGE 235, G-1 | SEE PAGE 235, H-1

SEE PAGE 232, B-5   SEE PAGE 232, C-5   SEE PAGE 232, D-5

SEE PAGE 116, B-1   SEE PAGE 116, B-1 & C-1   SEE PAGE 116, C-1 & D-1   SEE PAGE 116, D-1; 117, E-1   SEE PAGE 117, E-1

9-MZ-1029-S

Gulf of Mexico

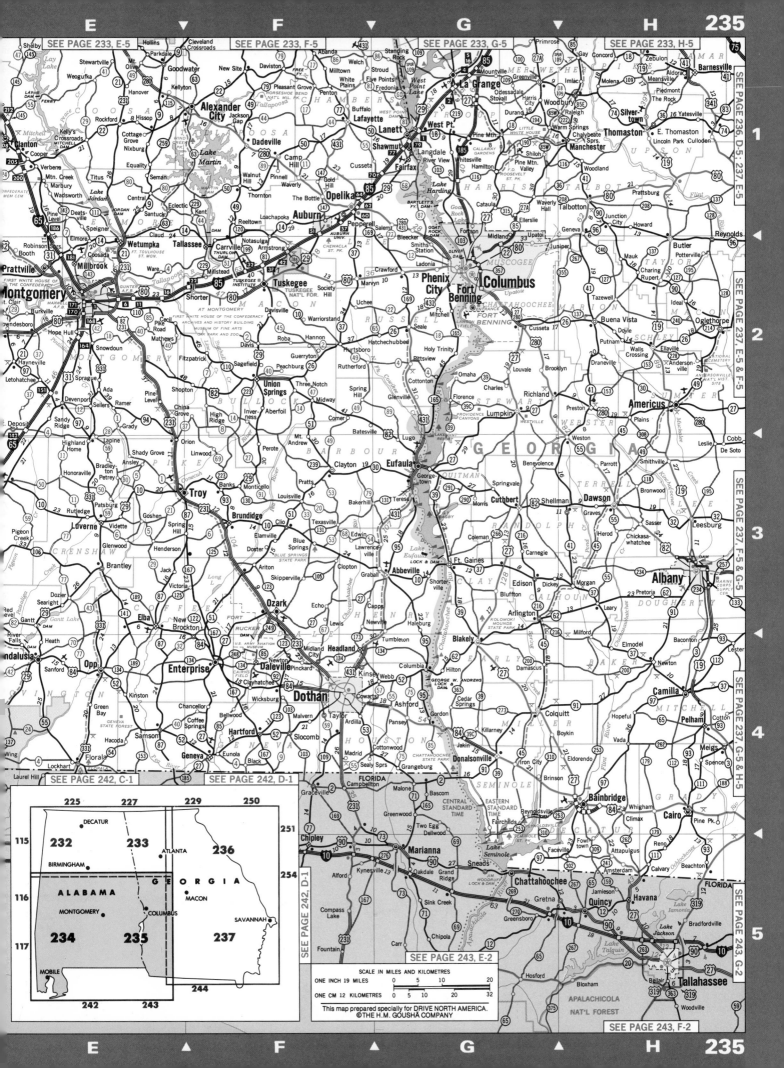

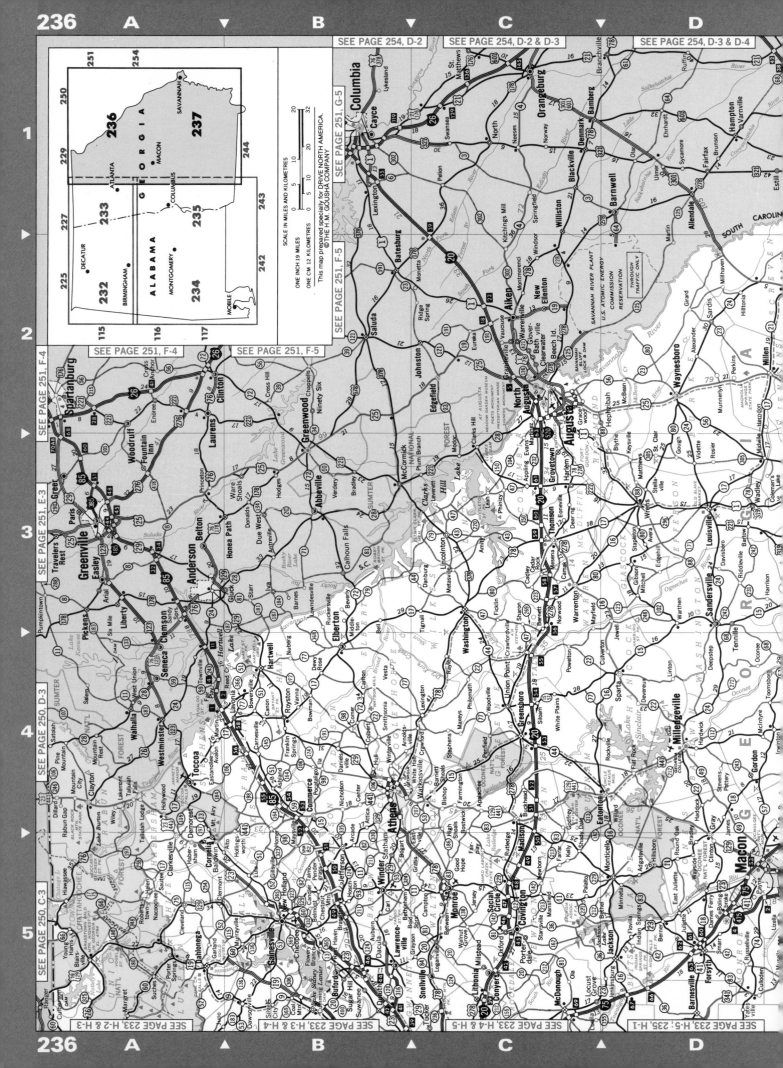

Old St. Augustine, Sparkling Miami and a Gateway to the Galaxy

Florida

Prehistoric Indian mounds, Spanish forts, frontier cabins, Georgian town houses, plantation homes, the Kennedy Space Center—such architecture is a reminder that Florida's treasures span several centuries and a fascinating spectrum of peoples and cultures.

St. Augustine (244, B-2), the oldest city in America, was founded as a Spanish military outpost in 1565. Thirty-five original buildings survive; 30 have been carefully reconstructed. Inside the 13-foot-thick walls of Castillo de San Marcos, built between 1672 and 1695, are guardrooms, powder magazines, living quarters and a prison. Zorayda Castle, erected in 1883 as a private residence, is a one-tenth-scale replica of the Alhambra Palace in Spain. St. Augustine's oldest residence (pre-1727) is built of coquina—a regional rock formed of solidified seashells.

In 1564, near the site of present-day **Jacksonville (244, B-3)**, French colonists established Fort Caroline. The outpost might have become America's first permanent settlement had Spanish attackers not destroyed it the following year. The National Park Service has reconstructed the fort and its moat from a 16th-century sketch. Jacksonville's Cummer Gallery of Art houses Renaissance portraits, rare tapestries and illuminated manuscripts along with paintings by Titian, Rubens and Goya.

Even though the Junior Museum in **Tallahassee (243, F-2)** is intended for children, adults too will enjoy the range of exhibits here. Forty acres of trails are part of the museum complex, as is Big Bend Pioneer Farm—11 hand-hewn log buildings, several dating from 1880. Visitors to nearby Wakulla Springs can ride a glass-bottom boat over the deepest of Florida's 17 major springs.

The Gulf of Mexico and neighboring Alabama squeeze northwestern Florida into a narrow panhandle. Here, traces of American prehistory have been preserved at **Fort Walton Beach (242, B-2)**, where a 13th-century Indian temple mound has been restored. Lumber baron William Henry Wesley created his latter-day monument, Eden, at nearby **Point Washington (242, C-2)** in 1895. The interior of the mansion reflects many styles, with European and American furnishings dating from the 1600s through the Victorian age. **Pensacola (242, A-2)** has been a naval base since President John Quincy Adams ordered a shipyard built here in 1826. The Naval Aviation Museum illustrates the story of flight through a variety of aircraft, scale models, and a Skylab command module.

Following the theme of Environment, Man and Time, the Florida State Museum in **Gainesville (244, C-4)** presents the history of Florida. Visitors can explore a re-created mangrove swamp and examine a paleontological site. Transportation is the main subject of the Antique Car Collection in **Silver Springs (244, D-3)**. Little-known vehicles such as the Rumpler (shaped like a boat on wheels) can be seen alongside such classics

as a 1932 Stutz Bearcat, a 1935 Duesenberg convertible and a carriage used in *Gone With the Wind*.

The mound-building culture of early North American Indians, which eventually reached as far north as Ontario, may have had its first location north of Mexico at **Crystal River Historic Memorial (244, D-4)**. Ceremonies were held here from the second century B.C. until the 15th century. Preserved structures include a temple mound standing 30 feet high and an excavated crypt.

A number of lovely springs and nature preserves lie within a short drive of **Ocala (244, D-3)**. Giraffes, rhinos and other African animals graze along the banks of tranquil Silver River in Silver Springs. Water hyacinths, considered a nuisance by many Floridians, bloom in lavender extravagance along the scenic Oklawaha River in Ocala National Forest.

Water ballets are featured at Weeki Wachee Springs west of **Brooksville (245, E-4)** performed in an auditorium 16 feet underwater. With controlled breathing (and the help of concealed air hoses), the swimmers perform for 30 minutes without resurfacing for air. Passenger boats cruise past lush foliage and myriad blossoming plants to a nature park where trained parrots and cockatoos display their skills, and hawks, owls and eagles perform aerial shows.

Riding at anchor in **St. Petersburg (245, F-4)** is the British warship used in the 1962 production of *Mutiny on the Bounty*. The Polynesian settings reproduced here feature a replica of the longboat in which Captain Bligh and 18 crewmen were set adrift by mutineer Fletcher Christian. The nine galleries of the St. Petersburg Museum of Fine Arts house a collection of European and American art from the 17th through the 20th centuries, including two authentic English period rooms. Natural history exhibits, including shell and mineral specimens, are among the main features of the Haas Museum. A 3,000-year-old Egyptian mummy and a 400-year-old cypress canoe are on view at the St. Petersburg Historical Museum.

Across the bay in **Tampa** is Busch Gardens/The Dark Continent, where more than 3,000 animals can be viewed close at hand from a monorail, a cable car or the Trans-Veldt Railway. Trained animals perform in the Stanleyville area; dolphin shows captivate audiences in a 1,200-seat amphitheater.

Plant Hall, the main building of the University of Tampa, is one of the most exotic-looking academic buildings in the country—modeled after the Alhambra in Spain, complete with silver domes and minarets. During its hotel days, rickshaws carried guests down the long, wide corridors. The distinguishing feature of Florida Southern College, in **Lakeland (245, F-3)**, is its seven monumental buildings designed by Frank Lloyd Wright.

A complex of magnificent buildings set in splendidly landscaped grounds in **Sarasota**

(246, C-5) forms a fitting memorial to John Ringling, the great circus magnate. The John and Mable Ringling Museum of Art, its centerpiece, has been described as the most beautiful art museum in the United States. It is a reproduction, on a colossal scale, of a 15th-century Italian villa. Its galleries hold one of the world's great collections of Baroque paintings. The museum also contains notable works by El Greco, Rubens, Rembrandt, Gainsborough and Reynolds. The Ringling mansion is a Venetian Gothic palace of pink stucco and glazed terra-cotta rising from Sarasota Bay. Completing the complex is the Museum of the Circus, a treasure house of big top memorabilia from ancient Rome to the present.

Visitors to Florida Cypress Gardens in **Winter Haven (245, F-3)** are met with a spectacular display of flowering plants—bougainvillea, camelias, gardenias, magnolias and azaleas. Each day four Water Ski Reviews feature precision waterskiing and water ballet. Amid idyllic landscapes at Bok Tower Gardens in **Lake Wales (245, F-3)** stands a 205-foot tower, built of coquina and marble. It houses a 53-bell carillon on which a 45-minute recital is given daily.

Walt Disney World near **Orlando (245, E-2)** is America's favorite attraction. The 43-square-mile complex includes not only the Magic Kingdom with its turreted castle and multitude of rides and shows, but also a complete resort area with hotels, restaurants, marinas and golf courses. This is also where Walt Disney's greatest dream, the Experimental Prototype Community of Tomorrow (EPCOT), is being transformed into reality. The plan for EPCOT includes Future World, a series of exhibits foreshadowing the future, and the World Showcase, an international exhibit on the cultures, traditions and accomplishments of mankind.

Sea World, south of Orlando, stars trained dolphins, sea lions and killer whales. A man-made tide pool enables visitors to view such creatures as sea anemones, starfish and crabs. Ringling Bros. and Barnum & Bailey Circus World, in nearby **Davenport (245, F-3)**, re-creates the sawdust-and-greasepaint atmosphere of the traveling circuses of yesteryear.

Kennedy Space Center on **Cape Canaveral (145, E-1)** is a gateway to the galaxy. At the

American alligators (above) bask in the midday Florida sun. Trapped and hunted for centuries, the species is making a slow but steady comeback in the southern United States.

Slowly, gracefully, Columbia (left) lifts off its launch pad at Kennedy Space Center.

Aboard a monorail "safari," visitors to Busch Gardens/The Dark Continent (right) explore a re-created African veldt where animals roam free.

Children of all ages celebrate Mickey Mouse's 50th birthday at Walt Disney World (below) near Orlando.

Fountains and replicas of classic and Renaissance sculptures adorn the John and Mable Ringling Museum of Art in Sarasota. Colonnaded loggias reminiscent of 15th-century Italy surround a garden court.

239

Park rangers patrol the subtropical world of the Everglades on water-skimming airboats.

Descendants of Ernest Hemingway's cats (above) roam the late author's Key West home. Sunset watchers (right) honor a Key West tradition.

Miami Beach's sparkling Hotel Row (below)

Visitor Center are displays of equipment that has been to outer space, rocks from the moon, and interpretive movies. Exhibits include a full-scale model of a lunar module and a Skylab Space Station. Buses transport visitors to the launch sites and the Vehicle Assembly Building, where an Apollo/Saturn rocket stands poised outside. Merritt Island National Wildlife Refuge—98,000 acres of saltwater lagoons, mangrove and grass marshes, woodlands and dunes—is nearby. Part of the refuge overlaps Cape Canaveral National Seashore, where visitors can swim and fish within sight of the Center's launch gantries.

Coconuts washed ashore from a Spanish wreck, it is said, were responsible for the palm trees of exclusive **Palm Beach (246, D-1).** On Coconut Row stands the white marble palace—now a museum—that railway magnate Henry Morrison Flagler called home. Early photographs of the area are on display, and the tycoon's private railway car can be seen on the grounds. In the handsome Norton Gallery and School of Art in West Palm Beach are more than 700 European and American paintings, including masterpieces of the early Italian Renaissance.

Rivers, bays, lagoons and canals make up much of **Fort Lauderdale (247, E-1),** a city of islands and a boater's haven. From the Bahia Mar Yacht Centre the *Jungle Queen* cruises past luxurious homes and manicured gardens. Alligator wrestling and animal shows are attractions en route. At Ocean World, just east, sea lions and porpoises perform.

Miami (247, F-1) itself has virtually no beach. But on Miami Beach, linked to the mainland by five causeways, an unbroken highway of shimmering sand, 7½ miles long, stretches to the horizon. Another of Miami's popular islands, or "keys," is Key Biscayne, reputedly discovered in 1497 by John Cabot. Its two-mile coastline is split into two public beach areas, located at opposite ends of the bay. The story of the world's oceans is told at

A 53-bell carillon is the haunting voice of Bok Singing Tower in Lake Wales.

Planet Ocean in seven multi-media theaters and with more than 100 exhibits, including a real iceberg. Another nearby aquatic attraction is the Miami Seaquarium, the world's largest tropical marine aquarium. Killer whales perform daily, with a supporting cast of sharks, sea lions and dolphins.

The late James Deering, co-founder of the International Harvester Company, built his monumental estate, Vizcaya, overlooking Biscayne Bay. A stone breakwater in the shape of a great barge, decorated with obelisks and statues that symbolize the pleasures and terrors of the sea, guards the private

A Fragile Wonderland Beneath the Waves

John Pennekamp Coral Reef State Park, a fragile underwater wonderland just off the east coast of Key Largo, preserves North America's only living coral reef. Skin and scuba divers can explore the history-shrouded skeletons of the reef's many sunken ships, or watch strikingly colored tropical fish glide among 43 varieties of brilliantly hued coral. A nine-foot bronze statue and symbol of peace, *Christ of the Deep*, overlooks this tranquil setting. Park rangers conduct special snorkeling programs to familiarize visitors with the 21-mile-long reef and its marine life. For those who prefer to stay dry, there are 2½-hour tours in glass bottom boats.

House and Gardens was home to John James Audubon while he painted the wildlife of the Florida Keys in 1832.

Everglades National Park is a 2,188-square-mile wilderness of freshwater grasslands, hammocks (low, wooded hills) and cypress stands that provides sanctuary for a remarkable mix of wildlife. The park protects part of the vast swampland created by Lake Okeechobee, 70 miles to the north. Spillage from the lake flows to the sea in a "river of grass" some 50 miles wide and less than a foot deep.

Visitors may enter the Everglades in one of three ways. South of the Tamiami Trail ("Alligator Alley"), a short loop road with a public tram service leads to the Shark Valley observation tower overlooking an area rich in birdlife. At **Everglades City (247, F-3)** is a ranger station where visitors with boats—canoes or small outboards—may embark on one of the most unusual trails in America, the 99-mile Wilderness Waterway. Most travelers, however, enter the park from Route 27, which leads southwest from Homestead to the main park visitor center. Alligators are the best-known Everglades residents, but crocodiles are also present, as well as panthers and endangered southern bald eagles. In saltwater lagoons, shy and secretive manatees graze on marine plants.

Big Cypress Swamp National Preserve, a primeval expanse of marshland edged here and there with broad belts of cypress trees, adjoins the Everglades to the northwest. Giant bald cypress—some 600 to 700 years old and 130 feet high—are protected in the Audubon Society's Corkscrew Swamp Sanctuary near **Immokalee (247, E-3)**.

Inventor Thomas A. Edison owned two of the earliest known prefabricated houses: built in Maine, they were transported by schooner to **Fort Myers (246, D-4)** in 1886. His home here is just as it was at the time of his death in 1931, and his laboratory is intact—even to the chemicals in the test tubes.

harbor. The 16th-century-style Italian Renaissance mansion—now the Dade County Art Museum—houses Deering's collection of mostly Italian furniture, sculptures, textiles, ceramics and other works of art spanning 18 centuries. Classical music wafts through the galleries of the Bass Museum of Art in Miami Beach, passing paintings by Botticelli, Rembrandt and El Greco. The Lowe Art Museum of the University of Miami at **Coral Gables (247, F-1)** specializes in Indian tribal art, Oriental porcelain and bronze.

South of Miami, Route 1 parallels Biscayne Bay, hidden from view by a series of opulent estates. More than 4,000 plant varieties, ranging from the beautiful to the bizarre, flourish in the Fairchild Tropical Gardens at Coral Gables. Monkey Jungle, at **Goulds (247, F-1)**, is a novel zoo park where orangutans, gibbons and chimpanzees swing through the trees above visitors' heads.

Homestead (247, F-1) is a gateway west to the Everglades and south to the Florida Keys. Just north of town is Coral Castle, a fascinating structure built of hand-hewn coral blocks—some weighing as much as 30 tons.

Nearby Orchid Jungle presents a vast and colorful array of these enchanting flowers in an approximation of their natural habitats.

Hundreds of coral reef and limestone islands, large and small, curve out from the southern tip of Florida. About 50 of these are linked by the Overseas Highway between Miami and Key West. **Bahia Honda (247, H-3)** is one of the loveliest of the keys; its crescent-shaped beach and alluring tropical palms are protected by a state park. Off **Key Largo (247, G-1)** lies John Pennekamp Coral Reef State Park, the first undersea park in the United States and a living coral reef.

Key West (247, H-4) is the southernmost point in the continental United States, just 90 miles from Cuba. Spanish, Caribbean and American influences combine to form a unique culture evident in the city's architecture and its cuisine—which features such delights as turtle steak, conch chowder and Key lime pie. The relaxed atmosphere of Key West has attracted artists and writers for decades. The Ernest Hemingway Home and Museum is where the novelist produced several of his most notable works. Audubon

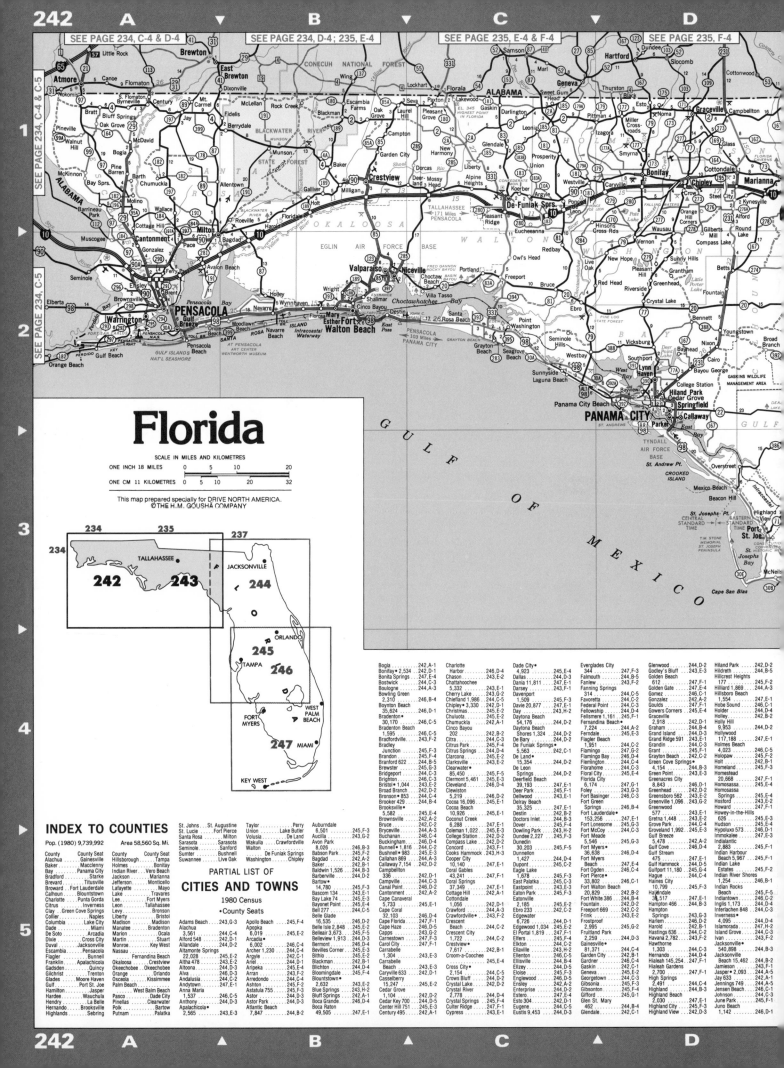

Florida

SCALE IN MILES AND KILOMETRES

ONE INCH 18 MILES — 0 5 10 20

ONE CM 11 KILOMETRES — 0 5 10 20 32

This map prepared specially for DRIVE NORTH AMERICA.
©THE H.M. GOUSHA COMPANY

INDEX TO COUNTIES

Pop. (1980) 9,739,992   Area 58,560 Sq. Mi.

PARTIAL LIST OF CITIES AND TOWNS

1980 Census — •County Seats

SEE PAGE 235, G-4 | SEE PAGE 235, H-4 | SEE PAGE 237, G-4 & G-5 | SEE PAGE 237, G-3 & G-4

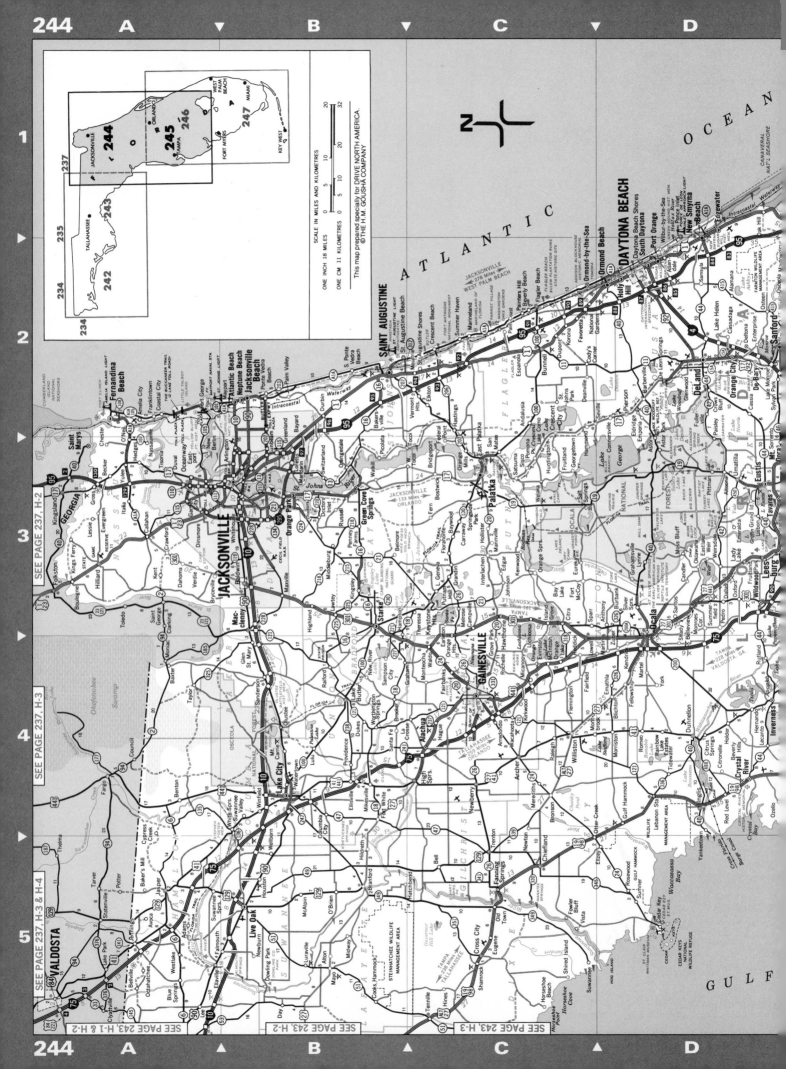

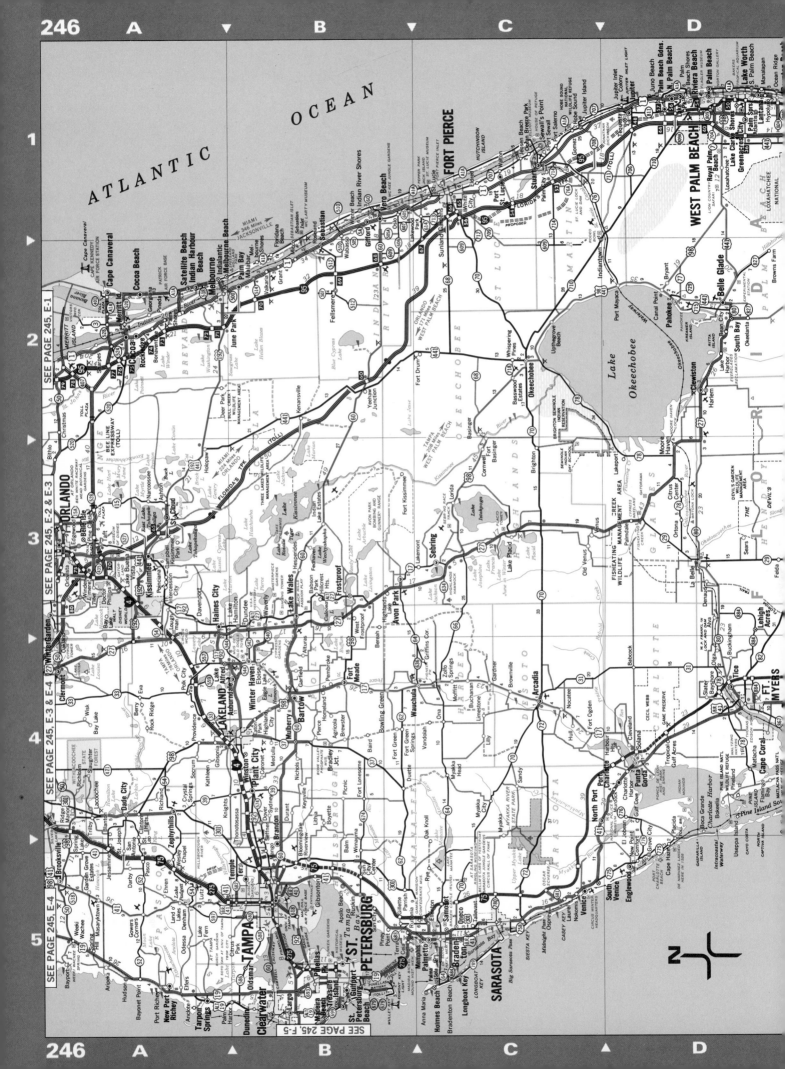

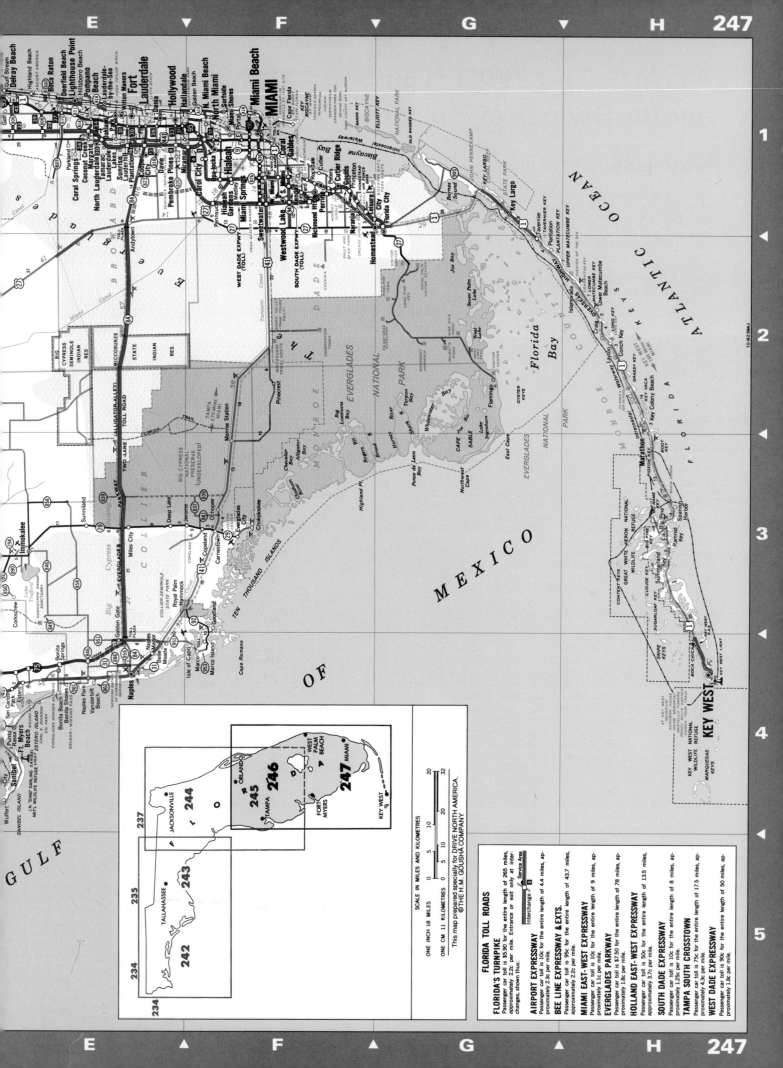

A Lost Colony, a First Flight and the Hazy Great Smokies

North and South Carolina

The most visited park in the United States, **Great Smoky Mountains National Park (250, D-2)**, crowns the Appalachian Mountains of North Carolina. At any season and in any weather, vistas of hazy, forested ridges stretching to each horizon inspire exhilaration and awe. The park's Oconaluftee Visitor Center, a restored pioneer homestead, shows how southern Appalachian settlers lived off the land until the early 20th century. Oconaluftee Indian Village in **Cherokee (250, D-2)** provides a similar representation of an 18th-century Cherokee Indian settlement. Cherokee is part of a reservation for descendants of those who escaped deportation to Oklahoma in 1838 along the "Trail of Tears." The story of this tragic 1,200-mile winter march is told at the Museum of the Cherokee Indian.

The Blue Ridge Parkway, one of the loveliest scenic routes in the United States, connects Smoky Mountain National Park with Virginia's lush Shenandoah Valley. Along the way, the parkway passes through Pisgah National Forest, a verdant refuge spread across the high spine of the Appalachians.

Creations of mountain craftsmen are displayed and sold near **Asheville (251, F-2)** in an airy gallery at the Folk Art Center. Mountain music enlivens the park in front of Asheville's city hall on Saturday evenings in summer. Novelist Thomas Wolfe's former home, memorialized in *Look Homeward, Angel*, is open to visitors.

The Piedmont is a region of forested hills between the Appalachians and the Coastal Plain. In 1766, Moravians from Pennsylvania pushed southward to this site and founded Salem. Old Salem today—a showpiece of clapboard, stone and half-timbered homes within modern **Winston-Salem (252, A-2)**—is an example of early town planning.

Three hundred years of North Carolina's history come to life at the Museum of History in **Raleigh (252, C-2)**, the state capital. One of its most treasured documents is the original charter by which King Charles II established the colony of Carolina in 1663. The galleries of the North Carolina Museum of Art contain masterpieces by Raphael and Goya, and numerous British and American paintings and sculptures. Fifty varieties of native trees shade the grounds of the State Capitol, a Greek Revival building raised in 1840.

The fertile soil of the Coastal Plain nurtures tobacco, sweet potatoes and peanuts. To the east, farmland gradually gives way to Tidewater lowlands, where broad rivers empty into wide bays. Sea breezes along the wave-battered Outer Banks helped launch the world's first powered flight by Wilbur and Orville Wright at **Kill Devil Hills (253, H-2)**. Near the field, reconstructions re-create the scene of the Wrights' 1901–03 camp and hangar. Wright Monument, a granite pylon rising above the dunes, marks the site from which the brothers launched nearly 1,000 glider flights in preparation for their historic triumph on December 17, 1903.

The turbulent waters and treacherous shoals of Cape Hatteras (right) have sunk so many ships that the area is known as "The Graveyard." Bleaching ship skeletons are still seen along its beaches.

Magnificent Biltmore— Vanderbilt's Home Was His Castle

George Washington Vanderbilt, grandson of railroad magnate Cornelius Vanderbilt, constructed Biltmore, the world's largest private home, on a broad Blue Ridge Plateau two miles south of Asheville, North Carolina. Almost 1,000 workers labored from 1890 to 1895 to build the 255-room mansion, and landscape the 40 acres of formal gardens set amid 12,000 acres of informal gardens and woodlands. (At one time the estate included more than 125,000 acres; part of the estate formed the nucleus of nearby Pisgah National Forest.) The main house, patterned after the châteaus of the Loire in France, is graced with Persian rugs, tapestries, a Wedgwood mantel, ancient Chinese vases, priceless antiques, and such objets d'art as an ivory chess set once owned by Napoleon. The ceiling of the cavernous Banquet Hall (*right*) arches 75 feet above the dining table. Over the elaborately carved triple fireplace are banners of the 11 great powers at the time of America's discovery. Outside, splendid gardens, walks and pools provide a fitting counterpart to the home, now a National Historic Site.

The mystery of the "Lost Colony" still puzzles historians and fascinates visitors to **Roanoke Island (253, H-2)**. Lying between the marshy mainland and the Outer Banks, this area was chosen by Sir Walter Raleigh as the site of the first English colony in North America. The colonists landed in 1585 but had vanished within three years, leaving behind only the inscription "Cro" carved in a stockade post. The riddle of their fate is posed each year in a musical drama staged at an outdoor theater overlooking Roanoke Sound and the presumed site of the settlement.

From Whalebone Junction south to Ocracoke Inlet, **Cape Hatteras National Seashore (253, H-3)** protects 70 miles of marshes and maritime forest, dramatic beaches and wild surf. Highway 12 snakes along this slim barrier past Bodie Island Lighthouse, which has alerted mariners to offshore shoals for more than a century. Cape Hatteras Lighthouse stands guard at Diamond Shoal, graveyard of more than 100 ships since the 17th century.

A ferry from Hatteras Island carries travelers to **Ocracoke Island (253, H-4)**. Sheltered by live oaks, cedars and loblollies, Ocracoke Village resembles a New England town with a semitropical air. The scalloped shoreline beyond was a landfall for Raleigh's colonists in 1585 and a refuge for the pirate Blackbeard, killed here by British seamen in 1718. Ocracoke is also known for its wild ponies,

believed to be descended from Spanish mustangs stranded in the 16th century.

The crown jewel of **New Bern (253, F-4)** is its magnificent Georgian-style Tryon Palace (1770), the seat of colonial government and the home of Governor William Tryon. In 1798 fire destroyed all but the basement and two wings. The present-day palace is a meticulous reconstruction based on original inventories and architectural plans.

Wilmington (255, H-1), on the Cape Fear River, is the chief port of North Carolina and permanent berth of the U.S.S. *North Carolina*, a memorial to North Carolinians who died in World War II. In Greenfield Gardens, a five-mile drive winds past millions of azalea and camellia blossoms. Glowing azaleas also frame the classical pillars of the Orton House, heart of a rich plantation created in 1725. The house itself is not open, but the gardens are a springtime delight.

A string of coastal islands and mainland beaches sweeps southward into South Carolina. **Myrtle Beach (255, G-2)**, with its 55-mile crescent of white sand known as the Grand Strand, is one of the East Coast's most popular resorts. Its boardwalk is a colorful midway of tourist attractions, and fishing from its pier is excellent. For golfers, there are more than 30 courses, carved from the wooded sandhills, within a half-hour's drive.

For two centuries, **Georgetown (255, F-3)** was the heart of the most productive rice-growing country in America. With maps,

Candy-striped Cape Hatteras Lighthouse (right), the tallest brick lighthouse in the country, stands sentinel at North Carolina's Diamond Shoals.

Aristocratic Charleston (below) is a coastal city of lovely gardens and attractive homes, examples of the best in pre-Revolutionary and antebellum architecture. Over three centuries it has survived war, earthquake and fire, as well as pirate attacks from the sea.

Magnificent stained glass glows in the Bob Jones University Art Museum (above), near Greenville, South Carolina.

tools and dioramas, the Rice Museum chronicles the rise and fall of the region's one-crop economy. Hopsewee Plantation, with its frame house of black cypress, is a typical Low Country rice plantation of the 18th century.

Charleston (255, E-4) retains a well cultivated air of the past: cobbled streets fragrant with jasmine and tea olive, palmetto-lined promenades, lacy wrought iron gates and walled gardens. Hub of the region known as the Low Country, Charleston grew rich by exporting rice and importing rum, sugar and slaves.

At Charles Towne Landing across the Ashley River from Charleston, South Carolina's first permanent English settlement (1670) has been reconstructed in a state park. Native wildlife is displayed in natural settings, and a replica of a 17th-century trading ship is moored in a creek. Fort Sumter guards the mouth of Charleston Harbor today just as it did in 1861, when the first shot of the Civil War was fired upon its five-foot-thick walls.

Many fine old plantations lie in Charleston's vicinity. The landscaped terraces, ornamental waterways and plantings of Middleton Place, begun in 1741, have survived two wars and a severe earthquake. English novelist John Galsworthy described the informal setting of Magnolia Gardens as "a miraculously enchanted wilderness." Boone Hall Plantation, which dates from a 1661 land grant, is renowned for its beautiful three-mile Avenue of Oaks.

Three different flags—Spanish, French and Scottish—flew over **Beaufort (254, D-5)** before British settlement was established here in 1710. It was during the community's golden age as an agricultural center, from about 1820 to 1860, that many of the finest homes and buildings were constructed on Bay Street and on the historic Point.

Columbia (254, C-2), the state capital, is a broad-avenued city in the heart of South Carolina. In the Columbia Museum of Art hang Renaissance paintings by Tintoretto and Botticelli. Southern arts and crafts are also emphasized—paintings, jewelry, ceramics and furniture—from all periods of the state's history. The Gibbs Planetarium, part of a science center, takes visitors on a simulated journey among the stars.

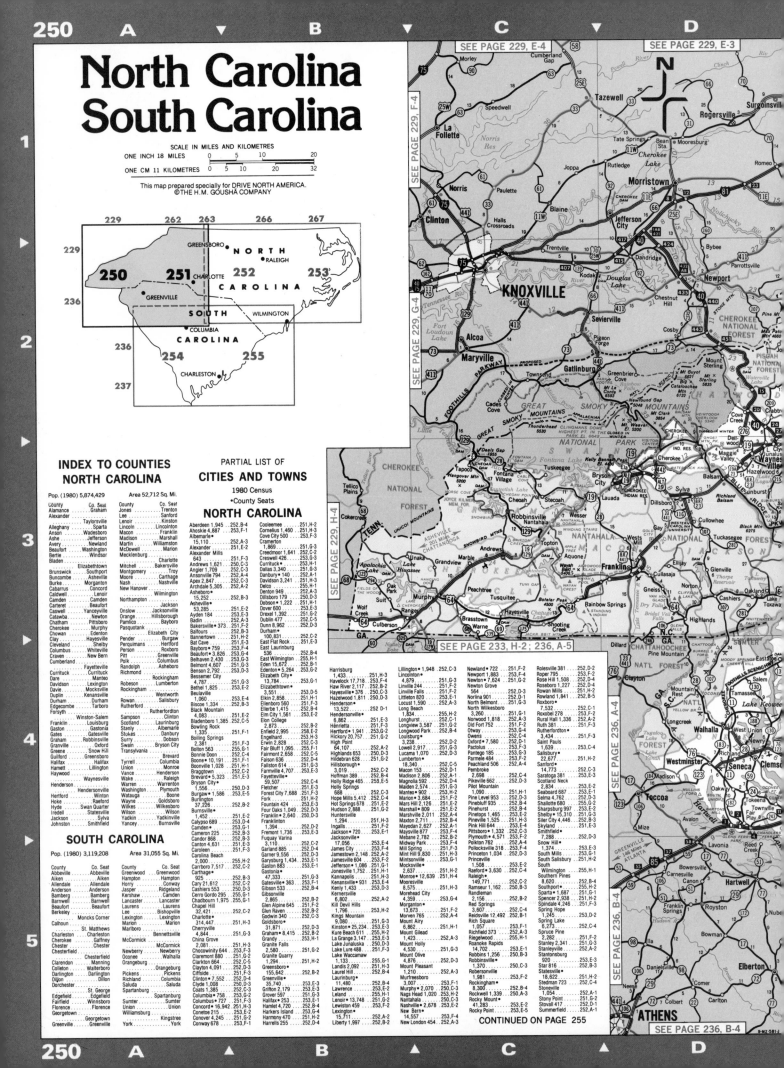

North Carolina
South Carolina

SCALE IN MILES AND KILOMETRES
ONE INCH 18 MILES 0 5 10 20
ONE CM 11 KILOMETRES 0 5 10 20 32

This map prepared specially for DRIVE NORTH AMERICA.
©THE H.M. GOUSHĀ COMPANY

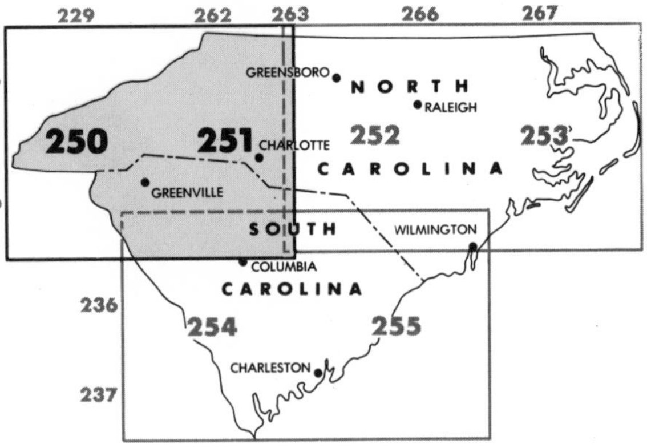

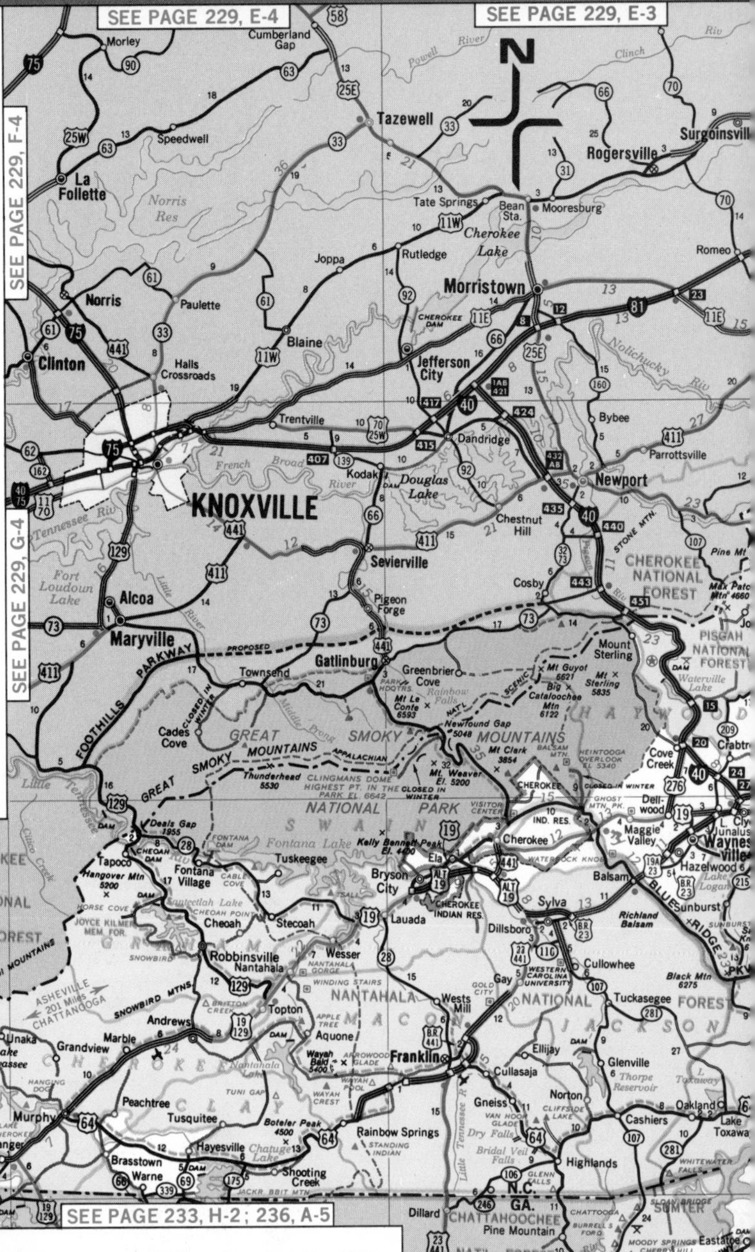

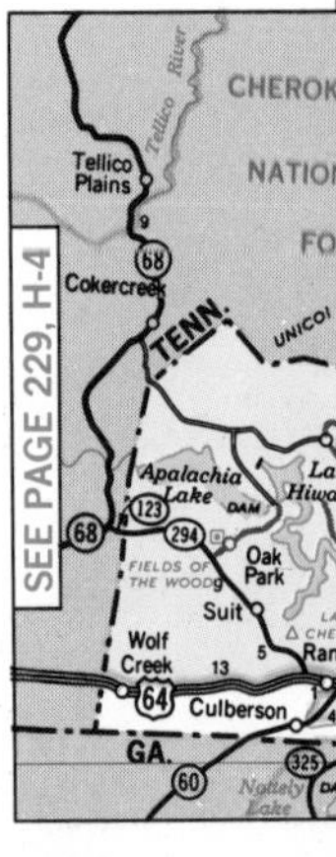

INDEX TO COUNTIES
NORTH CAROLINA

Pop. (1980) 5,874,429 Area 52,712 Sq. Mi.

County	Co. Seat
Alamance	Graham
Alexander	Taylorsville
Alleghany	Sparta
Anson	Wadesboro
Ashe	Jefferson
Avery	Newland
Beaufort	Washington
Bertie	Windsor
Bladen	Elizabethtown
Brunswick	Southport
Buncombe	Asheville
Burke	Morganton
Cabarrus	Concord
Caldwell	Lenoir
Camden	Camden
Carteret	Beaufort
Caswell	Yanceyville
Catawba	Newton
Chatham	Pittsboro
Cherokee	Murphy
Chowan	Edenton
Clay	Hayesville
Cleveland	Shelby
Columbus	Whiteville
Craven	New Bern
Cumberland	Fayetteville
Currituck	Currituck
Dare	Manteo
Davidson	Lexington
Davie	Mocksville
Duplin	Kenansville
Durham	Durham
Edgecombe	Tarboro
Forsyth	Winston-Salem
Franklin	Louisburg
Gaston	Gastonia
Gates	Gatesville
Graham	Robbinsville
Granville	Oxford
Greene	Snow Hill
Guilford	Greensboro
Halifax	Halifax
Hamett	Lillington
Haywood	Waynesville
Henderson	Hendersonville
Hertford	Winton
Hoke	Raeford
Hyde	Swan Quarter
Iredell	Statesville
Jackson	Sylva
Johnston	Smithfield
Jones	Trenton
Lee	Sanford
Lenoir	Kinston
Lincoln	Lincolnton
Macon	Franklin
Madison	Marshall
Martin	Williamston
McDowell	Marion
Mecklenburg	Charlotte
Mitchell	Bakersville
Montgomery	Troy
Moore	Carthage
Nash	Nashville
New Hanover	Wilmington
Northampton	Jackson
Onslow	Jacksonville
Orange	Hillsborough
Pamlico	Bayboro
Pasquotank	Elizabeth City
Pender	Burgaw
Perquimans	Hertford
Person	Roxboro
Pitt	Greenville
Polk	Columbus
Randolph	Asheboro
Richmond	Rockingham
Robeson	Lumberton
Rockingham	Wentworth
Rowan	Salisbury
Rutherford	Rutherfordton
Sampson	Clinton
Scotland	Laurinburg
Stanly	Albemarle
Stokes	Danbury
Surry	Dobson
Swain	Bryson City
Transylvania	Brevard
Tyrrell	Columbia
Union	Monroe
Vance	Henderson
Wake	Raleigh
Warren	Warrenton
Washington	Plymouth
Watauga	Boone
Wayne	Goldsboro
Wilkes	Wilkesboro
Wilson	Wilson
Yadkin	Yadkinville
Yancey	Burnsville

SOUTH CAROLINA

Pop. (1980) 3,119,208 Area 31,055 Sq. Mi.

County	Co. Seat
Abbeville	Abbeville
Aiken	Aiken
Allendale	Allendale
Anderson	Anderson
Bamberg	Bamberg
Barnwell	Barnwell
Beaufort	Beaufort
Berkeley	Moncks Corner
Calhoun	St. Matthews
Charleston	Charleston
Cherokee	Gaffney
Chester	Chester
Chesterfield	Chesterfield
Clarendon	Manning
Colleton	Walterboro
Darlington	Darlington
Dillon	Dillon
Dorchester	St. George
Edgefield	Edgefield
Fairfield	Winnsboro
Florence	Florence
Georgetown	Georgetown
Greenville	Greenville
Greenwood	Greenwood
Hampton	Hampton
Horry	Conway
Jasper	Ridgeland
Kershaw	Camden
Lancaster	Lancaster
Laurens	Laurens
Lee	Bishopville
Lexington	Lexington
Marion	Marion
Marlboro	Bennettsville
McCormick	McCormick
Newberry	Newberry
Oconee	Walhalla
Orangeburg	Orangeburg
Pickens	Pickens
Richland	Columbia
Saluda	Saluda
Spartanburg	Spartanburg
Sumter	Sumter
Union	Union
Williamsburg	Kingstree
York	York

PARTIAL LIST OF

CITIES AND TOWNS

1980 Census
•County Seats

NORTH CAROLINA

Aberdeen 1,945 . . 252,B-4
Ahoskie 4,887 . . . 253,F-1
Albemarle• 15,110 . . . 252,A-3
Alexander . . . 251,E-2
Alexander Mills 643 . . . 251,F-3
Andrews 1,621 . . . 250,C-3
Angier 1,709 . . . 252,C-3
Ansonville 794 . . . 252,A-4
Apex 2,847 . . . 252,C-3
Archdale 5,305 . . . 252,A-2
Asheboro• 15,252 . . . 252,B-3
Asheville• 53,285 . . . 251,E-2
Ayden 184 . . . 253,E-3
Badin . . . 252,A-3
Bakersville• 373 . . 251,F-2
Balfours . . . 252,B-3
Bannertown . . . 251,H-2
Bat Cave . . . 251,E-3
Bayboro• 759 . . . 253,F-4
Beaufort• 3,826 . . 253,G-4
Belhaven 2,430 . . 253,G-3
Belmont 4,607 . . . 251,G-3
Benson 2,792 . . . 253,D-3
Bessemer City 4,787 . . . 251,G-3
Bethel 1,825 . . . 253,E-2
Beulaville 1,060 . . . 253,E-4
Biscoe 1,334 . . . 252,B-3
Black Mountain 4,083 . . . 251,E-2
Bladenboro 1,385 . 252,C-5
Bowling Rock 1,335 . . . 251,F-1
Boiling Springs 2,381 . . . 251,F-3
Bolton 563 . . . 255,G-1
Bonnie Doon . . . 252,C-4
Boone• 10,191 . . . 251,F-1
Boonville 1,028 . . 251,H-1
Braggtown . . . 252,C-2
Brevard• 5,323 . . 251,E-3
Bryson City• 1,556 . . . 250,D-3
Burgaw• 1,586 . . 253,E-5
Burlington 37,226 . . . 252,B-2
Burnsville• 1,452 . . . 251,E-2
Calypso 689 . . . 253,D-4
Camden• . . . 253,G-1
Cameron 225 . . . 252,B-3
Candor 868 . . . 252,B-3
Canton 4,631 . . . 251,E-3
Caroleen . . . 251,F-3
Carolina Beach 2,000 . . . 255,H-2
Carrboro 7,517 . . . 252,C-2
Carthage• 925 . . . 252,B-3
Cary 21,612 . . . 252,C-2
Cashiers 553 . . . 250,D-3
Cerro Gordo 295 . . 255,G-1
Chadbourn 1,975 . 255,G-1
Chapel Hill 32,421 . . . 252,C-2
Charlotte• 314,447 . . . 251,H-3
Cherryville 4,844 . . . 251,G-3
China Grove 2,081 . . . 251,H-3
Chocowinity 644 . . 253,F-3
Claremont 880 . . . 251,G-2
Clarkton 664 . . . 252,C-5
Clayton 4,091 . . . 252,D-3
Ciffside . . . 251,F-3
Clinton• 7,552 . . . 252,D-4
Clyde 1,008 . . . 250,D-3
Coats 1,385 . . . 252,C-3
Columbia• 758 . . . 253,G-2
Columbus• 727 . . 251,F-3
Concord• 16,942 . 251,H-3
Conetoe 215 . . . 253,E-2
Conover 4,245 . . . 251,G-2
Conway 678 . . . 253,F-1
Cooleemee . . . 251,H-2
Cornelius 1,460 . . 251,H-3
Cove City 500 . . . 253,F-3
Cramerton 1,869 . . . 251,G-3
Creedmoor 1,641 . 252,C-2
Creswell 426 . . . 253,G-3
Currituck• . . . 253,H-1
Dallas 3,340 . . . 251,G-3
Danbury• 140 . . . 252,A-1
Davidson 3,241 . . 251,H-3
Delco . . . 255,H-1
Denton 949 . . . 252,A-3
Dillsboro 179 . . . 250,D-3
Dobson• 1,222 . . 251,H-1
Dover 600 . . . 253,E-3
Drexel 1,392 . . . 251,G-2
Dublin 477 . . . 252,C-5
Dunn 8,962 . . . 252,D-3
Durham• 100,831 . . . 252,C-2
East Flat Rock . . . 251,E-3
East Laurinburg 536 . . . 252,B-4
East Wilmington . . 255,H-1
Eden 15,672 . . . 252,B-1
Edenton• 5,264 . . 253,G-2
Elizabeth City• 13,784 . . . 253,G-1
Elizabethtown• 3,551 . . . 253,D-5
Elkin 2,858 . . . 251,H-1
Ellenboro 560 . . . 251,F-3
Ellerbe 1,415 . . . 252,B-4
Elm City 1,561 . . . 253,E-2
Elon College 2,873 . . . 252,B-2
Enfield 2,995 . . . 258,E-2
Engelhard . . . 253,H-3
Erwin 2,828 . . . 252,C-3
Fair Bluff 1,095 . . . 255,F-1
Fairmont 2,658 . . . 252,C-5
Faison 636 . . . 252,D-4
Fallston 614 . . . 251,G-3
Farmville 4,707 . . . 253,E-3
Fayetteville• 59,507 . . . 252,C-4
Fletcher . . . 251,E-3
Forest City 7,688 . 251,F-3
Fork . . . 251,H-2
Fountain 424 . . . 253,E-3
Four Oaks 1,049 . . 252,D-3
Franklin• 2,640 . . 250,D-3
Franklinton 1,394 . . . 252,D-2
Fremont 1,736 . . . 253,E-3
Fuquay Varina 3,110 . . . 252,C-2
Garland 885 . . . 252,D-4
Garner 9,556 . . . 252,D-3
Garysburg 1,434 . . 253,E-1
Gaston 883 . . . 253,E-1
Gastonia• 47,333 . . . 251,G-3
Gatesville• 363 . . . 253,F-1
Gibson 533 . . . 252,B-4
Gibsonville 2,865 . . . 252,B-2
Glen Alpine 645 . . 251,F-2
Glen Raven . . . 252,B-2
Godwin 340 . . . 252,C-3
Goldsboro• 31,871 . . . 252,D-3
Graham• 8,415 . . 252,B-2
Grandy . . . 253,H-1
Granite Falls 2,580 . . . 251,G-2
Granite Quarry 1,294 . . . 251,H-2
Greensboro• 155,642 . . . 252,B-2
Greenville• 35,740 . . . 253,E-3
Grifton 2,179 . . . 253,E-3
Grover 597 . . . 251,G-3
Halifax• 253 . . . 253,E-1
Hamlet 4,720 . . . 252,B-4
Harkers Island . . 253,G-4
Harmony 470 . . . 251,H-2
Harrells 255 . . . 252,D-4
Harrisburg 1,433 . . . 251,H-3
Havelock 17,718 . . 253,F-4
Haw River 2,117 . . 252,B-2
Hayesville• 376 . . 250,C-3
Hazelwood 1,811 . 250,D-3
Henderson• 13,522 . . . 252 D-1
Hendersonville• 6,862 . . . 251,E-3
Hėnrietta . . . 251,F-3
Hertford• 1,941 . . 253,G-2
Hickory 20,757 . . . 251,G-2
High Point 64,107 . . . 252,A-2
Highlands 653 . . . 250,D-3
Hildebran 628 . . . 251,G-2
Hillsborough• 3,019 . . . 252,C-2
Hoffman 389 . . . 252,B-4
Holly Ridge 465 . . . 253,E-5
Holly Springs 688 . . . 252,C-3
Hope Mills 5,412 . 252,C-4
Hot Springs 678 . . 251,E-2
Hudson 2,888 . . . 251,G-2
Huntersville 1,294 . . . 251,H-3
Ingalls . . . 251,F-2
Jackson• 720 . . . 253,E-1
Jacksonville• 17,056 . . . 253,E-4
James City . . . 253,F-4
Jamestown 2,148 . 252,A-2
Jamesville 604 . . . 253,F-2
Jefferson• 1,086 . 251,G-1
Jonesville 1,752 . . 251,H-1
Kannapolis . . . 251,H-3
Kenansville• 931 . 253,E-4
Kenly 1,433 . . . 253,D-3
Kernersville 6,802 . . . 252,A-2
Kill Devil Hills 1,796 . . . 253,H-2
Kings Mountain 9,080 . . . 251,G-3
Kinston• 25,234 . . 253,E-3
Kure Beach 611 . . 255,H-2
La Grange 3,147 . . 253,E-3
Lake Junaluska . . 250,D-3
Lake Lure 488 . . . 251,F-3
Lake Waccamaw 1,133 . . . 255,G-1
Landis 2,092 . . . 251,H-3
Laurel Hill . . . 252,B-4
Laurinburg• 11,480 . . . 252,B-4
Lawrence . . . 253,E-2
Leland . . . 255,H-1
Lenoir• 13,748 . . 251,G-2
Lewiston 459 . . . 253,F-2
Lexington• 15,711 . . . 252,A-2
Liberty 1,997 . . . 252,B-2
Lillington• 1,948 . 252,C-3
Lincolnton• 4,879 . . . 251,G-3
Linville 244 . . . 251,F-2
Linville Falls . . . 251,F-2
Littleton 820 . . . 253,E-1
Locust 1,590 . . . 252,A-3
Long Beach 1,834 . . . 255,H-2
Longhurst . . . 252,C-1
Longview 3,587 . . 251,G-2
Longwood Park . . . 252,B-4
Louisburg• 3,238 . . . 252,D-2
Lowell 2,917 . . . 251,G-3
Lucama 1,070 . . . 252,D-3
Lumberton• 18,340 . . . 252,C-5
Macon 153 . . . 252,D-1
Madison 2,806 . . . 252,A-1
Magnolia 592 . . . 252,D-4
Maiden 2,574 . . . 251,G-3
Manteo• 902 . . . 253,H-2
Marion• 3,684 . . . 251,F-2
Mars Hill 2,126 . . . 251,E-2
Marshall• 809 . . . 251,E-2
Marshville 2,011 . 252,A-4
Maxton 2,711 . . . 252,B-4
Mayodan 2,627 . . 252,A-1
Maysville 877 . . . 253,F-4
Mebane 2,782 . . . 252,B-2
Midway Park . . . 253,F-4
Mill Spring . . . 251,F-3
Mint Hill 9,830 . . . 251,H-3
Mintsonville . . . 253,G-1
Mocksville• 2,637 . . . 251,H-2
Monroe• 12,639 . 251,H-4
Mooresville 8,575 . . . 251,H-3
Morehead City 4,359 . . . 253,G-4
Morganton• 13,673 . . . 251,F-2
Morven 765 . . . 252,A-4
Mount Airy 6,862 . . . 251,H-1
Mount Gilead 1,423 . . . 252,A-3
Mount Holly 4,530 . . . 251,G-3
Mount Olive 4,876 . . . 252,D-3
Mount Pleasant 1,210 . . . 252,A-3
Murfreesboro 3,007 . . . 253,F-1
Murphy• 2,070 . . 250,C-3
Nags Head 1,020 . 253,H-2
Nantahala . . . 250,C-3
Nashville• 2,678 . 253,E-2
New Bern• 14,557 . . . 253,F-4
New London 454 . . 252,A-3
Newland• 722 . . . 251,F-2
Newport 1,883 . . . 253,F-4
Newton• 7,624 . . . 251,G-2
Newton Grove 564 . . . 252,D-3
Norlina 901 . . . 252,D-1
North Belmont . . . 251,G-3
North Wilkesboro 3,260 . . . 251,G-1
Norwood 1,818 . . . 252,A-3
Old Fort 752 . . . 251,F-2
Otway . . . 253,G-4
Owens . . . 252,C-4
Oxford• 7,580 . . . 252,D-1
Pactolus . . . 253,F-3
Pantego 185 . . . 253,G-3
Parmele 484 . . . 253,F-2
Peachland 506 . . . 252,A-4
Pembroke 2,698 . . . 252,C-4
Pikeville 662 . . . 252,D-3
Pilot Mountain 1,090 . . . 251,H-1
Pine Level 953 . . . 252,D-3
Pinebluff 935 . . . 252,B-4
Pinehurst . . . 252,B-4
Pinetops 1,465 . . . 253,E-2
Pineville 1,525 . . . 251,H-3
Pink Hill 644 . . . 253,E-4
Pittsboro• 1,332 . 252,C-3
Plymouth• 4,571 . 253,F-2
Polkton 762 . . . 252,A-4
Pollocksville 318 . . 253,F-4
Princeton 1,034 . . 252,D-3
Princeville 1,508 . . . 253,E-2
Raeford• 3,630 . . 252,C-4
Raleigh• 149,771 . . . 252,C-2
Ramseur 1,162 . . . 250,B-3
Randleman 2,156 . . . 252,B-2
Red Springs 3,607 . . . 252,C-4
Reidsville 12,492 . 252,B-1
Rich Square 1,057 . . . 253,F-1
Richfield 373 . . . 252,A-3
Riegelwood . . . 255,H-1
Roanoke Rapids 14,702 . . . 253,E-1
Robbins 1,256 . . . 250,B-3
Robbinsville• 1,370 . . . 250,C-3
Robersonville 1,981 . . . 253,F-2
Rockingham• 8,300 . . . 252,B-4
Rockwell 1,339 . . . 250,A-3
Rocky Mount• 41,283 . . . 253,E-2
Rocky Point . . . 253,E-5
Rolesville 381 . . . 252,D-2
Roper 795 . . . 253,F-2
Rose Hill 1,508 . . 252,D-4
Roseboro 1,227 . . 252,D-4
Rowan Mills . . . 251,H-2
Rowland 1,841 . . . 252,B-5
Roxboro• 7,532 . . . 252,C-1
Roxobel 278 . . . 253,F-2
Rural Hall 1,336 . . 252,A-2
Ruth 381 . . . 251,F-3
Rutherfordton• 3,434 . . . 251,F-3
Saint Pauls 1,639 . . . 253,C-4
Salisbury• 22,677 . . . 251,H-2
Sanford• 14,773 . . . 252,C-3
Saratoga 381 . . . 253,E-3
Scotland Neck 2,834 . . . 253,E-2
Seaboard 687 . . . 253,E-1
Selma 4,762 . . . 252,D-3
Shallotte 680 . . . 255,G-2
Sharpsburg 997 . . 253,E-2
Shelby• 15,310 . . 251,G-3
Siler City 4,446 . . . 252,B-3
Skyland . . . 251,E-3
Smithfield• 7,288 . . . 252,D-3
Snow Hill• 1,374 . . . 253,E-3
South Mills . . . 253,G-1
South Salisbury . . 251,H-2
South Wilmington . . . 255,H-1
Southern Pines 8,620 . . . 252,B-4
Southport• . . . 255,H-2
Sparta• 1,687 . . . 251,G-1
Spencer 2,938 . . . 251,H-2
Spindale 4,246 . . . 251,F-3
Spring Hope 1,245 . . . 253,D-2
Spring Lake 6,273 . . . 252,C-4
Spruce Pine 2,282 . . . 251,F-2
Stanley 2,341 . . . 251,G-3
Stanleyville . . . 252,A-2
Stantonsburg 920 . . . 253,E-3
Star 816 . . . 252,B-3
Statesville• 18,622 . . . 251,H-2
Stedman 723 . . . 252,C-4
Stoneville 1,054 . . . 252,A-1
Stony Point . . . 251,G-2
Stovall 417 . . . 252,D-1
Summerfield . . . 252,A-1

CONTINUED ON PAGE 255

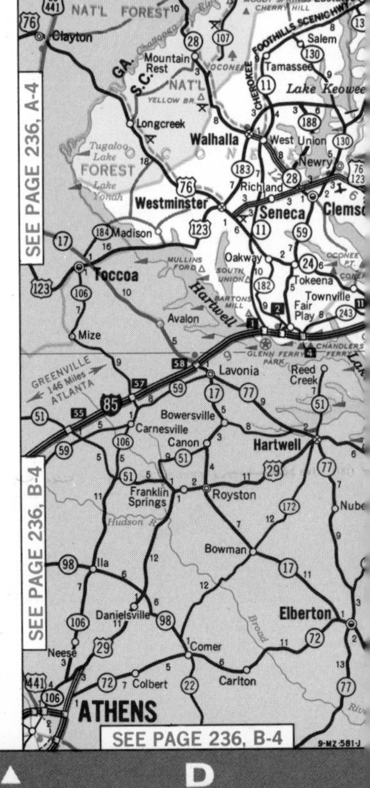

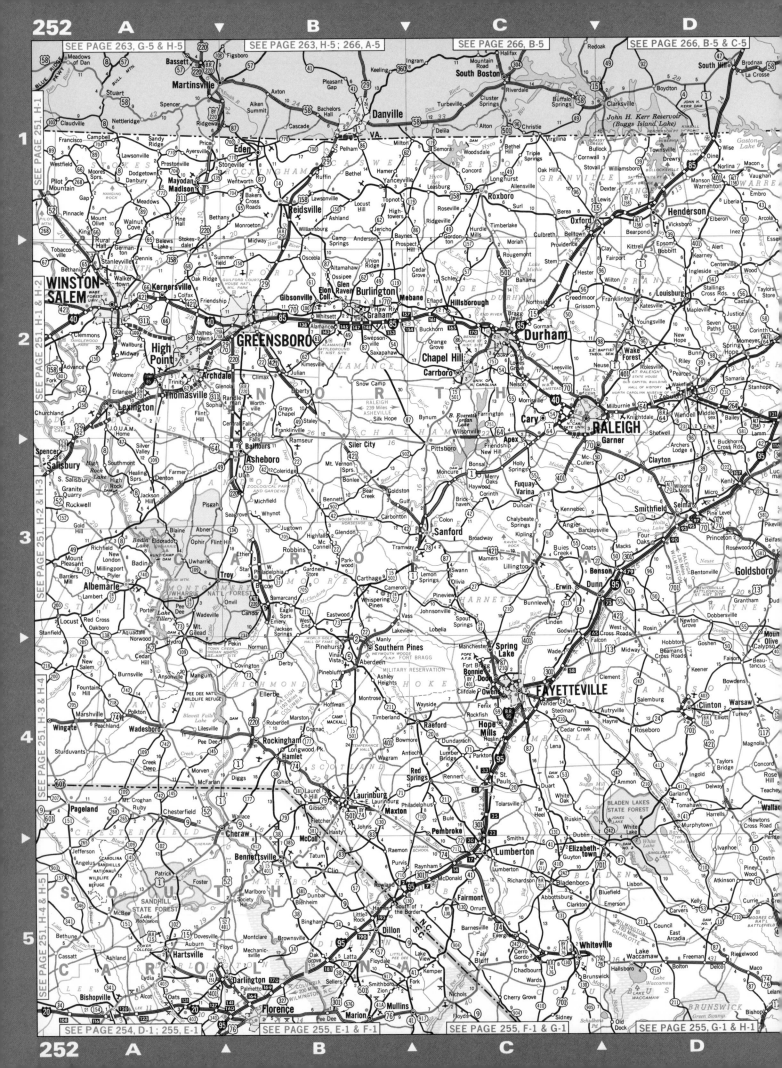

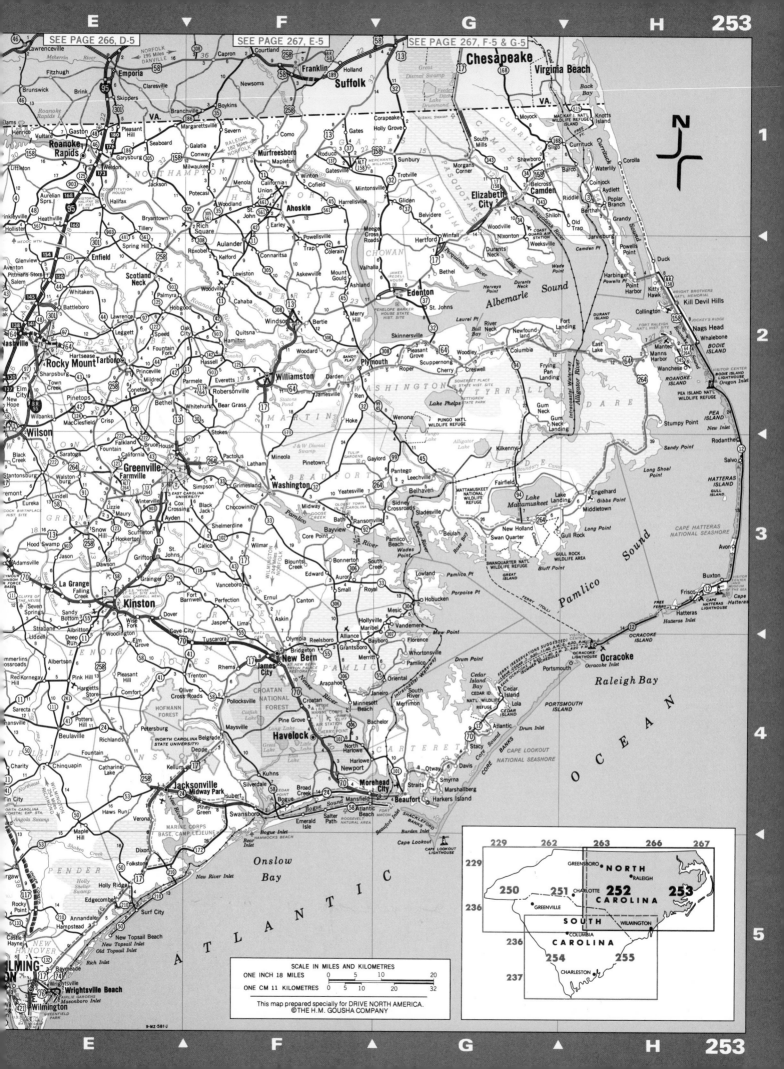

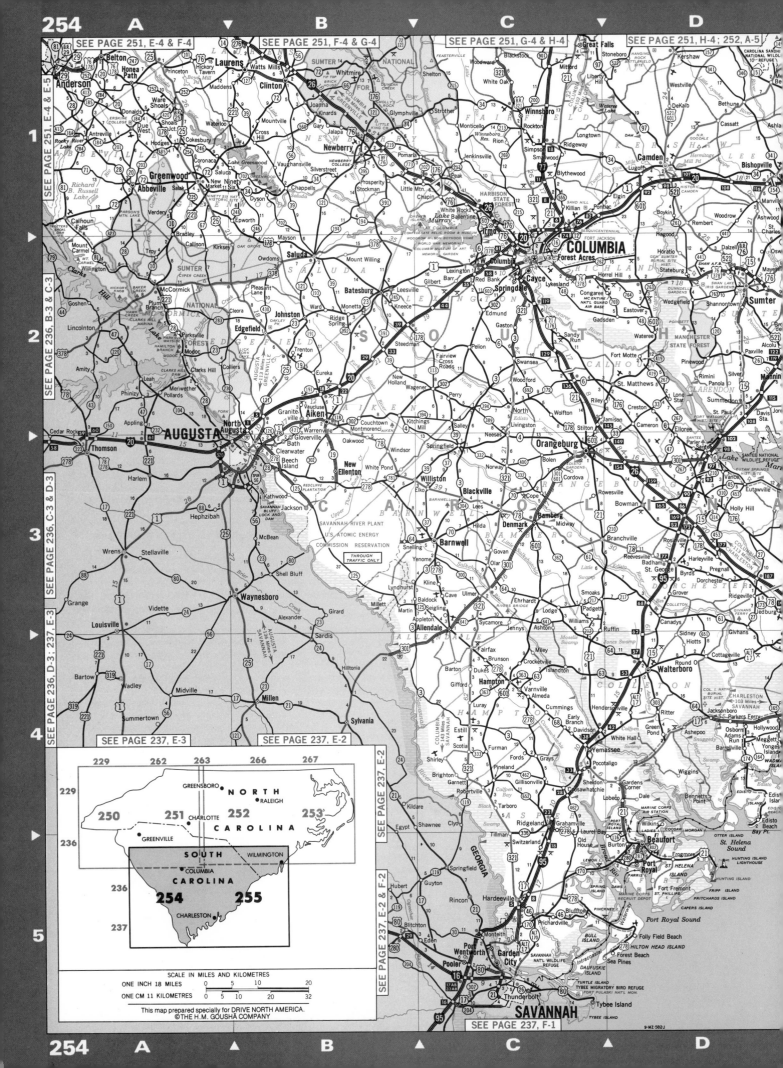

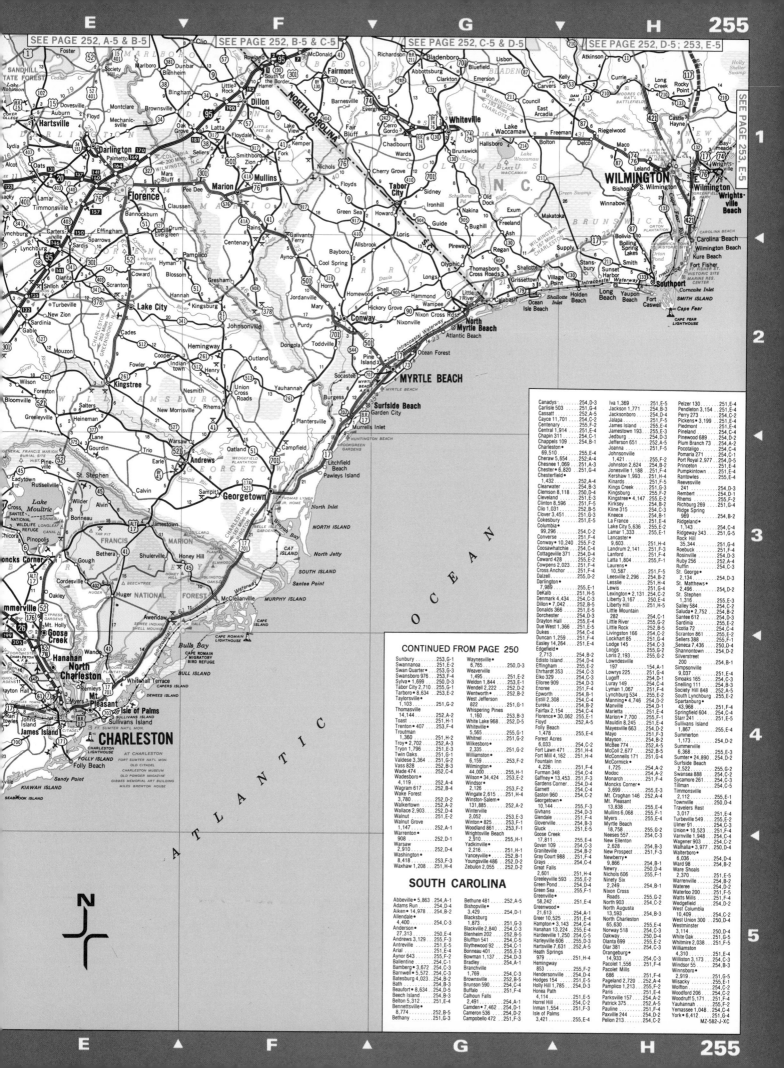

Of Mountains and Monuments, National Treasures and Tall Ships

West Virginia/Virginia/Maryland/Delaware

Mountain grandeur and a keen sense of history—these are the striking aspects of West Virginia. Much of this state's storied past can be glimpsed at the Cultural Center in **Charleston (263, E-1)**. The mahogany table upon which the Declaration of Independence was signed and the 35-star flag flown at Gettysburg during Lincoln's immortal address (1863) are among its many splendid exhibits. The Center is next to West Virginia's State Capitol, an elegant building that resembles the U.S. Capitol in Washington, D.C.

To the southwest lies the heart of the largest bituminous coalfield in the world. At **Beckley (263, E-3)**, visitors can board a motorized coal car and descend into the Beckley Exhibition Mine for a first-hand view of this natural resource and the industry it supports.

Monongahela National Forest, to the east, crowns the rugged Allegheny Mountains. Within its borders are parks and recreation areas, swimming beaches, trout streams, picnic groves and campgrounds. The restored logging cars and steam locomotive of the **Cass Scenic Railroad (263, H-1)** carry sightseers 11 miles to the summit of Bald Knob. Smoke Hole Canyon is typical of many beauty spots in the preserve. Here the south branch of the Potomac River has cut through the mountains a gorge so deep that the sun shines on the river only at midday. Seneca Rocks, so popular with climbers that it is nicknamed the "Face of 1,000 Pitons," is a jagged outcrop of quartzite that rises 1,000 feet above the North Fork Valley.

The Blue Ridge Mountains cradle the much-restored town of **Harpers Ferry (265, C-2)**, scene of John Brown's ill-fated raid in 1859. Brown's hope of a slave uprising withered in the face of a bayonet charge by federal troops; the fiery abolitionist was captured and later hanged.

A fine way to experience Virginia's **Shenandoah National Park (264, B-4)** is from one of the 64 scenic overlooks along Skyline Drive, which runs the length of the park. The overwhelming impression is of the vast blue Appalachians stretching to the horizon—and of an equally vast, gentle greenery of fields, farms and woods. Arching 215 feet over Cedar Creek, the limestone Natural Bridge is so strong that it carries a modern highway. In Luray Caverns cascades of frozen stone are massed together in hall after stunning hall.

South of Shenandoah National Park the Blue Ridge Parkway weaves through southwestern Virginia, a highland rich in history and natural beauty. Confederate heroes Robert E. Lee and "Stonewall" Jackson are buried in **Lexington (266, A-3)**, home of the historic Virginia Military Institute. South of **Roanoke (263, H-4)** lies the area known as Smart View, named for its "right smart view" of the Blue Ridge foothills.

Appomattox Court House National Historical Park (266, B-4) commemorates the end of the Civil War. More than 25 buildings and sites have been restored or reconstructed to their appearance in 1865 when, on April 9, Gen. Robert E. Lee surrendered the Army of Northern Virginia to Gen. Ulysses S. Grant.

Much of the character of **Charlottesville** stems from the University of Virginia. Thomas Jefferson was the designer of the "academical village," the hub of the present-day campus. The magnificent Rotunda (1826) was fashioned after the style of the Pantheon in Rome. Stately boxwood gardens grace Ash Lawn, the hilltop house constructed in 1799 for James Monroe, the fifth President of the United States.

Few historic residences so mirror their owners as does Thomas Jefferson's Monticello. He designed, built and remodeled this mansion over a period of 40 years, from 1768 to 1809. The house is filled with objects Jefferson loved, many original: rare books, paintings, exquisite furniture, and such gadgets as a silent butler that carried wine from cellar to table.

When **Richmond (266, D-3)** fell to Union troops in 1864 much of the city was razed. Many buildings that predate the Civil War still stand, however, mingled with the skyscrapers of the modern city. A first-century Roman temple in Nîmes, France, provided the inspiration for the State Capitol, completed in 1800. The country's largest collection of Confederate memorabilia is housed in the second White House of the Confederacy, official residence of President Jefferson Davis between 1861 and 1865. Documents and personal belongings in the Edgar Allan Poe Museum trace the tragic career of the famous American poet and author.

On May 13, 1607, **Jamestown (267, F-4)** became the first permanent English settlement in America. The colonists' early days were difficult, and most of the population perished from starvation or disease. But the settlement survived to become, for a short time, the political and cultural center of Virginia. The remains of the original site, all but abandoned in the 1700s, include the old church tower and the foundations of several buildings. Nearby is Jamestown Festival Park, a reconstruction of the primitive first settlement. Replicas of the settlers' vessels *Susan Constant, Discovery* and *Godspeed*—no bigger than modern pleasure boats—are moored in the James River.

Williamsburg (267, F-4) is America's best known and most beautifully restored Colonial town. Working from a detailed plan of the town as it was in 1782, teams of historians, archeologists, engineers and architects have restored more than 80 surviving buildings and reconstructed hundreds of others on their original sites. Formal English gardens surround the Governor's Palace, stately home of seven Colonial governors between 1720 and 1775. Carriages and oxcarts travel up and down the streets; costumed militia and fife-and-drum corps drill regularly on the Market Square Green.

The history and romance of the sea comes to life in the Mariners Museum in **Newport News (267, F-4)**, where twelve galleries contain dioramas of historic nautical events, hand-carved figureheads, ship fittings, armaments, antique tools, and seamen's journals. Nearby **Norfolk (267, G-5)** is the site of the country's largest naval base and a showplace of restored 17th- and 18th-century homes. Norfolk Botanical Gardens, known as the Gardens-by-the-Sea, are fragrantly alive with blossoming roses, azaleas, and rhododendrons. Across the James River rise the masonry walls of Fort Monroe (1834), the "Gibraltar of Chesapeake Bay." To the east, the sandy shoreline of **Virginia Beach (267, G-5)** extends for 28 miles along the Atlantic Ocean and Chesapeake Bay. The 2½-mile boardwalk, the surf, the boating and the fishing lure visitors year-round.

In 1759 George Washington settled on his estate, **Mount Vernon (265, E-4)**, married Martha Dandridge Custis and began the leisurely life of a gentleman farmer. The Mansion House, with its sweeping view of the Potomac and the Maryland hills beyond, is furnished with period pieces, many of them original. On the grounds are the gardens and outbuildings where the work of the plantation was carried out.

Most of what was Colonial **Alexandria (265, E-3)** is visible today in the section known as Old Town. Ramsay House (1724), the city's oldest dwelling, serves as a visitor center. In 1798 Washington held his last military review from the steps of nearby Gadsby's Tavern. Robert E. Lee spent part of his boyhood in the elegant Fitzhugh-Lee House, built in 1795. Overlooking the Potomac River and Washington to the west is Arlington National Cemetery and the gravesites of many notable Americans, including Presidents William H. Taft and John F. Kennedy.

As befits a nation's capital, **Washington, D.C. (265, E-3)** is a city of stately avenues, streets and squares, interspersed with impressive public monuments. Two of the most famous, the Washington Monument and the Lincoln Memorial, are separated by the 2,000-foot-long Reflecting Pool and the oval Rainbow Pool. Thomas Jefferson's circular,

West Virginia's Blue Ridge Mountains frame historic Harpers Ferry (left).

An 1896 rock crystal egg by Fabergé (below) glitters in the Virginia Museum of Fine Arts, Richmond.

Militia parade at Colonial Williamsburg (above).

The Virginia State Capitol Rotunda, Richmond.

domed memorial, similar to that of Monticello, stands in East Potomac Park. President Kennedy is commemorated by the impressive John F. Kennedy Center for the Performing Arts on the banks of the Potomac.

Perhaps America's greatest monument, the U.S. Capitol is the seat of American government—the Senate in one wing and the House of Representatives in the other. In the Great Rotunda with its 180-foot-high dome is a huge fresco by Constantino Brumidi. Statues

Flying Machines and Wooden Teeth in The Nation's Attic

Fondly called "the nation's attic, the Smithsonian Institution has spent more than 130 years accumulating its vast stockpiles of treasures—about 70 million cataloged items in a dozen different museums. The 44.5-carat Hope Diamond (*left*) dazzles visitors to the National Museum of Natural History. The 1903 Flyer used by the Wright Brothers in history's first manned powered flight is enshrined in the National Air and Space Museum. Art masterpieces from all periods hang in the National Gallery of Art, the Hirshhorn Museum and Sculpture Garden, and three other galleries. In the National Museum of History and Technology, Samuel Morse's telegraph equipment is displayed alongside such unusual exhibits as George Washington's wooden teeth.

of Presidents line its curved walls. Ornate frescoes also decorate the corridors of the Senate wing, the original Supreme Court chambers and the Statuary Hall, where famous figures represent each state. The Capitol's imposing beauty is complemented by the graceful 59-acre park in which it is set.

Every President except Washington has lived in the White House. Guided tours take in the State Dining Room and the Red, Blue, Green and East rooms on the ground and first floors. The furnishings include antiques and original pieces, but there are enough glimpses into the current President's life to remind visitors that this is not a museum.

The world's largest and richest library is contained in the Italian Renaissance-style Library of Congress. Its 80 million items include not only books, but music, maps, manuscripts, photographs, and the world's oldest motion picture—Thomas Edison's three-second *Sneeze*. Within the classical-style National Archives are the Declaration of Independence, the Constitution and the Bill of Rights, protected in helium-filled glass and bronze cases.

Its position on the city's second highest point makes the massive Washington Cathedral even more dramatic. Begun in 1907 (it is still not completed), it ranks as the world's fifth largest church. In striking contrast to the Gothic-style cathedral is the Islamic Center, an exotic touch of the Near East on Embassy Row.

Washington is a city of museums, and fascinating exhibits are found throughout the city. The Washington Dolls' House and Toy Museum holds a delightful collection of antique toys and games and authentically furnished dolls' houses. One of the world's finest collections of Renaissance books and manuscripts has been amassed at the Folger Shakespeare Library. Guided tours of the Federal Bureau of Investigation include a visit to the "Rogues Gallery" of criminals past and present.

Georgetown, the elegant residential suburb where many of Washington's diplomats live, is best seen on foot. Here visitors can shop for antiques, dine in chic restaurants and visit the Old Stone House, built in 1765 and the oldest house in Georgetown. The great, gargoyled Healy Building, with its tall clock tower, is the centerpiece of Georgetown University, founded in 1789.

Northeast of Washington is **Baltimore (265, E-2)**, Maryland's largest city and one of the country's busiest seaports. The oldest ship

Giant pandas (above), a gift from the People's Republic of China, romp in their pen—one of the many attractions at Washington's National Zoological Park.

in the U.S. Navy, the U.S.F. *Constitution* (1797), rides at anchor in the Inner Harbor. Clustered around the rejuvenated waterfront area are the Maryland Science Center, the National Aquarium, the Baltimore Maritime Museum and the pentagonal tower of the World Trade Center. Boat tours take visitors to Fort McHenry, which guards the harbor as it did during the War of 1812. On the night of September 13, 1814, the British bombardment of the fort inspired Francis Scott Key to write "The Star-Spangled Banner." A replica of the 30-by-42-foot flag that was "still there" the next morning hangs in the 1793 home of Mary Pickersgill, who sewed the original.

The National Historic Landmark District of **Annapolis (265, F-3)**, with its outstanding architecture, has been described as a museum without walls. Pleasure craft crowd the city's harbor; nearby Market Space is lined with shops and tempting restaurants. Annapolis is the home of the U.S. Naval Academy and St. John's College, chartered in 1784. On the campus stands the ancient Liberty tree, under which a peace treaty with local Indians was signed in 1652.

The cruise boat *Annapolitan* sails across the Chesapeake on all-day cruises to the restored fishing village of **St. Michaels (265, F-3)** and the Chesapeake Bay Maritime Museum. The bay is a seafood gourmet's paradise, offering fresh oysters, crabs, clams and terrapin. Wooden skipjacks still ply its waters—by law only sailing vessels are allowed to dredge for oysters in the bay.

The Delmarva Peninsula, between Chesapeake and Delaware bays and the Atlantic Ocean, abounds with salt marshes, harbors, coves and inlets, and some of the finest farmland in the East. Wide, tree-shaded streets and handsome old houses make **Easton (265, F-3)** one of the area's most attractive Colonial towns. In 1682 settlers put up a plain wooden meetinghouse which is still in use. In nearby **Wye Mills** visitors can buy cornmeal and flour from a gristmill that ground flour for Washington's army. During fall migration, as many as 100,000 Canada geese stop at **Blackwater National Wildlife Refuge**.

Ocean City (265, H-4) is Maryland's only resort on the Atlantic. A wide, three-mile-long boardwalk follows the sparkling beach. Barrier islands, built of sand thrown up by Atlantic storms, are strung along the coast.

Period elegance (above) graces the Winterthur Museum in Wilmington.

Three of Washington's most famous landmarks (left)—the Capitol, the Washington Monument and the Lincoln Memorial—loom through early morning haze. Star-shaped Fort McHenry (above), an eloquent reminder of the War of 1812, stands guard over Baltimore's inner harbor.

Chincoteague Island (265, H-5) is famous for its succulent oysters. Wild horses, believed to be descended from a shipwrecked Spanish herd, roam **Assateague Island**.

Farther up the coast in Delaware lies the fashionable resort town of **Rehoboth Beach (265, H-3)**. From June to September its boardwalk and wide, sandy beach are crowded with vacationers. Swimming, picnicking, boating and surf fishing are also popular at **Lewes,** founded in 1639 and known as "Delaware's Plymouth."

Delaware's Old State House in **Dover (265, G-2)** gives the town a distinctive dignity and charm. The nearby complex of government buildings on Capitol Square blends attractively with the old houses on the Green. Exhibits in the Delaware State Museum touch on the history and culture of the state. Especially interesting is the Eldridge Reeves Johnson collection of old talking machines and records.

The 1797 frigate Constellation is the historic centerpiece of Baltimore's waterfront.

Wilmington (265, G-1) has been an important shipping and industrial center since the 1700s. A highlight of the city's downtown renewal is the restored Grand Opera House (1871), now the Delaware Center for the Performing Arts. Old Swedes Church, one of the oldest in the United States, was consecrated in 1699. Recognizing the young country's need for gunpowder, E. I. du Pont built a powder mill in Wilmington in 1802 and founded what was to become a major American corporation. The Hagley Museum preserves the site, which traces American industrial development with working models and talking dioramas. Five generations of du Ponts have lived in nearby Eleutherian Mills, a Georgian mansion built in 1803. North of Wilmington stands Nemours (1910), the magnificent country estate of Alfred I. du Pont. Henry Francis du Pont transformed another estate, nearby Winterthur, into a treasure house of American art and architecture. The remarkable collection of furniture, antiques, paintings and decorative arts is arranged in 196 period rooms.

Delaware Maryland Virginia West Virginia

SCALE IN MILES AND KILOMETRES

ONE INCH 15 MILES 0 5 10 15

ONE CM 10 KILOMETRES 0 5 10 15 24

This map prepared specially for DRIVE NORTH AMERICA.
©THE H.M. GOUSHĀ COMPANY

INDEX TO COUNTIES

DELAWARE

Pop. (1980) 592,225 Area 2,057 Sq. Mi.

County	County Seat
Kent	Dover
New Castle	Wilmington
Sussex	Georgetown

MARYLAND

Pop. (1980) 4,216,446 Area 10,577 Sq. Mi.

County	County Seat
Allegany	Cumberland
Anne Arundel	Annapolis
Baltimore	Towson
Calvert	Prince Frederick
Caroline	Denton
Carroll	Westminster
Cecil	Elkton
Charles	La Plata
Dorchester	Cambridge
Frederick	Frederick
Garrett	Oakland
Harford	Bel Air
Howard	Ellicott City
Kent	Chestertown
Montgomery	Rockville
Prince Georges	Upper Marlboro
Queen Annes	Centreville
Saint Marys	Leonardtown
Somerset	Princess Anne
Talbot	Easton
Washington	Hagerstown
Wicomico	Salisbury
Worcester	Snow Hill

VIRGINIA

Pop. (1980) 5,346,279 Area 40,815 Sq. Mi.

County	County Seat
Accomack	Accomac
Albermarle	Charlottesville
Alleghany	Covington
Amelia	Amelia C.H.
Amherst	Amherst
Appomattox	Appomattox
Arlington	Arlington
Augusta	Staunton
Bath	Warm Springs
Bedford	Bedford
Bland	Bland
Botetourt	Fincastle
Brunswick	Lawrenceville
Buchanan	Grundy
Buckingham	Buckingham
Campbell	Rutsburg
Caroline	Bowling Green
Carroll	Hillsville
Charles City	Charles City
Charlotte	Charlotte Court House
Chesterfield	Chesterfield
Clarke	Berryville
Craig	New Castle
Culpeper	Culpeper
Cumberland	Cumberland
Dickenson	Clintwood
Dinwiddie	Dinwiddie
Essex	Tappahannock
Fairfax	Fairfax
Fauquier	Warrenton
Floyd	Floyd
Fluvanna	Palmyra
Franklin	Rocky Mount
Frederick	Winchester
Giles	Pearlsburg
Gloucester	Gloucester
Goochland	Goochland
Grayson	Independence
Greene	Stanardsville
Greensville	Emporia
Halifax	Halifax
Hanover	Hanover
Henrico	Richmond
Henry	Martinsville
Highland	Monterey
Isle of Wight	Isle of Wight
James City	Williamsburg
King and Queen	King and Queen C.H.
King George	King George
King William	King William
Lancaster	Lancaster
Lee	Jonesville
Loudoun	Leesburg
Louisa	Louisa
Lunenburg	Lunenburg
Madison	Madison
Mathews	Mathews
Mecklenburg	Boydton
Middlesex	Saluda
Montgomery	Christiansburg
Nelson	Lovingston
New Kent	New Kent
Northampton	Eastville
Northumberland	Heathsville
Nottoway	Nottoway
Orange	Orange
Page	Luray
Patrick	Stuart
Pittsylvania	Chatham
Powhatan	Powhatan
Prince Edward	Farmville
Prince George	Prince George
Prince William	Manassas
Pulaski	Pulaski
Rappahannock	Washington
Richmond	Warsaw
Roanoke	Salem
Rockbridge	Lexington
Rockingham	Harrisonburg
Russell	Lebanon
Scott	Gate City
Shenandoah	Woodstock
Smyth	Marion
Southampton	Courtland
Spotsylvania	Spotsylvania
Stafford	Stafford
Surry	Surry
Sussex	Sussex
Tazewell	Tazewell
Warren	Front Royal
Washington	Abingdon
Westmoreland	Montross
Wise	Wise
Wythe	Wytheville
York	Yorktown

WEST VIRGINIA

Pop. (1980) 1,949,644 Area 24,181 Sq. Mi.

County	County Seat
Barbour	Philippi
Berkeley	Martinsburg
Boone	Madison
Braxton	Sutton
Brooke	Wellsburg
Cabell	Huntington
Calhoun	Grantsville
Clay	Clay
Doddridge	West Union
Fayette	Fayetteville
Gilmer	Glenville
Grant	Petersburg
Greenbrier	Lewisburg
Hampshire	Romney
Hancock	New Cumberland
Hardy	Moorefield
Harrison	Clarksburg
Jackson	Ripley
Jefferson	Charles Town
Kanawha	Charleston
Lewis	Weston
Lincoln	Hamlin
Logan	Logan
Marion	Fairmont
Marshall	Moundsville
Mason	Point Pleasant
McDowell	Welch
Mercer	Princeton
Mineral	Keyser
Mingo	Williamson
Monongalia	Morgantown
Monroe	Union
Morgan	Berkeley Springs
Nicholas	Summersville
Ohio	Wheeling
Pendleton	Franklin
Pleasants	St. Marys
Pocahontas	Marlinton
Preston	Kingwood
Putnam	Winfield
Raleigh	Beckley
Randolph	Elkins
Ritchie	Harrisville
Roane	Spencer
Summers	Hinton
Taylor	Grafton
Tucker	Parsons
Tyler	Middlebourne
Upshut	Buckhannon
Wayne	Wayne
Webster	Webster Springs
Wetzel	New Martinsville
Wirt	Elizabeth
Wood	Parkersburg
Wyoming	Pineville

PARTIAL LIST OF

CITIES AND TOWNS

1980 Census

• County Seats

DELAWARE

Bellefonte 1,279 ... 265,H-1
Bethany Beach 330 ... 265,H-4
Blackbird ... 265,G-2
Blades 664 ... 265,G-4
Bowers Beach ... 265,H-3
Bridgeville 1,238 ... 265,G-3
Camden 1,757 ... 265,G-3
Cheswold 269 ... 265,G-2
Clayton 1,216 ... 265,G-2
Dagsboro 344 ... 265,H-4
Delaware City 1,858 ... 265,G-2
Delmar 948 ... 265,G-4
Dover • 23,512 ... 265,G-2
Ellendale 361 ... 265,H-3
Elsmere 6,493 ... 265,G-1
Felton 547 ... 265,G-3
Frankford 686 ... 265,H-4
Frederica 864 ... 265,H-3
Georgetown • 1,710 ... 265,H-4
Greenwood 578 ... 265,G-3
Harrington 2,405 ... 265,G-3
Hartley 106 ... 265,G-3
Kenton 243 ... 265,G-2
Laurel 3,052 ... 265,G-4
Leipsic 228 ... 265,G-2
Lewes 2,197 ... 265,H-3
Little Creek 230 ... 265,H-2
Middletown 2,946 ... 265,G-2
Milford 5,356 ... 265,H-3
Millsboro 1,233 ... 265,H-4
Milton 1,359 ... 265,H-3
New Castle 4,907 ... 265,G-1
Newark 25,247 ... 265,G-1
Newport 1,167 ... 265,G-1
Ocean View 495 ... 265,H-4
Odessa 384 ... 265,G-2
Rehoboth Beach 1,730 ... 265,H-3
Seaford 5,256 ... 265,G-4
Selbyville 1,251 ... 265,H-4
Smyrna 4,750 ... 265,G-2
State Road ... 265,G-1
Wilmington • 70,195 ... 265,G-1

MARYLAND

Aberdeen 11,533 ... 265,F-2
Annapolis • 31,740 ... 265,F-3
Baltimore 786,775 ... 265,E-2
Barton 617 ... 264,A-2
Bel Air • 7,814 ... 265,F-2
Berlin 2,162 ... 265,H-4
Bethesda ... 265,E-3
Betterton • 356 ... 265,F-2
Boonsboro 1,908 ... 264,D-2
Bowie 33,695 ... 265,E-3
Brunswick 4,572 ... 264,D-2
Burkittsville 202 ... 264,D-2
Cambridge • 11,703 ... 265,G-4
Catonsville ... 265,E-2
Cecilton 508 ... 265,G-2
Centreville • 2,018 ... 265,G-3
Chesapeake Beach 1,408 ... 265,F-4
Chesapeake City 899 ... 265,G-2
Chestertown • 3,300 ... 265,F-2
Church Creek 124 ... 265,F-4
Church Hill 319 ... 265,G-3
Clarksville ... 265,E-2
Clear Spring 477 ... 264,C-1
Clinton ... 265,E-3
Cockeysville ... 265,E-2
College Park 23,614 ... 265,E-3
Crisfield 2,924 ... 265,G-5
Cumberland • 25,933 ... 264,B-2
Deer Park 486 ... 261,H-3
Delmar 1,232 ... 265,G-4
Denton • 1,927 ... 265,G-3
East New Market 230 ... 265,G-4
Easton • 7,536 ... 265,F-3
Edgewood ... 265,F-2
Elkridge ... 265,E-2
Elkton • 6,468 ... 265,G-1
Ellicott City • ... 265,E-2
Emmitsburg 1,552 ... 264,D-1
Essex ... 265,F-2
Federalsburg 1,952 ... 265,G-4
Ferndale ... 265,E-3
Frederick • 27,557 ... 264,D-2
Friendsville 511 ... 261,H-3
Frostburg 7,715 ... 264,A-2
Fruitland 2,694 ... 265,G-4
Gaithersburg 26,424 ... 264,D-3
Galena 374 ... 265,G-2
Glen Burnie ... 265,E-3
Glyndon ... 265,E-2
Goldsboro 188 ... 265,G-3
Grantsville 498 ... 264,A-1
Greensboro 1,253 ... 265,G-3
Hagerstown • 34,132 ... 265,C-2
Halfway ... 265,C-2
Hampstead 1,293 ... 265,E-2
Hancock 1,887 ... 264,C-1
Havre de Grace 8,763 ... 265,F-2
Hebron 714 ... 265,G-4
Hurlock 1,690 ... 265,G-4
Hyattsville 12,709 ... 265,E-3
Indian Head 1,381 ... 265,E-4
Kennedyville ... 265,G-2
Kitzmiller 387 ... 261,H-3
La Plata • 2,484 ... 265,E-4
Laurel 12,103 ... 265,E-3
Laytonsville 195 ... 265,E-2
Leonardtown • 1,448 ... 265,F-5
Lexington Park 1,420 ... 265,F-5
Lonaconing ... 264,A-2
Manchester 1,830 ... 265,E-1
Mardela Springs 320 ... 265,G-4
Marydel 152 ... 265,G-2
Middletown 1,748 ... 264,D-2
Midland 601 ... 264,A-2
Millington 546 ... 265,G-2
Mount Airy 2,450 ... 265,E-2
Mount Savage ... 264,A-1
Mountain Lake Park 1,597 ... 261,H-3
New Market 306 ... 264,D-2
New Windsor 799 ... 265,E-2
North East 1,469 ... 265,G-2
Oakland • 1,994 ... 261,H-3
Ocean City 4,946 ... 265,H-4
Odenton ... 265,E-3
Owings Mills ... 265,E-2
Oxford 754 ... 265,F-4
Perryville 2,018 ... 265,F-2
Pikesville ... 265,E-2
Pittsville 519 ... 265,H-4
Pocomoke City 3,558 ... 265,G-5
Point of Rocks ... 264,D-2
Poolesville 3,428 ... 264,D-3
Port Deposit 664 ... 265,F-2
Potomac Park ... 264,B-2
Preston 498 ... 265,G-4
Prince Frederick • ... 265,F-4
Princess Anne • 1,499 ... 265,G-5
Queenstown 491 ... 265,F-3
Redhouse ... 261,H-4
Reisterstown ... 265,E-2
Ridgely 933 ... 265,G-3
Rising Sun 1,160 ... 265,F-1
Rock Hall 1,511 ... 265,F-3
Rockville • 43,811 ... 265,E-3
St. Michaels 1,301 ... 265,F-3
Salisbury • 16,429 ... 265,G-4
Savage ... 265,E-3
Severn ... 265,E-3
Sharpsburg 721 ... 264,C-2
Sharptown 654 ... 265,G-4
Silver Spring ... 265,E-3
Smithsburg 833 ... 264,D-1
Snow Hill • 2,192 ... 265,H-5
Solomons ... 265,F-4
Sparrows Point ... 265,F-2
Stockton ... 265,H-5
Sudlersville 443 ... 265,G-2
Sykesville 1,712 ... 265,E-2
Takoma Park 16,231 ... 265,E-3
Taneytown 2,618 ... 264,D-1
T.B. ... 265,E-4
Thurmont 2,934 ... 264,D-2
Timonium ... 265,E-2
Towson • ... 265,F-2
Union Bridge 927 ... 264,D-2
Upper Marlboro • 828 ... 265,E-3
Vienna 300 ... 265,G-4
Waldorf ... 265,E-4
Walkersville 2,212 ... 265,D-2
Westernport 2,706 ... 264,A-2
Westminster • 8,808 ... 265,E-2
Westover ... 265,G-5
Wheaton ... 265,E-3
Willards 540 ... 265,H-4
Williamsport 1,867 ... 264,C-2
Woodsboro 506 ... 264,D-2

VIRGINIA

Abingdon • 4,318 ... 262,D-5
Accomac • 522 ... 267,H-3
Alberta 394 ... 266,D-5
Alexandria 103,217 ... 265,E-3
Altavista 3,894 ... 266,A-4
Amelia C.H. • ... 266,C-4
Amherst • 1,135 ... 266,A-3
Appalachia 2,418 ... 262,B-4
Appomattox • 1,345 ... 266,B-4
Arlington • 152,599 ... 265,E-3
Ashland 4,640 ... 267,D-3
Axton ... 263,H-5
Bassett ... 263,G-5
Bedford • 5,991 ... 263,H-4
Belle Haven 589 ... 267,G-3
Berryville • 1,752 ... 264,C-3
Big Island ... 266,A-3
Big Stone Gap 4,748 ... 262,B-5
Blacksburg 30,638 ... 263,G-4
Blackstone 3,624 ... 266,C-4
Bland • ... 263,E-4
Bluefield 5,946 ... 263,E-4
Boones Mill 303 ... 263,H-4
Bowling Green • 665 ... 266,D-2
Boyce 401 ... 264,C-3
Boydton • 486 ... 266,C-5
Boykins 791 ... 267,E-5
Bridgewater 3,289 ... 264,A-4
Bristol 19,042 ... 262,C-5
Broadway 1,234 ... 264,B-4
Brodnax 492 ... 266,C-5
Brookneal 1,454 ... 266,B-4
Buchanan 1,205 ... 263,H-3
Buckingham • ... 266,B-3
Buena Vista 6,717 ... 266,A-3
Burkeville 606 ... 266,C-4
Cape Charles 1,512 ... 267,G-4
Capron 238 ... 267,E-5
Cedar Bluff 1,550 ... 262,B-4
Charles City • ... 267,E-4
Charlotte C.H. • 568 ... 266,B-4
Charlottesville • 45,010 ... 266,B-2
Chase City 2,749 ... 266,B-5
Chatham • 1,390 ... 266,A-5
Cheriton 619 ... 267,G-4
Chesapeake 114,226 ... 267,G-5
Chester ... 266,D-4
Chesterfield • ... 267,D-4
Chillhowie 1,269 ... 263,D-5
Chincoteague 1,607 ... 267,H-2
Christiansburg • 10,345 ... 263,G-4
Claremont 380 ... 267,E-4
Clarksville 1,468 ... 266,B-5
Cleveland 360 ... 262,C-4
Clifton Forge 5,046 ... 263,H-3
Clinchco ... 262,C-4
Clinchport 89 ... 262,B-5
Clintwood • 1,369 ... 262,C-4
Clover 215 ... 266,B-5
Coeburn 2,625 ... 263,C-4
Colonial Beach 2,474 ... 267,E-1
Colonial Heights 16,509 ... 266,D-4
Columbia 111 ... 266,C-3
Courtland • 976 ... 267,E-5
Covington • 9,063 ... 263,G-3
Craigsville 845 ... 266,A-2
Crewe 2,325 ... 266,C-4
Culpeper • 6,621 ... 264,C-4
Cumberland • ... 266,C-3
Damascus 1,330 ... 262,D-5
Dante ... 262,C-4
Danville 45,642 ... 266,A-5
Dayton 1,017 ... 264,A-4
Dendron 307 ... 267,E-4
Dillwyn 637 ... 266,B-3
Dinwiddie • ... 266,D-4
Drakes Branch 617 ... 266,B-4
Draper ... 263,F-4
Dublin 2,368 ... 263,F-4
Dumfries 3,214 ... 264,D-4
Dungannon 339 ... 262,C-5
Eastville • 238 ... 267,G-3
Edinburg 752 ... 264,B-3
Elkton 1,520 ... 264,B-4
Emporia • 4,840 ... 266,D-5
Ettrick ... 266,D-4
Exmore 1,300 ... 267,G-3
Fairfax • 19,390 ... 264,D-3
Fairlawn ... 263,F-4
Falls Church 9,515 ... 265,E-3
Falmouth ... 264,D-4
Farmville • 6,067 ... 266,C-4
Fieldale ... 263,H-5
Fincastle • 282 ... 263,H-3
Floyd • 411 ... 263,G-5
Franklin 7,308 ... 267,E-5
Fredericksburg 15,322 ... 264,D-5
Fries 758 ... 263,F-5
Front Royal • 11,126 ... 264,C-3
Galax 6,524 ... 263,F-5
Gate City • 2,494 ... 262,C-5
Glade Spring 1,722 ... 262,D-5
Glasgow 1,259 ... 266,A-3
Glen Lyn 235 ... 263,F-4
Gloucester • ... 267,F-3
Goochland • ... 266,D-3
Gordonsville 1,175 ... 266,C-2
Goshen 134 ... 266,A-2
Gretna 1,255 ... 266,A-5
Grottoes 1,369 ... 266,B-2
Grundy • 1,699 ... 262,D-4
Halifax • 772 ... 266,B-5
Hamilton 598 ... 264,D-3
Hampton • 122,617 ... 267,F-4
Hanover • ... 267,D-3
Harrisonburg • 19,671 ... 264,A-4
Haymarket 230 ... 264,D-3
Haysi 371 ... 262,C-4
Heathsville • ... 267,F-2
Herndon 11,449 ... 264,D-3
Highland Springs ... 267,E-3
Hillsboro 94 ... 264,C-3
Hillsville • 2,123 ... 263,F-5
Honaker 1,475 ... 262,D-4
Hopewell 23,397 ... 267,E-4
Hot Springs ... 263,H-2
Hurt 1,481 ... 266,A-4
Independence • 1,112 ... 263,E-5
Iron Gate 620 ... 263,H-3
Isle of Wight • ... 267,F-5
Ivor 403 ... 267,E-5
Jarratt 614 ... 266,D-5
Jonesville • 874 ... 262,B-5
Kenbridge 1,352 ... 266,C-4
Keysville 704 ... 266,B-4
Kilmarnock 945 ... 267,F-3
King and Queen Court House • ... 267,E-3
King George • ... 267,E-1
King William • ... 267,E-3
Lancaster • ... 267,F-3
Lawrenceville • 1,484 ... 266,D-5
Lebanon • 3,206 ... 262,D-5
Leesburg • 8,357 ... 264,D-3
Leona Mines ... 262,B-5
Lexington • 7,292 ... 266,A-3
Louisa • 932 ... 266,C-2
Lovettsville 613 ... 264,D-2
Lovingston • ... 266,B-3
Luneburg • ... 266,C-4
Luray • 3,584 ... 264,B-4
Lynchburg 66,743 ... 266,A-3
Madison • 267 ... 264,C-4
Madison Heights ... 266,A-3
Manassas 15,438 ... 264,D-4
Manassas Park 6,524 ... 264,D-3
Marion 7,029 ... 263,E-5
Martinsville • 18,149 ... 263,H-5
Mathews • ... 267,F-3
McKenney 473 ... 267,D-4
Meadowview ... 262,D-5
Middleburg 619 ... 264,C-3
Middletown 841 ... 264,C-3
Mineral 399 ... 266,C-2
Monterey • 247 ... 263,H-1
Montross • 456 ... 267,E-2
Mount Crawford 315 ... 264,A-4
Mount Jackson 1,419 ... 264,B-4
Narrows 2,516 ... 263,F-4
Natural Bridge ... 263,H-3
New Castle • 213 ... 263,G-3
New Kent • ... 267,E-3
New Market 1,118 ... 264,B-4
Newport ... 263,G-4
Newport News 144,903 ... 267,F-4
Newsoms 368 ... 267,E-5
Nickelsville 464 ... 262,C-5
Norfolk 266,979 ... 267,G-5
Norton 4,757 ... 262,C-4
Nottoway • ... 266,C-4
Occoquan 512 ... 264,D-4
Onancock 1,461 ... 267,G-3
Orange • 2,631 ... 266,C-2
Palmyra • ... 266,C-2
Pamplin 273 ... 266,B-4
Parksley 979 ... 267,H-2
Pearisburg • 2,128 ... 263,F-4
Pembroke 1,302 ... 263,F-4
Pennington Gap 1,716 ... 262,B-5
Petersburg 41,055 ... 266,D-4
Phenix 250 ... 266,B-4
Pocahontas 708 ... 263,E-4
Poquoson 8,726 ... 267,F-4
Port Royal 291 ... 267,E-2
Portsmouth 104,577 ... 267,F-5
Pound 1,086 ... 262,C-4
Powhatan • ... 266,C-3
Prince George • ... 267,E-4
Pulaski • 10,106 ... 263,F-4
Purcellville 1,567 ... 264,D-3
Quantico 621 ... 264,D-4
Radford 13,225 ... 263,F-4
Remington 425 ... 264,C-4
Reston ... 264,D-3
Rich Creek 746 ... 263,F-4
Richlands 5,796 ... 262,D-4
Richmond • 219,214 ... 266,D-3
Ridgeway 858 ... 263,H-5
Rivermont ... 263,H-3
Roanoke 110,427 ... 263,H-4
Rocky Mount • 4,198 ... 263,H-4
Roda ... 262,B-4
Round Hill 510 ... 264,C-3
Rural Retreat 1,083 ... 263,E-5
Rustburg • ... 266,A-4
St. Charles 241 ... 262,B-5
St. Paul 973 ... 262,C-5
Salem • 23,958 ... 263,G-4
Saltville 2,376 ... 262,D-5
Saluda • ... 267,F-3
Sandston ... 267,E-3
Scottsburg 335 ... 266,B-5
Scottsville 250 ... 266,B-3
Seven Pines ... 267,E-3
Shenandoah 1,861 ... 264,B-4
Smithfield 3,649 ... 267,F-4
South Boston 7,093 ... 266,B-5
South Hill 4,347 ... 266,C-5
Spotsylvania • ... 266,D-2
Springfield ... 264,D-3
Stafford • ... 264,D-4
Stanardsville • 284 ... 266,B-1
Stanley 1,204 ... 264,B-4
Staunton • 21,857 ... 266,A-2
Stephens City 1,179 ... 264,C-3
Stonega ... 262,B-4
Stoney Creek 329 ... 266,D-4
Strasburg 2,311 ... 264,B-3
Stuart • 1,131 ... 263,G-5
Suffolk • 47,621 ... 267,F-5
Surry • 237 ... 267,E-4
Sussex • ... 267,E-5
Tangier 771 ... 267,G-2
Tappahannock • 1,821 ... 267,E-2
Tazewell • 4,468 ... 263,E-4
The Plains 382 ... 264,C-3
Timberville 1,510 ... 264,B-4
Toano ... 267,F-3
Triangle ... 265,D-4
Troutdale 248 ... 263,E-5
Tysons Corner ... 264,D-3
Vansant ... 262,D-4
Victoria 2,004 ... 266,C-4
Vienna 15,469 ... 264,D-3
Vinton 8,027 ... 263,H-4
Virginia Beach 262,199 ... 267,G-5
Wachapreague 404 ... 267,H-3
Wakefield 1,355 ... 267,E-4
Warm Springs • ... 263,H-2
Warrenton • 3,907 ... 264,C-4
Warsaw • 771 ... 267,F-2
Washington • 247 ... 264,C-4
Waterford ... 264,D-3
Waverly 2,284 ... 267,E-4
Waynesboro 15,329 ... 266,B-2
Weber City 1,543 ... 262,C-5
West Point 2,726 ... 267,F-3
White Stone 409 ... 267,F-3
Williamsburg • 9,870 ... 267,F-4
Winchester • 20,217 ... 264,C-3
Windsor 985 ... 267,F-5
Wise • 3,894 ... 262,C-4
Woodstock • 2,627 ... 264,B-3
Wytheville • 7,135 ... 263,E-4
Yorktown • ... 267,F-4

WEST VIRGINIA

Accoville ... 262,D-3
Alderson 1,375 ... 263,F-3
Amherstdale ... 262,D-3
Anawalt 652 ... 263,E-4
Ansted 1,952 ... 263,E-2
Athens 1,147 ... 263,F-3
Barboursville 2,871 ... 262,C-1
Bayard 540 ... 261,H-4
Beckley • 20,492 ... 263,E-3
Belington 2,038 ... 261,G-4
Belle 1,621 ... 263,E-2
Benwood 1,994 ... 261,E-2
Berkeley Springs • 789 ... 264,C-2
Bethany 1,336 ... 261,F-2
Bethlehem 2,677 ... 261,E-2
Beverly 457 ... 261,G-5
Blacksville 248 ... 261,F-3
Bluefield 16,060 ... 263,E-4
Boomer ... 263,E-2
Bradshaw ... 262,D-4
Bramwell 989 ... 263,E-4
Bridgeport 6,604 ... 261,F-4
Bruceton Mills 296 ... 261,G-3
Buckhannon • 6,820 ... 261,F-4
Buffalo 1,034 ... 260,C-5
Burnsville 531 ... 261,E-5
Cairo 428 ... 261,E-4
Camden-on-Gauley 236 ... 263,F-1
Cameron 1,474 ... 261,F-2
Capon Bridge 191 ... 264,B-2
Caretta ... 262,D-4
Cass 148 ... 263,H-1
Cedar Grove 1,479 ... 263,E-2
Ceredo 2,255 ... 263,C-1
Chapmanville 1,164 ... 262,D-2
Charleston • 63,968 ... 263,E-1
Charles Town • 2,857 ... 264,C-2
Chattaroy ... 262,C-3
Chelyan ... 263,E-2
Chesapeake 2,364 ... 263,E-2
Chester 3,297 ... 261,F-1
Clarksburg • 22,371 ... 261,F-4
Clay • 940 ... 263,F-1
Clendenin 1,373 ... 263,E-1
Coalwood ... 262,D-3
Cowen 723 ... 263,F-1
Crab Orchard ... 263,E-3
Danville 727 ... 262,D-2
Davis 979 ... 261,H-4
Davy 882 ... 262,D-3
Delbarton 981 ... 262,C-3
Dunbar 9,285 ... 262,D-1
Durbin 379 ... 263,H-1
East Bank 1,155 ... 263,E-2
East Rainelle ... 263,F-2
Eccles ... 263,E-3
Eleanor 1,282 ... 262,D-1
Elizabeth • 856 ... 260,D-4
Elk Garden 291 ... 264,A-2
Elkhorn ... 263,E-3
Elkins • 8,536 ... 261,G-4
Ellenboro 357 ... 261,E-4
Fairmont • 23,863 ... 261,F-3
Fairview 759 ... 261,F-3
Farmington 583 ... 261,F-3
Fayetteville • 2,366 ... 263,E-2
Flatwoods 405 ... 261,E-5
Flemington 452 ... 261,F-4
Follansbee 3,994 ... 261,F-1
Fort Gay 886 ... 262,C-4
Franklin • 780 ... 261,H-5
Gary 2,233 ... 263,E-4
Gassaway 1,225 ... 261,E-5
Gauley Bridge 1,177 ... 263,E-2
Gilbert 757 ... 262,D-3
Glen Dale 1,875 ... 261,E-2
Glen Hedrick ... 263,E-5
Glen Jean ... 263,E-2
Glenville • 2,155 ... 261,E-4
Grafton • 6,845 ... 261,G-3
Grant Town 987 ... 261,F-3
Grantsville • 788 ... 261,E-4
Hambleton 403 ... 261,G-4
Hamlin • 1,219 ... 262,D-1
Harman 181 ... 261,H-4
Harpers Ferry 361 ... 265,C-2
Harrisville • 1,673 ... 261,E-4
Hedgesville 217 ... 264,C-2
Henderson 604 ... 260,C-5
Hillsboro 276 ... 263,G-2
Hinton • 4,622 ... 263,F-3
Holden ... 262,D-2
Hugheston ... 263,E-2
Hundred 485 ... 261,F-3
Huntington • 63,684 ... 262,C-1
Hurricane 3,751 ... 262,D-1
Huttonsville 242 ... 261,G-5
Iaeger 833 ... 262,D-3
Junior 591 ... 261,G-4
Kenova 4,454 ... 262,C-1
Kermit 705 ... 262,C-2
Keyser • 6,569 ... 264,A-2
Keystone 902 ... 263,E-3
Kimball 871 ... 263,E-3
Kingwood • 2,877 ... 261,G-3
Kistler ... 262,D-2
Leon 228 ... 260,C-5
Lewisburg • 3,065 ... 263,G-3
Littleton 335 ... 261,F-3
Logan • 3,029 ... 262,D-2
Lost Creek 604 ... 261,F-4
Lumberport 939 ... 261,F-3
Mabscott 1,668 ... 263,E-3
Madison • 3,228 ... 262,D-2
Mallory ... 262,D-3
Man 1,333 ... 262,D-3
Mannington 3,036 ... 261,F-3
Marlinton • 1,352 ... 263,G-2
Marmet 2,196 ... 263,E-2
Martinsburg • 13,063 ... 264,C-2
Mason 1,432 ... 260,C-4
Masontown 1,052 ... 261,G-3
Matoaka 613 ... 263,E-3
Maybeury ... 263,E-4
McMechen 2,402 ... 261,E-2
Meadow Bridge 530 ... 263,F-2
Middlebourne • 941 ... 261,E-3
Mill Creek 801 ... 261,G-5
Milton 2,178 ... 262,D-1
Minden ... 263,E-2
Monongah 1,132 ... 261,F-3
Montgomery 3,104 ... 263,E-2
Moorefield • 2,257 ... 264,A-3
Morgantown • 27,605 ... 261,G-3
Moundsville • 12,419 ... 261,E-2
Mount Gay ... 262,D-2
Mount Hope 1,849 ... 263,E-2
Mullens 2,919 ... 263,E-3
Naoma ... 263,E-2
New Cumberland • 1,752 ... 261,F-1
New Haven 1,723 ... 260,C-4
New Martinsville • 7,109 ... 261,E-3
Newburg 418 ... 261,G-3
Newell ... 261,F-1
Nitro 8,074 ... 262,D-1
Nutter Fort 2,078 ... 261,F-4
Oak Hill 7,120 ... 263,E-2
Oakvale 208 ... 263,F-4
Oceana 2,143 ... 262,D-3
Omar ... 262,D-3
Paden City 3,671 ... 261,E-3
Parkersburg • 39,967 ... 260,D-4
Parsons • 1,937 ... 261,G-4
Paw Paw 644 ... 264,B-2
Pennsboro 1,652 ... 261,E-4
Petersburg • 2,084 ... 264,A-3
Peterstown 648 ... 263,F-3
Philippi • 3,194 ... 261,G-4
Piedmont 1,491 ... 264,A-2
Pineville • 1,140 ... 263,E-3
Poca 1,142 ... 262,D-1
Point Pleasant • 5,682 ... 260,C-5
Princeton • 7,493 ... 263,E-4
Quinwood 460 ... 263,F-2
Rainelle 1,983 ... 263,F-2
Ranson 2,471 ... 264,C-2
Ravenswood 4,126 ... 260,C-4
Reedsville 564 ... 261,G-3
Rhodell 472 ... 263,E-3
Richwood 3,568 ... 263,G-2
Ridgeley 994 ... 264,B-2
Ripley • 3,464 ... 260,D-5
Rivesville 1,327 ... 261,F-3
Remney • 2,094 ... 264,B-2
Ronceverte 2,312 ... 263,G-3
Rowlesburg 966 ... 261,G-3
Rupert 1,276 ... 263,F-2
St. Albans 12,402 ... 262,D-1
St. Marys • 2,219 ... 261,E-3
Salem 2,706 ... 261,F-4
Seth ... 263,E-2
Shepherdstown 1,791 ... 264,C-2
Shinnston 3,059 ... 261,F-3
Sistersville 2,367 ... 261,E-3
Smithers 1,482 ... 263,E-2
Sophia 1,216 ... 263,E-3
South Charleston 15,968 ... 262,D-1
Spencer • 2,799 ... 260,D-5
Sprague ... 263,E-3
Star City 1,464 ... 261,G-3
Stonewood 2,058 ... 261,F-4
Summersville • 2,972 ... 263,F-1
Sutton • 1,192 ... 261,E-5
Switzer ... 262,D-3
Terra Alta 1,946 ... 261,G-3
Thomas 747 ... 261,H-4
Thorpe ... 263,E-4
Triadelphia 1,461 ... 261,F-2
Tunnelton 510 ... 261,G-3
Union • 743 ... 263,F-3
Verdunville ... 263,D-2
Vienna 11,618 ... 260,D-3
War 2,158 ... 262,D-4
Ward ... 263,E-2
Wardensville 241 ... 264,B-3
Wayne • 1,495 ... 262,C-2
Webster Springs • ... 263,G-1
Weirton 24,736 ... 261,F-1
Welch • 3,885 ... 263,E-3
Wellsburg • 3,963 ... 261,F-1
West Hamlin 643 ... 262,C-1
West Logan 630 ... 262,D-2
West Union • 1,090 ... 261,E-4
Weston • 6,250 ... 261,F-4
Westover 4,884 ... 261,G-3
Wharton ... 263,D-2
Wheeling • 43,070 ... 261,E-2
White Sulphur Springs 3,371 ... 263,G-3
Whitesville 689 ... 263,E-2
Williamson • 5,219 ... 262,C-3
Williamstown 3,095 ... 260,D-3
Winfield • 329 ... 262,D-1
Worthington 329 ... 261,F-3

DISTRICT OF COLUMBIA

Pop. (1980) 637,651

Washington 637,651 ... 265,E-3

MZ-577-J-XC

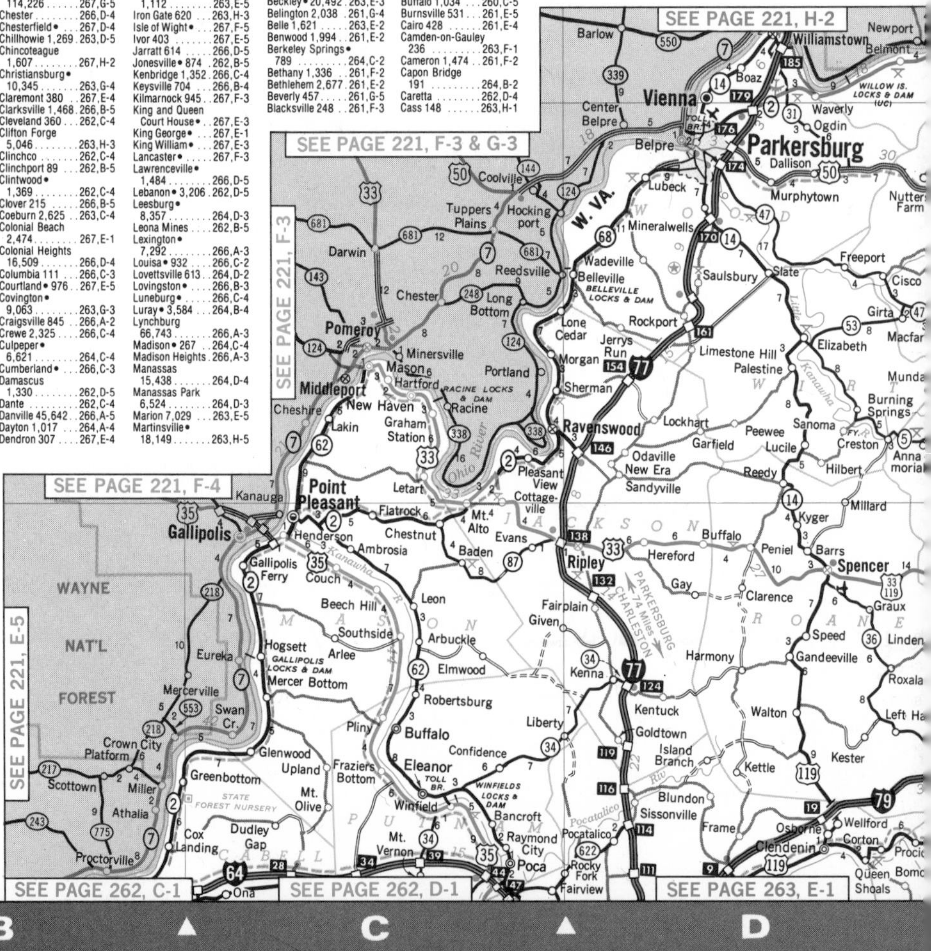

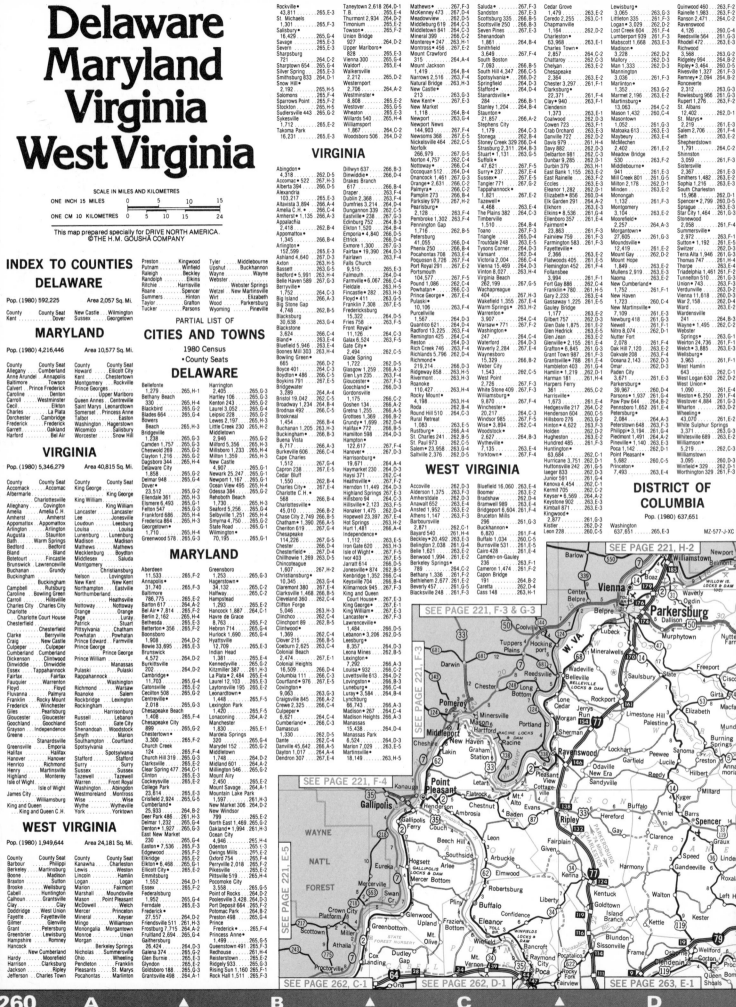

SEE PAGE 221, H-2
SEE PAGE 221, F-3 & G-3
SEE PAGE 221, F-3
SEE PAGE 221, F-4
SEE PAGE 221, E-5
SEE PAGE 262, C-1
SEE PAGE 262, D-1
SEE PAGE 263, E-1
Barlow
Vienna
Williamstown
Newport
Belmont
Boaz
WILLOW IS. LOCKS & DAM
Waverly
Ogdin
Parkersburg
Belpre
Center Belpre
Dallison
Coolville
Tuppers Plains
Hocking port
Lubeck
Murphytown
Darwin
Reedsville
Mineralwells
Wadeville
Belleville
BELLEVILLE LOCKS & DAM
Freeport
Saulsbury
Chester
Long Bottom
Pomeroy
Minersville
Mason
Hartford
RACINE LOCKS & DAM
Racine
Portland
Middleport
Cheshire
New Haven
Lakin
Graham Station
Letart
Ohio River
Lone Cedar
Jerrys Run
Morgan
Sherman
Rockport
Limestone Hill
Palestine
Elizabeth
Ravenswood
Lockhart
Garfield
Peewee
Lucile
Sanoma
Creston
Burning Springs
Point Pleasant
Kanauga
Gallipolis
Gallipolis Ferry
Henderson
Flatrock
Chestnut
Ambrosia
Mt. Alto
Baden
Evans
Pleasant View
Cottageville
Odaville
New Era
Sandyville
Reedy
Hilbert
Millard
Kyger
Buffalo
Peniel
Barrs
Spencer
Ripley
Hereford
Gay
Clarence
Graux
Speed
Linden
Gandeeville
Harmony
Roxala
W. VA.
WAYNE
NAT'L
FOREST
Beech Hill
Southside
Arlee
Hogsett
GALLIPOLIS LOCKS & DAM
Mercer Bottom
Leon
Arbuckle
Elmwood
Fairplain
Given
Kenna
Kentuck
Goldtown
Island Branch
Walton
Kettle
Kester
Eureka
Mercerville
Swan Cr.
Robertsburg
Buffalo
Liberty
Confidence
Crown City
Platform
Glenwood
Upland
Pliny
Fraziers Bottom
Eleanor
Greenbottom
Scottown
Miller
Athalia
Proctorville
Mt. Olive
Winfield
WINFIELDS LOCKS & DAM
Bancroft
Raymond City
Poca
Pocatalico
Rocky Fork
Fairview
Blundon
Sissonville
Frame
Wellford
Clendenin
Cox Landing
Dudley Gap
Mt. Vernon
Ona
Queen Shoals
PARKERSBURG 74 Miles
CHARLESTON

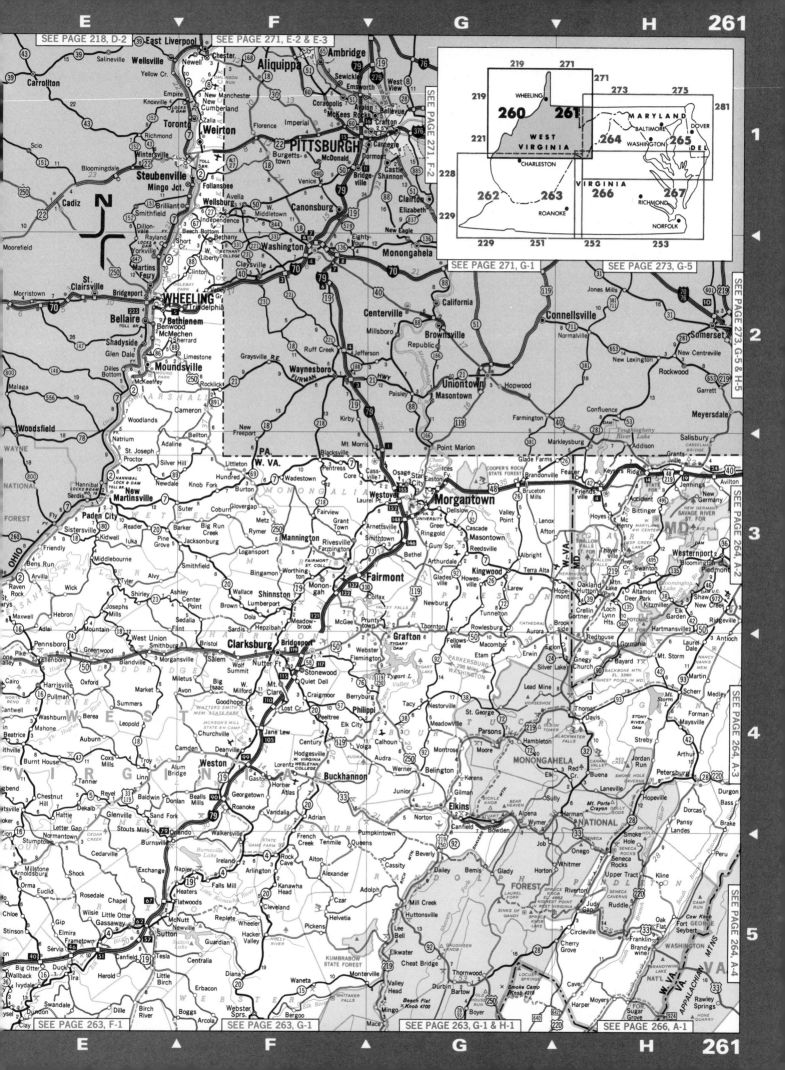

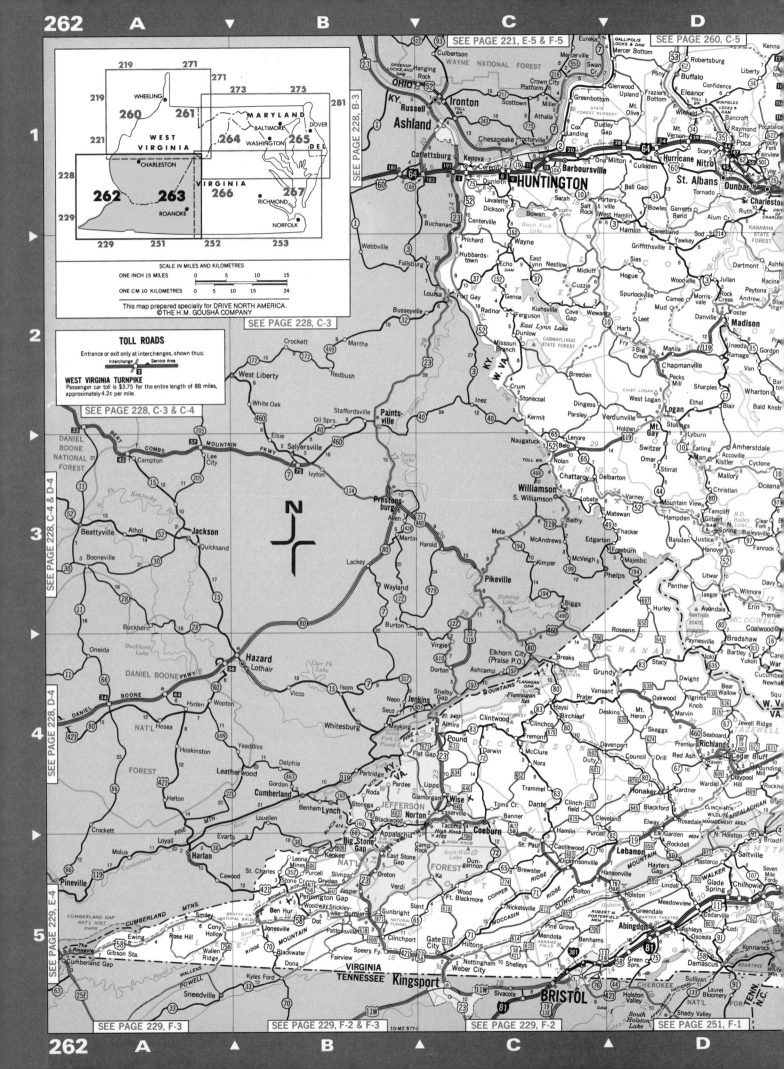

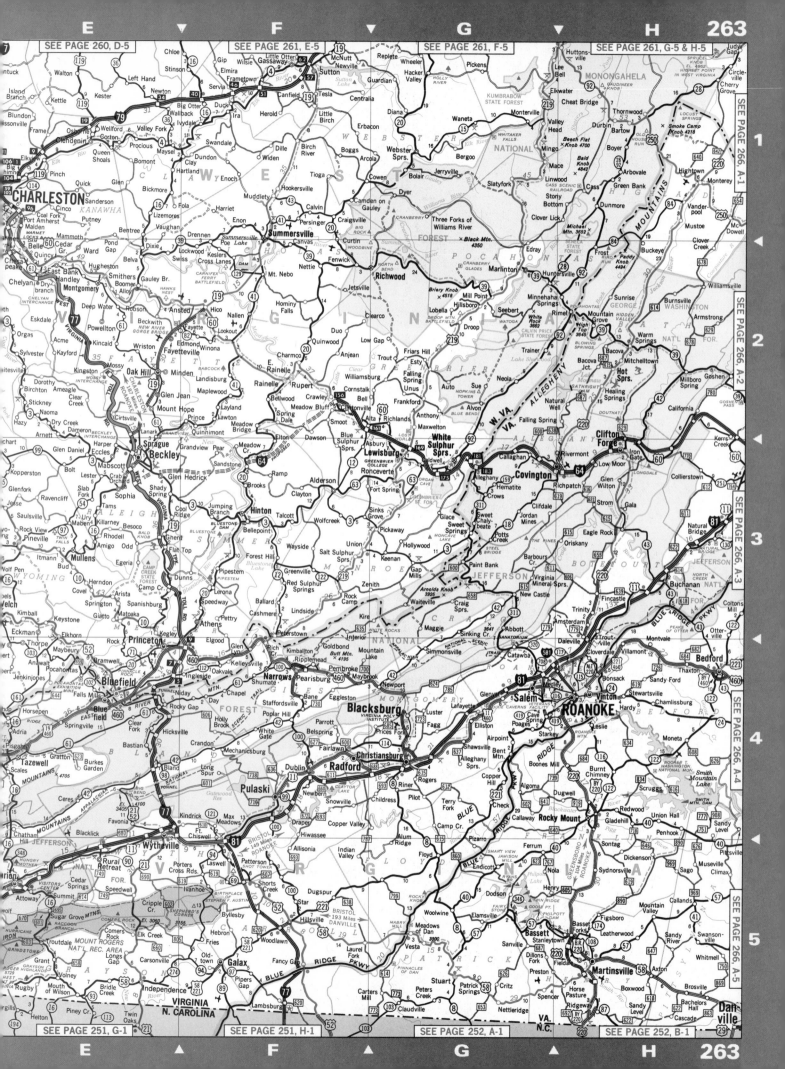

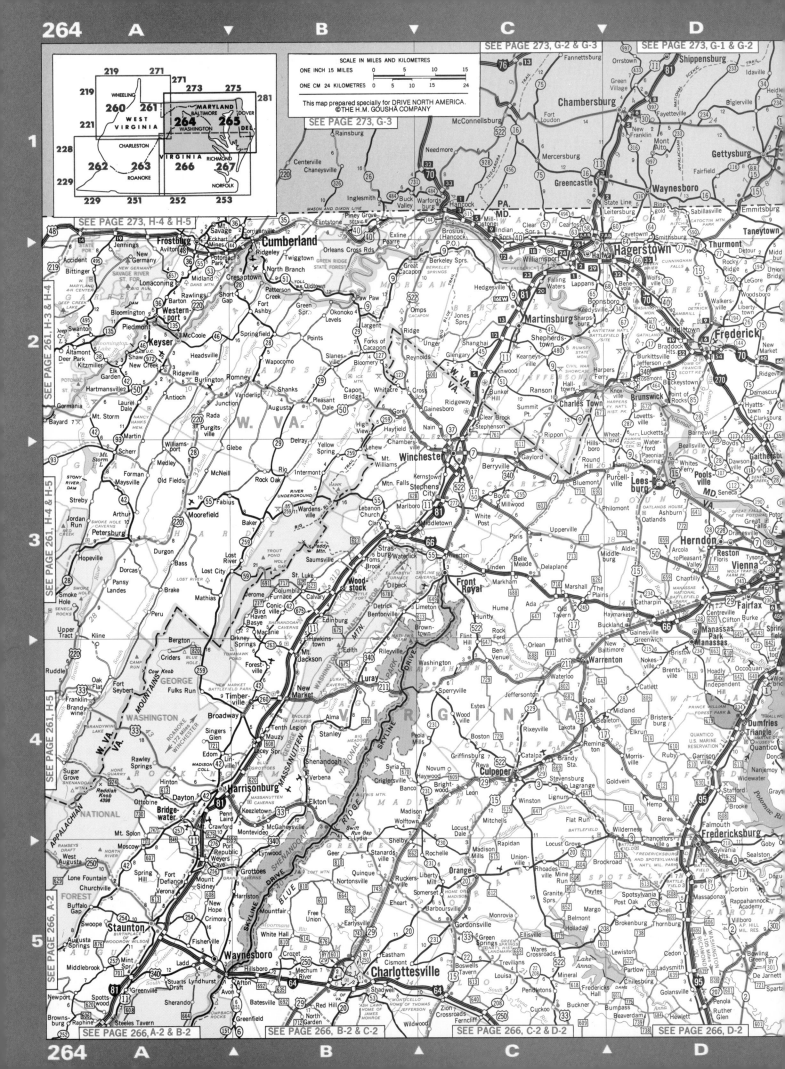

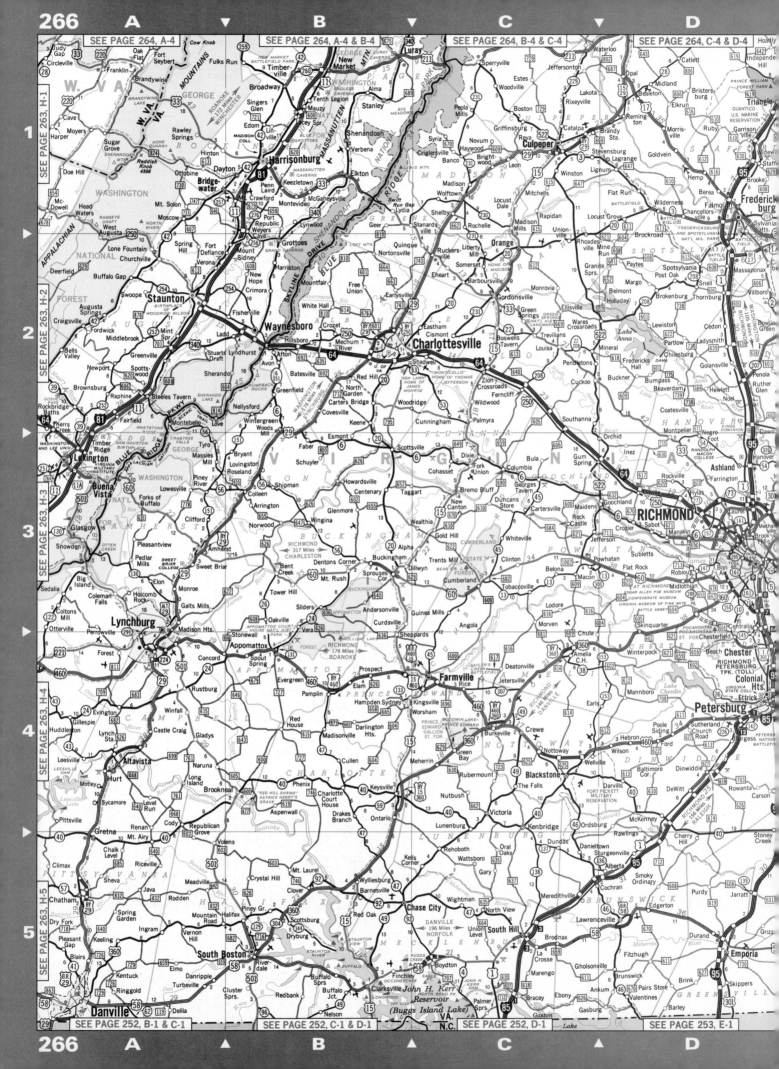

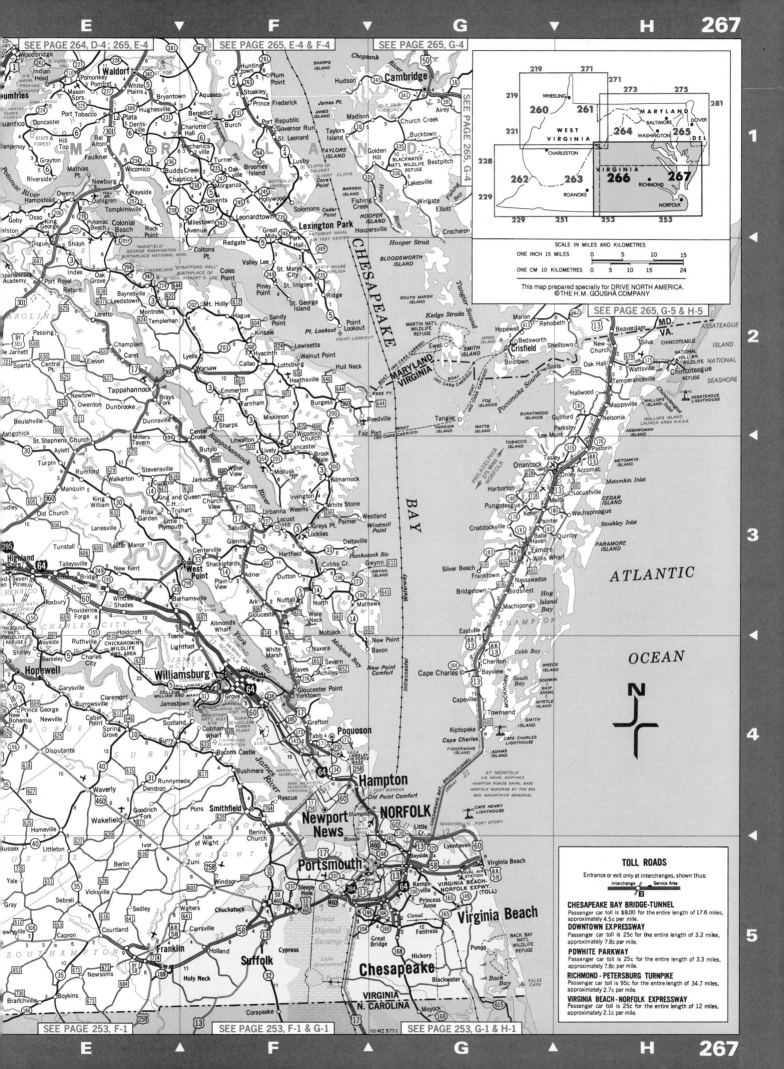

A Utopia for Freedom-Seekers and the Forge of Independence

Pennsylvania

Like the glorious quilts of its Amish settlers, Pennsylvania is a patchwork of colorful contrasts: wild and rugged Allegheny National Forest, Colonial battlefields and mill towns, the soaring skyline of Pittsburgh.

Philadelphia (275, G-2) is a living museum of Americana. Within the six-block area of Independence National Historical Park the Continental Congress met, the Declaration of Independence was adopted, the Liberty Bell rang out and the Constitution was written. Centerpiece of the park is Independence Hall (1732), where freedom from England was declared on July 4, 1776.

The "City of Brotherly Love" is also a city of museums and art galleries. The Franklin Institute, founded in 1824 as a gathering place for scientists and craftsmen, features Fels Planetarium, along with do-it-yourself exhibits on chemistry, physics, astronomy and computers. A broad range of the world's finest art hangs in the magnificent Philadelphia Museum of Art, whose classical portico looms above the Schuylkill River. The Pennsylvania Academy of the Fine Arts (1805), the oldest in the United States, is a treasure house of American art. Gathered in the Rodin Museum are 80 bronze casts; only the Musée Rodin in Paris contains a larger collection of the sculptor's works. The U.S.S. *Olympia* has been restored as a naval museum; it was launched in 1893 and saw action in the Spanish-American War.

In downtown Philadelphia venerable landmarks rub shoulders with modern glass-and-steel office towers, and cobblestone streets intersect broad boulevards. Society Hill comprises 25 blocks of historic homes and buildings, several open to the public. Nearby Elfreth's Alley, a narrow cobblestone lane, was laid out in 1704. Fairmount Park, threaded with scenic drives, walks, bicycle routes and bridle paths, covers more than 8,500 acres along both sides of the Schuylkill. The park provides a sylvan setting for a number of 18th-century mansions.

Beyond Philadelphia lie the history-rich valleys and villages of southeastern Pennsylvania. Washington's ragged and starving Continental Army encamped in **Valley Forge (275, G-2)** for the crucial winter of 1777–78. The Washington Memorial Chapel, the lofty bell tower, and a museum containing George Washington's campaign tent and headquarters flag face the Grand Parade where Baron von Steuben drilled the demoralized troops. A more peaceful time is remembered in the Mercer Museum at **Doylestown (275, F-2)**, where more than 40,000 tools used in pre-industrial America have been gathered. Visitors walking through the tall center court of this remarkable building will see a whaleboat, a canoe, a sled—even an early fire engine—suspended above them in a rich display of early American craftsmanship.

In Colonial days Pennsylvania was a haven of religious freedom where a number of utopian communities flourished. Moravians

Pennsylvania, plain and fancy: the Amish of Lancaster County (below); Philadelphia's colorful Mummers Parade (right).

who had fled religious persecution in Germany founded **Bethlehem (275, F-2)** in 1741 and lived here in a closed community for more than a century. The Widow's House (1768) is still a residence for widows and daughters of Moravian ministers, and peals from the sandstone Bell House once set the community's schedule. The self-sustaining community of **Ephrata Cloister (275, G-4)**—a celibate brotherhood and sisterhood and a married order of householders—operated a bakery, gristmill and farm. The buildings that survive are Germanic in character, made of wood and stone, with small dormer windows. Old Economy Village, near **Ambridge (271, F-2)**, was the third—and final—home of the Harmony Society, a pacifist sect founded in 1805 and disbanded 100 years later. In the midst of landscaped walks are the preserved home of founder George Rapp, the communal dining hall and dwellings, craft shops and workrooms.

Throughout the rolling countryside of eastern Pennsylvania can be seen the beautifully proportioned architecture, horse-drawn wagons and plain dress of the Pennsylvania Dutch. The Amish Farm and House in **Lancaster (275, G-4)** demonstrates the totally self-sufficient way of life practiced by these "Plain People." The outbuildings, barn and house are authentically equipped and furnished, and Amish vehicles (Conestoga wagon, sleigh, four-wheeled carriage) are on view. The Pennsylvania Farm Museum of Landis Valley houses more than 250,000 items illustrating rural life. Wheatland, a large 19th-century brick house on Route 23,

was the home of James Buchanan before and after he served as the only unmarried President of the United States (1857–61).

The dome of the State Capitol Building, modeled after St. Peter's Basilica in Rome, rises 272 feet to dominate the skyline of **Harrisburg (275, G-5)**. Beneath it is the great rotunda, a grand stairway of Italian marble and paintings depicting Pennsylvania history. The colony's original 1681 charter from Charles II is displayed in the William Penn Memorial Museum along with Indian artifacts, dioramas of birds and mammals, and antique furniture.

It was on the rolling hills of **Gettysburg National Military Park (273, H-1)** that Lee's Army of Northern Virginia engaged General George Meade's Army of the Potomac in the bloodiest battle ever fought in North America (1863). The defeat of Lee's forces was a turning point of the Civil War and cost 8,000 lives. At the Visitor Center is a 30-square-foot topographical map on which 625 lights depict troop movements and positions during the battle. The center also houses a vast collection of Civil War memorabilia—guns, sabers, uniforms, even the table on which General "Stonewall" Jackson's arm was amputated. Outside, a monument marks the spot where Lincoln delivered the Gettysburg Address.

Farmland, vineyards and 63 miles of ocean-like shoreline on Lake Erie are the scenic delights of the state's northwest corner. In a waterfront park in **Erie (270, B-2)** rests the brig U.S.S. *Niagara*, which won the Battle of Lake Erie under Commodore Oliver Hazard Perry in the War of 1812. A scenic

The genius of architect Frank Lloyd Wright is preserved in Fallingwater (above), the house he designed over a waterfall in Mill Run. Philadelphia office towers frame Constitution Place (left), where the United States was born. Hex signs decorate a 19th-century barn near Bird in Hand (below).

Chocolate Town, U.S.A.

Even the air smells like a candy bar in Hershey, the town that grew up around Milton Hershey's chocolate factory.

On a free Chocolate World tour (*right*) visitors pass animated displays depicting the cocoa bean's journey from tropical plantations to giant roasting ovens. Other attractions include the Hershey Museum of American Life, with Indian pottery, early fire-fighting equipment, Conestoga wagons and firearms dating from the American Revolution to World War II. Visitors will delight, too, in the magnificent Hershey Rose Gardens—and an amusement park called, not surprisingly, Hersheypark.

drive loops through Presque Isle State Park, a curving spit of land edged with fine beaches.

Western Pennsylvania was America's wild frontier when young George Washington, then a major in the Colonial Army, selected the scenic junction of the Monongahela, Allegheny and Ohio rivers as the site of **Pittsburgh (271, F-2)**. Soon coal was dug from its hills, blast furnaces sprang up, and the Iron City (later the Steel City) plunged headlong into the Industrial Age. Today Pittsburgh's smoky, industrial image is a thing of the past, following a dramatic post-World War II renaissance. Point State Park occupies the original site of Fort Pitt (1759); the city's modern skyline is dominated by the soaring 841-foot tower of the U.S. Steel Building. The Duquesne and Monongahela incline railways climb Mount Washington for breathtaking views of the "Golden Triangle."

In 1896 industrialist Andrew Carnegie turned from railroad-building to philanthropy. The Carnegie Institute was his gift to Pittsburgh, the city where he first became successful. Among the treasures in the Institute's Natural History Museum are the dinosaur, mineral and gem exhibits. The Museum of Art has an excellent collection of 19th- and 20th-century French art, Old Masters and contemporary works. The scion of another industrial family, Helen Clay Frick, founded the Frick Art Museum to house an impressive and wide-ranging collection of European paintings, sculptures, furniture, tapestries and Chinese porcelains. Pittsburgh's Buhl Science Center was one of the first such complexes in the country. "Sky Dramas" are presented in the Theater of the Stars.

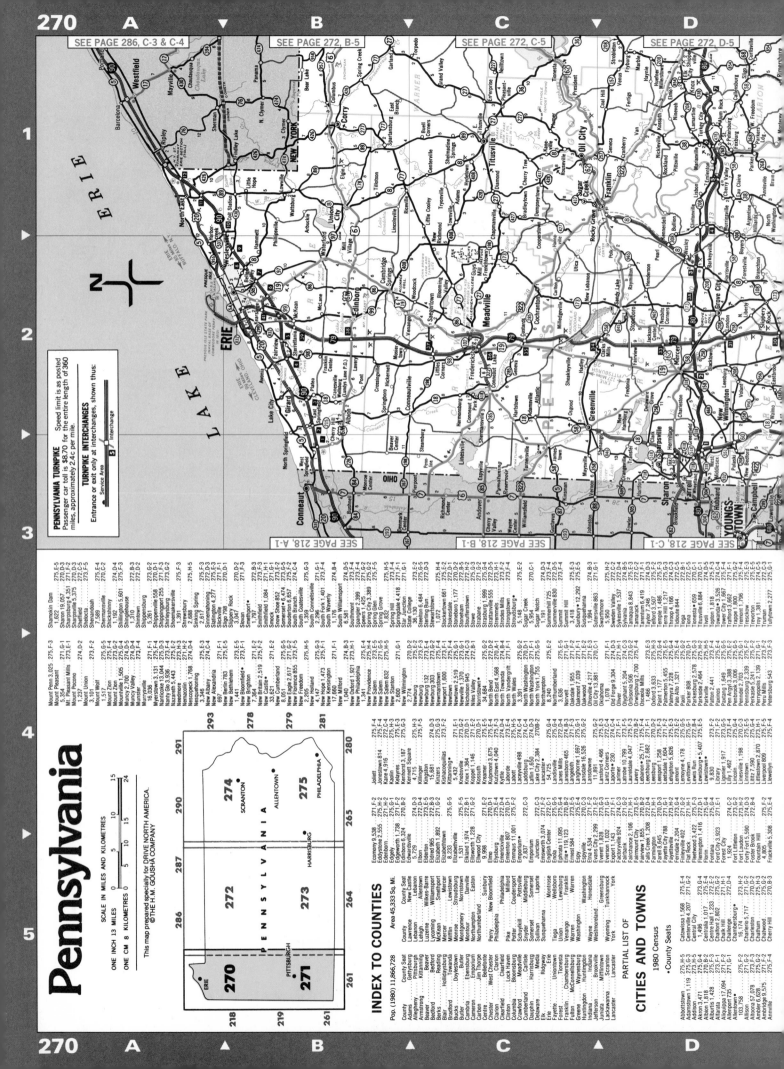

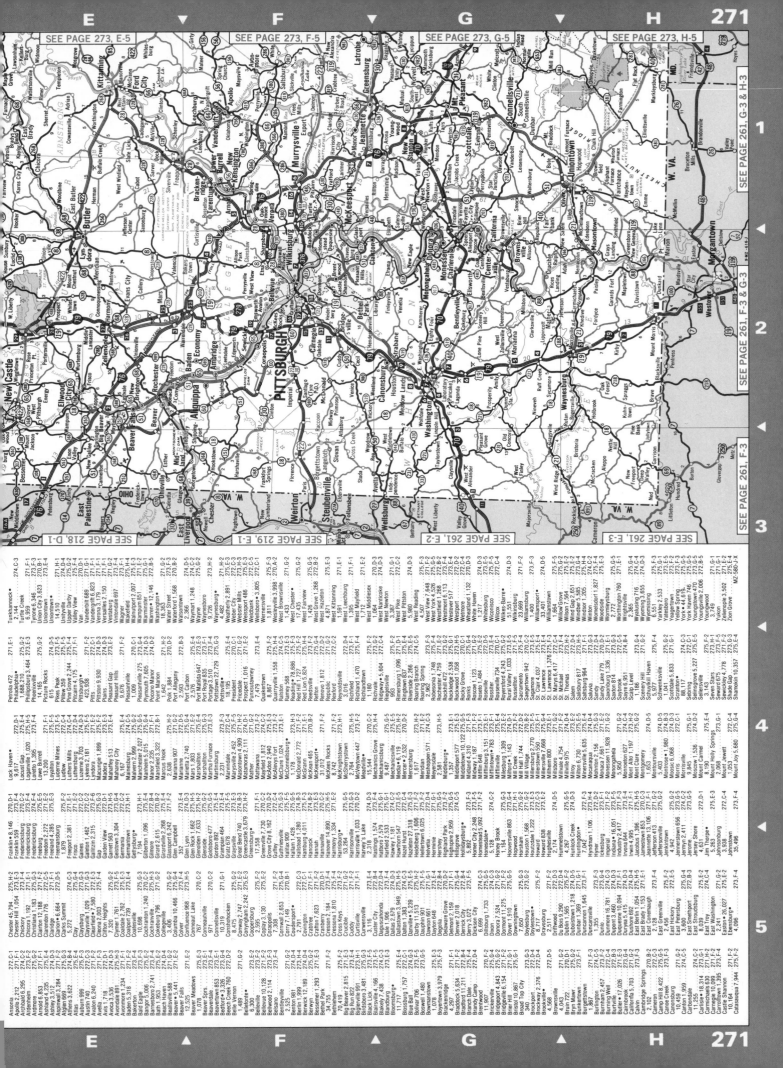

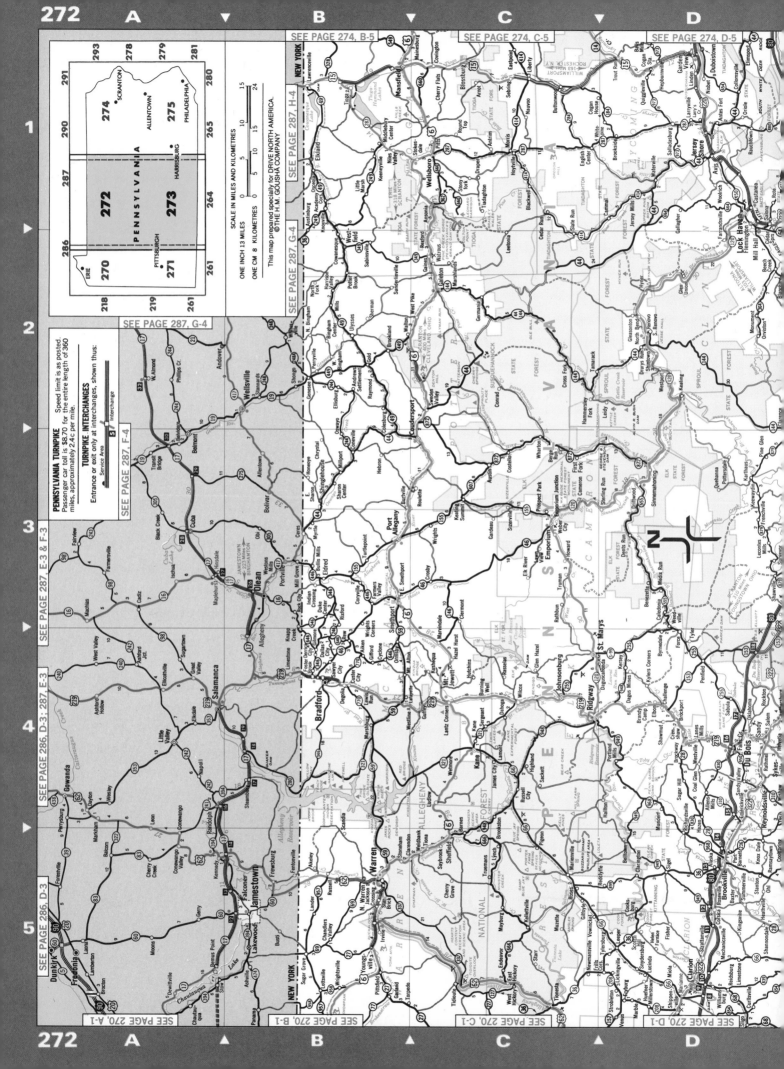

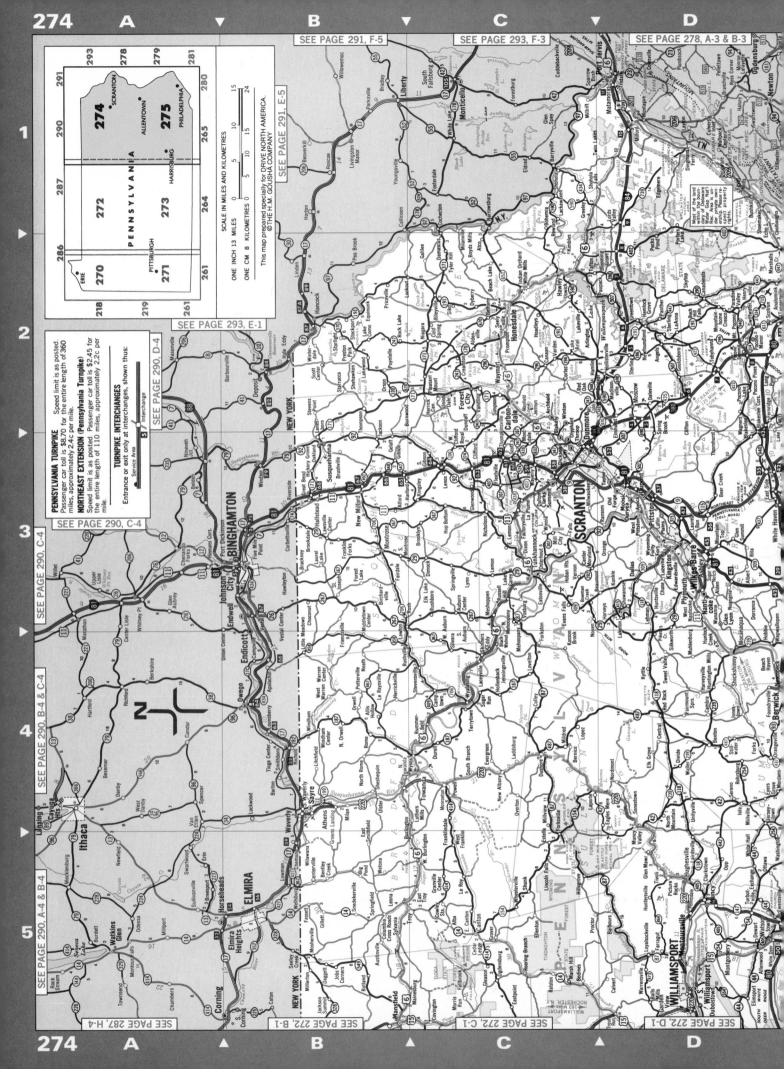

Fort Nonsense, the Halls of Academe and High-Rolling Atlantic City

New Jersey

Industrial vitality in the north, lovely coastal towns and pastoral farmland in the south—such is the scenic contrast that greets travelers in the "Garden State." New Jersey's largest city, **Newark (278, D-1)**, provides a glimpse of this unusual diversity. Founded in 1666 by Puritans from Connecticut, it is now one of the world's leading manufacturing centers. Yet on its outskirts Branch Brook Park blossoms with flowering cherry trees. Beginning in late April, these colorful trees put on a brilliant month-long display.

Thomas Edison spent 45 years of his life in **West Orange (278, D-2)**, and it was here that he developed many of his major inventions. The Edison National Historic Site preserves his chemical laboratory, machine shop and library, and a replica of Black Maria—the first motion picture studio. (The name derived from the black tar paper that covered its walls.) Edison's notebooks and many original models of his inventions, including the tinfoil phonograph (1877), are on display. Glenmont, Edison's 23-room Victorian home, stands on a ridge in nearby Llewellyn Park. The house contains almost all the original furnishings, as well as paintings, books and Edison memorabilia.

Great Swamp National Wildlife Refuge (278, D-3) is a wilderness of marsh, meadow and timberland and a favorite haunt of birdwatchers. It harbors one of the state's largest breeding areas for bluebirds. Visitors have spotted more than 200 other bird species here including green herons, mockingbirds and snow geese. Turtles, frogs and several varieties of nonpoisonous snakes also make their home in the swamp, which is crisscrossed by nature trails.

The courage and tenacity of George Washington and his troops is remembered at **Morristown (278, D-3)**, where the Continental Army spent the winter of 1779–80. George and Martha used the stately Ford Mansion, (1774) as headquarters. An adjacent museum recalls the Revolutionary Era through old prints and manuscripts, glass, pewter, silver and pottery displays, and dioramas. Reconstructed log cabins, originally built to house troops, can be seen in Jockey Hollow, four miles south. In the Wick House, it is said, Temperance Wick hid her horse in her bedroom to protect it from mutinous soldiers. Fort Nonsense, on a hilltop overlooking Morristown, was a key vantage point during the Revolutionary War. Its name was inspired by the legend that soldiers built the fort solely to keep themselves occupied.

Waterloo Village, near **Stanhope (278, C-4)**, was known as Andover Forge when the town supplied cannonballs and musket barrels to the Continental Army. Most of its surviving buildings date from the 18th century. In the houses, church, gristmill, inn and shops visitors can view nearly 50 rooms of antique furniture. South of Waterloo, the Stephens Section of Allamuchy Mountain State Park includes picturesque Saxton Falls

and the clear, rushing waters of the Musconetcong River.

Lawns and gardens, striking architecture and modern sculpture—and many miles of walks—welcome visitors to Princeton University, centerpiece of **Princeton (279, F-3)**. British and Colonial troops used Nassau Hall (1756) as a barracks and hospital during the Revolutionary War, and the Continental Congress assembled here in 1783. The pinnacled turrets of the magnificent University Chapel resemble those of a great Gothic cathedral. The Harvey Firestone Library is one of the largest open-stack libraries in the United States, with holdings that range from Babylonian cylinder seals, Egyptian papyruses and the earliest printed books to the papers of alumnus F. Scott Fitzgerald. Completed in 1965, the Woodrow Wilson School of Public and International Affairs has 59 graceful, quartz-faced columns with Italian travertine and gray glass walls. Its sculpture *Fountain of Freedom* memorializes the 28th President, who graduated from Princeton in 1879.

In 1758 the citizens of New Jersey petitioned for the building of winter barracks to billet British soldiers serving in the French and Indian War. Of the five built, a two-story stone structure in **Trenton (279, F-4)**, the state capital, is all that remains. It once housed 300 men and was used variously by British, Hessian (German mercenaries) and American troops. The brick Trent House (1719), believed to be the city's oldest, has been refurnished according to a 1726 inventory of the original contents. Governors Lewis Morris, Philemon Dickerson and Rodman Price lived here, and both Washington and Lafayette were guests. Fire destroyed much of the original 1792 State House in 1885; by 1889 it had been rebuilt into today's impressive gray limestone Renaissance structure. The New Jersey State Museum combines decorative and modern art, science exhibits and an outdoor sculpture garden.

Walt Whitman's former home in **Camden (279, H-5)** reveals the near-poverty in which this famous American poet passed his last eight years. His clothing, books, manuscripts and letters enrich the sparsely furnished Victorian frame house, now a museum. The Camden County Historical Society occupies more impressive quarters—Georgian-style Pomona Hall, built in 1726. The society's museum exhibits lighting devices, fire fighting equipment, toys and uniforms. The early American handiwork of weavers, candlemakers, coopers and blacksmiths is displayed in period shops.

Early colonists considered New Jersey's Pine Barrens unfit for farming and named it accordingly. This sandy, pine-covered wilderness of some 2,000 square miles once lay at the bottom of an ancient ocean. Today more than 20 species of orchids thrive here in the shade of pitch pine, white cedar and scarlet oak. Herons, egrets, migrating waterfowl and songbirds share the forest with

Princeton's handsome architecture is complemented by its park-like campus.

mink, beavers, gray foxes and white-tailed deer. **Lebanon State Forest (279, H-3)**, in the heart of the Barrens, is laced with sandy roads leading to campgrounds, picnic sites and nature trails. At **Wharton State Forest (281, F-2)**, less than three hours from Manhattan, canoeists can enjoy the quiet beauty of the Mullica River.

Highway 542 follows the Mullica west to **Historic Batsto Village (281, F-2)**, settled in 1760 by Swedes from Delaware (Batsto is a corruption of *baastoo*, Swedish for "bathing place"). The Swedish colonists, like many others, were attracted to the Pine Barrens for its iron ore bogs and seemingly endless supply of lumber. The village was one of the most important iron-making centers in Colonial America, producing kettles, stoves, nails and tools, and furnishing firearms and ammunition for the American Revolution. Batsto lay dormant, but intact, from 1870 until 1954, when the state acquired the land and began restoration of the town. Today the 36-room ironmaster's mansion sits on a hill overlooking the millpond; the post office, the general store, the gristmill and several other buildings are clustered nearby. The Batsto

Dunes fringe Island Beach State Park (upper left). Gingerbread and clapboard grace the Victorian resort of Ocean Grove (above).

Sightseers throng Atlantic City's famous boardwalk (left). High above the Hudson River loom the cliffs of the Palisades (below).

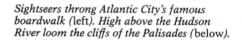

Natural Area, near the village, is a 150-acre wildlife preserve where visitors can view the many varieties of plants indigenous to the Pine Barrens.

Rich farmlands and quaint coastal towns provide much of the character of South Jersey, as this part of the state is often called. **Cape May (281, E-5)**, a narrow strip that separates Delaware Bay from the Atlantic, was settled by whalers from New England in the 1600s. When the whales began to disappear from local waters, many residents opened up their homes to visitors, initiating a tradition of seaside tourism for which Cape May has become famous. At the turn of the century, when the cool beaches of the Cape were a magnet to East Coast city dwellers, large Victorian resort hotels and handsome cottages sprang up. In 1976 the much-restored town was designated a National Historic Landmark. The J-shaped Chalfonte Hotel has survived since its opening in 1876

with most of its gingerbread ornamentation intact. Several 19th-century Presidents summered at Congress Hall, built in 1879 on the site of an 1812 inn. The Pink House (1879), festooned with elaborate "carpenter's lace," is an exuberant example of Victorian architecture.

Two miles west of the old town lies Cape May Point, the southern tip of New Jersey. A largely deserted beach stretches for miles along the shores of Delaware Bay here. Hosts of birds roost among its woods and dunes during spring and fall migrations. Cape May diamonds, bits of semiprecious quartz that have been polished by wind and water, are common. Sunbathing, shelling and fishing lure visitors to Cape May Point State Park, where Cape May Lighthouse has stood sentinel since 1859.

Up the coast, a remarkable variety of birds, including grebes, herons, loons and ibises, summer at **Stone Harbor Bird Sanctuary**

(281, F-5). The most unusual residents are cattle egrets, which can often be seen feeding on the backs of grazing livestock outside the park.

High rollers, low rollers and the merely curious flock to **Atlantic City (281, G-3)** to be dazzled by lavish casinos, floor shows and famous stars, or to enjoy its traditional pleasures—sandy beaches, jitneys (minibuses) and saltwater taffy. The city is the home of the 6½-mile-long wooden boardwalk (still the world's longest, widest and busiest), the historic Central Pier, and, the original Miss America Pageant. The Absecon Lighthouse dates from 1857 and has been restored as a marine environmental museum. Nearby Gardner's Basin is a colorful celebration of America's maritime heritage. Here visitors can see a 216-foot replica of the clipper *Flying Cloud* or spend three hours before the mast aboard the square-rigger *Young America*.

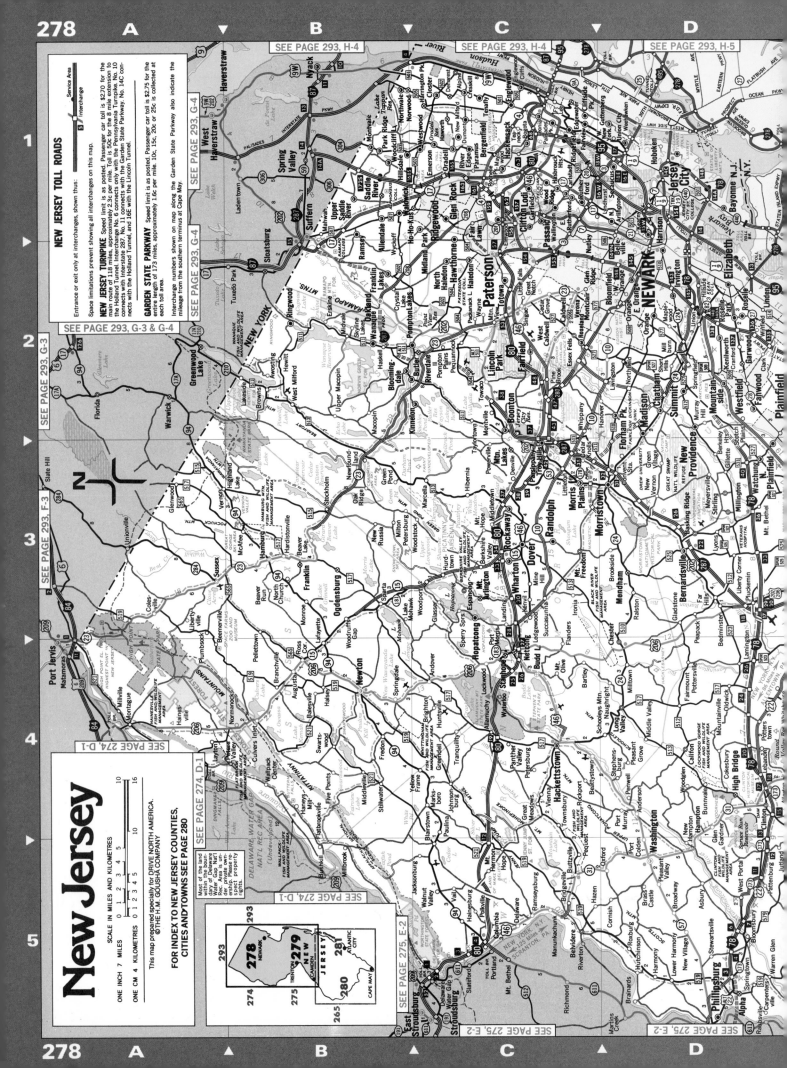

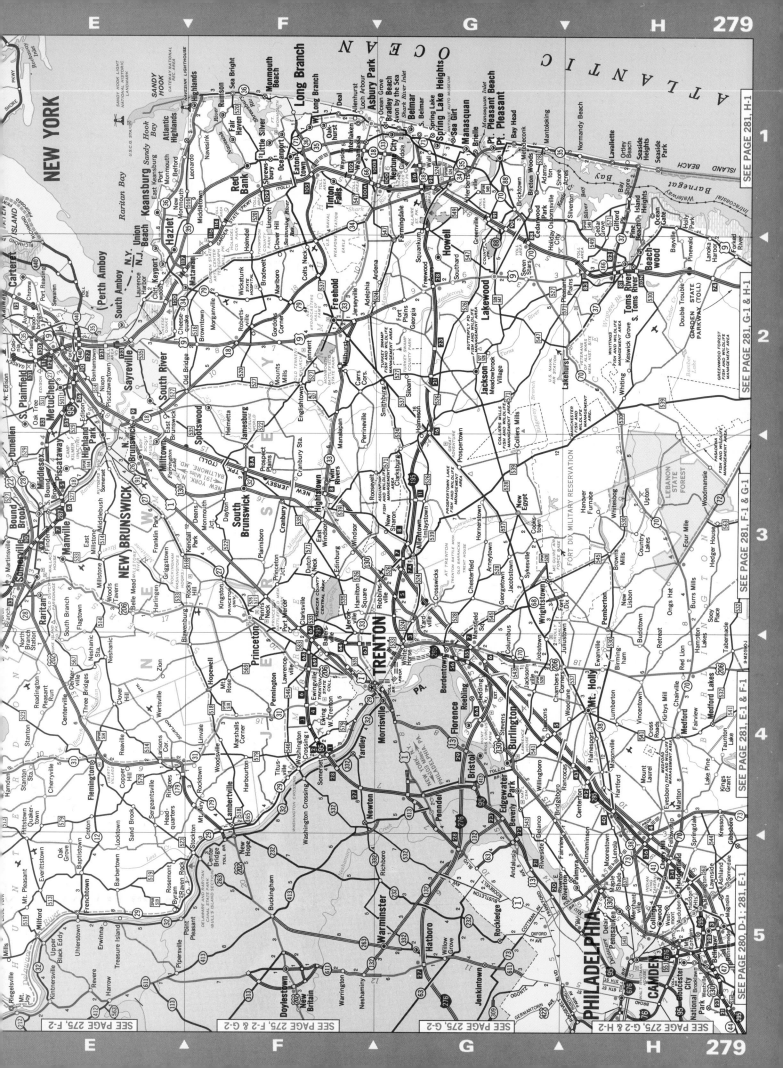

INDEX TO COUNTIES

Pop. (1980) 7,364,158 — Area 7,836 Sq. Mi.

County	County Seat	County	County Seat
Atlantic	Mays Landing	Mercer	Trenton
Bergen	Hackensack	Middlesex	New Brunswick
Burlington	Mount Holly	Monmouth	Freehold
Camden	Camden	Morris	Morristown
Cape May	Cape May C.H.	Ocean	Toms River
Cumberland	Bridgeton	Passaic	Paterson
Essex	Newark	Salem	Salem
Gloucester	Woodbury	Somerset	Somerville
Hudson	Jersey City	Sussex	Newton
Hunterdon	Flemington	Warren	Belvidere

PARTIAL LIST OF

CITIES AND TOWNS

1980 Census

• County Seats

† Includes Population of Whole (Town) Township

Absecon 6,859 ... 281,G-3
Adelphia ... 279,F-2
Allamuchy • †2,560 ... 278,C-4
Allendale 5,901 ... 278,B-1
Allenhurst 912 ... 279,F-1
Allentown 1,962 ... 279,G-3
Allerton ... 278,D-4
Alloway †2,680 ... 280,C-2
Almonesson ... 280,D-1
Alpha 2,644 ... 278,D-5
Alpine 1,549 ... 278,C-1
Anderson 892 ... 278,D-4
Andover 892 ... 278,C-4
Ardena ... 279,G-2
Asbury Park 17,015 ... 279,F-1
Ashland ... 281,E-1
Atlantic City 40,199 ... 281,G-3
Atlantic Highlands 4,950 ... 279,E-1
Atsion ... 281,F-1
Auburn ... 280,C-1
Audubon 9,533 ... 279,H-5
Augusta ... 278,B-4
Avalon 2,162 ... 281,F-5
Avon by the Sea 2,337 ... 279,G-1
Bakersville ... 279,F-4
Baptistown ... 279,E-5
Barbertown ... 279,E-5
Barnegat ... 281,H-1
Barnsboro ... 280,D-1
Barrington 7,418 ... 280,D-1
Basking Ridge ... 278,D-3
Bay Head 1,340 ... 279,G-1
Bay Shore ... 279,H-1
Bay Side ... 281,H-2
Bayonne 65,047 ... 278,D-1
Bayville ... 279,H-1
Beach Haven 1,714 ... 281,H-2
Beachwood 7,687 ... 279,H-2
Beattystown ... 278,C-4
Beaver Dam ... 280,D-4
Beaver Lake ... 278,B-3
Bedminster †2,469 ... 278,D-3
Beemerville ... 278,A-4
Belcoville ... 281,F-3
Belford ... 279,E-1
Belle Mead ... 279,E-3
Belleplain ... 281,E-4
Belleville 35,367 ... 278,D-1
Bellmawr 13,721 ... 280,D-1
Belmar 6,771 ... 279,G-1
Belvidere • 2,475 ... 278,C-5
Bergenfield 25,568 ... 278,C-1
Berkeley Hts. †12,549 ... 278,D-3
Berkshire Valley ... 278,C-3
Berlin 5,786 ... 281,E-1
Bernardsville 6,715 ... 278,D-3
Beverly 2,919 ... 279,G-4
Birmingham ... 279,H-4
Blackwood ... 280,D-1
Blackwood Terrace ... 280,D-1
Blairstown †4,360 ... 278,C-5
Blawenburg ... 279,F-4
Bloomfield 47,792 ... 278,D-2
Bloomingdale 7,867 ... 278,B-2
Bloomsbury 864 ... 278,D-5
Blue Anchor ... 281,E-2
Bogota 8,344 ... 278,C-1
Bonhamtown ... 279,E-2
Boonton 8,620 ... 278,C-2
Bordentown 4,441 ... 279,G-1
Bound Brook 9,710 ... 279,E-3
Braddock ... 281,E-2
Bradevelt ... 279,F-2
Bradley Beach 4,772 ... 279,G-1
Branchville 870 ... 278,B-4
Breton Woods ... 279,G-1
Bricksboro ... 281,E-4
Bricktown ... 279,G-1
Bridgeboro ... 279,G-4
Bridgeport ... 280,C-1
Bridgeton • 18,795 ... 280,D-3
Bridgeville ... 278,C-5
Brielle 4,068 ... 279,G-1
Brigantine 8,318 ... 281,G-3
Broadway ... 278,D-5
Brooklawn 2,133 ... 279,H-5
Browns ... 278,B-2
Browns Mills ... 279,H-3
Browntown ... 279,F-2
Budd Lake ... 278,C-4
Buddtown ... 279,H-4
Buena 3,642 ... 281,E-2
Bunnvale ... 278,D-4
Burlington 10,246 ... 279,G-4
Burrs Mills ... 279,H-3
Butler 7,616 ... 278,C-2
Buttzville ... 278,C-5
Byram ... 279,E-5
Caldwell 7,624 ... 278,C-2
Califon 1,023 ... 278,D-4
Camden • 84,910 ... 279,H-5
Cape May 4,853 ... 281,E-5
Cape May C.H. • ... 281,E-5
Cape May Point 255 ... 281,E-5
Carlls Corner ... 280,D-3
Carlstadt 6,166 ... 278,C-1
Carmel ... 280,D-3
Carneys Point ... 280,C-2
Carrs Cors ... 279,F-2
Carteret 20,598 ... 279,E-2
Cedar Brook ... 281,E-1
Cedar Grove ... 278,C-2
Cedar Grove ... 279,H-2
Cedar Run ... 281,H-2
Cedarville ... 280,D-3
Cedarwood Park ... 279,G-1
Centerton ... 279,H-4
Centerton ... 280,D-2
Centerville ... 279,E-4
Chairville ... 279,H-4
Chambers Corners ... 279,H-4
Chatham 8,537 ... 278,D-2
Chatsworth ... 281,G-1
Cheesequake ... 279,E-2
Cherry Hill †68,785 ... 279,H-5
Chesilhurst 1,590 ... 281,E-1
Chester 1,433 ... 278,D-4
Chesterfield †3,867 ... 279,G-3
Churchtown ... 280,C-2
Cinnaminson †16,072 ... 279,H-5
Clarksboro ... 280,D-1
Clarksburg ... 279,G-3
Clarksville ... 279,F-3
Clayton 6,013 ... 280,D-2
Clementon 5,764 ... 281,E-1
Clermont ... 281,F-4
Cliffside Park 21,464 ... 278,C-1
Cliffwood ... 279,E-2
Clifton 74,388 ... 278,C-1
Clinton 1,910 ... 278,D-4
Closter 8,164 ... 278,C-1
Clover Hill ... 279,E-4
Clover Hill ... 279,F-2
Colesville ... 278,A-3
Colliers Mills ... 279,G-3
Collingswood 15,838 ... 279,H-5
Cologne ... 281,F-3
Colonia ... 279,E-2
Colts Neck ... 279,F-2
Columbia ... 278,C-5
Columbus ... 279,G-4
Conovertown ... 281,G-3
Convent Station ... 278,D-3
Copper Hill ... 279,E-4
Corbin City 254 ... 281,F-4
Cranbury ... 279,F-3
Cranford ... 278,D-2
Cresskill 7,609 ... 278,C-1
Crosswicks ... 279,G-3
Croton ... 279,E-4
Culvers Inlet ... 278,B-4
Cumberland ... 281,E-3
Dayton ... 279,F-3
Deal 1,952 ... 279,F-1
Deepwater ... 280,C-2
Deerfield †2,523 ... 280,D-2
Delair ... 279,H-5
Delanco †3,730 ... 279,G-5
Delaware ... 278,C-5
Delmont ... 281,E-4
Demarest 4,963 ... 278,C-1
Dennisville ... 281,E-4
Denville †14,380 ... 278,C-3
Dividing Creek ... 280,D-4
Dorchester ... 281,E-4
Dorothy ... 281,E-3
Dover 14,681 ... 278,C-3
Downstown ... 281,E-2
Dumont 18,334 ... 278,C-1
Dunbarton ... 281,E-1
Dunellen 6,593 ... 279,E-3
Dutch Neck ... 279,F-3
East Brunswick †37,711 ... 279,E-2
East Keansburg ... 279,E-1
East Millstone ... 279,E-3
East Orange 77,025 ... 278,D-2
East Riverton ... 279,H-5
East Rutherford 7,849 ... 278,C-1
East Windsor †21,041 ... 279,F-3
Eatontown 12,703 ... 279,F-1
Edgewater 4,628 ... 278,C-1
Edgewater Park †9,273 ... 279,G-4
Edinburg ... 279,F-3
Edison †70,193 ... 279,E-2
Egg Harbor City 4,618 ... 281,F-2
Eldora ... 281,E-4
Elizabeth • 106,201 ... 278,D-2
Elm ... 281,E-2
Elmer 1,569 ... 280,D-2
Elmwood Park 18,377 ... 278,C-1
Elwood ... 281,F-2
Emerson 7,793 ... 278,C-1
Englewood 23,701 ... 278,C-1
Englewood Cliffs 5,698 ... 278,C-1
Englishtown 976 ... 279,F-2
Erma ... 281,E-5
Espanong ... 278,C-3
Essex Fells 2,363 ... 278,C-2
Estell Manor 848 ... 281,E-3
Estellville ... 281,F-3
Everittstown ... 279,E-5
Evesboro ... 279,H-4
Ewanville ... 279,H-4
Ewing †34,842 ... 279,F-4
Ewingville ... 279,F-4
Fair Haven 5,679 ... 279,F-1
Fair Lawn 32,229 ... 278,C-1
Fairfield 7,987 ... 278,C-2
Fairmount ... 278,D-4
Fairton ... 280,D-3
Fairview ... 279,H-5
Fairview ... 280,D-1
Fairview ... 279,H-4
Fairview 10,519 ... 278,C-1
Fanwood 7,767 ... 278,D-2
Far Hills 677 ... 278,D-3
Farmingdale 1,348 ... 279,G-2
Fellowship ... 279,H-5
Finderne ... 279,E-3
Flemington • 4,132 ... 279,E-4
Florence †9,084 ... 279,G-4
Florham Park 9,359 ... 278,D-2
Folsom 1,892 ... 281,E-2
Fords ... 279,E-2
Forked River ... 281,H-1
Fort Dix ... 279,H-3
Fort Lee 32,449 ... 278,C-1
Fort Plains ... 279,G-2
Four Mile ... 279,H-3
Franklin †31,358 ... 279,E-3
Franklin 4,486 ... 278,B-3
Franklin Lakes 8,769 ... 278,B-2
Franklin Park ... 279,E-3
Franklinville ... 280,D-2
Fredon †2,281 ... 278,B-4
Freehold • 10,020 ... 279,F-2
Freewood Acres ... 279,G-2
Frenchtown 1,573 ... 279,E-5
Garfield 26,803 ... 278,C-1
Garwood 4,752 ... 278,D-2
Georgetown ... 279,G-3
Gibbsboro 2,510 ... 281,E-1
Gibbstown ... 280,D-1
Gilford Park ... 279,H-1
Gillette ... 278,D-3
Glassboro 14,574 ... 280,D-2
Glen Gardner 834 ... 278,D-4
Glen Ridge 7,855 ... 278,D-2
Glen Rock 11,497 ... 278,C-1
Glendola ... 279,G-1
Glendora ... 280,D-1
Glenwood ... 278,A-3
Gloucester City 13,121 ... 279,H-5
Gordons Corner ... 279,F-2
Goshen ... 281,E-4
Gouldtown ... 280,D-3
Gravelly Run ... 281,F-3
Great Meadows ... 278,C-4
Green Bank ... 281,F-2
Green Creek ... 281,E-5
Greenville ... 279,G-2
Greenwich †973 ... 280,C-3
Grenloch ... 280,D-1
Guttenberg 7,340 ... 278,D-1
Hackensack • 36,039 ... 278,C-1
Hackettstown 8,850 ... 278,C-4
Haddon Heights 8,361 ... 279,H-5
Haddonfield 12,337 ... 279,H-5
Hainesburg ... 278,C-5
Hainesport †3,236 ... 279,H-4
Hainesville ... 278,A-4
Haledon 6,607 ... 278,C-2
Halsey ... 278,B-4
Hamburg 1,832 ... 278,B-3
Hammonton 12,298 ... 281,E-2
Hampton 1,614 ... 278,D-4
Hampton Lakes ... 279,H-4
Hanover †11,846 ... 278,D-2
Harbourton ... 279,F-4
Hardistonville ... 278,B-3
Harlingen ... 279,E-3
Harmony †2,592 ... 278,D-5
Harrington Park 4,532 ... 278,C-1
Harrison 12,242 ... 278,D-1
Harrisonville ... 280,C-2
Hartford ... 279,H-4
Harvey Cedars 363 ... 281,H-2
Hasbrouck Hts. 12,166 ... 278,C-1
Haskell ... 278,B-2
Haworth 3,509 ... 278,C-1
Hawthorne 18,200 ... 278,C-1
Hazlet †23,013 ... 279,E-2
Hedding ... 279,G-4
Hedger House ... 281,F-1
Helmetta 955 ... 279,F-3
Herbertsville ... 279,G-1
Hermon ... 281,F-2
Hesstown ... 281,E-3
Hewitt ... 278,B-2
Hibernia ... 278,C-3
High Bridge 3,435 ... 278,D-4
Highland Park 13,396 ... 279,E-3
Highlands 5,187 ... 279,F-1
Hightstown 4,581 ... 279,F-3
Hillsdale 10,495 ... 278,B-1
Hillside ... 278,D-2
Hoboken 42,460 ... 278,D-1
Ho-Ho-Kus 4,129 ... 278,C-1
Holly Park ... 279,H-1
Holmdel †8,447 ... 279,F-2
Holmeson ... 279,G-3
Hopatcong 15,531 ... 278,C-3
Hope †1,468 ... 278,C-5
Hopewell 2,001 ... 279,F-4
Hornerstown ... 279,G-3
Howell 25,065 ... 279,G-2
Hurdtown ... 278,C-3
Hurffville ... 280,D-1
Imlaystown ... 279,G-3
Indian Mills ... 281,F-1
Interlaken 1,037 ... 279,F-1
Irvington 61,493 ... 278,D-2
Iselin ... 279,E-2
Island Heights 1,575 ... 279,H-1
Jackson †25,644 ... 279,G-2
Jacobstown ... 279,G-3
Jamesburg 4,114 ... 279,F-3
Jefferson ... 280,D-1
Jenkins Neck ... 281,G-2
Jersey City • 223,532 ... 278,D-1
Jerseyville ... 279,F-2
Jobstown ... 279,G-4
Johnsonburg ... 278,C-4
Juliustown ... 279,H-3
Keansburg 10,613 ... 279,E-1
Kearny 35,735 ... 278,D-1
Kendall Park ... 279,E-3
Kenilworth 8,221 ... 278,D-2
Kenvil ... 278,C-3
Keswick Grove ... 279,H-2
Keyport 7,413 ... 279,E-2
Kingston ... 279,F-3
Kinnelon 7,770 ... 278,C-2
Kirbys Mill ... 279,H-4
Kresson ... 281,E-1
Lafayette †1,614 ... 278,B-4
Lakehurst 2,908 ... 279,H-2
Lakeside ... 278,B-2
Lakewood †38,464 ... 279,G-2
Lambertville 4,044 ... 279,F-4
Lamington ... 278,D-4
Lanoka Harbor ... 281,H-1
Larisons Corner ... 279,E-4
Laurel Springs 2,249 ... 281,E-1
Laurence Harbor ... 279,E-2
Lavallette 2,072 ... 279,H-1
Lawnside 3,042 ... 281,E-1
Lawrenceville ... 279,F-4
Layton ... 278,A-4
Lebanon 820 ... 278,D-4
Ledgewood ... 278,C-3
Leeds Point ... 281,G-3
Lenola ... 279,H-5
Leonardo ... 279,E-1
Leonia 8,027 ... 278,C-1
Liberty Corner ... 278,D-3
Lincoln Park 8,806 ... 278,C-2
Lincroft ... 279,F-1
Linden 37,836 ... 278,D-2
Lindenwold 18,196 ... 281,E-1
Linvale ... 279,F-4
Linwood 6,144 ... 281,F-3
Little Silver 5,548 ... 279,F-1
Littleton ... 278,C-3
Livingston †28,040 ... 278,D-2
Loch Arbour 369 ... 279,F-1
Lockwood ... 278,C-4
Lodi 23,956 ... 278,C-1
Long Branch 29,819 ... 279,F-1
Long Valley ... 278,D-4
Longport 1,249 ... 281,G-4
Loveladies ... 281,H-1
Lower Harmony ... 278,D-5
Lumberton †5,236 ... 279,H-4
Lyons ... 278,D-3
Madison 15,357 ... 278,D-2
Magnolia 4,881 ... 281,E-1
Mahwah †12,127 ... 278,B-1
Malaga ... 280,D-2
Manahawkin ... 281,H-2
Manalapan †18,914 ... 279,F-2
Manasquan 5,354 ... 279,G-1
Mansfield Square ... 279,G-4
Mantoloking 433 ... 279,G-1
Mantua †9,193 ... 280,D-1
Manunkachunk ... 278,C-5
Manville 11,278 ... 279,E-3
Maple Shade †20,525 ... 279,H-5
Marcella ... 278,C-3
Margate City 9,179 ... 281,G-3
Marksboro ... 278,C-4
Marlboro †17,560 ... 279,F-2
Marlton ... 279,H-4
Marmora ... 281,F-4
Marshalls Corner ... 279,F-4
Marshallville ... 281,F-4
Martinsville ... 279,E-3
Masonville ... 279,H-4
Matawan 8,837 ... 279,E-2
Maurice River †4,577 ... 281,E-4
Mauricetown ... 281,E-4
Mayetta ... 281,H-2
Mays Landing • ... 281,F-3
Mayville ... 281,E-5
Maywood 9,895 ... 278,C-1
McAfee ... 278,B-3
McKee City ... 281,F-3
Meadowbrook Village ... 279,G-2
Medford †17,471 ... 279,H-4
Medford Lakes 4,958 ... 281,E-1
Mendham 4,899 ... 278,D-3
Mercerville ... 279,F-3
Merchantville 3,972 ... 279,H-5
Metuchen 13,762 ... 279,E-2
Meyersville ... 278,D-3
Mickleton ... 280,D-1
Middle Valley ... 278,D-4
Middlebush ... 279,E-3
Middlesex 13,480 ... 279,E-3
Middletown ... 278,C-3
Middletown †62,574 ... 279,F-1
Midland Park 7,381 ... 278,C-1
Midvale ... 278,B-2
Milford 1,368 ... 279,E-5
Millbrook ... 278,B-5
Millburn ... 278,D-2
Millhurst ... 279,F-2
Millington ... 278,D-3
Millstone 530 ... 279,E-3
Milltown ... 278,D-4
Milltown 7,136 ... 279,E-3
Millville ... 278,A-4
Millville 24,815 ... 281,E-3
Milmay ... 281,E-3
Mine Hill †3,325 ... 278,C-3
Miramar ... 281,F-4
Monmouth Beach 3,318 ... 279,F-1
Monmouth Junction ... 279,F-3
Monroe ... 278,B-3
Monroeville ... 280,D-2
Montague †2,066 ... 278,A-4
Montclair 38,321 ... 278,C-2
Montvale 7,318 ... 278,B-1
Montville †14,290 ... 278,C-2
Moorestown 15,596 ... 279,H-4
Morganville ... 279,F-2
Morris Plains 5,305 ... 278,C-3
Morristown • 16,614 ... 278,D-3
Mount Arlington 4,251 ... 278,C-3
Mount Bethel ... 278,D-3
Mount Ephraim 4,863 ... 279,H-5
Mount Freedom ... 278,C-3
Mount Holly • †10,818 ... 279,H-4
Mount Laurel †17,614 ... 279,H-4
Mount Olive †18,748 ... 278,C-4
Mount Pleasant ... 279,E-5
Mount Rose ... 279,F-4
Mount Royal ... 280,D-1
Mountain Lakes 4,153 ... 278,C-3
Mountain View ... 278,C-2
Montainside 7,118 ... 278,D-2
Mountainville ... 278,D-4
Mullica Hill ... 280,D-1
Murray Hill ... 278,D-2
National Park 3,552 ... 280,D-1
Neptune City 5,276 ... 279,G-1
Nesco ... 281,F-2
Neshanic ... 279,E-4
Neshanic Station ... 279,E-4
Netcong 3,557 ... 278,C-4
New Brunswick • 41,442 ... 279,E-3
New Egypt ... 279,G-3
New Gretna ... 281,G-2
New Hampton ... 278,D-5
New Lisbon ... 279,H-3
New Milford 16,876 ... 278,C-1
New Monmouth ... 279,E-1
New Providence 12,426 ... 278,D-2
New Sharon ... 279,G-3
New Village ... 278,D-5
Newark • 329,248 ... 278,D-1
Newfield 1,563 ... 281,E-2
Newton • 7,748 ... 278,B-4
Nixon ... 279,E-2
Norma ... 280,D-3
Normandy Beach 279,H-1
Normanock ... 278,B-4
North Arlington 16,587 ... 278,D-1
North Beach ... 281,H-2
North Branch ... 279,E-3
North Branch Station ... 279,E-3
North Brunswick †22,220 ... 279,E-3
North Cape May ... 281,E-5
North Church ... 278,B-3
North Haledon 8,177 ... 278,C-2
North Plainfield 19,108 ... 278,D-3
North Wildwood 4,714 ... 281,E-5
Northfield ... 278,D-2
Northfield 7,795 ... 281,F-3
Northvale 5,046 ... 278,B-1
Norwood 4,413 ... 278,B-1
Nutley 28,998 ... 278,C-2
Oak Grove ... 279,E-5
Oakhurst ... 279,F-1
Oakland 13,443 ... 278,B-2
Oaklyn 4,223 ... 279,H-5
Oakville ... 281,F-3
Ocean City 13,949 ... 281,F-4
Ocean Gate 1,385 ... 279,H-1
Ocean View ... 281,F-4
Oceanport 5,888 ... 279,F-1
Oceanville ... 281,G-3
Ogdensburg 2,737 ... 278,B-3
Old Bridge †51,515 ... 279,E-2
Oldwick ... 278,D-4
Ongs Hat ... 279,H-3
Oradell 8,658 ... 278,C-1
Orange 31,136 ... 278,D-2
Ortley Beach ... 279,H-1
Osbornsville ... 279,G-1
Oxford †1,659 ... 278,D-5
Paisley ... 281,F-1
Palisades Park 13,732 ... 278,C-1
Palmyra 7,085 ... 279,H-5
Panther Valley ... 278,C-4
Paramus 26,474 ... 278,C-1
Park Ridge 8,515 ... 278,B-1
Parkertown ... 281,G-2
Parlin ... 279,E-2
Parsippany-Troy Hills †49,868 ... 278,C-3
Passaic 52,463 ... 278,C-1
Paterson • 137,970 ... 278,C-2
Pattenburg ... 278,D-5
Paulina ... 278,C-4
Paulsboro 6,944 ... 280,D-1
Peapack ... 278,D-3
Pellettown ... 278,B-3
Pemberton 1,198 ... 279,H-3
Pennington 2,109 ... 279,F-4
Penns Grove 5,760 ... 280,C-1
Penns Neck ... 279,F-3
Pennsauken †33,775 ... 279,H-5
Pennsville ... 280,C-2
Penny Pot ... 281,E-2
Penwell ... 278,D-4
Pequannock †13,776 ... 278,C-2
Pequest ... 278,C-5
Perth Amboy 38,951 ... 279,E-2
Peters Valley ... 278,B-4
Petersburg ... 281,F-4
Phillipsburg 16,647 ... 278,D-5
Pine Beach 1,796 ... 279,H-1
Pine Brook ... 278,C-2
Pine Hill 8,684 ... 281,E-1
Pinewald ... 279,H-2
Piscataway †42,223 ... 279,E-3
Piscatawaytown ... 279,E-2
Pitman 9,744 ... 280,D-1
Pittstown ... 279,E-5

CONTINUED ON PAGE 281

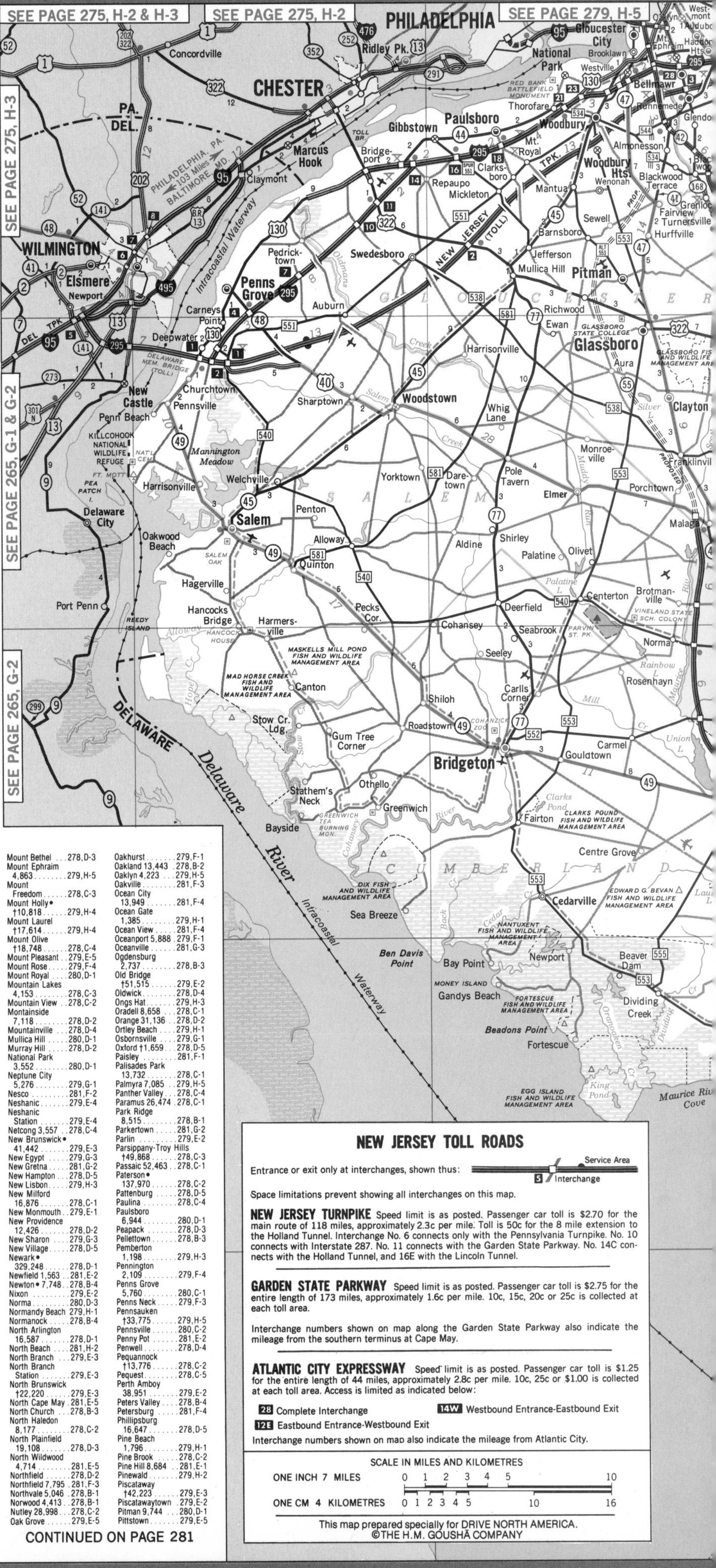

SEE PAGE 275, H-2 & H-3
SEE PAGE 275, H-2
SEE PAGE 279, H-5
SEE PAGE 275, H-3
SEE PAGE 265, G-1 & G-2
SEE PAGE 265, G-2
PHILADELPHIA
Gloucester City
Brooklawn
Westville
National Park
Ridley Pk.
Concordville
CHESTER
PA.
DEL.
Marcus Hook
Claymont
PHILADELPHIA, PA 103 Miles BALTIMORE, MD.
Gibbstown
Paulsboro
Bridgeport
Repaupo
Mickleton
Clarksboro
Thorofare
Woodbury
Mt. Royal
Bellmawr
Runnemede
Almonesson
Woodbury Hts.
Wenonah
Blackwood Terrace
Mantua
Sewell
Fairview
Turnersville
Hurffville
Barnsboro
Jefferson
Mullica Hill
Pitman
WILMINGTON
Elsmere
Newport
Swedesboro
Pedricktown
Penns Grove
Carneys Point
Deepwater
Auburn
Richwood
Ewan
GLASSBORO STATE COLLEGE
Glassboro
Aura
Harrisonville
New Castle
Penn Beach
Churchtown
Pennsville
Sharptown
Woodstown
Whig Lane
Clayton
DELAWARE MEM. BRIDGE (TOLL)
KILLCOHOOK NATIONAL WILDLIFE REFUGE
FT. MOTT
PEA PATCH I.
Delaware City
Mannington Meadow
Welchville
Yorktown
Daretown
Pole Tavern
Elmer
Monroeville
Franklinville
Porchtown
Malaga
Salem
Penton
Alloway
Aldine
Shirley
Palatine
Olivet
Oakwood Beach
Quinton
Hagerville
Port Penn
Hancocks Bridge
Harmersville
Pecks Cor.
Cohansey
Deerfield
Seabrook
Centerton
Brotmanville
VINELAND STATE SCH. COLONY
Norma
Seeley
Rosenhayn
MASKELLS MILL POND FISH AND WILDLIFE MANAGEMENT AREA
MAD HORSE CREEK FISH AND WILDLIFE MANAGEMENT AREA
Canton
Carlls Corner
Shiloh
Stow Cr. Ldg.
Roadstown
Gum Tree Corner
Bridgeton
Carmel
Gouldtown
Othello
Stathem's Neck
Greenwich
Bayside
Fairton
CLARKS POND FISH AND WILDLIFE MANAGEMENT AREA
Centre Grove
DELAWARE
Delaware River
Intracoastal Waterway
DIX FISH AND WILDLIFE MANAGEMENT AREA
Sea Breeze
NANTUXENT FISH AND WILDLIFE MANAGEMENT AREA
Cedarville
EDWARD G. BEVAN FISH AND WILDLIFE MANAGEMENT AREA
Ben Davis Point
Bay Point
Newport
Beaver Dam
MONEY ISLAND
Gandys Beach
FORTESCUE FISH AND WILDLIFE MANAGEMENT AREA
Dividing Creek
Beadons Point
Fortescue
EGG ISLAND FISH AND WILDLIFE MANAGEMENT AREA
King Pond
Maurice River Cove
NEW JERSEY (TOLL)
SALEM
CUMBERLAND
GLOUCESTER

NEW JERSEY TOLL ROADS

Entrance or exit only at interchanges, shown thus: Service Area, 5 Interchange

Space limitations prevent showing all interchanges on this map.

NEW JERSEY TURNPIKE Speed limit is as posted. Passenger car toll is $2.70 for the main route of 118 miles, approximately 2.3c per mile. Toll is 50c for the 8 mile extension to the Holland Tunnel. Interchange No. 6 connects only with the Pennsylvania Turnpike. No. 10 connects with Interstate 287. No. 11 connects with the Garden State Parkway. No. 14C connects with the Holland Tunnel, and 16E with the Lincoln Tunnel.

GARDEN STATE PARKWAY Speed limit is as posted. Passenger car toll is $2.75 for the entire length of 173 miles, approximately 1.6c per mile. 10c, 15c, 20c or 25c is collected at each toll area.

Interchange numbers shown on map along the Garden State Parkway also indicate the mileage from the southern terminus at Cape May.

ATLANTIC CITY EXPRESSWAY Speed limit is as posted. Passenger car toll is $1.25 for the entire length of 44 miles, approximately 2.8c per mile. 10c, 25c or $1.00 is collected at each toll area. Access is limited as indicated below:

28 Complete Interchange — 14W Westbound Entrance-Eastbound Exit

12E Eastbound Entrance-Westbound Exit

Interchange numbers shown on map also indicate the mileage from Atlantic City.

SCALE IN MILES AND KILOMETRES

ONE INCH 7 MILES: 0 1 2 3 4 5 10

ONE CM 4 KILOMETRES: 0 1 2 3 4 5 10 16

This map prepared specially for DRIVE NORTH AMERICA.

©THE H.M. GOUSHĀ COMPANY

A Taste of History, Wilderness and Broadway Glitter

New York

North America's biggest city is wall-to-wall activity. Pulsating with the energy of seven million people and served by the world's largest concentration of museums, restaurants, theaters and shops, **New York (293, G-5)** holds something for every visitor.

Still one of New York's most visible landmarks, the Empire State Building rises 1,472 feet from the street to the top of its television tower. Its 86th- and 102nd-floor observatories command spectacular views of the city and surroundings for a radius of 80 miles. Two of the world's tallest buildings, the twin 110-story towers of the World Trade Center, stand at the foot of Manhattan Island. In 58 seconds, elevators whisk visitors to a 107th-floor observation deck for extraordinary views of the entire metropolitan area.

The seven-block South Street Seaport Museum on the East River was part of a bustling port in the 19th century. Georgian buildings and the boats moored here re-create the atmosphere of the original "Street of Ships." The hub of Greenwich Village is Washington Square, gathering place for musicians, chess players and people-watchers of all kinds. The marble Washington Arch, centerpiece of the Square, was completed in 1895 to commemorate the centenary of George Washington's inauguration.

The Gothic spires of St. Patrick's Cathedral rise 330 feet between Fifth Avenue office towers. A magnificent 9,000-pipe organ and more than 70 stained glass windows grace the great church's interior. Across the street sprawls the 21-building Rockefeller Center. Guided tours take in the RCA Building's 70th-floor Observation Roof, the NBC television studios and a backstage look at Radio City Music Hall—the world's largest theater.

Fifth Avenue is New York's "Museum Row." The Museum of Modern Art, one of the first and finest of its kind, is dedicated to graphic arts and industrial design as well as to painting and sculpture. Major works by Rodin, Cézanne, Matisse and Dali are displayed with photographs by Steichen and mobiles by Calder. The Frick Collection, housed in the 1914 mansion of steel magnate Henry Clay Frick, emphasizes 14th- to 19th-century European paintings by such masters as Titian, Bellini, Rembrandt, Velázquez, Goya and El Greco.

The Metropolitan Museum of Art, on the eastern edge of Central Park, is a vast treasure house of more than three million objects representing the art of 50 centuries. Within the massive, Greek Revival-style building are paintings, drawings and prints, magnificent period rooms, sculpture, 18th- and 19th-century clothing, ancient jewelry and many other forms of decorative art as well as arms, musical instruments, mummies and a museum for children. Farther north on Fifth Avenue, the remarkable architecture of the Solomon R. Guggenheim Museum rivals the art treasures within. The cone-shaped building, designed by Frank Lloyd Wright, houses a quarter-mile, spiraling ramp where 19th- and 20th-century works are displayed.

Millions of minerals, jewels, plants, insects, mammals, fossils and human artifacts fill the 25-acre American Museum of Natural History. Reconstructed dinosaur skeletons and a 60-foot model of a blue whale are among the most popular exhibits; more than 200 display cases present birds and mammals in re-creations of their natural habitats. The adjacent Hayden Planetarium provides a fascinating view of the heavens.

One of the great pleasures of concert-going in New York is to promenade along the corridors of Avery Fisher Hall, where huge windows look out over Lincoln Center Plaza. The vast complex includes the renowned Juilliard School, the 3,800-seat Metropolitan Opera House, the New York State Theater and the Vivian Beaumont Theater, showcase for classical and experimental drama.

Towering above a patch of parkland along the East River is the United Nations—a fitting symbol for an international city. The 18-acre complex includes the glass-and-marble Secretariat, the General Assembly Building, the Conference Building with its famous Security Council Chamber, and the Hammarskjöld Library. One-hour guided tours are conducted in more than 20 languages.

Long Island, densely populated at its western end (the boroughs of Queens and Brooklyn), also abounds with farmland, elegant resort towns and lovely coastal scenery. One way to reach the 120-mile-long island is via the Brooklyn Bridge, the world's first great

*Stirring symbol of America, Lady Liberty (*right*) rises 300 feet above New York Harbor. The American Museum of Immigration circles the base.*

*Central Park (*below*) is New York's oasis of green and one of the world's great parks.*

A Tour of the Middle Ages

The Cloisters is an extraordinary museum of medieval art situated on a bluff high above the Hudson River. Within the cool stone rooms are statues, stained glass windows, frescoed walls, illuminated manuscripts, tomb effigies, altarpieces and magnificent tapestries. A recent acquisition is the 12th-century Bury St. Edmund's altar cross (*below*), carved from a single piece of walrus ivory.

Soaring 133 feet above the East River, the Brooklyn Bridge (above), has a surprisingly airy quality; it seems almost to float from its delicate-looking cables.

The lights of Broadway theaters (left) bathe Times Square in neon.

Wall Street towers (below) frame the Gothic brownstone Trinity Church. Its belfry holds three 18th-century English bells.

suspension bridge. Prospect Park embraces the splendid Brooklyn Botanic Garden with its Fragrance Garden for the Blind, Shakespeare Garden for Children, and Ryoanji Temple Stone Garden, a replica of the 15th-century original in Kyoto, Japan.

On Long Island's north shore lies the historic town of **Oyster Bay (292, A-4)** and Sagamore Hill, Theodore Roosevelt's summer White House from 1901 to 1909. The large North Room is a warm, personal retreat filled with Roosevelt's guns, hunting trophies and mementos. William K. Vanderbilt, Jr.'s 24-room estate in nearby **Centerport (292, B-4)**, now a museum, reflects the flamboyant life-style of its former owner.

The narrow, 32-mile barrier beach of **Fire Island (292, C-5)** is a roadless National Seashore, although a number of summer homes stand at its western end. Soft beaches of quartz and magnetite sand line the Atlantic shore, and the mixed terrain on the bay side is a haven for wildlife. Visitors can reach Sailor's Haven by ferry from Sayville, Watch Hill by ferry from Patchogue. Farther east lie the Hamptons, a string of popular summer resort towns and beaches.

Profits from the lucrative whaling trade built **Sag Harbor (293, E-4)** in the 19th century. Its Suffolk County Whaling Museum, in the 1845 home of whaler Benjamin Huntting, provides a fascinating record of the town's maritime past. In addition to whaling relics, harpoons, tools and logbooks, a superb collection of scrimshaw (whalebone and ivory carvings) can be viewed. The stark coastline of the extreme tip of Long Island at **Montauk Point (293, F-4)** is marked by a 1797 lighthouse. The crashing surf attracts artists and beachcombers; birdwatchers find the point a rewarding sanctuary for seabirds.

North of Manhattan, the New York Zoological Park, commonly called the Bronx Zoo, shelters a variety of animals that range from the familiar to the nearly extinct. Its naturalistic settings rely on deep moats and fenced-in enclosures instead of barred cages. The Children's Zoo has many animals that can be petted, and the remarkable World of Darkness building exhibits nocturnal animals in a simulated nighttime environment. The World of Birds features 25 replicated natural habitats, including desert and jungle settings and a 40-foot waterfall.

Gracious mansions dot both sides of the Hudson River between New York Harbor and Albany. Van Cortlandt Manor in **Croton-on-Hudson (293, H-4)**, begun in the 1680s, is the focal point of a restored estate once owned by one of New York's most influential families. The handsome Dutch manor house boasts many of the original furnishings, including a number of 18th-century family portraits. Author Washington Irving described Sunnyside, his home in **Tarrytown (293, H-4)**, as a "little old-fashioned stone mansion, all made up of gable ends, and as full of angles as an old cocked hat." Monument to a celebrity of a different sort, nearby Lyndhurst was the palatial estate of financier and "robber baron" Jay Gould. Intricate woodwork and marble fireplaces decorate the rooms; the stained glass windows are believed to be the work of Louis C. Tiffany.

Franklin D. Roosevelt spent much of his life in the comfortable 30-room mansion in **Hyde Park (293, G-2)** where he was born in 1882. Visitors can listen to a 30-minute "tape talk" by Mrs. Roosevelt describing the bedrooms, the living room, Dresden Room, dining room and private office. In the Roosevelt Library are ship models, naval prints, paintings, documents and the President's Room, scene of radio broadcasts and wartime talks with Allied leaders. Down the road, the Beaux Art-style Vanderbilt Mansion cost more than $2 million to decorate and furnish when it was built in 1896–98.

Farther up the Hudson near **Rhinebeck (293, H-2)** is the Old Rhinebeck Aerodrome, with its unique collection of antique aircraft. Visitors can enjoy air shows and "dogfights," or ride in an open-cockpit biplane. Fire-fighting apparatus from 1725 to 1926 is part of the unique collection at the American Museum of Fire Fighting in **Hudson (291, G-4)**. There is also a large art gallery featuring oil paintings, prints and the memorable folk art carving, *The Statue of a Fire Chief*.

Between the Hudson and the Delaware River to the west rise the 3,000 square-mile Catskill Mountains. Slide Mountain, near the center of **Catskill State Park (291, F-5)**, overlooks a splendid tapestry of peaks, valleys, lakes, rivers and waterfalls. Hiking trails and historic homes are the charms of **Hunter (291, G-4)**, where four ethnic festivals are held each year. **Woodstock (291, G-5)**, nestled in the mountains to the south, is a thriving center for artists, writers and musicians.

Kingston (293, G-2) was the first capital of New York State. The first State Senate (which adjourned hastily when it learned that a British force was approaching to burn the city) met in the Senate House (1676), now a museum. Kingston's Old Dutch Church serves one of the oldest congregations (founded in 1659) in the United States. In the churchyard lies George Clinton, first governor of New York, along with the graves of Revolutionary War patriots.

Albany (291, G-3), the state capital, is the oldest continuous settlement of the original 13 colonies (1624), and the site of the futuristic marble-and-glass Governor Nelson A. Rockefeller Empire State Plaza. The striking 12-building complex is as impressive as its name and includes a 44-story skyscraper with an observation deck, the bowl-shaped Performing Arts Center, and scores of fountains, reflecting pools and promenades. In striking contrast is the Romanesque-style New York State Capitol, completed in 1899. It took 13 years to complete the stone Million Dollar Staircase, where sculpted heads of 77 noted state and national figures are grouped with imps and angels. The ornate senate is considered one of the world's most beautiful legislative chambers.

From the late 1800s **Saratoga Springs (291, G-2)** was a magnet for wealthy devotees of thoroughbred racing, casino gambling and mineral water springs. Horse racing remains one of its main attractions and mineral baths can still be enjoyed at the bountiful Saratoga Spa State Park, along with golf, tennis and swimming. The Saratoga Performing Arts Center, summer home of the New York City Ballet, the Philadelphia Orchestra and the Spa Summer Theater, is also in the park. Bronze statues, stained glass and elegant furniture in the Casino (1871) recall its Victorian heyday. The "sport of kings" is celebrat-

ed in the National Museum of Racing with paintings, trophies, racing colors and sculptures of champions past and present.

Thirty miles long and dotted with nearly 200 tree-covered islands, **Lake George (291, G-1)** lies in the heavily wooded foothills of the Adirondack Mountains. The mountainous area between Bolton Landing and Hague is one of the most attractive stretches of its shoreline. Reconstructed Fort William Henry was originally built in 1755 by the British as a springboard for attacks against the French. To the north, Fort Carillon was raised by the French the same year, captured by the British in 1759, and renamed **Fort Ticonderoga (289, G-4)**. The superb reconstruction includes ramparts, bastions and barracks.

Lake Placid (289, F-3) has long been noted for winter and summer sports and for the many hiking trails through the rugged Adi-

rondack country. Memorial Highway climbs to the top of Whiteface Mountain, with its view of all 46 of the Adirondack High Peaks (those higher than 4,000 feet). These mountains are the roots of the oldest geological formations in North America; avalanche scars and rockslides mark their faces.

Where Lake Ontario meets the great St. Lawrence, the Thousand Islands crowd the waters in myriad shapes and sizes. Sightseeing boats leave from **Alexandria Bay (288, B-3)**, **Clayton** and several other river towns. An unusual attraction is Boldt Castle, a replica of a German Rhineland castle intended as a gift from a wealthy hotel owner to his fiancée. The castle was left unfinished after her sudden death in 1904. The Remington Art Museum in **Ogdensburg (288, C-2)** holds the world's largest collection of Frederic Remington's paintings, bronzes and sketches of the Old West. At the Erie Canal Village in

Like a set from a science-fiction movie, futuristic Rockefeller Empire State Plaza (above) crowns the skyline of Albany.

A stream draining into Seneca Lake has carved the chasm of Watkins Glen (right). The water here drops 600 feet in 1½ miles.

Treasures of Photography

The former home of George Eastman, father of modern photography, houses the International Museum of Photography at Rochester. The front of the museum is furnished much as it was when Eastman lived there (1905–1932), with antiques, books and paintings from his collection of Old Masters. Galleries throughout the rest of the house are filled with photographs and apparatus from the early daguerreotype era (1840s) to the present. A Giroux daguerreotype camera (circa 1839) and an Edison kinetoscope are two of the museum's treasures. The institution also owns major works by three renowned American photographers: Alvin Langdon Coburn, Lewis Hine and Edward Steichen. The adjacent Dryden Theater presents rare films from the museum's collection.

Hot-air balloons (above) make a splash of color in the sky above Glens Falls.

Boscobel (left), an 1808 mansion high above the Hudson River in Garrison, embodies the neoclassic ideas of Scottish architect Robert Adam, who contributed much to the development of American architecture. The house is now a museum furnished with English and American antiques. The grounds too are kept in an early 18th-century manner with herb, vegetable and flower gardens, brick paths, a "necessary" (privy), springhouses (used to keep dairy products cool) and gatehouse.

Rome (290, D-2) visitors can walk through the reconstructed village where canal digging began in 1817, or ride an 1840 horse-drawn packet boat along a section of the original waterway.

Cooperstown (291, E-3)—the "Village of Museums"—was founded in 1786 by the father of America's first novelist, James Fenimore Cooper. The bats, balls, gloves and uniforms of baseball's greatest heroes are enshrined in the National Baseball Hall of Fame here, where Abner Doubleday is believed to have invented the game in 1839. Exhibits of farming tools and methods in the Farmer's Museum bring to life rural America of the late 18th and early 19th centuries. A dozen buildings gathered from the surrounding countryside form a typical early rural community. Fenimore House, an imposing 1932 mansion overlooking Otsego Lake, contains an outstanding collection of folk art, paintings, sculptures and literary artifacts.

Corning (290, A-4), a southern gateway to the scenic Finger Lakes region, is also a world-famous glassmaking city. The Corning Glass Center presents the 3,000-year history of glass through its museum, science hall and Steuben factory, where visitors can watch craftsmen create magnificent pieces of cut, blown and etched glass. **Hammondsport (287, H-4)** is the commercial center of the state's wine industry. Taylor, Great Western and other wineries offer tours and tastings.

All of New York's Finger Lakes have their attractions, but **Cayuga Lake (290, A-3)**, with its sinuous, hilly shoreline and scenic highway, is one of the most striking. At the lake's southern end near **Ithaca (290, B-4)**, Taughannock Falls plummets 215 feet—33 feet more than Niagara.

New York's "Grand Canyon" is Genesee Gorge, a 600-foot sandstone gash and three waterfalls carved by the Genesee River. **Letchworth State Park (287, F-3)** contains the most spectacular stretch of the gorge. **Allegany State Park (287, E-4)** is the state's largest: 65,000 acres of unspoiled forests and lakes. The Chautauqua Institution, near the head of sparkling **Chautauqua Lake (286, C-4)**, was founded in 1874 as a center for religion, education and the arts. This internationally known resort attracts thousands of visitors to its courses and exhibitions.

Other waterfalls are higher, but none has the sheer grandeur and mesmerizing force of **Niagara Falls (286, D-2)**. The cascading waters of American, Bridal Veil and Horseshoe falls are spectacular by day. By night, bathed in a rainbow of lights, they are even more impressive. Visitors can experience the spectacle close-up by donning oilskins and riding the *Maid of the Mist*, or by exploring the walkways below Prospect Point and Goat Island. Other attractions in the area include the Native American Center for the Living Arts, the Schoellkopf Geological Museum, and Old Fort Niagara, built by French colonists in 1726.

Nearby **Buffalo (287, E-2)**, the second largest city in the state, is an industrial center and one of the Great Lakes' busiest ports. Five thousand years of art are represented in the Albright-Knox Art Gallery, with works by Degas, Rodin, Matisse and Picasso. The Buffalo Museum of Science, a favorite with children, has beautiful ancient Chinese ceramics, examples of African art, a dinosaur skeleton and Egyptian mummies.

New York

SCALE IN MILES AND KILOMETRES

ONE INCH 12 MILES 0 5 10 20

ONE CM 8 KILOMETRES 0 5 10 20 32

This map prepared specially for DRIVE NORTH AMERICA.

©THE H.M. GOUSHĀ COMPANY

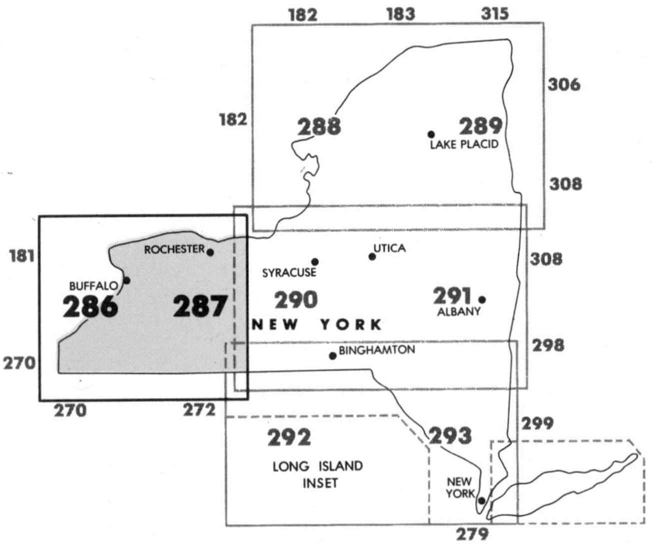
182
183
315
306
182
288
289
LAKE PLACID
308
181
ROCHESTER
SYRACUSE
UTICA
308
BUFFALO
286
287
290
291
ALBANY
NEW YORK
BINGHAMTON
298
270
270
272
292
293
299
LONG ISLAND INSET
NEW YORK
279

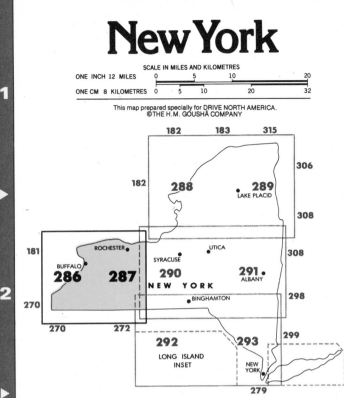

INDEX TO COUNTIES

Pop. (1980) 17,557,288 Area 49,576 Sq. Mi.

County	County Seat
Albany	Albany
Allegany	Belmont
Bronx	Bronx
Broome	Binghamton
Cattaraugus	Little Valley
Cayuga	Auburn
Chautauqua	Mayville
Chemung	Elmira
Chenango	Norwich
Clinton	Plattsburgh
Columbia	Hudson
Cortland	Cortland
Delaware	Delhi
Dutchess	Poughkeepsie
Erie	Buffalo
Essex	Elizabethtown
Franklin	Malone
Fulton	Johnstown
Genesee	Batavia
Greene	Catskill
Hamilton	Lake Pleasant
Herkimer	Herkimer
Jefferson	Watertown
Kings	Brooklyn
Lewis	Lowville
Livingston	Geneseo
Madison	Wampsville
Monroe	Rochester
Montgomery	Fonda
Nassau	Mineola
New York	New York
Niagara	Lockport
Oneida	Utica
Onondaga	Syracuse
Ontario	Canandaigua
Orange	Goshen
Orleans	Albion
Oswego	Oswego
Otsego	Cooperstown
Putnam	Carmel
Queens	Jamaica
Rensselaer	Troy
Richmond	St. George
Rockland	New City
St. Lawrence	Canton
Saratoga	Ballston Spa
Schenectady	Schenectady
Schoharie	Schoharie
Schuyler	Watkins Glen
Seneca	Waterloo
Steuben	Bath
Suffolk	Riverhead
Sullivan	Monticello
Tioga	Owego
Tompkins	Ithaca
Ulster	Kingston
Warren	Lake George
Washington	Hudson Falls
Wayne	Lyons
Westchester	White Plains
Wyoming	Warsaw
Yates	Penn Yan

PARTIAL LIST OF

CITIES AND TOWNS

1980 Census

• County Seats

Adams 1,701 .... 228,B-4
Addison 2,028 .... 287,H-4
Afton 982 .... 290,D-4
Akron 2,971 .... 287E-2
Albany• 101,727 .... 291,G-3
Albion• 4,897 .... 287,F-1
Alden 2,488 .... 287,E-2
Alexandria Bay 1,265 .... 288,B-3
Alfred 4,967 .... 287,G-4
Allegany 2,078 .... 287,E-4
Altamont 1,292 .... 291,G-3
Amityville 9,076 .... 292,B-5
Amsterdam 21,872 .... 291,G-2
Andover 1,120 .... 287,G-4
Angelica 982 .... 287,F-4
Angola 2,292 .... 286,D-3
Antwerp 749 .... 288,C-3
Arcade 2,052 .... 287,F-3
Ardsley 4,183 .... 292,A-4
Arkport 811 .... 287,G-4
Arlington 293,H-2
Athens 1,738 .... 291,G-4
Atlantic Beach 1,775 .... 293,H-5
Attica 2,659 .... 287,F-2
Auburn• 32,548 .... 290,B-2
Aurora 926 .... 290,B-3
Avoca 1,144 .... 287,H-4
Avon 3,006 .... 287,G-2
Babylon 12,388 .... 292,B-5
Bainbridge 1,603 .... 290,D-4
Baldwin 292,A-5
Baldwinsville 6,446 .... 290,B-2
Ballston Spa• 4,711 .... 291,G-2
Batavia• 16,703 .... 287,F-2
Bath• 6,042 .... 287,H-4
Bay Shore 292,B-5
Bayville 7,034 .... 292,H4-A4
Beacon 12,937 .... 292,G-3
Bellmore 292,A-5
Bellport 2,809 .... 292,C-5
Belmont• 1,024 .... 287,F-4
Bergen 976 .... 287,G-2
Bethpage 292,B-5
Binghamton• 55,860 .... 292,C-1
Black River 1,384 .... 288,C-4
Blasdell 3,288 .... 287,E-2
Bolivar 1,345 .... 287,F-4
Boonville 2,344 .... 290,D-1
Brentwood 292,B-5
Brewster 1,650 .... 293,H-3
Briarcliff Manor 7,115 .... 292,A-3
Brightwaters 3,286 .... 292,B-5
Broadalbin 1,415 .... 291,G-2
Brockport 9,776 .... 287,G-1
Brocton 1,416 .... 286,C-4
Bronx• (Part of N.Y. City) 1,169,115 .... 293,H-5
Bronxville 6,267 .... 292,A-4
Brooklyn• (Part of N.Y. City) 2,230,936 .... 293,H-5
Brownville 1,099 .... 288,B-4
Buchanan 2,041 .... 293,H-3
Buffalo• 357,870 .... 287,E-2
Galedonia 2,188 .... 287,G-2
Cambridge 1,820 .... 291,H-2
Camden 2,667 .... 290,C-1
Camillus 1,298 .... 290,B-2
Canajoharie 2,412 .... 291,F-2
Canandaigua• 10,419 .... 287,H-2
Canastota 4,773 .... 290,C-2
Candor 917 .... 290,B-4
Canisteo 2,679 .... 287,G-4
Canton• 7,055 .... 288,D-2
Carmel• 293,H-3
Carthage 3,643 .... 288,C-4
Cassadaga 821 .... 286,D-4
Castile 1,135 .... 287,F-3
Castleton-on-Hudson 1,627 .... 291,H-3
Catskill• 4,718 .... 291,G-4
Cattaraugus 1,200 .... 287,E-4
Cayuga Heights 3,170 .... 290,B-4
Cazenovia 2,599 .... 290,C-2
Cedarhurst 6,162 .... 292,A-5
Celoron 1,405 .... 286,D-4
Center Moriches 292,C-5
Centereach 292,C-4
Central Islip 292,B-5
Central Square 1,418 .... 290,C-1
Chateaugay 869 .... 289,F-1
Chatham 2,001 .... 291,H-4
Chester 1,910 .... 293,G-3
Chittenango 4,290 .... 290,C-2
Churchville 1,399 287,G-2
Clarence 287,E-2
Clark Mills 290,D-2
Clayton 1,816 .... 288,B-3
Cleveland 855 .... 290,C-2
Clifton Springs 2,039 .... 287,H-2
Clinton 2,107 .... 290,D-2
Clyde 2,491 .... 290,A-2
Cobleskill 5,272 .... 291,F-3
Cohocton 902 .... 287,G-3
Cohoes 18,144 .... 291,H-3
Cold Spring 2,161 .... 293,G-3
Cold Spring Harbor 292,B-4
Colonie 291,G-3
Commack 292,B-4
Cooperstown• 2,342 .... 291,E-3
Copiague 292,B-5
Corinth 2,702 .... 291,G-2
Corning 12,953 .... 290,A-4
Cornwall 293,G-3
Cornwall on the Hudson 3,164 .... 293,G-3
Cortland• 20,138 .... 290,C-3
Coxsackie 2,786 .... 291,G-4
Croghan 703 .... 288,C-4
Croton-on-Hudson 6,889 .... 293,H-4
Cuba 1,739 .... 287,F-4
Dannemora 3,770 .... 289,G-2
Dansville 4,979 .... 287,G-3
Deer Park 292,B-5
Delevan 1,113 .... 287,E-3
Delhi• 3,374 .... 291,E-4
Depew 19,819 .... 287,E-2
Deposit 1,897 .... 292,D-1
Dexter 1,053 .... 288,B-4
Dobbs Ferry 10,053 .... 293,H-4
Dolgeville 2,602 .... 291,E-2
Dryden 1,761 .... 290,B-4
Dundee 1,556 .... 290,A-4
Dunkirk 15,310 .... 286,D-3
Earlville 985 .... 290,D-3
East Aurora 6,803 .... 287,E-3
East Hampton 1,886 .... 293,E-4
East Hills 7,160 .... 292,A-5
East Islip 292,B-5
East Meadow 292,A-5
East Moriches 292,D-4
East Northport 292,B-4
East Patchogue 292,C-5
East Rochester 7,596 .... 287,G-2
East Rockaway 10,917 .... 292,H5-A5
East Syracuse 3,412 .... 290,C-2
Eden 287,E-3
Elbridge 1,099 .... 290,B-2
Elizabethtown• 659 .... 289,G-3
Ellenville 4,405 .... 293,G-2
Ellicottville 713 .... 287,E-4
Elmira• 35,327 .... 290,A-5
Elmira Heights 4,279 .... 290,A-5
Elmsford 3,361 .... 292,H4-A4
Endicott 14,457 .... 290,C-5
Endwell 290,C-5
Fair Haven 976 .... 290,A-1
Fairmount 290,C-2
Fairport 5,970 .... 287,H-2
Fairview 293,G-2
Falconer 2,778 .... 286,D-4
Farmingdale 7,946 .... 292,B-5
Fayetteville 4,709 .... 290,C-2
Fishkill 1,555 .... 293,H-3
Flanders 292,D-4
Floral Park 16,805 .... 292,A-5
Florida 1,947 .... 293,G-3
Flower Hill 4,558 .... 292,A-4
Fonda• 1,006 .... 291,F-2
Forestville 804 .... 286,D-3
Fort Covington 289,E-1
Fort Edward 3,561 .... 291,H-1
Fort Plain 2,555 .... 291,F-2
Frankfort 2,995 .... 291,E-2
Franklin Square 292,A-5
Franklinville 1,887 .... 287,E-4
Fredonia 11,126 .... 286,D-3
Freeport 38,272 .... 292,H5-A5
Freetown 293,E-4
Frewsburg 286,D-4
Friendship 287,F-4
Fulton 13,312 .... 290,B-1
Fultonville 777 .... 291,F-2
Garden City 22,927 .... 292,A-5
Geneseo• 6,746 .... 287,G-2
Geneva 15,133 .... 290,A-3
Glen Cove 24,618 .... 292,H4-A4
Glens Falls 15,897 .... 291,H-1
Glenpark 504 .... 288,B-4
Gloversville 17,836 .... 291,F-2
Goshen• 4,874 .... 293,G-3
Gouverneur 4,285 .... 288,C-3
Gowanda 2,713 .... 286,D-3
Granville 2,696 .... 291,H-1
Great Neck 9,168 .... 292,H5-A5
Great Neck Estates 2,936 .... 292,A-5
Green Island 2,696 .... 291,H-3
Greene 1,747 .... 290,C-4
Greenlawn 292,B-4
Greenport 2,273 .... 293,E-3
Greenwich 1,955 .... 291,H-2
Greenwood Lake 2,809 .... 293,G-4
Groton 2,313 .... 290,B-3
Hagaman 1,331 .... 291,G-2
Hamburg 10,582 .... 287,E-3
Hamilton 3,725 .... 290,D-3
Hammondsport 1,065 .... 287,H-4
Hampton Bays 292,D-4
Hancock 1,526 .... 293,E-2
Harriman 796 .... 293,G-3
Harrison 23,046 .... 292,H4-A4
Harrisville 937 .... 288,D-3
Hartsdale 292,A-4
Haverstraw 8,800 .... 293,G-4
Hempstead 40,404 .... 292,H5-A5
Herkimer• 8,383 .... 291,E-2
Herrings 170 .... 288,C-4
Hicksville 292,A-5
Highland 293,G-2
Highland Falls 4,187 .... 293,G-3
Hilton 4,151 .... 287,G-1
Holbrook 292,C-5
Holcomb 952 .... 287,H-2
Holley 1,882 .... 287,F-1
Homer 3,635 .... 290,C-3
Honeoye Falls 2,410 .... 287,G-2
Hoosick Falls 3,609 .... 291,H-2
Hornell 10,234 .... 287,G-4
Horseheads 7,348 .... 290,A-4
Hudson• 7,986 .... 291,G-4
Hudson Falls• 7,419 .... 291,H-1
Huntington 292,B-4
Huntington Bay 3,943 .... 292,B-4
Huntington Station 292,B-4
Hyde Park 293,G-2
Ilion 9,190 .... 291,E-2
Inwood 292,A-5
Irvington 5,774 .... 293,H-4
Island Park 4,847 .... 292,A-5
Ithaca• 28,732 .... 290,B-4
Jamaica• (N.Y. City) 292,H5-A5
Jamestown 35,775 .... 286,D-4
Jericho 292,H5-A5
Johnson City 17,126 .... 290,C-5
Johnstown• 9,360 .... 291,F-2
Jordan 1,371 .... 290,B-2
Keeseville 2,025 .... 289,G-2
Kenmore 18,474 .... 287,E-2
Kinderhook 1,377 .... 291,H-4
Kings Park 292,B-4
Kings Point 5,234 .... 292,A-4
Kingston• 24,481 .... 293,G-2
Lackawanna 22,701 .... 287,E-2
Lake Carmel 293,H-3
Lake George• 1,047 .... 291,G-1
Lake Grove 9,692 .... 292,C-4
Lake Placid 2,490 .... 289,F-3
Lake Pleasant• 291,F-1
Lake Success 2,396 .... 292,A-5
Lakewood 3,941 .... 286,D-4
Lancaster 13,056 .... 287,E-2
Larchmont 6,308 .... 292,H4-A4
Lattingtown 1,749 .... 292,A-4
Lawrence 6,175 .... 292,H5-A5
Le Roy 4,900 .... 287,F-2
Levitown 292,H5-A5
Lewiston 3,326 .... 286,D-1
Liberty 4,293 .... 293,F-2
Lima 2,025 .... 287,G-2
Lindenhurst 26,919 .... 292,B-5
Little Falls 6,156 .... 291,E-2
Little Valley• 1,203 .... 287,E-4
Liverpool 2,849 .... 290,B-2
Livingston Manor 293,F-2
Livonia 1,238 .... 287,G-2
Lloyd Harbor 3,405 .... 292,B-4
Lockport• 24,844 .... 287,E-1
Long Beach 34,073 .... 292,H5-A5
Lowville• 3,364 .... 288,C-4
Lynbrook 20,431 .... 292,H5-A5
Lyndonville 916 .... 287,F-1
Lyons• 4,160 .... 290,A-2
Lyons Falls 755 .... 288,C-5
Macedon 1,400 .... 287,H-2
Mahopac 293,H-3
Malone• 7,668 .... 289,F-1
Malverne 9,262 .... 292,A-5
Mamaroneck 17,616 .... 292,H4-A4
Manchester 1,698 .... 287,H-2
Manhasset 292,H5-A5
Manhattan (Part of N.Y. City) 1,427,533 .... 293,G-5
Manlius 5,241 .... 290,C-2
Marathon 1,046 .... 290,C-4
Marcellus 1,870 .... 290,B-2
Margaretville 755 .... 291,F-4
Marlboro 293,G-3
Massapequa 292,B-5
Massapequa Park 19,779 .... 292,B-5
Massena 12,851 .... 288,D-1
Mastic Beach 292,C-5
Mattituck 292,D-4
Maybrook 2,007 .... 293,G-3
Mayfield 944 .... 291,F-2
Mayville• 1,626 .... 286,C-4
Mechanicville 5,500 .... 291,H-2
Medina 6,392 .... 287,F-1
Mennands 4,012 .... 291,H-3
Merrick 292,A-5
Mexico 1,621 .... 290,B-1
Middleburgh 1,358 .... 291,F-3
Middleport 1,995 .... 287,E-1
Middletown 21,454 .... 293,F-3
Millbrook 1,343 .... 293,H-2
Millerton 1,013 .... 293,H-2
Mineola• 20,757 .... 292,A-5
Mineville 289,G-3
Mohawk 2,956 .... 291,E-2
Monroe 5,996 .... 293,G-3
Montgomery 2,316 .... 293,G-3
Monticello• 6,306 .... 293,F-2
Montour Falls 1,791 .... 290,A-4
Moravia 1,582 .... 290,B-3
Morrisville 2,707 .... 290,D-3
Mount Kisco 8,025 .... 292,H4-A3
Mount Morris 3,039 .... 287,G-3
Mount Vernon 66,713 .... 293,H-4
Naples 1,225 .... 287,H-3
Nassau 1,285 .... 291,H-3
Nesconset 292,B-4
New Berlin 1,392 .... 290,D-3
New City• 293,G-4
New Hartford 2,313 .... 290,D-2
New Hyde Park 9,801 .... 292,H5-A5
New Paltz 4,941 .... 293,G-2
New Rochelle 70,794 .... 292,H4-A4
New York• 7,071,030 .... 293,G-5
Newark 10,017 .... 290,A-2
Newark Valley 1,190 .... 290,C-4
Newburgh 23,438 .... 293,G-3
Newfane 287,E-1
Newport 746 .... 291,E-2
Niagara Falls 71,384 .... 286,D-2
Norfolk 288,D-2
North Bellmore 292,A-5
North Collins 1,496 .... 286,D-3
North Hornell 813 .... 287,G-4
North Syracuse 7,970 .... 290,C-2
North Tonawanda 35,760 .... 287,E-2
Nortport 7,651 .... 292,B-4
Norwich• 8,082 .... 290,D-4
Norwood 1,902 .... 288,D-2
Nunda 1,169 .... 287,G-3
Nyack 6,428 .... 293,H-4
Oakfield 1,791 .... 287,F-2
Oceanside 292,A-5
Ogdensburg 12,375 .... 288,C-2
Olcott 287,E-1
Old Field 829 .... 292,C-4
Olean 18,207 .... 287,E-4
Oneida 10,810 .... 290,D-2
Oneonta 14,933 .... 291,E-4
Orchard Park 3,671 .... 287,E-3
Oriskany 1,680 .... 290,D-2
Oriskany Falls 802 .... 290,D-2
Ossining 20,196 .... 293,H-4
Oswego• 19,793 .... 290,B-1
Otego 1,089 .... 291,E-4
Otisville 953 .... 293,F-3
Ovid 666 .... 290,A-3
Owego• 1,765 .... 290,B-5
Oxford 1,765 .... 290,D-4
Oyster Bay Cove 1,799 .... 292,H4-A4
Painted Post 2,196 .... 287,H-4
Palmyra 3,729 .... 287,H-2
Patchogue 11,291 .... 292,C-5
Pawling 1,996 .... 293,H-3
Peekskill 18,236 .... 293,H-3
Pelham 6,848 .... 292,A-4
Pelham Manor 6,130 .... 292,A-4
Penn Yan• 5,242 .... 290,A-3
Perry 4,198 .... 287,F-3
Phelps 2,004 .... 290,A-2
Philadelphia 855 .... 288,C-3
Philmont 1,539 .... 291,H-4
Phoenix 2,357 .... 290,B-2
Pine Bush 293,G-3
Pittsford 1,568 .... 287,G-2
Plainview 292,B-5
Plattsburgh• 21,057 .... 289,G-2
Pleasantville 6,749 .... 292,A-3
Port Byron 1,400 .... 290,B-2
Port Chester 23,565 .... 292,H4-A4
Port Henry 1,450 .... 289,G-4
Port Jefferson 6,731 .... 292,C-4
Port Jefferson Station 292,C-4
Port Jervis 8,699 .... 293,F-3
Port Leyden 740 .... 288,C-5
Port Washington 292,H5-A4
Portville 1,136 .... 287,F-4
Potsdam 10,365 .... 288,D-2
Poughkeepsie• 29,757 .... 293,H-2
Pulaski• 2,415 .... 288,B-5
Queens (Part of N.Y. City) 1,891,325 .... 293,H-5
Quogue 966 .... 292,D-5
Randolph 1,398 .... 286,D-4
Ravena 3,091 .... 291,G-4
Red Hook 1,692 .... 293,H-1
Rensselaer 9,047 .... 291,H-3
Rhinebeck 2,542 .... 293,H-2
Richfield Springs 1,561 .... 291,E-3
Richmondville 792 .... 291,F-3
Ripley 286,C-4
Riverhead• 292,D-4
Rochester• 241,741 .... 287,G-1
Rockville Centre 25,405 .... 292,H5-A5
Rome• 43,826 .... 290,D-2
Ronkonkoma 292,C-5
Roosevelt 292,A-5
Rosendale 293,G-2
Roslyn 2,134 .... 292,A-5
Rotterdam 291,G-3
Rouses Point 2,266 .... 289,G-1
Rye 15,083 .... 292,H4-A4
Sackets Harbor 1,017 .... 288,B-4
Sag Harbor 2,581 .... 293,E-4
St. George• (Part of N.Y. City) 293,H-5
St. James 292,B-4
St. Johnsville 2,019 .... 291,F-2
Salamanca 6,890 .... 287,E-4
Salem 959 .... 291,H-2
San Remo 292,B-4
Sands Point 2,742 .... 292,A-4
Saranac Lake 5,578 .... 289,F-3
Saratoga Springs 23,906 .... 291,G-2
Saugerties 3,882 .... 291,G-5
Savona 932 .... 287,H-4
Sayville 292,C-5
Scarsdale 17,650 .... 292,A-4
Schaghticoke 677 .... 291,H-2
Schenectady• 67,972 .... 291,G-3
Schoharie• 1,016 .... 291,F-3
Schuylerville 1,256 .... 291,H-2
Scotia 7,280 .... 291,G-3
Scottsville 1,789 .... 287,G-2
Sea Cliff 5,364 .... 292,A-4
Selden 292,C-4
Seneca Falls 7,466 .... 290,A-2
Setauket 292,C-4
Sherburne 1,561 .... 290,D-3
Sherman 775 .... 286,C-4
Sherrill 2,830 .... 290,D-2
Shortsville 1,669 .... 287,H-2
Sidney 4,861 .... 290,D-4
Silver Creek 3,088 .... 286,D-3
Silver Springs 801 .... 287,F-3
Sinclairville 772 .... 286,D-4
Skaneateles 2,789 .... 290,B-2
Sloan 4,529 .... 287,E-2
Sloatsburg 3,154 .... 293,G-4
Sodus 1,790 .... 290,A-2
Sodus Point 1,334 .... 290,A-2
Solvay 7,140 .... 290,B-2
South Corning 1,195 .... 290,A-5
South Fallsburgh 293,F-2
South Glens Falls 3,714 .... 291,H-1
South Huntington 292,B-4
Southampton 4,000 .... 293,E-4
Southold 293,E-4
Spencer 863 .... 290,B-4
Spencerport 3,424 .... 287,G-1
Springville 4,285 .... 287,E-3
Stamford 1,240 .... 291,F-4
Staten Island (Part of N.Y. City) 352,121 .... 293,G-5
Stillwater 1,572 .... 291,H-2
Stony Brook 292,B-4
Stony Point 293,G-4
Stottville 291,H-4
Suffern 10,794 .... 293,G-4
Sylvan Beach 1,243 .... 290,C-2
Syracuse• 170,105 .... 290,C-2
Tarrytown 10,648 .... 293,H-4
Theresa 827 .... 288,C-3
Ticonderoga 2,938 .... 289,G-4
Tonawanda 18,693 .... 287,E-2
Troy• 56,638 .... 291,H-3
Trumansburg 1,722 .... 290,B-3
Tuckahoe 6,076 .... 292,A-4
Tully 1,049 .... 290,C-3
Tupper Lake 14,478 .... 289,E-3
Tuxedo Park 809 .... 293,G-4
Unadilla 1,367 .... 290,D-4
Union Springs 1,201 .... 290,B-3
Utica• 75,632 .... 291,E-2
Valatie 1,492 .... 291,H-4
Valley Stream 35,769 .... 292,H5-A5
Vernon 1,373 .... 290,D-2
Vernon Valley 292,B-4
Victor 2,370 .... 287,H-2
Voorheesville 3,320 .... 291,G-3
Waddington 980 .... 288,D-1
Walden 5,659 .... 293,G-3
Wallkill 293,G-3
Walton 3,329 .... 291,E-4
Wampsville• 569 .... 290,C-2
Wantagh 292,B-5
Wappingers Falls 5,110 .... 293,H-3
Warrensburg 291,G-1
Warsaw• 3,619 .... 287,F-3
Warwick 4,320 .... 293,G-3
Washingtonville 2,380 .... 293,G-3
Waterford 2,405 .... 291,H-3
Waterloo• 5,303 .... 290,A-3
Watertown• 27,861 .... 288,B-4
Waterville 1,672 .... 290,D-2
Watervliet 11,354 .... 291,H-3
Watkins Glen• 2,440 .... 290,A-4
Waverly 4,738 .... 292,B-1
Wayland 1,846 .... 287,G-3
Webster 5,499 .... 287,H-1
Weedsport 1,952 .... 290,B-2
Wellsburg 647 .... 292,B-1
Wellsville 5,769 .... 287,F-4
West Carthage 1,824 .... 288,C-4
West Haverstraw 9,181 .... 293,G-4
West Winfield 979 .... 291,E-3
Westbury 13,871 .... 292,A-5
Westfield 3,446 .... 286,C-4
Westhampton Beach 1,629 .... 292,D-5
White Plains• 46,999 .... 292,H4-A4
Whitehall 3,241 .... 289,G-5
Whitesboro 4,460 .... 290,D-2
Whitney Point 1,063 .... 290,C-4
Williamson 287,H-1
Williamsville 6,017 .... 287,E-2
Williston Park 8,216 .... 292,A-5
Wilson 1,259 .... 287,E-1
Windsor 1,155 .... 292,D-1
Wolcott 1,496 .... 290,A-2
Woodmere 292,A-5
Woodridge 809 .... 293,F-2
Wurtsboro 1,128 .... 293,F-3
Wyandanch 292,B-5
Yonkers 193,351 .... 293,H-4
Yorktown 293,H-3
Yorktown Heights 293,H-3
Yorkville 3,115 .... 290,D-2
Youngstown 2,191 .... 286,D-1

MZ-532-J-XC

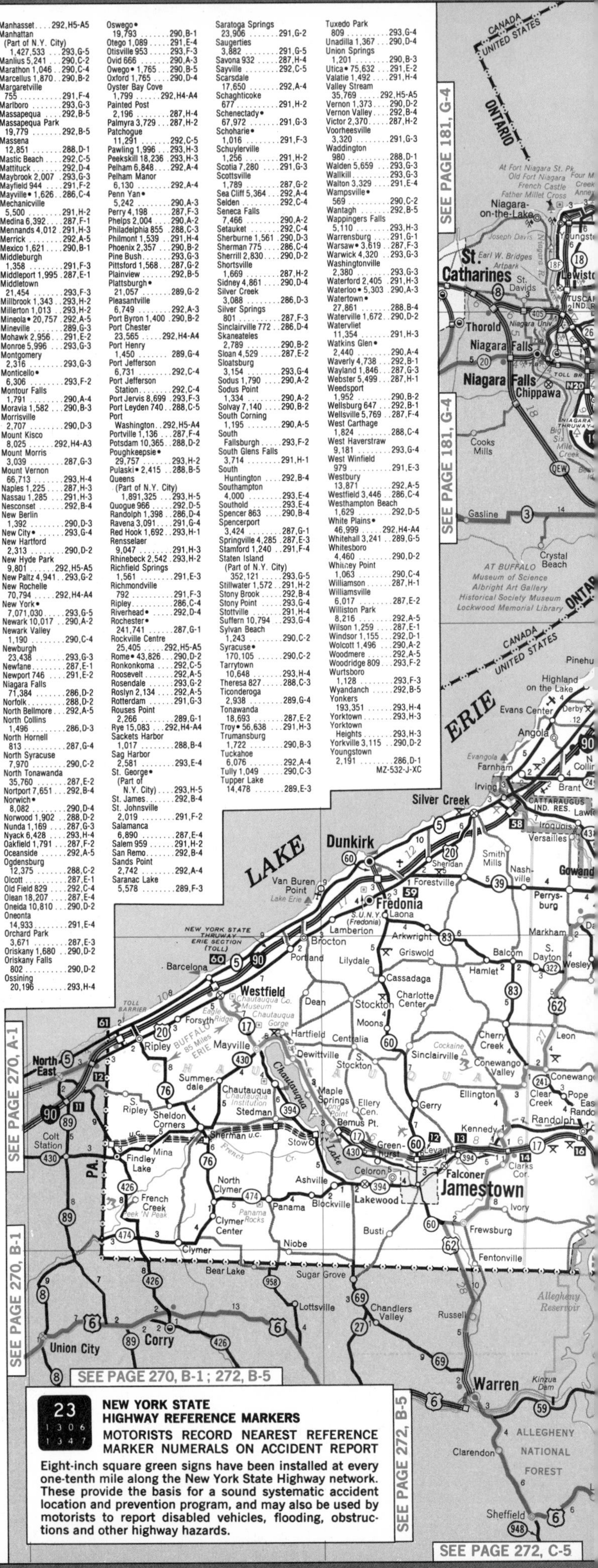
SEE PAGE 181, G-4
SEE PAGE 181, G-4
CANADA
UNITED STATES
ONTARIO
Niagara-on-the-Lake
St. Catharines
Thorold
Niagara Falls
Niagara Falls
Chippawa
AT BUFFALO
Museum of Science
Albright Art Gallery
Historical Society Museum
Lockwood Memorial Library
ERIE
LAKE
Silver Creek
Dunkirk
Fredonia
Van Buren Point
NEW YORK STATE THRUWAY ERIE SECTION (TOLL)
Barcelona
Brocton
Westfield
Ripley
Mayville
North East
Chautauqua
Sherman
Clymer
Panama
Lakewood
Falconer
Jamestown
Frewsburg
Union City
Corry
Warren
SEE PAGE 270, A-1
SEE PAGE 270, B-1
SEE PAGE 270, B-1 ; 272, B-5
SEE PAGE 272, B-5
SEE PAGE 272, C-5
ALLEGHENY NATIONAL FOREST
Sheffield

NEW YORK STATE HIGHWAY REFERENCE MARKERS

23 1306 1347

MOTORISTS RECORD NEAREST REFERENCE MARKER NUMERALS ON ACCIDENT REPORT

Eight-inch square green signs have been installed at every one-tenth mile along the New York State Highway network. These provide the basis for a sound systematic accident location and prevention program, and may also be used by motorists to report disabled vehicles, flooding, obstructions and other highway hazards.

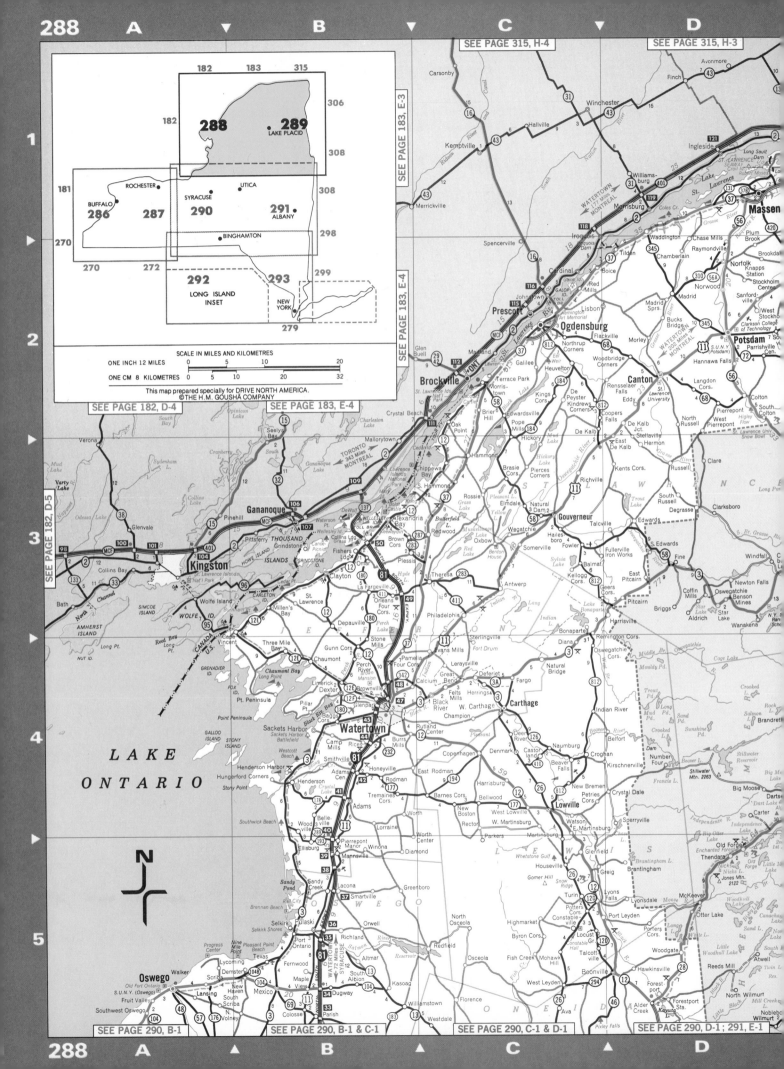

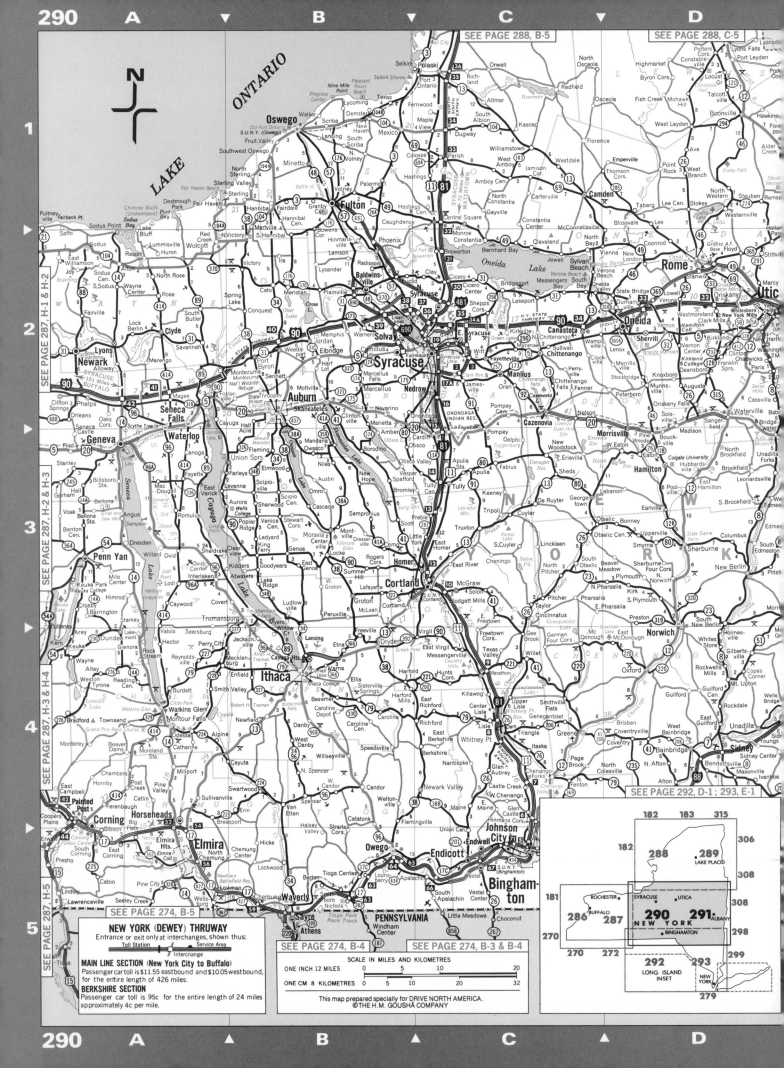

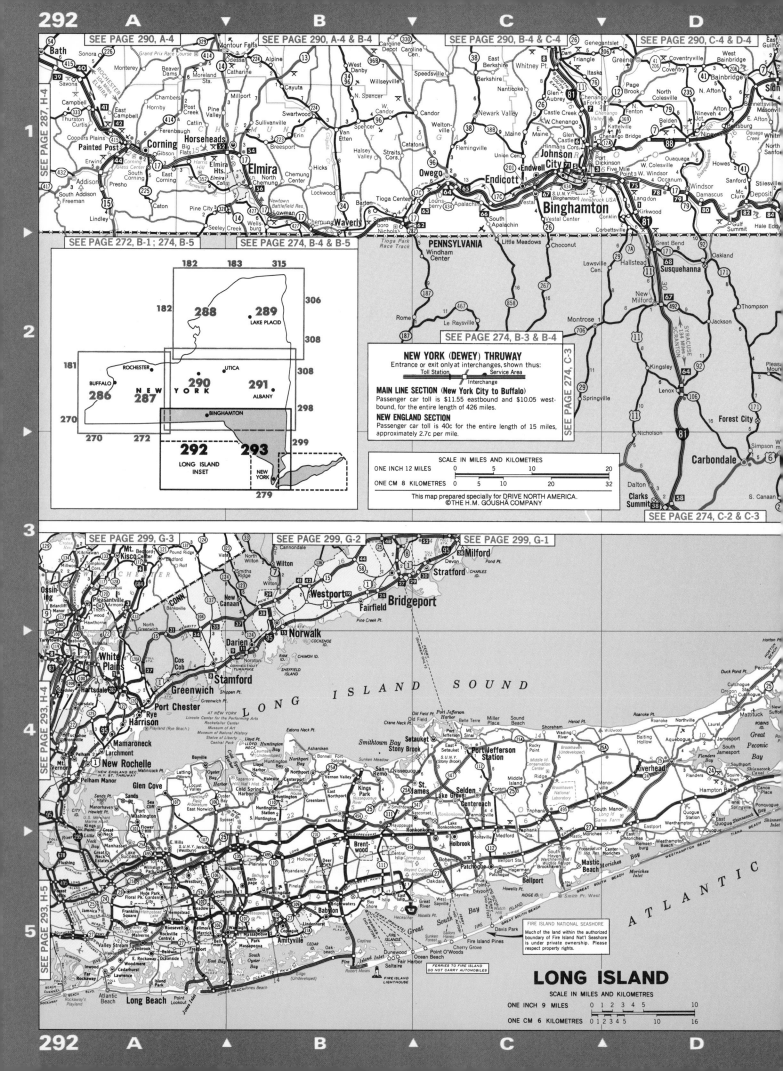

Lovely Seaports, a Famous Tea Party and Legends of Witches and Whalers

Massachusetts/Connecticut/Rhode Island

Lower New England—the states of Massachusetts, Connecticut and Rhode Island—has mountains, beaches, picturesque villages, summer resorts as old as America, and a variety of metropolitan culture. It was here that the Pilgrims first landed, and here that the fires of the Revolution were kindled.

Boston (302, C-4), home of the bean and the cod, honors the latter with an effigy of a codfish in the dignified State House. The building's gilded dome dominates historic Beacon Hill overlooking the Boston Common, on land originally owned by John Hancock. The gun alleged to have fired the first shot of the Revolution is displayed in the Archives Museum. In Boston Public Garden, next to the Common, carpets of colorful blooms surround a pond on which swan-shaped boats cruise.

That Boston appreciates its heritage more than most cities do is evident along the Freedom Trail, a series of sites central to the life of the city and the nation. The first site along the trail is Faneuil Hall (1742), used for so many political meetings that it became known as the Cradle of Liberty. Nearby Quincy Market, true to its beginnings, is a cornucopia of French crepes, Italian sausages, Danish cheeses, Greek pastries, German beer, Chinese noodles and American hot dogs. From the balcony of the Old State House (1713) on July 18, 1776, the Declaration of Independence was first read to the people of Boston (and is still read each July

4). Another crucible of conflict is the Old South Meeting House, where patriots met to plan the Boston Tea Party on December 16, 1773. Visitors can retrace the patriots' footsteps down Milk and Congress streets to the Boston Tea Party Ship and Museum, where displays include one of the chests thrown overboard that fateful night. The Paul Revere House is the city's oldest (1680); the silversmith who made the famous ride on April 18, 1775, lived here for 30 years. The lantern signal that warned Revere of the British march on Concord and Lexington shone from the steeple of Christ Church (1723), popularly known as "Old North."

Within musket range of Monument Avenue in Charlestown is Breed's Hill and the 221-foot Bunker Hill Monument, where a ragtag army of partriots engaged the British in the first major battle of the Revolution. One of America's greatest fighting ships, the U.S.S. *Constitution*, rides at anchor at the Charlestown Navy Yard. "Old Ironsides" (so named because cannonballs would not penetrate its copper-sheathed hull) was launched in 1797 and saw action in the War of 1812. The Bunker Hill Pavilion nearby stages a multimedia presentation called "Whites of Their Eyes."

One of Boston's most treasured institutions is the Museum of Fine Arts, whose Oriental collection is among the finest in the world.

Satan's Circle (right) casts an eerie glow in the Salem Witch Museum.

Classical, Egyptian, Near Eastern, American and European works complete the comprehensive collection. Symphony Hall is home not only of the Boston Symphony Orchestra, now over 100 years old, but also of the famous Boston Pops.

Rare and beautiful fish inhabit the 180,000-gallon ocean tank of New England Aquarium; the barge *Discovery* houses bottle-nosed dolphins and sea lions. The film "Boston and the Sea" is shown at the adjacent Museum of the American China Trade, a former sea captain's home. Exhibits in the Museum of Science, a "look-and-touch" museum for all ages, range from live animals to game-playing computers.

Cambridge, across the Charles River, is closely tied to the universities in its midst—Harvard, Radcliffe and the Massachusetts Institute of Technology. The city is a walker's haven where twisting streets, a bane to motorists, delight those on foot. Many of Henry Wadsworth Longfellow's best-known poems were written in an 18-room house that remains much the same as it was at the time of his death in 1882. Visitors to Harvard's venerable campus, founded in 1636, can tour six museums and art galleries.

The first shots of the American Revolution

Cape Cod (above) marches to a different drummer—and the beat is slow. Armed with bait and patience, surf fishermen play a waiting game with striped bass.

Meeting place and market since 1742, Faneuil Hall (right) was a gift to the people of Boston from merchant Peter Faneuil.

resounded at **Lexington (302, B-5)**, when local farmers skirmished with British troops (April 19, 1775). The line of the patriots is marked by an inscribed boulder bearing Captain John Parker's words: "Stand your ground; don't fire unless fired upon, but if they mean to have a war, let it begin here." After dispersing the patriots at Lexington, the redcoats marched to **Concord**, where they were met by armed "minutemen" alerted by Paul Revere. After heavy fighting the British were forced to retreat, demoralized and low on ammunition. The battle took place on the Old North Bridge over the Concord River and is commemorated by the famous Minute Man statue nearby. Concord is equally rich in literary history. The homes of Ralph Waldo Emerson, Louisa May Alcott and Nathaniel Hawthorne are open to the public. A cairn marks the site of Henry David Thoreau's cabin at Walden Pond.

The rockbound north shore of Massachusetts offers unusual history and beautiful scenery. **Salem (302, B-4)** was the scene, in 1692, of the notorious witchcraft trials which resulted in the execution of 19 innocent people. Signs showing a witch astride a broom direct visitors to the Courthouse where the trials were held, and to the home of Judge Jonathan Corwin. Rare books, manuscripts, and even a section of the tree from which the accused were hanged, are in the Essex Institute. The Peabody Museum was founded by sea captains who displayed treasures here from their voyages to the Orient. The China Trade comes to life in the Salem Seaport Museum, where visitors can venture on the simulated *Voyage of the India Star* in search of treasure.

Gloucester (302, B-3), too, is rich in sea lore. On the harborfront a famous bronze statue of a fisherman gazes out over the Atlantic—in memory of those who "went down to the sea in ships." Visitors to the Gloucester Fishermen's Museum can learn to caulk a boat, shave a mast or handle fishing gear. To the north, the rocky promontory of Cape Ann reaches into the Atlantic with 25 miles of spectacular coastline, six harbors and more than 20 sandy beaches. Seafood lovers can tour the New England Lobster Company north of **Rockport (302, A-3)** or browse among galleries and craft shops along the weather-beaten wharf.

Fighting the elements, sickness, and their own ignorance of the wilderness, the Pilgrims founded **Plymouth (300, D-3)** in 1620. Much of the spirit of these early years has been preserved or re-created in this historic town. Built in England and only slightly longer than a tennis court, the *Mayflower II* is a reproduction of the original. The simple architecture of the thatch-roofed First House and the 1627 House reflects the Pilgrims' way of life. South of town, Plimoth Plantation is a full-scale re-creation of the village as it was in 1627. At different seasons, "villagers" can be found shearing sheep, harvesting crops or preserving food.

The "bared and bended arm of Massachusetts"—this was Henry David Thoreau's metaphor for Cape Cod, the peninsula that thrusts out into the Atlantic from the eastern edge of the continent. Winding along Cape Cod Bay, Route 6A (the Cranberry Highway) passes shingled homes, salt marshes, country stores and the historic towns of Sandwich, Barnstable, Dennis and Brewster. The east-

"Old Ironsides" (above) was one of the first fighting ships built for the new navy ordered by President John Adams, alarmed at the depredations of American merchant ships by foreign privateers. The wooden square-rigger fought against the French, the British and the Barbary pirates.

Modern-day members of the Charlestown Militia re-enact the Boston Tea Party of two centuries ago, as they heave empty tea chests into Boston Harbor.

ern Cape is dominated by 28,000-acre **Cape Cod National Seashore (303, E-1)**, a sandspit world of beaches, sea cliffs and dunes clothed in bayberry and heath. Near its northern tip lies **Provincetown (302, D-2)**, part fishing village, part art colony, and awash with summer tourists.

Ferries from **Hyannis (303, E-2)** service the islands of **Martha's Vineyard (303, F-3)** and **Nantucket (303, G-2)**. For much of the 19th century, Nantucket was the whaling capital of the world. It was during this period that many of its captains' mansions were built and furnished with precious silks, Indian rugs, porcelains and Chinese furniture brought from the Orient. Martha's Vineyard, amazingly varied for its size, embraces soft sand beaches, scrub country, rolling farmland, cliffs, coves and tidal flats. Edgartown is perhaps the most picturesque of the Vineyard villages. It is noted for its white clapboard houses, built by 19th century whaling masters. Oak Bluffs' beloved carousel has delighted riders and onlookers alike for more than a century.

Old Sturbridge Village (300, D-3) is a re-creation of a 19th-century farming village and, like them, its center is a common graced by a white-steepled meetinghouse. The village's nearly 40 buildings include farmhouses, barns, a bank, cabinet shop, printing office, gristmill and tavern. All are authentic New England structures, restored and used for demonstrations of early arts and crafts, from candle dipping to barrel making. Old buildings also surround the village green of Storrowton in **West Springfield (300, D-4)**. Both restorations are working communities; daily chores are performed by guides in period dress.

Deerfield (300, B-4) was the last outpost on New England's frontier in 1669 and was twice devastated by Indian attacks. Its resettlement brought prosperity and a determination not to forget the past. Today visitors stroll down "The Street," a mile-long lane of elms and maples bordered by three centuries of carefully preserved houses and public buildings. Victims of the French and Indian raid of 1704 rest in a common grave beneath a grassy knoll in the Old Burying Ground.

Dense groves of pine and birch give the Berkshires of western Massachusetts their soft gray-green cover. In the fall the hills share with the rest of New England the glorious reds, oranges and yellows that cloak this region's peaks and valleys. **Mount Greylock (298, A-2)**, 3,491 feet, is the highest point in the state; an observation tower atop its summit provides a spectacular view of this autumn tapestry.

Stockbridge (298, C-2), with its picture-postcard setting, is the quintessential New England village. The illustrator Norman Rockwell lived and worked here, and many of the places and people in the area were models for his famous *Saturday Evening Post* covers. Chesterwood was the home of sculptor Daniel Chester French, creator of the bronze *Minute Man* and the marble *Abraham Lincoln*. His studio and gallery contain drawings, plaster casts and a revolving modeling table set on railroad tracks. Nearby **Tanglewood** is the summer home of the Boston Symphony Orchestra.

In **Campbell Falls State Park (298, D-2)**, a Massachusetts waterfall pours into a stream surrounded by evergreen forest in Connecti-

Mirror of a Maritime Past

Billowing sails, the ring of the caulker's mallet, the echo of voices from aloft—these are the sights and sounds of Connecticut's Mystic Seaport, a living museum of New England's maritime past. Seaport Street, on the waterfront, is lined with 19th-century shops: a shipsmith's workshop where whaling tools are forged, a loft where sails are cut and sewn, a carving shop (*right*), a cooperage, and a chandler stocked with goods to outfit ships for long voyages. Moored across the way are the whaler *Charles W. Morgan* (1841), the training ship *Joseph Conrad* (1882), and several other historic vessels. Exhibit buildings house displays of figureheads, scrimshaw, ship models, navigation aids and other marine artifacts.

cut. Farther south, the shallow, rippling Housatonic River flows through one of the finest pine groves in the East. Woodland paths at **Kent Falls State Park (299, E-2)** follow the waterfall as it cascades 200 feet and pauses in shallow pools. The river offers fine picnicking, fishing and canoeing where it wanders through **Housatonic Meadows State Park**.

Nearly every road through the Litchfield Hills is a scenic one, with waterfalls, covered bridges and tucked-away villages to delight the shunpiker. The streets of historic **Litchfield (299, E-2)** are lined with Colonial and Federal-style homes (built when the town was an important stagecoach stop) and no fewer than 10 churches.

Elizabeth Park in **Hartford (301, E-5)**, Connecticut's capital, is the site of the country's first public rose garden. More than 14,000 plants—in 1,000 varieties—bloom throughout summer. Some 47 permanent and visiting exhibits draw visitors to the Wadsworth Atheneum. Fine art, period costumes, firearms, furniture and a "tactile gallery" that invites touching, are the highlights. Two of New England's literary giants—Mark Twain and Harriet Beecher Stowe—made their homes in Hartford. The Mark Twain Memorial is a rambling Victorian Gothic residence

with an second-floor veranda that resembles the deck of a Mississippi riverboat. The simpler Stowe house is where the author of *Uncle Tom's Cabin* lived and worked.

New Haven (299, G-1), laid out in nine squares in 1638, is America's oldest planned city. The three churches that surround its green were all erected between 1812 and 1815. An eclectic mix of modern and Gothic-style architecture enlivens the campus of Yale University. Yale's Center for British Art contains the finest collection (outside England) of British paintings, prints, drawings, sculptures and rare books dating from the 1500s. Medieval manuscripts, John James Audubon's original bird prints and the letters of Mark Twain, Jack London and Ernest Hemingway are among the treasures of the Beinecke Rare Book and Manuscript Library. Charles Dickens described nearby Hillhouse Avenue as "the most beautiful street in America."

Rising six stories above the Connecticut River at **East Haddam (301, E-4)**, the 1876 Goodspeed Opera House reflects the style of steamboat saloons of the day and boasts a hand-painted backdrop of a river steamer. One of the greatest players to strut and fret his hour upon the stage was William Gillette;

Fresh from the bake pit, lobsters and clams have been steamed with sausages, corn, onions and potatoes over hot rocks and seaweed in that most traditional of New England rituals, the clambake.

America's past hangs upon Old Sturbridge Village (left) like a fine but faded coat.

Marble House (above) was where Mrs. O.H.P. Belmont threw Newport's most memorable party—at which the hundred "guests" were dogs in various forms of fancy dress.

Mystic, Connecticut, (left) resembles many a New England seaport of 100 years ago.

the actor built a 24-room, medieval-style castle downriver in **Hadlyme (301, F-4)**.

Whale Oil Row in **New London (301, F-3)** is a striking reminder of the town's whaling days. Four Greek Revival mansions, constructed in 1830, line a section of Huntington Street. Number Three houses the Tale of the Whale Museum and a fascinating collection of maritime artifacts, scrimshaw and ship's logs, and a fully rigged whaleboat. Early New England furniture, silver and toys, as well as ancient, classical and modern art, occupies the Lyman Allyn Museum.

The State of Rhode Island and Providence Plantations is America's smallest in area and longest in name, a region of winding lanes, neat farms and quiet beaches. Seeking a haven for "persons distressed in conscience," Roger Williams founded **Providence (301, E-1)**, its capital, in 1636. Benefit Street was built in the 1750s for the "common benefit" of citizens who wanted a street away from the river. Today its dignified old homes present a compelling record of urban New England. City Hall, designed in the "General Grant" (mansard Victorian) style, was raised in 1878. Another elegant reminder of the 19th century is the Arcade (1828), the country's first enclosed shopping mall. Rhode Island's State Capitol, built of white marble in the early 1900s, is one of the most beautiful in America. Its marble dome is second only to that of St. Peter's in size. Visitors to the Rhode Island School of Design's Museum of Art move through time—from the arts of ancient Egypt to galleries devoted to Greece and Rome, then to those of the Middle Ages, Renaissance and modern art.

For those who crave wild solitude in a heavily populated area—and don't mind insects—**Great Swamp Wildlife Management Area (301, F-1)** is an ideal retreat. A third of its 3,000 acres is actually dry land, from which visitors can observe game birds and animals and a variety of vegetation that ranges from arctic moss to orchids.

Few cities of its size can claim a more colorful history than **Newport (303, F-5)**. From its founding in 1639, the settlement was a haven for Colonial pirates and privateers, a major port for trade in rum, sugar and slaves, and a bustling fishing and shipbuilding center. In the late 1800s it became an opulent summer resort and social capital. The records, relics, art and artifacts of its history are well preserved in the city's mansions and museums.

Many of Newport's palatial "cottages" can be seen along the Cliff Walk, a spectacular promenade through the playground of the rich. The Elms, a chateau surrounded by park-like grounds, was built in 1901 for coal magnate Edward J. Berwind. In late afternoon, sunlight streams through the windows of William K. Vanderbilt's Marble House, reflecting off gold walls, bronze furniture and marble columns. His brother Cornelius built The Breakers, a Renaissance-style palace furnished with antique tapestries, massive chandeliers, stained glass, ornate fireplaces and a Great Hall that soars to a ceiling 50 feet above the floor.

An architectural gem in its own right, the Touro Synagogue is the oldest in the United States (1763), and its Georgian-style interior is considered by many to be the most beautiful. Hunter House (1748), on the historic Point, is one of the country's finest examples of Colonial architecture. At Newport harbor, visitors can board a replica of the historic sloop *Providence*.

More than 300 ponds, some excellent for fishing, are scattered throughout **Block Island (301, G-1)**, reached by ferry from Newport and Point Judith, Rhode Island; and from Groton, Connecticut. Old Harbor, home port of the island's fishing fleet, is a photogenic mélange of Victorian houses and saltweathered wharves. The flashing beacon of Southeast Light (1874) marks the 200-foot Mohegan Bluffs.

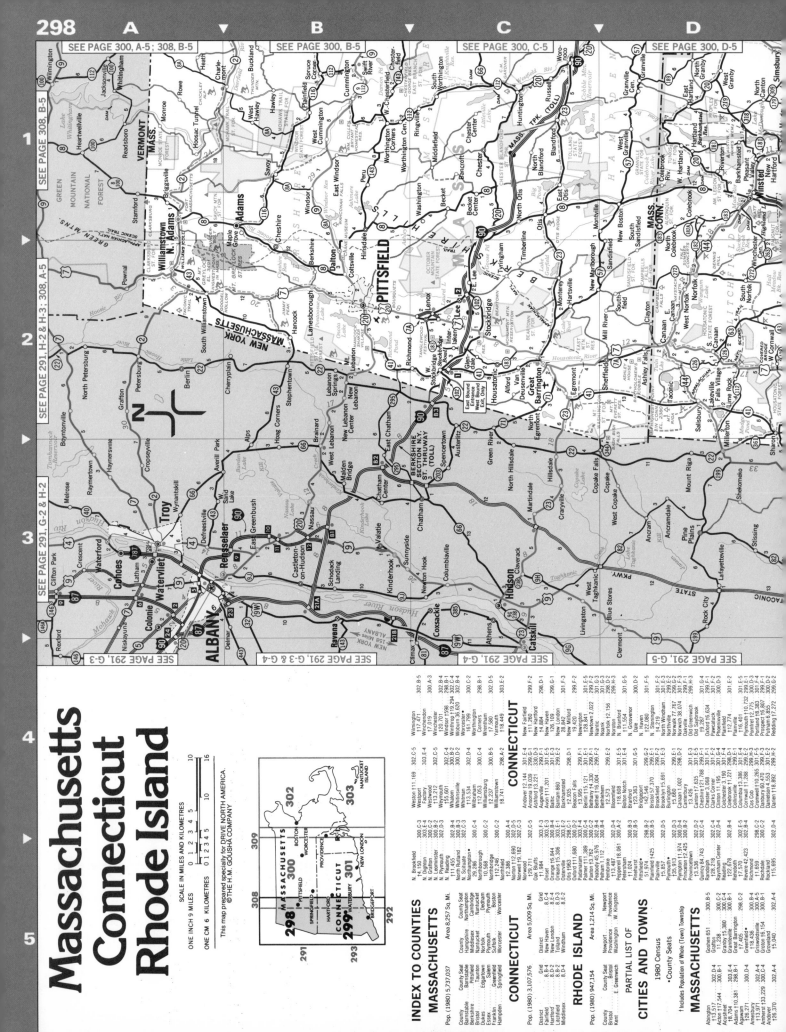

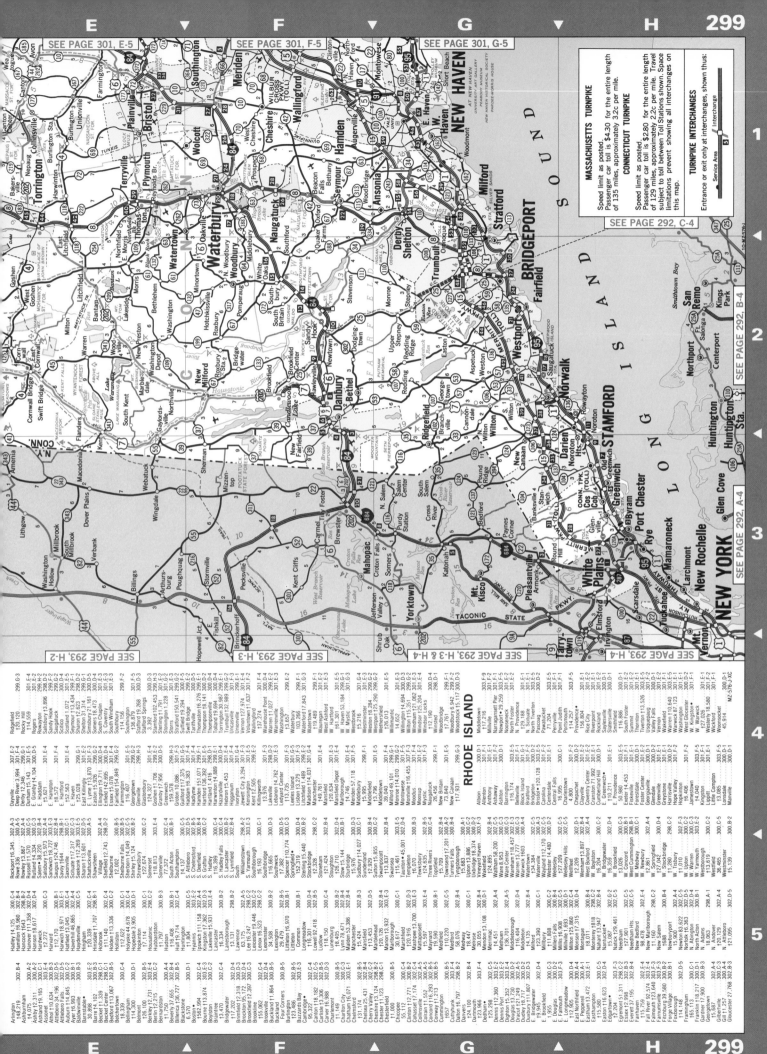

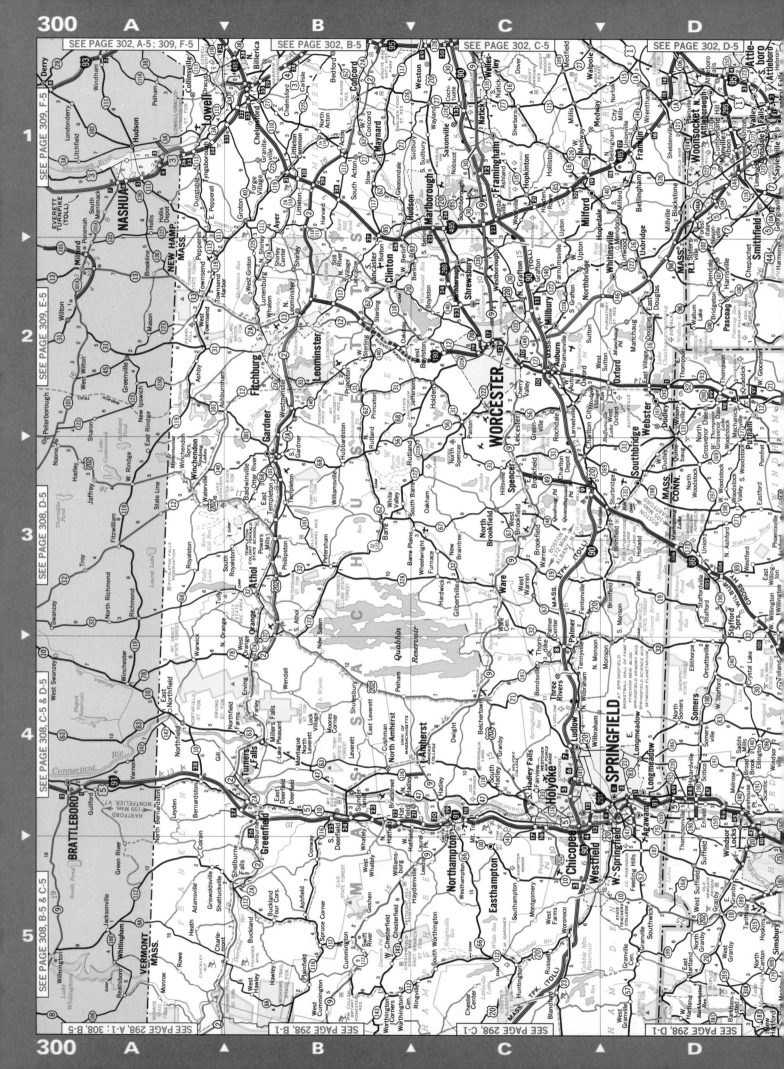

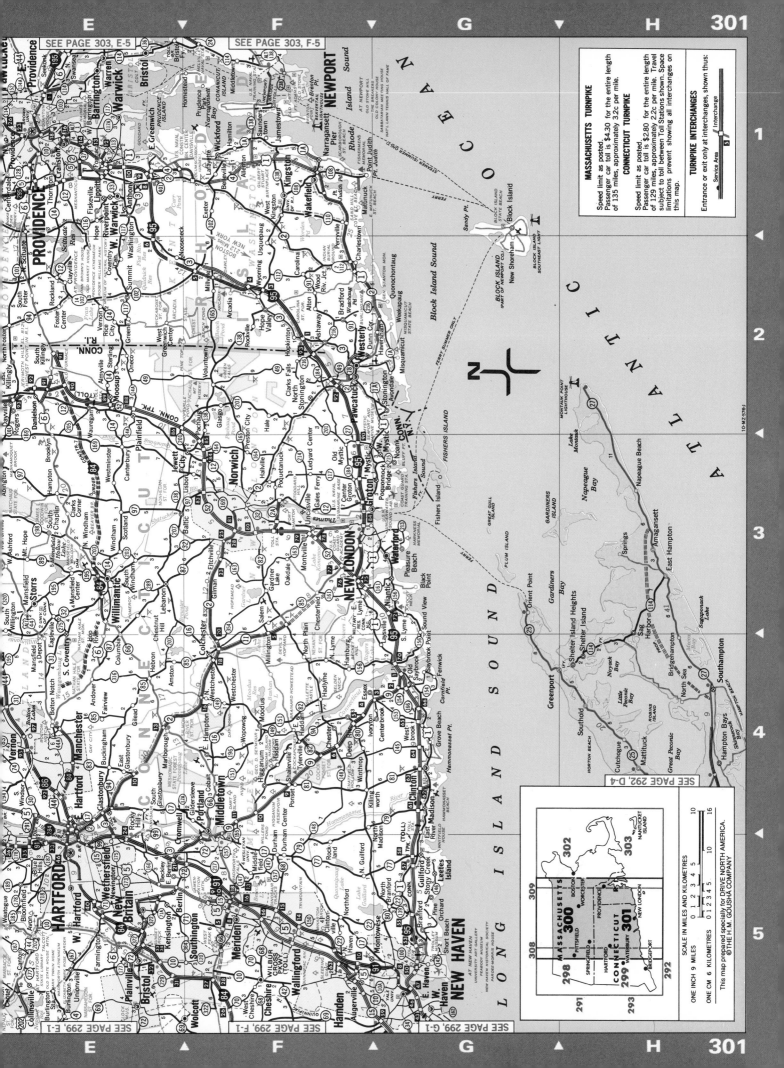

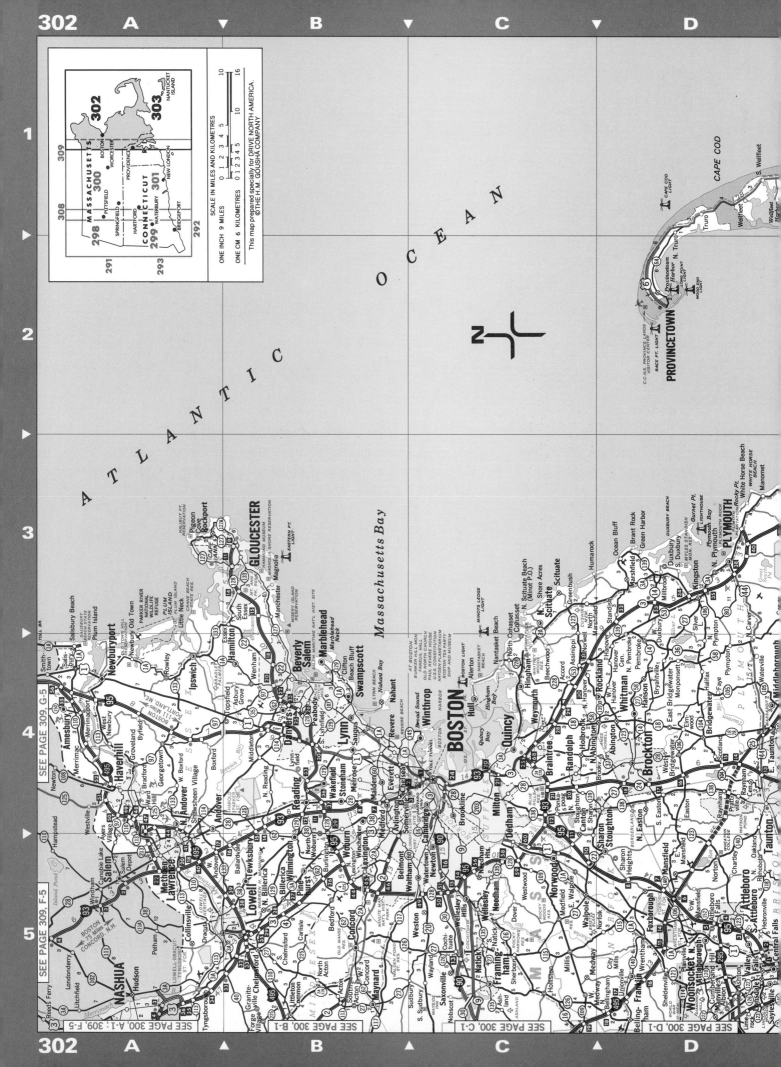

MASSACHUSETTS TURNPIKE

Speed limit as posted.
Passenger car toll is $4.30 for the entire length of 135 miles, approximately 3.2¢ per mile.

TURNPIKE INTERCHANGES

Entrance or exit only at interchanges, shown thus:

Service Area
Interchange

CAPE COD NATIONAL SEASHORE

Much of the land within the authorized boundary of Cape Cod Nat'l Seashore is under private ownership. Please respect property rights.

Cape Cod Bay

Nantucket Sound

NANTUCKET ISLAND

Nantucket

ATLANTIC OCEAN

NEW BEDFORD

FALL RIVER

PROVIDENCE

NEWPORT

MARTHA'S VINEYARD

RHODE ISLAND

STEAMER (SUMMER ONLY) NO AUTOS CARRIED

SEE PAGE 301, E-1

SEE PAGE 301, F-1

SEE PAGE 301, G-1

Granite, Green Mountains and a Northeast Kingdom

Vermont/New Hampshire

Vermont and New Hampshire personify New England: white towns surrounding elm-shaded greens, narrow cobbled streets along tangy waterfronts, rumpled patchworks of hills and river valleys.

The Battle of **Bennington (308, A-5)** was fought on August 16, 1777, when Americans under Gen. John Stark rallied to defeat a British force under Burgoyne. The Bennington Battle Monument, a 306-foot blue limestone obelisk, was dedicated in 1891 to commemorate this important victory. American and Hessian (German mercenary) soldiers who fell during the battle are buried in the cemetery of the Old First Church (1805), as is poet Robert Frost. Antique furniture and glassware, clothing, toys, pottery, and America's oldest flag (1776) combine to make the Bennington Museum one of the nation's most impressive regional museums.

Mount Equinox (3,816 feet) overshadows **Manchester (308, B-4)**, a resort town of modern summer houses and shuttered Colonial homes. Skyline Drive (a toll road) winds to the summit, providing sweeping views of Vermont, Massachussetts and New York. Other attractions include the Southern Vermont Art Center and the Museum of American Fly Fishing.

Steamtown, in **Bellows Falls (308, C-4)**, evokes 19th-century America with its 84 acres of steam locomotives, steam shovels and fire engines. Of all its attractions, the one most illustrative of life during the Steam Age is the 22-mile trip by steam-driven train through the picturesque Vermont countryside.

The State of Vermont was born in a tavern in **Windsor (308, C-3)** where delegates met to ratify a constitution in July 1777. The table around which they gathered is displayed in the Tap Room of Elijah's Tavern, now the Constitution House, along with period furniture. In 1846 the three-story American Precision Museum housed the Robbins, Kendall and Lawrence Armory and Machine Shop, the birthplace of the "American system"—the process of manufacturing using interchangeable parts.

The Ottauquechee River flows gently beneath the covered bridge in the center of the restored mill town of **Quechee (308, C-2)**, but downstream it roars though mile-long Quechee Gorge. Nearby **Woodstock**, with its historic green, covered bridge and handsome 18th- and 19th-century houses, is one of America's loveliest villages.

So much of **Proctor (308, B-2)** is made of marble, including an impressive bridge and the three-story Wilson Castle, that the town fairly glows. The Vermont Marble Company showcases rare and beautiful marbles, statues, bas-reliefs of all the U.S. Presidents, and a short movie on how marble is quarried and processed. Granite is produced at **Barre (306, D-5)**. A pinnacle on the brink of the Rock of Ages quarry—the world's largest—gives visitors a spectacular view of miners 350 feet

Clowns (left) and other merrymakers mingle with the crowds in Stowe on Village Night, but most come for the skiing (above). Below, much-photographed East Corinth, Vermont.

below carving out gigantic blocks with special jet torches.

The golden-domed Vermont State House in **Montpelier (306, C-5)** is set against the verdant backdrop of Capitol Hill. Dedicated in 1859, the third statehouse on the site resembles the Temple of Theseus in Athens. The rambling "Steamboat Gothic" Pavilion Office Building is a charming reproduction of the original 1876 landmark.

Tucked into a remote corner of Vermont's "Northeast Kingdom," **St. Johnsbury (307, E-4)** is a well-preserved reminder of the mill towns that once lined virtually every New England stream. The St. Johnsbury Athenae-

um (1871), an elegant Victorian building, houses one of the nation's oldest libraries and art galleries. The turreted Fairbanks Museum and Planetarium has a nearly complete collection of Vermont's extensive flora and fauna. Visitors to nearby Maple Grove, Inc. can tour one of the world's largest maple syrup factories.

From their hilltop setting in **Middlebury (308, A-1)**, the ivy-covered buildings of Middlebury College overlook church spires and tree-lined streets. A corner of France can be found on the campus at Lé Château, a castle-like language dormitory inspired by the Pavillon Henri IV at Fontainebleau. The

18 rooms of the Sheldon Museum include a nursery with toys and a faithful restoration of an old-time country store. Nearby, an 1872 factory now houses the Vermont State Craft Center at Frog Hollow.

Battery Park and the University of Vermont overlook the rejuvenated waterfront of **Burlington (306, B-4)**. To the west the Adirondacks of New York loom blue and hazy across the sparkling waters of Lake Champlain. To the northeast rises Mount Mansfield, center of the ski area that made **Stowe (306, C-4)** famous. South of Burlington, the Shelburne Museum is a unique village of 18th- and 19th-century buildings including homes, barns, a jail, railroad station, schoolhouse, lighthouse and a stagecoach inn, all carefully moved from their original sites and painstakingly restored.

One of the most panoramic and varied views in the East unfolds from the summit of **Jay Peak (306, D-3)**, reached by an aerial tramway. On a clear day it encompasses the skyline of Montreal to the north, the peaks of the Presidential Range to the east, and Lake Champlain and the Adirondacks to the west.

The best way to see New Hampshire's mountains is by driving through their notches, or gaps. **Dixville Notch (307, G-3)** is one of the wildest and most beautiful of all —a narrow, winding gorge surrounded by the jagged spurs of the Dixville Mountains.

Heavily forested **Franconia Notch State Park (307, F-5)** hosts a superb concentration of natural wonders: the Old Man of the Mountains, a 40-foot-high head carved out of Cannon Mountain by erosion; the Basin, a deep glacial pothole at the foot of a waterfall; and mountain-ringed Echo Lake, noted for its fine fishing and swimming. Footpaths and walkways lead from Highway 16 to the misty curtain of Glen Ellis Falls in majestic **Pinkham Notch**. West of **Glen (307, G-5)**, the Kancamagus Highway traverses the White Mountain National Forest, passing Loon Mountain, Sabbaday Falls and the Rocky Gorge and Lower Falls scenic areas.

Showman P. T. Barnum called the view from **Mount Washington (307, G-5)** "the second greatest show on earth." At 6,288 feet, it is the highest point in the Northeast; from its summit the other peaks of the Presidential Range roll toward the horizon. It was during one of the mountain's notorious storms, on April 12, 1934, that the strongest gust of wind ever recorded—231 mph—was registered.

The largest of New Hampshire's 1,300 lakes is Winnipesaukee, whose sapphire waters the Indians called "Smile of the Great Spirit." Sheltered in a snug horseshoe-shaped bay lies **Wolfeboro (309, G-2)**, a popular summer retreat since 1768. A four-mile drive passes lavish old homes set back amid towering pines, poplars and beeches. Another view

is from aboard the M/V *Mount Washington*, a 1,250-passenger cruise boat that makes 3¼-hour excursions on Lake Winnipesaukee.

Spread along a broad bend in the Merrimack River, tiny **Concord (309, F-4)** boasts several superlatives. The New Hampshire State Capitol here houses America's largest state legislature (424 legislators); the famous Concord stagecoach was the most familiar vehicle on the western frontier; and a local lawyer, Franklin Pierce, became the 14th President of the United States. One of two still-active Shaker communities is in nearby **Canterbury**. The original meetinghouse (1792), now a museum, reflects the importance in Shaker life of simplicity and careful workmanship.

The resorts of Hampton Beach, Great and Little Boars Head, Rye Beach, Seabrook Beach and Wallis Sands are strung along New Hampshire's 18-mile coast like beads on a string. The centerpiece of **Portsmouth (309, H-4)**—New Hampshire's only port—is Strawbery Banke, a 10-acre restoration dotted with the homes of sea captains, merchants and craftsmen. John Paul Jones, America's first naval hero, lived in the house that now bears his name, in 1777, while his sloop-of-war *Ranger* was being outfitted. Prescott Park, a waterfront garden filled with flowers and shrubs typical of Colonial America, is the scene of concerts, plays and art festivals.

Water cascades through the 800-foot-long Flume (above) in Franconia Notch State Park.

Nonhiking visitors have two ways of getting to the top of Mount Washington: by the toll road or on the colorful cog railway (left) with its chugging steam engine.

Vermont
New Hampshire

SCALE IN MILES AND KILOMETRES

ONE INCH 9 MILES | 0 1 2 3 4 5 10
ONE CM 6 KILOMETRES | 0 1 2 3 4 5 16

This map prepared specially for DRIVE NORTH AMERICA.
©THE H.M. GOUSHA COMPANY

PARTIAL LIST OF
CITIES AND TOWNS
1980 Census
•County Seats
† Includes Population of Whole (Town) Township

VERMONT

Merrimack . . . . . Concord
Rockingham . . . . . Exeter
Strafford . . . . . Dover
Sullivan . . . . . Newport

Washington . . . . . Montpelier
Windsor . . . . . Newfane
Windsor . . . . . Woodstock

INDEX TO COUNTIES
VERMONT

Pop. (1980) 511,456 | Area 9,609 Sq. Mi.

County	County Seat
Addison	Middlebury
Bennington	Bennington
Caledonia	St. Johnsbury
Chittenden	Burlington
Essex	Guildhall

County	County Seat
Franklin	St. Albans
Grand Isle	North Hero
Lamoille	Hyde Park
Orange	Chelsea
Orleans	Newport
Rutland	Rutland

NEW HAMPSHIRE

Pop. (1980) 920,610 | Area 9,304 Sq. Mi.

County	County Seat
Belknap	Laconia
Carroll	Ossipee
Cheshire	Keene

County	County Seat
Coos	Lancaster
Grafton	Woodsville
Hillsborough	Nashua

VERMONT

Addison †889 . 306,B-5
Albany 174 . . . 306,D-3
Alburg 496 . . . 306,B-2
Arlington
†2,184 . . . . 308,A-4
Ascutney 308,C-3
Bakersfield
†852 . . . . . 306,C-3
Barnard †790 . 308,C-2
Barnet †1,338 . 307,E-5
Barre 9,824 . . 308,C-3
Barton 1,062 . 307,E-3
Bellows Falls
3,456 . . . . 308,C-4
Bennington•
†15,815 . . . 308,A-5
Benson †739 . 308,A-2
Berkshire
†1,116 . . . . 306,C-2
Bethel †1,715 . 308,C-2
Bloomfield †188 .307,F-3
Bolton †715 . . 306,C-4
Bradford 831 . 308,D-1
Brandon †4,194 308,B-3
Brattleboro
11,886 . . . . 308,C-5
Bridgewater
†867 . . . . . 308,B-2
Bridport †997 . 308,A-1
Bristol 1,793 . 306,B-5

Brookfield †959 .308,C-1
Browning
†708 . . . . . 307,E-3
Brownsville . . . 308,C-3
Burke Hollow . . 307,E-4
Burlington•
37,712 . . . . 306,B-4
Cabot 259 . . . 306,B-4
Cambridge 217 .306,C-3
Cambridgeport . 308,C-4
Fairlee †770 . . 308,D-1
Felchville 308,C-3
Ferrisburg
2,117 . . . . . 306,B-5
Fletcher †626 . 306,C-3
Forest Dale . . . 306,B-3
Franklin †1,006 306,C-2
Georgia Center . 306,B-3
Glover †843 . . 306,D-3
Grafton †604 . 308,C-4
Granby †70 . . 307,F-4
Grand Isle
†1,238 . . . . 306,B-3
Granville †288 . 308,B-1
Greensboro †677 306,D-4
Groton †667 . . 306,D-5
Guildhall• †202 .307,F-4
Halifax †488 . . 308,C-5
Hancock †334 . 308,B-1
Hardwick 1,476 .306,D-4
Hartford †7,963 308,D-2

Craftsbury †844 306,D-4
Cuttingsville . . 308,B-3
Danby 1992 . . 308,B-3
Danville †1,705 .307,E-4
Derby Center
598 . . . . . . 307,E-2
Derby Line 874 .307,E-2
Dorset †1,648 . 308,B-4
Dummerston
†1,574 . . . . 308,C-5
Duxbury †877 . 306,C-5
East Barre . . . 306,D-5
East Montpelier
†2,205 . . . . 306,C-5
East Topsham
†767 . . . . . 306,D-5
Eden †612 . . . 306,D-3
Ely 308,D-1
Enosburg Falls
1,207 . . . . . 306,C-2
Essex Center . . 306,B-4
Essex Junction
7,033 . . . . . 306,B-4
Fair Haven
†2,819 . . . . 308,A-2
Fairfax †1,805 . 306,B-3
Fairfield †1,493 .306,C-3

Hartland †2,396 .308,C-3
Heartwellville . . 308,B-5
Highgate Center .306,B-2
Hinesburg
†2,690 . . . . 306,B-5
Holland †473 . 307,E-2
Hubbardton
†490 . . . . . 308,A-2
Huntington
†1,161 . . . . 306,C-4
Hyde Park • 475 306,C-4
Irasburg †870 . 306,D-3
Island Pond . . . 307,E-3
Isle La Motte
†393 . . . . . 306,B-3
Jacksonville
†252 . . . . . 308,B-5
Jamaica †581 . 308,B-4
Jeffersonville
491 . . . . . . 306,C-3
Jericho †1,340 . 306,C-4
Johnson 1,393 . 306,C-4
Lake Elmore . . . 306,C-4
Leicester 1803 . 308,B-1
Lincoln †870 . . 306,B-5
Londonderry
†1,510 . . . . 308,B-4
Lowell †573 . . 306,C-3
Ludlow 1,352 . 308,C-3
Lunenburg
†1,138 . . . . 307,F-4
Lyndon †4,924 .307,E-4
Lyndon Center . 307,E-4
Lyndonville
1,401 . . . . . 307,E-4
Manchester 563 308,B-4
Manchester
Center 308,B-4
Marshfield 301 306,D-5
Mendon †1,056 308,B-3
Middlebury•
†7,574 . . . . 308,A-1
Middlesex
1,235 . . . . . 306,C-5
Middletown Springs
†603 . . . . . 308,A-3
Milton 1,411 . 306,B-4

Monkton Ridge . 306,B-5
Montgomery
†681 . . . . . 306,C-3
Montpelier•
8,241 . . . . . 306,C-5
Moretown
†1,221 . . . . 306,C-5
Morgan †460 . 307,E-2
Morrisville
†1,448 . . . . 306,C-4
Morristown
2,074 . . . . . 306,C-4
Mount Holly
†938 . . . . . 308,B-3
New Haven
†1,217 . . . . 306,B-5
New Haven Jun. 306,B-5
Newbury †470 . 308,D-1
Newfane • 119 . 308,C-4
Newport • 4,756 306,D-2
Newport Center .306,D-2
North Bennington
1,685 . . . . . 308,A-5
North Hero•
†442 . . . . . 306,B-3
North Troy 717 . 306,D-2
North Westminster
310 . . . . . . 308,C-4
Northfield 2,033 306,C-5
Norton †184 . . 307,E-2
Norwich †2,398 308,D-2
Old Bennington
353 . . . . . . 308,A-5
Orange †752 . 306,D-5
Orleans 983 . . 306,D-3
Orwell †901 . . 308,A-2
Panton †537 . . 306,B-5
Pawlet †1,244 . 308,A-3
Peacham †531 . 307,E-5
Perkinsville 187 308,C-3
Pittsfield †396 . 308,B-2
Pittsford 666 . . 308,B-2
Plainfield 599 . 306,D-5
Plymouth †405 308,C-3
Pomfret †856 . 308,C-2
Post Mills 308,D-1
Poultney 1,554 . 308,A-3
Pownal †3,269 308,A-5

Proctor †1,998 .308,B-2
Proctorsville . . 308,C-3
Putney †1,850 . 308,C-4
Randolph 2,217 .308,C-2
Readsboro 402 .308,B-5
Richford 1,471 306,C-2
Richmond 865 . 306,B-4
Rochester
†1,054 . . . . 308,B-1
Roxbury †452 . 308,C-2
Royalton †2,100 308,C-2
Rupert †605 . . 308,A-4
Rutland•
18,436 . . . . 308,B-3
Ryegate Corner
†1,000 . . . . 307,E-5
St. Albans•
7,308 . . . . . 306,B-3
St. Albans Bay . 306,B-3
St. Johnsbury•
†7,938 . . . . 307,E-4
Salisbury †881 308,B-1
Saxtons River
593 . . . . . . 308,C-4
Searsburg †72 308,B-5
Shaftsbury
†3,001 . . . . 308,A-5
Sharon †828 . 308,C-2
Sheffield †618 .306,D-4
Sheffield †473 307,E-4
Shelburne
†5,000 . . . . 306,B-4
Sheldon †1,316 306,C-3
Sherburne Center
(Killington
P.O.) 308,B-2
Shoreham †972 308,A-1
Shrewsbury
†866 . . . . . 308,B-3
South Burlington
†10,679 . . . 306,B-4
South Hero
†1,188 . . . . 306,B-3
Springfield
†10,190 . . . 308,C-3
Stamford †773 .308,B-5
Stannard †142 .306,D-4

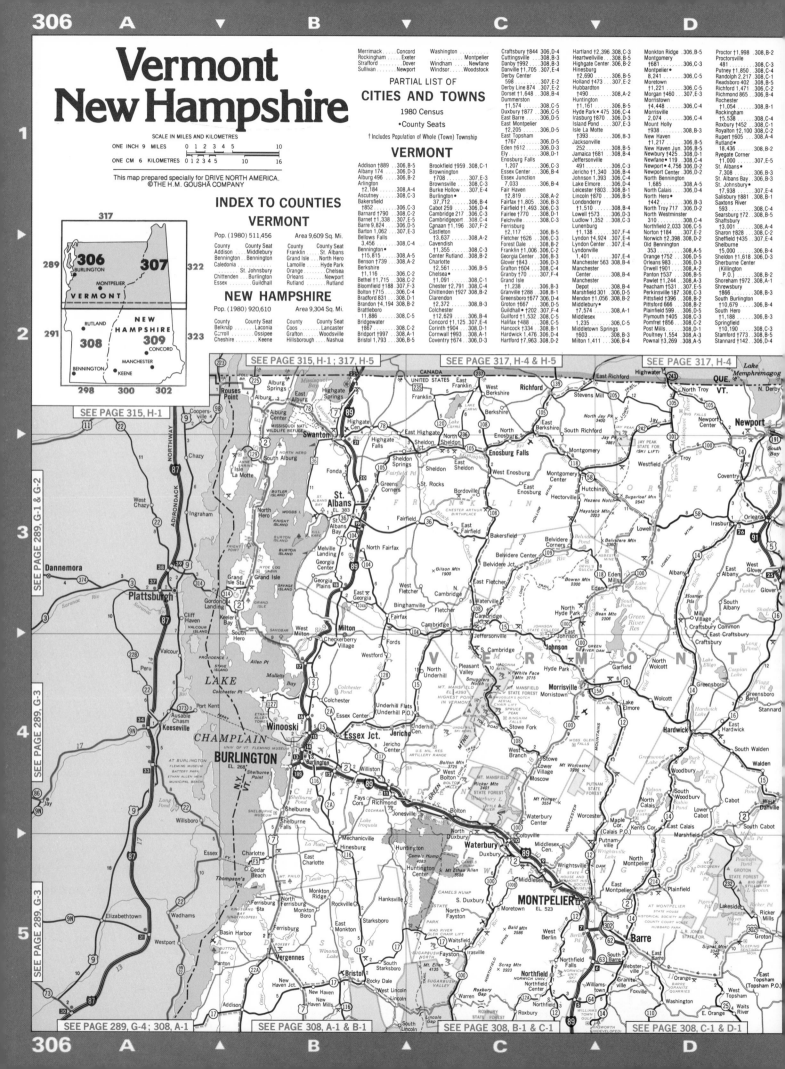

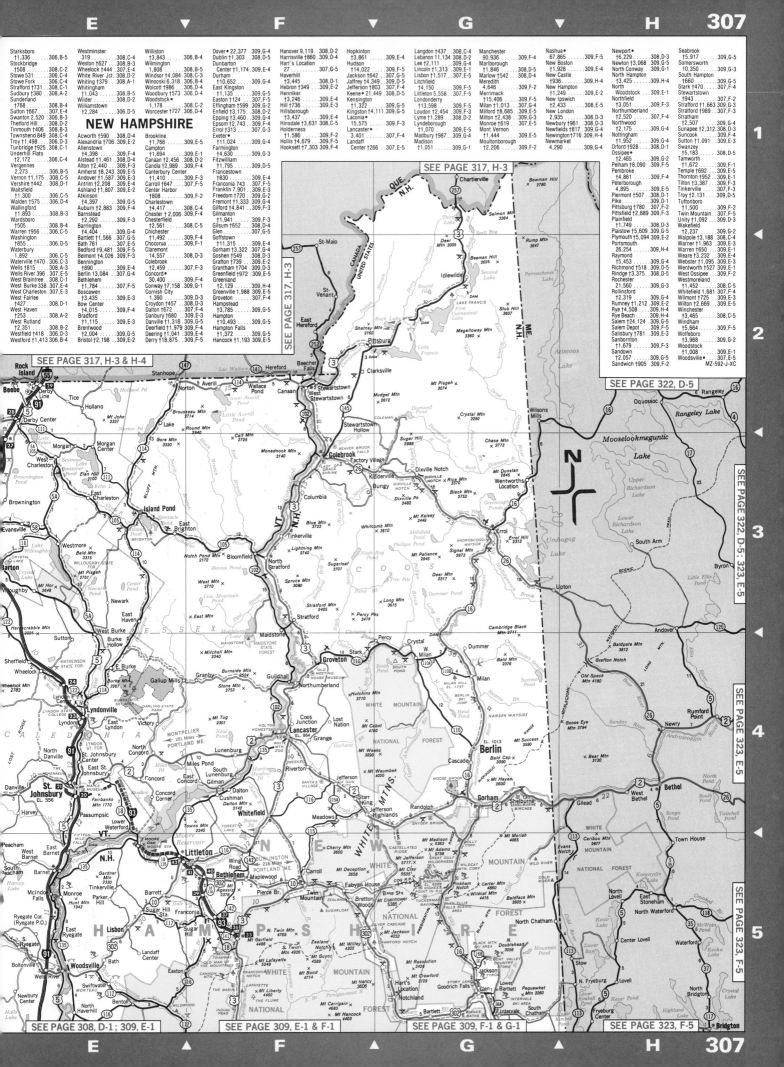

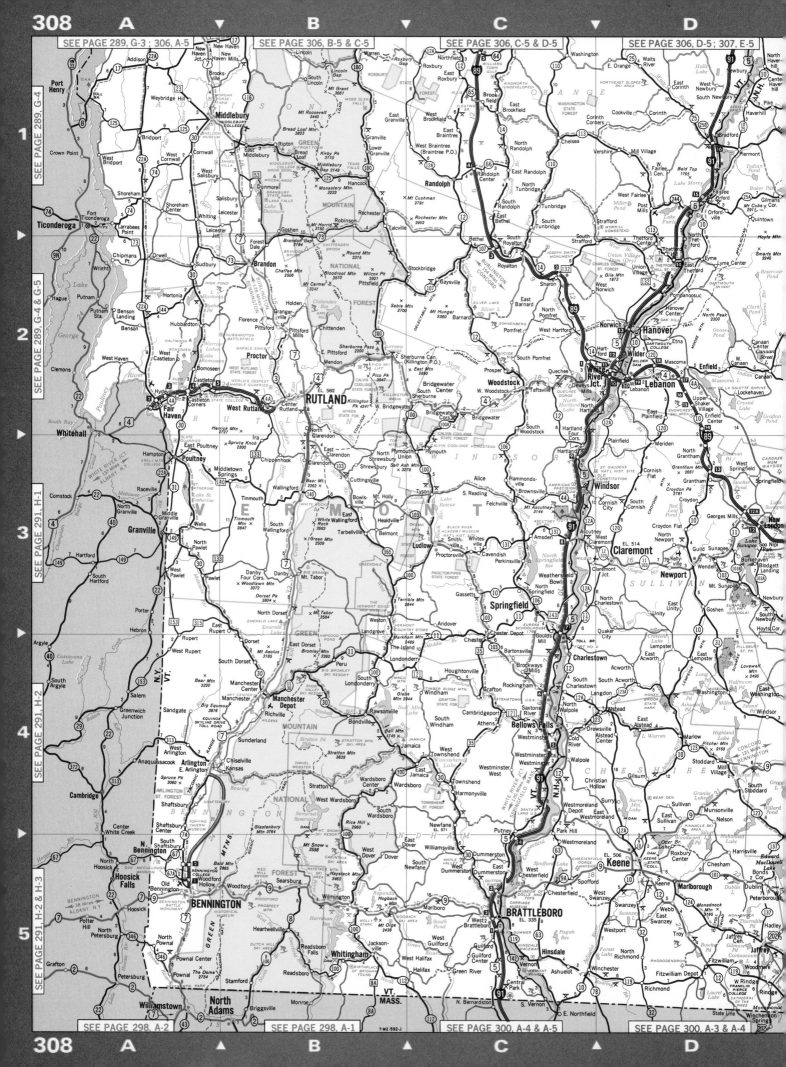

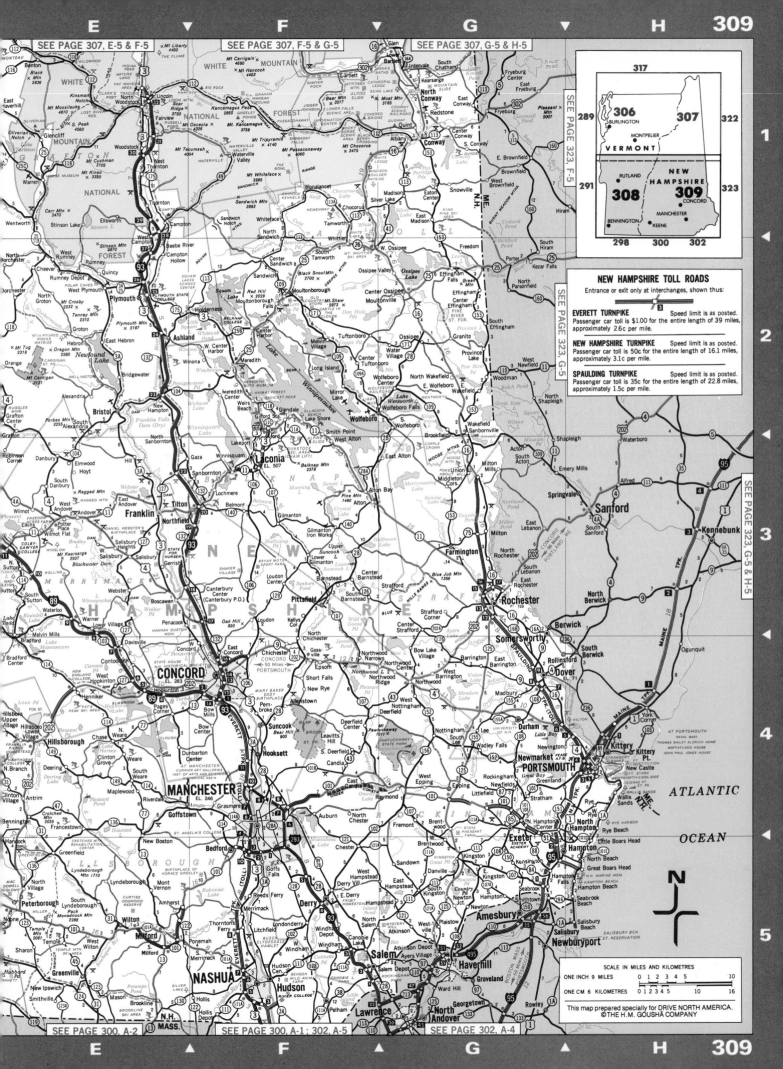

Gallic Warmth and 'joie de vivre,' Essences of *la Belle Province*

Québec

Canada's largest province is steeped in an atmosphere of old-world charm, of stone farmhouses and historic shrines. But it is also vibrantly modern, a place whose people—and arts—celebrate a unique heritage.

The city of **Hull (315, G-4)** was founded in 1800, more than two decades before Bytown (Ottawa), across the Ottawa River, began to grow. Northwest of the city stretches Gatineau Park, whose rolling hills embrace more than 200 kilometres of hiking and ski trails and a host of tranquil lakes.

South and east from Hull, traces of Canada's frontier days still linger along the banks of the Ottawa River. In summer, billowing sails are reflected in **Lac des Deux Montagnes (315, G-2)**, once a stopover for fur traders heading west. The picturesque village of **Saint-Eustache (315, G-2)** was the site of the decisive battle of the Rebellion of 1837; to this day the walls of the village church (1813) bear the marks of cannon shot.

Montréal (315, G-1), the largest city in *la Belle Province*, is a vivacious metropolis of almost three million people. Place Jacques-Cartier, in the heart of Old Montréal, was once a busy marketplace. Today the historic square is a realm of canopied gaiety, of outdoor cafés and quaint restaurants. Throughout the summer sidewalk artists sell their creations here, while local musicians lend a minstrel air. Historic buildings in the area include the domed Bonsecours Market (1849); the Auberge Le Vieux Saint-Gabriel, a restaurant dating (in parts) to 1688; and the Château de Ramezay, once the government seat of French Canada, now a museum of Québec history. Reconstructed Youville Stables (circa 1825) contains boutiques and workshops around a courtyard.

Uptown stands the magnificent Mary Queen of the World Cathedral. Thirteen bronze statues, patron saints of parishes that donated to the building's construction, dominate the facade of this 19th-century edifice. Opposite is Place Ville-Marie, a modern cross-shaped office tower that holds restaurants and fashionable boutiques in its concourse.

Montréal museums boast rich collections of art. The Museum of Fine Arts, Canada's oldest, holds works ranging from the Dutch and English masters to Picasso oils. Two life-size sculptures, Henry Moore's *Upright Motive No. 5* and Rodin's *Jean d'Aire* stand outside the nearby Dominion Gallery. McGill University's McCord Museum is a treasure house of Canadian social history.

Wooded slopes, undulating lawns and man-made Beaver Lake help make 500-acre Mount Royal Park a favorite year-round retreat and playground. The Mount Royal Art Center presents exhibitions in an old stone farmhouse; the park's 30-metre illuminated cross can be seen for 80 kilometres. Nearby St. Joseph's Oratory has evolved from the small chapel of a devoted lay brother into a world-renowned shrine that receives more than three million visitors annually.

Place Jacques-Cartier, Montréal

Successor to Expo 67, Man and his World holds a variety of fascinating pavilions whose themes range from humor to national achievements—all amid wide avenues, lagoons and gardens. La Ronde, on St. Helen's Island, sports a midway, bistros and rides. Nearby stands the Montréal Aquarium—home to penguins, sharks and brilliantly colored tropical fish—and the Montréal Military and Maritime Museum, housed in the arsenal of a fort built in 1820–24.

Fresh air, clear lakes and forested hills lure vacationers to the Laurentians, where resorts and inns offer water sports, horseback riding, tennis and golf in summer and superb alpine and cross-country skiing in winter. **Parc du Mont-Tremblant (315, E-2)**, with hundreds of kilometres of hiking, snowshoeing and cross-country ski trails, invites more rugged recreation.

Southeast of Montréal are the Eastern Townships (l'Estrie), the nine fertile counties that lie between the St. Lawrence lowlands and Québec's border with Vermont, New Hampshire and Maine. Ski hills here rival those of the Laurentians; in Lakes Memphrémagog and Massawippi anglers fish for ouananiche (landlocked salmon). Parc Safari Africain at **Hemmingford (315, H-1)** has one of the largest collections of exotic wildlife in Canada. Old-timers in the Canadian Railway Museum in **Saint-Constant (315, G-1)** include a locomotive that was built in 1887—and was one of the last steam engines to haul a CPR train, 86 years later.

Trois-Rivières (317, F-5), Canada's second-oldest city, was founded in 1634 at the confluence of two fur-trade routes, the St. Lawrence and the Saint-Maurice rivers. De Tonnancour House (1690), De Gannes House (1756) and several other early buildings still stand. North of town lie the remains of Les Forges du Saint-Maurice, the country's first iron foundry. A 65-kilometre scenic road cleaves **La Mauricie National Park (317, E-5)** and leads to campsites, beaches, boating and wildlife areas and scores of lakes.

Québec (317, E-3), the provincial capital, sits atop Cape Diamond, overlooking the St. Lawrence River. The heart of the city lies northwest of the historic Citadel, a massive, five-pointed fortress built atop the Cape in

Evening enfolds a typical rural Québec scene.

Québec's Château Frontenac (right) provides a backdrop for a smartly executed military review. Past and present are honored (below) on June 24, St. Jean Baptiste Day.

1820–32. To the southwest spreads the Plains of Abraham, where British troops led by Gen. James Wolfe defeated a French force under the Marquis de Montcalm in 1759, signaling the end of France's empire in the New World. Granite markers in National Battlefields Park commemorate key events of this most decisive battle in Canadian history. Nearby, the baronial towers of the Château Frontenac (1895), one of Canada's grand hotels, dominate the city skyline. Below the hotel's walls, a showcase for the architecture of New France has been created at Place Royale, where some 80 houses dating from the 17th and 18th centuries are being restored or rebuilt. *Bonhomme Carnaval*, a jovial giant snowman, rules over Québec's Winter Carnival in February. Streets then are lined with ice sculptures and there are parades, balls, and snowshoe races.

Only 40 kilometres from the bustle of Québec is the southern entrance to **Parc des Laurentides (316, D-3)**. This 8,000-square-kilometre wilderness (also known as

Sunlight glints through Percé Rock (above), Cartier's landfall in 1534.

Old Montréal's Notre Dame Church (below) is Canada's largest; its vaulted interior can accommodate 7,000 worshipers. The exquisite structure was decorated by French-Canadian artists including Osias Leduc and Victor Bourgeau. In Place d'Armes, winter snows blanket Philip Hébert's statue of de Maisonneuve, the founder of Montréal.

Réserve Faunique des Laurentides) has more than 1,500 lakes and some of the oldest mountains in the world. Caribou, once rare here, have been re-introduced to the area. One of several nature trails leads to a lovely 25-metre-high waterfall on the Noire River.

Its isolation ended in 1935 with the completion of the Montmorency Bridge, but **Ile d'Orléans (317, E-2)**, east of Québec, so preserves the province's rural past that the entire island is designated a historical site. Many islanders still cling to old customs, proud of the farms and villages that have stood here for more than two centuries. Some of the aged barns and fieldstone houses with their steep, Norman-style roofs are now restaurants, art galleries and theaters.

A shrine dedicated to Saint Anne in **Sainte-Anne-de-Beaupré (317, D-2)** attracts almost a million people each year, some merely curious, some hoping for a miraculous cure. Nearby **Parc du Mont Sainte-Anne**, one of eastern Canada's prime ski areas, has 29 downhill runs and 175 kilometres of cross-country ski trails.

Rich, fertile plains dotted with some 50 villages surround vast **Lac Saint-Jean (316, A-4)**. Behind them, ancient hills pile up far into the distance. Granite monoliths as big as

houses litter the north shore. The south shore supports dairy farms and unspoiled towns such as Hébertville, where charming 19th-century houses hug narrow streets.

The Gaspé Peninsula is a landscape of limestone cliffs, shingly beaches and fishing villages where cod is still dried on wooden racks along the beach. Inland, the magnificent Chic-Choc Mountains form a backdrop to deep river valleys and craggy gorges in **Réserve Matane (319, E-3)**. Farther east, one of the world's last herds of woodland caribou roams the slopes of 1,268-metre Mont Jacques-Cartier in **Parc de la Gaspésie (319,**

F-3). Most of a beautiful peninsula at the northeast tip of the Gaspé was set aside in 1970 as **Forillon National Park (319, G-3)**, a magnificent mix of seaside cliffs and forested headlands. Seals bask on offshore rocks and no fewer than six species of whales can be sighted in the waters off Forillon.

A cross erected in **Gaspé (319, G-3)** in 1934 commemorates Jacques Cartier's landing here four centuries earlier. A few kilometres from the beaches of **Percé (319, H-4)**, tens of thousands of gannets, murres, cormorants, puffins and gulls crowd the 100-metre-high cliffs of Ile de Bonaventure.

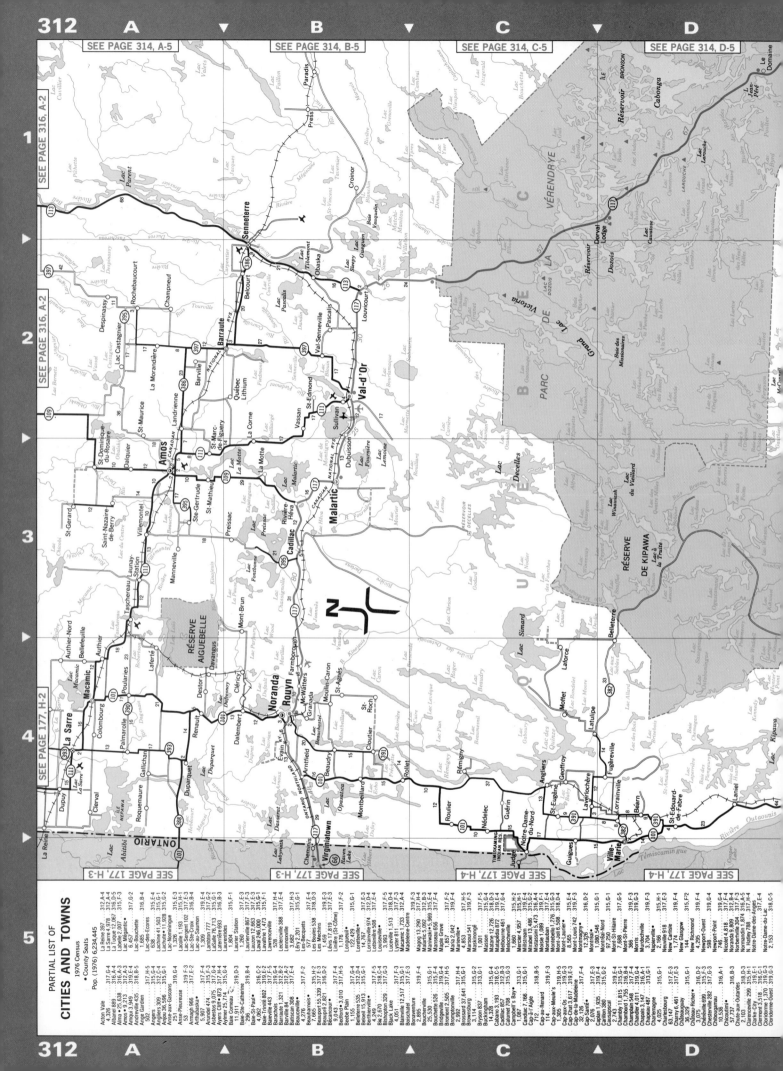

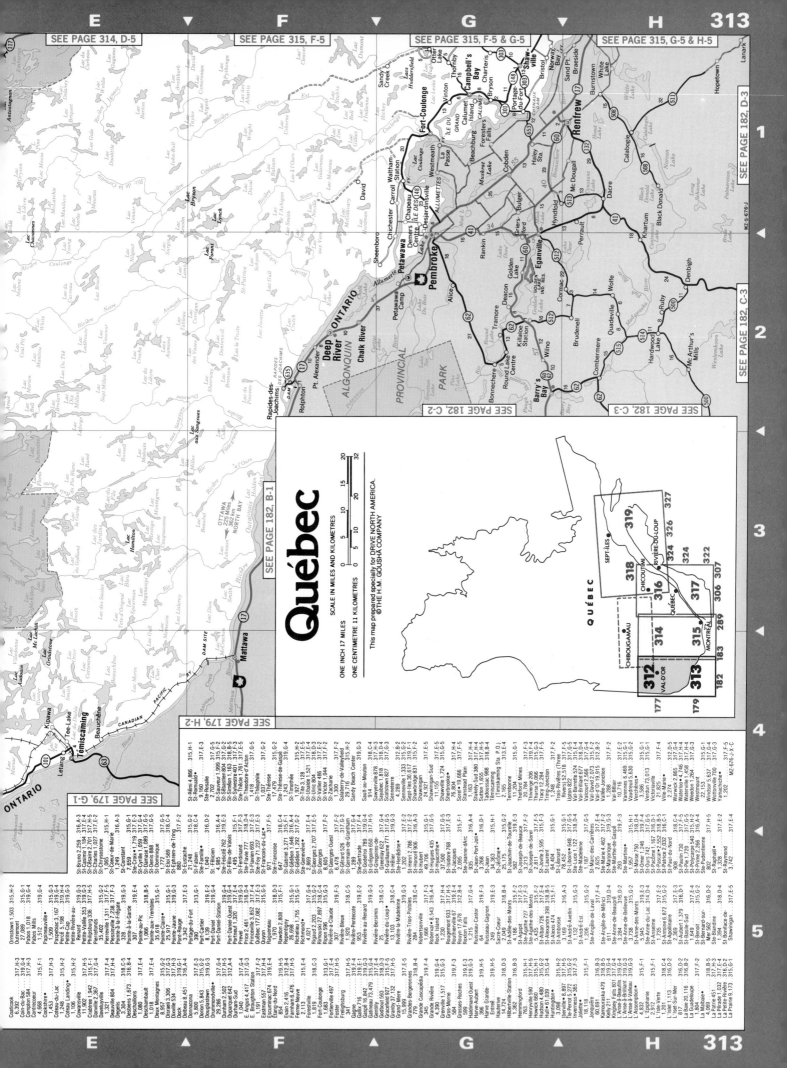

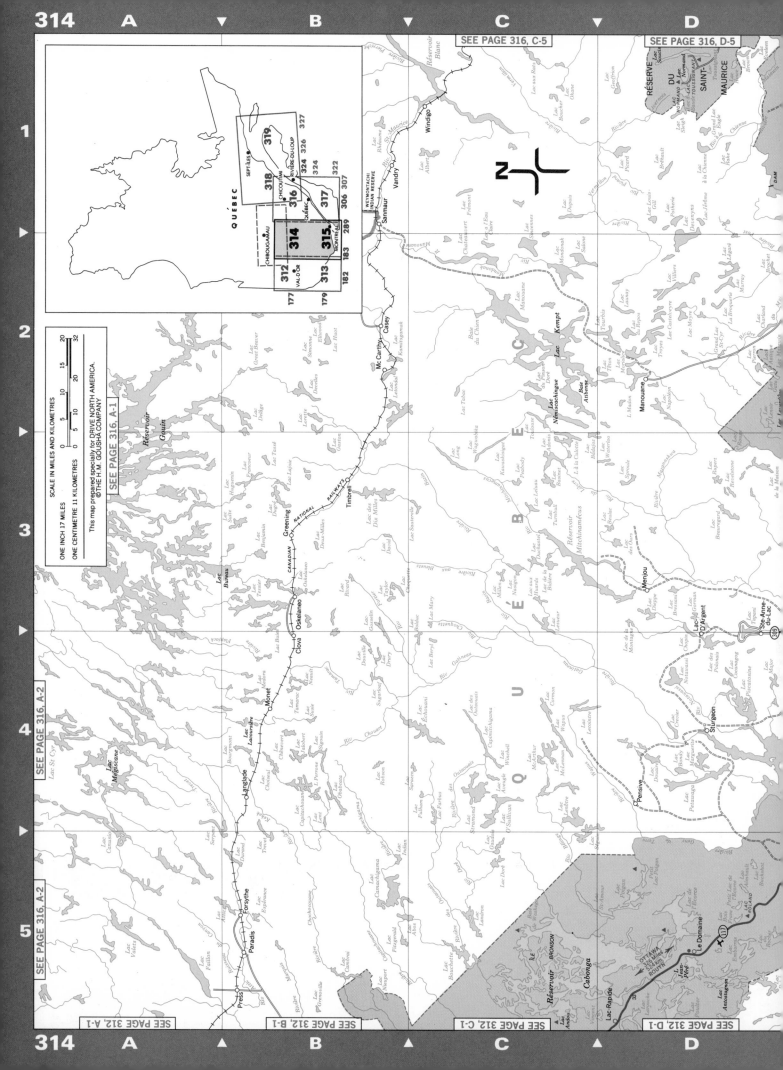

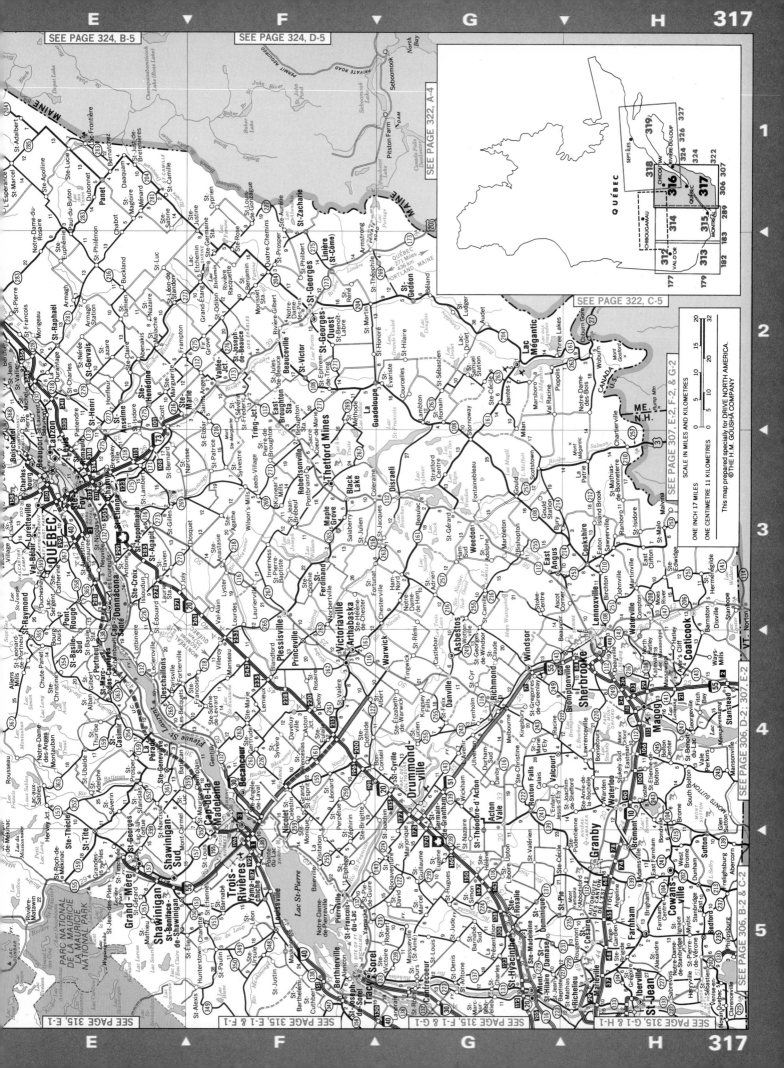

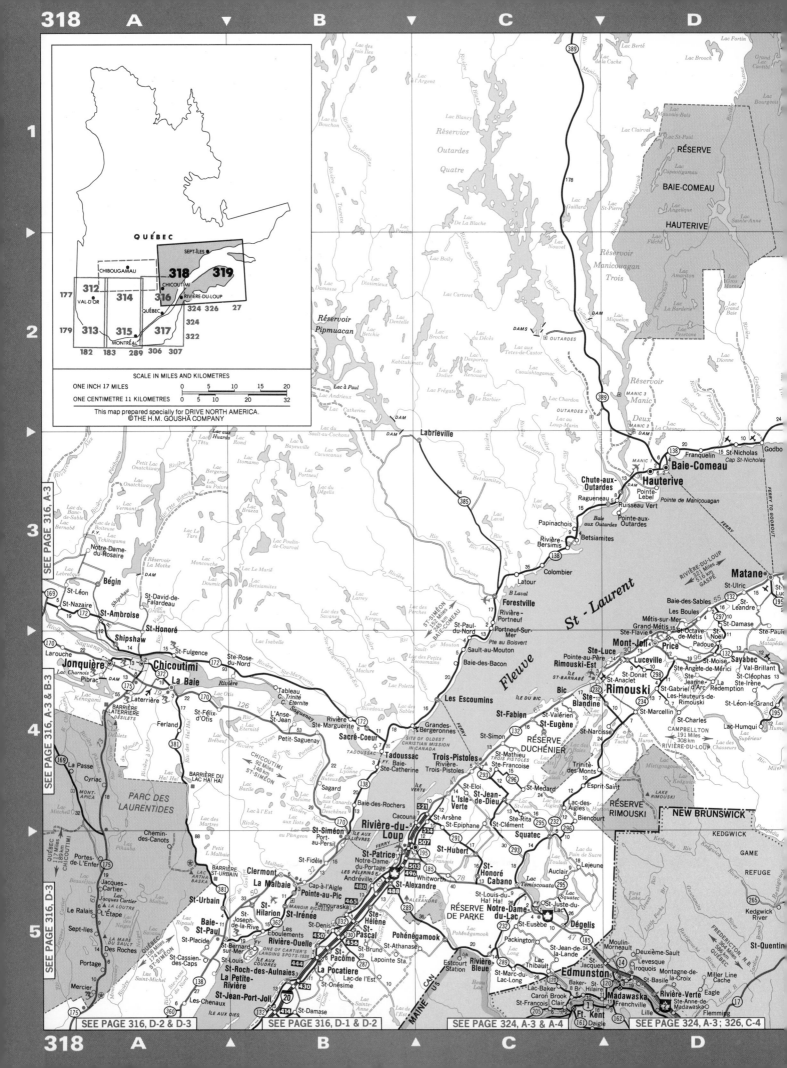

A Magnificent Maritime Realm of Loyalists, Acadians and Yankees

Maine/New Brunswick

The Pine Tree State, as Maine is called, is more than 85 percent forest. But it is the Atlantic that most travelers picture when they think of Maine. And it is this that beckons, with its foaming surf, secluded coves and island resorts, tidy fishing hamlets and Maine's most famous export—the lobster.

Southeast of Bangor lies the maritime realm of **Acadia National Park (325, H-3)**, which includes half of Mount Desert Island, named by Samuel de Champlain in 1604 for its barren heights. A paved road climbs 1,530-foot Cadillac Mountain—the highest peak on America's Atlantic Coast—to panoramas of islands, inlets and wave-worn headlands. A loop road includes Great Head, a sheer granite wall plunging 140 feet, and Thunder Hole, where the sea surges into a narrow chute with the force of a cannonball. **Bar Harbor** is a quaint resort town that for a century was the exclusive domain of the wealthy.

Sailors once whiled away long hours at sea creating scrimshaw—whalebone and ivory carvings—when Maine was a seafaring capital. Today this handiwork is displayed in the Penobscot Marine Museum at **Searsport (325, H-4)**. Harpoons, shipbuilding tools, charts and logbooks are also on view. Southwest lies **Rockland (323, F-2)**, site of the William A. Farnsworth Art Museum and Library. Works by three generations of Wyeths form part of the museum's collection of 19th- and 20th-century American paintings, prints, drawings and sculptures.

The cliffs of **Pemaquid Beach (323,G-3)** are among the most rugged in a state famous for them. Each spring the tidal Damariscotta River here teems with spawning alewives. Fort William Henry is a reconstruction of the 1692 stronghold built at Pemaquid by Sir William Phipps, first Royal Governor of Massachusetts. Fragments of English and European coins, pottery and tableware unearthed at Colonial Pemaquid, a treasure trove of 17th-century artifacts, are displayed here. The Age of Sail lives on at the Maine Marine Museum in **Bath (323, F-3)** through models, paintings, dioramas and photographs in 32 exhibit rooms—one designed for children urging them to "Please Touch."

Inland, on the Kennebec River, is **Augusta (323, E-3)**, Maine's capital since 1832. The granite State Capitol, capped by a gilded copper figure of Wisdom, dominates a 57-acre setting that also includes a 300,000-volume library and a museum and archives tracing Maine history. Benedict Arnold and Aaron Burr were among the famous figures who visited Fort Western (1754), the last Colonial fort in Maine, now a museum. Fine paintings and 19th-century furniture enhance the James G. Blaine House, built in 1830 by a man who became Speaker of the House of Representatives, Secretary of State and an unsuccessful candidate for the Presidency in 1884. **Hallowell (323, F-3)**, below Augusta on the Kennebec River, is a fascinating example of a 19th-century river port from

which ships once sailed for the West Indies.

Portland (323, G-4), the U.S. port nearest to Europe, is the state's major coastal city. Poet Henry Wadsworth Longfellow grew up in Portland's first brick house (1785), now a museum of Longfellow memorabilia. The nearby Victorian Mansion, a two-story brownstone with a magnificent "flying" staircase, is an opulent reminder of that age. Excellent examples of 19th- and 20th-century American art occupy three buildings of the Portland Museum of Art. In 1787 George Washington ordered the construction of the rubblestone Portland Head Light, one of four Colonial lighthouse towers still standing.

Scattered along Maine's southern coast are the picturesque shipbuilding-turned-resort towns of **Kennebunk (323, H-5)** and **Kennebunkport**. Nearby **Ogunquit**—Abnaki for "beautiful place by the sea"—is endowed

Maine's Mount Katahdin (above), seen from Chimney Point. Sloops and schooners (below) *bob in Camden's hill-girt harbor.*

with a 3-mile long white sand beach and the Cliff Walk, a historic promenade past rocky headlands and Victorian summer houses. Picturesque **York** holds among its charms the Elizabeth Perkins House (1732) with its protective "Indian shutters" and stenciled walls, and the Emerson-Wilcox House (1740). The Old Gaol, begun in 1719, is the oldest English civic building in the United States.

Across 92 miles of northern Maine winds the Allagash Wilderness Waterway, a forested chain of lakes and rivers that embraces 200,000-acre **Baxter State Park (324, D-4)**.

Baxter's sole concession to the automobile is a narrow, unpaved road; most of the park can be seen only from 75 miles of trails. Several paths lead to Mount Katahdin, at 5,267 feet the highest point in Maine. The Appalachian trail to Georgia—2,000 miles distant—begins nearby.

Coursing from New Brunswick's remote northwestern border with Maine to tidewater on the Bay of Fundy, the magnificent St. John River weaves through some of the most varied and enchanting scenery in the Maritimes. It is paralleled for most of

Delightful Atlantic puffins (left) summer on Grand Manan Island.

Franklin D. Roosevelt spent much of his youth on Campobello Island (below).

Fort Beauséjour was the scene of bitter fighting during the French and Indian War.

Fresh from the sea: herring is hung for curing near Seal Cove, New Brunswick.

its length by the Trans-Canada Highway. At **Hartland (328, B-1)**, it flows beneath the world's longest covered bridge (391 metres); hills flanking the river near **Woodstock** create one of the loveliest views in Atlantic Canada. Woodstock's hospitality is especially warm during Old Home Week, an annual July celebration that includes horse-pulling contests and harness racing. **Mactaquac Provincial Park (328, C-2)** has marinas, beaches, nature and hiking trails, playgrounds, an outdoor amphitheater, a rainy-day recreation center, and tent and trailer sites.The park's winter facilities include a toboggan run, lighted skating ponds, and snowshoe and cross-country ski trails.

Not far away the past seems rooted in the present at King's Landing Historical Settlement, an old-time community of more than 60 buildings in **Prince William (328, C-2)** that re-creates life along the St. John River between 1820 and 1890. Draft animals and costumed staff tread dirt lanes, visitors quaff beer in the cosy taproom of the King's Head Inn, and women weave and spin, churn butter and make soap in historic houses where cheery fires welcome guests.

Downstream lies **Fredericton (328, D-2)**, wrested from the wilderness by Loyalists in 1783. The "City of Stately Elms," now the provincial capital, is home to the nation's oldest provincial university (1785), Canada's first astronomical observatory (1851) and

its first engineering school (1854). The Beaverbrook Art Gallery features a superb collection of British and Canadian paintings, including works by Gainsborough, Turner, Hogarth and the Group of Seven.

The five-kilometre Loyalist Trail in **Saint John (329, E-4)** is a journey into the history of one of North America's oldest cities. The walk leads past the Old Loyalist Burial Ground (its first gravestone dates from 1784), the bustling, block-long Old City Market (1876), the Loyalist House, with its 1818 Duncan Phyfe tables and elegant swooning sofas; and Barbour's General Store, a faithful re-creation of an 1800s shop with cracker barrels and spice racks. An outstanding nautical collection at the New Brunswick Museum includes ship models and supplies and equipment from the clipper ship *Marco Polo*. Twice daily some of the world's highest tides (up to 15 metres) rush into the Bay of Fundy, forcing the roiling waters *upstream* over Reversing Falls Rapids.

Three blockhouses were built in 1812 to defend **St. Andrews (328, C-4)** against American privateers—who never did attack. The lone surviving blockhouse and battery of cannons, a national historic site, guards the harbor entrance to this charming resort town. Whales, seals, lobsters and eels inhabit the sheltered waters of Passamaquoddy Bay, and its sandy fringes yield a rich offering of marine life at low tide—periwinkles, sand dol-

lars, starfish and moon snails. Offshore lies **Campobello Island (328, C-5)**, where President Franklin D. Roosevelt summered. His 34-room Dutch Colonial "cottage" (a wedding gift from his mother) is the centerpiece of Roosevelt-Campobello International Park. Ferries from **Black's Harbour (328, C-4)** on the mainland service the Grand Manan Islands, whose towering cliffs are home to thousands of nesting seabirds—a sight that astonished naturalist John James Audubon in 1833.

Battered by the waves of the Bay of Fundy, the steep, sculptured cliffs of **Fundy National Park (329, F-3)** are indented with scores of coves and inlets. The 207-square-kilometre park rises from the craggy coast to the Caledonia Highlands—a plateau of rolling maple hills full of tumbling brooks and rivers, placid lakes and meadows. In the dense forests moose, white-tailed deer, bears and bobcats find shelter. Outside the park at Hopewell Cape stand top-heavy columns of soft red rock, called "flowerpots," capped by balsam fir and stunted black spruce.

Old Acadian dykes near **Sackville (329, G-2)** hem the 20,000-acre Tantramar marshes, dubbed the "world's biggest hayfield." In 1755 the marshes became a battleground as British troops and New England volunteers captured French-held Fort Beauséjour near **Aulac (329, G-3)**.The stronghold's restored foundations and stone casements, built after the 1755 siege, are visible today. **Shediac (329, G-2)**—the self-proclaimed "Lobster Capital of the World"—stages a week-long festival in mid-July with parades, folk songs and dances, sports events and lobster dinners. Shediac has several inviting beaches on the Northumberland Strait; their waters are among the warmest north of Virginia.

A 25-kilometre sweep of sandbars shelters tidepools and salt marshes in **Kouchibouguac National Park (327, G-5)**. Peat bogs here are estimated to be 6,000 years old, and marram grass and false heather anchor rippling coastal dunes. The park's quiet tidewater lagoons offer fine swimming.

Rich in Acadian tradition, northeastern New Brunswick has always looked to the sea for its livelihood. A ritual blessing of the fishing fleet, symbolic of Christ's blessing of the fishermen of Galilee, is a highlight of the annual Acadian Festival in **Caraquet (327, G-3)** each August. Residents of the Village Historique Acadien, a re-created pioneer community between Caraquet and Grande Anse, live much as their forbears did—tending cattle and crops.

321

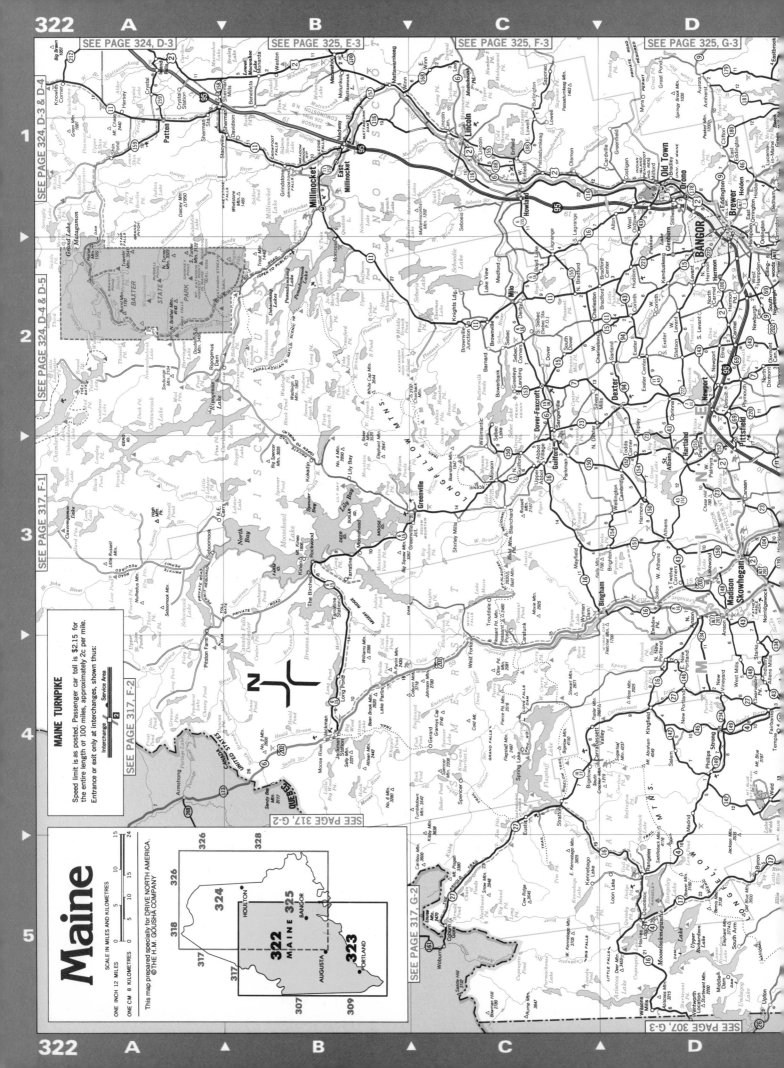

SEE PAGE 324, D-3 & D-4

SEE PAGE 324, D-4, D-5

SEE PAGE 317, F-1

SEE PAGE 317, F-2

SEE PAGE 317, G-2

SEE PAGE 317, G-2

SEE PAGE 307, G-3

MAINE TURNPIKE

Speed limit is as posted. Passenger car toll is $2.15 for the entire length or 100 miles, approximately 2c per mile.

Entrance or exit only at interchanges, shown thus:

Interchange ■ Service Area

Maine

SCALE IN MILES AND KILOMETRES

ONE INCH 12 MILES

ONE CM 8 KILOMETRES

This map prepared specially for DRIVE NORTH AMERICA.
© THE H.M. GOUSHA COMPANY

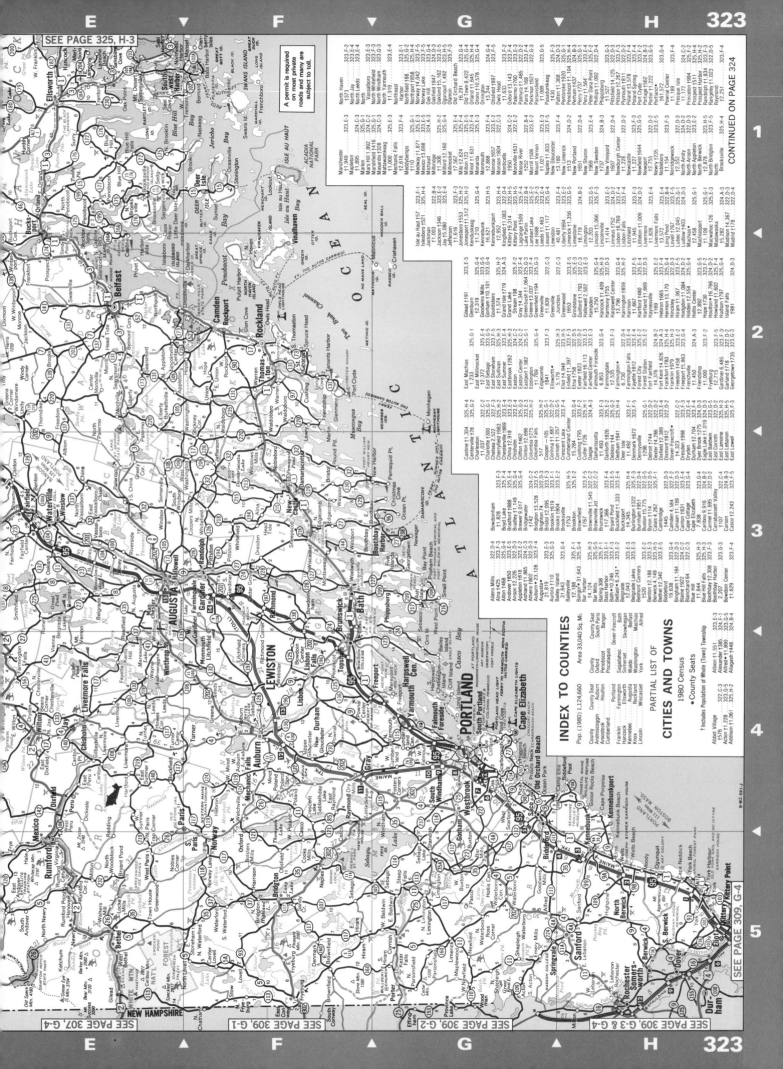

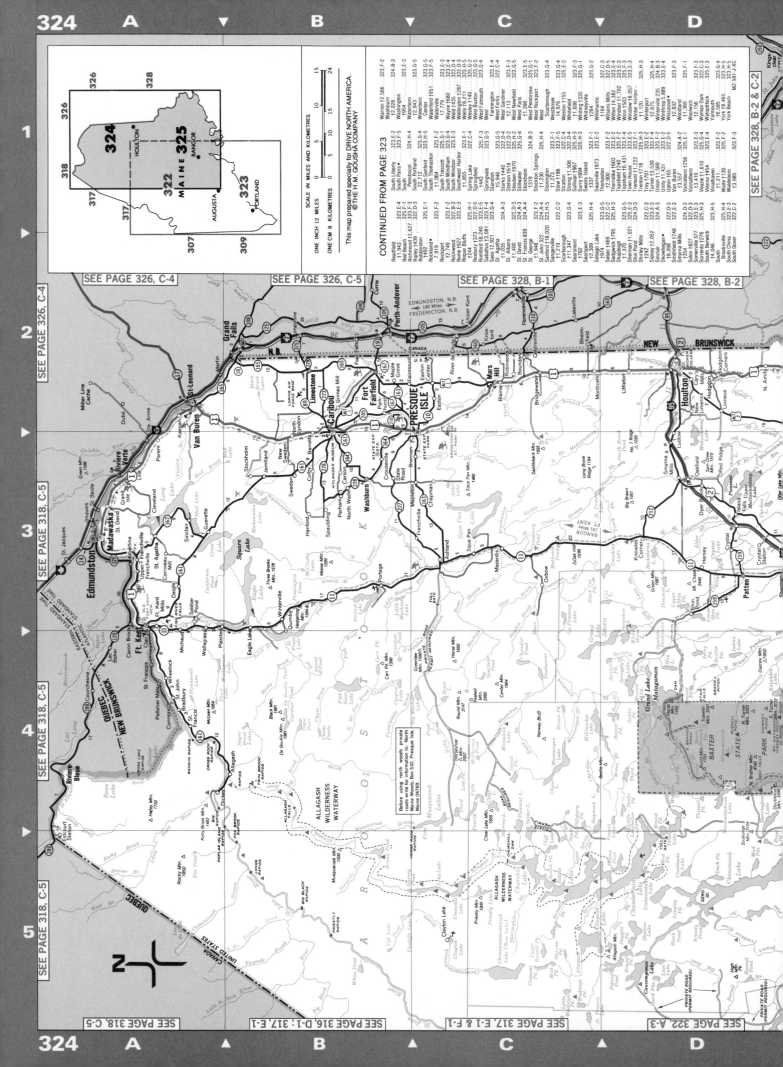

SEE PAGE 326, C-4 · SEE PAGE 326, C-5 · SEE PAGE 328, B-1 · SEE PAGE 328, B-2

SEE PAGE 326, C-4
SEE PAGE 318, C-5
SEE PAGE 318, C-5
SEE PAGE 318, C-5

SEE PAGE 316, D-1; 317, E-1
SEE PAGE 317, E-1 & F-1
SEE PAGE 322, A-3

SCALE IN MILES AND KILOMETRES
© THE H.M. GOUSHA COMPANY
This map prepared specially for DRIVE NORTH AMERICA.

ONE INCH 12 MILES
ONE CM 8 KILOMETRES

CONTINUED FROM PAGE 323

Readfield 323.E-4
Red Beach 325.F-1
Richmond 12,627 323.F-3
Ripley 1439 323.E-3
Robbinston 1492 322.D-3
Rockland• 7,919 323.F-5
Rockport 7,749 323.F-5
Rockwood 322.B-3
Rome 1627 323.F-3
Roque Bluffs 325.H-1
11,855
Roxbury 1373 323.E-5
Rumford 18,240 322.D-5
Sabattus 13,081 323.F-4
Saco 12,921 323.G-4
St. Agatha 1974 324.A-2
St. Albans 1035 323.E-3
St. David 322.D-2
St. Francis 839 324.A-3
St. George 323.G-4
St. John 322.C-2
St. John 322 324.A-2
Sanford 18,020 323.H-5
Scarborough 11,230 323.G-4
Sebago Lake 11,230 323.F-4
Sebec 1469 323.E-2
Sedgwick 1795 325.H-3
Shapleigh 322.G-4
Sherman 16,431 325.H-3
Sherman 11,021 323.G-5
Shin Pond 324.D-3
Shirley Mills 323.E-3
Trenton 1718 325.H-3
Troy 1701 323.F-3
Turner 11,539 323.F-4
Union 11,369 323.F-5
Unity 11,431 323.F-3
Van Buren 324.A-2
Vanceboro 1256 325.F-1
Vassalboro 323.F-3
Vazie 11,610 325.G-2
Vienna 1454 323.E-3
Vinalhaven 14,046 323.H-5
Waite 1130 325.H-4
Waldoboro 5,889 323.G-4
Waldo 322.F-3

Warren 12,566 323.F-2
Washburn 324.B-3
Washington 1954 323.F-5
Waterboro 12,943 322.G-4
Waterboro Center 323.G-5
Waterford 1951 323.F-5
Waterville 1,064 323.F-2
Wayne 1680 323.F-3
Weld 1435 322.D-4
Wellington 1287 322.D-3
Wells 18,211 322.H-5
Wesley 1140 325.H-3
West Burton 322.D-4
West Falmouth 323.G-4
West Farmington 2,113 322.E-4
West Gardiner 323.F-3
West Newfield 322.G-4
West Paris 322.E-5
West Pembroke 325.H-1
Weston 1155 325.G-1
Westbrook 14,976 323.G-4
Whitefield 323.F-3
Whitefield 1,606 323.F-3
Whiting 1335 325.H-1
Whitneyville 1264 325.H-3
Willimantic 1337 323.F-1
Wilsons Mills 322.C-4
Wilton 14,382 322.E-4
Windsor 11,702 323.F-3
Winn 1500 325.G-1
Winslow 18,057 323.F-2
Winter Harbor 325.H-3
Winterport 11,222 325.G-2
Winterport 323.G-3
Winthrop 12,052 323.F-3
Winthrop 5,889 324.A-2
Wiscasset 12,832 323.F-3
Woodland 11,369 324.A-2
Woolwich 1554 323.F-3
Wyman Dam 322.D-3
Woolpocack 1454 323.E-3
Yarmouth 323.G-4
York 16,585 322.H-5
York 18,465 325.H-5
York Beach 13,985 322.H-5

NEW BRUNSWICK
NEW BRUNSWICK
QUEBEC
CANADA
UNITED STATES
ALLAGASH WILDERNESS WATERWAY
BAXTER STATE PARK

Before using north woods, private roads write for information to North Maine Woods, Box 532, Presque Isle, Maine 04769

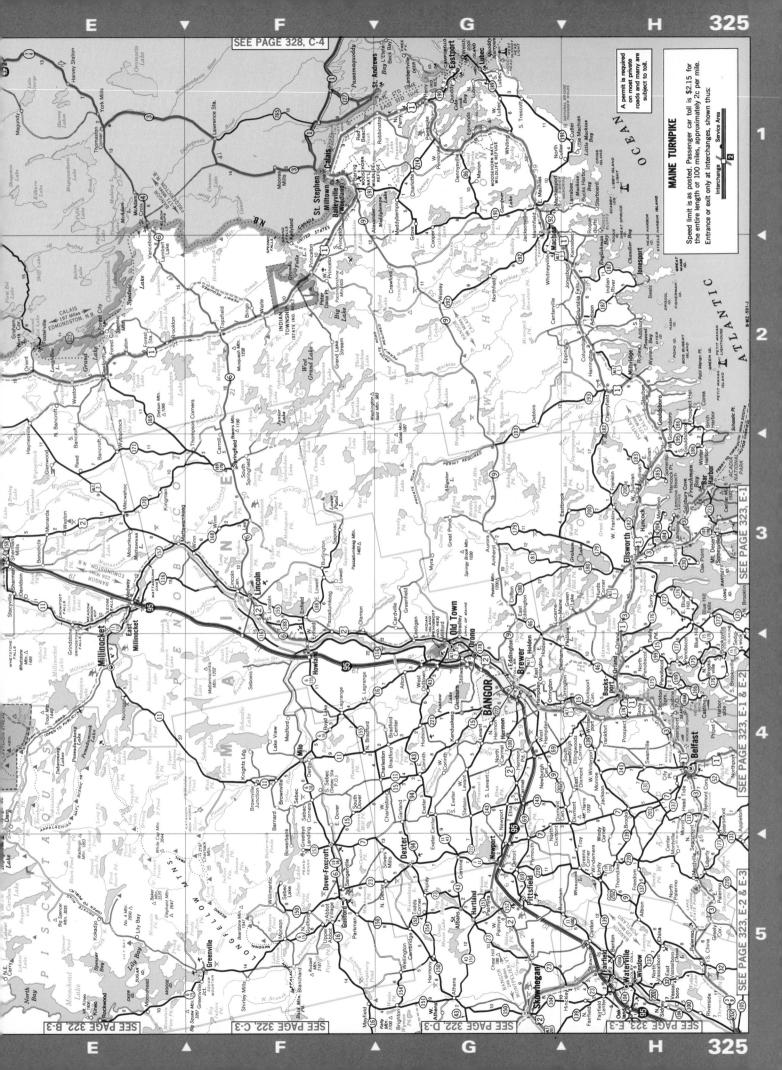

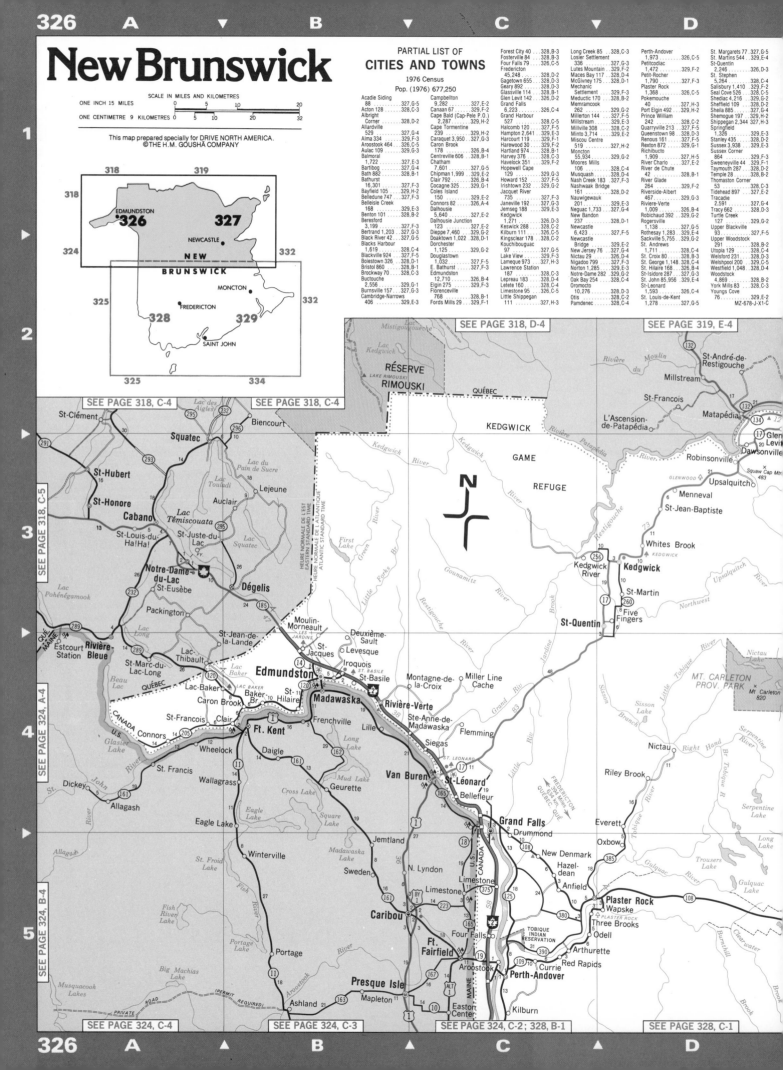

New Brunswick

ONE INCH 15 MILES
ONE CENTIMETRE 9 KILOMETRES

SCALE IN MILES AND KILOMETRES

This map prepared specially for DRIVE NORTH AMERICA.
©THE H.M. GOUSHA COMPANY

PARTIAL LIST OF CITIES AND TOWNS

1976 Census
Pop. (1976) 677,250

Place	Map ref.
Acadie Siding 88	327,G-5
Acton 128	328,C-3
Albright Corner	328,D-2
Allardville 529	327,G-4
Alma 334	329,F-2
Aroostook 464	326,C-5
Aulac 109	329,G-3
Balmoral 1,722	327,E-3
Bartibog 882	327,G-4
Bath 882	328,B-1
Bathurst 16,301	327,F-3
Bayfield 105	329,H-2
Belledune 747	327,F-3
Bellisle Creek 168	329,E-3
Benton 101	328,B-2
Beresford 3,199	327,F-3
Bertrand 1,203	327,G-3
Black River 42	327,G-6
Blacks Harbour 1,619	328,C-4
Blackville 924	327,F-5
Boiestown 326	328,D-1
Bristol 860	328,B-1
Brockway 70	328,C-3
Buctouche 2,556	329,G-1
Burnsville 157	327,G-4
Cambridge-Narrows 406	329,E-3
Campbellton 9,282	327,E-2
Canaan 67	329,F-2
Cape Bald (Cap-Pele P.O.) 2,287	329,H-2
Cape Tormentine 239	329,H-2
Caraquet 3,950	327,G-3
Caron Brook 178	326,B-4
Centreville 606	328,B-1
Chatham 7,601	327,G-5
Chipman 1,999	329,E-2
Clair 792	326,B-4
Cocagne 325	329,G-1
Coles Island 150	329,E-2
Connors 365	326,A-4
Dalhousie 5,640	327,E-2
Dalhousie Junction 123	327,E-2
Dieppe 7,460	329,G-2
Doaktown 1,022	328,D-1
Dorchester 1,125	329,G-2
Douglastown 1,032	327,F-5
E. Bathurst 1,277	327,F-3
Edmundston 12,710	326,B-4
Elgin 275	329,F-3
Florenceville 768	328,B-1
Fords Mills 29	329,F-1
Forest City 40	328,B-3
Fosterville 84	328,B-3
Four Falls 79	326,C-5
Fredericton 45,248	328,D-2
Gagetown 655	328,D-3
Geary 892	328,D-3
Glassville 114	328,B-1
Glen Levit 142	327,E-3
Grand Falls 6,223	326,C-4
Grand Harbour 527	328,C-5
Halcomb 120	327,F-5
Hampton 2,641	329,E-3
Harcourt 119	329,F-1
Harewood 30	329,F-2
Hartland 974	328,B-1
Harvey 376	328,C-3
Havelock 351	329,F-2
Hopewell Cape 129	329,F-2
Howard 152	327,F-5
Irishtown 232	329,G-1
Jacquet River 467	327,F-3
Janeville 192	327,G-3
Jemseg 188	329,E-3
Kedgwick 1,271	326,D-3
Keswick 288	328,C-2
Kilburn 111	326,C-5
Kingsclear 178	328,C-2
Kouchibouguac 97	327,G-5
Lake View	329,F-3
Lameque 973	327,H-3
Lawrence Station 187	328,C-3
Lepreau 183	328,D-4
Letete 160	328,C-4
Limestone 95	326,C-5
Little Shippegan 111	327,H-3
Long Creek 85	328,C-3
Losier Settlement 336	327,G-3
Lutes Mountain	329,F-2
Maces Bay 117	328,D-4
McGivney 175	328,D-1
Mechanic Settlement	329,F-3
Meductic 170	328,B-2
Memramcook 262	329,G-2
Millerton 144	327,F-5
Millstream	329,E-3
Millville 308	328,C-2
Minto 3,714	329,E-2
Miscou Centre 519	327,H-2
Moncton 55,934	329,G-2
Moores Mills 106	328,C-3
Musquash 36	328,D-4
Nash Creek 183	327,F-3
Nashwaak Bridge 161	328,D-2
Nauwigewauk 201	329,E-3
Neguac 1,733	327,G-4
New Bandon 237	328,D-1
Newcastle 6,423	327,F-5
Newcastle Bridge	329,E-2
New Jersey 76	327,G-4
Nictau 29	326,D-4
Nigadoo 799	327,F-3
Norton 1,285	329,E-3
Notre-Dame 282	329,G-2
Oak Bay 254	328,C-4
Oromocto 10,276	328,D-3
Otis	328,C-2
Pamdenec	328,C-4
Perth-Andover 1,973	326,C-5
Petitcodiac 1,472	329,F-2
Petit-Rocher 1,790	327,F-3
Plaster Rock 1,368	326,C-5
Pokemouche 40	327,H-3
Port Elgin 492	329,H-2
Prince William 242	328,C-2
Quarryville 213	327,F-5
Queenstown 98	328,D-3
Renous 161	327,F-5
Rexton 872	329,G-1
Richibucto 1,909	327,H-5
River Charlo	327,E-2
River de Chute 42	326,C-5
River Glade 264	329,G-3
Riverside-Albert	329,G-3
Riviere-Verte 1,009	326,B-4
Robichaud 392	329,G-2
Rogersville 1,138	327,G-5
Rothesay 1,283	329,E-4
Sackville 5,755	329,G-2
St. Andrews 1,711	328,C-4
St. Croix 80	328,C-3
St. George 1,148	328,C-4
St. Hilaire 168	326,B-4
St-Isidore 287	327,G-3
St. John 85,956	329,E-4
St-Leonard 1,593	326,C-4
St. Louis-de-Kent 1,278	327,G-5
St. Margarets 77	327,G-5
St. Martins 544	329,E-4
St-Quentin 2,246	326,D-3
St. Stephen 5,264	328,C-4
Salisbury 1,410	329,F-2
Seal Cove 526	328,C-5
Shediac 4,216	329,G-2
Sheffield 105	328,D-2
Sheila 885	327,H-3
Shemogue 197	329,H-2
Shippegan 2,344	327,H-3
Springfield	329,E-3
Stanley 435	328,D-2
Sussex 3,938	329,F-3
Sussex Corner 864	329,F-3
Sweeneyville 44	329,F-1
Taymouth 287	328,D-2
Temple 28	328,B-2
Thomaston Corner 53	328,C-3
Tidehead 897	327,E-2
Tracadie 2,591	327,G-3
Tracy 662	328,D-3
Turtle Creek 127	329,G-2
Upper Blackville 93	327,F-5
Upper Woodstock 291	328,B-2
Utopia 129	328,C-4
Welsford 231	328,D-3
Welshpool 200	329,C-5
Westfield 1,048	328,D-4
Woodstock 4,869	328,B-2
York Mills 83	328,C-3
Youngs Cove 76	329,E-2

MZ-678-J-X1-C

SEE PAGE 318, D-4   SEE PAGE 319, E-4   SEE PAGE 318, C-4   SEE PAGE 324, C-4   SEE PAGE 324, C-3   SEE PAGE 324, C-2; 328, B-1   SEE PAGE 328, C-1

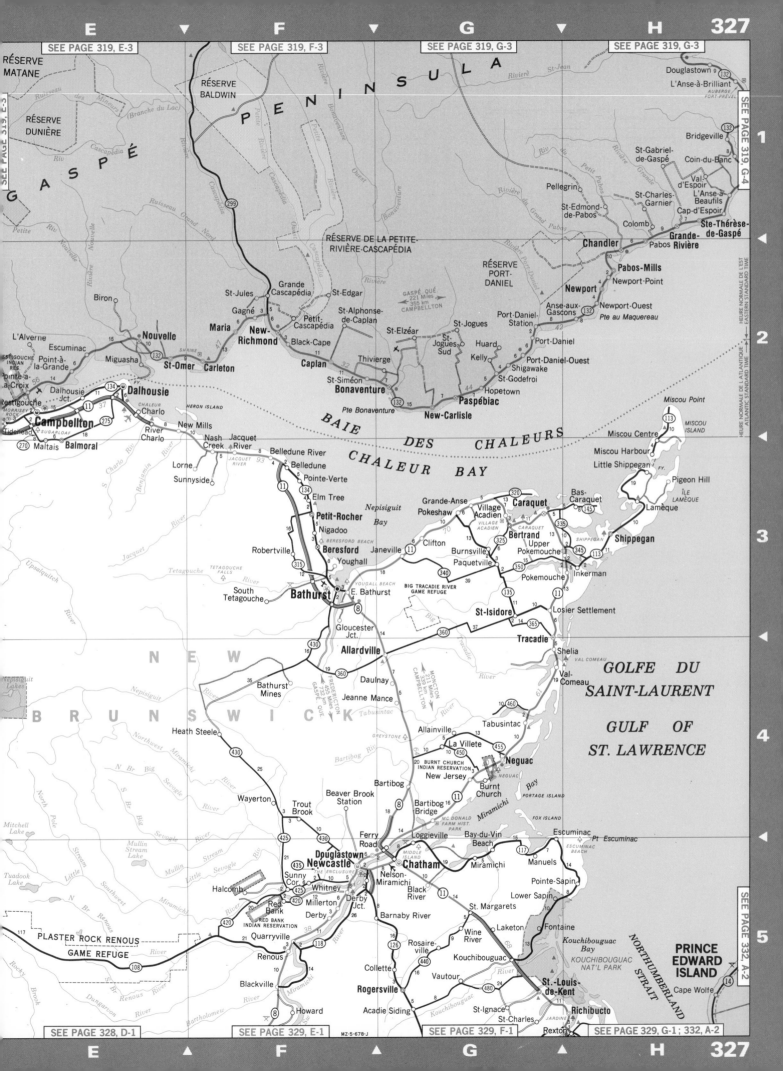

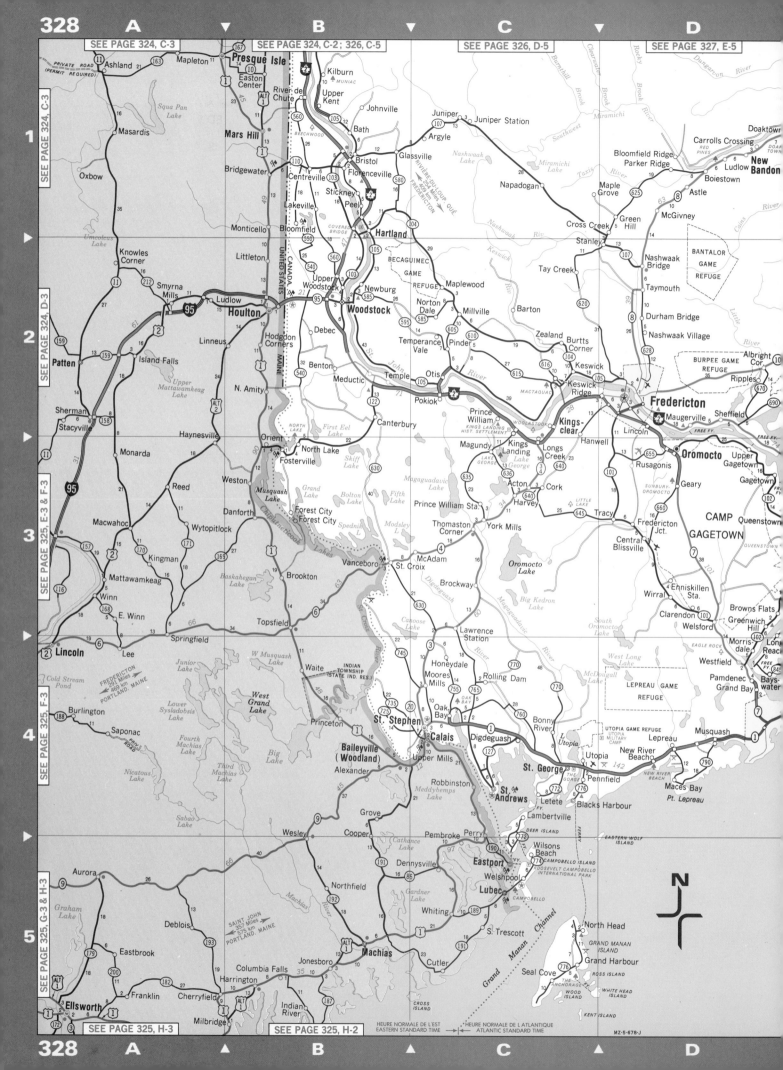

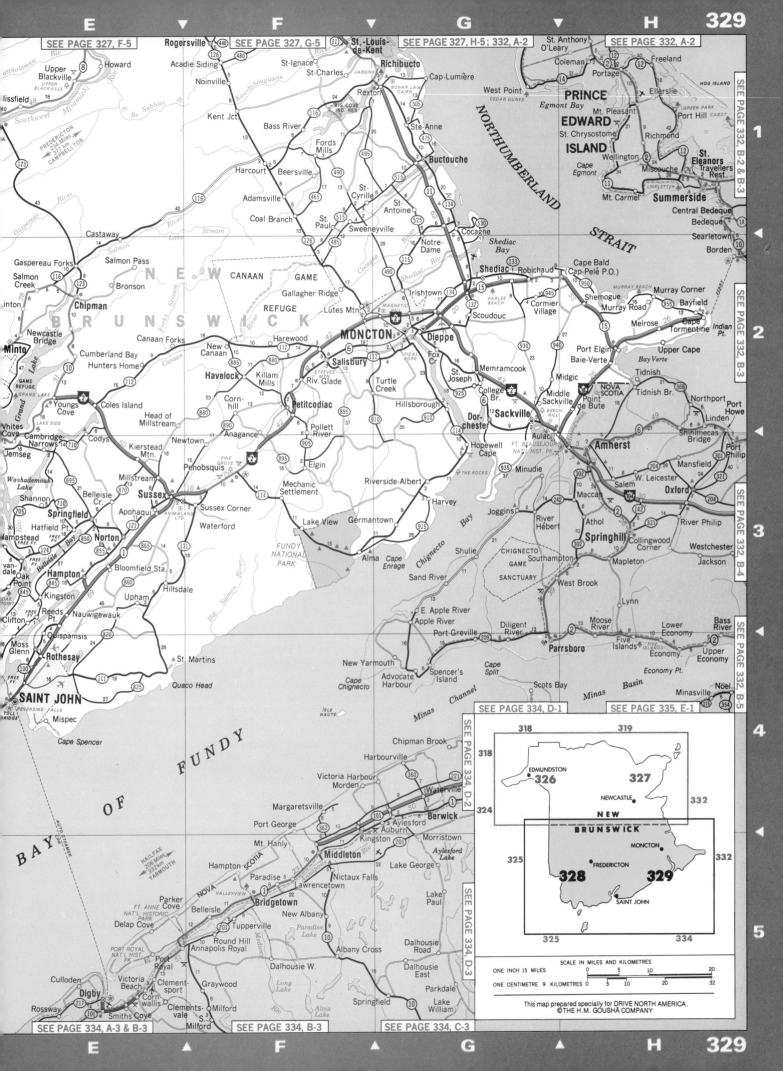

Windjammers, Rumrunners and a 'Garden' on the Gulf

Nova Scotia/Prince Edward Island

Nowhere in Nova Scotia are visitors more than 60 kilometres from salt water, and Nova Scotian lore is alive with tales of rumrunners and ghostships, of buried treasure and sleek, seaworthy schooners. This seafaring heritage is perhaps best preserved in **Halifax (335, E-5)**, the capital and commercial center of the province. Here modern buildings now flank North America's first naval dockyards, begun in 1759 under the supervision of Capt. James Cook. *Bluenose II*, a replica of the famous fishing schooner built in Lunenburg, offers two-hour harbor tours. On a hill above stands the Citadel, a huge star-shaped stronghold built in 1828–56. For 150 years cannon fire from the Citadel's battlements has signaled the stroke of noon. Near the waterfront is the stone residence (circa 1800) of Nova Scotia's lieutenant-governor, and Province House, Canada's oldest legislative building (1819). Downtown, visitors can stroll through the graceful Public Gardens, opened in 1867. At Point Pleasant Park, shady pathways skirt the ruins of five batteries built in 1762; the Prince of Wales Martello Tower has been fully restored.

Southwest of Halifax, the "Lighthouse Route" winds along a coastline rich in the traditions and loveliness of the sea. Picturesque **Peggy's Cove (335, E-3)**, possibly the most photographed village in Canada, is at the mouth of St. Margarets Bay, where New England-bound rumrunners loaded bootleg liquor during Prohibition. Just west of here treasure hunters have sought pirate bullion—some say Captain Kidd's—on Oak Island near **Mahone Bay (334, D-3)** since 1795. On stormy nights, legend has it, the ghostly hulk of the American privateer *Young Teazer*, sunk in 1813, cruises the bay in flames.

One of Nova Scotia's most famous ports is **Lunenburg (334, D-3)**, where shipbuilders and sailmakers still ply their trades. The town has produced *Bluenose* (1921), whose likeness graces the Canadian dime, and the tall ship used in the 1962 film *Mutiny on the Bounty*. The rumrunner *Reo II* and the *Teresa and Connor* (1938), last of the Grand Banks fishing schooners, are moored at the Fisheries Museum of the Atlantic. Huge crowds at the Lunenberg Fair—the Nova Scotia Fisheries Exhibition and Fishermen's Reunion—annually watch boat races and contests of fish filleting, scallop shucking, cable splicing and net mending.

Kejimkujik National Park (334, C-3), was created in 1969 to preserve both its Indian petroglyphs and some of Nova Scotia's finest inland countryside, where island-dotted lakes are surrounded by forested hills. With longer, hotter summers than most of the province, Kejimkujik is a haven for wildlife. Ribbon snakes, Blanding's turtles and southern flying squirrels—found nowhere else in the Maritimes—abound here. The park also has one of the most varied reptile and amphibian populations in eastern Canada, and its rivers support trout and perch.

Skillful shucking (right) reveals the succulent heart of a Digby, Nova Scotia, scallop. Cape Breton's Cabot Trail (below) curves around headlands, clings to the edges of craggy cliffs, and threads dark gorges.

On the Bay of Fundy stands **Port Royal National Historic Park (334, B-3)**, site of the first successful French settlement in the New World (1605). Nearby **Annapolis Royal** preserves a 1708 powder magazine at Fort Anne National Historic Park. The fort—the most fought-over place in Canada—was built by French colonists in the 1630s and secured by British forces in 1710 after 14 bitter sieges.

A small historic park in **Grand Pré (334, D-2)** stands where, in 1755, a notice was read banishing the Acadians from Nova Scotia for refusing to swear allegiance to England. A bronze statue of *Evangeline*, the fictional heroine of Longfellow's epic poem about the Acadian expulsion, is also in the park.

The **Springhill (332, A-4)** Miners' Museum tells of this coal-mining town's courage in the face of disaster. Mining equipment here ranges from "teapot lights" to breathing apparatus. A diary, letters of trapped men, and other relics of Springhill's three worst mine accidents are also displayed. A museum tour includes a 108-metre descent into the depths of a mine.

Canada's oldest Highland games, at **Antigonish (333, E-4)**, is a festival of caber tossing, broad jumping and shot-putting. At St. Francis Xavier University, Scottish crests line the walls of the Hall of Clans. South of town, travelers can savor the pace of 19th-century community life in restored Sherbrooke Village, once a wealthy port and gold-mining town. Guides in period costume conduct tours of village homes, a smithy, a general store and a courthouse.

Cape Breton Island's famed Cabot Trail dips and turns for 296 kilometres along the coast past gypsum bluffs, verdant gorges and wave-tossed headlands and coves. Much of this lovely highway weaves through **Cape Breton Highlands National Park (333, G-2)**. Wooded hills rise steeply behind a magnificent sandy shore at **Ingonish Beach**, the park headquarters. In the remote heart of the park is the Everlasting Barren—a rugged expanse of muskeg, ponds and stunted, wind-gnarled spruce.

Southwest of the park lies the lovely Margaree Valley and **Margaree Island National Wildlife Area (333, F-2)**. Common terns, black guillemots and great cormorants nesting on 20-metre-high cliffs greet visitors to this gentle sanctuary. Some of the best salmon pools in Canada line the Margaree River, and the Margaree Salmon Museum at **North East Margaree** displays anglers' and poachers' rods and *flambeaux*—torches used for night fishing. Near **Baddeck (333, G-3)**, sailboats tack and reach on Bras d'Or Lake during the Bras d'Or Yacht Club Regatta in August. *Beinn Bhreagh*, the former summer home of Alexander Graham Bell, overlooks Baddeck Bay. A museum in nearby Alexander Graham Bell National Historic Park contains some of Bell's papers, replicas of early telephone equipment and such ingenious Bell inventions as an early iron lung and a hydrofoil boat.

The massive fortifications of **Louisbourg (333, H-3)**, whose garrison was once one of the largest in North America, loom near the easternmost tip of Cape Breton Island. Reduced to ruins by the British in 1758, Fortress Louisbourg has risen anew: old streets and cellars have been unearthed, and buildings have been reconstructed with the tools and techniques of 250 years ago.

Inland, away from the beaches, Prince Edward Island (above) is a study in green.

Sightseers stroll the cobbled streets of Halifax's Historic Properties (left), where privateers and press-gangs once roamed.

Colorful textiles take shape in a Charlottetown craft shop (below).

The Gulf of St. Lawrence laps against Prince Edward Island National Park (below).

Canada's smallest province, Prince Edward Island is also one of its prettiest and most popular. Its rolling green hills, striking red cliffs and crescent-shaped beaches of gleaming white sand attract millions to this "Garden of the Gulf."

The jewel of the island is **Prince Edward Island National Park (332, C-2)**. Some of Canada's finest beaches are here, backed by dunes carpeted with marram grass. The park, never more than two kilometres wide, extends for 40 kilometres along the island's north shore. Near **Cavendish (332, B-2)** stands Green Gables, the farmhouse immortalized in Lucy Maud Montgomery's *Anne of Green Gables*. Outside the park, at **South Rustico (332, C-2)**, egg crates, fish and cracker barrels, and a potbellied stove add old-time flavor to Jumpin' Jack's, an 1800s country store. West at **Port Hill (332, B-2)**, a cupola crowns the restored James Yeo, Jr. Homestead, built about 1865 and now part of Green Park Provincial Park. Displays in an

interpretive center relate the story of wooden shipbuilding on the Island.

Visitors to the Woodleigh Replicas at **Burlington** take an unusual journey through Old England. Stone-and-concrete models—some large enough to enter—include Shakespeare's birthplace, the Tower of London, the 14-room Anne Hathaway cottage, and Dunvegan Castle, complete with antique furnishings and a dungeon.

The look of the past is everywhere at the Villages des pionniers acadiens (Acadian Pioneer Village) in **Mt. Carmel (332, A-3)**. The re-created 1800s settlement has among its exhibits a barn, a school, a rectory and log houses. Acadian music, dances, handicrafts and traditional island dishes are also featured. East, on scenic Lady Slipper Drive, is **Summerside (332, B-3)**. Celebrants at the mid-July Summerside Lobster Carnival enjoy a festive blend of parades and picnics, livestock and agriculture exhibits, lobster dinners and harness racing.

Victorian homes line quiet, tree-lined streets in **Charlottetown (332, C-3)**, the province's capital and Canada's birthplace. The Fathers of Confederation met for the first time in a high-ceilinged room in the Georgian-style Province House in 1864. The adjacent Confederation Centre of the Arts is a memorial to the nation's founders. The two-block-long complex contains a museum, a library, an art gallery and a 1,100-seat theater where Canada's colorful folk troupe, Les Feux-Follets, often performs. *Anne of Green Gables* is staged here during the Charlottetown Festival. Beaconsfield, an impressive Victorian mansion (1877) housing the P.E.I. Heritage Foundation, overlooks Charlottetown harbor and tranquil Victoria Park. Nearby Government House (1834), a white colonial building, is the residence of the province's lieutenant-governor.

Across the harbor French colonists founded Port la Joie (present-day **Rocky Point**) in 1720. After capturing the site in 1758, the British built Fort Amherst here. Its earthworks are preserved in a national historic park. Nearby, visitors can wander among the birchbark wigwams of a reconstructed 16th-century Micmac Village and examine hunting and fishing implements and a 200-year-old birchbark canoe.

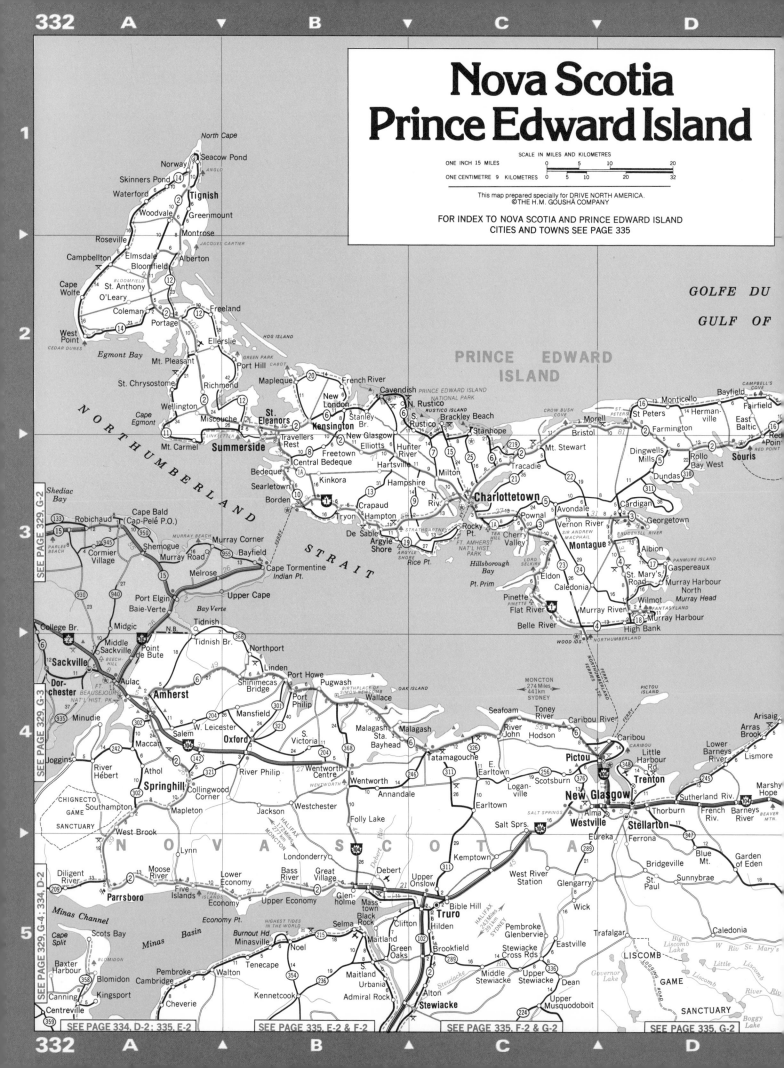

CABOT STRAIT

Cape St. Lawrence Meat Cove Cape North
Capstick
Aspy Bay White Point Cape Egmont
Pollett Cove Cape North South Harbour Neils Harbour
Pleasant Bay Black Brook Cove

CAPE BRETON HIGHLANDS
NATIONAL PARK

Cap Rouge Presqu'île Ingonish
North Bay Ingonish
Ingonish Beach South Bay Ingonish
Chéticamp Ingonish Ferry Cape Smoky
Point Cross Wreck Cove
Grand-Étang Birch Plain
Breton Cove
Belle-Côte Kingross North Shore

CAPE BRETON
ISLAND

Margaree Harbour Indian Brook St. Ann's Bay
Margaree Valley
Margaree Forks North River Bridge English-town Big Bras-d'Or Sydney Mines New Waterford
N.E. Margaree Egypt
Dunvegan St. Ann's New Victoria Dominion
S.W. Margaree S. Gut St. Ann's N. Sydney Glace Bay
Inverness Finlayson GAELIC COLLEGE Reserve Mines Donkin
Scotsville Upper Margaree Big Harbour Ross Ferry Westmount Port Morien
Strathlorne ALEXANDER GRAHAM BELL NAT'L HIST. PARK Sydney Birch Grove
Middle River Baddeck Leitches Cr. Sydney River Homeville
Hunters Mtn. Mira Road
Mabou Nyanza Beaver Cove East Bay Mira
Brook Village FIRST AIR FLIGHT IN BRITISH EMPIRE Main-à-Dieu
L'Ainslie S. Side Bucklaw ESKASONI INDIAN RESERVE Ben Eoin Albert Bridge SCATARIE ISLAND
Port Hood Little Narrows Iona Eskasoni Marion Bridge Cape Breton
PORT HOOD ISLAND Whycocomagh Grand Narrows Louisburg
WHYCOCOMAGH INDIAN RESERVE Big Pond FORTRESS OF LOUISBOURG NATIONAL HISTORICAL PARK
Orange-dale Gabarus Gabarus Bay

Cape George Malagawatch Bras d'Or Lake Victoria Bridge
Ballantynes Cove Judique Irish Cove
Cape George Glendale Loch Lomond Fourchu
Georgeville Kingsville Loch Lomond
Malignant Cove Lakevale Queensville St. Georges Channel Soldiers Cove
Crystal Cliffs Creignish West Bay St. Esprit
Troy Grand River
St. Georges Bay Havre Boucher Cleveland St. Peters L'Ardoise
Antigonish Port Hastings BATTERY
Heatherton Tracadie Auld Cove Grand-Anse
James Riv. Sta. Lower South River Monastery Port Hawkesbury
Melford JANVRIN ISLAND
Glen Alpine Fraser Mills Sand Point Petit de Grat Bridge
Lochaber Alder River Arichat MADAME ISLAND
New-town Roman Valley Boylston Chedabucto Bay
Aspen Giant Lake BOYLSTON
Smithfield Salmon River Lake Guysborough Port Shoreham Canso
Melrose Ogden Queensport Cape Canso
Stillwater Country Harbour Cross Roads Stormont Halfway Cove Hazel Hill
Sherbrooke Goldboro Charlo Cove Cole Cove Whitehead
Goldenville Larrys River
Port Bickerton Seal Harbour New Harbour

SAINT- LAURENT
ST. LAWRENCE

MAGDALEN ISLANDS AUTO STEAMER
EAST POINT East Pt. Elmira

N

ATLANTIC OCEAN

PRINCE EDWARD ISLAND
CHARLOTTETOWN
332 333
329 SYDNEY
TRURO
NOVA SCOTIA
334 335
HALIFAX

SEE PAGE 335, H-2

HALIFAX 243 Miles
391 km SYDNEY

MZ-5-678-J

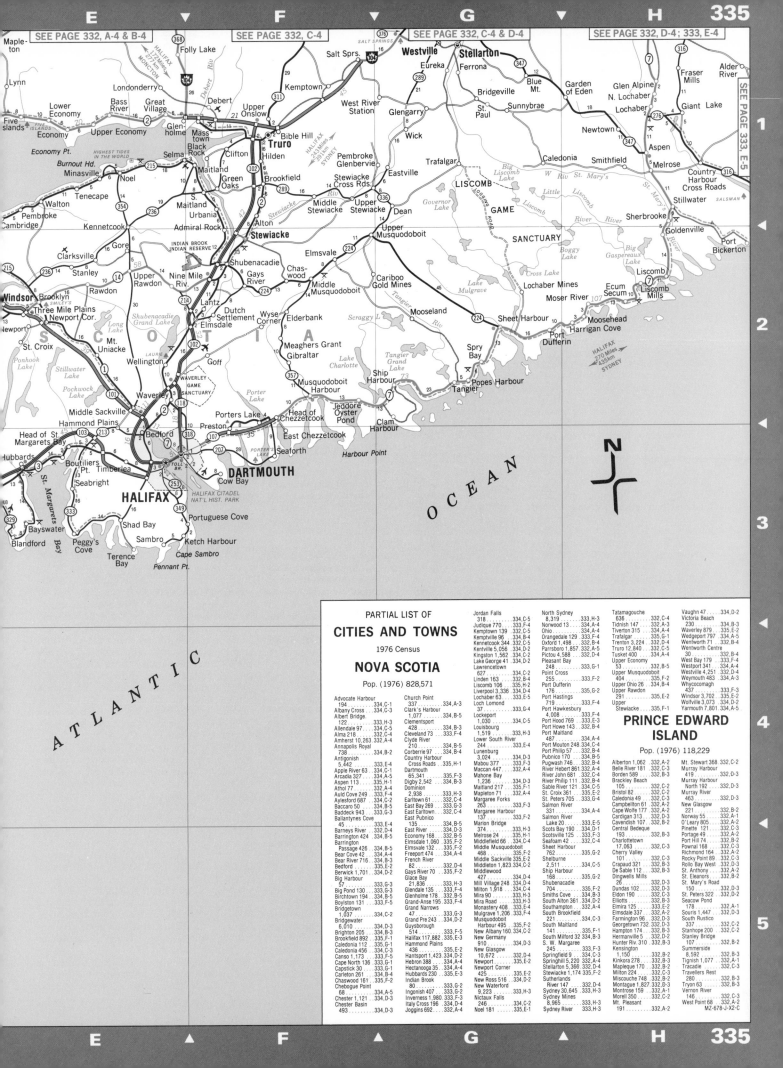

PARTIAL LIST OF CITIES AND TOWNS

1976 Census

NOVA SCOTIA

Pop. (1976) 828,571

Advocate Harbour 194 .... 334,C-1
Albany Cross ... 334,C-3
Albert Bridge 122 .... 333,H-3
Allendale 97 ... 334,C-5
Alma 218 ... 332,C-4
Amherst 10,263 .332,A-4
Annapolis Royal 738 .... 334,B-2
Antigonish 5,442 .... 333,E-4
Apple River 63 .334,C-1
Arcadia 327 ... 334,A-5
Aspen 113 ... 335,H-1
Athol 77 ... 332,A-4
Auld Cove 249 .333,F-4
Aylesford 687 ... 334,C-2
Baccaro 50 ... 334,B-5
Baddeck 943 ... 333,G-3
Ballantynes Cove 45 ... 333,E-4
Barneys River .332,D-4
Barrington 424 .334,B-5
Barrington Passage 426 ... 334,B-5
Bear Cove 42 ... 334,A-4
Bear River 716 ..334,B-3
Bedford ... 335,E-2
Berwick 1,701 ..334,D-2
Big Harbour 57 ... 333,G-3
Big Pond 130 ...333,G-3
Birchtown 194 ..334,B-5
Boylston 131 ...333,F-5
Bridgetown 1,037 ... 334,C-2
Bridgewater 6,010 ... 334,D-3
Brighton 205 ...334,B-3
Brookfield 892 ..335,F-1
Caledonia 112 ..335,G-1
Caledonia 456 ..334,C-3
Canso 1,173 ...333,F-5
Cape North 136 .333,G-1
Capstick 30 ... 333,G-1
Carleton 261 ...334,B-4
Chebogue 161 ..335,F-2
Chebogue Point 68 ... 334,A-5
Chester 1,121 ..334,D-3
Chester Basin 493 ... 334,D-3

Church Point 337 .... 334,A-3
Clark's Harbour 1,077 .... 334,B-5
Clementsport 428 ... 334,B-3
Cleveland 73 ...333,F-4
Clyde River 210 ... 334,B-5
Corberrie 97 ...334,B-4
Country Harbour Cross Roads .335,H-1
Dartmouth 65,341 ...335,F-3
Digby 2,542 ...334,B-3
Dominion 2,938 ... 333,H-3
Earltown 61 ...332,C-4
East Bay 269 ...333,G-3
East Earltown...332,C-4
East Pubnico 135 ... 334,B-5
East River ... 334,D-3
Economy 168 ...332,B-5
Elmsdale 1,060 .335,F-2
Elmsvale 132 ...335,F-2
Freeport 474 ...334,A-4
French River 82 .... 332,D-4
Gays River 70 ..335,F-2
Glace Bay 21,836 ... 333,H-3
Glendale 135 ...333,F-4
Glenholme 178 .332,B-5
Grand-Anse 195 .332,D-4
Grand Narrows 47 ... 333,G-3
Grand Pre 243 ..334,D-2
Guysborough 514 ... 333,F-5
Halifax 117,882 .335,E-3
Hammond Plains 436 ... 335,E-2
Hantsport 1,423 .334,D-2
Hebron 388 ... 334,A-4
Hectanooga 35 ..334,A-4
Hubbards 230 ...335,E-3
Indian Brook 80 .... 333,G-2
Ingonish 407 ...333,G-2
Inverness 1,980 .333,F-3
Italy Cross 196 .334,D-4
Joggins 692 ...332,A-4

Jordan Falls 318 .... 334,C-5
Judique 770 ...333,F-4
Kemptown 139 ..332,C-5
Kemptville 96 ..334,B-4
Kennetcook 344 .332,C-5
Kentville 5,056 .334,D-2
Kingston 1,562 .334,C-2
Lake George 41 .334,C-2
Lawrencetown 627 ... 334,C-2
Linden 163 ... 332,B-4
Liscomb 106 ...335,H-2
Liverpool 3,336 .334,C-4
Lochaber 63 ...335,E-5
Loch Lomond 37 .... 333,G-4
Lockeport 1,030 ... 334,C-5
Louisbourg 1,519 ... 333,H-3
Lower South River 244 ... 333,E-4
Lunenburg 3,024 ... 334,D-3
Mabou 377 ... 333,F-3
Maccan 447 ...332,A-4
Mahone Bay 1,236 ... 334,D-3
Maitland 217 ...335,F-1
Mapleton 71 ...332,A-4
Margaree Forks 263 ... 333,F-3
Margaree Harbour 137 ... 333,F-2
Marion Bridge 374 ... 333,H-3
Melrose 24 ...335,H-1
Middlefield 66 .334,C-4
Middle Musquodoboit 468 ... 335,F-2
Middle Sackville 335,E-2
Middleton 1,823 .334,C-2
Middlewood 427 ... 334,D-4
Mill Village 248 .334,D-4
Milton 1,918 ...334,C-4
Mira 90 ... 333,H-3
Mira Road ...333,H-3
Monastery 408 ..333,E-4
Mulgrave 1,206 .333,F-4
Musquodoboit Harbour 495 ...335,F-2
New Albany 160 .334,C-2
New Germany 910 ... 334,D-3
New Glasgow 10,672 ... 332,D-4
Newport ...335,E-2
Newport Corner 425 ... 335,E-2
New Ross 516 ...334,D-2
New Waterford 9,223 ... 333,H-3
Nictaux Falls 246 ... 334,C-2
Noel 181 ... 335,E-1

North Sydney 8,319 ... 333,H-3
Norwood 13 ... 334,A-4
Ohio ... 334,A-4
Orangedale 129 .333,F-4
Oxford 1,498 ...332,B-4
Parrsboro 1,857 .332,A-5
Pictou 4,588 ...332,D-4
Pleasant Bay 248 ... 333,G-1
Point Cross 255 ... 333,F-2
Port Dufferin 176 ... 335,G-2
Port Hastings 719 ... 333,F-4
Port Hawkesbury 4,008 ... 333,F-4
Port Hood 769 ..333,F-3
Port Howe 143 ..332,B-4
Port Maitland 487 ... 334,A-4
Port Mouton 248 .334,C-4
Port Philip 57 ..332,B-4
Pubnico 170 ...334,B-5
Pugwash 746 ...332,B-4
River Hebert 861 .332,A-4
River John 681 .332,C-4
River Philip 111 .332,B-4
Sable River 121 .334,C-5
St. Croix 361 ..335,E-2
St. Peters 705 ..333,G-4
Salmon River 331 ... 334,A-4
Salmon River Lake 20 ... 333,E-5
Scots Bay 190 ..334,D-1
Scotsville 125 ..333,F-3
Seafoam 42 ...332,C-4
Sheet Harbour 762 ... 335,G-2
Shelburne 2,511 ... 334,C-5
Ship Harbour 168 ... 335,G-2
Shubenacadie 704 ... 335,F-2
Smiths Cove ...334,B-3
South Anton 361 .334,D-2
Southampton 224 .332,A-4
South Brookfield 221 ... 334,C-3
South Maitland 141 ... 335,F-1
South Milford 32 .334,B-3
S. W. Margaree 245 ... 333,F-3
Springfield 9 ...334,D-3
Springhill 5,220 .332,A-4
Stellarton 5,366 .332,D-4
Stewiacke 1,174 .335,F-2
Sutherlands River 147 ... 332,D-4
Sydney 30,645 ..333,H-3
Sydney Mines 8,965 ... 333,H-3
Sydney River ...333,H-3

Tatamagouche 636 ... 332,C-4
Tidnish 147 ...332,A-3
Tiverton 315 ...334,A-4
Trafalgar ...335,G-1
Trenton 3,224 ..332,D-4
Truro 12,840 ...332,C-5
Tusket 400 ... 334,A-4
Upper Economy 53 ... 332,B-5
Upper Musquodoboit 404 ... 335,F-1
Upper Ohio 26 ..334,B-4
Upper Rawdon 291 ... 335,E-2
Upper Stewiacke ...335,F-1
Vaughn 47 ... 334,D-2
Victoria Beach 230 ... 334,B-3
Waverley 879 ...335,E-2
Wedgeport 797 .334,A-5
Wentworth 71 ..332,B-4
Wentworth Centre 30 ... 332,B-4
West Bay 179 ...333,F-4
Westport 341 ...334,A-4
Westville 4,251 .332,D-4
Weymouth 483 ..334,A-3
Whycocomagh 437 ... 333,F-3
Windsor 3,702 ..335,E-2
Wolfville 3,073 .334,D-2
Yarmouth 7,801 .334,A-5

PRINCE EDWARD ISLAND

Pop. (1976) 118,229

Alberton 1,062 .332,A-2
Belle River 181 .332,C-3
Borden 589 ...332,B-3
Brackley Beach 105 ... 332,C-2
Bristol 82 ... 332,C-3
Caledonia 49 ...332,C-3
Campbellton 61 .332,A-2
Cape Wolfe 177 .332,A-2
Cardigan 313 ...332,C-3
Cavendish 107 ..332,B-2
Central Bedeque 193 ... 332,B-3
Charlottetown 17,063 ... 332,C-3
Cherry Valley 101 ... 332,C-3
Crapaud 321 ...332,B-3
De Sable 112 ...332,B-3
Dingwells Mills 26 ... 332,D-3
Dundas 102 ...332,C-3
Eldon 190 ... 332,C-3
Elliotts ... 332,B-3
Elmira 125 ...332,E-2
Elmsdale 337 ...332,A-2
Farmington 96 ..332,D-3
Georgetown 732 .332,D-3
Hampton 174 ...332,B-3
Hermanville 5 ...332,D-2
Hunter Riv. 310 .332,B-3
Kensington 1,150 ... 332,B-3
Kinkora 278 ...332,B-3
Maplequa 170 ..332,B-2
Milton 224 ...332,C-2
Miscouche 748 .332,B-2
Montague 1,827 .332,D-3
Montrose 159 ..332,A-1
Morell 350 ...332,C-2
Mt. Pleasant 191 ... 332,A-2

Mt. Stewart 368 .332,C-2
Murray Harbour 419 ... 332,D-3
Murray Harbour North 192 ... 332,D-3
Murray River 221 ... 332,D-3
New Glasgow 221 ... 332,B-2
Norway 55 ... 332,A-1
O'Leary 805 ...332,A-2
Pinette 121 ...332,C-3
Portage 49 ...332,A-2
Port Hill 74 ...332,A-2
Pownal 168 ...332,C-3
Richmond 164 ..332,A-2
Rocky Point 89 .332,C-3
Rollo Bay West .332,D-3
St. Anthony ...332,A-2
St. Eleanors ...332,B-2
St. Mary's Road 337 ... 332,C-3
St. Peters 322 .332,D-2
Seacow Pond 178 ... 332,A-1
South Rustico ...332,C-2
Stanhope 200 ...332,C-2
Stanley Bridge 107 ... 332,B-2
Summerside 1,447 ... 332,B-3
Tignish 1,077 ..332,A-1
Tracadie 280 ...332,C-2
Travellers Rest 280 ... 332,B-3
Tryon 63 ... 332,B-3
Vernon River 146 ... 332,C-3
West Point 68 .332,A-2

MZ-678-J-X2-C

An Enchanting Island of Cliffs, Capes and Colorful Outports

Newfoundland

Canada's youngest province, anchored in bountiful but often stormy waters, is populated by a hardy folk wedded to the sea. More than half of Newfoundland's residents live in coastal fishing villages and outports whose colorful names—Tickle Cove, Blow Me Down, Come by Chance, Happy Adventure—enliven the provincial map.

One of Newfoundland's most dramatic sights is the huddled, mist-shrouded form of Gros Morne, a forbidding landmass on the ragged fringes of Bonne Bay. This 806-metre peak—Newfoundland's second highest—dominates **Gros Morne National Park (338, B-2)**, a magnificent stretch of the Long Range Mountains. Along the park's 100-kilometre coastline rise sheer cliffs and wave-battered headlands. Tidal pools swarm with marine life, and sand dunes tower up to 12 metres high. Between the sea and the mountains lies a low coastal plain threaded by rivers flowing through bog and grassland. Inland, the park is a mix of deep ponds flanked by near-vertical cliffs, highland tundra and waterfalls so powerful and high (some more than 100 metres) that water evaporates into mist before it can reach the land below. Newfoundland caribou graze treeless barrens, and gyrfalcons—one of 175 bird species sighted here—wheel and dip on mountain air currents. A branch of the main highway into Gros Morne skirts the Tablelands, a wasteland of ocher-brown volcanic rocks that comprises one of Canada's strangest landscapes.

North of Gros Morne, at **Port au Choix (338, B-1)**, vestiges of Canada's prehistory can be glimpsed. An interpretive center preserves relics of the "red paint people" who roamed the region more than 4,000 years ago. Also displayed are artifacts of Dorset Inuit who inhabited nearby Pointe Riche about A.D. 100. In their footsteps came the Vikings, who founded a settlement at **L'Anse aux Meadows (338, C-1)** around A.D. 1000. This carefully excavated site on Newfoundland's most northerly point holds the remains of seven buildings, a smithy and two cook pits. Iron rivets have been unearthed here, along with the floorboard of a Norse boat and a soapstone flywheel (used for spinning) that is the earliest European tool discovered in North America.

Farther south, the Humber River roars through a narrow gorge, then flows into **Sir Richard Squires Memorial Park (338, B-2)**, where vaulting salmon can be seen bypassing nine-metre-high Big Falls by means of fish ladders. To the west is **Corner Brook (338, B-2)**, whose Bowaters mill produces some 400,000 tons of paper annually. A side trip leads to **Blow Me Down Provincial Park (338, A-2)**, where (legend says) pirate treasure lies buried. Steep wooden stairs climb a rock overhang to a lookout tower that gives onto the Bay of Islands.

Newfoundland's interior is a sparsely settled wilderness that supports the province's pulp and paper industry. **Grand Falls (338,**

C-3) churns out more than 700 tons of newsprint daily. The Mary March Museum here exhibits photographs of early logging operations in the province and a mural of a Beothuk Indian village (by the early 1800s the Beothuks, a nomadic tribe, had been hunted to extinction by European settlers). In the early years of transatlantic flight, **Gander (338, C-2)** was the "Crossroads of the World." One of the first international airports was established here by the British in the mid-1930s, and served as a base for the wartime Atlantic Ferry. Among the treasures in the modern terminal's aviation museum is a wooden propeller from the twin-engine Vickers Vimy biplane that made the first nonstop transatlantic flight (June 1919, from St. John's to Clifden, Ireland).

Mammoth icebergs—some as high as 50 metres—drift past **Twillingate (338, C-2)** from Labrador and Greenland each summer. Visitors to the Twillingate Museum walk through rooms furnished with antiques and stocked with old tools, clothing and household articles. A collection of arrowheads, knives and cooking utensils are remnants of a Maritime Archaic culture that lived here some 3,500 years ago.

Terra Nova National Park (339, F-1), easternmost of Canada's national parks, overlooks Bonavista Bay. Atlantic breakers roll to the foot of its headlands, and sheltered beaches yield to undulating forests and bogs where moose, black bear and lynx roam. Humpback and pilot whales ply the bays and channels, and giant squid lurk in the depths of Bonavista Bay. Sailing enthusiasts can canoe on freshwater ponds or enjoy yachting and powerboating on saltwater inlets; fishing enthusiasts can cast for trout and salmon, or for saltwater species such as cod, mackerel, herring and squid. When the weather warms, Sandy Pond is a popular swimming area. During the day, interpreters conduct nature walks along park trails. In the evening, informative talks are given on subjects ranging from ecology to folklore. **Salvage (339, F-1)**, at the tip of the Eastport Peninsula near Terra Nova, is one of Atlantic Canada's oldest settlements. In a restored century-old frame house, the Salvage Fisherman's Museum displays a telling collection of local artifacts and fishing gear. The floor of a kitchen is covered with canvas—in accordance with an old Newfoundland custom.

Newfoundlanders of Port au Port Peninsula (above) trace their ancestry to 18th-century French fishermen.

The colorful cityscape of St. John's (right).

Remains of a 2,000-year-old Viking settlement, possibly the Vinland of Norse sagas, have been unearthed at L'Anse aux Meadows (left).

The flip of a humpback's tail greets whale-watchers in Trinity Bay (below).

Like many early Newfoundland settlements, **Trinity (339, G-2)** was harassed by pirates and French warships; the remains of fortifications and guns can still be seen. North America's first Court of Admiralty was held here in 1615, and the continent's first smallpox vaccination administered in 1800 by medical missionary John Clinch. Ship models dating from the 1830s and British Admiralty bluebacks (nautical charts) are displayed at the Trinity Museum. Farther north lies the busy fishing port of **Bonavista (339, G-1)**, where John Cabot may have landed in 1497. A few kilometres north stands a lighthouse that has faithfully guided fishermen around Cape Bonavista for more than a century. Water erosion at nearby Spillers Cove has formed an unusual double grotto called The Dungeon.

From the Burin Peninsula, fleets head for the storied Grand Banks, which teem with fish drawn by the meeting of the Labrador Current and the warm Gulf Stream. The Southern Newfoundland Seamen's Museum in **Grand Bank (338, C-4)**, in the former Yugoslav Pavilion of Expo '67, houses fishing gear, charts and photographs depicting the region's maritime past. At nearby **Fortune (338, C-4)**, ferries service the windswept islands of St. Pierre and Miquelon, French holdings since Jacques Cartier claimed them in the 16th century.

The Avalon Peninsula is linked to the rest of Newfoundland by a narrow land bridge. At **Placentia (339, F-4)**, bordered by two

Brooding cliffs, deep fjords and bright fishing villages such as Port de Grave (above) give the coastline of Conception Bay its special character.

best explored on foot, along streets that once echoed the footsteps of merchants, sailors and privateers. Historic Water Street may be the oldest commercial thoroughfare in North America: European sailors bartered, bought and sold on this site as early as 1500. St. John's Harbor is home port to the schooner *Norma and Gladys*, a floating museum devoted to fishing and marine conservation. Near the harbor entrance, brightly colored houses perch precariously on the flanks of 152-metre-high cliffs guarded by the silent guns of Signal Hill. This windswept headland, now a national historic park, was the scene of the last encounter between French and British troops on North American soil (September 18, 1762). Fortress-like Cabot Tower was raised in 1897–1900 to commemorate both Cabot's discovery of Newfoundland in 1497 and Queen Victoria's Diamond Jubilee. A nearby monument marks where Guglielmo Marconi received the first transatlantic wireless message, from Cornwall, England, in 1901. On the south side of the harbor entry lie the remains of 18th-century Fort Amherst, and overlooking Quidi Vidi Lake is a British battery restored to appear much as it did in 1812. The St. John's Regatta, possibly North America's oldest annual sports event, has been held on the lake since 1826. In the Newfoundland Museum visitors can see the caribou skin coat worn by Shanawdithit, last of the Beothuks, as well as a host of fascinating displays ranging over 7,000 years of the Island's history.

Barren and beautiful **Cape Spear (339, H-3)**, 10 kilometres south, is the easternmost point in North America. One of Canada's oldest lighthouses (1833) stands near the modern tower that replaced it in 1955. The serrated coast between Cape Spear and Cape Race is a graveyard of ships and a birdwatcher's delight. Petrels, puffins, gulls, murres and kittiwakes virtually fill the sky and honeycomb the cliffs of the **Witless Bay Bird Sanctuary (339, H-4)**. Charter boats circle its three small islands.

fjords that extend 10 kilometres inland, stands Castle Hill National Historic Park. Here in 1693 French colonists built Fort Royal, ceded two decades later to the British in the Treaty of Utrecht. The remains of guardrooms, barracks, a powder magazine and the foundations of an English blockhouse can be seen in the inner fort. A plaque at **Argentia** commemorates the Atlantic Charter, signed by Churchill and Roosevelt aboard a British warship anchored here in August 1941. Off the tip of Cape St. Mary's looms **Bird Island (339, E-5)**, a vast half-dome awash with nesting gannets, murres and kittiwakes.

A string of quiet fishing villages lies along the east coast of Trinity Bay. Fame came to **Heart's Content (339, G-3)** in July, 1866, when the *Great Eastern* steamed into port trailing in its wake the first successful trans-atlantic telegraph cable. The old relay station, now a museum, displays telegraph equipment from this period.

Across the peninsula on Conception Bay is **Harbour Grace (339, G-3)**, settled about 1550 and fortified some 60 years later by buccaneer Peter Easton, the "Pirate Admiral." The Customs House, which houses the Conception Bay Museum, stands on the site of Easton's fort. Boat models, antique furniture, early photographs and exhibits chronicling the history of transatlantic flight highlight the collection. Between Harbour Grace and Portugal Cove the Conception Bay shoreline changes character as the deep, fjord-like inlets of the north shore give way to harborless cliff faces and gravel beaches.

Signal Hill dominates the entrance to **St. John's (339, H-3)**, Newfoundland's capital and a city with a vivid past. Old St. John's is

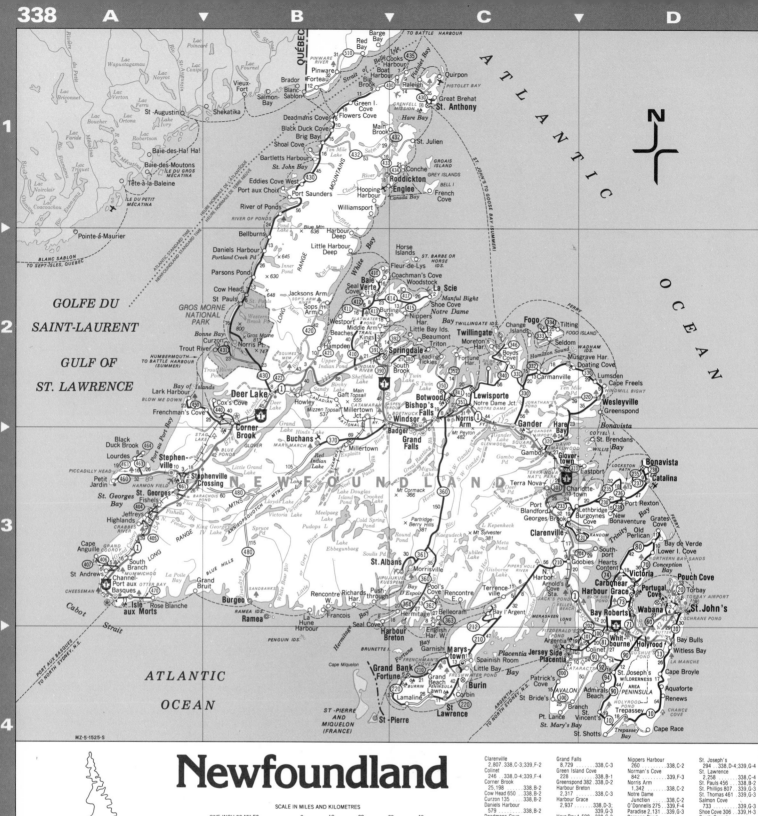

Newfoundland

SCALE IN MILES AND KILOMETRES

ONE INCH 30 MILES

ONE CENTIMETRE 19 KILOMETRES

0 10 20 30 40
0 10 20 30 50 64

This map prepared specially for DRIVE NORTH AMERICA.
© THE H.M. GOUSHA COMPANY

PARTIAL LIST OF
CITIES AND TOWNS

1976 Census
Pop. (1976) 557,725

Aquaforte
172 . .338,D-4; 339,G-5
Arnold's Cove Sta.
1,160 . 338,C-3; 339,F-3
Avondale 937 . . 339,G-4
Badger 1,160 . . . 338,B-2
Baie Verte
2,528 . . . . 338,B-2
Bauline 163 . . . . 339,H-3
Bay Bulls
1,104 338,D-4;339,H-4
Bay de Verde
749 . . 338,D-3; 339,G-2

Bay l'Argent
474 . . . . 338,C-3
Bay Roberts
4,072 338,D-3;339,G-3
Bellburns 148 . . 338,B-2
Belleoram 536 . . 338,C-3
Bishop's Falls
4,504 . . . . 338,C-2
Black Duck Cove
159 . . . . 338,B-1
Bonavista
4,299 338,D-3;339,G-1
Botwood 4,554 . . 338,C-2

Boyds Cove
422 . . . . 338,C-3
Brig Bay 174 . . 338,B-1
Buchans 2,078 . 338,B-3
Burgeo 2,474 . . 338,B-3
Burin 2,892 . . . 338,C-4
Calvert 436 . . . 339,G-4
Cape Anguille
130 . . . . . . 338,A-3
Cape Broyle
711 . . 338,D-4;339,G-4
Cape Freels 95 . 338,D-2
Cappahayden
87 . . . . . . 339,G-5
Carbonear
5,026 338,D-3;339,G-3
Carmanville 911 . 338,C-2
Catalina
1,129 .338,D-3;339,G-1
Cavendish 340 . 339,G-3
Change Islands
535 . . . . . 338,C-2
Channel-Port Aux
Basques 6,187. 338,A-3

Clarenville
2,807. 338,C-3;339,F-2
Colinet
246 . .338,D-4;339,F-4
Corner Brook
25,198 . . . . 338,B-2
Cow Head 650 . . 338,B-2
Curzon 135 . . . 338,B-2
Daniels Harbour
579 . . . . . . 338,B-2
Deadmans Cove
33 . . . . . . 338,B-1
Deep Bight 209 . 338,F-2
Deer Lake
4,546 . . . . 338,B-2
Donovan's 41 . . 339,H-3
Dunville 1,909 . 339,F-4
Eddies Cove West
436 . . . . . . 338,B-1
Englee 989 . . . 338,B-1
Fermeuse 631 . . 339,G-5
Flat Rock 743 . . 339,H-3
Flowers Cove
436 . . . . . . 338,B-1
Fogo 1,103 . . . 338,C-2
Forest Field 42 . 339,G-4
Fortune 2,406 . . 338,C-4
Fox Harbour
627 . . . . . . 339,F-4
Frenchman's Cove
321 . . . . . . 339,F-4
Freshwater
1,426 . . . . . 339,G-4
Gambo
533 . . 338,C-3;339,E-1
Gander 9,301 . . 338,C-2
Georges Brook
350 . 338,D-3;339,F-2
Glovertown
2,176. 338,C-3;339,G-3
Goobies
167 . . . . . . 339,F-3
Grand Bank
3,802 . . . . . 338,C-4
Grand Beach 93 . 338,C-4

Grand Falls
8,729 . . . . . 338,C-3
Green Island Cove
228 . . . . . . 338,B-1
Greenspond 382 . 338,D-2
Harbour Breton
2,317 . . . . . 338,C-3
Harbour Grace
2,937 . . . . 338,D-3;
. . . . 339,G-3
Hare Bay 1,598 . 338,C-3
Hearts Content
634 . 338,D-3;339,G-3
Highlands 189 . . 338,A-3
Holyrood
1,610 . . . 338,D-4;
. . . . 339,G-4
Isle aux Morts
1,270 . . . . 338,A-3
Jeffreys 287 . . 338,A-3
Jersey Side
1,027. 338,C-4;339,F-4
Kelligrews . . . 339,G-3
La Scie 1,256 . . 338,C-2
Lance Cove 274 . 339,G-3
Lawn 1,025 . . . 338,C-4
Lewisporte
3,782 . . . . 338,C-2
Little Bay . . . 338,C-4
Long Pond . . . 339,G-3
Lourdes 987 . . 338,A-3
Lumsden 597 . . 338,D-2
Makinsons 413 . 339,G-3
Marystown
5,915 . . . . 338,C-4
Mitchells Brook
152 . . . . . . 339,G-4
Mobile 150 . . . 339,H-4
Mount Carmel
437 . . . . . . 339,G-4
Mount Pearl
. . . . 339,H-3
Musgrave Harbour
1,530 . . . . 338,C-2
New Bridge 67 . 339,G-4

Nippers Harbour
260 . . . . . . 338,C-2
Norman's Cove
842 . . . . . . 339,F-3
Norris Arm
1,342 . . . . 338,C-2
Notre Dame
Junction 275 . 338,C-2
O'Donnells 275 . 339,F-4
Paradise 2,131 . 339,H-3
Parsons Pond
544 . . . . . . 338,B-2
Petit Jardin . . 338,A-3
Petty Harbour
824 . . . . . . 339,H-3
Placentia
2,209 338,C-4;339,F-4
Port Saunders
691 . . . . . . 338,B-2
Port Union 678 . 339,G-1
Portugal Cove
1,527 338,D-3;339,H-3
Pouch Cove
1,543 . . . . 339,H-3
Ramea 1,226 . . 338,B-3
Renews
436 . 338,D-4;339,G-5
River of Ponds
290 . . . . . . 338,B-1
Roddickton
1,234 . . . . 338,B-1
Rose Blanche
766 . . . . . . 338,A-3
St. Albans
2,040 . . . . 338,C-3
St. Andrews
304 . . . . . . 338,A-3
St. Anthony
2,987 . . . . 338,C-1
St. George's
1,976 . . . . 338,A-3
St. John's
85,576 . . . 338,D-3;
. . . . 339,H-3

St. Joseph's
294 . .338,D-4;339,G-4
St. Lawrence
2,258 . . . . 338,C-4
St. Pauls 456 . . 338,B-2
St. Phillips 807 . 339,G-3
St. Thomas 461 . 339,G-3
Salmon Cove
733 . . . . . . 339,G-3
Shoe Cove 306 . 339,H-3
South Branch
425 . . . . . . 338,A-3
South Brook
828 . . . . . . 338,B-2
Springdale
3,513 . . . . 338,B-2
Stephenville
10,284 . . . 338,A-3
Stephenville Crossing
2,207 . . . . 338,A-3
Swift Current
417 . . . . . . 339,E-3
Torbay
2,908 . . . . 338,D-3;
. . . . 339,H-3
Trepassey
1,427 338,D-4;339,G-5
Trout River
784 . . . . . . 338,B-2
Twillingate
1,404 . . . . 338,C-2
Upper Island Cove
1,851 . . . . 339,G-3
Victoria
1,767 338,D-3;339,G-3
Wabana
4,824 338,D-3;339,G-3
Wesleyville
1,167 . . . . 338,D-2
Whitbourne
1,268 338,D-4;339,F-4
Windsor 6,349 . 338,C-2
Witless Bay
888 . . . . 338,D-4;339,H-4

MZ-1525-J-XC

City Maps

Monuments and museums, restaurants and nightlife, sky-high buildings and eye-catching fashion—these are the delights of North America's cities. In the following pages "In-and-Out" maps show the way into, around and through 18 Canadian and 106 U.S. cities, and special "Close-up" maps focus on the downtown areas of 12 of the continent's greatest cities.

Close-up: Vancouver

Alberta

Calgary

Edmonton

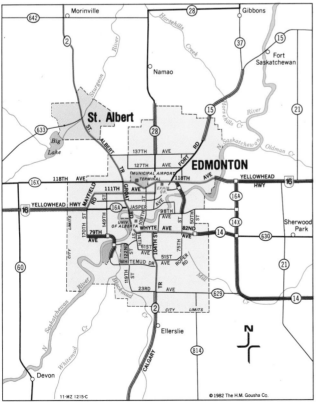

British Columbia

Vancouver

Victoria

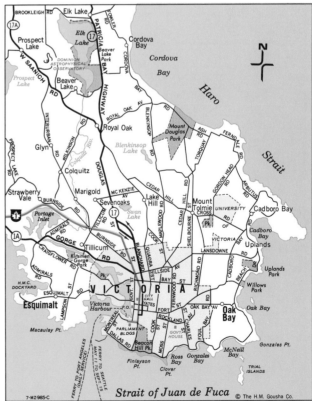

Manitoba

Brandon

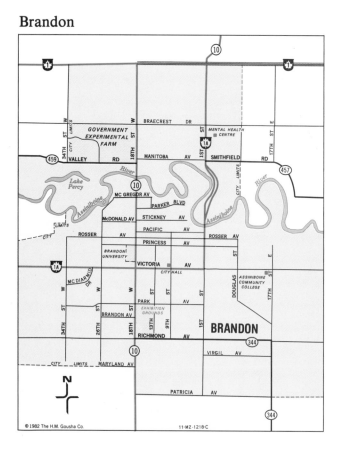

Winnipeg

New Brunswick

Saint John

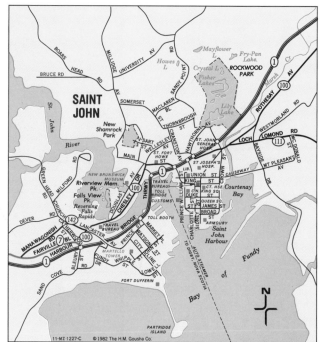

Newfoundland

Saint John's

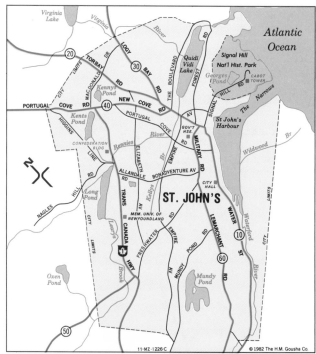

Nova Scotia

Halifax

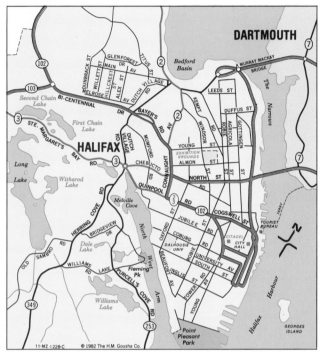

Ontario

London

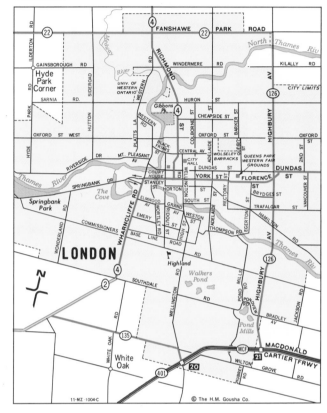

Ontario

Hamilton

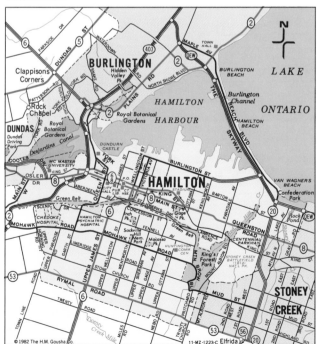

Ottawa

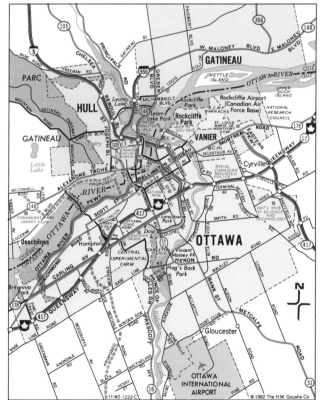

Close-up: Toronto

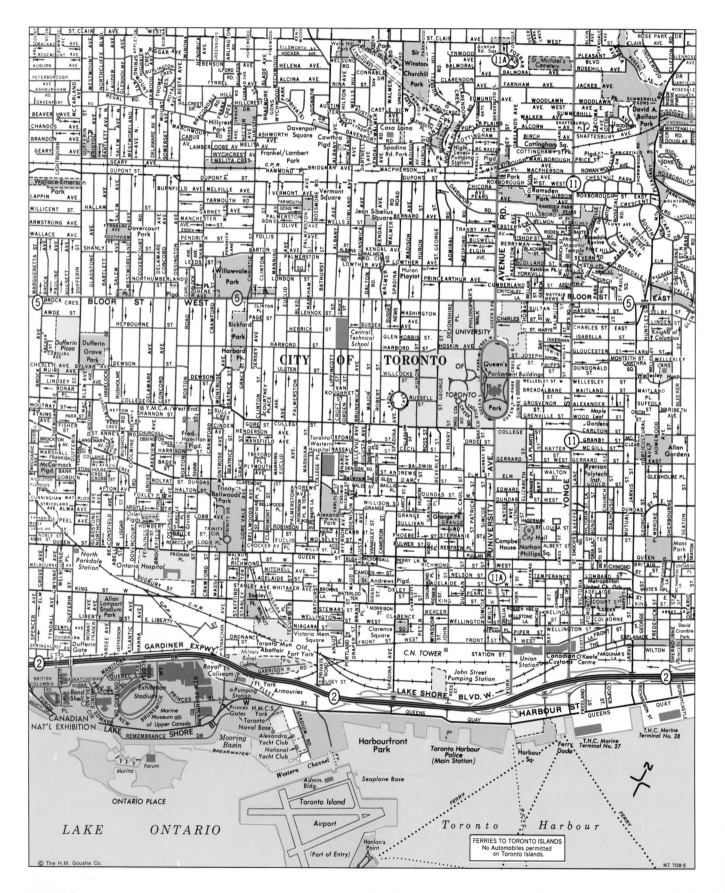

© The H.M. Gousha Co.

MZ 708-S

Ontario
(continued)

Toronto

Prince Edward Island

Charlottetown

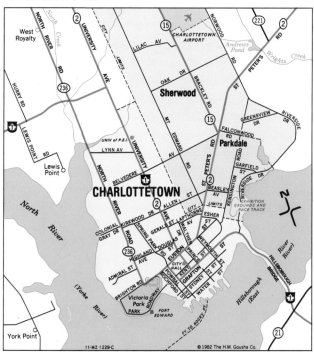

Québec

Québec

Close-up: Montréal

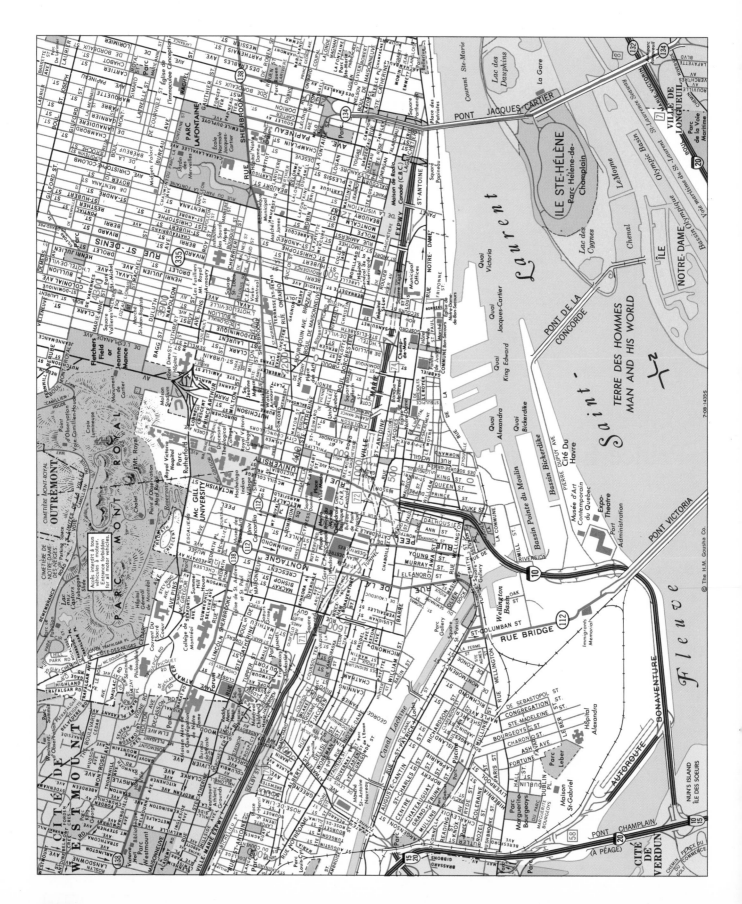

Québec
(continued)

Montréal

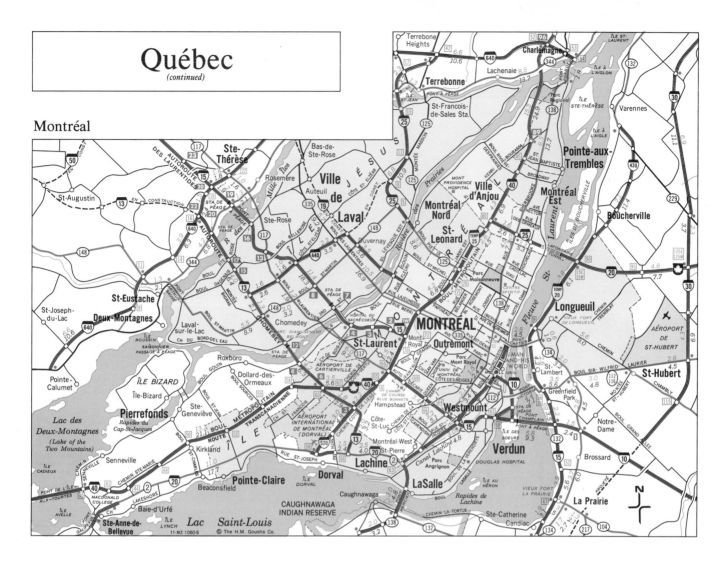

Saskatchewan

Saskatoon

Regina

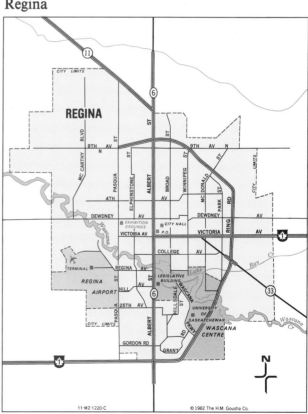

Alabama

Birmingham

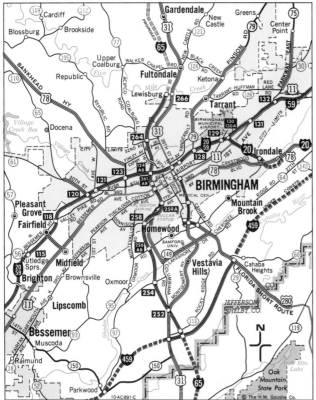

Mobile

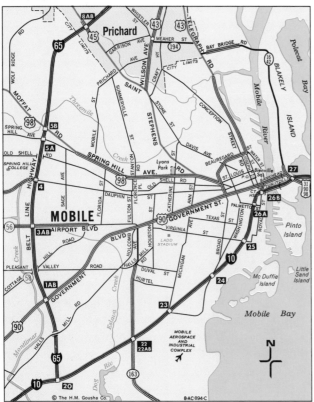

Arizona

Phoenix

Arkansas

Little Rock

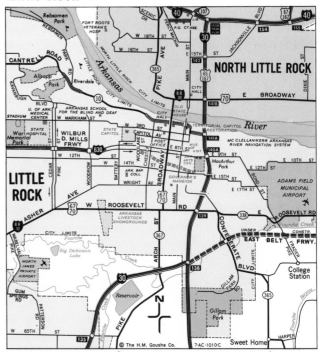

348

California/Close-up: Los Angeles

Los Angeles

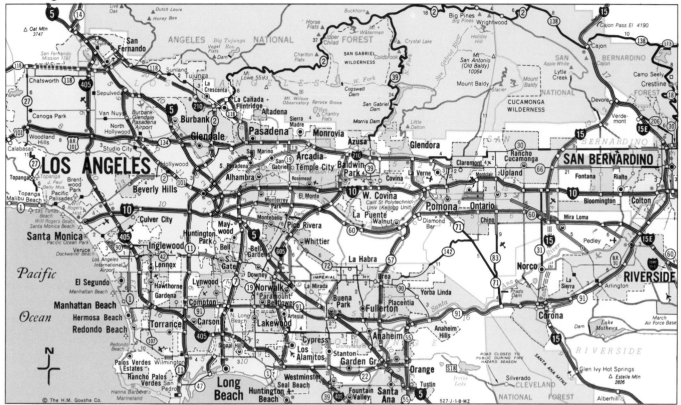

Downtown Los Angeles

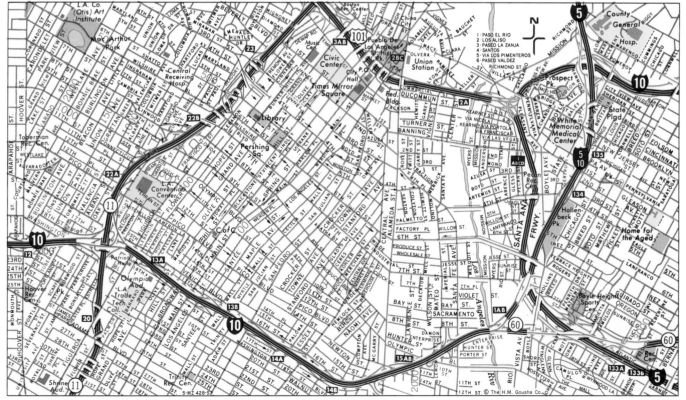

Close-up: San Francisco

San Diego

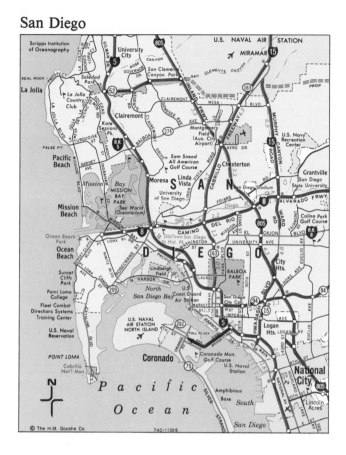

Colorado Springs

San Francisco

Denver

Bridgeport

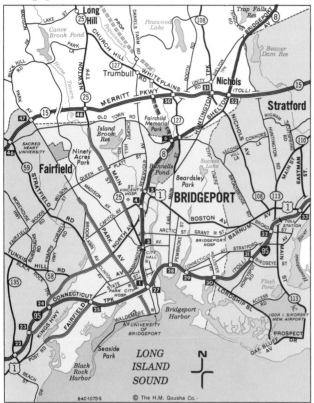

New Haven

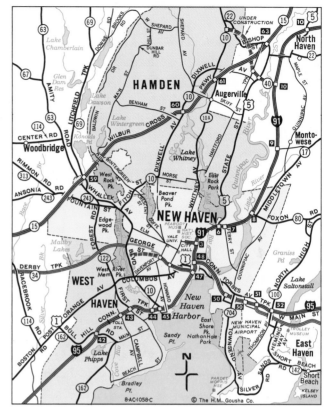

Delaware

Hartford

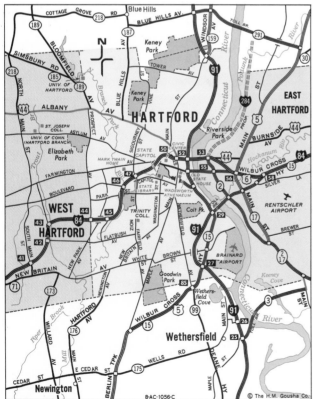

Wilmington

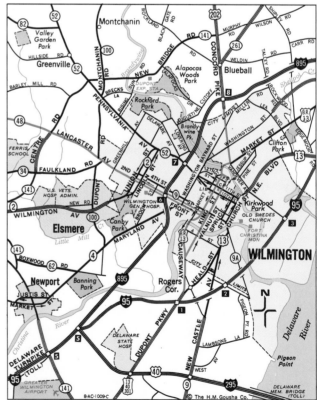

District of Columbia

Washington

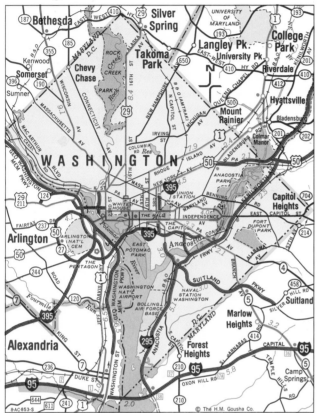

Florida

Fort Lauderdale

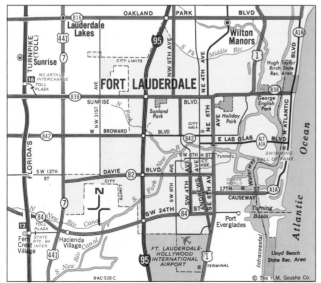

Jacksonville

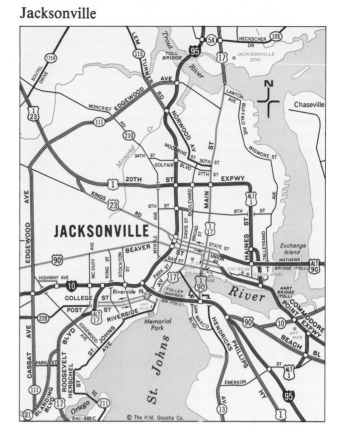

Miami

Close-up: Washington, D.C., Miami

Downtown Washington, D.C.

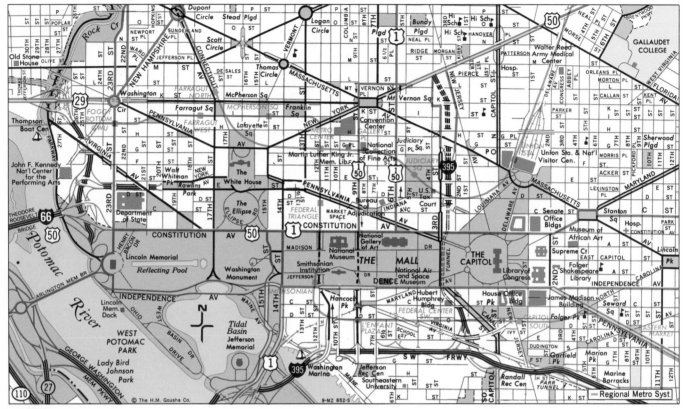

Downtown Miami

Florida
(continued)

Orlando

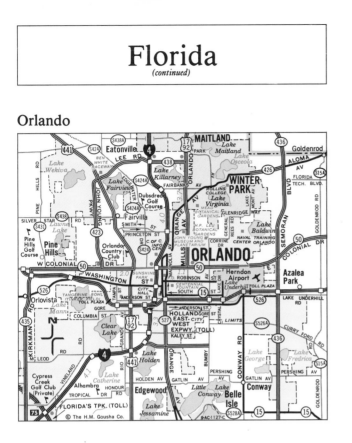

Pensacola

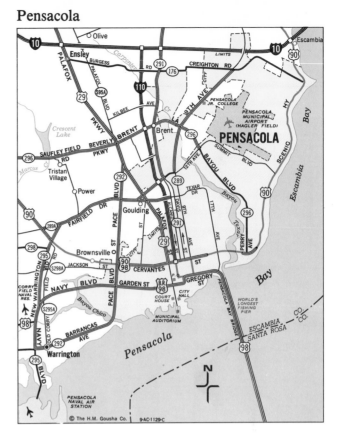

Tampa, St. Petersburg

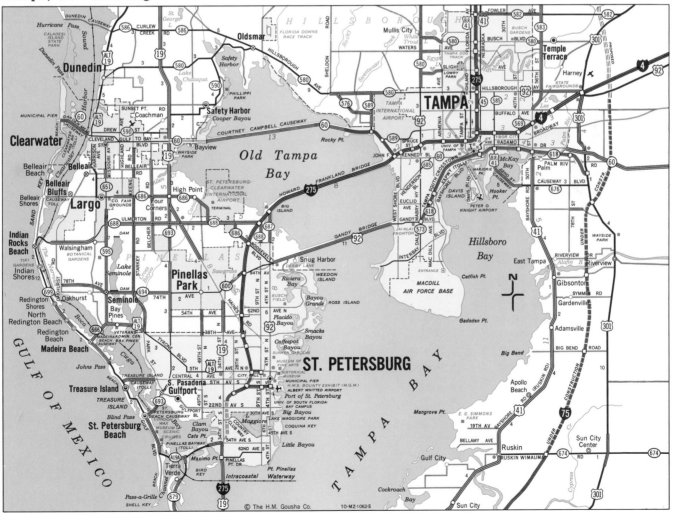

Florida
(continued)

West Palm Beach, Palm Beach

Idaho

Boise

Georgia

Atlanta

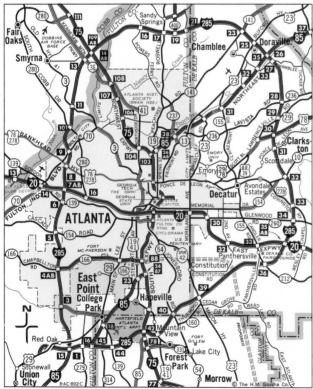

Illinois

Chicago

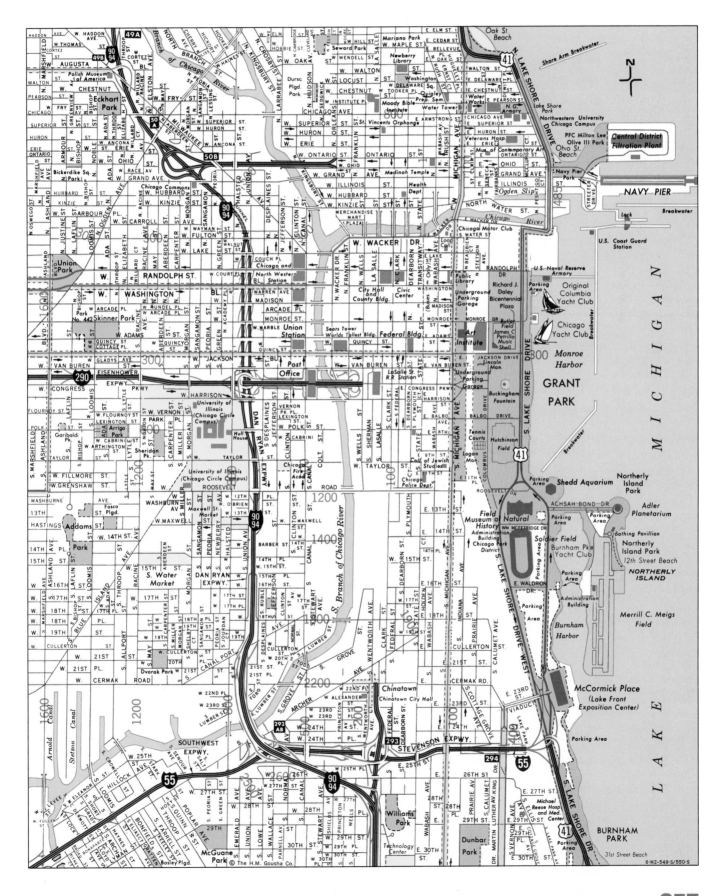

Illinois-Iowa

Quad Cities

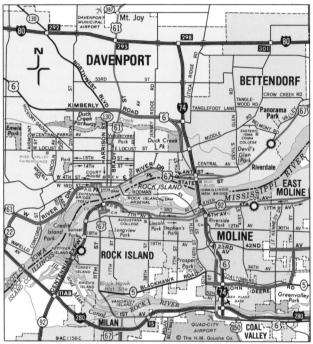

Indiana

Fort Wayne

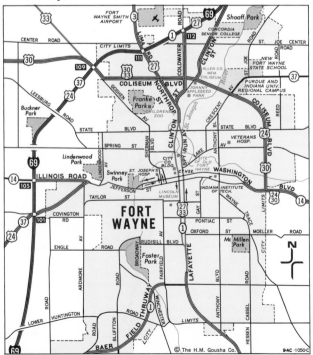

Iowa

Des Moines

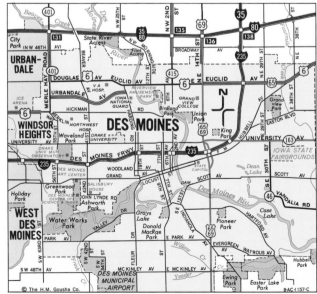

Kansas

Wichita

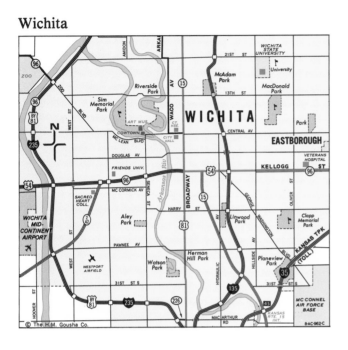

Louisiana

Baton Rouge

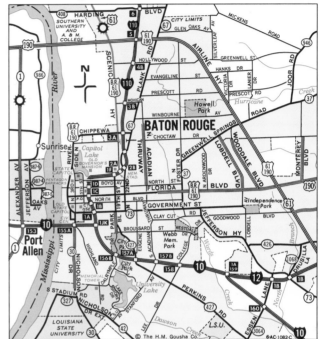

Kentucky

Louisville

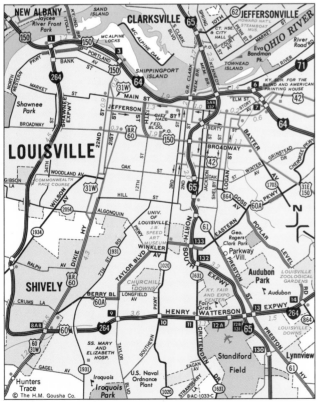

New Orleans

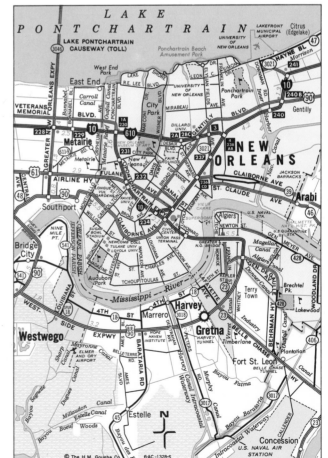

359

Maine

Portland

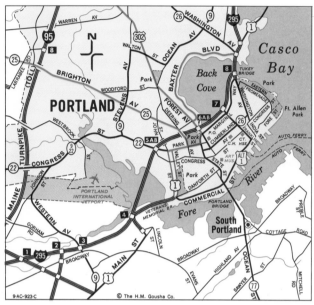

Maryland

Baltimore

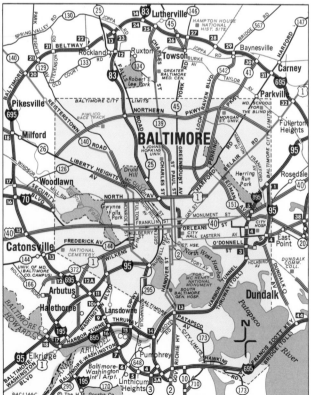

Massachusetts

Boston

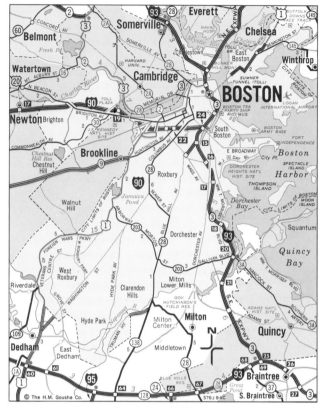

Springfield

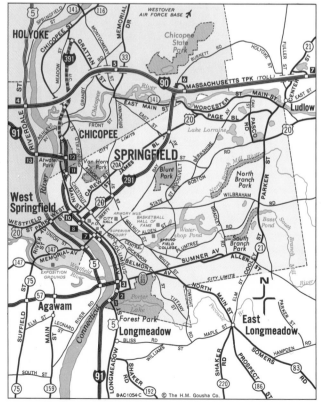

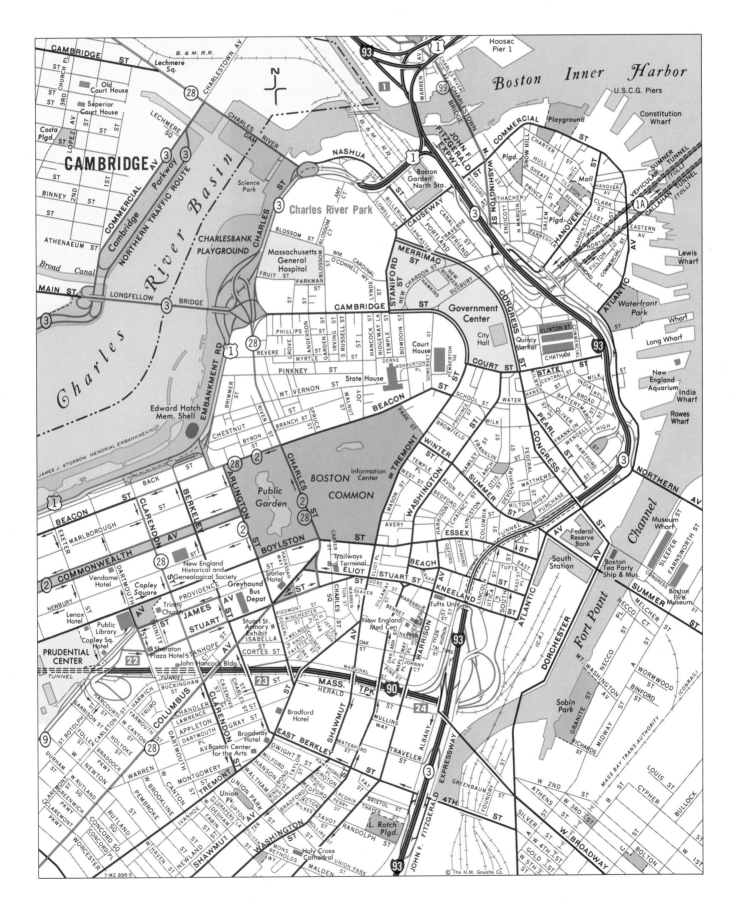

Massachusetts
(continued)

Worcester

Michigan

Detroit

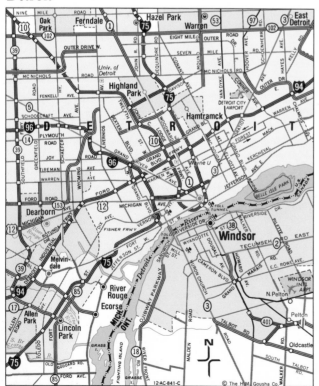

Flint

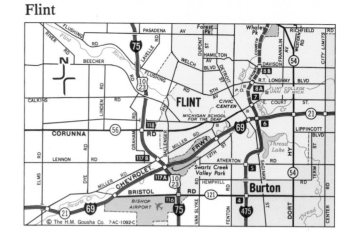

Grand Rapids

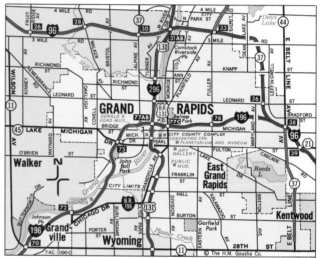

Minnesota

Minneapolis, St. Paul

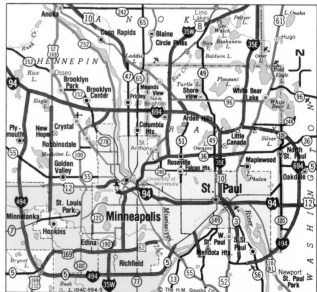

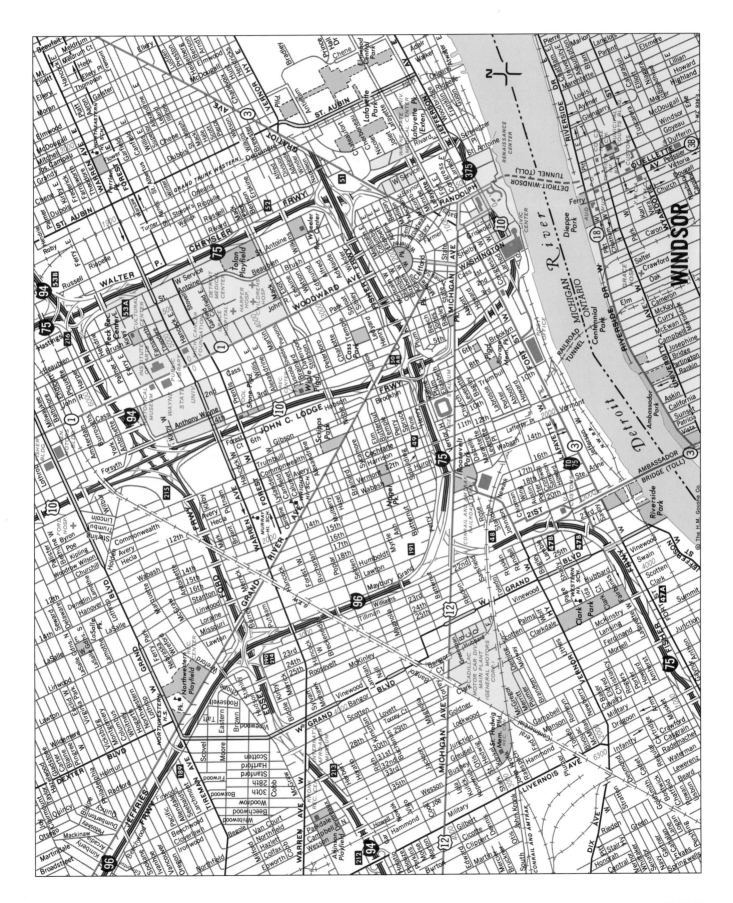

Mississippi

Jackson

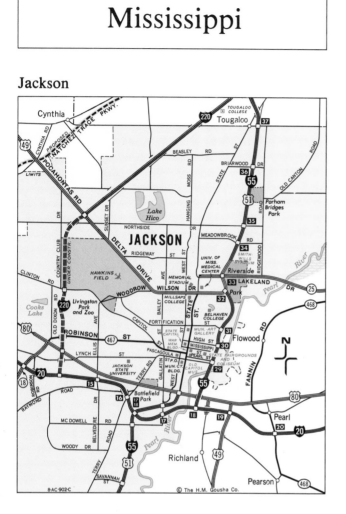

Missouri

Columbia

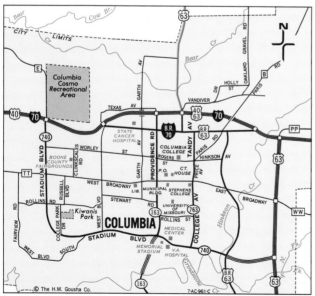

Kansas City

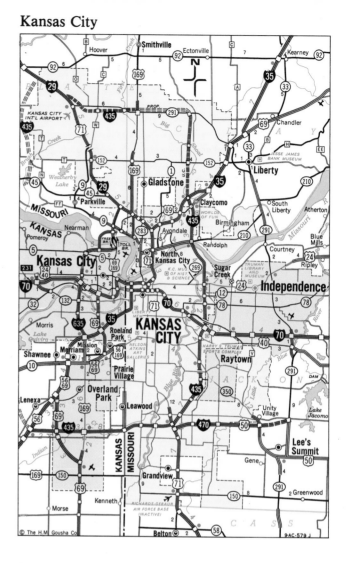

St. Joseph

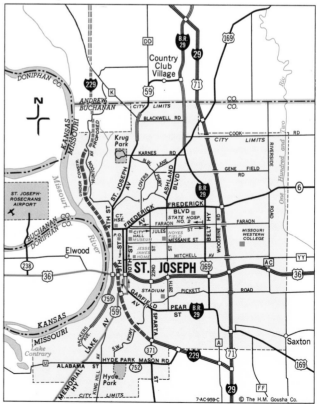

Missouri

St. Louis

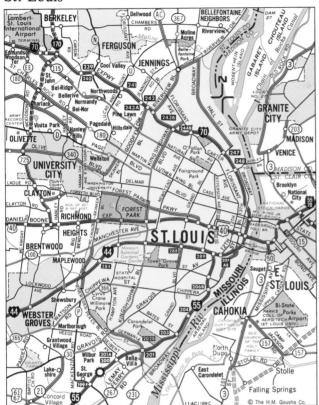

© The H.M. Gousha Co.

Montana

Great Falls

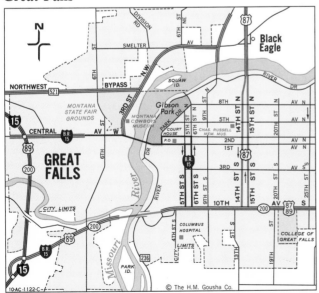

© The H.M. Gousha Co.

Helena

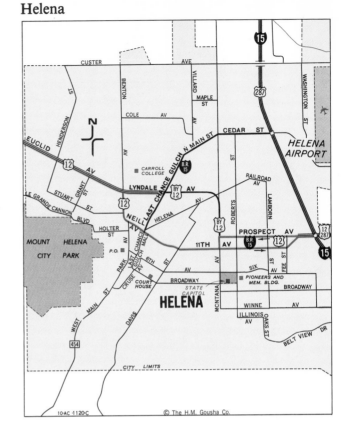

10-AC-1120-C   © The H.M. Gousha Co.

Nebraska

Fremont

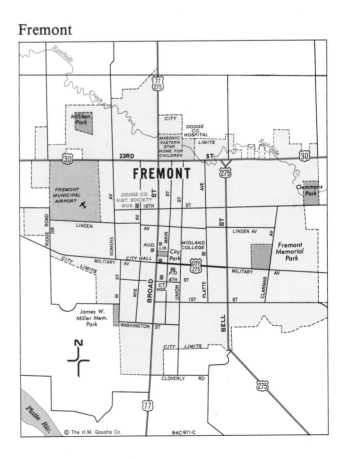

© The H.M. Gousha Co.   8-AC-971-C

Nebraska
(continued)

Nevada

Lincoln

Las Vegas

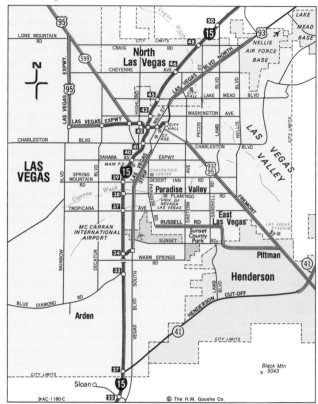

Omaha

Reno

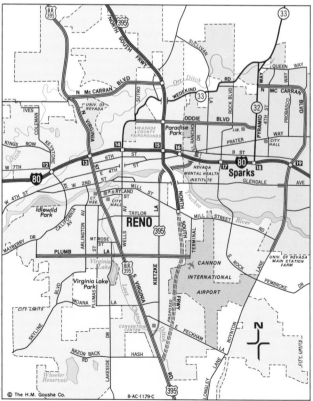

New Hampshire

New Jersey

Concord

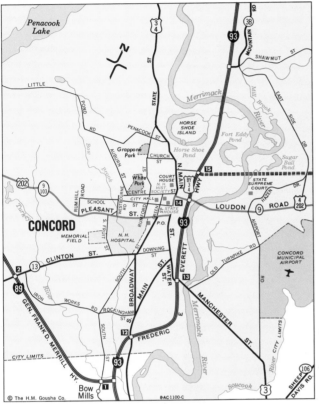

Atlantic City

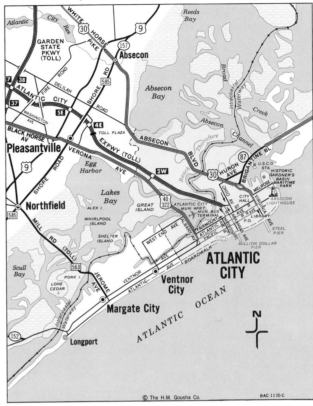

Manchester

Trenton

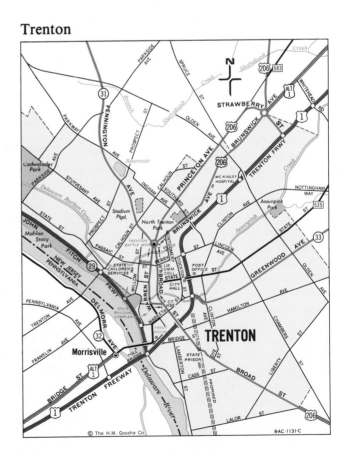

New Mexico

Albuquerque

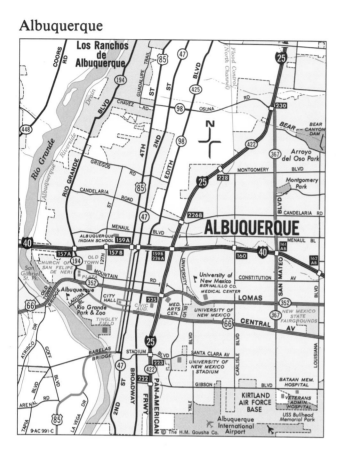

Santa Fe

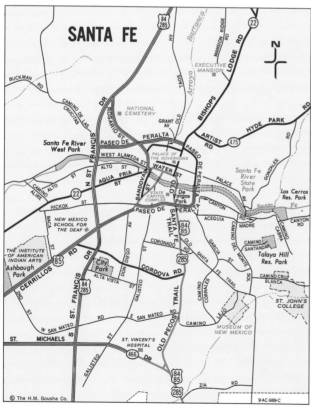

New York

Albany

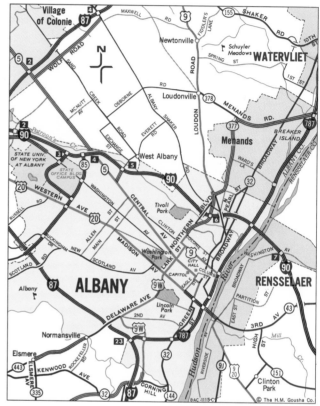

Buffalo

New York

Rochester

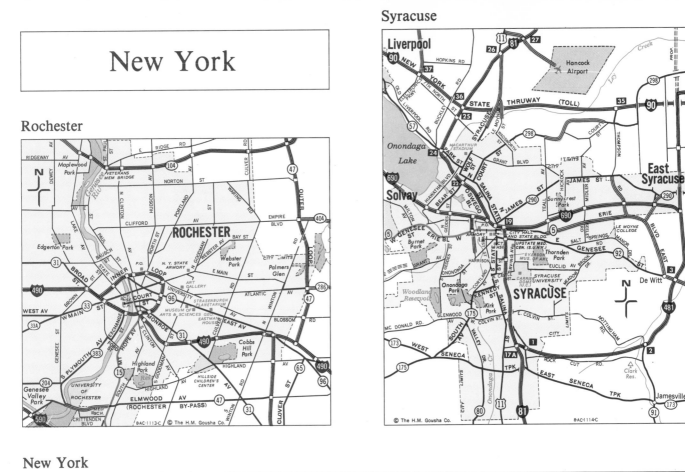

Syracuse

New York

Close-up: New York

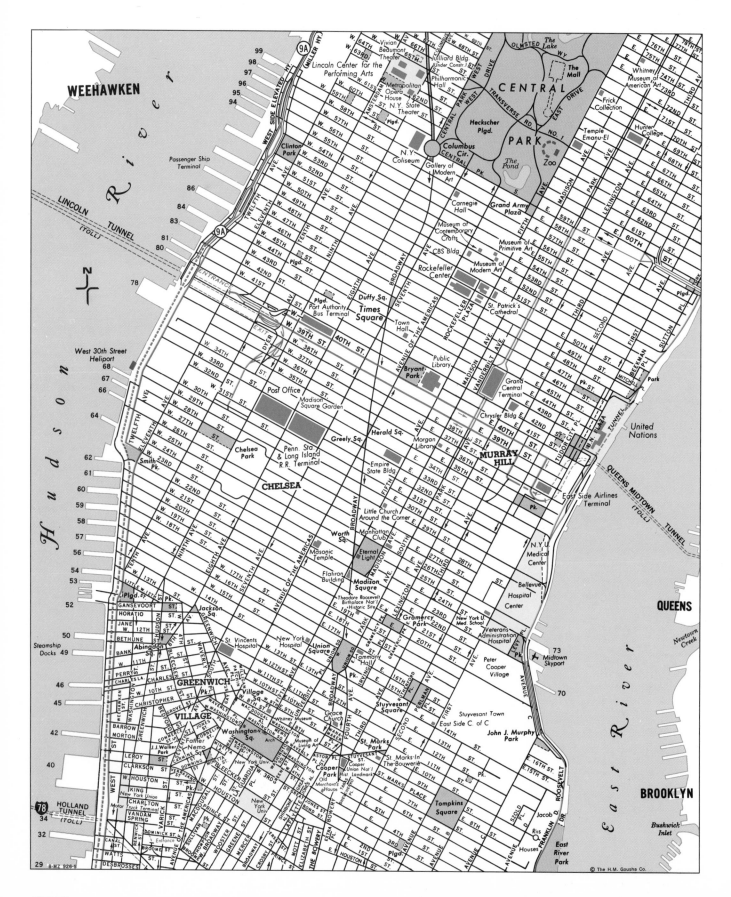

Utica

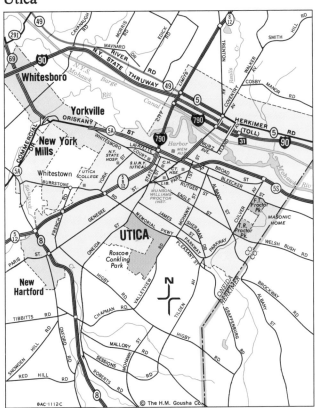

Greensboro

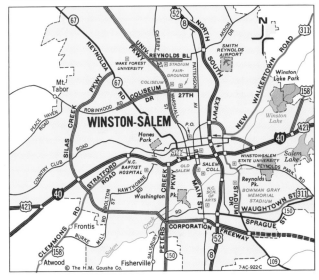

Winston-Salem

North Carolina

North Dakota

Charlotte

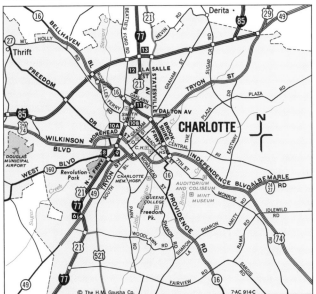

Grand Forks

Ohio

Akron

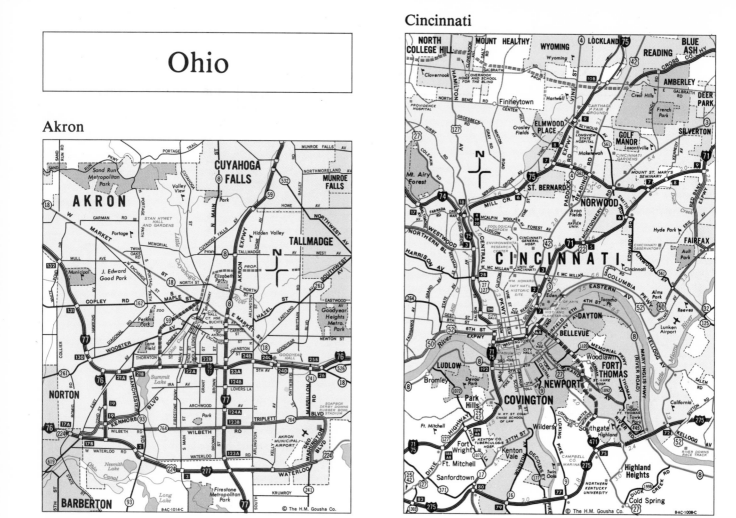

Cincinnati

Cleveland

Ohio

Toledo

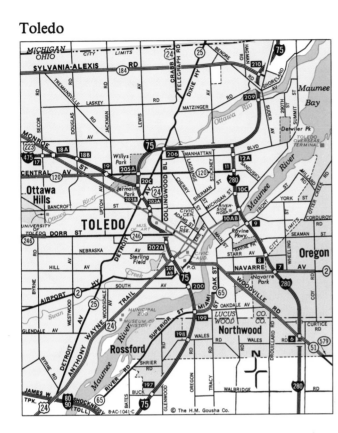

Oklahoma

Oklahoma City

Lawton

Tulsa

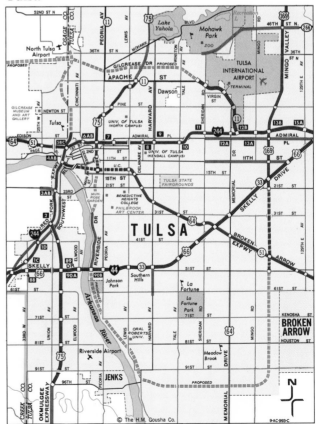

Oregon

Pennsylvania

Portland

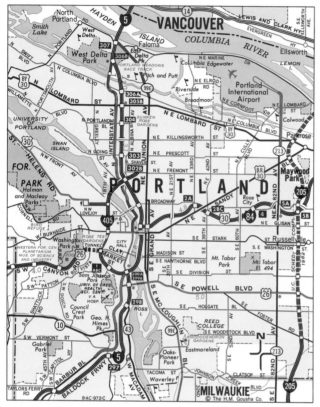

Erie

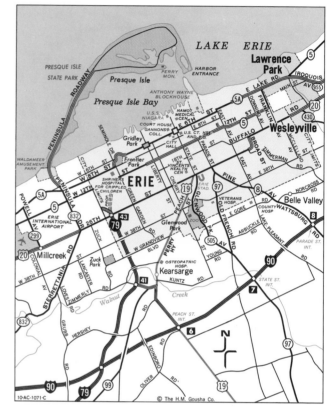

Salem

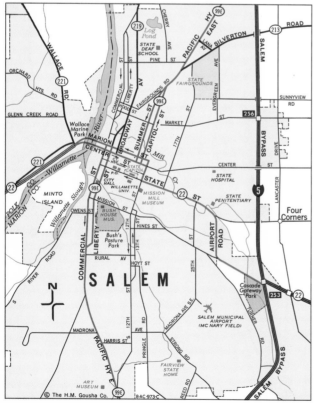

Harrisburg

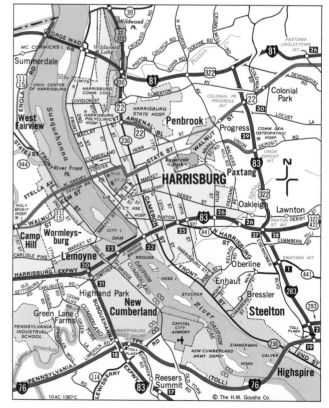

Close-up: Philadephia

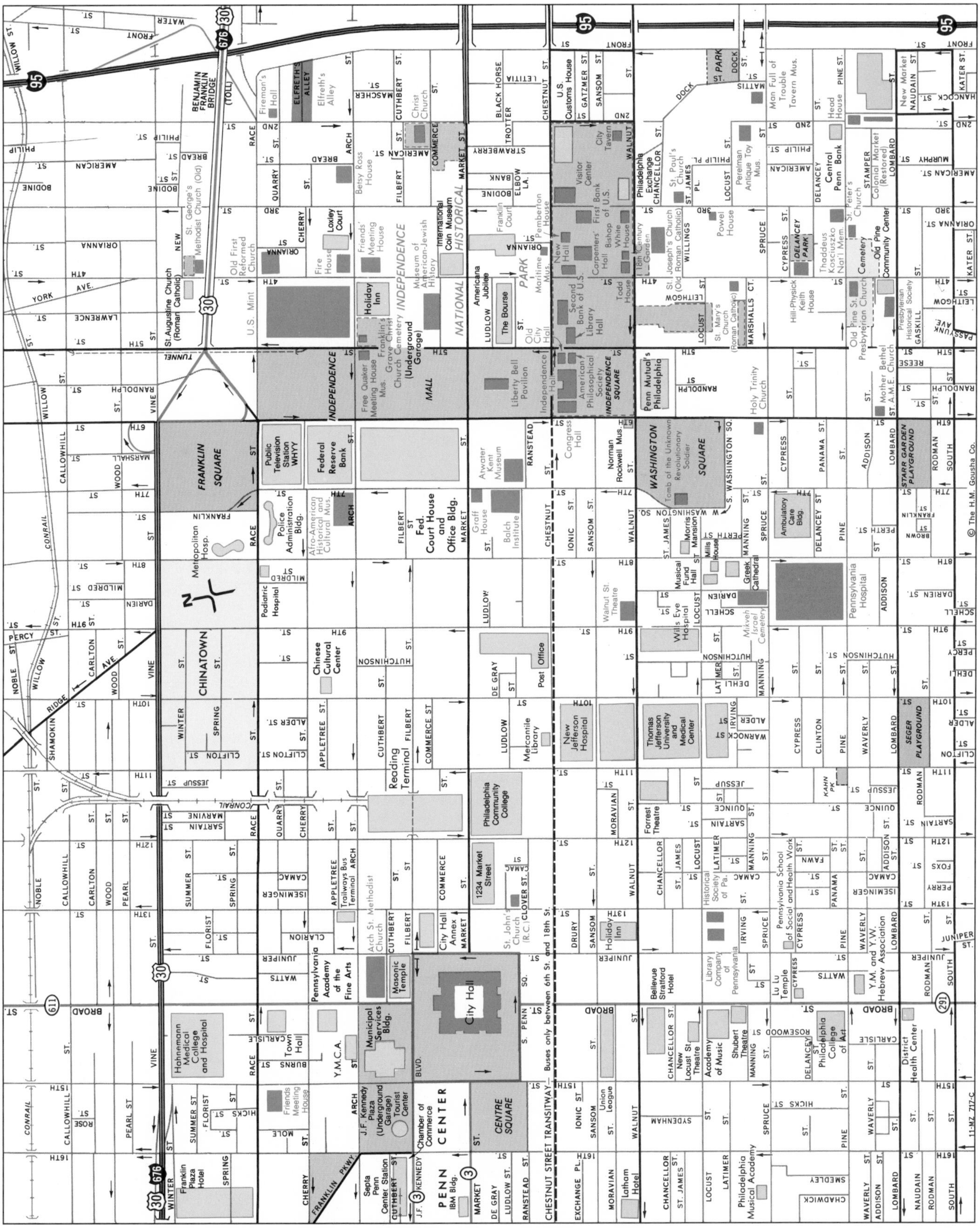

Pennsylvania

(continued)

Philadelphia

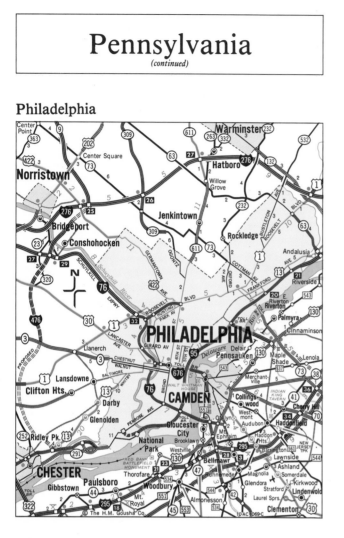

Scranton

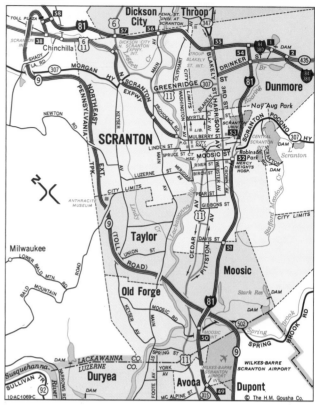

Pittsburgh

Rhode Island

Providence

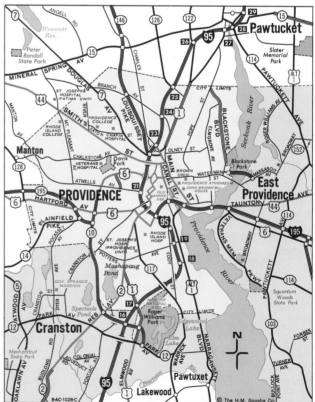

South Carolina

Charleston

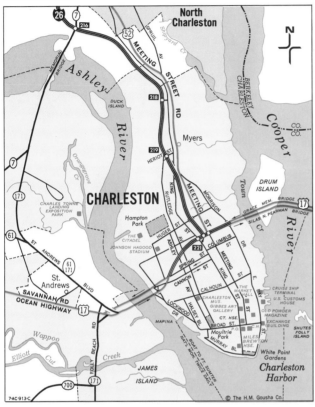

Columbia

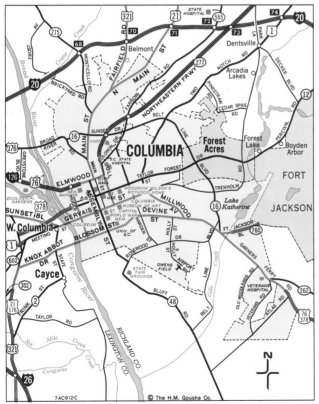

South Dakota

Rapid City

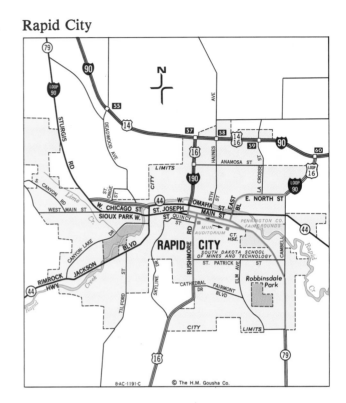

Tennessee

Chattanooga

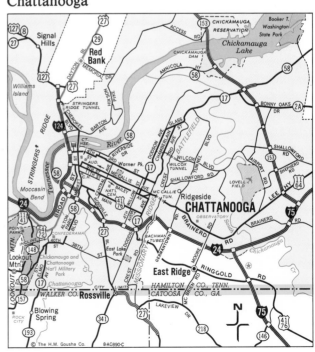

Tennessee
(continued)

Knoxville

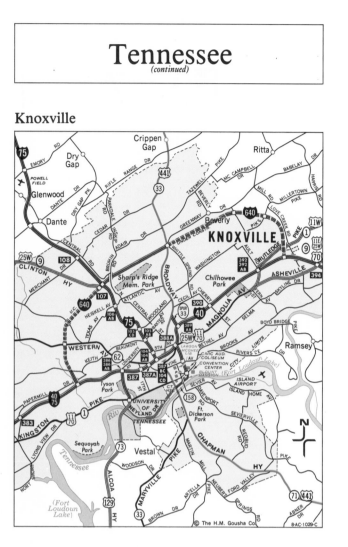

Nashville

Texas

Memphis

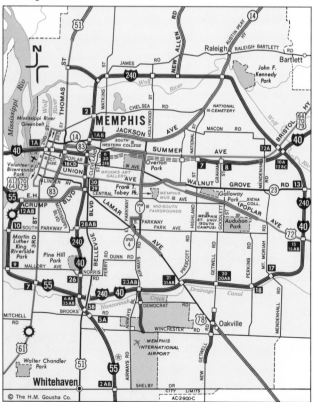

Amarillo

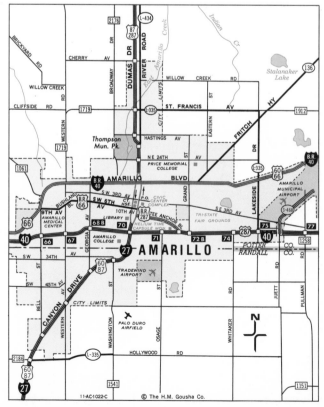

Texas

Austin

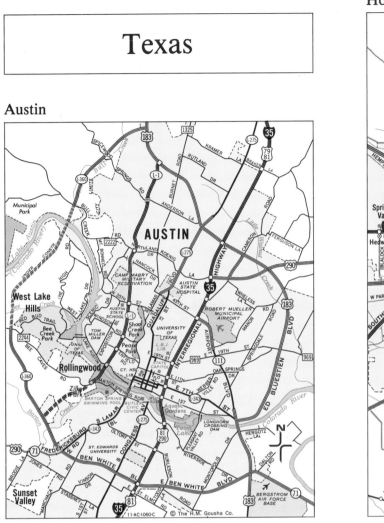

Houston

Fort Worth, Dallas

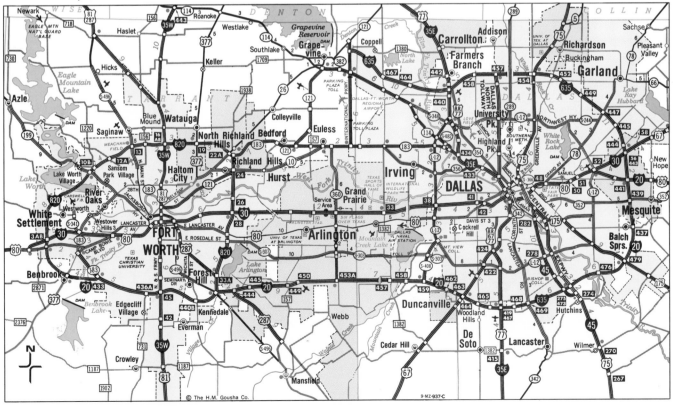

Texas
(continued)

San Antonio

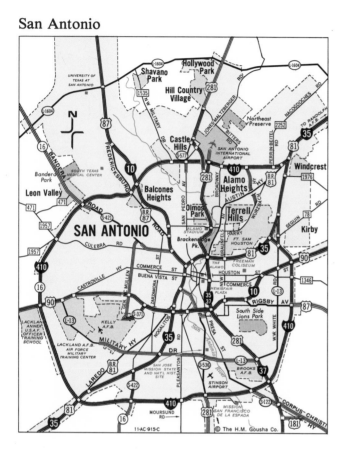

Wichita Falls

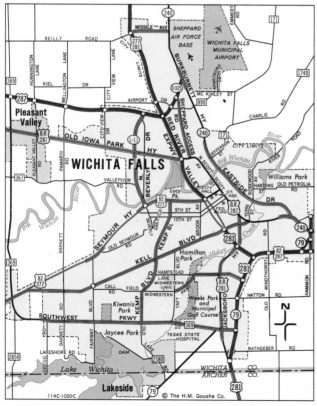

Utah

Salt Lake City

Vermont

Burlington

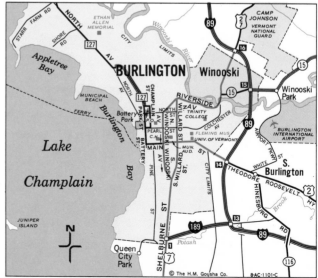

Virginia

Norfolk

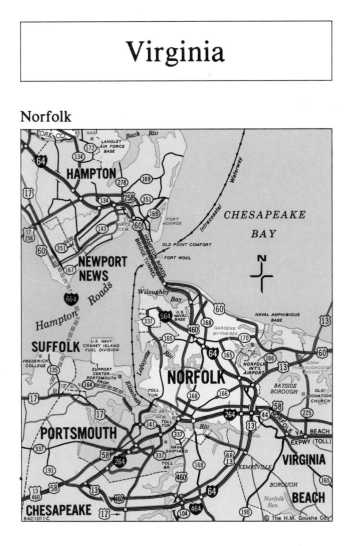

Washington

Olympia

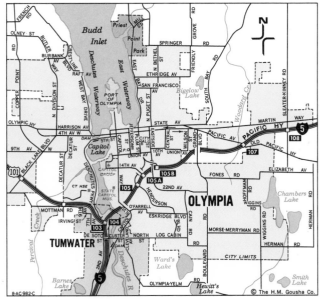

Seattle, Tacoma

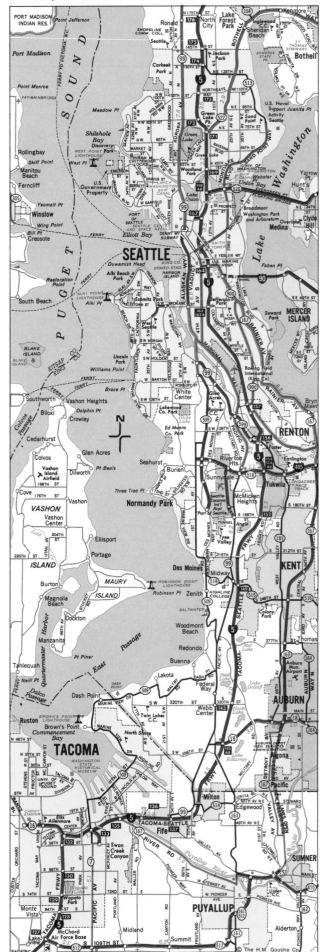

Washington
(continued)

Spokane

Wisconsin

Milwaukee

West Virginia

Charleston

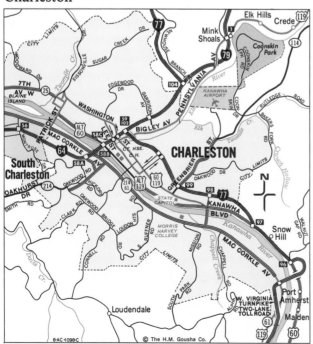

Wyoming

Cheyenne

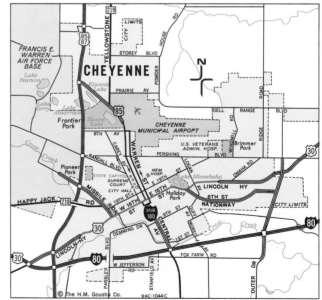

City Map Index

Canadian Cities

United States Cities

Picture Credits

Credits are from left to right, top to bottom with additional information as needed.
1 MS; **2–3** Grant Heilman Photography; **7** D. Hallinan/MS; **8** Paul von Baich (2); **8–9** R. Wayne Towriss; Karl Sommerer; **9** Neil Newton/MS (top); Eberhard Otto/MS; **12** Don McPhee; Brian Stablyk; **12–13** Ken Straiton/MS; **13** Allan Harvey/Masterfile; MPM; John de Visser/Masterfile; **20** Eberhard Otto/MS (top); Andy Levin/BS; Glen Tooke/Image Finders; **20–21** Patrick Morrow/Photo Graphics; **21** Robert N. Smith; Susanne M. Swibold; **26** Photri; Rene Pauli/SA; Bill Ross/Image Finders (middle); Roberts/MS; **27** Russell Lamb/SA; **36** David Stoecklein; Ed Cooper/SA; Courtesy C. M. Russell Museum, Great Falls, Montana; Monserrate Schwartz/SA; Craig Aurness/Image Finders; **52** Roberts/MS; **52–53** Tom Tracy/IBC; **53** David Muench (top); Paul Fusco/Magnum; David Muench; **54** Rene Burri/Magnum; David Muench; **54–55** Bill Ross/Image Finders; **55** © Four By Five/Michele Burgess; **64** Craig Aurness/Image Finders (top); Chuck O'Rear/Image Finders; Eberhard Otto/MS; **66** Russell Lamb; Grant Heilman Photography; **66–67** Rene Pauli/SA; **67** Brian Stablyk; Adrian Atwater/SA; **76** Frances Cochran/Image Finders; **76–77** Ray Manley/SA; David Muench/SA; **77** © Four By Five/Bill Fletcher; Colour Library/MS; **84** Kent & Donna Dannen; **84–85** Gene Ahrens/SA; **85** Jerry Jacka; Ray Manley/SA; Robert Glander/SA; **94** Roberts/MS; © Four By Five/Bob Llewellyn; Ed Cooper/SA; **95** Bob Taylor; National Cowboy Hall of Fame & Western Heritage Center, Oklahoma City, Oklahoma; Chuck O'Rear/Image Finders; **108** Matt Bradley (top); Harry Redl/BS; **109** Tony Ray Jones/Magnum; John Messina/BS; David Muench (2); **118** Roberts/MS; David Muench; **119** Tom Ebenhoh/BS; Kent & Donna Dannen; Alan Pitcairn/Grant Heilman Photography (middle); Matt Bradley; **142** Matt Bradley; Jim Brandenburg/Bruce Coleman Inc.; **143** Alvis Upitis/BS; MPM (2); Dan McCoy/BS (bottom right); **150** Kent & Donna Dannen; Erwitt/Magnum; Charles Moore/BS; **151** David Muench; Grant Heilman Photography; Kent & Donna Dannen; **160** F-11; **160–161** Menno Fieguth; **161** G. J. Harris; Mennon Fieguth; John de Visser/Masterfile; **166** Henry Kalen; Richard Vroom/Reader's Digest; Henry Kalen; **166–167** Eberhard Otto/MS; **167** Henry Kalen; Malak; Henry Kalen; **172** Victor Last; **172–173** SMI; **173** SMI; John de Visser/Masterfile; © Dan Gibson/SMI; Lowry Photography; **184** Robert Carr/Bruce Coleman Inc.; **185** Dick Pietrzyk/MS; R. Malace/MS; Doug Wilkins; Greenfield Village & Henry Ford Museum; Courtesy Michigan Travel Bureau; **192** MPM; Wisconsin Division of Tourism; Wolf von dem Bussche/IBC; **192–193** Wisconsin Division of Tourism; **193** The Circus World Museum, Baraboo, Wisconsin; **200** Lloyd Ostendorf; SA; MS; **200–201** © Four By Five/Bob Llewellyn; Deere & Company; **201** David Green/Bruce Coleman Inc.; Museum of Science & Industry, Chicago; **208** Alvis Upitis/SA; **208–209** Roger H. Pelham; **209** William Holmes McGuffey Museum, Miami University, Oxford, Ohio; Tony Linck/SA (middle); James Blank/MS; **222–223** John Iacono/Sports Illustrated © Time Inc.; **223** Nashville Area Chamber of Commerce; David Muench; Stern/BS; Bill Strode/BS; **230–231** State of Alabama; **231** Wendell Metzen/Southern Stock Photos; MS; Jim Amos/Photo Researchers Inc.; Robert Glander/SA; **238–239** NASA/Photri; **239** David Muench; Jim Tuten/Southern Stock Photos; Porterfield Chickering/Photo Researchers Inc.; Ringling Museum of Art; **240** James A. Kern; John Launois/BS; Bok Tower Gardens; MPM; **241** Signy Spiegel/BS; Photo Researchers Inc.; **248** The Biltmore Company; **248–249** David Muench; **249** Kent & Donna Dannen (top); South Carolina Department of Parks, Recreation and Tourism (middle); Bob Jones University, S.C.; **256–257** Peter Gridley/MS; **257** Virginia Museum Photograph; © Four By Five/David White; MPM (middle left); Smithsonian Institution; Lee Boltin (bottom); **258** F. Schroeder/SA; **258–259** Photri; Jim Howard/MS; **259** Courtesy The Henry Francis du Pont Winterthur Museum; Photri; **268** Camerique; Photri; **269** Andy Levin/BS; Harold Corsini/Western Pennsylvania Conservancy; Jane Latta; Hershey Foods Corporation; **276** MS; **276–277** SA; **277** Virginia Martin/MS; Michael Abramson/BS; SA; **282** Andy Levin/BS; The Metropolitan Museum of Art, The Cloisters Collection, 1963; **282–283** Brian Stablyk; Van Bucher/Photo Researchers Inc.; **283** MS; John de Visser/IBC; **284** Geoffrey C. Clifford/BS; John de Visser/IBC; R. G. Hyde; **285** R. Krubner/MS; Boscobel; **294** MPM; Cary S. Wolinsky/Stock Boston (middle left); Bullaty Lomeo; **295** MPM (2); **296** MPM; **296–297** Old Sturbridge Village; **297** Dr. Wayne Tester; Fred Ware/BS; F. H. Wood/SA; **304** MPM (2); **304–305** MS; **305** Eric Sanford Photography; H. Russell/SA (bottom); **310** © Four By Five/Mia & Klaus; Joane Plouffe (middle right); © George Zimbel/SMI; **311** Yves Tessier; Hellmut Schade; MPM (middle); George S. Zimbel; **320** Henry A. Harding; Fred Sieb; **321** G. J. Harris; MPM; Hellmut Schade; Malak; **330** Chris Reardon; Gwen Walker; **331** MPM; George S. Zimbel (top right); Malak (middle); David Ainley; **336** © Michael Kohn/SMI (top right); © Derek Trask/SMI; © Jeff Goodyear/SMI; **337** © Harold Clark/SMI; Malak; **384** Ross Stojko/Image Finders.

Cover: Paul von Baich (2); Eberhard Otto/MS; Hälle Flygard; Eberhard Otto/MS; Roberts/MS; E.L. Simmons/IBC; SPU/Masterfile.

Highway 17 near Nipigon, Ontario